THE
MID-ATLANTIC
REGION

THE
MID-ATLANTIC
REGION

The Greenwood Encyclopedia of
American Regional Cultures

Edited by
Robert P. Marzec

Foreword by William Ferris, Consulting Editor

Paul S. Piper, Librarian Advisor

GREENWOOD PRESS
Westport, Connecticut • London

Library of Congress Cataloging-in-Publication Data

The Mid-Atlantic region : the Greenwood encyclopedia of American regional cultures / edited by
   Robert P. Marzec ; foreword by William Ferris, consulting editor.
      p.   cm.
   Includes bibliographical references and index.
   ISBN 0–313–33266–5 (set: alk. paper)—ISBN 0–313–32954–0 (alk. paper)
   1. Middle Atlantic States—Civilization—Encyclopedias.   2. Middle Atlantic States—Social
life and customs—Encyclopedias.   3. Popular culture—Middle Atlantic
States—Encyclopedias.   I. Marzec, Robert P.   II. Series.
   F106.M586   2004
   974'.003—dc22   2004056059

British Library Cataloguing in Publication Data is available.

Library of Congress Catalog Card Number: 2004056059
ISBN: 0–313–33266–5 (set)
        0–313–32733–5 (The Great Plains Region)
        0–313–32954–0 (The Mid-Atlantic Region)
        0–313–32493–X (The Midwest)
        0–313–32753–X (New England)
        0–313–33043–3 (The Pacific Region)
        0–313–32817–X (The Rocky Mountain Region)
        0–313–32734–3 (The South)
        0–313–32805–6 (The Southwest)

First published in 2004

Greenwood Press, 88 Post Road West, Westport, CT 06881
An imprint of Greenwood Publishing Group, Inc.
www.greenwood.com

Printed in the United States of America

The paper used in this book complies with the
Permanent Paper Standard issued by the National
Information Standards Organization (Z39.48–1984).

10 9 8 7 6 5 4 3 2 1

CONTENTS

Contents

FOREWORD

Region inspires and grounds the American experience. Whether we are drawn to them or flee from them, the places in which we live etch themselves into our memory in powerful, enduring ways. For over three centuries Americans have crafted a collective memory of places that constitute our nation's distinctive regions. These regions are embedded in every aspect of American history and culture.

American places have inspired poets and writers from Walt Whitman and Henry David Thoreau to Mark Twain and William Faulkner. These writers grounded their work in the places where they lived. When asked why he never traveled, Thoreau replied, "I have traveled widely in Concord."

William Faulkner remarked that early in his career as a writer he realized that he could devote a lifetime to writing and never fully exhaust his "little postage stamp of native soil."

In each region American writers have framed their work with what Eudora Welty calls "sense of place." Through their writing we encounter the diverse, richly detailed regions of our nation.

In his ballads Woody Guthrie chronicles American places that stretch from "the great Atlantic Ocean to the wide Pacific shore," while Muddy Waters anchors his blues in the Mississippi Delta and his home on Stovall's Plantation.

American corporate worlds like the Bell system neatly organize their divisions by region. And government commissions like the Appalachian Regional Commission, the Mississippi River Commission, and the Delta Development Commission define their mission in terms of geographic places.

When we consider that artists and writers are inspired by place and that government and corporate worlds are similarly grounded in place, it is hardly surprising that we also identify political leaders in terms of their regional culture. We think of John Kennedy as a New Englander, of Ann Richards as a Texan, and of Jimmy Carter as a Georgian.

Because Americans are so deeply immersed in their sense of place, we use region like a compass to provide direction as we negotiate our lives. Through sense of place we find our bearings, our true north. When we meet people for the first time, we ask that familiar American question, "Where are you from?" By identifying others through a region, a city, a community, we frame them with a place and find the bearings with which we can engage them.

Sense of place operates at all levels of our society—from personal to corporate and government worlds. While the power of place has long been understood and integrated in meaningful ways with our institutions, Americans have been slow to seriously study their regions in a focused, thoughtful way. As a young nation, we have been reluctant to confront the places we are "from." As we mature as a nation, Americans are more engaged with the places in which they live and increasingly seek to understand the history and culture of their regions.

The growing importance of regional studies within the academy is an understandable and appropriate response to the need Americans feel to understand the places in which they live. Such study empowers the individual, their community, and their region through a deeper engagement with the American experience. Americans resent that their regions are considered "overfly zones" in America, and through regional studies they ground themselves in their community's history and culture.

The Greenwood Encyclopedia of American Regional Cultures provides an exciting, comprehensive view of our nation's regions. The set devotes volumes to New England, the Mid-Atlantic, the South, the Midwest, the Southwest, the Great Plains, the Rocky Mountains, and the Pacific. Together these volumes offer a refreshing new view of America's regions as they stretch from the Atlantic to the Pacific.

The sheer size of our nation makes it difficult to imagine its diverse worlds as a single country with a shared culture. Our landscapes, our speech patterns, and our foodways all change sharply from region to region. The synergy of different regional worlds bound together within a single nation is what defines the American character. These diverse worlds coexist with the knowledge that America will always be defined by its distinctly different places.

American Regional Cultures explores in exciting ways the history and culture of each American region. Its volumes allow us to savor individual regional traditions and to compare these traditions with those of other regions. Each volume features chapters on architecture, art, ecology and environment, ethnicity, fashion, film and theater, folklore, food, language, literature, music, religion, and sports and recreation. Together these chapters offer a rich portrait of each region. The series is an important teaching resource that will significantly enrich learning at secondary, college, and university levels.

Over the past forty years a growing number of colleges and universities have launched regional studies programs that today offer exciting courses and degrees for both American and international students. During this time the National Endowment for the Humanities (NEH) has funded regional studies initiatives that range from new curricula to the creation of museum exhibits, films, and encyclopedias that focus on American regions. Throughout the nation, universities with regional studies programs recently received NEH support to assist with the programs that they are building.

The National Endowment for the Arts (NEA) has similarly encouraged regional initiatives within the art world. NEA's state arts councils work together within regional organizations to fund arts projects that impact their region.

The growing study of region helps Americans see themselves and the places they come from in insightful ways. As we understand the places that nurture us, we build a stronger foundation for our life. When speaking of how she raised her children, my mother often uses the phrase "Give them their roots, and they will find their wings." Thanks to *American Regional Cultures*, these roots are now far more accessible for all Americans. This impressive set significantly advances our understanding of American regions and the mythic power these places hold for our nation.

William Ferris
University of North Carolina
at Chapel Hill

PREFACE

We are pleased to present *The Greenwood Encyclopedia of American Regional Cultures*, the first book project of any kind, reference or otherwise, to examine cultural regionalism throughout the United States.

The sense of place has an intrinsic role in American consciousness. Across its vast expanses, the United States varies dramatically in its geography and its people. Americans seem especially cognizant of the regions from which they hail. Whether one considers the indigenous American Indian tribes and their relationships to the land, the many waves of immigrants who settled in particular regions of the nation, or the subsequent generations who came to identify themselves as New Englanders or Southerners or Midwesterners, and so forth, the connection of American culture to the sense of regionalism has been a consistent pattern throughout the nation's history.

It can be said that behind every travelogue on television, behind every road novel, behind every cross-country journey, is the desire to grasp the identity of other regions. This project was conceived to fill a surprising gap in publishing on American regionalism and on the many vernacular expressions of culture that one finds throughout the country.

This reference set is designed so that it will be useful to high school and college researchers alike, as well as to the general reader and scholar. Toward this goal, we consulted several members of Greenwood's Library Advisory Board as we determined both the content and the format of this encyclopedia project. Furthermore, we used the *National Standards: United States History* and also the *Curriculum Standards for Social Studies* as guides in choosing a wealth of content that would help researchers gain historical comprehension of how people in, and from, all regions have helped shape American cultures.

American Regional Cultures is divided geographically into eight volumes: *The Great Plains Region*, *The Mid-Atlantic Region*, *The Midwest*, *New England*, *The Pacific Region*, *The Rocky Mountain Region*, *The South*, and *The Southwest*. To ensure that cultural elements from each state would be discussed, we assigned each state to a particular region as follows:

The Great Plains Region: Kansas, Nebraska, North Dakota, Oklahoma, South Dakota

The Mid-Atlantic Region: Delaware, District of Columbia, Maryland, New Jersey, New York, Pennsylvania, West Virginia

The Midwest: Illinois, Indiana, Iowa, Michigan, Minnesota, Missouri, Ohio, Wisconsin

New England: Connecticut, Maine, Massachusetts, New Hampshire, Rhode Island, Vermont

The Pacific Region: Alaska, California, Hawai'i, Oregon, Washington

The Rocky Mountain Region: Colorado, Idaho, Montana, Utah, Wyoming

The South: Alabama, Arkansas, Florida, Georgia, Kentucky, Louisiana, Mississippi, North Carolina, South Carolina, Tennessee, Virginia

The Southwest: Arizona, Nevada, New Mexico, Texas

Each regional volume consists of rigorous, detailed overviews on all elements of culture, with chapters on the following topics: architecture, art, ecology and environment, ethnicity, fashion, film and theater, folklore, food, language, literature, music, religion, and sports and recreation. These chapters examine the many significant elements of those particular aspects of regional culture as they have evolved over time, through the beginning of the twenty-first century. Each chapter seeks not to impose a homogenized identity upon each region but, rather, to develop a synthesis or thematically arranged discussion of the diverse elements of each region. For example, in turning to the chapter on music in *The Pacific Region*, a reader will discover information on Pacific regional music as it has manifested itself in such wide-ranging genres as American Indian tribal performances, Hawaiian stylings, Hispanic and Asian traditions, West Coast jazz, surf rock, folk scenes, San Francisco psychedelia, country rock, the L.A. hard-rock scene, Northwest "grunge" rock, West Coast hip-hop, and Northern California ska-punk. Multiply this by thirteen chapters and again by eight volumes, and you get a sense of the enormous wealth of information covered in this landmark set.

In addition, each chapter concludes with helpful references to further resources, including, in most cases, printed resources, Web sites, films or videos, recordings, festivals or events, organizations, and special collections. Photos, drawings, and maps illustrate each volume. A timeline of major events for the region provides context for understanding the cultural development of the region. A bibliography, primarily of general sources about the region, precedes the index.

We would not have been able to publish such an enormous reference set without the work of our volume editors and the more than one hundred contributors that they recruited for this project. It is their efforts that have made *American Regional Cultures* come to life. We also would like to single out two people for their help: William Ferris, former chairman of the National Endowment for the Humanities and currently Distinguished Professor of History and senior associate director for the Center for the Study of the American South, University of North Carolina at Chapel Hill, who served as consulting editor for and was instrumental in the planning of this set and in the recruitment of its volume editors; and Paul S. Piper, Reference Librarian at Western Washington University, who in his role as librarian advisor, helped shape both content and format, with a particular focus on helping improve reader interface.

With their help, we present *The Greenwood Encyclopedia of American Regional Cultures*.

Rob Kirkpatrick, Senior Acquisitions Editor
Anne Thompson, Senior Development Editor
Greenwood Publishing Group

INTRODUCTION

A standard assumption in today's world of globalization greatly influences how current sensibilities understand the presence of distinct and different regions that exist in an otherwise totally modernized (read unified and connected) landscape. The term "region" and the notion of "regionalism" bring to mind thoughts of "backwardness," "isolationism," "insularity," or at best generate images of the "exotic" and "quaint." Now that the twentieth century has come to a close, and people have grown accustomed to the presence of such integrative wonders as the Internet, such normalizing apparatuses as the television set, and such familiar sights as the supermarket and fast food chains, it becomes increasingly difficult—and even odd—to think in terms of singular events, places, and cultures that exist alongside the overpowering world of mass production. Yet the current reality, for all its fascination with cosmopolitanism, nationalism, and even internationalism, owes its creation to the distinctiveness of regional cultures that once defined the terrain of human reality (a distinctiveness that, in many ways, continues to this day).

The tension between the global and the local characterizes much of the mid-Atlantic region. The mid-Atlantic region of the United States is an expansive and complicated section of America that contains within it an astounding diversity of cultures, trends, and ideas that it would be more appropriate to refer to it as a "multi-regional" space. In the course of reading these chapters, one is struck not only with the heterogeneity of the region but also with the impossibility of uncovering any single factor or feature that would serve as the region's most fundamental quality. The centuries of mid-Atlantic development, both pre- and post-European arrival, are distinguished and made rich by this multiplicity of regional cultures. Collecting events of the past in writing in order to provide a comprehensive study thus poses certain problems. The putting in writing of history necessarily involves the act of creating a narrative—and narratives about the past generally seek to support the views of the present. In a world accustomed to accepting processes of globalization at face value, this makes the retrieval of local cultures a more complicated task than it might once have been. Regions in this sense become important, not out of some cavalier interest in "local color," but because of the alternatives the local offers the present global world and its tendency to swiftly homogenize regions. We see this argument proven a surprising number of times in each of the thirteen chapters included in this anthology, regardless of the topic of discussion and extent of its horizon.

In this sense, the topics of the chapters carry greater weight and are more far-reaching than one might immediately presume. The subject matter of each of the chapters has a value in and of itself, of course. Music, for instance, holds an aesthetic value for the realm of culture—in the sense of one of its general aims being entertainment and pleasure. But the reader will quickly discover the extent to which each of these topics also has a value that transcends their immediate context. As Christine M. Battista reveals with great astuteness, music has a significance of a kind that spreads to social and political arenas. In her words, "music has been used as a tool for freedom, as a way of expressing and celebrating heritage, as a method of communication, as an instrument that helps in the revival of values, and even as a powerful form of resistance." Music was used as a form of communication for early Native Americans, as a spiritualism that expressed a particular tribe's beliefs; it served as a vehicle for the sacred and the secular for both Native Americans and Christians; at times it functioned as political criticism, such as Francis Hopkinson's satire of the British government during the American Revolutionary War in his "Battle of the Kegs"; as "high art," music served as the backdrop for the pageantry of the wealthy; as "folk music" it operated as a means of class commentary and opposition; as both "art" and "folk music" it provided a real outlet for the early women's movement; and music also gave power to minority identities historically denied access to mainstream America. As the twentieth century saw the rise of greater commercialism, music, as with many of the other arenas of creativity and production discussed in this volume, began to confront economic forces of homogenization. Many popular artists from the 1920s onward found themselves coming under the demands of marketing strategies and contending with the transformation of new musical forms into mass-produced trends—such as the corporate genre-categorization of ethnic music in the 1920s and 1930s, and the hegemony of ragtime and jazz by white musicians who began to perform the compositions of African Americans. In the current age of mass-marketing and multimillion-dollar contracts, the growing influence of such forces seems an inevitable fact of life. Some, however, like the contemporary folk artist Ani DiFranco, who is able to sidestep these forces as much as possible (she produces material on her own label, "Righteous Babe Records"), offer a real alternative to these widespread pressures of monopolization.

Likewise, as Emily Workman profoundly reveals, fashion plays an important role as "political and social catalyst" in the mid-Atlantic region. Workman highlights as well the impossibility of categorizing fashion—as if styles of dress were the sole property of any single community, or as if any overarching model could exist that would define the "essence" of mid-Atlantic fashion. Early Dutch settlers, for instance, incorporated clothing ideas from Native Americans. The exigencies of seasonal changes equally engendered new designs. European influences, such as Charles I's "cavalier" style, mixed with these new and shifting mid-Atlantic contexts, to develop a rich and hybrid world of dress. The borders of fashion were not closed. Diverse cultural differences took root, but also underwent an active trans-mutation between different European nations, and between Europeans and Native Americans. Fashion could also be about control, materially acting out the impulse to dominate a region in the process of the Europeanization of the Americas. The seventeenth-century fur trade was a case in point. Settlers along the Hudson River manipulated and eventually monopolized this Indian economy, provoking a war with the Iroquois. This imbrication of fashion to the world of politics soon ex-tended to the world of capitalist development. The fur trade bestowed great wealth on the middle class Dutch, who not only sold the furs domestically, but established a high-demand market in Europe as well. This was intense consumption and mar-keting, of a kind that nearly brought about the extinction of a species—making the rise of a fashion trend also a matter of environmental significance.

This "interrelational" character of these topics is made apparent in each of the chapters. In the chapter on literature, Russell Leo's discussion of the Red Record (the "Wallum Olum") of the Lenni Lenape people (the Delaware Indians)—the earliest literary work of the Mid-Atlantic—powerfully underscores these affilia-tions by examining the Red Record's complex and rich affiliations. Not only a work of literature, the Red Record is a work of human production that holds widespread significance: it serves as a foundational historical document for the Lenni Lenape, delineating the development of the Lenapian culture; it is an epic poem, relating the story of a devastating flood; it functions as a moral work, marking the intro-duction of evil to the human world; it operates as a catalog and chronicle of past leaders, giving information on the migration of peoples from Asia across the Bering Strait and into the mid-Atlantic region; and it is a work of art, full of physical de-pictions in the form of hieroglyphs. Leo reveals this literary text to be "the cul-tural, political, and spiritual history of a group of people rendered in writing." Any attempt to artificially compartmentalize this work would not only be irresponsi-ble, it would recklessly reduce its considerable power as an artifact.

The issue of compartmentalization affects each of the topics presented here. From ethnicity to literature, from architecture to ecology, from to fashion to food, these fields of cultural production cannot be isolated from one another. Moreover, such attempts at isolation can have detrimental effects, as the chapter on ecology makes acutely manifest when discussing the Chesapeake Bay, and its important relationship to what environmentalists refer to as "riparian forests." These are areas of forest land that border bodies of water—streams, rivers, marshes, and shorelines. The trees pro-vide shade that keeps stream water cool, thus enabling it to retain oxygen; this oxy-genation in turn allows for the growth of beneficial algae; the canopy of leaves captures rainfall and filters out unhealthy dust from construction; and the roots of the trees filter out fertilizers and other pollutants that spread from farmlands and cities. Riparian forests thus function as a barrier that stands between the environ-ment and the everyday activities of humanity, keeping healthy the expansive network of rivers and streams that serve as the "circulatory system" of the Chesapeake. The isolationist philosophy of seeing all land in terms of private property, therefore, has the potentially disastrous affect of turning the riparian forest of an individual's backyard into a matter of "personal use." Such widespread tendencies to isolate and compartmentalize erase the *relational* nature of the environment—in this case the complex and ecologically crucial connections of trees to the surrounding biosphere. Years of this world view have led to the suffering of entire ecosystems.

The chapters also emphasize a related but equally important issue: the dominance of one world view over another. To return for a moment to the example of the Red Record, this work also reveals what is crucial to any historical study of regional cultures worthy of the name. The document, which informs us of the regional culture of the Lenni Lenape, ends with the introduction of an entirely different culture—the colonists from Europe. As such, it is a narrative that ends in the face of a new and absolutely *other* narrative, one that will not only bring new people and ideas to the region, but one that will also change the whole historical movement of the region. The important point to recognize here is that it would be equally reckless and limiting to try to discover a single foundation or origin to the mid-Atlantic region as whole. Though the historical record of humanity's existence in the region is replete with the maneuvers of cultures laying claim to "origins" in their attempts to justify ownership of the region to the exclusion of all others, such attempts only reveal what is truly at work: the confrontation—sometimes peaceful, sometimes hostile—of multiple and divergent narratives, upon which cultures found themselves. The violent encounter between the Lenni Lenape and the Europeans marks only the first in what would become a series of brutally decisive confrontations. Later cultural narratives, such as those that represented the area of the mid-Atlantic (and America in general) as empty "virgin" land, gave great force to the removal and general erasure of regional cultures such as the Algonquians, the Mohawks, the Senecan, and other tribes. Moreover, narratives had the power to physically carve lines into the very landscape of the Mid-Atlantic. In the formidable ethnicity chapter, Kathryn Wilson mentions one of the most historically significant of these: the Mason-Dixon line that divided the Mid-Atlantic throughout the antebellum and civil war period: "While Philadelphia and western New York were hotbeds of abolitionist activity, the slave system was retained in West Virginia, Maryland, and Delaware." Cultural regions thus arise, more often than not, out of these struggles for territorial domination, struggles which involve the empowering of certain narratives and world views over others.

Gathering a collection of essays on the historical formation of a region as expansive and diverse as the Mid-Atlantic consequently poses certain problems. One soon realizes that in the face of such diversity, a full representation of the region is impossible. The chapters in this volume will provide the reader with a strong and substantial introduction to their topics. The resource guides at the end of each, and the volume resource guide offer further avenues for exploration. Even so, obviously not all meaningful events, people, and works can be mentioned. Nor can each be given equal weight. With this awareness, the very question of what makes a work or event "meaningful" or "important" comes on stage and demands that it be given serious consideration. If it is true that cultures come to power in and through the rise of *their* narratives over the narratives of *others*, then it is also true that cultures will install criteria that will support rather than weaken the narratives that justify their supremacy. In other words, what one culture finds "meaningful" and "important" may be radically opposed to how another culture measures its reality. This means that ideas of importance rest upon particular and not universal standards. A traditional historical survey of "great classics" of mid-Atlantic literature, for instance, might overlook the Revolutionary War writings of Jupiter Hammon, who was born a slave on Long Island in New York, and became one of the first well-known published black writers in America. In the face of the overwhelming narrative of the day, a narrative that supported slavery, Hammon's works would have been deemed less valuable. In this sense his writing has value of another kind, for it functions as a counter-narrative, thereby challenging the dominant culture that denies importance to his very existence, and to the existence of his fellow slaves.

The awareness of these and similar narrative/cultural struggles gives great weight to the very idea of "regionalism." A figure like Jupiter Hammon writes in and from out of his specific historical context. As such, his work reflects the region in which he lived—in both a historical and a locational sense of this word. A "region" is therefore a name for a geographical area as well as a moment in time. And it goes without saying that regions are always changing. Some of these changes occur suddenly, as with the violent ascendence of one culture over another, or with the exhilaration of a less peremptory cultural exchange, as with the start of a new mode of musical composition. Other times these changes occur slowly, as when a certain narrative that has come to power is able to maintain its dominion through the course of many years. Ethnicity, for instance, involves "not only . . . the settlement of diverse groups, but also . . . their interaction with one another." Differences based on race, nation, religion, language, and so on, are "invested with meaning and symbolically elaborated." In this sense ethnicity, like culture itself, is not static, but stems from a process of "interaction and encounter, accommodation and conflict." Ethnicity is therefore always a matter of hybrid identities: Italian American, Korean American, Mexican American. In sum, larger global cultural narratives of identity that define different nations encounter one another in local spaces, and in the process bring new, specifically regional forms of identity into existence.

As mentioned above, cultural encounters can result in the erasure of multiple narratives by a single narrative that then becomes dominant—what might be called a "grand narrative." In other instances, peoples' interactions involve another kind of complexity that reveals more deeply the fundamental differences in narratives and how these narratives influence the ways in which people see and think. Negotiations between different cultural groups, Wilson points out, involves a movement "back and forth between different understandings of property, language and writing, social customs, and notions of reciprocity." These interactions occur in spaces that cannot be clearly located in either culture, for in the very creative process of negotiation, the interactions create new spaces, ones that do not exist in the normal reality of the everyday in either culture. These contradictory spaces can function as the most powerful opportunity for creativity. In the historical document, however, they more frequently ended in misunderstandings that incited acts of colonization—for reasons of prejudice stemming from the unquestionable faith in the narratives of one's home culture. As Wilson argues, "While Europeans valued linear time, property ownership and individualism, Native Americans operated with circular notions of time and space and communal/use-based notions of land incompatible with European ideas of individual rights and private property. . . . The Lenape did not own land. . . . Property was use-based; if you needed an axe . . . you used it and when you no longer needed it, it could be used by another." It was not always the case, however, that the citizens of the more dominant culture never underwent changes in these interactions with what was fundamentally different: "Many of the settlers developed an affinity for the indigenous way of life, adopted Indian dress, learned Indian languages, and formed alliances."

The presence of multiple cultural influences extend beyond the common understanding of the region's history. English as a language, for instance, was not at all the only, or even at times the dominant language spoken in areas of the region. German was a prominent language throughout the nineteenth century. Parts of Pennsylvania and Maryland were in fact bilingual, with German-language publications produced throughout the region, and German textbooks used in schools in Lancaster, Pennsylvania. In the Baltimore of the 1880s and 1890s, "fully one third of the population spoke German." It was only from the rise of anti-German sentiment with World War I that the language's hold on the area waned. Such language factors were, and continue to be, significant factors in the region's heterogeneity and hybridity. Hybridity owes its fact to patterns of immigration and migration, as Rebecca Roeder makes apparent in her informative chapter on language. The formation of Anglo American English dialects stems from patterns of settlement and movement—African American migration from the south to the north, European migration from east to west, Hispanic immigration from the southwest, and so on. Because of these movements, and because of factors such as cultural supremacy, the language of the Mid-Atlantic is now homogenized. But it must also be thought of as having different dialect regions, with language patterns and expressions continually evolving and changing to this day, especially in cities. To this degree the English language has, through the kind of linguistic development that is particular to the region, picked up words from a variety of cultures. Place names such as Roanoke, Manhattan, and Massachusetts that tend to be thought of as "typically American" in fact come from Native American languages, as do terms such as moose, racoon, skunk, squash, hickory, pecan (which were each elements of the environment unfamiliar to English colonists). In some peculiar instances, dialects can persist in the face of larger grand-narrativizing forces. Smith Island, located in the Chesapeake Bay, Maryland has been an isolated enclave of small islands for 300 years. Even today Smith Island is only accessible by boat, and the inhabitants speak a dialect that stands in opposition to its surrounding territory.

Different areas within the mid-Atlantic region offered different possibilities. New York, being close to the religious restrictions of New England Puritanism, differed from Pennsylvania's religious tolerance and political freedom. William Penn, Pennsylvania's founder, aggressively advertised his state throughout the British Isles and in Protestant Europe, depicting the state as a region in which people could be left alone by church and state. Nevertheless, as the environment chapter reveals, despite this promise of diversity, Pennsylvania was economically reified as a business venture. The very *landscape* of the state, furthermore, underwent a transformation that was based, in part, upon Penn's schematic layout of the city of Philadelphia, a plan that affected the development of future cities across not only the Mid-Atlantic, but America at large. Landscape changes of this kind also substantially affected the ecology of the region. Changes in the past that seemed innocuous at the time had a profound impact on the future of the region. Geographical arrangements not only gave rise to such phenomena as the social split between townspeople and farmers, but also informed current situations of ecological destruction. The turning of land into private property and the rise of urban sprawl, for instance, has led to the attenuation of sections of the land that are crucial to the survival of not only wildlife populations, but also the very water supply that mid-Atlantic inhabitants rely on today.

William Penn's ideal of freedom from church and state thus did not mean an end to cultural domination among the citizens of Pennsylvania, and the region at large. Native Americans living in the region are a case in point, as Timothy Finnegan persuasively relates in the art chapter: "the Delaware Indians inhabiting the present-day New York City and New Jersey area did not have the ability to protect their traditional territory. Beginning in 1737 with the Walking Purchase, Pennsylvania settlers effectively took over this territory along the coast, and eventually relocating these tribes to reservations in eastern Oklahoma. Their location directly on the mid-Atlantic coast was also the first point of contact between the Native Americans and Europeans where adoption of European manufactured goods were immediately adopted by the Delaware, further blurring knowledge of what was traditional art production and what was European influenced." Preserving the heritage of one's cultural art production was a major issue for many constituents of the Mid-Atlantic. The Iroquois, for instance, held greater political strength than the Delaware Indians. As an organized nation, they operated on a larger land area, which "had the effect of delaying the disruption of their art traditions through relocation by the United States government." And like music, artistic production could be a matter of direct activism as well. Early-twentieth-century photographer Jacob Riis, for instance, produced works of social realism that documented the working poor of the cities. He traveled from city to city, lecturing and showing his pictures of poverty-stricken urban life in an attempt "to change the situation of the people he met and photographed."

Equally important is the subject of food, which underwent changes and transformations that parallel each of the discussions of narrative contestation mentioned above. As Robert F. Moss and Caffilene Allen show in the food chapter, the Lenni Lenape were also expert fishermen and taught European "newcomers how to catch oysters, clams, and fish." The entire Chesapeake Bay crabbing industry arguably owes some credit to the southern regional tribes of the Susquehanna, Nanticoke, and Wicomico, who "not only showed Europeans how to make cornbread and hominy but also how to catch crabs, which is today one of the most important food-related activities in the Chesapeake area." As with the corporatization of music production, food also underwent a similar encapsulation within the "grand narratives" of big business. As a major center of vegetable production, the Mid-Atlantic became "the birthplace of some of the first and largest American industrial food processors." One of the first was the Campbell Soup Company, which began in 1869 marketing a line of canned tomatoes, vegetables, jellies, and condiments before becoming known, after 1897, for its mass production of condensed soups. It has now become an international conglomerate, bringing in over "$6 billion in revenue from its worldwide operations." The rise of the supermarket is a story of a similar nature, with grocery chains such as A&P purchasing dozens of local independent stores at a time, and adopting a "cash-and-carry" model that eliminated the old style "store credit" sale for its customers. Independent stores attempted to combat the onslaught of these large firms by deploying "a range of counterattacks, from promoting their superior customer service to attempting to prosecute the chains through the courts for anti-competitive behavior." These efforts were largely unsuccessful: "By the 1920s, chain groceries had firmly established themselves in the market. In the 1930s, they further consolidated their position by increasing the size of the stores and the number of products carried, creating the first 'supermarkets,' the model for grocery shopping that dominates the market to this day." Supermarkets now account for over 90 percent of "all retail sales of fresh produce and grocery items in the Mid-Atlantic"—a grand-narrative phenomenon of a type that is reflected across the board of cultural production in the Mid-Atlantic.

The incredible amount of diversity and the ongoing war between narratives is further highlighted in the chapters on architecture, film, folklore, sports and recreation, and religion. Mid-Atlantic architecture, Ian Morley argues, is a combination of the regional and the "international" in its commingling of everything from Greek revival and other European classical styles to high modernism. Older styles, moreover, intermingle with the new, with classical architecture, for instance, influencing architects throughout the nineteenth and early twentieth centuries. Buildings owe their existence to the indivisible relations between changing aesthetic perceptions, corporate attitudes, economic factors, land development practices, and general philosophical world views, as well as to technical advancements. With the sports chapter, we see that even this arena of cultural activities cannot so easily be isolated in terms of its "entertainment" value. Lacrosse is a prime example. As a game it was played by a number of tribes in North America, with different versions of the game tied to the different regions of the Southeast, the Great Lakes, and the Iroquois. For the Iroquois federation (of the Mohawk, the Oneida, the Onondaga, the Cayuga, the Seneca, and then later, the Tuscarora Indians), the game carried religious significance, and was thought to be, as Geoffrey Griffin points out, "a gift from the Creator." The games sometimes held importance in the care of the sick: "There were often rituals and ceremonies before and after games which were sometimes played to aid in the healing of the sick."

Narrative clashes are further highlighted powerfully by Jeremy Bonner in the religion chapter, which reveals the extent to which the diversity of religious practices in the mid-Atlantic region underwent substantial transformations from the pluralism of the early republic, to the later decline of Protestantism and subsequent rise of Catholicism. The chapter also addresses the relation of political factors on religion—such as the influences that Franklin Roosevelt's New Deal and then the civil rights movement of the 1960s had on Catholicism—showing that religious practices, like all the other topics discussed in this volume, cannot be compartmentalized from their socio-political context.

Only a glimpse of the many cultures that immigrated to the region will make apparent the absurdity of imposing any single narrative on the region as a whole. From the appearance on Native American soil of early British and French colonists who would soon bring with them mass numbers of slaves from various African regions, to later Swedish, German, Irish, and Welsh migration; from the arrival of a great many Italians, Hungarians, Lithuanians, Poles, Russians, Slovaks, and Ukrainians, after 1870, to the movement into the region of Cubans, Mexicans, Puerto Ricans, and other Spanish-speaking peoples in the late 1950s and early 1960s; and from the immigration of Chinese, Japanese, Korean, and other Asians to the most recent influx of South Asians such as Hindus and Muslims from India that bring with them a mix of Indian and British cultural influences, the Mid-Atlantic continues to reflect a decentered reality. But as we have seen, this list should by no means give the false indication that different constituencies and their cultural narratives were, or are now given equal representation and status. The many examples of narrative warfare will hopefully make this apparent. Narrative warfare, moreover, continues in our present context. At the dawn of the twenty-first century, the Mid-Atlantic offers the promise of continuing cultural expansion, a richness that stems from the fact of its multi-regional constitution. Nevertheless it also faces the threat of regional erosion—economically, environmentally, ethnically, socially, and politically—from a variety of homogenizing orders. In this "information age" the site of this contestation will be the landscape of narrative production. The question is whether the narratives most widely produced will seek to efface (or rigidly compartmentalize and economically exploit) the abundance of regional diversity, or whether they will foster attitudes of cultural and economic integration and regional uniqueness.

ARCHITECTURE

Ian Morley

The history of America is littered with the architectural remnants of days gone by, the country's search for national identity in its infant years, the expression of national power and all that modern society symbolizes. In the modern era, the mid-Atlantic cities have been pivotal in this process, particularly with regard to the evolution of many architectural styles and building types. In addition, the metropolises of the region and the United States at large symbolize both the best and worst of modern urban living, high and low standards of living, and associated problems. Cities like New York and Washington, D.C., are known the world over for their edifices, such as high-rise offices and public buildings, and their environments. Yet this global reputation it has gained from its famous buildings sometimes overshadows the fact that the area has its own distinct architectural identity. The local context has very much affected the development of the region's architecture, resulting in a wide range of styles and building types that any visitor to the region can today enjoy. For example, the influx of Europeans from the seventeenth century onward has resulted in many European building forms found in America, such as the huge barns in rural areas which derive from the agricultural buildings of Germany and England. Another example is the diversity of architectural styles in almost every city of the region: Baroque style buildings near neo-Gothic, neoclassical, and Greek revival. Such localized influences have created great diversity in mid-Atlantic architecture, making a homogenized view of the region a near impossibility.

PRECOLONIAL ARCHITECTURE

Before European colonization, the mid-Atlantic region was inhabited by Native Americans who formed part of an Indian group that spread geographically from Virginia in the south to New England and Canada in the north. Indeed, prior to the arrival of Europeans the Indian population lived in a highly developed society with rules, customs, languages, beliefs, culture, and built forms. By the time Europeans first set foot on North American soil, hundreds of Indian nations existed, many often living in relative proximity to each other where sources of food were plentiful. While these groups varied in many ways across America, certain architectural traditions were prevalent within particular regions. The Indian dwelling in particular developed in regional forms due to the influence of a number of factors: distinct regional climates, the availability of different building materials, and also, significantly, because of the different ways of life of various groups and the development of their particular rules of behavior.

Archaeological evidence in the form of large earth mounds highlights that Indians have lived in Delaware for thousands of years. Although little is known about the early American Indians, studies in other regions of the country have suggested that the pattern of these burial mounds might follow alignments to the setting of the sun at particular solstices. In West Virginia, too, Native American Indian earth mounds can be seen; hence, residents often refer to local Indian tribes as the mound builders. In other parts of the region stone monoliths have been found which also suggest more historic human activity; but it is with Native Americans that the first major architectural developments and regional design character emerged, although sadly much of this architecture has been lost or altered due to colonial and postcolonial influences.

While earth mounds still can be seen, much has been done by museums to show representations of Native Indian buildings, typically pole-framed structures erected from natural materials like tree bark, wood, rocks, reeds, grass, reeds, and snow—abundantly available materials that concurrently allowed the Indians to fortify their belief in the spirit of the land and its resources. These materials also suited the nomadic Indian lifestyle. They could be quickly found, and they were easy to use for the purpose of building structures that were not necessarily designed for longevity, as it was often necessary to be mobile in order to find food. But historical records have shown that the Indians did create elaborate house structures, described subsequently, along the St. Lawrence River in New York State. Some houses still remain because of land rights given to the Indians by the colonizing English and French that allowed the Iroquois peoples to continue their traditional lifestyles away from European cultural intervention. However, "social progress" in other parts of the Atlantic region has meant that many Indians were killed, many buildings destroyed, and much of their heritage lost.

While it might be assumed that the lack of modern industrial technology dictated the size, shape, and form of American Indian structures, in reality sociocultural factors were more important. Thus within the mid-Atlantic region evidence has been found of longhouses, huge frame structures (supported by poles) that could be up to 328 feet in length, with the length being determined by social codes (appearing from the fifteenth century) which necessitated that all people of the same group live under the same roof. Typical longhouses have been estimated to be about 98 feet long and 20 feet wide, within which the cultural and social solidarity of the group could be encouraged.

Erected from sapling posts, the longhouse frame was so strong that a sleeping area could be provided above the ground level—a helpful design trait during the cold winters of the region when temperatures can become very cold. The rounded roof was often 16 feet or more in height and covered the living areas given to each family, usually facing toward each other across a central aisle which allowed for easy communication. A totem pole marked the entrance doorway. However, by the 1800s the impact of European architecture on the Atlantic Indian groups and their architecture was noticeable as longhouses began to appear with gables—a response to government pressure, traders, and missionaries who forced contemporary western design styles upon the Native Americans despite the modern built forms having no cultural meaning to them.

Archaeologists working in the Mid-Atlantic have discovered that in the more permanent indigenous settlements not only did the Indian population continue to use sapling posts and bark for the frames and exterior of structures, but the shape of buildings differed a little from the longhouse form. Whereas a longhouse was oval in shape, in the permanent settlements buildings were usually more circular, forming wigwams (up to 20 feet in diameter and erected by placing animal skins over a wooden frame) within which one or two families would live. Easy to erect, with the doorway positioned eastward to the morning sun, the dwelling was perfectly suited to both the nomadic tribes and the less traveled groups of indigenous people who farmed as much as hunted and gathered. However when it was necessary for many families to live together, structures more similar in shape to the longhouse were built.

EUROPEAN INFLUENCE ON THE DEVELOPMENT OF MID-ATLANTIC REGION CITIES

One means by which a region can express a sense of cultural identity is through the arrangement and development of its towns and cities. The Atlantic region has a number of prominent cities, many of which have developed due to the conscious employment of urban planning. For example, Washington, D.C., was a deliberately planned capital city; Buffalo was deliberately laid out according to the 1804 plan by Joseph Ellicott (although much subsequent growth was a response to industrial developments); Philadelphia developed from a plan by a Quaker; and nineteenth-century suburbs were planned in many places. The Mid-Atlantic's cities form an urban culture distinct to the region. Notable aspects of the architecture of New York City, Washington, D.C., Philadelphia, Pittsburgh, and Baltimore merit a closer look.

New York

Urban life in the mid-Atlantic region has existed for centuries, and no one place more typifies the cultural, economic, political, environmental, and social development of the region than New York. As a place of settlement, New York, or New Amsterdam as it was known, has existed for nearly 400 years. New York, originally a colony owned by the Dutch West India Company, began its growth as a modern metropolis in the nineteenth century when wave upon wave of immigrants from Europe and elsewhere arrived, in so doing swelling the city to unprecedented population levels. In 1789 New York's population was approximately 33,000, by 1820 it was about 250,000, and by 1850 it had risen to approximately 500,000. By about 1900 more than 3 million people of varying nationalities lived and worked within its bounds. This growth led the city to be marked by an enormous assortment and intensity of life. Subsequent immigration in the early 1900s compounded social diversity and pushed New York's population to 7 million by 1930.

By the early 1900s New York was arguably the greatest American city. Its rise to prominence was a consequence of many factors: the construction boom, the growth of high-rise structures, the growth in the city's broad demography, and the merging of the once independent boroughs (Queens, Staten Island, the Bronx, and Brooklyn) in 1898 into one city. All these factors gave a unique flavor to life in New York, which encapsulated both the best and worst of modern American urban living. Architecture played a significant role in this process, as did nineteenth-century engineering developments. The opening of the New York State Barge Canal (from 1825) and Oswego Canal encouraged a series of social and economic changes that transformed the city and the surrounding region: the canals helped the westward movement of settlers, gave access to the rich land and natural resources west of the Appalachians, and helped make New York the greatest commercial city in the country. By 1900 New York had the world's longest suspension bridge (the Brooklyn Bridge, 1869–1883, by John Augustus Roebling), the world's longest subway system, and many of the world's tallest buildings.

Washington

In 1789, when George Washington was sworn in as the first U.S. president, the ceremony took place in New York. In 1790 Congress decided that a new capital city was necessary, and so begins the story of Washington, D.C., as the political and administrative heart of America, to be built on a site "not exceeding 10 miles square" somewhere in the Potomac region formerly part of the states of Maryland and Virginia, an area first explored by the Spanish but colonized initially by mainly English Catholics. This choice of site as the permanent seat of the U.S. government, with its virtues of freedom and equality, whether a deliberate choice or not by George Washington, was symbolically placed between Virginia and Maryland, two of the largest slave-holding states in America at that time. Thus this placement influenced not only the mid-Atlantic states, but the southern states as well. A Frenchman, Pierre L'Enfant (1754–1825), designed the new settlement. What L'Enfant created, much of which is still evident today, was a plan of Baroque inspiration and reflected his personal ambition to create a city of such scale and beauty that it would increase the wealth (in the broadest sense) of the nation.

The resultant form of Washington, D.C., reflecting the spirit of freedom and independence, was distinctly European but different from other mid-Atlantic cities that were distinctly European, for example, Philadelphia. Washington, D.C., was Baroque—the Baroque symbolizes authority and energy, the traits of young America. New roadways were to be broad, many up to 160 feet in width, perfectly straight in form, radiating from each other in geometric patterns that led to and from prominent public structures. L'Enfant's buildings were to be Baroque in design too, some placed at the ends of the central axes along monumental pathways known as malls. Such planning and architectural measures helped radiate a great sense of order and power of the people, power of the country, and the power of democracy in the fledgling nation, as distinct from European expressions of autocracy.

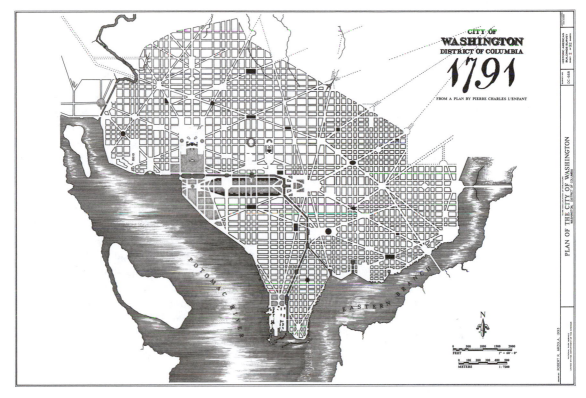

Pierre Charles L'Enfant's original plan of Washington, D.C., reflected his ambition to create a city of great scale in the Baroque style. Courtesy Library of Congress.

Philadelphia

As Pennsylvania's capital, Philadelphia has managed to handle the forces of modern industrialization, economics, and politics yet still retain a sense of charm usually found in much smaller settlements. Originally part of land used by Lenni Lenape Indians, the area first received European settlers in the seventeenth century. By the mid-1700s Philadelphia was a major colonial center with a population that consisted largely of Quakers. The further arrivals of immigrants, such as the Irish and Scots, not only swelled the size of the settlement but added Catholicism and Presbyterianism to the local religious melting pot. By the 1770s Philadelphia's population was in excess of 30,000; so diverse was this demographic composition that religious groups represented in the city were Anglicans, Baptists, Catholics, German Reform, Jews, Methodists, Presbyterians, and Quakers—Quaker meetinghouses can be seen throughout the settlement. Furthermore, these groups helped Philadelphia develop as a seat of education thanks to the establishment of a college (now the University of Pennsylvania), academy, and charitable school in 1755. The Scots in particular played a fundamental role in founding educational institutions not only in the city, but throughout the state, region, and nation.

Philadelphia was the most extensively "preplanned" American settlement of its time, thanks to William Penn (1644–1718), a Quaker, who as first governor of

Pennsylvania proposed a "greene country towne" (1681). Laid out in a grid form, a model for subsequent communities in America, the city had several distinct features, including blocks of land of similar size and shape which presented a sense of uniformity in all subsequent urban development for many decades to come. John Reps in *The Making of Urban America* (1965) has suggested that the Great Fire of London (1666), which Penn experienced at first hand, was an influence on the urban form of Philadelphia and he thus endeavored to create a safe and clean city in his 1681 plan. Given the cramped environment of London and the fire crisis, open space was to be a major element in Penn's plan. Five squares were laid out, including Washington Square (1682). However, due to his religious convictions, it might be assumed that Penn also endeavored to create a place of social equality. By employing a perfect grid form, Penn was able to create plots of land of the same size and shape. All plots of land were standardized. In Penn's society all landowners had equal amounts of land; no one had more than anyone else. Philadelphia society would therefore be one of equality. The grid was thus both practical and an extension of his social views about what society should be like. Its use perhaps suggests that Penn was influenced by contemporary English and Irish urban developments—for example, the laying out of a new garrison, Londonderry in Northern Ireland, and plans for London such as those by Sir Christopher Wren after the Great Fire in 1666, which were based on straight street urban forms. Regardless of the sources of inspiration, its use subsequently allowed Philadelphia to develop with a distinct urban form which contributes to the mid-Atlantic urban culture.

Pittsburgh

The built environment of the Pittsburgh region of Pennsylvania is an archetypal modern American industrial townscape, saturated with architecture of strength, variety, and invention. Pittsburgh originated as a French fort, Fort Duquesne (1754), and then became the British Fort Pitt (1858). Much of the historic architecture seen elsewhere in the state is not found in Pittsburgh, due to the Great Fire of 1845, which decimated the settlement, and to a wholesale demolition policy implemented by the city government in the 1940s and 1950s. The pre–Great Fire spirit and tenacity of the early industrial workers survived, though, and was even amplified as the city rebuilt itself, becoming the industrial core of the North prior to the Civil War. Today the city is still known as a heavy industrial center, a place with both tough working-class neighborhoods and salubrious suburbs; but regardless of where one lives in the city, the values of home, family and neighborhood, and hard work still give Pittsburgh its distinct identity. Pittsburgh has numerous modern edifices, like the 256-meter U.S. Steel Tower (1970). Another wonderful building is the neo-Gothic Cathedral of Learning (1926–1936, Charles Klauder), a 163-meter-high building that is part of the University of Pittsburgh. Not only impressive from the outside due to its size and 2,500-plus window spaces, the interior of the University of Pittsburgh tower was designed in seventeen styles by numerous architects to represent the different nationalities comprising the city's population. This influence of local demography on the composition is somewhat typical of architecture in other parts of the mid-Atlantic region. As in Philadelphia, education has played a vital cultural and architectural role in the development of Pittsburgh and the region at large.

The built environment of the Pittsburgh region of Pennsylvania is an archetypal modern American industrial townscape.

Today the mid-Atlantic region is home to many renowned colleges and universities. Another institution of note is the Davis and Elkins College in Randolph County, West Virginia. Founded in 1904 in a rural location, the college, which is affiliated to the Presbyterian Church, thus reflecting the heritage of the local area, today has a campus with twenty buildings situated in proximity to two historic mansions, Halliehurst (1890) and the French-style Graceland (1892).

Baltimore

Baltimore's architecture has also been greatly influenced by industry. Immigrants from Ireland, Britain, Germany, France, and the Caribbean have played a significant role as well, in helping to augment the city's size (its population grew from 26,500 in 1800 to 509,000 in 1900) and culture, evident in the variety of building styles in the city. Technology and industry have been influential as well. Iron and steel framing at the end of the nineteenth century allowed the city skyline to increase in height. Churches that once dominated the skyline, like Maximilian Godefroy Unitarian Church (1817, the country's first), were to be replaced by high-rise offices. The use of iron on the expanding railways soon led to its employment on a mass scale. Consequently, iron began to appear as a major ingredient of the city's architecture. By the mid-1800s Baltimore took on local and national architectural prominence as the city was central in the American adoption of iron-front buildings, subsequently developed into the steel and glass high-rise buildings that characterized twentieth-century America. Iron is literally everywhere in Baltimore. It is difficult to underestimate the railroad's influence on architecture in Maryland

and elsewhere. For instance, one of the city's most prolific and influential architectural firms, Niernsee and Neilson, began in the Baltimore and Ohio Railroad office. Importantly too, the railway created a new building type in the city, the railroad station, which was to emerge with its own distinct style—the "railroad style" based on the design of Italian villas. While America from the mid–nineteenth century was architecturally evolving toward Gothic forms of design, the railroad helped maintain the classical idiom in places such as Baltimore.

One of the difficulties of writing about architectural and regional identity for an area such as the Mid-Atlantic is that historically local contexts have been so influential. Baltimore, by way of example, contains more eighteenth-century buildings in a neoclassical style than do other parts of Maryland, a result of fashion within the settlement when it was economically and culturally powerful in the colonizing of the state. Of note too, the general architectural style in the city also moves away from the European as is particularly evident in Pennsylvania, for example, and toward finding an American style. Despite being European in origin Baltimore's neoclassical style is not truly European due to alterations by skilled designers such as Benjamin Henry Latrobe, who was striving to create an American style. Latrobe gave the city a masterpiece in the design of the Cathedral (1814–1818). His form of neoclassical style was also taken by his students and his colleagues into the state, which reinforced the neoclassical as America's own. Neoclassicism, embodied in brick and stone classical forms, was perfect for the new nation. A more simplified version of it, the Greek Revival, became the first truly national style in America. These buildings and others earned Baltimore a reputation for being a city of the monumental and beautiful.

Industrial developments have been noted as an influence on Baltimore's architectural development, but industry also affected the built form of the Mid-Atlantic in other ways. Most early industrial activity used water, and not steam, as the primary source of power. The large number of fast-flowing waterways in the region, for example, in eastern Maryland, provided a continuous and free source of power for industrial machines. Such natural supplies of power acted as an incentive for many industrialists to move inland to create factories and mills. As more people moved inland, to construct or to work in the plants, farmers in turn arrived in order to earn a living providing food to the growing urban centers and their markets. Upon the completion of the mill buildings, further construction occurred as workers required houses close to their place of employment. As a consequence, factory villages circled many larger settlements, like Maryland's capital, Baltimore. The harbors of coastal settlements also had to expand to cope with pressures put on them.

BUILDING TYPES

European traditions influenced the Mid-Atlantic's churches, municipal buildings, commercial centers, and sports facilities in different ways.

Churches

Gothic Style

Church architecture in nineteenth-century New Jersey developed along different lines than in neighboring states. The Gothic style was widely adopted throughout New Jersey, but with a slightly different form of design. Most New Jersey churches in the Gothic style contain the pointed-arch window, called a lancet, a principal feature of the Gothic form everywhere, yet the lancet sets the New Jersey churches apart from those of other American states as it was used in some instances prior to the Gothic period (from the 1820s and 1930s) in America. By way of example, many churches dating from the late eighteenth and early nineteenth centuries have lancet windows, including the stone Reform Church in Neshanic (1772) and the six Reform Churches in Bergen County (erected between 1773 and 1819). However, the churches built by Puritans, Presbyterians, and Quakers in the 1800s rejected the use of lancets, possibly due to perceived liturgical or denominational significance attached to the style. Yet other denominations, like the Jewish and Episcopalian faiths, used the arched window form, which can be viewed at the wooden Zion Lutheran Church in Saddle River (1820), the Greek revival Episcopal church (1836) in Piscataway, and the Presbyterian church in Kingwood (1837).

The arrival of the High Gothic in New Jersey church design, with its pinnacles, traceries, buttresses, and lancets, came later than in other areas of the region, such as Washington, D.C., and New York, and the state also lacked a Catholic church until the mid–nineteenth century due to the dominance of Protestantism. Yet the cultural connection with Europe, particularly England, was still strong in this part of the nation, and by the 1830s the influence of the English Gothic country home is evident in New Jersey and places such as Pennsylvania. House design will be discussed subsequently.

Before 1830, Gothic features in New Jersey churches were limited to the church windows. After 1830, many church buildings began to incorporate more traditional Gothic features. St. Andrew's in Mt. Molly (1843) is a perfect example. Its form suggests an opening of the Gothic in New Jersey, a move to compositions with towers, pinnacles, and the like. John Notman's church in Glassboro (1846) also highlights the move to a fuller Gothic design, and the success of these two buildings and others led other denominations to adopt the style. From the mid–nineteenth century both Methodists and Presbyterians began constructing churches in Gothic styles, albeit in a slightly more English style than others with Romanesque elements (pre-Gothic) being commonly used in the composition. The style remained popular in the state well into the twentieth century, as the Chapel at Princeton University (1928) testifies.

Church Building Materials

Churches in New Jersey used wood as well as stone as the primary building material. Wood was used where matters of economy were of great significance. Today New Jersey has a large number of nineteenth-century wooden churches. With a charm all their own, these churches are an integral part of the architectural and social fabric of the state. St. Peter's (1849) in Spotswood, one of the earliest wooden

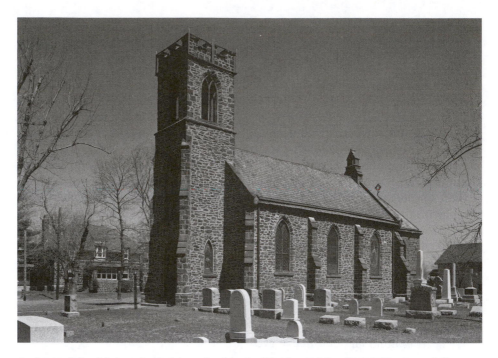

Architect John Notman's Gothic-style church, Glassboro, New Jersey. Courtesy Library of Congress.

board-and-batten constructed churches in America, St. James Episcopal Church (1859) in Hackettstown, St. John's in Boonton (1863), and the Church of the Holy Cross in North Plainfield (1868) all stand as landmarks in the architectural and cultural development of New Jersey.

New Jersey's proximity to New York City has strongly affected the development of the state. The impact of the arrival of Europeans, first from the Netherlands and Sweden, was to prove dramatic in New Jersey in that it eroded the local Indian culture that existed before; equally important was the English annexation of the New Netherlands colony in 1664. The English, many of whom were Quakers, were to greatly influence the subsequent development of the state, particularly in church design (e.g., the brick-built, Georgian-style Old St. Mary's Church from 1703 in Burlington) and meetinghouses. These early colonial buildings were often small in scale, rectangular in plan, and domestic in character, being simply designed and built from wood, reflecting the principles of simplicity and equality promoted by the Quaker faith. However, by the mid–nineteenth century some buildings, for example the 1853 meetinghouse in Hector, adopted pointed-arch windows, highlighting the dominance of an English style, the Gothic, in Atlantic church design.

Church Design in West Virginia

As a settlement with a history of 300 or so years, Charlestown, West Virginia, has a broad and colorful history. The city has an extraordinary variety of church and synagogue buildings, a positive reflection of the religious freedom encouraged and enjoyed by the early colonizers and city fathers. Among the most notable are

St. Philip's Episcopal Church (originally 1670), the first church in the colony, St. Michael's Episcopal Church (1761), and the French Protestant Church (1844–1845). The French as well as the English were vital in shaping West Virginia's architecture, as many French Protestants settled there to escape from religious persecution during the reign of King Louis XIV. As a consequence the French influence in building design can be seen. Most early churches in West Virginia were brick-built, whereas in other places wood was the material of choice. Significantly too, early Episcopal churches often have a grander design than buildings of other denominations (i.e., they were larger, had thicker walls, were erected from bricks, and often had a tower), as emphasis was placed on providing an environment respectful to Prayer Book worship and church activities.

West Virginia's Church architecture is distinct, partly due to the influence of geography on the developing cultures in the area. While many of the state's settlers were Scots, Germans, Welsh, Irish, and Dutch, and thus came from different religious denominations, the role of the Appalachian Mountains played a central role in the cultural development of the state. For example, east of the mountains, where the land is flatter, the Episcopal Church dominated. Those in the rugged west of the state included Presbyterians, Methodists, and Baptists. The people in the east were generally wealthier than those in the west, and so their churches were often larger and brick-built. In the industrial east brick construction was commonplace for a variety of building types (including homes). In the west, with its large forested areas, wood construction was more practical and affordable. The state's geography thus gives West Virginia its own characteristic building types. For example, during the 1850s a large number of covered bridges were constructed over the inland rivers. Many of these bridges no longer exist, but visitors can still visit the Philippi (1852) and Barrackville (1853) covered bridges (by Lemuel and Eli Chenoweth), as well as the covered bridges at Carrollton (1855–1856, by Emmett and Daniel O'Brien). Some of these structures are 500 feet or so in length.

Public Buildings in the Mid-Atlantic, Early to Present

Buffalo

Cities like Buffalo, located close to the U.S.-Canada border, house a number of public edifices of note that contribute to the mid-Atlantic region's architectural identity. Buffalo has a variety of old and new industrial buildings, churches and cathedrals, low-rise and high-rise edifices. Cities such as Buffalo have been architecturally shaped by local economic contexts, booming and expressing themselves architecturally in dramatic fashion when the local economy was in good shape, yet building much less, and on a smaller scale, in times of economic depression when corporate downsizing often meant the loss of many jobs. Buffalo's major contribution to the region's design character is the City Hall scheme, which pays homage to the indigenous peoples of the region. At 115 meters high, the City Hall is a large building, but its impact on the eye results not just from its size, but also from its impressive Art Deco style, a 1930s adaptation of commercial skyscraper design to the housing of government offices.

The structure is covered in rich detailing that illustrates the local history of the settlement, particularly that of the Iroquois Indian people who lived in the area prior to urbanization by Europeans; transport (the development of the Erie Canal); foreign relations (U.S.-Canada); and the industrial endeavors of the local citizens. The detailing both inside and outside the edifice adds to the monumental character for the onlooking eye. For example, upon entering the building the visitor notices the richly decorated lobbies and corridor spaces, and the piers that terminate in large sculptured figures. The exterior of the building is also adorned with sculpture, some in classical (Greek and Roman) form with mythical figures symbolizing the past and present spirit of the citizens and city, some designed in the style of local indigenous tribes' motifs, not only to beautify the structure but also to highlight the significance of Native American history to the area.

The effect of the completion of the City Hall was immense in Buffalo and inspired further construction of Art Deco styled buildings in the immediate vicinity. Thus the City Hall must be viewed as the anchor for a substantial civic design project in the center of the city. By the mid-1930s the eastern side of Niagara Square had been filled with federal and state buildings, in so doing establishing a monumental group of governmental buildings, an idea first suggested at the start of the previous decade. Like so many urban design projects in America and elsewhere, planned projects become real only after a prominent public structure has been perceived as successful to the city leaders and citizens, thus inspiring subsequent architectural development in the vicinity.

The mid-Atlantic region has sometimes been a test-bed in the deliberate revival of design styles among public buildings. For example, the design and construction of the Buffalo Psychiatric Center (1870–1896) by Stanford White and H.H. Richardson has been widely recognized as Richardson's first major example of reviving the Romanesque in America. Richardson's further use of the style was fundamental to developing the architectural character of the city at the end of the nineteenth century.

New Jersey

Once the third largest port in the New World, the city of Burlington, New Jersey, has architecture that reflects its past significance. As the first known settlement in New Jersey (dating from 1624), Burlington has a long heritage. Some forty historical monuments remain within its boundaries today, including the building of the oldest fire company (1795), the county's oldest residence (1685), the state's oldest library (1758), and the Episcopal Church (1703). The state capital, Trenton, which was established by Quakers from England, is also full of architectural wonder and historical delight. As an important place in the American Revolution, the city saw much fighting. After passing a charter in 1792, the settlement established a local government who did much in the following century to ensure the continued development of the city. The growing political aspirations of the corporation were also reflected architecturally in its first City Hall, erected in 1837 in a simple late Georgian style when the population was about 5,000. A second, larger City Hall in a Baroque style typically seen in Europe and America at the turn of the twentieth century was subsequently built. Other places in New Jersey also built new buildings to cope with the increasing demands of public administration. One good example is the 1881 City Hall in Hoboken, which demonstrated the town's growth as a center of industry and transportation. Designed by Francis Himpler in the Second Empire style, the structure is architecturally significant for its huge front with classical detailing, typical of civic architecture in the late nineteenth century. The City Hall was enlarged in 1911. Two wings at the front and a prison unit at the rear were added, and the roof was converted into a mansard (after the French designer François Mansart) style. Lewis Broome's City Hall (1894–1896) in Jersey City is also a fine example of a late-nineteenth-century public building. In addition, the Hudson County Courthouse in Jersey City show's the willingness of New Jersey administrations to erect large public buildings in a Greek form. Erected in 1910, this granite edifice by Hugh Roberts was composed in a classical manner with Corinthian columns, a rusticated ground-floor level, and a cupola.

New York City

One of the first and most prominent of New York's public buildings was the Federal Hall National Memorial, also known as the Custom House, designed by Itheil Town and Alexander Davis, who formed one of America's earliest and most influential architectural partnerships (1829–1835). Erected from 1833 to 1844 this Parthenon-inspired, Greek revival–style structure was important in extending the appeal of European classical styles in not just the region but the nation. Sitting on a raised site, the Custom House stands as a formidable piece of design. The history of the Custom House has been covered in detail by Willensky and White in the *AIA Guide to New York City*; in many respects its story reflects not just of the history of New York or the mid-Atlantic region but also that of the nation itself, as George Washington was sworn in as the first U.S. president on the Federal Hall's balcony.

The use of classical architecture in New York, and elsewhere in America, continued throughout the nineteenth century and into the start of the twentieth century in part due to the influence of the City Beautiful Movement, which was created by designers, architects, and landscapers inspired by classical forms and the ordered, clean environment of the 1893 Columbian World's Fair in Chicago (plan by Daniel Burnham). Public buildings in particular erected at that time used classical styles. For example, the New York Public Library (1897–1911, by Carrere and Hastings) used a Beaux-Arts style, and two structures of an entirely new building type, the rail station, also used classical idioms. New York was to be blessed by two of the most finely designed railway buildings in America, the monumental city gates known as Pennsylvania Station (1902–1911), a product of Charles McKim, one of America's foremost designers, and Grand Central Station (1903–1911 by Reed and Stem).

New York City's Grand Central Station (1903–1911, by Reed and Stem) remains one of America's most finely designed and culturally revered railway buildings. Courtesy Library of Congress.

Pennsylvania

Philadelphia's architecture is as diverse as the city's past. The city has been significant at times in the adoption of national styles; for example, it helped establish the Greek revival style in the early nineteenth century. In terms of political importance, no city, with the exception of Washington, D.C., can rival Philadelphia, and while the doctrine of democracy is seen to radiate from Washington, D.C., it really began in Philadelphia, for the city is the birthplace of the political system in America. Independence Hall, erected (from 1732) in a Georgian style (essentially an English style, although its use for this building must have helped people increasingly see it as an American style too), stands as a symbol of a nation coming forth. Designed by Andrew Hamilton and Edmund Wooley, the edifice must be viewed as one of the birthplaces of the American nation. Situated near Independence Hall are more public buildings that are visually impressive to the eye but that were designed in context, that is, in the same style as earlier buildings nearby, most notably the Old City Hall (1790–1791, by David Evans), designed in a Georgian style; Congress Hall (1787–1789); one of America's oldest banks, the United States Bank (1795–1797, by Samuel Blodgett and James Windrim); and one of the nation's mints. Further examples of Georgian style in Philadelphia include Carpenters' Hall (1770–1774 by Robert Smith), Owen Biddle's 1804 Quaker Meeting House, the Powel House (1765–1766), and the President's House (from the 1760s). By the early 1800s, though, this style was being replaced by the Greek-revival form, used for the Merchant's Exchange (1832–1834, William Strickland), for instance, which helped to popularize the style regionally.

Washington, D.C.

The history of public building in Washington, D.C., is central to its growth, for it helped instill public confidence in land investment at numerous times when general development in the city was slow. One of the most significant of the city's edifices is the Capitol. A massive structure that was erected between 1793 and 1868. Assembled in a tasteful neoclassical form using the Corinthian order, thus invoking visions of historic democratic Greece, the Capitol was constructed using a system of stone-bearing masonry, on top of which is placed the huge dome that was designed by Thomas Walter between 1851 and 1863. Sitting on the top of the dome (287 feet high, 135 feet wide) is a large bronze statue, *Freedom*, by Walter. The centers of the main elevation, that is, the principal facade of the building, and the east and west side walls of the Capitol are covered by huge porticos behind which are placed the entrance doorways. Steps lead from the ground to the entrances due to the building being raised above ground level. Decoration is simple but elegant on the walls of the Capitol, with rustication used on the lower ground floor and sculpting being employed to create friezes within the pediments of the porticos. A sculpture by Luigi Persico occupies the east central pediment of the Capitol; positioned directly under the dome, it shows the figure of America together with Justice and Hope standing at the altar of Liberty.

One of the oldest federal buildings in Washington, D.C., is the United States Treasury Department building, another classically (Greek) formed structure. The building was commissioned in 1836 and was originally designed by Robert Mills,

The Capitol, erected between 1793 and 1868, symbolizes many aspects central to the evolution of modern America. In a prominent position, atop its 287-foot dome, is Thomas Walter's bronze statue, *Freedom*. Courtesy of the Washington, D.C., Convention and Tourism Corporation.

architect of the the Washington Monument and the city Patent Office Building. Erected beginning 1836 on a site originally reserved for a national church or pantheon for national heroes in L'Enfant's city plan, the Patent Office stands as one of the country's finest Greek revival–style edifices and was important in influencing the use of Greek forms for both public and private buildings in the following years. Other buildings in Washington, D.C., with a similar design include St. Elizabeth's Hospital by Thomas Walter (opened 1855), John Russell Pope's classically formed Temple of the Scottish Rite (1910), and the Corinthian Supreme Court building of 1935 (Cass Gilbert, 1859–1934), which is one of interwar America's largest public edifices. Other styles abound as well. These include, by way of example, the deconstructionist American Institute of Architects Headquarters (1973, by the architectural group TAC), the Hirshhorn Museum (1974, by Gordon Bunshaft), I. M. Pei's stylistically challenging National Gallery East Wing (1974–1978), and Maya Lin's stone Vietnam War Memorial (1982), to name a few. A good starting point for a study of the city's architecture is the American Institute of Architects' *Guide to the Architecture of Washington D.C.*

West Virginia

In an environment, rural and urban, as diverse as that of the mid-Atlantic region, and influenced by so many different contexts in its development, it is important to examine the form of both domestic and public buildings. As discussed in the previous section, variations in design occurred throughout the developing region after the first colonists arrived. Charlestown, for instance, has buildings that are more Scottish and Palladian in style, in contrast to the English Gothic found in cities farther north.

It was noted earlier that West Virginia has its own distinct character within the larger regional spirit. Charlestown, the state capital, highlights this difference. Numerous buildings in Charlestown date from circa 1770, a time when the settlement was economically flourishing as a place of industry and commerce. Buildings from this time include the Museum (1773), one of the oldest in the country, the Old Exchange and Provost Dungeon (1771), and the Heyward-Washington House (1772). Charlestown not only had Georgian-style buildings but also others that showed the influence of Italian Renaissance designer Andrea Palladio (1508–1580) and Scottish architect Robert Adam (1728–1792), designs used by the very affluent (even by regional standards) to establish their own style in the region. Adam's influence can be seen in the Nathaniel Russell House. Later buildings in the town however tended to follow the regional and national pattern, that is, searching for a suitable general style for public edifices that tended prior to the mid-1800s to be largely Greek revival in nature.

Sports Stadiums

Arriving immigrants brought with them sports and games from Europe and elsewhere, and as the population grew so did the need for sports structures in which to hold major sports events. While some sports have a European origin, others are

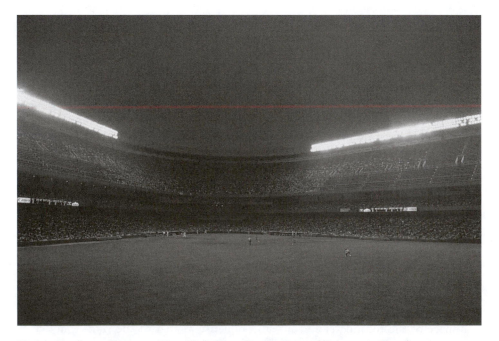

Yankee Stadium. Courtesy New York State Department of Economic Development.

distinctly American and have contributed to forging the American spirit. When thinking of city architecture, sports stadiums and arenas comprise a significant, if sometimes ignored, building type. For fans of baseball, New York's Yankee Stadium in the Bronx (opened 1923) and Shea Stadium (opened 1964), the home of the New York Mets, in the Flushing Meadows district, stand out as particularly good examples, although today most cities in the mid-Atlantic region have major sporting facilities similar to these. As with many other aspects of cultural life in the region, New York takes a leading position. Within the Flushing Meadows district is the world's largest tennis stadium, Arthur Ashe Stadium, which is part of a huge tennis complex used for the U.S. Open Championship each year. Fans of American football in the city can spend their time at Giants Stadium. The stadium was built in 1976 and was used for the 1994 World Cup soccer championships. Not all sports facilities are outdoors, and for any sports fan a visit to Madison Square Garden (opened 1968) in the midtown area of Manhattan is a must. With 20,000 seats, fans can flock to watch the New York Knicks basketball team or see other sports like ice hockey. Indoor arenas have also been erected throughout the region and these buildings frequently host music events that contribute to the region's cultural vibrancy.

The Beginnings of Modernism

Although some classically inspired public building continued, by the 1920s and 1930s, the seeds of modernism were starting to grow in the region. High-rise buildings in particular appeared in the Mid-Atlantic's larger cities; it was not until the 1950s that high-rise building was used for housing, having been used primarily for office buildings up to that time. Today, many of the region's office buildings are known throughout the world, as are its museums, none more so than Frank Lloyd Wright's 1959 building for the Guggenheim Foundation in New York.

Frank Lloyd Wright

Located on a site at Fifth Avenue between Eighty-eighth and Eighty-ninth Streets, the Guggenheim sits on its urban site in majestic fashion. Described as

[Wright's] great swansong, the Solomon R. Guggenheim Museum of New York, is a gift of pure architecture—or rather of sculpture. It is a continuous spatial helix, a circular ramp that expands as it coils vertiginously around an unobstructed well of space capped by a flat-ribbed glass dome.[1]

Such was the success of the design of the building that critics have said that it overpowers the art inside. For an architect there maybe can be no better criticism! But it is true that Wright's building, with its synchronization of shapes—circles, ovals, squares, arcs, triangles—puts the designer's personal imprint on modernist architecture with its purely rigid forms. Wright had in fact rewritten modernism in his building. In New York the rectilinear grid plan of Manhattan had also been broken by the soft, curving facade of the museum. Inside, the curving, almost endless space of the rotunda presented visitors with a unique platform to view modern art. Guggenheim's wishes had been fulfilled. With his design, Frank Lloyd

Frank Lloyd Wright's design of the Guggenheim Museum earned him a leading position in the architectural world. Photograph by David Heald. © The Solomon R. Guggenheim Foundation, New York.

Wright had earned a position of immortality in architectural circles, a response to the excitement and reaction the building creates in those who see and visit it. His other buildings in the region include the expressionist modern classic, Fallingwater House (from 1934 to 1948) originally designed as a residence for the Edgar Kaufmann family, but now open to the public at Mill Run, Pennsylvania. With its sharp horizontal planes and organic design into a waterfall and rock ledges, Fallingwater also earned Wright international fame.

Other Modernist Architects

The modern style of the Guggenheim stimulated further modernist architecture in New York City, the state of New York, and the mid-Atlantic region. One particularly noted modernist architect in the region was Louis I. Kahn (1901–1974), who often designed in a style similar to Wright's. Prominent works in the Mid-Atlantic by Kahn include the First Unitarian Church in Rochester, New York (1959–1967), the Bath House in Trenton, New Jersey (1954–1959), and the Norman Fisher House (1960), Esherick House (1967–1972), and Erdman Hall Dormitories (1960–1965), all in Pennsylvania. Noted modern architect I. M. Pei (b. 1917), mentioned earlier, designed the Javits Convention Center (1979–1986) in New York City, the Everson Museum of Art (1968) in Syracuse, and the Johnson Museum of Art (1973) in Ithaca, all in New York State. Elsewhere in the region, in Baltimore, Maryland, for instance, Pei designed the World Trade Center. Another well-known contemporary architect is Frank Gehry, who has also worked in Maryland. Gehry's work can be seen in a new town called Columbia, a settlement of about 90,000 people, where he designed the Rouse Company in 1974. Modernism pioneers Frank Lloyd Wright and Ludwig Mies van der Rohe (1886–1969) have buildings in the state as well. Wright designed two houses in Maryland, the Joseph Euchtman House (1939) in Baltimore and the R. L. Wright House (1953) in Bethesda. Mies van der Rohe, famous for his high-rise apartment building designs, designed the Charles Center, part of Baltimore's attempt to architecturally drag itself out of the industrial depression that had blighted the city and its economy on and off since the 1930s. Other notable architectural pieces in the state are the Salisbury School (1972–1977) by Hardy-Holzman-Pfieffer at Salisbury and the Zamioski House (1893) by Hugh Newell Jackson at the Eastern Shore.

New Jersey, a highly industrial, urbanized state, has many examples of modern design, which was used as part of the state's modernizing process, often at the cost of removing historic buildings. In the twentieth century much of the state's rural and urban environment was radically transformed and much modern building took place. Modern twentieth-century buildings of note include Louis I. Kahn's Bath House in Trenton (1954–1959), Richard Rodger's Pennsylvania Technology Center in Princeton (1982), and the Gordon Wu Hall by Robert Venturi in Princeton (1983). Significantly, local Native American tribes have also contributed to the modern townscape and economy, having developed hotels and casinos on their land after 1978 when gaming was legalized in New Jersey. Profits from the casinos are often used by the Native American groups for community betterment and to establish new schools, colleges, community centers, and businesses.

Airports

Modern life, not just modern architecture, has influenced mid-Atlantic living. Air travel as well as rail travel has affected the appearance of towns and cities. Upon any journey to a large airport in the region, such as John Fitzgerald Kennedy (JFK) Airport, one may be taken aback by the variety and size of the airport buildings. Terminal Two (opened 1962) by Finnish American architect Eero Saarinen (1910–1961) stands out architecturally not just in New York but also in the region and beyond. Designed with soaring concrete vaults which resemble the wings of a bird in flight, this building highlights Saarinen's ability as a modern master of architecture. With its huge open interior, all fittings were designed in context with each other so as to establish one large composition. Sylvia Hart Wright in the *Sourcebook of Contemporary North American Architecture* (1989) superbly described the terminal building as being

> surely one of the world's most dramatic airline terminals. Few straight lines here: approached head on, its curving contours uncannily suggest a bird in flight. Inside, the main lobby's soaring, swooping walls, its carefully modeled staircases, seating areas, and many other features are a blend of graceful sculptural forms selected to suggest the excitement of the trip.

High-Rise Offices and Apartments

By about 1900 the United States of America was not merely a nation but a superpower. Since gaining its independence from the British, America had been settled from east to west, its land had been crossed by rail lines, its industrial might had grown to previously unimaginable proportions, and its cities were growing to new scales. New wealth produced a demand for construction and thus new architectural forms. One of the ways this manifested itself in the Mid-Atlantic was through the introduction of a new vertical scale in urban settlements. Today one particular city, New York, and high-rise buildings (skyscrapers) are almost synonymous. Few places in the world can rival New York for tall buildings. Because New York has so many edifices of note, it is difficult to select just a few for detailed description. This section highlights a small sample of high-rise buildings of differing forms, erected in different periods, and some of the individuals who have made major contributions to the design of the city.

Office Buildings

While New York is famed for its tall structures, Chicago was the first city to build skyscrapers. One of the earliest and most cherished high-rises in New York is the Flat Iron Building, a commercial office tower designed in 1902 by Daniel Burnham, the architect and planner pivotal to the success of the 1893 Columbian World's Fair in Chicago. Located at the intersection of Broadway, Fifth Avenue, and Twenty-third Street, the Flat Iron, so called due to its shape on a thin triangular site, is considered the city's oldest remaining skyscraper, and stands at a height of 285 feet. Constructed with a steel frame, this building helped bring to New York and the mid-Atlantic region the idea of quickly constructing high-rise office buildings, and must be viewed within the context of the development of the skyscraper in America, such is its importance. The building helped pave the way for the later, and higher, structures that typify the skylines of New York and other large cities in the region today. The Flat Iron was followed by the Metropolitan Life Building (1907–1909 by Le Brun), the neo-Gothic Woolworth Building (1910–1913 by Cass Gilbert, 762 feet high), the Art Deco Chrysler Building (1928–1930, William Van Alen, 77 floors high), the Empire State Building (1931 by Shreve, Lamb, and Harmon, 1,252 feet high), Rockefeller Center (1930–1940), the United Nations Headquarters (1952 by Harrison), and the Seagram Building (1954–1958 by Frank Lloyd Wright and Philip Johnson); the list is seemingly endless.

Multistory office buildings dominate downtown and midtown Manhattan, although circumstances in recent years have raised many questions about their future. While few in New York deny the need for high-rise office buildings, due to a high demand for land and lack of space, the terrorist attacks of September 11, 2001, on the World Trade Center towers (designed by Minoru Yamasaki, 1970–1977) have left many doubts in the minds of New Yorkers regarding the city's past willingness to build structures of immense height. On the other hand, this creates a huge dilemma for New York: no other city in the world is as much defined by its high-rises as New York. But why is New York such a high-rise settlement? A number of answers can be given, including:

- Technical and industrial progress in America and elsewhere at the end of the nineteenth century, such as developments in understanding load-bearing (that is, construction in which walls and columns, for example, support the weight of ceilings, and stresses in structural systems), the use of the steel frame (pioneered by William Le Baron Jenney), and the introduction of the elevator have allowed for the erection of buildings of great height.
- Corporate attitudes influencing aesthetics. Large businesses wished to locate their offices or headquarters in big cities, and to be near the stock exchanges and large pools of labor.
- A practical need. Companies with their many departments needed large amounts of space, preferably within the same building in order to operate efficiently and for purposes of convenience. In Manhattan, where land is limited in supply and expensive to buy, the only way to solve this problem was, and still is, to build high.

- The high cost of land, and the fact that plots established in the colonial era were often small in New York, makes it extremely problematic now to plan and design wide buildings.
- Competition and prestige, influenced by available economic capital, which allows large companies to plan and build grandiose structures, which in turn enhances the company name.
- Changing aesthetics in the twentieth century including a trend toward increasing building heights for some building types.

While economics have played a major role in New York City's development of the high-rise, in effect the city is central to the culture of the high-rise, and the high-rise central to the culture of the city. For example, the history of the tallest buildings in the world centers upon New York, but high-rise buildings have been used in New York and other mid-Atlantic cities as not just for offices but also apartments. Centrally located apartment buildings provide a solution for people who want to live at the urban core and not in the often physically distant suburbs. With late twentieth- and early twenty-first-century cultural changes increasingly promoting an urban life, there has been a growth in apartment building for both the affluent and less well-off as originally envisaged by mod-

Forty-second Street skyline, New York City. New York State Department of Economic Development.

ern architectural pioneer Le Corbusier. With easy access to places of employment, transport nodes, and public amenities, central urban living has become increasingly popular in the mid-Atlantic region. In New York and elsewhere apartment buildings punctuate the skyline. Developments in modernist thought by designers such as Mies van der Rohe, Le Corbusier, Philip Johnson, and Walter Gropius helped constructors see the high-rise building as a means to provide "communities in the sky." Yet, notably, much standardization has resulted in apartment building design after Gropius's groundbreaking Lake Shore Drive project (1948–1951) in Chicago, although the modernist notion of "towers in parks," the idea of putting green space around buildings, did influence the city government of New York and its public housing program. Stylistically at least, because modernism was promoted by designers as an "international style," a globalized architectural form, often regional culture was given little consideration in the design process for offices and apartments in the mid-Atlantic region. Hence they tend to look the same.

High-Rise Apartments

Richard Plunz has highlighted high-rise apartment historical development within the mid-Atlantic region, particularly as a means for the rich to literally be above the problems of living at ground level (noise, crime, traffic, etc.). As noted before, technology and available capital made high structural building possible in the large industrial cities, and the problems of urban life contributed to the demand for apartments in these settlements. But as the cost of land increased due to the demand for development, coupled with transportation developments, many of the rich left the city for suburban districts and left behind a legacy of luxury apartments too expensive for the less wealthy in urban society. Many of these apartments, particularly in older urban districts, quickly became filled with working-class families who would share the property with other families in order to pay the rent. In such situations the quality of the buildings often deteriorates, speeding up the exit of wealthier people in the building who in turn are replaced by poorer tenants. Thus the social composition of the building alters. Such transitions are particularly common in times of economic hardship. Like other cities, New York has its own morphology of land use, social classes, and ethnic groups, with different districts having building types found in the homelands of the immigrants. Today the older districts of the city where many immigrant groups still reside are subject to urban renewal projects that take a variety of forms, including creating affordable housing opportunities for the less well-off in society, installing public art schemes and new commercial facilities, improving housing amenities and infrastructure, and establishing community and cultural centers within the neighborhoods that help reflect the needs and composition of the local population. Shopping malls have also been used as agents of urban renewal in some instances to stimulate local economic growth.

Residential Houses

While many of the mid-Atlantic states contribute to the regional vernacular design, it is important to note that in many instances they have been shaped by very local contexts which even today give them a distinct visual character. Delaware, by way of example, was first colonized by Swedes in the late 1630s. Upon arriving in America the Swedes quickly built a fort, not only to protect themselves in "New Sweden" (today called Wilmington), but also to protect their river trade and establish a communication link with other colonies in the mid-Atlantic region. By the end of the 1600s the Swedes had also built churches in their colony and houses elsewhere in the region (most noticeable by the steep overhanging roof design). At this point, the British had arrived in the area from England and British colonies in nearby states.

Just as the Swedes left an imprint on the architectural development of Delaware, so too did the British. Milton, for example, dates from 1672, and some of Delaware's finest colonial and Victorian houses are found in the small town. In keeping with the colonial style, houses were designed with wrap-around porches while nineteenth-century buildings followed developments in England and frequently used the Gothic form as inspiration, as their turrets and arched window shapes highlight. Such designs were far more elaborate than those of the early colonial period, when buildings such as the Holt House (1665) in Lewes were simply formed from wood, with a small number of windows and a pitched roof. However, significantly, any visitor traveling south through Delaware will be aware of the changes in the state's colonial architectural forms. Buildings in the north were symmetrically formed, simple in design, and followed the Georgian style. The chimney, for instance, was positioned at the end of the rooftop. In areas where the Dutch and Germans settled—and in Pennsylvania, where many early German colonists (Catholics) settled due to the lower cost of land—houses were designed with gabled rooflines and chimneys at the center. In southern Delaware houses were more federalist in form and more formal in appearance. Structures were built from red brick and not wood, chimneys and windows being symmetrically arranged to form a highly ordered front elevation. Annapolis, Maryland, also highlights the mid-Atlantic region's built diversity, and it is in the city that the architectural identity of Maryland first emerged (after 1694 when it became the state capital). Many British Baroque-influenced buildings remain and Georgian styles can also be seen, such as at Hammond-Harwood House (1774)—a recognized colonial masterpiece. Other well-designed edifices in Annapolis include those belonging to the Carroll family. Houses dating from 1768 in Mount Clare, the 1803 Homewood House and 1812 Mansion, are well worth a visit as well. Pennsylvania houses, like those in Maryland, were subject to an English design influence, particularly from the mid–nineteenth century. The north of Pennsylvania in particular is littered with homes of an English style, many in an English Gothic cottage style built for local oil and lumber entrepreneurs as monuments to their industrial success. In

The Hammond-Harwood House (1774), in Annapolis, Maryland, is a recognized colonial masterpiece and an excellent example of the Baroque and Georgian influences of the time. Courtesy Library of Congress.

the 1870s Pennsylvanians also took notice of the use of terracotta tiles and half-timbered and stucco walls being used by English architects in new manor houses for the very wealthy. It is from this period that English Queen Anne elements filter into the American vernacular, and fine examples can be seen in the north of the state, for example in Oil City.

As with Delaware, Maryland's location arguably influenced the development of its vernacular design. The south of Maryland has styles more in keeping with the southern states of America. One of the first public buildings, the 1676 State House at St. Mary's in southern Maryland, incorporated materials, principally brick and iron (for the frames of the casement windows), that were typical of the planter aristocracy houses of the South, and many houses from the 1700s incorporate southern American elements, including buildings in the colonial (Georgian) style in the east of Maryland. With their gardens outside and staircases inside, these homes are a marvel. Later versions of these homes, built of stone and with a Germanic design influence, such as the 1740 Hager House in Hagerstown, can be seen in the west of Maryland.

Whereas styles in the south of Maryland display an influence from the southern states of the country, to the north of Maryland styles are more similar to those found in the northern industrial states. As a consequence Maryland today has an architectural culture that is particular to the state. Known as "America in Miniature," Maryland is not only cosmopolitan in cultural terms. Significantly, these structures reflect the range of influences upon people coming into the state. For instance, the state had some of the earliest Catholic settlements in the eastern United States as many Catholics left England from the 1630s on to avoid persecution. Upon landing in Maryland they set about erecting a Catholic cathedral.

Delaware, particularly Kent County, has a large number of historic structures from the eighteenth and nineteenth centuries. The towns of Smyrna and Milford have a number of beautiful buildings in the Georgian style. Allee House (1753) in Smyrna, for example, is one of the state's best old farmhouses. State Street in Dover is full of Victorian-style houses, built for those who had profited from the local peach crops, and the Old State House (1792) has been restored to its original interior design with a rare geometrically formed stairwell. New Castle County in Delaware also has many architectural pieces worthy of mention. These include the Georgian-style Collins-Sharp House (1774), George Read II House (1801, also in a Georgian style that emerged as a development of the colonial design form), the brick Hales-Byrnes House (mid–eighteenth century), and the Wilson-Warner House (1769, in a Georgian style unique to Delaware). The Georgian style was especially popular in the region's economically flourishing areas where a new social system with a strong middle class emerged. This could be seen all over the eastern United States in fact, and was particularly evident in the southern mid-Atlantic region in the 1700s where the early colonial social structure greatly weakened with economic development. The middle classes emulated the upper classes, and their homes imitated the Georgian mansions the wealthy built, albeit on a smaller scale. These flourishing communities in turn erected churches, schools, colleges, and other public buildings that, like the houses, reflected the Georgian style.

New Jersey is especially rich in houses, churches, and industrial buildings dating from the early colonial years. The four corners of New Jersey are awash with historical buildings, including early nineteenth-century lighthouses along the coast and Llewellyn Park in Essex (home of Thomas Edison)—the first planned and landscaped suburb in America, which dates from the 1850s. Another fine piece of nineteenth-century landscape architecture and community planning is found at Sudbrook Park near Baltimore. Designed in 1889 by Frederick Law Olmsted, the founder of landscape architecture and planning movements in America, Sudbrook Park demonstrates how his design principles could translate socially and not just aesthetically into community planning. Sudbrook Park was a wealthy middle- and upper-class community, and architecturally the buildings reflect the social status of the inhabitants. However, their vernacular forms, with their Queen Anne–style shingles and colonial revival styles, were designed in context with each other to provide a visually harmonious built environment. The homogenous character of the environment thus enhances Sudbrook Park's importance and possibly provided a model to City Beautiful Movement designers at the end of the 1800s and the start of the 1900s for how to create visual and social order within the perceived environmental chaos of industrial American cities. In the later twentieth century these nineteenth-century suburbs were also inspirational in the development of mass suburbanization in America. Other developments in the Mid-Atlantic should not be ignored in the national history of housing, such as Stein and Wright's Sunnyside Gardens (New York, 1924) and their scheme for Radburn, New Jersey, on which modern American suburbanization is based. The community of Greenbelt, Maryland, with its unique physical organization, is also worthy of mention. In cultural terms, these schemes not only added to the urban flavor of the region, they also acted as models for municipal urban development projects across the nation.

Prevalent Styles in Residential Design

The individual states within the mid-Atlantic region developed their own distinct vernacular styles of home design. A number of styles were prevalent before c. 1900, including the colonial, Georgian, federal (used only in the south), Jacobean revival, classical/Greek revival, Gothic revival, Italianate, and Romanesque styles. The colonial style, sometimes referred to as Dutch colonial, was employed as late as 1800, particularly in coastal regions of the Mid-Atlantic; it is easy to identify due to its steeply sloping gambrel roof, similar to a French mansard rooftop. The style was used by Dutch and English settlers and their descendants, and underwent a revival in the twentieth century, often with the addition of bay windows, which were not found in original colonial buildings. The size of the Dutch colonial buildings varied greatly, some having two floors and others three, and chimneys have been found in a variety of positions along the rooftop. Building materials also varied from place to place, as brick, wood, and stone, and variations thereof, were employed as and when necessary. One of the few remaining buildings from the early colonial period is the Old Dutch House, New Castle, Delaware.

Replacing the colonial style was the Georgian style, used for both public buildings and houses. The roofs of Georgian-style buildings were not as steep, and the chimneys were larger. Also characteristic were the use of a cornice, the more common use of brick as a building material, and different window shapes (straight, multipaned, sometimes with wood surround) being positioned symmetrically along the main elevations, often in accord with the central axis of the building (usually marked by an entrance doorway). Some of the design features of Georgian architecture were also evident in the federal style, a simple form used only in the southernmost parts of the Mid-Atlantic (c. 1830s) where the influence of southern regional cultures was more pronounced. In more northern regions the Adam style was employed at this time. Examples of buildings in the Adam style, which was very British in form, can be seen in Franklin, Pennsylvania. Features include a regular mass and plan to the building, symmetrically arranged windows around the main doorway (at the center of the ground floor, next to which are stone columns and above which is an elliptical fan), and the use of sash windows (with six small panes in each sash—a product of technological developments at that time).

The use of Greek revival styles has already been highlighted during the descriptions of public buildings. Greek revival houses can be identified by their simple mass, rectangular plan, shallow roofs, and pediment at the front of the building. Entablatures usually consisted of a cornice, frieze, and architrave and were frequently continued around all four elevations just below the roof level. Houses in this style are particularly rectilinear and angular in form. The style, however, varied somewhat between its first use at the very end of the eighteenth century and its decline in popularity by the mid–nineteenth century, a consequence of wider societal influences. For instance, the pure early Greek revival form was widely adopted in the early 1800s, when political and military tension between England and America was high, as the style was not perceived to be associated with England; styles perceived as "English," on the other hand, were rejected. However, as the ill-feeling toward the English dissipated, Greco-Roman style became popular, reflecting a revival in English architectural fashion.

Just as the developments in England influenced mid-Atlantic house design and the adoption of Greco-Roman styles, the English influence encouraged the widespread use of the Gothic. Some of the first buildings in America in the Gothic revival form appeared in Pennsylvania by about 1830, the products of Alexander Jackson Davis, who based his designs on the English cottage vernacular. The use of the Gothic brought a new ornate sensitivity to mid-Atlantic architecture. The early Gothic homes, built for affluent members of society, were often expensive to build due to their elaborate detailing, for example, their gabling and eaving. Toward the end of the nineteenth century an offshoot of the Gothic emerged, known widely as the Romanesque. This style was used sparingly in house design and public design. It was used, for instance, in symmetrical and asymmetrical compositions, and it could be used with vertical elements. This style is most noticeable by its window shape (round arched) and rusticated stonework, and was partly stylistically developed in the region by H. H. Richardson, a pioneer of true American architectural forms, whose public work was a major influence on the City Beautiful Movement by the end of the 1800s.

From the 1840s to the 1880s Italian influences were popular in the house design of the wealthy. For those wishing to avoid the rigidity of the Greek revival, or the heavy decoration of the Gothic, the Italianate offered a perfect solution. Particularly common in New York State, these houses were often painted gray, blue-gray, or pale yellow-green, were designed with double door entrances, large overhanging eaves, wide cornices, round headed windows (with curved wooden or brick arches), and cast-iron ornamental brackets on the supports of the porch, and were sometimes formed with a front gable, towers, cupolas, and bay windows. A mid-Atlantic Italianate house is easy to identify not only for the reasons given above but due to its shape—a square form.

Rural Buildings: Barns and Log Houses

In the Mid-Atlantic, famous for its industrial heartland and large urban settlements, it is easy to overlook rural influences on regional vernacular designs such as barns and farmhouses. While it is not possible to describe every type of rural building found in the region, this section provides some insight into its architecture and the distinctive regional culture that it expresses. Barn buildings, multipurpose structures used for storing foodstuffs and machinery and for processing or sheltering animals, are a particularly significant aspect of the mid-Atlantic region's unique architectural identity.

When European immigrants arrived in America they brought with them their agricultural traditions, which included not only particular farming methods but also individual ways of rural living. While the modern barn is greatly standardized in form, historically this was not the case in the Mid-Atlantic, as each immigrant group brought the barn-building traditions of their mother country upon settling in the New World. The Swedes, Italians, Dutch, Germans, Swiss, Ukrainians, and English all drew upon their European rural traditions, including barn design. Research by Thomas Hubka at the University of Wisconsin–Milwaukee has shown that barn design is an amalgam of a number of factors associated with immigration: the number of settlers, their nationality, their date of arrival in America, and their geographical location. As a consequence of these factors, local, regional, and national differences were common in colonial and postcolonial America. Significantly, many traditional European barn types, particularly the English and German ones, acted as models for immigrant groups who collectively helped to make a new barn tradition: the American barn. As the colonial process continued in the eighteenth and nineteenth centuries, slowly the English and German traditions not only merged but were embraced by the wider rural society to form the modern American tradition: that can be seen across the country today. Nowhere is this new American tradition more evident than in the mid-Atlantic region. The archetypal American barn, known as a gambrel barn and is identifiable by its double-sloping roof, is a development of medieval European (English and German) barn buildings.

A number of reasons have been suggested as to why the largely English barn form and German barn construction traditions dominated in the mid-Atlantic region. The English barn, a grain threshing/hay storing barn, was designed with a width of three bays, a depth of one bay, and with a central drive, erected from heavy timbers with mortise and tenon construction. Reasons for its dominance are the larger size of the English population in America and the continuation of English social and political customs after the founding period of the colony. However, in parts of the mid-Atlantic region, such as southwestern Pennsylvania, where Germanic peoples settled, another barn tradition emerged. Larger than the English version and more structurally advanced, the German barn differed due to the different system of farming employed by the Germanic peoples. For example, while the English barn was small and had other small buildings positioned nearby (outbuildings, each used for the different operations of a farm), the Germans had

Side elevation of a German-style barn in Chester County, Pennsylvania. Courtesy Library of Congress.

no outbuildings, as their system of farming was more centralized and thus all farm operations could take place under one roof. Why did the German barn become popular? In short, it was a highly practical design. Nevertheless, diverse barn designs persisted as different immigrant groups, such as the Dutch and Italians, continued their own farming traditions.

Farms consist not only of a collection of barns and other utility buildings but also the farmhouse where the family resides. Historic mid-Atlantic farmhouses may incorrectly be seen as wood frame structures built from local materials which evolved into Georgian-style buildings based on the English country house. Particularly influential to the emerging Atlantic farmhouse vernacular were the Dutch, who designed with symmetrical front elevations and sloping (gambrel) roofs, also used in barn design. As with the development of barns, ethnic affiliations influenced farmhouse design and construction methods, particularly in the early colonial period, but given the colonial setting it was often necessary to adapt to the new way of life and surroundings. Distinct architectural traditions became shared, ultimately weakening previously distinct ethnic associations in rural building during the eighteenth and nineteenth centuries. This was particularly true, for example, in colonial Virginia for the rural house made of wood. However, some ethnic traditions persisted more strongly in the rural context. Germans often lived in clusters, which allowed them to maintain their culture and identity, architecturally expressed, for example, by their distinct floor plan and methods of construction.

Terry Jordan in *American Log Buildings: An Old World Heritage* (1985) argues that cultural geography also influenced the success of some ethnic groups in maintaining their vernacular designs. With regard to the Swedes, among the first European settlers of the mid-Atlantic region, their designs persisted in the region due to the success of their construction and settlement methods, coupled with their possession of cultural preadaptation in the form of log building techniques well suited to the American frontiers. For these reasons Jordan notes the longevity of Swedes' log-cabin design in the region, and their successful adaptation of building traditions brought by German, Scots-Irish, and British settlers. The Germans in particular quickly adapted to the new environment by drawing upon not only their own vernacular designs but also those of other immigrant groups. Yet even among German colonists differences in design resulted in the seventeenth century—the result not of different regional cultures in Germany, as they all came from the same parts of the country (the center and south)—but due to differences in wealth between the Germans in urban Virginia and rural Virginia and Pennsylvania. The poorer Pennsylvanians and Virginians were unable to afford brick chimneys, for example, while the wealthier Germans placed their chimneys toward the center of the floor plan, as in the central-southern German houses called *stubes*. By about 1800, though, this building plan altered due to increased wealth, as the traditional German house was abandoned for a new style with a central passage (in an *I*-shaped plan). Visually the "new" buildings were Georgian in style, and this growth in Georgian homes provides strong evidence of the economic and cultural growth of the region. This development lessened the influence of the mother country in the push to attain the status of an independent nation.

Buildings of War and Defense

The American Civil War left an indelible mark on the mid-Atlantic region not only in cultural terms but also architecturally, in terms of buildings foregrounding the need for fortification. In New Jersey, British barracks dating from the 1750s at Trenton still remain, and in Delaware, Fort Delaware, located on marshy Pea Patch Island close to Delaware City, and now part of a state park, can be visited. Originally dating from about 1819, when it was constructed to help repel the British, the present fortification dates from 1848 to 1859 and is shaped in a pentagon form covering about six acres of land. The fort was not always used as a military stronghold. During the Civil War it served as a prison to accommodate captured or surrendered Confederate troops. Its remote location was considered ideal to deter escape attempts yet close enough to southern naval bases to

The Pentagon

A more modern military building worthy of special attention is the Pentagon, home of the U.S. Department of Defense, constructed in a five-sided form (five concentric rings named A, B, C, D, and E) with reinforced outer concrete walls. While a visitor to Washington, D.C., may be amazed at the scale of L'Enfant's plan and the enormity of the Washington Monument, the Capitol, and the Supreme Court, these are tiny in comparison to the thirty-four acres covered by the Pentagon—the world's largest office building (erected 1941–1943). Despite its huge size the building was erected in only sixteen months due to America's involvement in World War II, during which there was a practical need to bring together many government departments under the same roof as quickly as possible. Nearly 13,000 people worked on constructing the building. Today, more than 23,000 employees, both military and civilian, work there.

facilitate the handing over of prisoners when necessary, and its 32-foot-high walls strong enough to withstand any potential attack. At its peak as a prison, 12,000 prisoners were held at the fort—a population almost equal to that of the state's largest city at the time, Wilmington.

Pennsylvania, in part because of its strategic location on the Delaware River, also has its fair share of military buildings. One somewhat unusual military structure is Fort Mott in Pennsville, Salem County. Erected originally in 1872 and reconstructed in the 1890s due to the threat of a war with Spain, the fort was built to protect the mouth of the Delaware and thus the city and industries inland to the north. The gun towers date from 1902. Consisting of a central column of concrete and riveted steel supports, its top section provides an observation tower with 360 degree views of the surroundings. The stairs to the observation point wind around the steel structure. It is one of only a handful of such buildings from the era that remain in New Jersey. An old lighthouse also survives close to the port.

CONCLUSION

Despite their relatively small size, each mid-Atlantic state has developed its own distinct sense of history and culture, which has in turn shaped its architecture. The geography of the region has also influenced life within it, and natural features such as the Appalachian Mountains and the Allegheny Front have helped shape the design styles developed in states such as West Virginia and Pennsylvania. In New Jersey and New York as well, geography has influenced the production of a varied range of architectural characters and styles. It is easy to suppose that the architecture of the Mid-Atlantic must be dominated by developments in the largest and most cosmopolitan cities in the region—New York and Washington, D.C. Such an assumption, though, is erroneous, as the region has a myriad of architectural forms, arguably, in a historical context at least, as a design response to the unfolding and interaction of cultural processes in an ethnically diverse area. Groups of immigrants brought to the region their own vernacular forms and building traditions, and once settled they formed distinct social groups within which networks formed. Such interaction allowed stylistic forms to evolve and for the material culture of the group to be expressed and displayed. In time this helped establish a regional system of culture, identity, and exchange along with competing socioeconomic interests which were to ultimately be deployed across the entire country. In architectural terms these individual forces help shape the emerging national styles.

Much of the architectural development within the Mid-Atlantic has influenced the development of architecture nationally. Many building types were first developed in the region, a notable example being the railroad station, and the region too has been significant in developing the high-rise office building that so dominates the skyline of modern American cities. Many of the world's most famous modern architects have worked in the region, including Frank Lloyd Wright, I. M. Pei, Louis I. Kahn, Eero Saarinen, Richard Rogers, Frank Gehry, Alvar Aalto, and Daniel Burnham; the list is almost endless. Thus, for both its past and present activity mid-Atlantic architecture has national importance.

RESOURCE GUIDE

Printed Sources

Gallery, John Andrew. *Philadelphia Architecture: A Guide to the City*. Boston: MIT Press, 1984.

Gray, Christopher. *New York Streetscapes: Tales of Manhattan's Significant Buildings and Landmarks*. New York: Harry N. Abrams, 2003.

Hart Wright, Sylvia. *The Sourcebook of Contemporary North American Architecture: From Postwar to Postmodern*. New York: Van Nostrand Reinhold, 1989.

Herman, Bernard. *Architecture and Rural Life in Central Delaware, 1700–1900*. Knoxville: University of Tennessee Press, 1987.

Jordan, Terry. *American Log Buildings: An Old World Heritage*. Chapel Hill: University of North Carolina Press, 1985.

Knepper, Cathy. *Greenbelt, Maryland*. Baltimore: Johns Hopkins University Press, 2001.

Kostof, Spiro. *A History of Architecture: Settings and Rituals*. New York: Oxford University Press, 1985.

Lanier, Gabrielle, and Bernard Herman. *Everyday Architecture of the Mid-Atlantic: Looking at Buildings and Landscapes*. Baltimore: Johns Hopkins University Press, 1997.

Mitchell, Alexander. *Washington Then and Now*. Thunder Bay: Thunder Bay Press, 2000.

Mullins, Lisa. *Colonial Architecture of the Mid-Atlantic*. Harrisburg: National Historic Society, 1987.

Nabokov, Peter, and Robert Easton. *Native American Architecture*. Oxford: Oxford University Press, 1988.

Plunz, Richard. *A History of Housing in New York*. New York: Columbia University Press, 1992.

Web Sites

The Architect of the Capitol
http://www.aoc.gov/

Architecture for Kids: A History of American Houses
http://www.takus.com/architecture/

The Architecture of Washington, D.C.
http://www.geocities.com/CapitolHill/2233/

Craftsman Perspective, Mid-Atlantic Arts and Crafts Architecture
http://www.craftsmanperspective.com/docs/midatlantic.html

Frank Lloyd Wright
http://www.franklloydwright.org

The Great Buildings Collection
http://www.greatbuildings.com
Provides information on a thousand buildings and hundreds of architects.

The New Jersey Churchscape
http://www.njchurchscape.com

Old Swedes Church
http://www.oldswedes.org/

University of Delaware Library, Historic Homes in the Mid-Atlantic and New England
http://www2.lib.udel.edu/usered/elunch/fall98/histhomes.htm

Special Collections/Architecture Libraries/Archives

New York Public Library
498 5th Avenue
New York, NY 10018
Phone: 212-930-0830
http://www.nypl.org

Please note that state chapters and regional offices of the American Institute of Architects contain some archive collections of work within the locality. Additionally, universities and college libraries contain local history sections that include some details of local architectural history and practices.

Paul J. Gutman Library
Philadelphia University
Schoolhouse Lane
Philadelphia, PA 19144
Phone: 215-951-2840
http://www.philau.edu/library/

Samuel Paley Library
Temple University
13th Street
Philadelphia, PA 19122
Phone: 215-204-8257

Videos/Films

New York: The Center of the World. Pt. #8. Dir. Ric Burns. Warner Home Video, 2003.

Festivals

Annual Annapolis by Candlelight
Historic Annapolis Foundation
18 Pinckney Street
Annapolis, MD 21401
http://www.annapolis.org

Organizations

Historic Annapolis Foundation
18 Pinckney Street
Annapolis, MD 21401
http://www.annapolis.org

Maryland Historical Trust
100 Community Place
Crownsville, MD 21032-2023
http://www.MarylandHistoricalTrust.net

Mid-Atlantic Center for the Arts
1048 Washington Street
P.O. Box 340
Cape May, NJ 08024
http://www.capemaymac.org

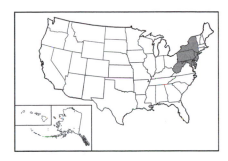

ART

Timothy Finnegan

The art produced within the mid-Atlantic region has been in a constant state of change and development. From ancient Native American cultures to the present, the Mid-Atlantic can be viewed as a heterogeneous intersection, where artists and their traditions are exposed to new cultures and new traditions, which bring with them new materials and ways of manipulating them. Coupled with fluctuating sources of patronage, artists will adapt over time to these changing social conditions within the region, producing artwork that informs us of their immediate life experiences within a specific community and nation.

Several consistent points of contact are evident when one looks at this region of the country across time. In addition to those forces that shape individual artists in the day-to-day production of their work, other guiding forces also govern art production for any given art period or movement: materials, patronage and cultural contact—each of which are inseparable and react together. These forces are not all equal in significance at every stage of artistic production. Some periods of art history in this region might be influenced more by the availability of materials, rather than an interaction with another culture. As more people come in contact with different cultures as a result of technological developments, the resources available to an artist will dramatically increase.

EARLY NATIVE ART PRODUCTION

Two of the oldest cultures that occupied part of the Mid-Atlantic were the Adena and Hopewell cultures. From approximately 1000 B.C.E. to 700 C.E. they inhabited much of the land from the Great Lakes region to the Gulf of Mexico, including West Virginia, Pennsylvania, and western New York. The Adena culture was the oldest, spanning the years between 1000 B.C.E. and 100 C.E., with the Hopewell achieving dominance between 100 B.C.E. and 600 C.E. The materials used to make art, which were found mainly at burial sites, reflect the function of trade between members of these cultures. Trade from one region to another facilitated the flow of raw materials used for artistic production.

The seminomadic lifestyle of these people was based around the seasonal availability of food. Planned travel, usually north-south, was organized to hunt migrating wildlife and gather local foodstuffs. This movement, sometimes via river routes or established walkways, kept them in contact with other nomadic tribes which increased the likelihood of trading materials from region to region. The art objects that have been found through archaeological excavation of burial sites around eastern Ohio, which took place from the early nineteenth to the twentieth century, were made of materials that originated in the Great Lakes region and in the Gulf of Mexico.

A Hopewell site in the Ross County-Scioto River valley in Ohio, called Mound City by archaeologists, contained many burial mounds. The Hopewell may have chosen this particular site for habitation and mound making as a result of its geological and biological diversity. The surrounding area had fertile soil, deposited from the flowing river, and abundant wildlife. This fertile area, rich in food and carving materials allowed their culture, and its art, to thrive.

Art materials found at Mound City included copper, mica, and carved pipestone. These raw materials were imported from various places within the established territory of the Hopewell. Although archaeologists know little about where the artists were turning these materials into art objects, the art, made of materials from distinct and distant areas, comments on their importance to the culture.

Copper had been mined in the Great Lakes region since 3000 B.C.E. and reached its high point in 1500 B.C.E. The copper trade between Native cultures of the Great Lakes region to the middle Atlantic region existed until the sixteenth century. Mica from the eastern Tennessee area was also traded throughout the region. The copper and mica found at the Hopewell site were formed into flat designs, commonly called ornaments, in shapes that might suggest vegetation and flower motifs. Since the copper and mica shapes were alike in design, having similar thicknesses and similar silhouettes, the difference in the nature of each material must have played a significant role in their use. The dense quality of the copper in contrast to the reflective sheets of mica, signify multiple meanings for a repeated symbol.

The pipestone, a hard stone native to the mound region, was carved into smoking pipes. The carving is thought to have been done by sharp flint stones, with abrasives then rubbed on the stone to create a smooth surface. In form, the Hopewell pipes were exclusively zoomorphic (in the form of animals), and as such they are referred to as effigy pipes. In some cases, the eyes of the animal were made of inlaid freshwater pearls. Since the Hopewell, as noted above, inhabited an area with many varieties of wild animals, their adoption of effigies may serve to identify the pipe's owner to a specific animal clan. This type of signification was also thought to be the case for pipes and ladle effigies of later Native cultures.

In addition to the materials listed above, other objects have been found in mounds from western New York State, showing evidence of pottery, beadwork, and textile traditions. The pottery was produced from grit-tempered paste obtained from rivers in the area. The beads, saltwater quahog clam shells, originated in either the Gulf or the southeastern or northeastern coastal areas. Little is known about the production of textiles of this period, as we are only aware of the tradition through a secondary source: the surface texture of the pottery.

On one expedition, an Iroquois skeleton was found on what is referred to as the "Squawkie Hill Mound," situated on the north bank of the Genesee River near Mount Morris in Livingston County, New York. Around the neck of the skeleton were shell beads, possibly saltwater clam shells, plus many disc-shaped beads no bigger than 1/16 of an inch thick. At another mound, called the Genesee Mound, located 4.5 miles north of Squawkie Hill, a pottery vessel was uncovered. It stands 6¾ inches high and is made of grit-tempered paste with a pointed bottom. This pointed shape efficiently transfers heat from the fire into the vessel's contents. The opening has a constricted neck that allows for easier handling of the vessel when full. This neck also keeps the contents from spilling when carrying the vessel. The surface texture of the vessel was created by textiles which were wrapped around a wooden paddle and pressed or tapped onto the soft clay or paste. The resulting pattern becomes permanent once the pot has been fired.

The Grave Creek Mounds of Grave Creek, West Virginia, were built by the Adena culture. These mounds (dating from around 500 B.C.E. to 100 C.E.), measure approximately 72 feet high and 164 feet across. Although there are a limited number of objects associated with this particular mound, the mound itself, as a permanent structure, is a testament to the successful nature of the connections created throughout the Hopewell culture by its traders and artists.

Overlapping historically with the Hopewell were five tribes whose confederacy and contact with early settlers left a rich art tradition which continues to the present. Beginning between 100 B.C.E. and 100 C.E. and extending to the late eighteenth century, five tribes—Seneca, Cayuga, Oneida, Onondaga, and Mohawk—inhabited what is now New York, Pennsylvania, Ontario, and Ohio by controlling the trade of fur along the Delaware, Ohio, and Susquehanna rivers. A confederacy joining these five tribes, called the League of Iroquois or the Great Peace, was created between the early fifteenth century and the late sixteenth. This was an attempt to unite the separate and sometimes warring tribes by arranging annual meetings where sachems, or tribal leaders, would discuss and try to resolve conflicts.

Iroquois pictographs—pictures that stand for a word or phrase—were produced to communicate information to other tribal nations. As Father LaFitau, a Jesuit missionary writing in 1724, described the scenario: "When an Indian returns from war and wishes to make his victory known to the neighboring nations through whose country he passes . . . he supplies the lack of an alphabet by those characteristic symbols which distinguish him personally; he paints on a piece of bark, which is raised on a pole by a place of passage [trail], or he cuts away some pieces from a tree trunk with his hatchet, and after having made a smooth surface, traces his portrait and adds other characters, which give all the information he desires to convey."[1] Although Father LaFitau's description leaves much room for speculation about the "symbols" and "characters" that were used, these pictographs

Collections of Native American Art

Much of what we know about early Native American art comes from descriptions of French Jesuit missionaries or nineteenth-century collectors. The collectors were working for newly established historical museums in America. Directors of these museums noticed the decimation of tribal Indians through relocation, death from disease, and wars with the colonists. Their collection of artifacts was an attempt to preserve Native culture before its extinction. At the time, Native American cultures and their arts were little understood by the historians, archaeologists, and collectors. It is problematic that these incomplete collections are sometimes used as a benchmark to define what is "traditional" or significant about a certain tribe's art.

highlight the artist's role in the Iroquois nation as well as the importance of contact between cultures. The artist was a mediator who could present the Nation's political messages or agenda, through personalized symbols.

The Iroquois created many forms of woven textiles, but the most common technique used before European contact was finger weaving. Although the term makes the process sound simple, this technique lent itself to an abundant variety of complex weaving styles. Most of the textiles that survived were in the form of belts, sashes, or burden straps, which were tightly woven straps that acted as a belt which would hold items tight to ones body for transport. In most cases, regional materials such as milkweed fiber, bast, nettle, Indian hemp, and slippery elm were used in their production. Other local raw materials, such as porcupine quills, and moosehair were incorporated into the weaving process to add color and decoration. One raw material, the decorative quahog clam shell, was obtained through trade routes established by the ancient Hopewell culture, tribes from the northeastern coastal areas.

Another raw material, marine shell, had special status within the weaving and textile tradition. Wampum belts, decorated with the marine shells, were made to document or solidify the process of verbal communication between individuals or tribes, after they discussed treaties or proposals. The belts or strings would then be exchanged between the leaders if an agreement was reached. This exchange of wampum was a symbolic reference to the act of exchanging words. The colors of the beads were a deep purple-to-black or white and were usually made into geometric designs. This geometric pattern, for example, could refer to one individual or a group who was involved in the conversation. This pattern would then be connected, by a line which symbolized a path or chain, to another in the conversation. In this way, wampum, like the pictographs, connected the Iroquois artist to the policies and politics of the nation and acted as a link between cultures.

In the early eighteenth century, Iroquois politics would turn to the emerging American colonies, especially Pennsylvania, to try and preserve their independence and access to important waterways for hunting and travel. As an organized nation, covering a large land area, the Iroquois carried political strength when dealing with the colonists. This had the effect of delaying the disruption of their art traditions through relocation by the United States Government. Unfortunately, the Delaware Indians inhabiting the present-day New York City and New Jersey area did not have the ability to protect their traditional territory. Beginning in 1737 with the Walking Purchase, Pennsylvania settlers effectively took over this territory along the coast, eventually relocating these tribes to reservations in eastern Oklahoma. Their location directly on the mid-Atlantic coast was also the first point of contact between the Native Americans and Europeans where European manufactured goods were immediately adopted by the Delaware, further blurring knowledge of what was traditional art production and what was European influenced. This early disruption of their culture meant that few traditional artifacts made within this region were left behind.

This convergence of European cultures and Native American cultures, beginning in the seventeenth century, altered the use of art materials and designs. Italian and Bohemian glass quickly replaced the marine shells, moosehair, and porcupine needles as decorative elements. Machined cotton and wool replaced the Indian hemp for textile manufacture. As evident in a late-nineteenth-century Iroquois hat,[2] the traditional geometric patterns were sometimes replaced with French floral designs and the style of construction is influenced by Scottish Glengarry bonnets. As we will see later, the reclaiming of Indian artistic traditions that were discontinued or disrupted by colonial influence emerges in the twentieth century from the work of artists, educational institutions, and museums.

Again we find from this new colonial presence, the first European immigrants who began producing sculptures and paintings, which we call folk art, were not artists. The majority of individuals who made the transatlantic voyage to the colonies in the seventeenth century were laborers and craftspeople. Established artists working in the large cities of Europe and England did not need to travel to find work. They secured patronage from their state or wealthy individuals who were connected to the wealth of international trading. There was no need to leave their financial security as well as risk the dangerous long voyage into a socially and economically undeveloped land.

Folk Art

The definition of "folk art" is heavily debated. There has not been a consensus among art historians that describes folk art as coming from a specific school, style, movement, region, or time period. Generally, this tradition is defined through two elements: the artist is outside of the tradition of academic training and has raw materials for the art that are accessible and inexpensive. Academic training can be considered as structured learning process within an institution. At most, the new immigrants received training in manual jobs as apprentices. Apprentices would learn the craft of masonry or carpentry, for example, from an artisan who was considered a skilled craftsperson. Some folk artists had no experience as apprentices but worked with materials such as wood or metal in the process of maintaining their family farm in the country. In either case, folk art is closely related to the daily life of the people who are making it, and the techniques that they use are learned from practical experience. It is also worth noting that most immigrants from Europe did not adopt techniques or materials that were in use by the Native Indians. Although Native Americans were sometimes the subject of the art in colonial times, European traditions would define most of the artistic production until the end of the nineteenth century.

Gravestones

The earliest form of colonial sculpture in the mid-Atlantic region during the eighteenth century can be seen in carved gravestones. Gravestones filled a practical need for the colonists, and stone cutters or masons would be commissioned to produce the markers. The grave of Mary Price, carved in 1766 by David Jeffries of Elizabethtown, New Jersey, shows images frequently seen on the local stone, quarried from Newark.

The most common type of stone used for gravestones was slate. The material's inherent flatness, its easy removal from quarry sites in sheets, and its abundance in the region, were economical advantages that kept processing costs low. Although slate is fragile, especially when carving surface marks with hammers and chisels, importing a stronger stone like marble from Italy was prohibitively expensive. The term carved, as opposed to sculpted, has been applied to the folk artist, which suggests rough cutting by an unskilled maker. Contrary to this implication, there is a great amount of skill needed by the artist in order to incise slate. One needs an intimate knowledge of the nature of the stone to be a successful carver. The existing examples of the shallow, yet intricate, relief work, demonstrate expertise in manipulating slate's brittle structure which is not suited for three dimensional carving. These gravestones are an excellent example of how local materials influenced the art of the region.

The typical iconography, or visual imagery, used by Jeffries and other artists, conveyed ideas about death and life. The winged cherub or weeping angel was often found in the half circle at the top of a monument. This was associated with the existence of angels in the Christian faith who would carry the soul into heaven, hence its presence at the top of the stone to suggest this upward movement. The hourglass below the cherub suggests the passage of time, eventually leading to death. The floral pattern around the heart-shaped field, possibly a grape vine, suggests the natural growth of life or a connection to wine as the blood of Christ. The stylized form which is commonly interpreted as a heart, symbolizes the affection and love family members had for the deceased. Most markers of this period contained circular, scroll-like motifs that visually connect the inscribed text of the deceased name, her family relations and date of death, to a historical document, like a death certificate written on paper, or left in the family Bible.

Weathervanes

In addition to masons, early folk art was made by metal workers. Their art appeared primarily in the form of weathervanes. These objects had practical and religious purposes like the grave markers, while some were connected to the commerce and politics of the region. The city of Philadelphia and its surrounding area was a productive farming area. Weathervanes were used, most importantly, to help one predict the weather patterns of the area as wind direction along with temperature fluctuations and cloud conditions could impart enough information to prepare for storms or dry weather. These vanes were produced by craftspeople and purchased by individuals, businesses, and organizations, some of whom requested custom configurations for aesthetic or advertising purposes. While folk art was not typically financially supported through patronage or commissions, vanes connected to ongoing commercial enterprises sometimes increased the vane's longevity, leaving a tradition of artifacts for us to study and appreciate today.

One vane was constructed for a mill built in Upland, later renamed Chester, Pennsylvania.[3] The advertisement consisted of the initials of the owners, William Penn, Samuel Carpenter, and Caleb Pussey, along with the mill's construction date, 1699. As a business owner and future statesman, Penn's patronage can be seen as the beginning of a long history of government funded projects. Although the vane is small in scale and has little visual imagery, its maker adopts calligraphic styles current at the time to create a formally balanced image. George Washington also commissioned a vane, the Dove of Peace, from Philadelphian Joseph Rakestraw in 1787, for Mount Vernon. Washington not only ordered the work himself, but he also included specific formal requirements, such as inclusion of an olive branch in its mouth, and that it be the actual size of a dove as well as not having the supporting pole extend above the bird in order to make it look more realistic. Even for such a small commissioned work, its production cost was an issue for Washington, which suggests that weathervanes were not appropriate vehicles for art. It also suggested the lack of funds earmarked for commissions by the government at this early stage of the nation's economic growth. Although not a vane, the political banner "Protect Home Industries" of William and Thomas Howard, Charlestown, Chester County, Pennsylvania, shows a more personalized vision of the relationship between the craftspeople and the political environment of the 1840s.[4] This political statement, made up of forged bar iron shaped into numerous tools that were welded on an iron-framed grid, creatively became a political voice in the presidential campaign of

Ship Figureheads

In the mid-Atlantic region, carving of wooden ship figureheads was an important industry for coastal areas. All figureheads from this time were carved from local pine, an abundant, light, and inexpensive material that is soft enough to allow for easy manipulation. Almost all were painted, sometimes white, to imitate European sculptures made of expensive Italian marble. They were not carved in the round, meaning on all sides, as the back of each figurehead needed to be firmly attached to the ship's bow. The carver, therefore, emphasized the two sides, port and starboard, and the forward facing line that made the profile. The figures themselves were representations of women, statesmen, or animals, usually in the form of birds. Although most manufacturing was done in New England, James Randolph of Baltimore, Maryland, produced many for large ships that were built along the coast. One figurehead for the *Seaman's Bride*, a vessel built in Baltimore in 1851, was in the shape of an eagle.

Patroon Portrait Painters

The business and political patrons of folk art had their counterpart in the private sector. Along the Hudson River, north of New York City, were several unknown artists, labeled "Patroon portrait painters" after the Dutch Patroon system of landownership. This system was organized by the West India Company, and it granted large areas of land to males who were connected to the company. As a result, wealth was generated from working the land, which was then used by the land owners to hire artists to paint portraits of the landowners. Portraiture had a long tradition in the Netherlands and these newly arrived patroons were able to continue that tradition in America. These artists secured the patronage of the Patroons from 1715 to approximately 1730. Nothing is known about the artist's training or experience, but the portraits show a knowledge of mezzotint prints that were in circulation throughout the larger cities in the colonies. By studying the three dimensional shading, perspective differences of foreground and background figures of the prints, the folk painters had a visual guide, or manual, that was used as a substitute for academic training or exposure to a master artist

The intent of the paintings were to "take a likeness" of the sitter, by showing the face of the sitter in a frontal manner, rather than a more dynamic, three-quarter-view of the face. This approach is seen in the oil painting of Magdalena

Douw (Gansevoort) of approximately 1729.[5] This frontal pose of Magdalena emphasizes her facial features, yet her body beneath the floral dress seems twisted as her shoulders face left and her feet are facing forward. With the exception of this inconsistent representation of her anatomy, this large, vertical painting (51 by 33 inches) is in the tradition of the Flemish painter Sir Anthony Van Dyck (1599–1641). Van Dyck, like the Patroon painters, places the sitter's face far above the viewer's eyes, forcing the viewer to look up at the portrait. Van Dyck's extensive portraiture of the English nobility was copied via mezzotint prints which were available in the colonies. The objects in the painting are attributes of the sitter's gender. Although she is obviously literate, with book in hand, the fruit on the table, representing powers of reproduction from Christian iconography, suggests that the sitter's role is that of a mother. Also, by including the uncultivated landscape behind her, women's connection to the process of nature could be suggested. Similar to Magdalena's portrait, the painting of Moses Levy,[6] who lived from 1665 to 1728, connects him with images that signify his gender. Shown half-length, he is dressed in formal attire while, in the background, his ships are at sea. He is connected to commerce, possibly international trade, and rather than being controlled by nature's forces, he is taming them as the dog sits patiently by his side.

Folk Painters

Although the "Patroon" painters found employment within a small area, the Folk painter as itinerant, or wandering, artist becomes the standard after the American Revolution. With trade and commerce expanding, entrepreneurs were establishing small businesses in more remote regions of the colonies. Creating a more widespread demand for inexpensive "likenesses." Micah Williams (1782–1837), a self-taught itinerant artist, worked in New Brunswick, Matawan, and Freehold, New Jersey. His materials were pastel and paper, which were inexpensive and easy to transport. Williams could also complete a pastel portrait much quicker than one with oil paint.

Another itinerant artist, Jacob Maentel (1763–1863), was born in Germany and immigrated to Philadelphia around 1810. There is no record of Maentel having exposure to art training while in Germany. Instead, his connection to the culturally secluded German population in Pennsylvania (referred to as Pennsylvania "Dutch" by the local English-speaking population who mistakenly derived the word from "Deutsch," which means German) affected his painting style. The German Quaker tradition shunned a grandiose idea of self that most other immigrant populations shared. This translated into fewer individuals desiring likenesses of themselves. But Maentel did manage, whether from his unflattering silhouette style or by incorporating his portraiture with the birth certificate of the sitter, to commission full-length portraits of many German community members. In his *Boy with Rooster*, a sense of the individuality of the sitter is lessened by the use of a sharp half-face pose, so the viewer is not looking eye to eye with the sitter. No personal possessions are shown, although the rooster in the boy's arms could be his to raise, nor other specific property markers are used in the background. Maentel did customize some portraits by signing the painting in the Pennsylvania German fraktur style in an effort to complement the sitter's birth record also produced in the fraktur style.

This German fraktur style is a decorative type of lettering script integrated with images called "Fraktur-schrift." This style was used for documents that recorded births, marriages, baptisms, weddings, bookmarks, and house blessings. The documents were mainly produced by teachers, but sometimes the family members would add their own decoration to the page. The materials used were quill pen and brush to apply the paint made of "a mixture of whiskey and varnish composed of cherry tree gum diluted in water."[7] The birth certificate of Marie Portzline, June 11, 1820 shows several common images such as birds, usually grouped in symmetrical pairs, circular barn symbols, interlaced patterns, floral designs, and heart-shaped borders that would usually contain text. This German painting tradition began to decline in the early nineteenth century, when printing presses, products of the Industrial Revolution, mass-produced illustrated certificates in the fraktur style.

European Influence on Mid-Atlantic Artists

Beginning in the late eighteenth century, artists and patrons would start to favor established European trends rather than the local or rural trends noted above. As Philadelphia's immigrant population grew, more artists with knowledge of European techniques arrived, who then found employment as itinerant painters. These new arrivals influenced other artists by their techniques which appeared to "better" exemplify the idea of a "likeness." In addition, political and wealthy individuals involved in changing a British Colony into a self-determining nation saw colonial status (and therefore its art) as subservient to that of nationhood. European nations were seen as models of "proper" culture, especially artistic, which was emulated while folk art of the colonial period was marginalized.

As the son of a Swedish portrait painter, John Hesselius (1728–1778) immigrated to Maryland in 1711, moving to Philadelphia in 1735. In 1750, his career as itinerant artist began as he traveled within Maryland and Virginia, painting portraits of wealthy plantation owners. He eventually settled near Annapolis in Anne Arundel County, Maryland, after marrying a wealthy widow. His inclusion into an influential family, allowed him access to wealthy patrons. He was influenced by British painter John Wollaston, who was in Annapolis from 1753 to 1754. Both used mezzotints for compositional references, but Wollaston would also learn directly from examining European master works from a trip to London. This knowledge would be available to Hesselius in the finished product of Wollaston's works that he completed while in Annapolis. Hesselius, via Wollaston, drew from the sixteenth-century Venetian tradition of adding elaborately folded drapery, seen in *Charles Calvert*, painted in 1761. The attempt to convey complex folds through the blue fabric draped over the arm of Charles fall short in comparison to English and European standards. Also not as convincing are the foreshortening attempts of Charles' right arm and the slave's kneeling leg position, yet these attempts were close counterparts to the European standard.

In contrast to the preoccupation with portraiture in smaller cities like Baltimore, some artists in Philadelphia used images that reflected political changes within the new nation. William Russell Birch (1755–1834), an engraver, immigrated to Philadelphia in 1794 from England, bringing his mezzotint and printing tradition with him. Birch completed a series of twenty-nine engravings titled *The City of*

America's First Black Professional Artist

Another itinerant painter to work in the Maryland area was Joshua Johnston (c. 1763–1824). Johnston was actively painting portraits in Baltimore from 1796, beginning with his first published advertisement announcing his arrival in town in order to find sitters, in the *Baltimore Intelligencer* newspaper. Other than census or city directories, records of his history are scant, but they conclude that Johnston was a freed slave who established a living as America's first known, black, professional portrait artist. With Baltimore's black population growth, and the city's Abolition Society, free blacks found assistance establishing wage-earning occupations. Johnston's movement from Fells Point, a less-than-prosperous part of town, to a wealthier neighborhood whose inhabitants were known abolitionists, helped Johnston establish sufficient patronage.

Joshua Johnston was well acquainted with other artists in the area, most notably the Peale family, which included Charles Willson Peale (1741–1827) and his seventeen children (named after famous European master painters), along with his nephew Charles Peale Polk (1767–1822). Johnston called himself a "self-taught genius" in a 1798 advertisement, so any training from Peale might only be in exposure to these European masters, whose paintings could have been seen in Rembrandt and Raphaelle Peale's museum. Some scholars have suggested that Johnston was actually owned and then freed by the Peale family. His approach to portraiture was similar to that of the Peales and others from this period. He showed men with books and women with sprigs from nature, yet he imposed his own style by producing forty-six full-length portraits of young children. One such painting, *The Westwood Children*, circa 1807, shows the three young boys of the Westwood family. The tenderness of the brothers, who hold delicate cut flowers and fruit from nature, is contrasted with the family dog who displays its own fondness for nature by holding a bird in its jaws.

Philadelphia in the State of Pennsylvania North America as It Appeared in the Year 1800.

This series was a combination of city street maps and fourteen street scenes organized in pairs of two. These pairs were designed to show the city in a physical state of change. Each pair presented a contrasted theme such as "The [finished and empty] house intended for the President of the United States in Ninth-street" against "An unfinished [and empty] house, in Chestnut street." The maps would act as a guide for locating each scene. The street scenes, in pairs of two, would show workers within the city constructing a "new" urban center or citizens at leisure enjoying the parks and public monuments. In the pairing of the "State-House Garden, Philadelphia" plate with the "Gaol, in Walnut Street Philadelphia," activities of work and leisure are clear as workers remove the old jail in the foreground with the new jail gleaming in the background, and the garden scene is filled with walking couples. Technically, these engravings display a thorough knowledge of perspective as figures are understood to move and exist in three dimensional space. In making these engravings, Birch absorbed the new efforts to change rural colonialism into a unified nation by contrasting the old, outdated Philadelphia with the new urban center.

Philadelphia's growth created a wealthy class of patrons who financially supported artists and purchased European works for their collections, which were viewed and studied by local artists. One such patron, Robert Gilmore Sr., was keenly interested in supporting artists who tended to follow European developments. He lent European master works to local museums, while his Philadelphia home was the social gathering place for several artists in the community. In 1858 he helped sponsor and participated in the Baltimore and Ohio Railroad "Artists' Excursion," where a large group of artists and patrons traveled along the route to record and document the views outside the train windows. Some of the many local artists he supported were William Rush, Charles Grafly, Thomas Cole, Thomas Doughty, and Thomas Sully.

William Rush

William Rush (1756–1833), born in Philadelphia, was possibly the most striking case of a folk wood-carver trained as an artisan's apprentice who then developed into a sculptor of the European tradition. He served his apprenticeship, which ended around 1780, under Edward Cutbush. Between 1780 and 1800, Rush was making ship figureheads, none of which have survived. Rush made his transition via access to the Pennsylvania Academy of Fine Arts (PAFA) collection of master European replicas, as well as studying from French-born Jean Antoine Houdon, whom visited Philadelphia in 1785. Rush's *Water Nymph and Bittern* of 1809, which was commissioned by the Philadelphia Water Works, was carved of local pine, as no sources of marble suitable for large-scale sculptures had been found in America at this time. Although the pine was painted white, resembling the treatment of the figureheads to resemble marble, this work successfully shows neoclassical techniques in the figure's pose.

Rush applies neoclassicism in his *Nymph* sculpture. The Nymph's tight-fitting clothes that show the form of the figure underneath is sometimes referred to as the "wet drapery" technique. This sculptural treatment was used by ancient Greek artists, and was known to most European artists through the Elgin collection held at the British Museum. The collection contains pediment sculptures that were taken from the Parthenon building on the Greek Acropolis. Underneath the drapery, the figure's standing posture is clearly seen. The posture has an *S*-shaped curve that occurs naturally when one stands, with one leg bearing most of the body's weight while the other is bent and relaxed, forcing the hips and shoulders to tilt. This curved stance is another neoclassical element used by Rush. The one major difference between Rush's work and that of the European masters was his singular use of wood, rather than marble.

This circumstance, where no American artist had the resources or skill to produce a major piece of sculpture from marble, was partly due to the lack of a standardized academic art tradition in America similar to those in Europe. With this in mind, William Rush and Charles Willson Peale (see below) helped found the PAFA. Established in 1805 in Philadelphia, this institution and its founders worked toward "the cultivation of the Fine Arts, in the United States of America, by introducing correct and elegant copies from works of the first masters, in sculpture and painting and by thus facilitating the access to such standards . . . and otherwise assisting the studies and exciting the efforts of the artists, gradually to unfold, enlighten and invigorate the talents of our Countrymen."[8] To fulfill this function, the academy ordered plaster casts made from sculptures from the Louvre in 1806 to use for study. For most academic instructors, study consisted of having their students copy the plaster casts in pen-and-ink drawings.

Charles Willson Peale

In addition to the academy's collection, Charles Willson Peale also founded his own private museum. With the intent of building a public museum with governmental support, he turned local and regional events into expressions of national identity. After employment as a saddle-maker's apprentice, itinerant portrait painter, and clock repairer, he went to London to study painting under the former Philadelphian Benjamin West (1738–1820). John Hesselius also trained Peale to paint. In 1776 Peale was connected to the city's "revolutionary artisan community," painting portraits of Philadelphia's wealthy class. After 1780 he became interested in the concept of a museum where he desired to "contain the entire world 'in miniature.'"[9] Much of Peale's "world" centered on his knowledge of natural history and art museums of Europe, and the international scientific language (Latin) used to categorize nature. For Peale, these connections, rather than Native American history or folk art, determined what should be contained within a museum that would represent America as a "civilized" country.

Peale's museum interest and his painting came together in the *Exhumation of the Mastodon* of 1806–1808. This painting includes portraiture and elements of landscape as well as documenting an event of historical significance. There are close to twenty identified portraits in this painting. Among them are Peale, some of his family, friends, the owner of the land on which the mastodon bones were found, and the leading ornithologist of the day, Alexander Wilson. The landscape in the background, which takes up almost half the painting, is part of a French tradition that was just becoming popular in American painting. His use of the genre of landscape painting was no doubt influenced by West, who adopted the tradition before moving to England. The painting of the removal of the mastodon's bones from a pit in Shawangunk, New York, was intended to hang next to the reassembled bones in his museum. The painting gives us a wealth of information about how Peale positioned himself as an employer, builder of the nation's natural history via the assembly of the mastodon's bones, and a member of the nation's intelligentsia.

The Peale family also organized a 1795 exhibit, in association with the PAFA, at the Philadelphia State House that included Dutch still-life paintings. Both Raphaelle and James Peale adopted European still-life painting, beginning its acceptance and legitimacy for America artists. William Harnett (1848–1892) (studied in New York City) continued this tradition in his early paintings, and then later adopted the French trompe l'oeil (to deceive the eye) style, after several years abroad in Munich. With this trompe l'oeil approach, Harnett does not allow the paint to reveal any evidence of brushstrokes, and objects are painted in their true size, always having sharp shadows from a consistent but imaginary light source. Harnett's *After the Hunt* of 1885 emphasizes visual details, but it is not just simple imitation. As Harnett said, "In painting from still life I do not closely imitate nature. Many points I leave out and many I add . . . I always group my figures, so as to try and make an artistic composition, I endeavor to make the composition tell a story."[10]

Regional Artists and European Standards

Although European influences were gaining popularity with most painters, marble sculptural production was still unable to rival European standards, even after the formation of the PAFA. This created a crisis for regional artists from Philadelphia and New York who were competing for commissions against European artists at the end of the eighteenth century. As a result, European, not American, sculptors were being selected for large state government commissions (for instance, the Italian Antonio Canova was commissioned to carve George Washington for the new North Carolina State Capitol). In addition, artists began to travel to Europe for training and commissions that would allow them to develop different techniques needed for producing new images, and working with new materials.

Hiram Powers (1805–1873), born in Vermont, traveled to Washington and New York City to fulfill portrait bust commissions of President Andrew Jackson, John C. Calhoun, and Daniel Webster. With money from these commissions, he and his family were able to move to Florence, Italy, in 1837, never to return. Much earlier, Benjamin West (1738–1820), born in Springfield, Pennsylvania, with the financial help of Reverend William Smith, left Philadelphia in 1760 for Italy. West would eventually end up in England as a court painter for the monarchy. Thomas Crawford (1813–1857) of New York City left for Rome, Italy, in 1835, to study under neoclassical sculptor Bertel Thorvaldsen, eventually setting up his own studio there making marble busts.

When the U.S. government did award commissions to Americans, they were working exclusively in European workshops. Crawford, while in Rome, was awarded commissions from the U.S. Government, resulting in the creation of the pediment sculpture *Progress of Civilization* and the statues *History* and *Justice*, to be placed in the Senate; bronze doors for the House and Senate; and the bronze figure *Freedom* for the Capitol Dome. William Henry Rinehart (1825–1874), from Union Bridge, Maryland, who began as a stone cutter of marble, quarried from his family farm, moved to Baltimore in 1846. He then left for Florence in 1855, settling in Rome in 1858. There, he catered to traveling Americans who would order marble busts while on their Grand Tour (an educational trip through Europe that emphasized its ancient architecture and art). Ironically, Rinehart was only able to receive patronage from Americans while they were abroad. By placing his workshop on a visible site in Rome along the highly trafficked route of the Grand Tour, he designed a successful marketing strategy that was unavailable in Philadelphia or New York City. George Grey Barnard (1863–1938), born in Bellefonte, Pennsylvania, was in Paris in 1883 and studied at the Ecole des Beaux-Arts. Although he returned to Washington Heights, New York, in 1894, where he received a commission for the Pennsylvania State Capitol Building in Harrisburg, he completed the work in Europe. The effects of this trend in patronage bypassed development of a support system that would encourage regional uniqueness. Unfortunately, even artists who remained in America could not avoid the trend to emulate European influences.

Erastus Dow Palmer (1817–1904), born in Pompey, New York, was one exception to this trend of the artist learning abroad. With very little academic training, and without traveling to Europe until late in his career, Palmer produced one of the first large-scale marble sculptures that did not conform to the neoclassical trend. From his studio in Albany, New York, in 1857, he produced *The White Captive* using a singularly American theme, and a real rather than ideal form of the human figure. The theme is not from Greek or Roman mythology, but one of westward American expansion. The white woman is understood to be held captive by Native American. In the tradition of "captive narratives," written by colonists who were assimilated into American Indian tribes after periods of war, Palmer alludes to his country's recent history. The woman captive is not presented as an ideal image, but as a contemporary individual with broad shoulders and unkempt hair and having angular, rather than smooth, outlines. Only the *S*-curved stance and the use of marble resembles the neoclassical ideal. Overall, Palmer was mainly interested in making sculpture that expressed his own country. This piece was made in response to American ex-patriot Hiram Power's famous *Greek Slave*, which was made in Italy.

With the exception of the unique Palmer, other sculptors who remained in America gained experience by joining national organizations and by competing for inclusion in international exhibitions held in American cities. The format of these international exhibitions required large numbers of sculptors and assistants to produce large-scale temporary works. This practice, performed locally, gave an apprentices exposure to accomplished artists, thus increasing their chances of obtaining public commissions. Karl Bitter (1867–1915), born in Germany, immigrated to New York City in 1889. He was well trained in constructing appropriate sculptures for the exhibitions, and to fulfill public commissions. Bitter's extensive workshop experience in Germany and Vienna gave him technical skills in clay sculpting and stone carving. In America, he gained experience by working with architect Richard Morris Hunt on large-scale sculptures connected to well-funded architecture projects. These architectural projects, and his activity in the National Sculpture Society, earned him the experience to acquire privately and publicly funded commissions for public monuments. His skills also led him to be named director of sculpture at the Buffalo Pan-American Exposition of 1901, whose purpose was to "display the abundance of natural resources in the United States and to dramatize their use in the development of her industry."[11]

Charles Grafly (1862–1929), born in Philadelphia, began his artistic career as an apprentice carver at John Struthers's stone yard, and then studied at the PAFA. Traveling to Paris in 1888 for four years of study at the Ecole des Beaux-Arts and the Academie Julian, he returned to teach at the PAFA in 1892, until his death in 1929. He participated in the Paris and Buffalo Expositions of 1900 and 1901, respectively. His use of allegorical themes is evident in his *In Much Wisdom* of 1902, with a snake and mirror acting as wisdom's symbols, yet his treatment of the woman's figure does not imply a neoclassical ideal form but a realistic, common figure that might have been influenced from his figure study classes at the PAFA.

Landscape

In the nineteenth century, the region's development in painting, which expanded from portraiture to include landscape painting, took a different course than that of sculpture. The region's landscape painters were still influenced by European styles, but because of the ease of obtaining painting materials and the ability of individuals to sketch outdoors without the need of apprentices, workshops, or expensive materials that hindered American sculptors, painters were freer to establish distinct regional styles. The painters were also guided by the unique subject matter of the American wilderness.

The landscape tradition in America begins with scenes of nature at popular tourist sites made by immigrants from England who settled in the mid-Atlantic region. William Guy Wall (1792–1864) of New York City and John Hill (1770–1850) of Philadelphia collaborated on a series titled *Picturesque Views of*

American Scenery between 1820 to 1825. Scenes like Wall's *Landscape: Bakers Falls, New York* reflected the interest urban artists, and the merchants who would patronize them, had in the region's geological wonders. This interest was partly due to the idea that, in the wake of the Industrial Revolution, the undeveloped forests of the country were close to extinction. The threat that the wild landscape would disappear caused a reaction on the part of many artists to document nature in its "pure" state. In addition, writers such as Archibald Alison commented on the grand historical nature of America's landscape. Painters, similarly, began creating landscapes of uninhabited wilderness with a romantic sense of wonder and awe. The region's painters would look to America's own natural geography instead of the distant neoclassical tradition for subject matter.

Hudson River School

The recording of this unique American identity in the mid-Atlantic region began with the Hudson River School. This school consisted of artists who painted the landscape of the Hudson River valley including the mountains of the Catskills and Adirondacks in New York State. These landscape paintings were highly sought after by urban merchants of the time.

Thomas Doughty

Thomas Doughty (1793–1856), born in Philadelphia, was one of the first artists in America to exclusively paint landscapes. He was financially supported by the patronage of Robert Gilmor Jr., and was exposed to Dutch and English landscape traditions through Gilmor's collection. He was also aware of the French master of landscape painting Claude Gellee, whose paintings were sentimental landscapes where trees, lakes, and mountains were placed in specific areas to keep the scene balanced and tranquil. The approach used by Doughty added a small amount of Romanticism, which meant that he used images to conjure strong feelings in the viewer. In his *In Natures Wonderland* of 1835, he added a single figure dwarfed by the surrounding scene. The viewer was intended to experience the scene through the eyes of this figure, to be enveloped by the landscape. The classical balance is seen in the centered pond, flanked by the cliff on the left with the tree on the right.

Thomas Cole

Thomas Cole (1801–1848) changed several elements of Claude's formula when composing his landscapes. Cole, who immigrated from England to Ohio in 1820, and later lived in Philadelphia from 1823 to 1825, briefly studied at the PAFA. In 1824 he moved to New York City, where he began painting as an itinerant portrait painter north of the city. During his travels he was exposed to the natural beauty of northern New York's scenery. Instead of using the calming scenes favored by Doughty, Cole added irregular and sometimes threatening landscape elements to ignite feelings of fear and awe in the viewer. In his *Schroon Mountain, Adirondacks*, the view is from above, looking down a great valley, bordered by two dead trees wreaked by the unforgiving forces of nature. The sky is menacing with stormy clouds moving in.

Although Cole's naturalistic landscapes quickly changed into ideal representations that emphasized allegorical themes over the landscape, others painters followed Cole's lead, painting scenes inspired by landscapes such as Schroon Mountain.

Other Landscape Painters

Asher B. Durand (1796–1886) was an engraver's apprentice in Newark, New Jersey, from 1812 to 1817, moving to New York City in 1817 to produce banknotes, portraits, and landscapes. In 1840 Durand traveled throughout Europe on the Grand Tour and studied the European master painters that hung in the major museums. Durand, unlike Cole or Doughty, was very conscious about letting nature itself, not the artist, dictate the painting. His interest in Ralph Waldo Emerson's transcendentalism allowed his ego to shrink away so that he could connect completely with the spirit he felt within nature. His outdoor sketches were often used as starting points for his paintings, creating an immediate connection with his subject. He created less formal arrangements with random groupings of trees, cliffs, and rocks, as seen in *Study from Nature: Rocks and Trees* of the mid-1850s.

Landscape paintings were also used as advertising by the growing railroad industries, who commissioned artists to produce scenic "postcards" of views from their train's travels. William Louis Sonntag (1822–1900), born in East Liberty, Pennsylvania, was an active painter of West Virginia's territory. Under commission by the Baltimore and Ohio Railroad, he painted scenes along the train route from Baltimore, Maryland, to Harper's Ferry, West Virginia, then to Wheeling. His *Mountain Lake Near Piedmont, Maryland* of 1860 is similar to Durand's paintings with the centered pond and small figures with their backs to the viewer, yet the purpose of the commissioned project produces a new approach. The landscape is of wilderness tamed. The cabin in the background signifies the encroachment of civilization, consistent with the expansion of the national rail system, unlike Durand's earlier solitary hiker arriving upon an untouched vista.

Similarly, the Delaware Railroad commissioned an 1855 calendar advertisement. George Inness (1825–1894), a map engraver by trade in New York City, submitted *The Lackawanna Valley* to fulfill the contract. In contrast to idyllic scenes of the fast-vanishing wilderness, his image showed the recently industrialized valley of Scranton, Pennsylvania, with its railroad roundhouse, labor yards, smokestacks, and burned tree stumps. This vision was certainly a cogent representation of a possible scene along the route, which also showed the machinery and destruction that made rail travel possible. This image, not surprisingly, was rejected by the railroad president since it was not the idyllic scene he

---

Durand and Landscape

In the mid-nineteenth century, American landscape painting had much to do with the formation of the idea of a coherent nation. While the art of the Hudson River School painters largely depicts an idealized, prelapsarian state of nature in the region, Asher B. Durand acknowledged the advance of technology as part of a symbiotic relationship in the American landscape. Paintings such as *View of the Hudson River Valley* (1851) and *Progress, or The Advance of Civilization* (1853) present an ideological view of an ideal nationhood in which nature and culture were perfectly balanced. *Progress* uncritically depicts the evolution of transportation (from wagon to barge and canal to steamboat and train) as if it were seamless. The landscape serves as supportive background to this civilizing, technological process, with Indians on the left watching the rise of the new American order, and Euro-American settlers on the right working as active citizens of this order.[12]

hoped would help sell train tickets. Inness's approach to this commission reflected his attitude toward the new industrial growth in America. Inness, who studied the landscapes of the French Barbizon school while in Paris, was loosely connected to the Hudson River School painters. He was spiritually and emotionally connected to nature's beauty. His use of materials created soft tones of color in his images to elicit emotion in the viewer. His glazing technique, using many layers of turpentined thinned oil with a light brown tint, created a translucent, almost mystical rendering of nature.

In contrast to the landscape tradition, the Long Island regionalist William Sydney Mount (1807–1868), born in Setauket, New York, produced genre paintings, or scenes from ordinary life of the Long Island area. Instead of traveling, as the Hudson River School painters did, he painted what he knew around his community. Mount's connection to his local community was exceptional because he was one of the few American artists never to travel to Europe. Exposed to Dutch genre paintings exhibited in New York City, he adopted this style to record precise and convincing figures surrounded by diffuse lighting.

Realism

Photography

With the rise of the Industrial Revolution in America and Europe during the nineteenth century, technology itself entered the art world in the form of photography. The impact of this new medium would be far-reaching, ultimately threatening long-standing ideas of idealism that permeated artistic academies. The technology, codeveloped by Louis-Jacques-Mande Daguerre (1787–1851) of France and William Henry Fox Talbot (1800–1877) of England, quickly spread through America after Daguerre made his invention public in 1839. First, the Daguerreotype permitted inexpensive portraits compared to the expense of commissioned paintings. As a result, many portrait studios opened in urban areas. The work closely followed the established style of portrait painting. The first Daguerreotype portrait studio in America was opened in New York City in 1840 by Alexander Wolcott and John Johnson. Mathew Brady (1823–1896) opened his portrait studio in New York City in 1844 and organized groups of photographers to document the aftermath of Civil War battles. Daniel Freeman (1868–1919), a black photographer active in Washington, D.C., from 1881 to 1919, opened his studio in 1885. Freeman was the founder of the Washington Amateur Art Society and taught photography at Frelinghuysen University. As Mount did with painting, Freeman actively documented his own community, using this new technology. Sometimes he added allegorical themes, similar to those in neoclassical sculpture, to align his photographs with the other traditional art mediums.

In addition to studio businesses, amateur photographers in Philadelphia and New York influenced changes in technique and style in work produced throughout the region. Organized into local clubs, members exchanged images with other regional and international clubs. This practice kept members aware of current trends throughout the country and abroad.

Alfred Steiglitz

One member of the Philadelphia Photographic Society, Alfred Steiglitz (1864–1946), born in Hoboken, New Jersey, rebelled against the "hobby" aspect of the clubs and left his position as editor of *Camera Notes* in 1902. Steiglitz organized the Photo-Secession Movement. He held that photography was an art form that must do more than just reproduce images. He "saw what others were doing was to make hard cold copies of hard cold subjects in hard cold light. I did not see why a photograph should not be a work of art."[13]

Steiglitz's idea of photographic art, and art in general, was that it should "get to the nature of the thing."[14] He wanted the viewer of his work to directly experience the subjects he photographed. For example, his *The Hand of Man* showed a locomotive, traveling through an industrial train corridor, as it belched coal smoke and steam. Steiglitz positioned the viewer in the cold "underworld" of industrial machinery, which was a 360-degree turn from the picturesque view of Sonntag's *Mountain Lake Near Piedmont, Maryland*. As Inness did with his paintings, Stieglitz captured changes to the natural world brought about by technology, using a new technology to make his point. Interestingly, Steiglitz's most important contribution to the arts in the region was his activism as patron and gallery owner. In this capacity, he sponsored America's foremost modern artists in the first three decades of the twentieth century, as noted later.

Thomas Eakins

Taking a different perspective on the uses of photography, Thomas Eakins (1844–1916) of Philadelphia experimented with the medium as a scientific rather than aesthetic tool, in the studies of human locomotion and physiognomy he incorporated into his exclusively figurative paintings. As an academician, Eakins studied at PAFA and took anatomy lessons at Philadelphia Medical College. He studied life drawing instead of the more customary painting in Europe. His mentor, Jean Leon Gerome (1824–1904), was known for his highly descriptive and factual representations. In his early portraits, like *Max Schmitt in a Single Scull* of 1871, Eakins used photographs of the area to extract details of the surroundings. For *Swimming Hole*, he used more photographic details from an 1883 plate to include landscape and bathing figures. Eakins's comfort with new ideas extended beyond adopting the new technology of the camera. As an instructor at the PAFA, he rejected the long-standing academic tradition of drawing from plaster casts, using live, nude models instead. He insisted that his students establish a connection between themselves and the sitter. In *The Thinker: Louis N. Kenton*, action is restrained, but the figure becomes introspective, and Eakins almost conveyed the very thoughts of the sitter.

Eakins was also a teacher at the Art Students League in New York. This institution was instrumental in training and developing artists, from Eakins's day through the present. Almost every American artist of note has taken classes there. In return for a small class fee, students received training from the country's best artists-turned-teachers. The students who passed through this institution contributed to almost every artistic style since the beginning of the twentieth century. This influence led to New York City's increasing domination of the mid-Atlantic region's art scene.

The Artist-Reporter

The influence of photography extended beyond amateur and artistic circles, entering the world of journalism. Urban newspaper editors, hoping to capture the feelings and immediacy of current events, tried to present daily articles that would appeal to a reading public who was quickly becoming familiar with photographs. Because the technology of photography was not sophisticated enough to be applied to newspaper printing presses, artist-reporters were hired to strengthen the appeal of written stories. In the Mid-Atlantic, artist-reporters were used by the *Philadelphia Press, Philadelphia Inquirer, New York World*, and *New York Herald* newspapers. These artist-reporters were exposed to the realities of inner-city life. Some of them incorporated the techniques and subject matters used for the newspaper stories into their paintings and drawings, challenging the powerful European and American academy systems.

Artist Robert Henri, born Robert Henry Cozad (1865–1929), became a vocal opponent of academic and impressionistic styles. He urged artist-reporters to paint the urban realities of New York City. Henri grew up in Atlantic City, New Jersey, and attended the PAFA in 1886, where he studied life-drawing under its director, Eakins, before moving to New York City in 1887. In 1902 he was an instructor at the New York School of Art. Partly influenced by Eakins's connections to his sitter, Henri's painting technique, seen in *Laughing Child*, was to quickly apply strokes of thick paint in order to capture the fleeting spirit of the sitter. This fast-paced, spontaneous technique was the precise training some of his pupils later received while drawing on-the-spot sketches of events as reporters.

Henri's innovative teaching mantra—"Work with great speed. Have your energies alert, up and active. Finish as quickly as you can"—[15] clashed with the philosophy of conservative members of New York's artistic community. The jurors considered these new experimental paintings unfinished and unsophisticated, and they did not select any of the work for their shows. As a chosen jury member for the National Academy of Design's annual salon exhibition, Henri rebelled against the decisions made by the academy's hanging committee after they rejected works submitted by several of his students. The resulting skirmish prompted Henri and his followers, some of whom were also rejected by the judges, to plan the now famous 1908 Independent Exhibition at Macbeth Galleries in New York. Of the eight painters in the show, two Philadelphian artist-reporters, John Sloan (1871–1951) and William Glackens (1870–1938), would be key participants in the eight-member Ashcan School. Although their styles were somewhat different, all eight members felt the need to break from the academic tradition as they attempted to capture both the spirit and subject matter of the urban life they experienced. The Ashcan School artists painted the scenes of the inner-city life of Philadelphia and New York as they experienced it. Painting common scenes and individuals in a rapid and spontaneous manner established what was considered to be an honest connection between the artist and the subject matter. This style was in direct opposition to the analytical methods taught in the established art academies of the time.

John Sloan, who worked at the *Philadelphia Inquirer* and studied at the PAFA, agreed with Henri's assessment that a new vitality was needed in American art. Of the three Philadelphians in the Ashcan School, Sloan effectively documented a

Native American Arts and John Sloan

John Sloan's politics influenced his support for Native American arts. He organized the 1931 Exposition of Indian Tribal Arts in an attempt to put Indian artists "on the map" of American culture. Through the exposition, Sloan wanted to "[a]waken public appreciation so as to encourage the Indians to continue to create and develop their art."[16] He also wanted to counter the common understanding of Indian art as primitive and lacking aesthetic value. In the catalog, Sloan noted, "no other objects in this exhibition, are as familiar in conception, from a European point of view, as the delicate [Hopewellian] figurines. . . . [A Hopewellian figurine] has its own style, but the idiom is one which we can understand without effort."[17]

sense of community within contemporary urban life. In his *Sixth Avenue and Thirtieth Street* of 1907, which hung at the Macbeth exhibition, the bustling street scene shows different classes of people going about their daily lives. The woman in a simple white dress, who carries a bucket of beer purchased from the back door of a bar, walks in the opposite direction from a fashionably dressed woman. This simple pairing illustrates visible class issues in the community. Using a seemingly random street corner, Sloan, as a Socialist Party member, used this painting and others to depict a progressive ideal of political activism through his experiences of public life.

William Glackens worked at the *Philadelphia Press* before moving to New York in the late 1890s to become a freelance illustrative artist for several magazines. His stylistic background aligned him with the Ashcan School, but his marriage into a wealthy family disconnected him from his original economic class. Some of his subjects were wealthy individuals. His *At Mouquin's*, depicting an upscale restaurant, showed lawyer Jim Moore with an unidentified woman friend posing for the artist. This format was more in line with the tradition of portraiture mentioned above than with compelling contemporary events.

Working at the same time as the painters of the Ashcan School, Jacob Riis (1849–1914) produced even more radical breaks from earlier traditions with the social realism of his photo documentation of the urban working poor. From Riis's journalistic background as a police reporter for the *New York Tribune*, he was exposed to urban slum communities. Shocked by the poverty, he began to expose these horrible living conditions in order to instigate social reform. He revealed scandalous scenes like *Tenement Interior in Poverty Gap: An English Coal-Heaver's Home*, to which he added text that further described the photograph. Traveling from city to city giving lectures and showing his scenes of urban life, he was an active liberal political progressive who attempted to change the situation of the people he met and photographed.

Jacob Riis, *Tenement Interior in Poverty Gap: An English Coal-Heaver's Home*. Courtesy Library of Congress.

Modernism

Although the members of the Ashcan School did not come as close as Riis in effecting change in New York's inner city, several members were involved in the groundbreaking Armory Show Exhibition in New York City in 1913. This show was initially an attempt to assemble American artists and display their work in a European museum–style environment, with a few European artists, for the visual consumption of the public. Even though it ultimately became a showcase of European artists who shocked the public with its new style of modernism, the exhibit's attempt to package a concept of the state of the arts foreshadowed the significant role museums would play in artistic development in the twentieth century.

Before the mid-Atlantic region's large museums and galleries were established, in the tradition of Robert Gilmore Sr., Alfred Steiglitz, as art patron, established the "291" gallery in 1908. In addition to exhibiting contemporary modern European artists like Auguste Rodin (1840–1917) and Henri Matisse (1869–1954), Steiglitz also patronized local artists, promoting their works and encouraging their unique styles. His encouragement reflected his desire to educate the masses on the meaning of modern art.

Steiglitz's support of Arthur Garfield Dove (1880–1946) helped establish an abstract tradition for American artists. Dove used his connection to nature as a starting point for his painting style. Instead of presenting a particular site or singular area like the Hudson River School artists, his paintings told the story of a union between the essence of nature, found anywhere, and the artist. One title used by Dove for a series, *Nature Symbolized*, emphasizes the non–site-specific concept of nature that informed his work. Raised in Geneva, New York, from the age of five, he graduated from Cornell in 1903 and subsequently moved to New York City, where he was an illustrator for *Century*, *Cosmopolitan*, and *Life* magazines. After meeting Henri, he decided to leave his job and focus more on painting. His early works showed the influence of Paul Cezanne that he developed after a two-year stay in Paris. But after summering at a Connecticut farm, nature's processes became his focus, as seen in the piece *Plant Forms*. At his early one-person shows at Steiglitz's 291 gallery in 1912, and continuing at the annual shows that followed, Dove was befriended by Duncan Phillips. Phillips financially assisted Dove throughout his career, with monthly stipends of $50, and eventually amassed a large collection of Dove's work. These paintings constituted a majority of his collection, the Phillips Memorial Gallery in Washington, D.C.

The Arensberg Circle

A contemporary of Steiglitz, Walter Arensberg, born in Pittsburgh in 1878, was also an active patron. He not only served as a social and financial patron, but ac-

Jacob Riis

Jacob Riis did not consider himself an artist. His photographs were not meant to express his inner feelings or emotions, nor were they to be an expression of an acquired or learned skill. Above all, they were intended to be part of a campaign for social reform to alleviate the sanitation, education, and housing problems caused by slum life. He originally employed professional photographers to accompany him into the urban slums, but when they began to refuse to enter these communities, he began taking his own pictures.

tively assisted in the production of art as well. He opened his New York City apartment as a social gathering place for American and European artists and writers. His patronage attracted regional as well as international artists who were connected to many different styles and movements. From his patronage, Arensberg collected a large number of works produced by those he sponsored. Like Phillips's collection in D.C., Arensberg's works were eventually willed by his family to the Philadelphia Museum in 1950.

The most prominent artist in this circle was Marcel Duchamp (1887–1968). Born in France, he, along with Francis Picabia (1879–1953), moved to New York City in 1915. Together they established the Dada movement in New York City. Dada was an international movement that began in Switzerland in 1916. Its members mocked established artistic and social conventions by creating art that emphasized absurdity. In New York, Duchamp's version of the movement was to react against the European trend of that time, which proposed that art should appeal to the senses. Instead, Duchamp emphasized art for the mind. Duchamp's readymades were ordinary objects, transformed into art by the will of the artist. These sculptures, like *In Advance of the Broken Arm* of 1915, disregarded the art tradition of skillful material manipulation from the artist's hands in creating a beautiful object. The viewer had to make the connection between the object and representation. Morton Schamberg (1881–1918) of Philadelphia, another Dadaist, produced *God*, a plumbing trap affixed to a wood miter box. Instead of using regional materials, designing sculptures for specific patrons, or using familiar concepts with familiar objects, their art was designed to break the notions of familiarity and expectation that the viewer had about art. Many Dadaists turned their backs on familiar media and techniques to create this break and to push the boundaries of what was a possible artistic form.

A member of the Arensberg circle, but not connected to Dada, Charles Demuth (1883–1935) was a regionalist painter of the buildings in the industrial city of Lancaster, Pennsylvania. A student at the PAFA from 1905 to 1911, he later painted landmarks of his hometown in a Precisionist style. Precisionists painted objects using areas of unmodulated color which was contained by straight-edged lines. This technique emphasized the flat surface of the canvass, not an illusion of three-dimensional space. In Demuth's *Modern Conveniences* he incorporated intrusive lines that flattened the composition. Charles Sheeler (1883–1965) of Philadelphia was another Precisionist who made still-life paintings of objects obtained from local folk art collector Dr. Henry Chapman Mercer. His collection contained many items from the local Pennsylvania German population. Sheeler and Demuth collaborated on photographic excursions of barns in the Bucks County area. Sheeler studied the photographs to create the Precisionist sharp, flat edge seen in his *Bucks County Barn* of 1923.

Joseph Stella (1877–1946), born in Muro Lucano, Italy, immigrated to New York in 1896, and became a U.S. citizen in 1923. Stella visited West Virginia in 1907 and Pittsburgh in 1908 to draw miners and factory workers. Later, Stella incorporated the energetic movement of Italian Futurism with the subject matter of New York's industrial growth seen in the new skyscrapers. In his *Voice of the City of New York Interpreted* (1920–1922), he adopted a spiritual connection, previously reserved for the awe inspired by the landscape and nature, to the growing urban city. In the city, he recalled, "Many nights I stood on the bridge . . . a defenseless prey to the surrounding swarming darkness—crushed by the mountainous black impenetrability of the skyscrapers—here and there lights resembling suspended falls of astral bodies . . . shaken by the underground tumult of trains in perpetual motion, like the blood in the arteries. . . . I felt deeply moved, as if on the threshold of a new religion or in the presence of a new DIVINITY."

Social Realism

Life in New York City was experienced differently by the black population in Harlem. New York City was a magnet for African Americans leaving the South between World War I and World War II. This movement from the South, where jobs were scarce and conditions intolerable for most rural blacks, to the North, where the demand for industrial labor grew, was called the Great Migration. The city's black population grew from approximately 92,000 in 1910 to 328,000 in 1930. This growing community created a new awareness of black identity. This awareness was expressed in art, literature, and philosophy, and known as the Harlem Renaissance.

The WPA and Art

The government-financed Works Progress Administration of Franklin D. Roosevelt put millions of Americans to work during the depression. One subdivision, the Public Works of Art Project, was a program established in 1934 to fund mural production in America. In 1935, another subdivision, the Federal Art Project, was created, which expanded the type of art production to be funded. Easel painting, sculpture, and other media were included. By 1936, the project employed 6,000 artists, more than half living in New York. Artists would have to submit finished works to the government to receive a stipend of around $23 a week. From 1935 to 1941, this type of government patronage, during a time of great hardship, kept the artistic culture in New York City and the country alive. This funding was the critical element credited to supporting the social realists of the 1930s, and the abstract expressionists of the 1940s, considered to be the most influential American artistic movement of the twentieth century.

Photographer James VanDerZee was active in Harlem from 1920 to the 1980s. As a portraitist and street photographer, he documented the happenings of the area. By photographing wealthy black property owners, like Harry Wills in *Donner Party with Boxer Harry Wills* of 1926, VanDerZee created a visual record of the African American's rise into the upper classes. He also took photographs in clubs that were used as places to organize and create change within the local community, as there were few opportunities outside of Harlem for its residents to be politically active.

The parents of painter Jacob Lawrence (1917–2000) were among the millions to actually make the migration. From South Carolina, Lawrence's family moved to Atlantic City, where Jacob was born. They later moved to Easton, Pennsylvania, then to Philadelphia, and finally settled in Harlem in 1930. Lawrence was enrolled in an arts-and-crafts program there where he was instructed by Charles Alston, who eventually became one of the most influential artists in Harlem. This auspicious meeting opened many doors for Lawrence in the art community. Lawrence later enrolled in the Works Progress Administration (WPA) program as a result of the help given by another Harlem artist, Augusta Savage (1892–1962). This allowed him, like most artists during the depression years, to continue working.

With the assistance of the WPA, Lawrence created his sixty-panel *Migration Series* during 1940 and 1941. This series documented events that happened during

Jacob Lawrence's silkscreen print of an African American woman and man sitting at a table reading before a window showing street a scene (1988). Courtesy Library of Congress.

the long journey endured by black families who traveled northward. Painted on hardboard, not canvas, the images conveyed strong emotions by distorting and simplifying visual reality. Lawrence's intentional simplification made the images understandable to people of all ages and cultures. The titles of each piece, usually a descriptive sentence, supported each panel's emotional content as well as giving the viewer information about the struggles of the migration (for example, "They were very poor" and "In every home people who had not gone North met and tried to decide if they should go North"). There was never any reference to neoclassical or academic treatments of this singularly American subject.

In a fashion similar to Lawrence's social commentaries, the social realism of other New York–based artists of the 1930s like painters Reginald Marsh (1898–1954), Isabel Bishop (1902–1988), and Ben Shahn (1898–1969), and photographer Berenice Abbott (1898–1991) was inspired by the Ashcan painters. The Ashcan painters supplied the tradition of the subject matter of the urban streets, which was adopted in Marsh's description of New York's Bowery scene and Bishop's figures in public spaces, showing the disastrous effects of the depression on the city's inhabitants. Abbott and Shahn incorporated themes of socialist politics into their work, by using images of individuals which imparted empathy with workers' rights and social reform.

Abstract Expressionism

With a resounding shift in subject matter, abstract expressionism disrupted this realist imagery during the late 1940s and the 1950s. It favored an abstract style that reflected the inner emotions of the artist. This approach to art production, although begun in New York City, was not concerned with the visible environment of a particular location, but the inner world that existed within everyone's subconscious. Abstract expressionism, or action painting, was partly influenced by Mexican muralists, an awareness of psychoanalytical theory, and the Surrealist movement. The Mexican muralists Diego Rivera (1886–1957), Jose Clemente Orozco (1883–1949), and David Alfaro Siqueiros (1896–1974), although realist and socialist inspired, supplied emotional energy, large-scale paintings, and new techniques of paint application for the abstract expressionists.

De Kooning and Pollock

Two representatives of the school were Willem de Kooning (1904–1997) and Jackson Pollock (1912–1956). De Kooning, born in Rotterdam, Holland, studied at the Rotterdam Academy and immigrated to New York City in 1926. As a student of the academy, he was a figure painter and portraitist by training. While in New York, he manipulated the human figure into an abstract form with doodle-like application of paint in his woman-series piece *Woman VI*. These doodles derived from contact with Andre Breton's Surrealist movement followers who were in New York City during the early 1940s. The Surrealists emphasized a drawing technique, called automatic drawing, that was not guided by the artist's thoughts. For de Kooning, the abstracted women were vague expressions he had of gender at the time, where the figures conveyed his feelings of ambivalence toward women. The outcome of his irritation turned into a disturbing visual image. This working out of inner emotions through the process of painting was encouraged by exposure to psychology and personal therapy, as both de Kooning and Pollock had personal therapists. De Kooning's technique of paint application, slow and deliberate, was never evident in his works since they appeared to have been completed quickly. His connection to action painting resided only in the finished painting, looking like it was produced with energy and movement, not from his application technique.

Pollock, however, was the most notable painter who used movement and action in his application of paint to the canvas. Influenced by the Mexican muralists, Pollock began using large canvasses that rivaled the size and visual impact of the mural. After working as a helper in a mural workshop in New York City under Siqueiros in 1936, Pollock began to accumulate information he later transferred to his art. Siqueiros chose new synthetic paints like Duco, used to paint automobiles, to provide an alternative to the traditional materials found in the academies and schools. New methods of applying paint through spraying, dripping, and scraping were encouraged. The painting surfaces were laid on the floor, and the mural designs began with accidental marks of color, from which the images followed.

Pollock's imagery came from his subconscious. He was led to therapy in 1939 after he acknowledged both his alcoholism and his failure at figural drawing after studying at the Art Students League while under Thomas Hart Benton (1889–1975). His Jungian therapist encouraged spontaneous, free associating drawing as a therapeutic tool. As a result, Pollock began using mythological themes, which he learned were supposedly part of his collective unconscious, as subject matter. Images like *Totem Lesson 1* of 1944, *Moon Woman* of 1942, and *She Wolf* of 1943 were his attempts to paint abstractions of ideas that all people collectively share, without the need to adhere to the rules of drawing.

It was his Guggenheim-commissioned mural of 1944 that fueled his movement into a new style of action. At 7 by 11 feet, and completed almost overnight, it was placed on the floor, and literally attacked by the artist with his materials. Using large brushes to make flowing forms, the process was more emotive, gestural, and dynamic than contemplative in order to meet the deadline set by the patron Peggy

Guggenheim. This process was recalled by Pollock in the late 1940s when he began producing his infamous drip paintings in his Long Island studio barn. These abstractions of paint-dripped color were made by waving a soaked brush or stick of enamel paint over the canvas with a rhythmic sweeping motion of the arm. Interestingly, both de Kooning's and Pollock's paintings were very traditional in the ways that the artists consciously created balanced compositions. They kept key motifs or repeated shapes away from the four corners of the canvas, creating avenues to guide the viewer's gaze within the painting, in a very structured, yet highly intuitive way.

Abstract expressionism defined a major change in the art world. Its dramatic departure from established tradition created a media sensation. Like no time in the past, art made news in America. From a *Time* magazine interview that dubbed "Jack the Dripper" the greatest painter in the world, to his tragic death from driving his car, while drunk, off the road near his Long Island home, Pollock's paintings were seen as the battleground of his troubled life. Art was not only turning personal and emotional but it was being bought by international corporations, especially this abstract art that the corporations considered nonpolitical. The final result was that New York City, not Europe's Paris, became the new art capital of the Western world.

Some aspects of abstract expressionism continued and formed new movements. Color field painters such as Barnett Newmann (1905–1970) and Mark Rothko (1903–1970) adopted de Kooning's large areas of color and Pollock's large canvasses. While Newmann added vertical lines over large areas of pure color, Rothko juxtaposed varying colors, in the form of squares with undefined edges, that created spiritual transitions from one color to the other. Both still used the large canvasses as well. Ironically, in the tradition of modernism, abstract expressionism soon became something to rebel against. Artists, looking back to Marcel Duchamp, adopted Conceptual art, using an intellectual rather than a purely visual or emotional approach to producing their works. This approach would transform the modern era into the postmodern.

The sculptural equivalent to the abstract expressionistic painters was David Smith (1906–1965). Never trained in art at school, Smith came to sculpture from his experience as a welder in an automobile plant in 1925 and then a locomotive factory during World War II. Moving to New York City in 1926, he studied at the Art Students League under John Sloan. After exposure to a photograph of Picasso's metal sculptures of 1928 in the French art magazine *Cahiers d'Art*, he began experimenting with the aid of his industrial tools and skills. He, like Pollock, added new industrial materials and techniques to art production. Using a welding torch, steel, and iron, he rejected the chisel, marble, and bronze tools legitimized by the academic art establishment. Most of his sculptures were designed for placement outdoors, especially after moving from his Brooklyn Terminal Iron Works studio to Bolton Landing, New York, in 1940. Some pieces used the landscape as a starting point, much like de Kooning's use of the female figure, like *Hudson River Landscape* of 1951. This work had some elements that could be interpreted as objects in nature, like flowing water and an expanding vista, but the overall impression was a subjective one, coming from Smith's intimate relationship with nature and his surroundings at Bolton Landing. His larger works, produced as a series, like his totem or Cubi series, were imposing structures that created their own landscapes and were less informed by the natural landscapes they inhabited. All abstract in form, the sculptures successfully defined themselves as balanced and expressive, much like Pollock's paintings.

Pop Art

Pop art was a direct reaction against abstract expressionism. Artists turned to popular culture and media for materials and subject matter. The medium used was not connected to the feelings of the artist. It was also, in most cases, devoid of any direct social commentary. This lack of personal involvement by the artist was exemplified by Robert Rauschenberg (b. 1925). Rauschenberg's mixed media combined elements of collage, painting, and sculpture. These elements, seen in his *Skyway* of 1964, had no relationship to one another and did not reveal Rauschenberg's personality. In short, there were a lot of separate images used, but there was never any subject that unified the im-

Postmodernism and the Art of Popular Culture

Modernist artists looked to art itself for new ideas on how to create, like emphasizing the flatness of the painting (Demuth), using color itself as a way to communicate emotion (Rothko), or applying paint onto the canvas in such a way as to express personal emotion and the human gesture involved in the act of painting (Pollock). They produced art with a concern for design and strove for a sense of originality. Postmodernism, which began in the 1960s, used popular consumer culture from around the world, driven by technology, as a source for images and ideas. One effect of postmodernism was a movement away from the strongly personal aspect of abstract expressionism toward a more impersonal artwork. Some artists treated art-making as a mechanical process of reproduction, incorporating found images from the mainstream media into their art. Others assembled their art with a sense of play and embraced chance. Conversely, some artists adopted these postmodern techniques in order to create artistic expression for previously marginalized voices, groups, and perspectives. As a result, the viewer's ability to discern a definitive meaning of a postmodernist work from the visible object matter was called into question. Multiple readings and contextualized viewings of the artwork became much more common.

ages. Jasper Johns (b. 1930) applied the same distanced position in his art, insisting that the artwork be just another object where he "thought it was of no particular interest that [an image] was one thing or another or something else."[18] His painting *Flag* of 1954 created a stir when the question arose whether it was a painting of a flag or a flag made into a painting.

Using the same detachment, Andy Warhol (1928–1987) called his studio the "Factory," and employed other people to produce his art. He used the repetitive and mechanical process of silkscreen printing, commonly used in the mass production of signs, T-shirts, and advertising, to remove the personal connection between the artist and the finished art object. He reproduced images of famous popular heroes like Marilyn Monroe and Elvis with no interest in producing a one-of-a-kind original likeness or portrait. Frank Stella (b. 1936) abandoned the brushstroke, so apparent in de Kooning's work, by showing no trace of brush marks on the surface of his paintings. Stella used assistants and students to paint the works, and he never signed the completed artwork.

In Harlem during the early 1960s, Romare Bearden (1912–1988) began using collage not with detachment in mind but to represent a spiritual connection he felt emanating from his Harlem community. His use of collage placed him in the art historical tradition of Picasso and Braque, while his use of urban black photographs allowed him to "redefine the image of man in the terms of the Negro experience I know Best."[19] His *Prevalence of Ritual: Baptism* of 1964 suggested a complex reading of the importance of religion in his African American experience. The human figures were composites of religious African art objects and contemporary individuals, symbolizing the African influence in contemporary black society. Bearden's figural distortions were a conceptual device that he used to convey an improvisational, jazzlike, visual rhythmic pattern of images. He also used this device to convey emotions by emphasizing certain body parts over others. Bearden's collage technique was guided by a playful attitude, allowing him to creatively assemble many disparate images into a single cohesive one.

Installation and Performance Art

Some artworks were made specifically for museum or gallery spaces. In collaboration with the major museums in New York, especially the Museum of Modern Art (MOMA) and the Metropolitian Museum, artists were given the opportunity to transform entire rooms with their art. Installation art, pioneered by Duchamp, tended to "take over" most of the physical space of a gallery or museum room. The work usually incorporated the actual structure of the gallery as part of the art piece. This technique was an attempt by the artist to overwhelm the viewers' senses with a variety of objects and images. With work experience as a commercial artist in New York, Barbara Kruger (b. 1945) used texts and images that were printed directly on the walls and floors of the gallery in her *Untitled* of 1991. As a postmodernist, Kruger also used images from print media and juxtaposed them with a written text to raise issues about gender and consumerism in twentieth-century culture.

This connection between artist and institutional space was questioned by the performance artists of the 1960s. From the 1960s to the present, these artists perform their art message in the form of dance, music, spoken words, sounds, and images that would often take place in public places as a rejection of the now institutional space that musuems have become. Usually performed in theaters or on street corners, once the performance was finished, the artwork ceased to exist. Carolee Schneemann's (b. 1939) *Meat Joy* of 1964 was performed in New York City and used touch, smell, taste, and sound by having actors rub dead animal carcasses and blood over their bodies while appearing to enjoy the activity. Performance art, from the 1960s to the present, has been a rejection of the pop art emphasis on mass-media images and the art object as a thing that can be bought and sold.

Neo-Pop

Commodity art (or Neo-pop), which began in the East Village of New York City, during the late 1980s and into the 1990s, continued pop art's fascination with the images of mass media. The movement itself was promoted by editors working for influential art magazines such as *Artforum*, who in turn packaged the art as legitimate by including it in their pages. Focusing on the idea that American culture was based on the buying and selling of commodities, Jeff Koons (b. 1955) placed ads in art magazines to advertise himself as a commodity. Artists as well as editors of art magazines like *Artforum*, *Art News*, and *Art in America*, all published in New York City, took advantage of the financial climate of the 1970s to the early 1990s, in which inflation encouraged cash investment. Art was sellable as never before, sometimes not for its aesthetic qualities, but for its pragmatic investment potential.

New York galleries, in addition to magazines, created new movements and established new artistic careers by featuring artists who gained popularity through the media. These artists were then scooped up by major museums like the Metropolitan Museum of Art, MOMA, and the Whitney Museum of American Art for retrospective shows. The museum directors and curators, like the artists noted above, were capitalizing on the new marketability of art to promote the museum itself.

While artists like Koons were interested in the commodification of the art object and the marketing system of the galleries, museums, and magazines, other New York artists were turning to different materials not associated with the slick advertising of new products. Slack artists used secondhand objects and personal trash to counter artistic consumerism. Karen Kilimnik (b. 1955) built installations using discarded materials to create an unfinished and disorderly space. These spaces, seen in her *Madonna and Backdraft in Nice*, reflect her own self-described personality as a "slob," as well as provide a commentary on the ordered and precise world one experiences within the traditional gallery or museum.

The Guerrilla Girls

From the 1980s to the present, the anonymous political activist group Guerrilla Girls took artwork, in the form of broadsheets, directly to the streets of New York City. As the self-proclaimed "conscience of the art world," these artists began protesting sexism and racism in the art world by making posters and affixing them to buildings and other city objects around Manhattan. This choice of placement was part of their message, that women artists and artists of color have been ignored and, as a result, are excluded from participation in the male-dominated vocation of art production that appears in galleries and museum collections. Their gallery space, though not by choice, was the street. Their messages, like those in *The Advantages of Being a Women Artist* and *When Racism and Sexism Are No Longer Fashionable*, use fonts that resemble familiar, easy-to-read newspaper type. Their use of humor makes the subject matter of the posters less intimidating and more approachable for the viewer on the street. As an organization of artists, they have received funding from individual donors from around the world. They also can be hired, usually by academic institutions, for lectures which they attend wearing gorilla masks to protect their artistic careers from backlash and to assert that the criticisms are not coming from particular individuals but from all women who live within a patriarchal society. The postmodern concept of anonymity is not a result of their detachment from their work, but is a result of their intense passion and commitment to the politically progressive agenda intended to create societal change.

Modern Technology and Art

Other contemporary artists are instead using technology as a tool in the creative process, and as raw material in their art production. Julian Laverdiere (b. 1971), who was born in 1971 in the Adirondacks and currently lives in New York City, focuses on technological developments that have changed our society from an industrial into an information era. Laverdiere has produced mixed media assemblages like *First Attempted Trans Atlantic Telegraph Cable Crossing* (2000), which attempts to impart a romantic view of technology's evolution by placing a model of a ship which sank as it was laying the cable across the ocean in a mausoleum-like tomb. This presentation encourages the viewer to relate positively to technology's progression. In contrast, Jennifer Eun Cho (b. 1958) disassembles technology in an aggressive, retaliatory way. In *Haystack* of 1999, she "harvests" toxic fumes and coiled filaments from within compact discs, by melting them and then assembling the remnants. Cho's interaction with technology, which mimics a farmer's interaction with the land and nature, reflects the importance of technology in our current culture. Other artists, such as Andy Mezensky (date of birth unknown) of Baltimore, use materials that are not so technologically advanced, but are as important in our contemporary environment. Recycling machines found in public works facilities, Mezensky reassembles them and adds organic, anatomical shapes that are cast in bronze. This combination of the underground, unseen network of machinery and the bronzed flesh reveals our intimate connection to the machines of our culture which we never see or experience first hand.

While Mezensky deals with the unseen technology, other artists are more apt to use electronic media such as video and the computer in their work. Those who create electronic art are breaking new ground in artistic creation, as it is unrelated to traditional artistic production, and tends to have little commodity value. Because of this, many commercial galleries did not support this new medium until the mid-1990s when the Soho Guggenheim began retrospectives of individual artists' work and then MOMA's "Video Spaces: Eight Installations" exhibition. Artists like New York City's Bill Viola (b. 1951) have created rich environment installations controlled by computers. In Viola's *Slowly Turning Narrative*, several video monitors and projectors with elaborate sound systems and mirrors deliberately created an environment of sensory overload for the viewer.

Technology has also allowed many artists to work in collaborative productions. Acting like a new artists' society or a new "school," the World Wide Web has connected artists to one another, as well as to the public, as no other gallery, patron, newspaper, or magazine could do in the past. This caused an increase in community-based projects like those established by the Baltimore Museum of Art, which invited artists to work with the local community over several months to create a work that would be the focus of other public programs organized by the museum. In addition, the Contemporary Museum of Baltimore organized an exhibition of mid-Atlantic artists, who used sailcloth as their primary material. The results, including work by Baltimore's digital artist Lew Fifield, were exhibited in conjunction with the 1999 Baltimore Waterfront Festival.

Past and Present

As some artists have adopted technology to travel in virtual space beyond their local community, Native American artists have traveled back in time in an effort to reestablish discontinued artistic traditions that were once part of their culture. Traditional art materials and designs have been incorporated into contemporary art by many Native artists in an attempt to keep their cultural history alive. This union of past with the present is seen by artists such as Peter Jones (b. 1947) of the Onondaga tribe, who has rekindled the tradition of Iroquois pottery. This pottery tradition, for reasons unknown, was no longer practiced after 600 C.E. With no written or oral traditions to refer to, Jones looked to surviving pieces of pottery in museums and collaborated with other Native sculptors to try and re-create the process. His vessels draw on those found at the Squawkie Hill Mound with the pointed bottom, scalloped upper rim, and textures made by shells and fabric. Jones also makes clay works that comment on contemporary issues such as gaming resorts on Indian reservations and other relevant social issues. Similarly, Richard Glazer Danay (b. 1942) of the Mohawk tribe uses a traditional Mohawk cross-hatching design for part of the brim decoration of his *Mohawk Headdress*. Forms suggesting the "false face" masks are also used. Contemporary materials replace the traditional, with a construction worker's hard hat for the feathered headdress and acrylic paint for vegetable dyes.

With this union of past with present we have come full circle, in some respects, from the Native American tradition to the contemporary and back again. Along this path, we have found the arts of the mid-Atlantic region to be constantly changing and adapting to certain forces. Artists' exposure to the changing sources of patronage, available materials, and teachers influence the type of art produced. In turn, the art produced has given us glimpses into certain areas of the region, through visual documentation of its territory and people. In addition, the art has given us glimpses of the internal visions and expressions of the artists themselves. These glimpses will hopefully give meaning to the actions of artists in the past so that we can understand the new artistic visions of the present.

RESOURCE GUIDE

Printed Sources

Baigell, Matthew. *A Concise History of American Painting and Sculpture*. Rev. ed. New York: HarperCollins, 1996.

Baltimore Museum of Art. *American Paintings 1750–1900, from the Collection of the Baltimore Museum of Art*. Baltimore: Baltimore Museum of Art, 1983.

Bearden, Romare, and Harry Henderson. *A History of African-American Artists from 1792 to the Present*. New York: Pantheon Books, 1993.

Davidson, Abraham A. *Early American Modernist Painting, 1910–1935*. 2nd ed. New York: Da Capo Press, 1994.

Dempsey, Amy. *Art in the Modern Era: A Guide to Styles, Schools and Movements 1860 to the Present*. New York: Harry N. Abrams, 2002.

Fineberg, Jonathan. *Art Since 1940: Strategies of Being*. Upper Saddle River, NJ: Prentice Hall, 1995.

Gerdts, William H. *The East and the Mid-Atlantic: Art Across America—Two Centuries of Regional Painting, 1710–1920*. New York: Abbeville Press, 1990.

Guerrilla Girls. *Confessions of the Guerrilla Girls*. New York: HarperPerennial, 1995.

Harvey, David. *The Condition of Postmodernity: An Inquiry into the Origins of Cultural Change*. Cambridge, MA: Blackwell, 1990.

Hollander, Stacy C., and Brooke Davis Anderson, eds. *American Anthem: Masterworks from the American Folk Art Museum*. New York: Harry N. Abrams, 2001.

King, J.C.H. *First Peoples, First Contacts: Native Peoples of North America*. Cambridge: Harvard University Press, 1999.

Lovejoy, Margot. *Postmodern Currents: Art and Artists in the Age of Electronic Media*. 2nd ed. Upper Saddle River, NJ: Prentice Hall, 1997.

Novak, Barbara. *American Painting of the Nineteenth Century: Realism, Idealism, and the American Experience*. 2nd ed. New York: Harper and Row, 1979.

Pearlman, Bennard B. *Painters of the Ashcan School: The Immortal Eight*. New York: Dover Publications, 1979.

Stokstad, Marilyn, ed. *Art History*. Rev. ed. Vol. 2. New York: Harry N. Abrams, 1999.

Wade, Edwin L., ed. *The Arts of the North American Indian: Native Traditions in Evolution.* New York: Hudson Hills Press, 1986.

Weidman, Gregory R., ed. *Classical Maryland, 1815–1845: Fine and Decorative Arts from the Golden Age.* Baltimore: Maryland Historical Society, 1993.

Whitney Museum of American Art, ed. *Two Hundred Years of American Sculpture.* New York: David R. Godine, 1976.

Willis, Deborah. *Reflections in Black: A History of Black Photographers, 1840 to the Present.* New York: W. W. Norton, 2000.

Web Sites—Museums, Collections, and Resources

American Folk Art Museum
2 Lincoln Square Columbus Ave.
New York, NY 10023
http://www.folkartmuseum.org

Folk art from the colonial period to the twentieth century.

Andy Warhol Museum
Pittsburgh, PA 16483
http://www.warhol.org

Over 4,000 works in all media accompanied by educational information on the artist.

Art Students League
West 57th St.
New York, NY 10019-2104
http://www.theartstudentsleague.org

Offering student exhibitions and faculty lectures on anatomical drawing and art historical subjects.

Baltimore Museum of Art
10 Art Museum Dr.
Baltimore, MD 21218-3898
(410) 396-4930
http://www.artbma.org

The permanent collection contains work from Andy Warhol, Jasper Johns, Robert Rauschenberg, and Barbara Kruger.

Corcoran Museum of Art
17th St.
Washington, DC 20006-4804
http://www.corcoran.org

This collection has artwork from Rembrandt Peale, William Glackens, Thomas Cole, William Sydney Mount, Hiram Powers, and Joshua Johnson.

Guerrilla Girls
http://www.guerrillagirls.com

Get involved with progressive politics, or just have fun, while you learn about racism and sexism in the arts. The site has access to all the Guerrilla Girls posters.

Huntington Museum of Art
2033 McCoy Rd.
Huntington, WV 25701
http://www.hmoa.org

Regional cultural center with extensive art programs for children and adults.

Metropolitan Museum of Art
1000 Fifth Ave. at 82nd St.
New York, NY 10028-0198
(212) 570-3828
http://www.metmuseum.org

Over 3,000 works of American art.

Museum of Modern Art, Queens
33 St. at Queens Blvd.
Long Island City, NY 11101
http://www.moma.org

Online "exhibition" of fourteen images by Jasper Johns and six images by Willem de Kooning.

National Gallery of Art
Constitution Ave. NW
Washington, DC 20565–0001
(202) 842-6176
http://www.nga.gov

Online tours of major themes in American art, such as landscapes, and individual artists such as Jackson Pollock.

Peabody Art Collection
Maryland State Archives
350 Rowe Blvd.
Annapolis, MD 21410
http://www.mdarchives.state.md.us

The Annapolis Collection contains 700 works of art, most of which can be viewed online. The Peabody Collection contains 1,400 art objects, specializing in nineteenth- and early-twentieth-century American paintings, with most available online.

Philadelphia Museum of Art
26th St. at Benjamin Franklin Pkwy.
Philadelphia, PA 19103
http://philamuseum.org

Extensive holdings of Pennsylvania German art and an extensive collection of work by Thomas Eakins and Marcel Duchamp.

The Phillips Collection
1600 21st St., NW
Washington, DC 20009
http://www.phillipscollection.org

Collection has extensive holdings of Jacob Lawrence, Arthur Garfield Dove, and Thomas Eakins.

PS1 Contemporary Art Center
22–25 Jackson Ave.
Long Island City, NY 11101
mail@ps1.org
http://www.ps1.org

Contemporary online projects (zexe.net) and online tours.

Seneca/Iroquois National Museum
774-814 Broad St.
Salamanca, NY 14779
seniroqm@localnet.com
http://www.senecamuseum.org

Hundreds of ancient and contemporary cultural and art objects from the Iroquois Nation.

Solomon R. Guggenheim Museum
1071 Fifth Ave. (at 89th St.)
New York, NY 10128-0173
www.guggenheim.org

Whitney Museum of American Art
945 Madison Ave. at 75th St.
New York, NY 10021
http://www.whitney.org

ECOLOGY AND ENVIRONMENT

Robert P. Marzec,
with Daniel Malerk

The notion of living inside an extended community of relationships and obligations, stretching from the bioregion to the biosphere, represents a new vision of personal and global security that is in sharp contrast to the detached, mechanistic view of the past, with its emphasis on dominance, control, subjugation, self-interest, and autonomy. . . . Reintegrating ourselves back into the temporal and spatial contours of the local biome and the earth's biosphere will require a leap of human consciousness, a fundamental transformation of our sense of self and our relationship to the world around us.
—Jeremy Rifkin, *Biosphere Politics*

History and ecology go hand in hand. To understand the environment of the Mid-Atlantic, it is necessary to have knowledge of a variety of broad historical and political factors that affected the region through the centuries and made it what it is today. The mid-Atlantic region we know today emerges with the rise of the Atlantic world of exploration and colonization, which includes English and European expansion and settlement. Studying this expansion reveals that economy and ecology also go hand in hand. As we will see, precolonial Native Americans held a very different economic, and thus ecological, relationship to the land. Although Indians and Europeans engaged in similar activities that affected the environment (such as clearing the forests for purposes of farming), intense economic development on the part of Europeans demanded that the land be "improved" to produce a "higher yield" than was common with Indian cultivation. Coupled with the philosophical and religious outlook that the land needed to be "subdued" by humanity, improvement practices began to change the environment of the region—slowly at first, then more dramatically as European colonization spread further inland. In this sense, the past and the present also go hand in hand, for this view of the land that governed European settlement became the ground plan that largely determines the status of the environment and our ecological outlook today.

Recognizing these large patterns of development, however, need not necessarily result in the imposition of a single grand perspective upon the landscape that would reduce the complexities of different regions by homogenizing the Mid-Atlantic under some artificially imposed global order. The role of geography cannot be denied in an attempt to understand the character of different regions, and the way in which regions can only be approached in terms of their *distinct relation* to one another. This means developing an awareness of the intricate ecological relations of soil quality to forests and streams, and the connection these have to the quality of fish and wildlife that live and thrive in bay areas miles away. This means too that it is equally important to understand that the region cannot be thought of as "developing naturally," as if the influences of various cultures and their political agendas have had nothing to do with the ways in which humanity has had a profound effect on the environment. As with any region of the United States, or the globe for that matter, various cultural centers of power have influenced, and continue to exert an influence on, the areas they "discover" and eventually colonize. Native Americans, the English, the Dutch, the French, and others have all affected the status of the region, though not equally. We must consequently acknowledge as well the extent to which European nations have taken steps, more often than not massively aggressive steps, to control and dominate the region for purposes of their own ascendency. Understanding the history of the environment means having an awareness of how Western ideological, symbolic narratives of "the virgin land," "the growth of the republic," "frontier expansion," and so on, have all laid the groundwork for *particular* ecological and environmental possibilities. And because the agendas of these various cultural centers continue to have an impact on human development into the twenty-first century, so to do they continue to impact the environment of the Mid-Atlantic.[1]

PHYSICAL DESCRIPTION

The mid-Atlantic region of the United States consists of the following states of New York, Pennsylvania, New Jersey, Delaware, Maryland, and West Virginia, as well as the District of Columbia. The region's total landscape of nearly 163,000 square miles makes up roughly 5 percent of the continental United States and holds 15 percent of the U.S. population. In terms of land mass, large cities do not cover much of the mid-Atlantic region, but they do compose some of the more important population concentrations and metropolitan areas of the country, with New York, Washington, D.C., Philadelphia, Pittsburgh, and Baltimore being among the largest. These major cities generate the greatest percentage of revenue for the area, a staggering 60 percent for the region as a whole. This capital and job base is found primarily along the coastal plain, or in the case of Pittsburgh, near the concentration of the Ohio, Allegheny, and Monongahela rivers. The majority of the mid-Atlantic population tends to center in these five cities, although population in the region did grow overall by 20 percent between 1967 and 1995.

The mid-Atlantic region is diverse, both culturally and geographically. There are several natural resources that are abundant and vital to life in the region. Agricultural land, wetland areas, wildlife habitats, forests, and rivers and streams are all crucial to the survival of the region. Each of these are taken increasingly for granted in this technologically governed information age. The Mid-Atlantic boasts some of the more notable natural resources in the United States, which makes it all the more important that the public develop a strong understanding of the intricacies and delicate nature of the region as a whole.

Mountains and river basins are two of the more impressive landscape features of the mid-Atlantic region. The Appalachian Mountains take up much of the western portion of the region, while in the east, coastal plains stretch to the Chesapeake Bay. The Chesapeake Bay system itself is arguably the region's most important and central ecological feature. As with any ecological region, the bay does not end with its own geographical limits, but extends beyond these confines in the form of its watershed—the various rivers and streams that flow into the bay, and the expansive wetlands and forests that filter out pollutants and serve as habitats for migratory birds and fish that make the bay their primary home. The bay watershed is so large that it extends throughout the entire District of Columbia and into every state in the region except New Jersey. Recent research has revealed that the Bay was actually formed 35 million years ago by a meteor, and became the shallow waterscape that we know today when the last ice age ended 10,000 years ago.[2]

Forests account for over half of the region's land cover. At one point human development practically eradicated these forests, but trees have been able to regenerate over the course of the last century. Still, urban expansion and agricultural development threaten forests once more, carving them up into smaller sections. By doing this, new patterns and structures in the landscape develop, which change the status of ecosystems. Urban or more populated areas are mainly situated along or near the coastal region (New York City, Philadelphia, Baltimore), but roads, both urban and rural, now cover a shocking 25 percent of the entire region. While this provides easier access for humanity, it fragments the environment and simultaneously changes ecosystems and adds pollutants to areas unfamiliar to these toxins. Along those same patterns, agricultural land covers around another 25 percent, and also impacts the environment, although, as we shall see, in different ways. Water quality and aquatic habitat are also essential to the mid-Atlantic region and its landscape. There are hundreds of water disruptions throughout the Mid-Atlantic, which in turn disrupt aquatic ecosystems. Numerous factors include problems like population density, road density, agriculture, and the distances between human settlements and these bodies of water. Indirect impacts can be characterized as air and water pollution from urban areas, and invasions from animals looking to move their habitats because of these ecological changes. Agricultural land is also prone to soil erosion and runoff from pesticides and fertilizers, mostly found in eastern Pennsylvania, Maryland, and parts of West Virginia and Delaware. Not incidentally, these same areas of the Mid-Atlantic are among some of the most water polluted in the nation.

The east coastal plan contains many shallow inland bays and tidal rivers. More than 64,000 square miles of land drain into the Chesapeake Bay—the nation's largest estuary. The Delmarva peninsula, about 180 miles long, separates the Chesapeake Bay from Delaware Bay and the Atlantic Ocean, and extends from Delaware through Maryland to Virginia (hence the name). The eastern part of the peninsula is characterized by sand beaches and level, regular land; the west coast is more jagged and marshy. Agriculture, fishing, poultry raising, and tourism are the main industries. The mid-Atlantic region thrives with such an odd balance of few heavily populated areas and great amounts of rural areas due to its surrounding environmental counterparts, which are depended on heavily. Three essential river basins those of the Delaware, Potomac, and Susquehanna rivers—provide much of the region's drinking water as well as water for consumption outside the mid-Atlantic. First, the Delaware River basin, which extends between Hancock, New York, and Delaware Bay, is the longest free-flowing (undammed) river east of the Mississippi. Providing roughly 6.3 billion gallons of water every day for residential, commercial, and industrial use, the Delaware River basin has a total population of 7.3 million. An additional 9.9 million people rely on it for their water. In addition, the Delaware River basin serves major industries such as dairy and poultry farming, fishing, and even tourism.

Second, and just as important, is the Potomac River basin, which extends from Maryland into Pennsylvania, Washington, D.C., and finally into West Virginia. While serving roughly 4.6 million people (3.7 million from Washington, D.C., alone), the Potomac River basin's waters are also vital for agriculture, forestry, and fossil fuel production, especially coal. The Mid-Atlantic's third river basin, arguably the most vital, is the Susquehanna River basin. Draining over 27,000 square miles in Maryland, Pennsylvania, and New York, the Susquehanna's mainline stream of river is the longest commercially nonhazardous river in North America. With a population of only 4.1 million people, it is the smallest river basin in terms of the amount of drinking water it supplies, but it has a larger drainage area than the other two river basins combined. The Susquehanna River basin accounts for 43 percent of the Chesapeake Bay's drainage area, as well as half of the fresh water flowing into the Chesapeake Bay. With this kind of drainage and flowing water, it should come as no surprise that this river basin experiences a major flood on an average of once every twenty years, a cause for added stress for the region in terms of cleanup and economic loss.

The mid-Atlantic region also enjoys a wealth of mountainous territory. Part of the Appalachian Mountain range runs through the heart of the Mid-Atlantic, with the most famous consisting of the ranges in Pennsylvania and the Appalachian Highlands area of New York. These ranges are more commonly known in the Mid-Atlantic as the Allegheny Mountains. The north end of the region is heavily glaciated, and thus gives central New Yorkers the Finger Lakes, so called because of their appearance together in succession in the landscape of New York. In Pennsylvania, the Allegheny Mountains combine with the Pocono Mountains, a popular resort area that offers such activities as skiing and other winter sports. In addition to their economic importance in terms of tourism, the Pocono Mountains provide important wildlife habitat.

The Appalachian Mountains date back to prehistoric times. A look at some of the rock samples collected from the Allegheny region has provided scientists and historians alike with evidence that the Appalachians were formed during "land plate collision." The birth of the Appalachian range (possibly some 480 million years ago) marks the first of several mountain-building plate collisions that led the way to the formation of Pangaea, the ancient super continent, with the Appalachians being at the center of this massive geological landscape. Because North America and Africa were originally connected, the Appalachians are thought to have been part of the same mountain chain as the Atlas Mountain range, which lies in Morocco. The mountains on the western border of the Mid-Atlantic are

An artist paints a view of the Appalachian Mountains, c. 1940. Courtesy Library of Congress.

known for their scenic quality and have numerous state parks, especially in West Virginia. Coal mines in West Virginia and steel mills in Pittsburgh flourished for a time due to the abundant minerals found in the mountains and surrounding areas, but continuous industrial development has taken its toll on these areas. The Appalachian Mountains extend all the way to the state of West Virginia (and beyond)—the section of the Mid-Atlantic furthest to the west. Nicknamed the "Mountain State" and the "Panhandle State," West Virginia lies in the very heart of the Appalachian highlands.

The northern part of the region consists entirely of New York State, which along the eastern coast begins with a series of islands (Manhattan Island, Staten Island, and Long Island) and stretches over 300 miles to reach the shores of Lake Erie. The Atlantic coastal plain of New York differs from the middle of the state (the plateau region of the Appalachian Mountains discussed above), which differs as well from the western portion of the state, a lowland area that flows out of the interior plains. The geography of the state is highly heterogeneous, from the rocky cliffs of the Palisades along the New York/New Jersey shore, to the upstate Thousand Island region along the St. Lawrence River, to Taughannock Falls on Cayuga Lake (one of the Finger Lakes), to well-known Niagara Falls in the west.

Directly and indirectly, and positively and negatively, human activity has affected the environment of the Mid-Atlantic more than anything else since Europeans began to cross the Atlantic five centuries ago. Humanity tends to group and structure the land for its own purposes, and the condition of the landscape itself is usually not preserved after human colonization takes place. For example, although humans create the size and shape of agricultural fields, regional patterns of topography, soils, and overall land geography equally impact agricultural production. The co-constitution of humans and environmental geography is extremely relational in the mid-Atlantic region, mainly because of the unique land resources. The dependency in the relationship between the landscape of the Mid-Atlantic and humanity has created a cornucopia of land patterns and designs.

THE NATIVE AMERICAN ERA

During the era of Paleoindian America (10,000–7,000 B.C.E.) the Laurentide Ice Sheet still covered most of Canada. With the melting of this ice sheet came episodic runoff, which led to gullying of the watersheds, with alluvial fans flowing along the floodplain margins. Heavy sedimentation built up along the valley floors from 6500 to 3200 B.C.E. Arable ground cover increased after 2800 B.C.E. Dense forests developed in the humid Northeast, and evidence of Indian settlements at this time is rare, except along the coasts. Nevertheless, economic activity began to develop, and from 1000 to 500 B.C.E., more definite patterns emerged. These patterns included cultivated crops, pottery technology, the development of the bow and arrow, and food trading. An intensified

Taughannock Falls on Cayuga Lake reflects but one aspect of New York's profoundly heterogeneous environment. New York State Department of Economic Development.

gathering economy, coupled with continuing agricultural customs, had begun by 400 C.E. In the period 900–1500 C.E., riverine trade networks, a common system of agriculture, and broadly shared ideas and beliefs unified the settlements from the Gulf coast to the Great Lakes.

Despite the prevalent world view of the early French and English colonialists, the North American landscape was not a "virgin land" in the early 1600s. Native Americans had thrived on the land for thousands of years. The descendants of Asian peoples that crossed the Bering Straits some 15,000 years ago, they were creating farming towns when Europe was in the Dark Ages. In fact, the oldest documented site of "prehistoric" Native American antiquity is Meadowcroft Rockshelter, located near Pittsburgh, Pennsylvania.[3] Many of these archaeological sites can be found throughout the Mid-Atlantic and the continental United States. The mass migration and settlement of these Paleoindians reflect their ability to successfully develop extensive big-game hunting. In the mid-Atlantic region, Paleo-indian peoples tended to settle in deciduous woodlands, most likely hunting white-tailed deer, and further north, caribou. Even so, European settlers saw Indians as savages who had no right to the land, and viewed America as an empty space for establishing new frontier settlements.

Excavated sites indicate that the landscape of the Neolithic period of Native American culture included several categories of development: (a) short-term sites used for hunting and plant collecting; (b) homesteads of one to several families; (c) hamlets of ten to twenty houses; (d) villages of 30 to over 300 houses, enclosed by palisade or earthwork; and (e) ceremonial towns, ranging in size from 12 to over 200 acres, and including up to 1,000 houses. Karl W. Butzer describes how this "Mississipian" network extended from the Great Plains to the Northeast: "In upstate New York, the Iroquois, a peripheral offshoot of the Woodland tradition, shifted from small, oval houses to great longhouses during the 13th century, indicating a change from nuclear to extended residences, with up to two dozen units; from then until about A.D. 1500 they congregated into increasingly large villages, supported by relatively intensive agriculture and by hunting, fishing, and plant gathering within a large territorial radius." When the early French explorers landed on the East Coast, they introduced European diseases to a Native American population that had no immunity to such foreign viral influences. Plagues such as smallpox, measles, scarlet fever, and whooping cough killed off whole regions of Indians. After the French explorer Jacques Cartier's visit to the St. Lawrence River in 1535, the Iroquois agricultural settlement disappeared, most likely as a result of the introduction of these diseases. Smallpox and measles annihilated up to two-thirds of the Huron and Iroquois; similar population destruction occurred from the sixteenth to the eighteenth centuries in the Southeast, thereby dramatically reducing the Native American influence on the landscape.

Even so, the many thousands of years of Indian settlement left their mark on the mid-Atlantic landscape of today. The areas now known as New York, Pennsylvania, and New Jersey all contained Indian settlements. Many Indians lived along the seaboard from Maryland to Georgia. The Indian population reached its greatest density in the Chesapeake Bay region.[4] Fur-trading posts and British forts were originally built in areas that once were important nodes of Indian settlement, including Albany and Pittsburgh. Core Indian territory, with its established settlements in prime locations, was thus highly attractive to the European settlers who would soon colonize the landscape. In this sense the mid-Atlantic region was not the "virgin" environment often referred to by Europeans and those today who yearn for a return to a "golden age" of land ecology. Indians had modified the land extensively through the years. They cleared forests by burning the undergrowth and deadening large trees (by making incisions in the wood) for farming. They combined farming with hunting and fishing. And when plots of land became worn out, they made new openings or moved entire villages to new areas with fertile soils.

The ecological approaches taken by Native Americans differ markedly from those of the European colonists who eventually came to dominate the region. Indian communities were sometimes nomadic, having developed a close ecological relation to the seasonal changes of the environment. In contrast, most European settlements, from cities to farming communities were geographically fixed. Indian farming methods were also different, such as the planting of more than one crop in a single field, and using mounds to plant seeds, which guarded against soil erosion. Moving from one habitat to another during seasonal changes also meant the hunting of only those species that were plentiful, ensuring that no single species would be subject to extinction from overuse. Europeans constantly criticized the Indians for "improper use" of the land—because they did not establish permanent land development schemes or turn the land over for profit and capitalist development. Indians did not adequately "subdue the soil," as Genesis 1:28 advised the European Christians.[5]

THE EARLY COLONIAL ERA TO THE TWENTIETH CENTURY

In the wake of Columbus's voyage to America, the mid-Atlantic region came under the influence of a vast "Atlantic circuit" comprising a complex and unequal union between four continents (North America, South America, Europe, and Africa) that were home to a wide variety of ethnic groups and cultural traditions. The entire Atlantic coast became a theater of exploration and rivalry for Atlantic European nations. Economic, geopolitical, and agricultural interests were all tied together in this theater, and these factors provide a general summation of three main stages of development in the region: seafaring along the coast, the conquering of coastal areas, and the subsequent agricultural cultivation of the coastal landscape. From this sprung village communities, and eventually larger towns. Jamestown in particular is considered to be a significant early focal point for the development of regional societies in the United States.

French settlements grew up along the St. Lawrence River, ultimately extending into the Thousand Islands region of upstate New York, to Lake Ontario and Lake Erie, through to Detroit, and as far south as New Orleans. Moving out from New England, the British also established settlements along the St. Lawrence and in the Thousand Islands region, competing with the French and the Indians for domination of the area. New England, New York, and Philadelphia became geographical concentrations of power and population that still hold dominion today. Strong geographically specific habits and cultures unfolded. Numerous "guides to the wilderness," such as that written by Judge William Cooper (father of James Fenimore Cooper), appeared in the early 1800s. Cooper ridiculed aristocratic English and Irish settlers who "wasted energy" cutting down trees and rooting out stumps to produce a "neatly manicured" landscape that matched the English countryside. He advised his readers to burn the forests and immediately plant on the scorched land, so as to quickly bring in a substantial harvest. This philosophy became prevalent, buttressed by the belief that there would always be more land to cultivate.

Cultivation practices were marked by the desire for economic gain, rather than a concern for the status of the land. Settlers engaged in heavy deforestation, plundered the riches of the land, and moved on. Present-day habits of highway development and abandonment of urban areas that have outlived their usefulness are deeply rooted in colonial American practices: "Mobility—the willingness to abandon places when they had served a particular purpose—was the key to success, whether success was defined in economic or social terms. And the passion for mobility has left its distinctive marks on the American landscape: a chronic inclination to spend money on public roads; an uncritical admiration for the latest machines of transportation, whether steamboats, or speeding locomotives, or fast cars, or jet aircraft; and the unromantic willingness to abandon things that had outlived their immediate usefulness."[6] European settlers thus set in motion a new environmental use, and consequently a new pattern of environmental historical development, that placed its emphasis on settlement rather than itinerancy, on the turning of land into a commodifiable resource for intense development, and on the view that, above all, the proper relation to the land—which "justified" confiscating land from the Indians—was one of mastery. Such beginnings—"all of which increased considerably the intensity of the human load on the environment"—no doubt influenced the attenuated status of the environment in the twenty-first century.[7]

William Penn's "Holy Experiment"

Though this outlook was widespread, the British settlers of mid-Atlantic North America were not homogeneous. The Northeast contained two dominant cultural regions: the puritan theocracy of New England, and the Pennsylvania culture region. In the early nineteenth century, New England culture began to spread into the mid-Atlantic area of northern New Jersey and through the Catskills and Adirondacks of New York, then along the Erie Canal and the northwestern tip of Pennsylvania. Upstate New York eventually became an extension of New England. The Roman and Greek place-names that punctuate upstate New York (e.g., Ithaca, Rome, Brutus) are an indication of New England's embrace of classical republican democracy. Such names are practically absent from Pennsylvanian towns. The Pennsylvania "hearth" of British and German settlers started with a small settlement on the Delaware River, then developed its own migration stream of pioneers that spread throughout the lower half of Pennsylvania and northern Maryland, and beyond. Unlike the rigid theocracy that dominated New England and its expanding culture, the Pennsylvanian hearth was not dominated by a single religious world view or a single political outlook. The area became known in Europe and England as a haven for religious diversity and as a site for political experimentation. Despite this promise of tolerance, Pennsylvania was nonetheless economically reified as a business venture. William Penn's "Holy Experiment" was, perhaps more than anything, a vast investment site, making a great deal of money for Penn and his followers: "Penn mounted a large-scale advertising campaign throughout the British Isles and in parts of Protestant Europe, touting Pennsylvania as a tolerant place where settlers would be left alone by church and government—provided only that they paid for their land and obeyed the laws. From 1700 onward, migrants flooded to Pennsylvania through the new port of Philadelphia, soon to become the biggest city in North America."[8]

Substantial German and Swiss colonization in the area today known as the "Pennsylvania Dutch" country introduced large-scale farming to the area. Unlike that of New England, Pennsylvanian soil was rich and fertile, making the area an ideal location for agricultural development. The landscape is still characterized by large, cathedral-like barns based on a style of design imported from Switzerland. Large barns and expansive farmland have come to define the American farmstead and the environment of not only Pennsylvania, but much of the Midwest as well. This individual family-oriented approach to colonizing the land directly opposed the common European practice of the day, in which farmers were clustered in rural villages, with their fields in outlying areas. The new geographical arrangement led to a social split between townspeople and farmers. This philosophy of individualism continues to inform the nature of the environment in the Mid-Atlantic, and affects the situation of ecological attenuation.

Penn's experiment influenced urban development as well. His grid plan for Philadelphia—which was drawn up before the city was even built—was a radical departure from the old European forms. Unlike New England towns—such as Boston, which is similar in design to the meandering street progression of London, England—Penn's plan required that all streets be wide, and laid out at sharp right angles. This rigid layout system became a major model for towns and cities throughout the United States. Penn's Philadelphia plan included parks and gardens, but as property values rose through the years, gardens were destroyed and trees were chopped down to make way for new development. Washington, D.C., was formed according to a similar plan by Major Pierre L'Enfant, who overlaid the landscape with a right-angled grid coupled with circles and spokes. The widespread use of preplanned grids for towns and cities, a tablelike view from above that is imposed on the landscape regardless of its geographical features, arguably "paved the way for the acceptance of Jefferson's idea of a gridded land division system for the rural lands of the whole Northwest Territory." No doubt this spatial orientation affected the Land Ordinance of 1785, which was the beginning of the federal government's role in turning the "virgin land" of the Western Frontier into a commodifiable territory made available for private ownership.[9]

Economic Exploitation

To the west of Washington, D.C., a major coal industry would soon develop. West Virginia boasts a coal tradition that dates back to the time of its birth as a separate state in 1863. In 1742, John Peter Salley took an exploratory trip across the Allegheny Mountains and reported an outcropping of coal along a tributary of the Kanawha River. He named this tributary the Coal River, and his report became the first reference to coal in what is today West Virginia. While coal was known to exist throughout most of West Virginia, no extensive mining took place until the mid-1800s. Until that time, there was little incentive to exploit coal as a resource because of the great abundance of wood and a lack of manufacturing industries. Small amounts of coal were used by crossroads blacksmiths or by the settler whose cabin stood near an outcrop. In 1810, settlers in and around Wheeling began to use coal obtained from a nearby mine to heat their homes and places of work. By 1817, coal began to replace charcoal as a fuel for the numerous Kanawha River salt furnaces. By 1836, the coal fields of western Virginia had received so much attention that the state's foremost geologist, Professor William B. Rogers, was sent to visit the mines and analyze the coal in eight counties. The total coal production in 1840 for the state was about 300,000 tons, of which 200,000 tons was used in the Kanawha salt furnaces. Between 1840 and 1860 many coal companies were organized, and corporations were created under the laws of Virginia for the purpose of encouraging financial investments from foreign countries. Following the Civil War, rising industrial interest in the state's mineral resources brought a new era of development and growth for the coal industry. The industry spread to new cities and towns, and by 1880 there were extensive operations in nearly all of West Virginia's counties. Of the numerous coal fields that grew up in West Virginia, a few are of particular interest. One of the larger is the Fairmont Field, developed around the rich Pittsburgh seam. The first marketed Pittsburgh coal in western Virginia was produced around 1852 from a mine near the present city of Fairmont. Production and marketing success of the field increased, and in 1901 the Fairmont Coal Company was formed. West Virginia's southern coal fields were not opened until about 1870, though they were known to exist much earlier. Over the course of the next three decades, operations were consolidated into large companies, and Pocahontas Fuel Company, organized in 1907, soon dominated the other companies in McDowell County.

As the coal industry grew, mining methods and laws changed rapidly. In the earliest days, local farmers and slaves surface-mined the coal, using picks and shovels. The coal was dug out, shoveled into baskets and sacks, and carried away. Later, sleds, wheelbarrows, and carts came into use in deep mining, hauled by oxen, mules, goats, dogs, and sometimes men. Progress in mechanization was slow, as operators did not want to pay for expensive new equipment, and miners feared being replaced by it. By 1890, however, electric coal cutting, loading, and hauling machines came into use. After 1936, mechanization went forward very rapidly, with shuttle cars, long trains, conveyor belts, and other large mining machinery coming into common use. Large-scale surface mining did not start until 1914, with two peaks occurring in coal production—in 1927 (146,088,121 tons) and 1947 (173,653,816 tons). Since most of the mines were located far from established towns, the coal companies built their own towns and provided inexpensive homes, a company store, a church, and often recreation facilities for the miners and their families.

Private rural land ownership is a characteristic of the Mid-Atlantic and the American landscape at large (as opposed to England and Germany, where the countryside is open to the public). The rise of the automobile would further enforce the enclosed nature of an individualistic-oriented social system. The automobile would demand an additional change to the environment in the form of roads, which slowly began to connect outlying areas to towns and cities. Lines of circulation were mostly "natural roads" (as opposed to the few military roads that appeared during the American Revolution) up until the late eighteenth to early nineteenth century. Congress would not order a general transportation survey until 1807. The

Coal mines in West Virginia flourished for a time from the abundant minerals found in the mountains and surrounding areas, but continuous industrial development has taken its toll on these areas. Courtesy Library of Congress.

automobile, of course, made travel to greater distances possible, but also introduced phenomena such as jammed metropolitan arteries and urban sprawl, both of which, as we shall see, now greatly threaten the ecology of key areas of the Mid-Atlantic.

Practical highways would not develop on the rural landscape of the Mid-Atlantic until the twentieth century. Several factors went into the development of the national roadway system. Even though the United States could applaud itself for having the best railway system in the world by 1900, its roads were another story. Political interest groups, such as the National League for Good Roads (founded in 1892), pushed for improvements. But a key factor—the beginning of free rural mail delivery by the Post Office in 1891—made it necessary to improve the quality of highways. Then in 1916, the lobbying of groups such as the American Automobile Association helped to bring about the passage of the Federal Highway Act, which required that states establish highway departments in order to obtain federal funds for highway construction.[10] But an integrated network of roads would not be called for until World War I, when railroads could not meet the demand for troop movement and material needs. At this time Baltimore became an important seaport for freight moving in convoys from manufacturing cities in the Midwest. Maryland was the first state to begin licencing for motor vehicles to generate income for road improvement. A national defense highway system was created in the wake of World War I, with the Highway Act of 1921 requiring every state to designate 7 percent of its road mileage as "primary" and thus eligible for federal money. In 1939, New York City's streetcar line was reduced from 1,344 miles to 337. New York, in fact, touted that it had created the first road to be constructed exclusively for automobiles: "the Long Island Motor Parkway . . . was completed in 1911 by William Vanderbilt to speed the wealthy from Long Island estates toward Manhattan."[11] In the midst of the Cold War, President Eisenhower argued that a new road system needed to be built, establishing the 1956 Highway Act with the following argument: "too many roads were congested, poor roads inflated transportation costs for business, and, finally, existing highways were inadequate for the evacuation of cities threatened by nuclear attack."[12] Railroads and other forms of public transportation were no longer considered viable alternatives to automobile transportation.

Deforestation

As mentioned above, deforestation played a major role in the transformation of the environment of the mid-Atlantic region. Clearing forests was part of the colonial world. No farmland could be established without first creating treeless plots of land. No winter could be survived without wood to burn as fuel. Wood also served as the major material for building houses, fences, furniture, and ships. The log cabin was a predominant feature of the landscape, appearing first among the Swedish immigrants living in the Delaware region. Deforestation occurred throughout the Mid-Atlantic. Trees were cleared either by cutting (more common in the north and known as "Yankee clearing"), or by girdling (the removal of a band of bark completely from the circumference of a tree, which eventually kills the tree).

This relationship of humans to the forests was "the basic element of American geography and history for the first two and a half centuries of settlement."[13] It was taken for granted as the first step in the "improvement" of untamed land. It was more than a matter of occupational necessity; the clearing of the forests was a reflection of the pioneer structure of feeling, a philosophical outlook that gave credence to the world of colonialism: "the 'war of the woods,' as one settler called it, heightened the heroic nature of the pioneer endeavor." These clearings had a dramatic effect on the animal population. Intense hunting of bear and buffalo, and even deer, almost led to the extinction of these creatures. Animals such as wolves were considered dangerous and hunted because it was thought they needed to be exterminated. Clearing forests for the purpose of settlement fractured the landscape, dividing large wooded territories into smaller parcels: "animals that required large forested areas (such as bears) declined in number, and those that could live, or even thrive, in proximity to humans and human settlements (for example, racoons) increased."[14]

Because the war on the forest was accepted as a matter of course, no records on the process were kept for roughly the first two centuries of European encroachment. Records were not available until 1850, but it is estimated that over 113.7 million acres of forest land had been cleared by that year. An additional 39.7 million acres were cleared in the next decade alone. Between 1860 and 1909, 150.8 million acres of forests were removed for the purposes of farmland cultivation.[15] This dramatically changed the landscape of the region, which had formerly been occupied by some 12 million Native Americans, "the bulk of whom lived in forests." It is important, though, to realize that although the original forests may no longer exist, regrowth has brought back about 60 million acres in the United States since 1910. Nonetheless, increased urbanization and other forms of development continue to threaten this ecologically crucial component of the landscape. The loss of forests negatively affects the environment in many ways, contributing to floods, soil erosion, loss of animal habitat, species endangerment, and poorer drinking water.

The Erie Canal extends across 364 miles of New York State, linking Lake Erie to the Hudson River. Courtesy New York State Department of Economic Development.

Acres of forest lands were also cut down as part of the process of industrialization in the Mid-Atlantic. Maryland was a major exporter of iron goods. The large ironworks established there needed wood to make charcoal to use as fuel. Ironworks for the domestic market existed in Philadelphia and York, Pennsylvania. Philadelphia was also a major ship building center (along with Boston). The iron mill town was born in eastern Pennsylvania in the 1840s. The Great Lakes region in upstate New York saw the rise of steamboats. The desire for navigable waterways led to a period of significant canal construction. The longest, and one of the earliest, is the Erie Canal, which extends 364 miles across New York, linking Lake Erie to the Hudson River. Canals also linked coal mines in eastern Pennsylvania to Philadelphia and New York City.[16]

The railroad network was improved and expanded during the latter half of the nineteenth century, as railroads blanketed the eastern half of the nation. Railroads augmented the movement of resources and equipment and decreased travel time between regions, facilating the construction of iron and steel mills in areas like Philadelphia, Pittsburgh, and Shenango, Pennsylvania. Coal mines were developed in West Virginia and western Pennsylvania. Pittsburgh and Steelton, Pennsylvania, became known for their iron and steel, and Schenectady, New York, for its electrical machinery. Oil production went hand in hand with these industrial developments. Major oil production began in the 1860s in northwestern Pennsylvania. By 1880, long-distance pipelines connected Appalachian oil fields to Buffalo, New York City, and Philadelphia. New Jersey saw the rise of major refining districts in the early part of the twentieth century, and the production of petrochemicals began in the 1920s. These multiple courses of development have all played a role in the changing status of the environment and its complex ecosystems.

THE MID-ATLANTIC ENVIRONMENT TODAY

The factors listed above give only a small indication of the environmental and ecological status of the mid-Atlantic region in the early twenty-first century. Striking a balance between humanity and the land is an issue now acutely decisive for the future of the land. Sometimes it is not a matter of human incursion when it comes to environmental distress. Geological hazards such as landslides, earthquakes, subsidence, and floods have been studied extensively, for instance, in West Virginia. Several factors contribute to triggering landslides, the most important being heavy rains, clay soil, and steep slopes. Some studies indicate that there are nearly 500,000 landslides in the state, with damage estimates suggesting $30 million annually. Earthquakes are not common in West Virginia, but since 1758 dozens have occurred in the Appalachians and been felt in the state. Subsidence, which is defined as the collapse of the ground surface over a void, whether natural or man-made, is a continuing problem in West Virginia. Pennsylvania also experiences similar trouble. Floods are common in West Virginia because of heavy rains and narrow stream valleys. Some floods are also man-made, such as the Buffalo Creek disaster in 1972 when an earthen dam broke. While there have been some protests against man-made dams in the region because of problems such as these, man-made dams still dominate many of West Virginia's waterways.

Water is the most essential mineral resource in West Virginia; it is indispensable for human consumption, navigation, recreation, agriculture, industry, the generation of electricity, and a host of other uses. West Virginia's residents use about 25 to 30 billion gallons of water per day, most of which is returned almost imme-

Potomac River overflowing its banks near Harpers Ferry, West Virginia, 2001. Photograph Janet Ward. Courtesy NOAA.

diately to the creeks and rivers. Locating sources of potable water is one of the most important challenges faced by environmental geologists. The geologist must be knowledgeable about the rock types and structure in order to properly locate well sites to provide for the needs of households or developments. The pollution of surface and ground water is a constant problem in West Virginia, primarily due to sewage and acid mine drainage. Large sewage treatment plants and small septic tank systems are regulated by the state's health department; their use is increasing, although they are expensive. Acid mine drainage has been studied extensively and again, treatment is improving, but the costs are considerable.

New Jersey has similar resource and environmental problems. Like West Virginia and other mid-Atlantic states, New Jersey depends on diminishing supplies of locally derived materials and resources, but the state also differs significantly from other areas. Most notably, the Musconetcong Valley region in northern New Jersey is central to the state's continuing development. The Musconetcong Valley's drainage system, which lies within the region known as the Highlands, remains vital to the state's residents. The Highlands, located in northern New Jersey and southeastern New York, are so named because of the plateau-like landscape. In New Jersey alone, this plateau takes up one-eighth of the land mass and drains one-sixth of the state. The valley surfaces in the Highlands are on average 1,000 feet above sea level, and the area's rivers flow in a southwestern direction. In addition to its landscape, the Highland area is unique where climate and weather are concerned. The Musconetcong Valley region is somewhat colder in winter and summer than nearby regions due to its higher elevation.

The Importance of Watersheds

The Mid-Atlantic's environment has been greatly affected by human presence. In terms of the region's current environmental status, and the importance of striking a humanity/land balance, nothing provides a better example in understanding this vital relationship than the Chesapeake Bay. This is an immense multiple-state area of the landscape that also helps to reveal how the mid-Atlantic region as a whole is interconnected.

The Chesapeake Bay receives its water from the "Bay watershed"—an expansive six-state, 64,000-square-mile drainage basin. As already noted, Delaware, Maryland, Pennsylvania, Virginia, West Virginia, and the entire District of Columbia make up this watershed. The watershed is the largest in the United States, and one of the world's most productive estuaries. Thousands of small creeks, springs, streams, and rivers flow into the bay. It is also North America's most biologically diverse estuary, supporting some 3,600 species of animals, fish, and plants. In addition, it is a source of food and shelter for twenty-nine waterfowl species, and over 1 million waterfowl spend each winter in the basin.[17] Conserving the water supply affects not only those living on the bay; every inhabitant of the six-state watershed area lives only a few minutes from one or more of the thousands of streams that drain into the bay.

One key issue facing mid-Atlantic environmentalists today is the deforestation of this watershed. Currently, less than 60 percent of the watershed is forested, which directly affects the bay's water supply (see sidebar on Riparian Forests).[18] There are more than 100,000 miles of streams and shoreline in the watershed. Unfortunately, almost 50 percent of this streamside area has degraded, or been converted to urban and other land uses. The degradation of water grass beds in the bay, which disappeared widely in the 1970s and 1980s, has also resulted in the decline of one of the bay's most important species, the blue crab. Crabs use the grasses as sources of shelter after molting when their shells are soft, because at that time they are vulnerable to predators. Striped bass also fell to a dangerously low level in the bay in the 1980s. The bass, along with herring and shad, are migratory fish. They migrate to freshwater to spawn, then return to the ocean as adults. The construction of dams through the years has blocked important fish passages, contributing to the decline of these species. However, four of the largest dams, all situated along the Susquehanna River, have been reopened to migratory fish. These and other dams have either been breached, or "fish ladders" have been introduced to ensure that these species of fish—some of which, like shad, migrate all the way to Binghamton, New York—will have access to their former migratory corridors.

The ecology of the bay and its multi-state watershed needs to be carefully kept in balance. Attention must be paid to the ways in which all areas of the land in the region affect one another. It is not only pollution from factories that should attract our concern. Even nutrients that farmers add to their crops can adversely affect the equilibrium of the region as a whole. The by now unquestioned philosophy that argues that a higher crop yield is more efficient and productive for the economy and our food supply needs to be reconsidered in the context of this balance. In fact, next to sewage, nutrients in the form of fertilizers are the main pollutants of the bay today. The bay itself is an invaluable source of fish and other wildlife because of its size and shallow water level. The shallowness of the bay allows sunlight to penetrate under water, which makes for an incredibly rich environment. However, overfertilization, which produces higher crop yields, also produces harmful agricultural runoff. Coupled with sewage, the unnatural intensity of these nutrients makes the algae in the bay overbloom, and too much algae in turn blocks sunlight. The lack of sunlight drastically changes the amount of area-specific organisms. Even though chemicals such as nitrogen and phosphorus have been reduced to some extent in the last fifteen years, such nutrient pollutants affect the entire ecosystem of the bay. In the year 2003, the bay saw the lowest harvest ever of oysters.

Nutrient pollutants stem from what are called "point sources"—specific locations or points of pollutant entry (a pipe, for example, from a factory). There are some 305 significant municipal wastewater treatment plants that affect the bay watershed. Over the course of the last decade and a half, environmental conservation efforts have helped convince 73 of these plants to implement nutrient removal technology. The Chesapeake Bay Program hopes to see that number increase to 153 by 2010. Phosphorous and nitrogen loads have been reduced by 52 percent and 31 percent, respectively, since 1985. However, the watershed's population is expected to increase by at least 14 percent by the year 2020, which will make it all the more difficult to further decrease these loads, let alone maintain the current levels. Toxic chemicals such as chromium, copper, DDT, lead, mercury, nickel, silver, and many others also continue to contaminate the bay, harming plants, animals, and humans. The Anacostia River in Maryland, the Elizabeth River in Virginia, and Baltimore Harbor are some of the key areas that pose a serious threat.

The Delaware Estuary also faces similar threats. The bay is bordered by New Jersey on the northeast and by Delaware on the southwest, and the estuary, approximately 133 miles, extends to Pennsylvania, New Jersey, and Delaware, through which the Delaware River flows. An estuary is a body of water where fresh water from rivers and streams mixes with ocean salt water. As with the Chesapeake Bay, this transition from land to sea makes the Delaware Estuary an important habitat. Home to the largest population of horseshoe crabs in the world, the estuary also provides habitat for migratory birds, as well as feeding and spawning grounds for fish, shellfish, and marine mammals. It is just as important for filtering pollutants and sediments from land, while also operating as a buffer to flooding and erosion. The Delaware Estuary is the world's largest freshwater port, and is also home to one of the greatest concentrations of heavy industry in the

The Delaware Estuary is the world's largest freshwater port and also home to one of the world's greatest concentrations of heavy industry. Courtesy NOAA.

world. Levels of nutrients are two to three times greater in the Delaware Estuary than they are elsewhere in the mid-Atlantic region, whereas the Chesapeake Bay has the highest oxygen depletion. As with the Chesapeake, the Delaware Estuary is polluted by metals, especially arsenic, nickel, mercury, and zinc. And it contains harmful concentrations of hydrocarbons, pesticides, DDT, and polychlorinated biphenyls (PCBs). In the Environmental Protection Agency's assessment of the mid-Atlantic region's estuaries, tests of over 3,000 fish from seventy-six sites revealed that edible portions of 65 percent of fish and shellfish contained levels of metals and organic toxicants high enough to present risk to human consumers. This constitutes a real problem, for commercial fishing enterprises have come to depend on the bay for its large annual yield of clams, crabs, lobsters, and oysters. Moreover, organic contamination of the Delaware River increased from 1990 to 1997.

These changes to the Delaware Estuary and the Chesapeake Bay area are mostly the result of increasing human population: "Most of the changes are traceable to the increasing presence of humans. Population in the mid-Atlantic estuarine watersheds has grown from 13 million in 1950 to 21 million in 1990, and is estimated to be 25 million by 2020."[19] Similarly, the bay watershed's population was a little over 11 million in 1970; in 2000 the population was close to 16 million, roughly a 38 percent increase. Population in the D.C. metropolitan area has also mushroomed, with that of Loudoun County, Virginia, alone (30 miles northwest of D.C.) increasing 96.8 percent in only ten years (1990–2000). By the year 2020, the bay watershed population is expected to be in the area of 17.8 million—an increase of 300 new residents a day. Such development will have a substantial impact on the land and its forests: "A total of 1.7 million new homes are projected to be built in the watershed by 2020, potentially consuming more than 600,000 additional acres of forest and farmland."[20]

The Delaware Estuary is part of the Delaware River basin—an immense 13,539-square-mile area of the Mid-Atlantic that extends far north, above Hancock, New York, and the Schuykill River, and as far south as Cape Henlopen, Delaware. Some 50 percent of the basin's total land area is in eastern Pennsylvania, including the cities of Philadelphia, Reading, and Pottstown, and more than 23 percent of the basin lies in New Jersey. As one of the world's largest concentrations of heavy industry, the estuary requires vigilance in maintaining the quality of its resources. Drinking water for the majority of the residents in the region comes from the Delaware River and its tributaries. Since the founding of the Delaware Estuary Program in 1988 (which includes the Environmental Protection Agency, and the states of Delaware, Pennsylvania, and New Jersey), quality standards and tighter controls have helped to ensure that the water is cleaner than it was three decades ago (helped in part by the Clean Water Act, passed by Congress in 1972).[21] At one point the estuary was so severely polluted that "little or no oxygen remained in the water to support fish populations. Untreated municipal sewage and industrial waste led to low dissolved oxygen levels in the more industrialized areas. . . . Gaseous odors, released from sewage in the water, tarnished ships, sickened sailors, and turned nearby houses yellow in color."[22] At one point, the striped bass was almost eliminated from the rivers between Wilmington, Delaware, and Philadelphia, Pennsylvania. The striped bass spends most of its life in salt water, but needs to migrate to freshwater areas such as rivers to spawn. Because oxygen levels were so low in the estuary, bass

The Importance of Horseshoe Crabs

The Delaware Estuary is home to the world's largest population of horseshoe crabs. Misnamed, horseshoe crabs are actually more closely related to spiders and insects, belonging to the phylum "arthropod," which contains the three major classes of insects, arachnids, and crustaceans. The horseshoe crab is one of the oldest species on the planet; some 350 million years old, they predate even the dinosaurs and flying insects. Even though they have no immune system, they have an uncanny ability to fight off infection and survive in seawaters that are virtually "bacterial soup." Although unable to develop antibodies, horeshoe crabs contains compounds that bind to and immobilize bacteria and viruses. Blood clots form when they encounter the bacterial toxin called endotoxin, which acts as a signal that the crabs are are wounded. The clots prevent further bleeding and act as a physical barrier against infection.

Because of their reaction to endotoxin, horseshoe crabs serve a vital role for the medical industry. Endotoxin is of the greatest concern in the process of sterilization because of its ability to withstand steam sterilization. Pharmaceutical and medical device industries use an extract from the blood of the horseshoe crab to ensure that vaccines and medical devices are free of endotoxin and bacterial contamination. Their blood has come to play a vital role in ensuring that human medical injections are safe. The horseshoe crab is not harmed in this process. Laboratory scientists are careful to extract only 30 percent of a single crab's blood, which regenerates in a week after the crab is returned to the water.

The horseshoe crab is also essential to migratory birds stopping along the East Coast. A decline in their number will directly affect shorebirds and sea turtles. Each spring, the horseshoe crabs come onto the beaches to lay their eggs. Eggs not buried become an essential source of food for the shorebirds that stop to feed along the way. The Delaware Estuary is "the largest stop-over for shorebirds in the Atlantic Flyway and is the second largest staging site in North America."[23] Anywhere from half a million to a million birds stop in the estuary in their northward migration.

could not travel beyond this area to reach the rivers. Other human influences, such as dams, posed a different form of obstruction. As with the Chesapeake, the Clean Water Act made it possible for ecologists to locate pollution point sources. Pollution control measures over the past twenty-five years have addressed this problem, bringing the population of striped bass back to the region. Even so, toxic chemicals, oil spills, and human development still pose a problem, with storm water runoff being one of the most serious pollution problems. Not all fish found in the estuary are safe to eat. Though banned in the late 1970s, PCBs are still found in the tissues of white perch and cannel catfish. These and other toxic substances have long-term effects, and many species of fish still carry unhealthy levels of pollutants, which, among other health concerns, can increase the risk of cancer in humans. Swimming is also an issue in the estuary, which still contains sections that pose risks to human health.

Another important watershed in the mid-Atlantic region is located in New York, tied to the Great Lakes region. As with the Chesapeake and the Delaware bays and watersheds, Lake Ontario and Lake Erie and their watersheds are very important to the ecology of the area. The watershed for this section of the land contains a network of waterways that provide 58 million gallons of drinking water every day to more than 500,000 people living in the metropolitan areas of Buffalo and Rochester, in addition to rural areas in the counties of Genesee, Monroe, Ontario, Orleans, and Wayne. Marshland terns and river otters, in addition to a diversity of other fish and wildlife species, make their habitat in this region.

When examining regional environmental issues, more than simply the kind of widespread connections between land areas that we have laid out needs to be considered. Even more expansive than the watershed of the Chesapeake Bay is the bay's airshed, which includes all the states of the mid-Atlantic region as well as all

The Importance of Riparian Forests

Since the massive decline of forest lands during the sixteenth to the nineteenth centuries, new growth over the last century and a half has replaced much of what was lost. However, agricultural, city, and suburban expansion over the last three decades now threatens the forests again. Shoreline residential development and heavy boat traffic leave shorelines unforested, and contribute to shoreline erosion. This loss is not merely a matter of preserving some aesthetic idea of a beautiful landscape. Forests are essential to the survival of our ecosystem.

Of particular importance are the riparian forests, which are a functional last line of defense against agricultural production and urban development. Riparian areas are sections of the land that border bodies of water—streams, rivers, marshes, and shorelines. They serve as a transition between the aquatic and the terrestrial environment. One crucial ecological factor to grasp in developing an understanding of the environment is the fundamental connection between sections of the land normally thought to function apart from one another. A stream, for instance, cannot be seen as isolated from its indissoluble relationship to what lies around it. Fish, for instance, would not be able to survive without riparian forests. These areas of the land are especially important to the mid-Atlantic region, for the Chesapeake Bay, although located entirely in Maryland, exists as an ecosystem because of the many streams and rivers that flow throughout not only the state of Maryland, but Pennsylvania, western New York, and even the eastern most tip of West Virginia. This expansive multistate area forms the "circulatory system" of the Chesapeake. Healthy streams and rivers are critical to keeping the bay healthy and restoring its nutrients.

The riparian forests offer a diversity of habitat for important amphibians, reptiles, and waterfowl. Many species of birds use the streams as travel corridors and nesting sites; the shorelines offer spawning habitats for trout, shad, herring, alewife, and striped bass. The fish, in addition to insects and crustaceans, find shelter in small pool areas created by fallen trees. The roots of the trees themselves stabilize stream banks, limiting soil erosion. Leaves are a food source for insects, who are in turn eaten by fish and birds. Riparian forests thus serve as a foundation for the food web, creating a natural shade canopy that keeps the water cool, enabling streams to retain more dissolved oxygen, thereby encouraging the growth of beneficial algae and aquatic insects. The canopy of the leaves also captures rainfall, which filters out unhealthy dust from wind erosion, construction, and farm machinery. The roots of the trees take up fertilizers and other pollutants that spread from farmlands and cities, keeping them from pouring into the stream. In the process called "denitrification," riparian forest floor bacteria convert harmful nitrate to nitrogen gas, which is released into the air. All in all, some 30–90 percent of pollutants and sediment can be reduced by this buffer system. Without this area of the land, the entire ecosystem would suffer.

of Ohio, most of Kentucky and North Carolina, a third of Tennessee, and portions of New Hampshire, South Carolina, and Canada. Airborne toxins from agriculture, automobile emissions, industry, and power generating facilities are deposited directly into the bay. Research indicates that 32 percent of the nitrogen load in the bay stems from these multistate atmospheric pollutants.

In addition to the mid-Atlantic forests, wetlands are also an important ecological feature of the region. Because of the bay watershed, wetlands extend from Delaware to West Virginia, and from Maryland to New York—over 1.5 million acres (about one and a half times the size of Delaware). Wetlands are important because they contribute to soil production and plant growth, and provide fish and wildlife habitats. They help maintain freshwater flow by filtering out pollutants and sediments, and serve to moderate the effects of floods and droughts. However, wetlands in the states listed above are now far below their precolonial levels: "Maryland has lost 73 percent of its original 1.13 million acres, Delaware 54 percent of its original 480,000 acres, West Virginia 24 percent of its original 134,000 acres, and Pennsylvania . . . 56 percent of its 1.13 million aces."[24]

The Importance of Environmental Organizations

Despite the growing threat of pollution and urban expansion to the environment, multistate concern at the government level for the decline of the Chesapeake Bay has grown. The Chesapeake Bay Program was founded in 1983, and has partners in Maryland, Pennsylvania, Virginia, and the District of Columbia. The organization includes representatives from federal and local governments, the Environmental Protection Agency, and citizen advisory groups. The program has focused on the restoration of the bay's finfish, shellfish, grasses, and other aquatic life and wildlife, helping in the process to bring about considerable advances in estuarine science.

The attention paid to the bay in the past twenty years has also brought about more awareness of the effect that ecological degradation—especially tree loss—would have on the environment. American Forests, a national organization, examined urban tree loss in the D.C. metropolitan area. They calculated that trees in the metropolitan area annually remove 20 million pounds of pollution from the air, a benefit worth $50 million each year. The organization also analyzed the extent to which trees absorb storm water, lessen erosion, and reduce peak flow: "Urban trees . . . retain 949 million cubic feet of water. If these trees were lost and replaced by impervious surfaces, building equivalent retention facilities would cost the region $4.7 billion."[25] Organizations such as American Forests point to the need to convince state and local governments that they must incorporate this kind of awareness into their strategic planning. In the watershed, ecological studies show that for maximum ecosystem resiliency, forest buffers should exist on at least 70 percent of all shorelines and streambanks. The current minimum requirement for the buffers themselves is 35 feet, but ecologists have shown that wider buffers serve a greater variety of functions, and scientific literature recommends a buffer of at least 75 to 150 feet.[26] This means that at least 30,000 miles of forest buffers need to be restored, in addition to ensuring that already-existing buffers remain.

The Pennsylvania Chesapeake Bay Advisory Council, the Natural Resources Conservation Service of the United States Development Agency, the Chesapeake Bay Foundation, the Farm Service Agency, the Farm Bureau, and other county forestry boards and conservation groups have participated in watershed planning and restoration. Moreover, the Chesapeake Bay Program has led to agreements among Virginia, Maryland, Pennsylvania, the District of Columbia, the Chesapeake Bay Commission, and the Environmental Protection Agency. These agreements to address environmental degradation have generated comprehensive documents that have become "an international model for large-scale ecosystem management."[27] It is hoped that nearly 10,000 miles of forest buffers will be restored by 2010. This is an indication of the length of time and the degree of commitment required to resolve key environmental problems we face at the beginning of the twenty-first Century. Unfortunately, continuing urban sprawl—one of the most significant factors contributing to environmental degradation throughout the mid-Atlantic region—may eventually undermine all these efforts of the past twenty years: "there is a clear correlation between population growth and associated development and environmental degradation in the Chesapeake Bay system."[28] The technology exists to solve these problems, but funding shortages and the habitual lifestyles of the population continue to retard these and other greatly needed environmental programs.

Urban Pollutants

Runoff from impervious surfaces is not only a matter of oil and gas leaking from cars onto parking lots, or too many fertilizers and pesticides applied to lawns, or sediment and other pollutants from construction sites. Groundwater supplies are replenished when rainwater is able to soak back into the ground. When too much of the land becomes impervious to rainwater, the water runs off into nearby rivers and streams and is carried away, and the groundwater supply begins to diminish. Sprawl from New York City, Philadelphia, Baltimore, and Washington, D.C., not only affects the entire ecology of key parts of the Mid-Atlantic, but also compromises the ability of the land to support life.

Air pollution is also an important issue in the mid-Atlantic region. While pollution sources and circulation patterns change over time, the phenomenon of acid raid—which damages the soil and the life cycles of plants and animals—is a consistent problem in every state of the region. The burning of fossil fuels is the major cause of acid rain. Factories and power plants burn coal and oil to produce electricity for homes throughout the region. Gasoline (another fossil fuel) from cars, trucks, and airplanes adds to air pollution. The pollutants in the smoke and fumes from these sources rise into the atmosphere to mix with clouds, and eventually fall

Urban Sprawl

One of the key problems that has led to environmental degradation is a phenomenon known as urban sprawl. Most of the people in the mid-Atlantic region live in the urban corridor between the District of Columbia and Philadelphia, in the New York City metropolitan area, and in the Pittsburgh area. Overall population growth in the region is highest in the coastal plain, near the ocean and the estuaries, as opposed to the western areas of the region such as western New York. As with all ecological issues, the phenomenon of urban sprawl needs to be considered in terms of its contextual relations to conventional human practices and technological and economic development.

Urban sprawl directly increases the use of automobiles. Because sprawl tends to form in large housing-only sections, this forces the population to rely chiefly on automobiles to travel between the home and recreation areas, shopping areas, and work places—all of which lie beyond the dense area of housing development. These lengthier commutes contribute to the increase in air and water pollution; to the loss of farmland, open fields, forests, and wetlands; and to heavier flooding and traffic congestion. Even though tougher emission standards have decreased the amount of pollution a single car produces, the number of cars continues to grow, along with the distance people travel. More sprawl, which creates more traffic, also leads to the construction of more road surfaces, parking lots, parking garages, and so forth. These impervious surfaces cannot absorb chemical pollutants and runoff, which means that excessive pollutants will drain into local water bodies: "According to the Center for Watershed Protection, more than 30 different studies have documented that streams, lakes, and wetland quality decline sharply when the area of impervious surfaces located in upstream watersheds exceeds 10 percent of total land area."[29]

back to the earth in the form of acid rain. The Environmental Protection Agency conducted a survey of streams throughout the Mid-Atlantic from 1996 to 1997, and is currently compiling a report that will give specifics on affected areas within the region. But other regions also have an effect on the air of the Mid-Atlantic. Central Pennsylvania extending east to the Pocono Mountains and all the way south through western Maryland and northern West Virginia contain the highest levels of nitrate pollution. This is a regional pattern that stems from prevailing western winds a carrying air pollutants from other regions.

Environmentalists and organizations devoted to water preservation, watershed regeneration, fish and wildlife preservation, riparian forest renewal, and land stewardship in general have recognized the dangers of urban sprawl. Organizations such as the Sierra Club have begun to campaign for alternative, public-transportation projects, and encourage protection of open space, for the creation of healthy communities. They cite environmentally-friendly developments that use "smart-growth ideas to protect open space, and . . . urban green spaces to link neighborhoods to each other and to their natural surroundings."[30] One example is the Hoboken Waterfront Project in Hoboken, New Jersey, which is restoring a waterfront park that will then be linked up to a coastal trail. Another fine example is Rochester, New York's Renaissance 2010 plan—a downtown development scheme that consciously safeguards open spaces, waterways, parks, and urban forests from suburban sprawl. However, the potential for urban and suburban sprawl to encroach into buffer zones, fields, forests, and wetlands continues to be an ongoing debate. Although awareness of the ecological effects of urban sprawl has grown, many activist groups seek more environmentally friendly policies for the region.

Population Expansion

Another environmental factor is population expansion, which has been an increasing problem since World War II. The cities, countryside, and suburbs of the Mid-Atlantic have seen an explosion of development that has recast traditional human settlement patterns. The countryside of America, the space that served as the raison d'être for European immigration to the New World, with its mythological promise of an agricultural utopia, has practically lost its hold on the American consciousness, materially and ideologically. More and more people live and work in suburban settings. This influx and expansion unfortunately results in unhealthy and unchecked land-use practices. In Philadelphia "and virtually every other major metropolitan area, countless uncoordinated development decisions have caused expansion at a far faster rate in land consumption than in population growth."[31] Public services such as the financing of road and sewer extensions and other infrastructure issues increase pressure on public dollars, which never go far, and which, in terms of underdevelopment, adversely affect minority urban areas.

Pollutants

Increased population growth also means more pressure on the production of foodstuffs. Pesticides and other pollutants have become the standard for "efficient productivity" and higher yields on many farms. This plays havoc with the equilibrium of ecosystems of farmlands, and other side effects, such as pesticide contaminated runoff, threaten to destroy natural resources. For instance, the groundwater supplies of Long Island and the Baltimore and D.C. areas are now in jeopardy. Natural resources such as the flow of water remain largely unacknowledged by policy makers. These and other crucial ecological issues have failed to enter into the consciousness of the public at large.

CONCLUSION: THE FUTURE OF THE MID-ATLANTIC ENVIRONMENT

In 1948, in Donora, Pennsylvania, smog levels had risen to such an extent as to be life-threatening. Widespread reporting of these levels led to public awareness of the need to clean up the air. However, according to Henry L. Diamond and Patrick F. Noonan, founders of the Sustainable Use of Land Project, no similar event has galvanized public concern for the land. They cite the discovery of the toxic waste dump in the Love Canal neighborhood of Niagara Falls, New York, as the only event that has come close to generating a similar widespread concern for environmental issues. Controversies over landfills, billboards, airports, and new highways remain local concerns for the most part, and fail to establish an environmentally concerned citizenry at the national level that would have any effect on the agenda of corporations and government policy makers. The very political and legal system for making decisions about land use is more than fifty years behind the times: "Today, many communities continue to rely on a legislative framework that was created for a very different pre–World War II America. As a result, the planning and growth management mechanisms in force in most states in the 1990s are woefully out-of-step with the times."[32]

Beginning with the economic downturn of the 1990s and continuing into the early twenty-first century, American citizens have become increasingly wary of governmental regulations, including environmental ones. As we have seen throughout this chapter, individualism and private property have been ideological driving forces from the time of the first European settlers. Such deeply rooted lifestyles make it all the more difficult to address land depletion and ecological degradation: "In the 1950s, the vast interstate highway system was designed in part to meet civil defense objectives during the Cold War, to be able to evacuate cities and move military equipment around the country."[33] The vast highway system created after World War II has led to unprecedented increases in traffic volume and subsequent congestion, further constraining natural resources and open spaces.

A supportive environment depends on a healthy equilibrium among forests, soils, wildlife, waters and estuaries, minerals, and more. What is needed is an extensive inventory of resources. Urban expansion and thoughtless use of land for purposes of producing the highest yield with no consideration given to the destruction of soil and ecosystems have an effect on this equilibrium: "As most land is privately held, private landowners must be galvanized to assure a healthy land base. . . . Without the stewardship of property-owning corporations and individual landowners, the future of the American landscape is bleak." Diamond and Noonan argue that through education, tax incentives, and similar benefits, habitats and damaged lands can be restored. But this is only the first step. Alliances between segmented groups also need to be formed: "A constituency for better land use is needed based on new partnerships that reach beyond traditional alliances to bring together conservationists, social justice advocates, and economic development interests. These partnerships can be mobilized around natural and cultural resources that people value."[34]

The American ideology that yokes ideas of freedom with upward economic and social mobility, with the ability to purchase and live on individually oriented, private land, and with the idea of expansion as a sign of personal progression, has heavily influenced the nature of humanity's relation to the environment: "The freedom vested in private enterprise and property ownership created landscapes filled with contradictory, sometimes conflicting, land uses, frequent change, and uneven sprawl into the countryside."[35] Suburbia reflects this ideology—a craving for things new and large, which results in the desire for maximum personal space in suburban areas (for those who can afford it) and the abandoning of urban residential areas throughout the Mid-Atlantic. As the upwardly mobile (who are then replaced by the poor) leave cities in favor of the suburbs, the landscape outside the city changes. By the 1970s large shopping malls and retail stores had all but replaced downtown city shopping areas. Public transportation, which could serve the public in getting to downtown shops and forms of entertainment that were within walking distance from one another, could no longer adequately serve the vaster spatial orientations of malls, theaters, grocery stores, and restaurants that began to overtake the environment. Automobiles, which fit well into the ideology of individual liberty, were consequently necessary if one was to exist in this new environment: "the autonomy and privacy of the automobile embodied the suburban expression of individual freedom and economic mobility."[36]

This widespread development in the landscape has also had deleterious effects on the social environment. In what has been referred to as the "great American enclosure movement," African Americans from the South after the Civil War migrated to cities in the North (Baltimore, Philadelphia, New York, Buffalo) in search of jobs and a chance to lay claim to the American promise of private property. Slavery may have been abolished, but its effects lingered, economically and socially disbarring African Americans from the opportunities available to other Americans, which left them little choice but to settle in abandoned and rundown neighborhoods. The 1970s would see the migration of many poor Latin Americans to inner-city neighborhoods as well.

Since World War II, with the development of the interstate highway system, individual means of transportation have come to far outweigh public transportation, such as busses and trains. Outlying areas throughout the mid-Atlantic region— such as the growing metropolitan areas of D.C., Baltimore, Philadelphia, Pittsburgh, Harrisburg, New York City, and others—formerly too remote for practical housing development are now made accessible by automobile. Greater traveling distances are a common fact of public life. The Piedmont region of Maryland, Pennsylvania, and Virginia, and the mid-Atlantic coastal plain of Maryland and Delaware, contain some of the most-threatened farmland areas in the United States: "Maryland, Virginia, and Pennsylvania rank among the top-10 states in terms of production per acre of farmland. Unfortunately, harmful sprawl development is consuming some of the nation's best agricultural lands."[37] The bay watershed region of the mid-Atlantic states alone lost 1.12 million acres of agricultural land between 1985 and 2000. Federal transportation policy remains devoted, for the most part, to highway construction. Increasing roadway construction has deleterious ecological effects. Moreover, building more roads does not necessarily result in less congestion, but only ends by attracting more drivers, resulting in worse traffic jams and longer commutes: "Communities with the highest amounts of road-building actually have higher amounts of congestion."[38]

Prosperity in industry does come with plenty of environmental concerns. The Mid-Atlantic's relatively dense population and economic development continue to create stress on the region's natural resources, particularly its river basins and estuaries. There is no easy solution to these possible environmental disasters, but education is critical to public understanding of these problems and a collective effort to reverse these trends. Part of the problem stems from economic dependencies on manufacturing industries. For example, man-made pollution from industry is picked up by local rivers and streams that flow into bigger bodies of water. This industrial waste blocks other needed nutrients.

Land pollution is a factor in the deteriorating ecological system of the region, but air pollution is another big worry. The coal industry thrives in this region, with West Virginia and Pennsylvania among the top five coal-producing states in the nation. Considering West Virginia's small size, it is easy to see why there are so many concerns about the health of its citizens. West Virginia is in the bottom of the five states in terms of landmass, but as pointed out above, remains in the top five in coal production. Of course, this is not an easy problem to solve, considering that coal accounts for 20 to 25 percent of the total energy used and more than 50 percent of the electricity generated in the United States. The Department of the Interior has attempted to implement new technology to cut the nation's dependence on coal, mainly because of the environmental damage that coal mining causes. Coal with high sulfur content is damaging because it produces an acidic drainage after it has been produced for energy, and this in turn contributes to acid rain in the region. In the long run, cleaning up processes and controlling pollution end up costing consumers in the mid-Atlantic region more than standard mining processes. These new processes may be inconvenient to some in the industry, but they remain vital to helping the environment.

Changes in the environment are a direct effect of humanity's changing relationship to the land. In the early 1800s, over 80 percent of the American labor force was employed on farms. The first true American suburb was created in 1814, when steam ferry service across the East River linked Brooklyn with Manhattan. At that moment in history, Brooklyn was still an agrarian settlement, with a population of fewer than 5,000 people: "Its development, foreshadowing that of suburban America in general, depended on low cost, convenient mass transit that linked the suburban home with the place of employment." But by 1890, Brooklyn had a population of 800,000 and had grown into the nation's fourth largest city; the mass migration from rural to urban areas was under way. Such development has had a strong and irreversible impact on the environment: "During a period of rapid development between 1954 and 1971, Long Island suffered a loss of 47 percent of its wetlands."[39] And according to the American Farmland Trust, the United States in general loses close to 1 million acres of farmland and open space each year. Such intense development has a direct effect on the American taxpayer: "from 1988 to 1998, destruction caused by flooding cost American taxpayers more than $473 billion in local, state and federal funds."[40]

There are alternatives in the works to this type of expansion in the mid-Atlantic region, alternatives that consider the distinct relational nature of ecosystems, and humanity's involvement in these relations. Some cities have invested money in public transportation systems, as Washington, D.C., has done with its "metro." These alternatives greatly reduce the amount of carbon monoxide released into the atmosphere, and also reduce the amount of travel time for commuters who would normally be stuck in traffic. Washington, D.C., generated nearly $15 million in surrounding private development between 1980 and 1990, with 40 percent of the area's retail and office space built within walking distance of metro stations. In addition, the 1998 Transportation Equity Act for the Twenty-First Century "provides nearly $630 million for transportation enhancements, which include greenways, bike trails, and easements for open space." And increased attention to the value of wetlands resulted in the North American Wetlands Conservation Act of 1999.[41]

Despite this legislation and the work of environmental organizations, regions are still immensely threatened. The Chesapeake Bay remains on the federal list of impaired waters. And much needs to be done in terms of human awareness to improve the Delaware Estuary as well: "If one quart of oil were spilled into the Delaware Estuary, the resulting oil slick would cover two acres, or 87,120 square feet of water surface."[42] Development in many areas of the Mid-Atlantic continues to threaten parklands, natural landmarks, and the delicate balance of ecosystems. Harriman State Park in Rockland County, New York, is one such place. Situated between the New York/New Jersey Highlands and the Hudson River, much of the county over the past twelve years has been given over completely to development. Environmental concern at the local level is on the rise, however. County and town officials, along with the Trust for Public Land, have implemented measures to protect and conserve some of the remaining undeveloped land in the county, in particular Harriman State Park. "Growth. Expansion. Progress. For two centuries, they have been synonymous. And they have been the American way. Until now. The consequences of unbridled, haphazard growth—traffic congestion, air pollution, overcrowded schools, lost farmland, forests and open space—are forcing us to reconsider how and where we build."[43]

Perhaps one of the most sobering facts in all of this is that 49 percent of Americans now live in areas with unsafe smog pollution. In this sense, the Mid-Atlantic mirrors problems that all Americans face. Not only that, nations around the globe are hurt by increases in air pollution that contribute to atmospheric greenhouse gases, leading to rising sea levels and other severe environmental problems. This larger context can help to develop an awareness of the importance of the local relational context of ecological systems. Cultivating a strong familiarity with the environment from the standpoint of its ecological interconnectedness, as well as understanding how local bioregions relate to the global biosphere, not only helps us to understand the nature of the mid-Atlantic region, but also offers the possibility of a more stable future for all of the region's inhabitants—human or otherwise.

RESOURCE GUIDE

Printed Sources

Anderson, Terry L., and Bruce Yandle. *Agriculture and the Environment: Searching for Greener Pastures*. Stanford, CA: Hoover Institution Press, 2001.

Conzen, Michael P., ed. *The Making of the American Landscape*. Boston: University of Chicago Press, 1990.

Diamond Henry L., and Patrick F. Noonan. *Land Use in America*. Washington, D.C.: Island Press, 1996.

Hays, Samuel P., *A History of Environmental Politics Since 1945*. Pittsburgh: University of Pittsburgh Press, 2000.

Jackson, Richard H. *Land Use in America*. New York: Halsted Press, 1981.

Opie, John, ed. *Americans and Environment: The Controversy Over Ecology*. Lexington, MA: D.C. Heath, 1971.

Rifkin, Jeremy. *Biosphere Politics: A New Consciousness for a New Century*. New York: Crown, 1991.

Simpson, John Warfield. *Visions of Paradise: Glimpses of Our Landscape's Legacy*. Berkeley: University of California Press, 1999.

Web Sites

Chesapeake Bay Journal
http://www.bayjournal.com

Chesapeake Bay Program
http://www.chesapeakebay.net/baynews.htm

The Sierra Club Report on Sprawl, September 2000
http://www.sierraclub.org/sprawl

Trust For Public Land
http://www.tpl.org/

U.S. Environmental Protection Agency. *Mid-Atlantic Integrated Assessment (MAIA)*
http://www.epa.gov/maia

ETHNICITY

Kathryn Wilson

The Mid-Atlantic may very well be the most ethnically diverse region in the United States. A dynamic middle ground between the Northeast, South, and Midwest, the region has been shaped by three centuries of complex and dynamic interactions between various cultural and racial groups. Prior to European settlement, the region was home to diverse Native American groups who regularly interacted with and recognized differences among each other. The region's several major ports and industrial centers made it a continuing destination for a staggering array of immigrants from around the globe. Ethnic differences have also been a salient factor in the development of regional cultures and subcultures.

Ethnicity in the Mid-Atlantic has been shaped not only by the settlement of diverse groups, but also by their interaction with one another. Indeed, ethnic identity in this context must be understood by what sociologists refer to as "differential identity," that is, identity that emerges from, and is understood and expressed across, perceived differences. These differences may be based in race, nation, religion, language, or some combination of all of these. When these differences are invested with meaning and symbolically elaborated, they structure social relations and identities in an emergent fashion within specific cultural environments. In this way ethnic identity is not a static entity but a strategic process based on interaction and encounter, accommodation and conflict, on the identification of groups, as well as ethnic groups' own senses of self. Ethnicity in this region, as across the United States, has often been an offspring of immigration and the crossing of cultural and geographic boundaries—the arrival of the global in the local. Ethnicity in this context is expressed as a hybrid or hyphenated identity, such as Italian American, Korean American, and Mexican American, for example. In the politics of contemporary ethnicity, these hyphenated identities signal a sense of self that transcends national boundaries (by crossing them through immigration from one country to another) and points to the continued presence of the global in the regional or local setting through the maintenance of ethnic traditions and identities.

NATIVE AMERICANS

Ethnicity in the Mid-Atlantic did not begin with the arrival of European immigrants; rather, native groups inhabiting the region prior to contact also perceived differences among themselves that can be understood as ethnic differences, based in culture and language. At the time of European settlement, native populations in the Mid-Atlantic fell into two primary language groups: the Algonquian and the Iroquoian. Primary Algonquin groups in the region included the Lenni Lenape. The three traditional Lenape divisions (Munsee, Unami, and Unalactigo) were based on differences in dialect and location. Other Algonquin groups included the Mahican in Pennsylvania, the Shawnee in Pennsylvania and West Virginia, and the Nanticoke and Piscataway in the Chesapeake region. Iroquois groups dominating New York and northern Pennsylvania included members of the Six Nations: Cayuga, Mohawk, Oneida, Onondaga, and Seneca, later joined by the Tuscarora. The original homeland of the Iroquois was in upstate New York between the Adirondack Mountains and Niagara Falls. Through conquest and migration, they gained control of most of the northeastern United States and eastern Canada. At its maximum in 1680, their empire extended south to the Chesapeake, west as far as Kentucky, and north to lower Michigan, southern Canada, and northern New England west of the Connecticut River.

In addition to major language/culture distinctions, new hybrid tribal identities emerged when disease and war fragmented native groups, leading to the consolidation of some tribal groups. The Susquehannock, for example, were a formidable group concentrated primarily in Pennsylvania, but ranging from the Potomac River in northern Virginia to southern New York, who absorbed many neighboring groups. The Susquehannock lived in a number of large, fortified villages (perhaps as many as twenty) that stretched along the Susquehanna River and its branches across Pennsylvania into southern New York.

Many Native American groups were known by names that came from outside the group itself—from Europeans or other native groups. Susquehannock appears to have been an Algonquin name meaning the "people of the Muddy River" (Susquehanna). Several names for Susquehannock were commonly used by early settlers. The French called them *Andaste*, from their Huron name *Andastoerrhonon*. The Dutch and Swedes used the Delaware name *Minqua*, meaning "stealthy" or "treacherous." The Powhatan in northern Virginia may have called them the *Pocoughtaonack* or *Bocootawwanauke*.

Shawnee came from the Algonquin word *shawun (shawunogi)*, meaning "southerner," and referred to their original location in relation to the Great Lakes Algonquin. Delaware was not a Native American name but rather created by an English sea captain who wished to honor Sir Thomas West, Third Lord de la Warr and the first governor of Virginia. English colonists later used "Delaware" to designate the bay, the river, and the native peoples who lived there. The Delaware called themselves Lenape, translated either as "original people" or "true men." The Swedish form was Renape. For many Algonquin, the Lenape were the "grandfathers," a term of great respect stemming from the widespread belief that the Lenape were the original tribe of all Algonquin-speaking peoples. The Iroquois were named by their enemies: the Algonquin called them the *Iroqu (Irinakhoiw)*, "rattlesnakes," and the French added the suffix "-ois." The Iroquois called themselves *Haudenosaunee*, meaning "people of the longhouse." These varieties of naming practices point to the various lenses through which Native American identity was viewed, depending on perspective. Naming was one critical way to acknowledge salient cultural differences, claim authenticity, or assimilate the colonized.

Although distinct culturally and linguistically, Algonquin and Iroquoian societies did share some common characteristics. Both were predominantly peoples of the Late Woodland period, nonmigratory societies that depended primarily on hunting, fishing, and agriculture for sustenance. Beans, squash, and corn were the primary crops cultivated by women, while men hunted wild game. Both groups based kinship and identity on matrilineal clans, such as the Bear, Wolf, Turkey, and Turtle clans, which cut across village or settlement lines. Clothing was made from deerskin, and decorated with shell beads, porcupine quills, feathers, and other ornaments. Tattoos were common for both sexes. Older men wore their hair long, although warriors sported an erect scalp lock known as a Mohawk, although it was common to most of the eastern tribes.

The Lenape were not a single tribe, but a set of independent villages. There was no central political authority, and Lenape sachems (leaders) usually controlled only a few villages at a time. Most Lenape villages were not fortified and were comprised of round and oblong wigwams. Unlike the Algonquin tribes, the Iroquois lived in communal clan-based longhouses. These longhouses were sometimes over 200 feet in length and covered with elm bark. Villages were fortified and permanent, moving only for defensive purposes or when the soil became exhausted (about every twenty years).

In many ways, warfare and conquest were the Iroquois raison d'être, including the practice of torture. But the most distinctive feature of the Iroquois was their political system, the Iroquois League. The League was constituted through an elaborate system of checks and balances, based on 114 wampums and reinforced by a funeral rite known as the "Condolence." (Wampum are small beads made from polished shells and fashioned into strings or belts; they were used by certain Native American peoples as jewelry or currency at the time of European colonization and were often exchanged as part of treaty and other negotiations. The word "wampum" comes from the Narragansett word for "white shell beads.")

The council was composed of fifty male sachems and each tribe's representation was set: Onondaga fourteen; Cayuga ten; Oneida nine; Mohawk nine; and Seneca eight. All decisions of the council had to be unanimous. There was also a hierarchy among members; Mohawk, Onondaga, and Seneca were addressed as "elder brothers" or "uncles," while Oneida, Cayuga, and Tuscarora were "younger brothers" or "nephews."[1]

The Iroquoian empire incorporated thousands of non-league peoples during the 1650s. Political power was retained by the original Iroquois; those incorporated remained second-class citizens who were members not of the League, but of the "Covenant Chain," a terminology first suggested by the Dutch at a treaty signed with the Mohawk in 1618. By 1677 the Iroquois had extended membership in the chain to the Mahican and Delaware, and later to other Algonquin and Siouan tribes. Essentially, the Covenant Chain was a trade and military alliance that gave the Iroquois full authority to represent its members with Europeans, without direct representation in the League council. Thus, the Iroquois' Six Nations, through their dealings with European settlers, came to represent all native peoples in a way that increasingly effaced internal differences between Indians in their interactions across a more dramatic ethnic difference.

EARLY COLONISTS

Native-European Contact

Early European settlement in the Mid-Atlantic included the Dutch in New York, the Swedes in Pennsylvania and Delaware, and the English in Pennsylvania, Delaware, and Maryland. Many of these early settlements were commercial ventures attempting to mine the riches of the New World. Swedes established New Sweden along the Delaware in 1638 for the purposes of trading beaver fur with Native Americans. They forged trading relationships with the Lenni Lenape and built Fort Christiana along the Delaware River. Eventually they were forced to cede their colony to the Dutch (who subsequently ceded it to the English in 1664).

Further north, the Dutch West India Company explored territories in North America between 1624 and 1664. Numbering only a few thousand, they settled primarily in the lowlands of what became the states of Delaware, New Jersey, and New York. In 1626 the settlement of New Amsterdam was established at the mouth of the Hudson River and trade outposts created on the Hudson, Mohawk, and Delaware rivers. Trading posts, towns, and forts were created up and down the Hudson River. Probably the most successful trading post was established at Fort Orange, site of present-day Albany, located at the confluence of the Hudson and Mohawk rivers.

Dutch

The Dutch set the tone of early New York as a seafarers' town full of taverns, smugglers, and diverse human comings and goings. They also left their mark on the landscape in the form of stone gabled houses and fortified structures: Dutch settlers erected a stockade wall at what was then the northern edge of New Amsterdam, which later evolved into Wall Street, and the Dutch villages of Haarlem and Breukelen, now the New York City areas of Harlem and Brooklyn. Early Dutch farms, called *bouweries*, provided the name for the section of the city that would later be known as the Bowery. The influence of the Dutch Reformed Church represents the primary Dutch contribution to the culture of the region, along with holiday traditions such as New Year's Day and the St. Nicholas tradition.

European settlement shaped the contours of ethnicity in the region through contacts with Native peoples. William Penn, the Quaker founder of Pennsylvania, sought peaceful relations with the indigenous Lenape. The Dutch fared less well—suffering attacks from Mohawks, and, in the 1630s and early 1640s, carrying on a series of violent campaigns against the area's Native Americans, which created a tense and volatile situation between European settlers and Native Americans in that area.

In large measure, however, initial native-European interaction was characterized by coexistence and accommodation as the two sides pursued the fur trade and land sales with each other. When Dutch encountered Mohawk or Swedes and English interacted with Lenni Lenape, they encountered in the other a fundamental difference, not only in terms of language and culture but of underlying worldview as well. These differences informed early negotiations between the groups, which involved moving back and forth between differential understandings of property, language and writing, social customs, and notions of reciprocity. In Pennsylvania, where Penn sought peaceful coexistence with Indians, natives exchanged wampum, while Europeans transcribed proceedings in writing. Encountering the other, each group had to inhabit a "middle ground," a sphere of accommodation, which, according to historian Richard White, was "in between cultures, peoples, and in between empires and the nonstate world of villages," where "diverse peoples adjust their differences through what amounts to a process of creative, and often expedient, misunderstandings."[2] While initial contact represented an exploratory encounter with this diversity, pervasive misunderstandings, shaped by perceptions of essential racial difference, ultimately fueled European colonization, with tragic consequences for native populations.

While Europeans valued linear time, property ownership, and individualism, Native Americans operated with circular notions of time and space and communal/use-based notions of land incompatible with European ideas of individual rights and private property. The Lenape did not own land, differentiating only family hunting territories in the winter. Property was use-based; if you needed an axe, for example, you used it, and when you no longer needed it, it could be used by another.

Spiritual practices drove the two groups apart and together. Indigenous populations believed in a spiritual world in which the natural, human, and spirit worlds coexisted. Lenape religious ceremonies were centered around a dedicated "big house." Priests could interpret dreams or tell the future; others were able to heal the sick. While the Lenape did possess an idea of an afterlife for the dead, it did not resemble the bleak concepts of heaven and hell—a lack of moral clarity that troubled many Europeans. Locating themselves within a clear spiritual hierarchy that located the supernatural, human, and natural worlds as distinct from one another, many Europeans regarded indigenous spiritual practices as witchcraft.

The work of missionaries, particularly the Moravians, created some spiritual middle ground. In Pennsylvania and New York, these Pietists from Germany sought conversions among native peoples. Like other Europeans, they recognized fundamental differences with Indians but tended to de-emphasize inequalities between the two societies. Believing in the equality of all people before God, and in the individual's communication with God, they did win some converts. Although it is difficult to gauge how fully the "praying Indians" embraced a Christian worldview, they did convert, ultimately creating a category of Indian ethnicity.

Trade remained a primary point of interchange between Europeans and indigenous people. An exchange of ideas and identities as well as goods, trade led to important transformations in Native American life and slowly altered native material culture. The incorporation of European techniques and materials into native art, for example, engendered a blossoming of artistic forms as well as a reshaping of those forms along European lines. By 1750 the Lenape sported silver nose rings and clothing decorated with bright cloth purchased from European traders. Glass and metal beads were incorporated into elaborate beadwork. Clay receptacles increasingly resembled metal cooking pots. Once they began trade with the Dutch, the Mahican abandoned many of their traditional weapons and quickly embraced firearms. On the other hand, trade with Europeans was fundamentally unbalanced: Native Americans traded raw goods, such as furs, for finished European goods, such as weapons, tools, and other metalwork. This imbalance slowly created a dependence on trade in European finished goods, and had a devastating effect on native cultures, circumscribing their options in dealing with the expansion of European settlement.

Contact with Native Americans also changed some Europeans when they came into close contact with Native Americans in the western backcountry. Many of these settlers developed an affinity for the indigenous way of life, adopted Indian dress, learned Indian languages, and formed alliances. Frontier negotiators such as Conrad Weiser and Kiontwogky (also known as Cornplanter), the son of a Seneca woman and a Dutch trader from Albany, inhabited deeply hybrid lives between the two cultures.

Throughout the eighteenth century, race and ethnicity increasingly came to play a role in Native-European diplomacy as accommodation broke down. The increasing encroachment of Europeans on Indian lands led to violence in the regional western frontier, and shifting alliances during European wars (such as the French and Indian War) engendered a culture of retaliatory violence both between different tribes and between Native Americans and Europeans. Increasingly, Europeans, especially those settlers along the backcountry, saw Native Americans as a different race, as a savage nation with which they were at war. Violent incidents peppered the New York and Pennsylvania backcountry. A massacre of the Moravian-influenced Christian Indians at Conestoga, outside Lancaster, Pennsylvania, in 1763 illustrated the degree to which white settlers' attitudes toward Indians had become increasingly monolithic so that they did not differentiate between different kinds of Indians.[3] These attitudes, and the imperialistic practices they engendered, erased the particular, localized nuances that had governed Indian-European negotiations and alliances early on, as well as the more hybrid cultural and personal interchanges between the two groups, reducing interaction to one of homogenized conflict and overt racism.

This violence and its consequences ultimately displaced the Native American populations of the Mid-Atlantic. Under pressure of white settlement, the Lenni Lenape moved westward to Wyoming Valley, to the Allegheny, and finally to eastern Ohio. Many fought for France in the French and Indian War and for the British in the Revolutionary War. Eventually they ended up on reservations in Oklahoma and Ontario. In the United States, much of the Iroquois' homeland was surrendered to New York land speculators in a series of treaties following the Revolutionary War. Despite these developments, most Seneca, Tuscarora, and Onondaga avoided removal during the 1830s, remaining in New York. There are also sizable groups of Mohawk, Oneida, Cayuga, and Caughnawaga still in the state. Most of the Oneida, however, relocated in 1838 to a reservation near Green Bay, Wisconsin. The Cayuga sold their New York lands in 1807 and moved west to join the Mingo in Ohio, subsequently ceding their Ohio lands to the United States to relocate to the western Indian Territory in 1831. A few New York Seneca moved to Kansas briefly, only to join the others in northeast Oklahoma and become the modern Seneca-Cayuga Tribe of Oklahoma.

Iroquois Indians, 1914. Courtesy Library of Congress.

COSMOPOLITANISM, IMMIGRATION, AND NATIVISM

Characterized by several major watersheds—the Chesapeake, Delaware, and Hudson bays—and several major ports—Philadelphia, New York, and Baltimore—the Mid-Atlantic was a major destination for European immigrants over three centuries. Pennsylvania in particular, with its explicit statement of religious tolerance and freedom, actively solicited immigration from a variety of European countries early on. Many sought refuge there and spread throughout the region to Maryland, Delaware, and New York. New York was likewise diverse from the beginning, attracting not only a small number of Dutch settlers, but also people of diverse European origins seeking to benefit from the prosperity of the empire's thriving mercantilism.

Life in port cities such as Philadelphia was characterized by a great degree of cosmopolitanism, with international residents from France, Spain, and Poland joining English settlers, African slaves, and Native American emissaries. Foreign merchants, immigrants, exiles, diplomats, and statesmen all passed through Philadelphia and participated in the political and literary culture of the city. As the first capital of the new nation, Philadelphia was home to many foreign diplomats. It was also a republican beacon for revolutionary exiles from Latin American countries seeking independence from Spain, such as Francisco Miranda and Manuel

Torres, who took up residence in Philadelphia and New York City. There they continued their political activities, publishing newspapers and organizing for Latin American independence. As late as the late nineteenth century, Philadelphia and New York were centers of independence activity for Cubans and Puerto Ricans. Not all diversity was located in the cities, however; a wide array of European settlers staked their claim in the rural areas of the region, along the western frontier or "backcountry" in the eighteenth century.

Germans

The largest and most visible ethnic group in the mid-Atlantic region throughout the eighteenth and early nineteenth centuries was German. Germans settled primarily in rural areas of the Mid-Atlantic, cultivating farmland throughout the region. Most Germans came from specific regions in German-speaking Europe: the southern Rhine, Bavaria, Alsace, Switzerland, and the Palatinate. Some came seeking religious freedom, such as the Amish, Mennonites, and other plain Anabaptist sects. But these groups made up only 10 percent of the German immigrant population during that period. Others were poor farmers, laborers, or craftsmen who came as indentured servants and worked their way to freedom.

Most Germans in the eighteenth century arrived through the port of Philadelphia, moving north to New York and south through Maryland. In New York, they settled the Upper Hudson and Mohawk River valleys. In Maryland, they moved into the western counties of Frederick, Washington, and Carroll. By 1790, 86 percent of all Maryland Germans lived in these backcountry counties and made up 44 percent of the total population of those counties. In Pennsylvania, where most Germans lived in the counties clustered around Philadelphia, the German presence was even more pronounced. They spread west through the central part of the state, establishing centers at Lancaster and York, and by the time of the Revolutionary War, they were settled throughout the state, making up one-third of the commonwealth's population and constituting the largest ethnic minority in the region.

Although German immigrants came from different parts of Germany and spoke different dialects of the language, they came to embrace a German ethnic identity in the context of the United States through their interactions with one another and English-speaking immigrants. This ethnicity had expression not only in folk culture and arts, but in the emergence of a distinctive German dialect known as Pennsylvania Dutch, the term *Dutch* being a corruption of

A young Pennsylvania Amish man who has not yet let his beard grow according to the customs of his church (1942). Courtesy Library of Congress.

Deutsch, which is German for "German." This dialect resulted from the interaction and fusion of various German dialects over many decades, as well as interactions with the English language.

Language retention was a dominant characteristic of German ethnicity in the Mid-Atlantic, and German was maintained as an active everyday language throughout the nineteenth century, when parts of Pennsylvania and Maryland could be considered effectively bilingual. German-language publications flourished throughout the region, and school in Lancaster, Pennsylvania, was taught in German—a concern of the Pennsylvania legislature in 1839 when it approved German as an official language of school instruction. More than half of the immigrant population of Baltimore in 1870 had come from Germany, and in the 1880s and 1890s fully one-third of the city's population spoke German. Baltimore's public schools were bilingual.[4] World War I impacted the development of German language and ethnicity; in the face of anti-German sentiment, use of German as a daily language fell off dramatically.

In addition to farming, German immigrant occupations continued to embrace the *gesellschaft*, or craftsman, traditions of their country of origin, leading to a florescence in German American folk art. Quilting, weaving, basket making, painted furniture, pottery, and other decorative arts bore and still bear the recognizable traits of Pennsylvania German aesthetics: bright primary colors such as blue, red, and yellow; and simple decorative motifs such as angels, tulips and other flowers, stars, hearts, birds, and geometrical figures. Pottery made from red clay and utilizing *sgrafitto* and slip-trailing techniques, known as redware, was common and is still produced today. Fraktur, which flourished from 1750 to 1850, is another familiar form of Pennsylvania German folk art. Fraktur refers both to a style of writing and to an art form. Fraktur writing was based on a loose imitation of bold, rigid Gothic lettering, and was produced primarily by schoolmasters and clergymen in German communities. The style of illumination was utilized to illustrate marriage and birth certificates (*taufschein*), hymnals, books, and other important documents. These folk arts have become some of the most visible symbols of German ethnicity into the twenty-first century, embodied in the lifestyle of the Amish, but they also infused the visual arts of the region as a whole, from the painted furniture displayed in museums, to the quilts sold at shops and auctions, to the popular, mass-produced hex signs that dot the regional landscape.

This landscape was influenced heavily by the expression of German ethnicity in vernacular architecture. Banked barns in the German style, known as "Pennsylvania barns," characterize farmsteads in central Pennsylvania and throughout the region. These barns are characterized by building on a mound of earth (the "bank") to create two levels, one for livestock and the other for storage. German settlers also built a distinctive three-room house, which was later effaced by the building of a symmetrical Georgian outer façade, while retaining the inner three-room floor plan, signaled by an "off-center" chimney, a building technique that spoke to Germans' attempts to assimilate to an Anglo majority. Germans also contributed the technique of log construction for buildings as well as the iconic design of the famous Conestoga wagon that transported so many pioneers west.

German ethnicity survives today primarily as a culture of memory, located in public enactments of ethnicity, the commodities of the tourist industry, and the quaint regional folklore of the "Pennsylvania Dutch," or embedded in the mem-

Ethnic events, like this German Oktoberfest in New York State, are broadly popular and draw diverse Americans into invented ethnic celebrations. Courtesy New York State Department of Economic Development.

ories of individual families. Some singing societies survive, such as the Arion Singing Society of Central New York, originally organized in 1896 to promote German culture and activities in the area. Now called the German American Society of Central New York, it works to promote German heritage and traditions. "Oktoberfests" celebrate German identity through music, folk arts, and, of course, beer. One of the oldest and largest of the German American clubs in Philadelphia, the Cannstatter Volksfest-Verein, was founded in 1873 for the purpose of celebrating the customs and traditions of their homeland, especially the annual harvest festival held in the town of Bad Cannstatt. The annual fest is held today on Labor Day weekend and draws thousands of people, both German Americans and others, to observe and participate in the event. The club also continues its charitable fraternal tradition providing support for German language schools, hospitals, nursing homes, and orphanages, as well as to specific individuals in need.

Welsh and Scots-Irish

Germans were joined on the mid-Atlantic frontier by the Scots-Irish and the Welsh. Welsh immigrants arrived in the region in the late seventeenth century. From 1682 to 1700, the Welsh were the largest immigrant group in Pennsylvania, constituting approximately one-third of the colony's population in 1700.[5] Many were Quakers seeking religious freedom; others were Baptist, Anglican, or Presbyterian. The bulk of these immigrants settled in a tract of land northwest of Philadelphia created by William Penn as a Welsh "barony." Although short-lived, the barony left its mark on the region through the retention of Welsh place names, such as Bryn Mawr, Tredyffrin, Bala Cynwyd, and Gwynedd. Poor harvests in Wales renewed Welsh immigration to the region in the 1790s, and in the nineteenth century many skilled Welsh workers traveled to Oneida and Utica counties in New York and to the coal and iron regions of northeastern Pennsylvania. The development of the steel industry also led to the settlement of Welsh communities in the late nineteenth century in cities such as Sharon, Johnstown, and Pittsburgh in western Pennsylvania. Smaller Welsh populations were also scattered throughout West Virginia, Maryland, and Delaware.

Most Welsh ultimately assimilated to the larger English population over time, with Welsh ethnicity largely maintained through language and other expressive traditions. Language was preserved in the Welsh-language press, which flourished in the late nineteenth century in Pennsylvania and New York, and to a lesser extent in Welsh language churches. Literary and musical traditions were another rich arena of ethnic expression. The *Eisteddfod*, an oral performance contest featuring oral poetry, recitations, and vocal music, was an important expressive tradition that reached its height in the late nineteenth century, particularly in the coal regions of Pennsylvania. The *Gymanfa Ganu*, a choral music festival, is another important Welsh musical tradition, often focused on hymn singing. Traditionally held on St. David's Day, March 1, present-day *Gymanfa Ganu* festivals are held in Pennsylvania, Maryland, and New York, feeding a national contest held annually in May.

Another British ethnic group to settle in the region was the Scots-Irish. Scots-Irish is a term that is used to refer to groups who, displaced from their land in Scotland, relocated first to poor rural counties of Northern Ireland, and later to America after a 1740 famine in Ulster once again forced them to move. Overwhelmingly Presbyterian, the Scots-Irish often came to colonial America in family or congregational groups. Many were middle-class farmers and craftsmen. Arriving in Philadelphia, they made their way westward to Lancaster and Harrisburg, then further west to the Cumberland Valley forty to fifty miles west of Philadelphia, and finally south to the foothills of the mountains in Western Maryland.

A major component of Scots-Irish identity was religious, and their Presbyterian faith left a lasting impression on the religious makeup of the region. The first presbytery in America was founded in Philadelphia in 1706 and by 1718 there were thirteen Presbyterian churches in Pennsylvania. By the 1730s, the Scottish ministers could no longer fill the demand for pastors and Presbyterian ministers began to be trained and educated at American schools. Their brand of Protestantism served as the foundation for the Baptist and Methodist faiths of today.

Often located on the outskirts of European settlement in western Pennsylvania and Maryland, the Scots-Irish found themselves inhabiting a "buffer zone" between English and Native Americans. The group also entertained a reputation for violence and anti-authoritarian attitudes. Many Scots-Irish settlers in western Pennsylvania were squatters, a practice that got them into trouble with both the Quaker government and displaced Native Americans. Scots-Irish settlers, for example, were often embroiled in conflicts with Native Americans along the backcountry frontier, and they constituted the majority of rural farmers involved in the infamous Whiskey Rebellion of 1794. Over the years, Scots-Irish have been both celebrated and derided as scrappy, stubborn pioneers with a taste for whiskey and a distaste for government interference.

Finding western Pennsylvania increasingly inhospitable, the Scots-Irish migrated southwest along what came to be known as the Great Pennsylvania Wagon Road, formerly the Iroquois' Great Warriors Path. The Great Warriors Path led from Iroquois headquarters around the Great Lakes through central Pennsylvania, into western Maryland around Hagerstown, across the Potomac River through the Shenandoah Valley of Virginia to North Carolina and eventually Georgia. This migration led to the development of another distinctly regional culture, that of the southern Appalachian Mountains, where Celtic patterns of music and speech shaped cultural practice to a large degree. As such, much of Scots-Irish culture has ceased to be viewed as an ethnic culture per se and, in its interactions with African and other cultures, has come to constitute "American" folk culture.

Irish

Although the Mid-Atlantic witnessed some early immigration from Ireland throughout the colonial era, primarily Protestant, the critical mass of Irish immigrants arrived in the nineteenth century, shortly before and after 1846. Known as the "Famine Generation," these Irish immigrants were largely Catholic and rural in origin, settling in mid-Atlantic cities like New York, Baltimore, and Philadelphia. They clustered primarily in working-class slums: in Baltimore, the Irish settled at Fells Point and Locust Point; in Philadelphia in Northern Liberties and Southwark. In New York City, the Irish came to define the infamous neighborhood known as Five Points. In addition to settlement in cities, Irish immigrants also settled the patch towns of the anthracite regions of Pennsylvania where they formed a core of the mineworker population.

Irish immigration patterns were unique in that the majority of Irish immigrants were young single women. These women sought to escape the confining gender roles of the old country, working in sewing or as domestics. More than 60 percent of Irish-born workingwomen labored as servants. Most Irish-born men were unskilled laborers in canals, railroads, and general construction. They sought work in the coal mines of western Maryland and northeastern Pennsylvania, laid track for the B&O and Pennsylvania railroads, and dug the Chesapeake, Erie, and Ohio canals. They worked at livery stables and in the shipbuilding and ironworks industries in Baltimore. In Philadelphia, some skilled Irish workers labored as handloom weavers in the textile factories. Work for most Irish men was seasonal, unsettled, and dangerous—leading to a high incidence of desertion or disappearance due to accidents. Many Irish newspapers of the period feature ads from women seeking to find their lost husbands. As a result, a large percentage of Irish American households were female-headed during this period.[6]

Irish ethnicity was shaped not only by national origin and culture, but also by religious and racial difference. Predominantly Catholic among a Protestant majority, the Irish suffered discrimination and negative stereotyping. Attitudes inherited from Britain constructed the Irish as racially other than white—dirty, dissolute, and inherently violent. In many popular images of the time, Irish men were portrayed as pugnacious and monkeylike, the women as large-boned drudges. While the fabled "No Irish Need Apply" signs may not have actually existed, Irish immigrants certainly did experience employment discrimination, sometimes explicit and sometimes implicit. A perusal of employment ads from the penny papers of the day reveals phrases like "native Americans only," which were intended to exclude Irish workers. These attitudes also took a specifically American form in concerns about the threat that the Irish and other Catholic immigrants (including some from Germany) posed to American democracy, attitudes that were held by prominent men such as Horace Bushnell and Samuel Morse. The popular belief was that the Catholic faith bound the Irish in loyalty to the Pope and foreign monarchies.

While such anti-Irish sentiment was a national phenomenon, it was concentrated in cities such as those in the Mid-Atlantic, where many Irish had settled. In New York City, Philadelphia, and Washington, D.C., nativist riots targeted Irish neighborhoods and churches throughout the 1840s and 1850s. For example, during several rounds of riots in 1844 in Philadelphia, nativist mobs attacked several Catholic churches in Irish neighborhoods, burning one, St. Augustine's, to the ground. A year later, the Native American Party was formed by the "Know-Nothings" in New York, and held their first convention in Philadelphia.

Irish ethnicity was shaped in part by this climate of discrimination. Some have argued that hostility helped shape a high degree of ethnic solidarity among Irish Americans, reflecting both the discrimination that Irish Catholics faced and a belief that their economic security depended on internal unity. Fraternal organizations, inherited from the old country, such as the Ancient Order of Hibernians and the Sons of St. Patrick, offered assistance to new immigrants and helped to create an ethnic community infrastructure. They also supported struggles of labor and working-class identity. In the patch towns of the anthracite region, for example, many of the infamous "Molly Maguires" were members of the Order. The violent drama of the coalfields was not only a conflict between labor and capital, but an ethnic conflict as well, inflected by prevailing negative attitudes about the Irish as violent rabble-rousers, and a targeting of their community institutions by law enforcement.[7]

In the cities, working-class identity was also a key component of Irish ethnicity. Many Irish men found work in egalitarian group situations: on labor gangs, construction crews, or as longshoremen. The Irish were prominent in the working-class culture of nineteenth-century cities, forming fire companies and participating in street gangs. Irish Americans also often took the lead in supporting labor unions, and labor leaders such as Elizabeth Gurley Flynn, the "rebel girl," helped build the modern labor movement. In 1907 Flynn became an organizer for the Industrial Workers of the World and organized garment workers in Pennsylvania, silk weavers in New Jersey, and restaurant workers in New York. The novelist Theodore Dreiser described her as "an East Side Joan of Arc." Irish men were also likely to seek government employment (as police officers for instance) or to find jobs under contractors who held city contracts or in public utilities such as public transportation. Politically active, the Irish came to dominate the political establishment in New York and Philadelphia, through the police and city government. One grandson of Irish immigrants, Al Smith, who was born in New York City's Lower East Side in 1873, rose through Tammany Hall to be elected governor of New York. With a distinctively working-class, ethnic, "Lower East Side" style, Smith became the first Roman Catholic to win the nomination of a major party for president in 1928.

The racial attitudes the Irish encountered also shaped their relations with other minority ethnic groups, particularly African Americans. They worked to reshape perceptions of their racial difference and create themselves as "white." Participation in cultural forms such as minstrelsy, one of the most popular cultural entertainments of the nineteenth century (Abraham Lincoln himself attended minstrel shows) allowed the Irish to "black up" and at the same time they removed the cork, to emphasize their "whiteness." Thus they actively distanced themselves from African Americans and from the stigma of racial Otherness.

African Americans

African Americans were also some of the earliest residents of the Mid-Atlantic. Most if not all arrived as slaves. Contrary to popular representations of slavery, which locate it primarily in the antebellum South, slavery did exist in the Mid-Atlantic, as it did throughout much of the North, until the early nineteenth century. The Mid-Atlantic was unique in that it encompassed both states that were "free" during the antebellum era, as well as those where slavery lingered until the end of the Civil War.

Slavery in the Mid-Atlantic was of a different quality than in the lowland South, where the presence of large-scale plantation agriculture engendered a distinct African American community and culture. In the North, most farms and households contained only a handful of slaves, many of whom lived and worked in close proximity to white masters and indentured servants. Many masters hired their slaves out. In some cases, masters kept only a portion of the slave's wages, which allowed some slaves to save money and buy their freedom. One such slave was Absalom Jones, who purchased his freedom, was ordained as a minister, and became one of the most influential free black leaders in late-eighteenth-century Philadelphia. With Richard Allen, another self-freed slave from Delaware, he founded the Free African Society and two black churches, St. Thomas Episcopal and Mother Bethel A.M.E. Church.

The presence of Quakers in the Mid-Atlantic, particularly Pennsylvania, led to early advocacy for abolition of slavery in the eighteenth century. The Pennsylvania Abolition Society, founded in 1774 by a group of Quakers, was instrumental in the passage of an abolition act by the Pennsylvania legislature in 1790. The New York State legislature voted to end slavery nine years later. In both cases, the legislation outlined a gradual abolition of slavery. In New York, for example, those who were slaves in 1799 would not be freed until they were twenty-five (women) or twenty-eight (men) years old, by 1827. In fact, New Yorkers could be legally enslaved as late as 1841 within the terms of the act.

Abolition led to the formation of large and visible free black communities in Philadelphia and New York City; Philadelphia's free black community was the largest in the nation in the early nineteenth century. These communities were home to a diverse range of African Americans from all walks of life. By the early nineteenth century, Philadelphia's black community was characterized not only by an elite group of lawyers, businesspeople, and ministers, but also a defined middle class of mechanics, domestics, and caterers. The black elite worked with white Quakers and others for the abolition of slavery, but they also formed separate institutions within their community such as churches, literary societies, Masonic lodges, and schools. In Philadelphia, the Institute for Colored Youth educated

In the late 1800s the African American elite classes in Pennsylvania had separate Masonic lodges, such as this group from the Grand Lodge of Masons No. 2, c. 1897. Courtesy Library of Congress.

black children beginning in 1837, and the Banneker Institute, a literary and debating society named for Maryland mathematician/scientist Benjamin Banneker, was founded in 1854.

Despite emancipation and the gains of the free black community (or in some cases because of them), racism was still a salient factor in the antebellum North. Throughout the decades preceding the Civil War, free blacks were subject to escalating discrimination and violence. Commentators accused the black elite of aping white manners in a ridiculous fashion, and racist images circulated throughout the popular press. In 1836, the New York Women's Anti-Slavery Society in Buffalo barred blacks from membership. Blacks were disenfranchised by the Pennsylvania state constitution in 1837. Violent riots targeted black homes, businesses, and pedestrians in cities throughout the region in the 1830s, 1840s, and 1850s. Blacks were banned from public transportation and most public assembly rooms, libraries, and restaurants.

Differences across the Mason-Dixon line divided the Mid-Atlantic during the antebellum and civil war period. While Philadelphia and western New York were hotbeds of abolitionist activity, the slave system was retained in West Virginia, Maryland, and Delaware. Western New York, known as the "burned-over district" because of its strong evangelical and reform impulses, was especially influential, and liberal, reform-minded cities such as Rochester provided an active base for abolition activities. Frederick Douglass, a former slave and prominent abolitionist, made his home in Rochester, publishing his newspaper the *North Star* there and offering his home as a stop on the Underground Railroad. William Wells Brown lived in a less welcoming Buffalo from 1836 to 1844.[8]

The Underground Railroad mapped routes all throughout Pennsylvania, New Jersey, and New York, north to Canada. Rochester, conveniently located close to the Canadian border, served as one of the last stops in the Underground Railroad. Albany, Syracuse, Rochester, and Buffalo all contained many Underground Railroad stops. Philadelphia, where William Still and his interracial Philadelphia Vigilance Committee operated, was an important transfer point for fugitive slaves. The passage of the Fugitive Slave Law in 1857 heightened tensions along the Mason-Dixon line. Free blacks living in border communities of southern Pennsylvania were especially vulnerable to capture and reenslavement. The enforcement of the law was dramatic and divisive in these communities, often exploding in violence. Such was the case of an 1851 riot that erupted in Christiana, Pennsylvania, when slave catchers attempted to transport a captive.

After the Civil War, emancipation in the south transformed African American life in the North as southern blacks sought to improve their lives through migration to the northern states, including those in the Mid-Atlantic. This historic movement, known as the Great Migration, swelled the African American populations of cities of Washington, D.C., Philadelphia, Pittsburgh, New York, Buffalo, and Baltimore at the turn of the twentieth century. Many came to work in the burgeoning steel industries or in the mines of West Virginia and Pennsylvania. In Washington, D.C., federal jobs were a main attraction. From 1900 to 1920, northwest Washington, D.C., was home to the largest black community in the country, inhabited by a prosperous black middle class and anchored by a range of churches, newspapers, black-owned businesses, and other civic institutions. Howard University, and the surrounding neighborhood known as Shaw, became a center for African American intellectuals and artists and nurtured figures such as Duke Ellington, Paul Laurence Dunbar, Langston Hughes, Alain Locke, Mary Church Terrell, and Thurgood Marshall.

Later, during the 1920s and 1930s, New York City became another center of black literary, social, and cultural life. The neighborhood of Harlem emerged as a mecca for African American artists and intellectuals, supporting visual artists and writers such as Aaron Douglass, Ralph Ellison, Langston Hughes, Richard Wright, and Zora Neale Hurston. The famed Cotton Club showcased the talents of renowned black musicians such as Cab Calloway and Duke Ellington. These artists formed a cultural movement, known as the Harlem Renaissance, that expressed a kind of cultural nationalism, articulated by thinkers such as Alain Locke, which affirmed the equality of African Americans through artistic and intellectual achievement.

African Americans were not always welcome up north: all throughout the 1910s, riots targeted recent arrivals from the South, and the Ku Klux Klan was active in Pennsylvania and New York during what has been referred to as the nadir of race relations. Rigid segregation, particularly of residential areas and schools, remained the norm. African Americans, disillusioned by the disappointments of life in the North, mobilized against this racism, campaigning against lynching and segregation. Once again, the mid-Atlantic region was a center of black political activity.

The NAACP had its roots in the so-called Niagara Movement (named for its genesis in western New York) which, under the leadership of W.E.B. DuBois, renounced Booker T. Washington's accommodation policies (Washington himself had grown up in Malden, West Virginia, where his family worked in the salt mines). After the Springfield race riot of 1908, white liberals joined with the nucleus of Niagara "militants" and founded the NAACP the following year.

African American struggles continued throughout the second half of the twentieth century in the wake of the gains of the civil rights movement and the rise of "Black Power." In major metropolitan areas of the mid-Atlantic region, steel, railroad, and manufacturing industries were on the decline, leading to a mass exodus from the cities, loss of jobs, and a general erosion of the urban economic base. These trends affected the large populations of African Americans who had come to settle in these cities. Race riots were common in major cities throughout the mid- to late 1960s, and African Americans in the Mid-Atlantic continually have renewed the struggle for civil rights, filing employment discrimination suits and seeking to desegregate schools and neighborhoods, among other activities.

INDUSTRIALISM AND IMMIGRATION

African American migration and German and Irish immigration were just the beginning of the Mid-Atlantic's burgeoning diversity, which blossomed in the second half of the nineteenth century during a great wave of immigration from southern and eastern Europe. The rapid industrialization in the region, which drew African Americans north, also drew large numbers of European immigrants to work in mills, mines, factories, and sweatshops across the region. After 1870 Ukrainians, Poles, Hungarians, Slovaks, Russians, Lithuanians, and Italians arrived in large numbers through the ports of New York, Philadelphia, and Baltimore. Many passed through Ellis Island; New York City was a major destination for immigrants and the Lower East Side the quintessential immigrant neighborhood. Whatever their port of entry, however, they dispersed throughout the region, settling where work could be found, not only in large cities, but also in mid-size cities and towns. Italians, Poles, Hungarians, and other eastern Europeans joined Irish and Welsh in the anthracite and bituminous coal regions of Pennsylvania and West Virginia. Hungarians, Poles, and Slovaks comprised the majority of workers in the steel mills of western Pennsylvania and New York (although the industry drew all groups). Italians made up the largest ethnic group in New Jersey's silk industry and West Virginia's glass industry. In manufacturing cities, ethnic enclaves emerged as immigrants settled in neighborhoods around dominant industries. These enclaves were formed in part through chain migration, whereby groups immigrated and settled near one another, clustering along shared familial, village, or regional lines. Italian American identity, for example, was based in part on a sense of connection to *paesani*, members of the same village in Italy, as well as family/kin ties. Immigrants formed distinct neighborhoods, such as "Little Italies," which supported a sense of familiarity and eased the adaptation of immigrants to a new cultural setting.

Whether they settled in large cities or small towns, immigrants had to adjust to life in the United States, and many institutions within immigrant communities were aimed at easing this cultural and economic transition. Italian immigrants, for

Italian American clam seller on Mulberry Street, New York City, c. 1900. Courtesy Library of Congress.

example, found work through professional labor brokers known as *padrones*. Working on contract, Italians dug tunnels, laid railroad tracks, constructed bridges and roads, and erected the first skyscrapers. As early as 1890, 90 percent of New York City's public works employees were Italian. Ethnic banks also catered to the financial needs of the community, often along Italian regional lines.

Mutual assistance through the formation of fraternal and other organizations was aimed at providing an economic support system to new immigrants. Additionally, fraternals helped preserve ethnic culture through calendar celebrations involving ethnic food, music, dance, costume, and language. Some of the fraternal organizations had their origins in the old country, such as the Slovak/Czech *sokols*, or gymnasiums, which offered sports activities and more, sponsoring language classes and cultural events such as plays and dances. Italian mutual societies also played an important role in community life, offering a safety net and social arena: sponsoring events and conventions, and clubs for games such as bocce. Many of these fraternals were based in the village identities immigrants carried from Italy. In other cases, they were new creations that emerged in the American context, such as the Sons of Italy. In Polish communities, fraternal organizations such as the Polish Roman Catholic Union, Polish National Alliance, Union of Polish Women, and the Polish Falcons flourished and served a variety of important community functions. Like other mutual aid societies, they offered life insurance services and culturally specific social outlets. Fraternals performed an important civic function as well, creating leadership in the ethnic community. In Italian American communities, for example, fraternals promoted a leadership infrastructure, known as the *prominenti*, who represented the ethnic group to the larger community and promoted the visibility and involvement of the ethnic community in the political realm. Such larger advocacy efforts worked to distill regional differences from the old country into a larger ethnic identity. The ethnic press also played an important role in community formation, as foreign language newspapers and magazines reported on issues of concern to the community.

Many of these immigrant groups were predominantly Catholic, and the church played another central role in community life. By the late nineteenth century, the Catholic Church hierarchy, dominated by Irish Americans, resisted the formation of ethnic parishes important to Poles, Italians, and others who wished to worship in their native tongue. For many faithful Polish Catholics, the move from home parishes in the old country into the multiethnic Catholic community in the United States was a difficult transition. Although some Polish immigrants attended churches in German or Czech American parishes, early on Polish immigrants began to establish their own parish churches. Between 1873 and 1922, Polish Americans established thirty-four parishes in Greater Buffalo and western New York, for example. Italian Americans founded ethnic parishes as well, and were largely responsible for the presence of Catholicism in West Virginia. Italian folk traditions such as processions and annual *festas* in honor of village patron saints expressed both religious faith and ethnic identity; devotion to saints was also expressed through the creation of shrines and home altars.

Jewish Immigration

Religion was also central to the experience of Eastern European Jews who fled anti-Semitic pogroms to seek refuge and a new life in the Mid-Atlantic. In America they joined previous generations of German Jewish immigrants who, unlike the recent arrivals, were educated bourgeoisie. Jewish enclaves formed in many cities, the largest being the Lower East Side in New York City and South Philadelphia. *Shuls*, or synagogues, and religious schools dotted many a street corner in these neighborhoods. As with other immigrant groups, mutual assistance was an important value expressed through the creation of numerous voluntary organizations, known as *farein* or *landsmanschaft*. One of every four Jews in New York City belonged to a *landmanschaft* in the early twentieth century, for instance. These organizations provided financial assistance, insurance benefits, and burial services, and sent remittances to hometowns back in the old country. They also provided immigrants with a chance to pray and socialize together.[9] Language was another strong component of Jewish ethnicity, expressed in the circulation of Yiddish newspapers such as New York City's *Forward*, and the growth of Yiddish theater throughout the region.

Most eastern European Jewish immigrants came from rural peasant backgrounds and sought unskilled labor in the United States. A large number labored in the garment trade; 40 percent of Jewish immigrants in Philadelphia, for example, worked in garment sweatshops (often owned by German Jews). Others were peddlers and shopkeepers, or workers in other industries such as cigar making. These strong working-class associations, combined with traditions of activism in the old

A scene in early New York City, the Jewish ghetto, Hester Street. Courtesy Library of Congress.

country, supported the growth of labor activism, socialism, and anarchism in Jewish communities. Like the Irish, Jewish immigrants played a central role in the growth of organized labor. For example, the young Jewish women who worked in the garment trade in New York took the lead in labor organizing, particularly after the Triangle Shirtwaist Factory fire of 1911, which galvanized the emerging garment workers' unionizing efforts as young women organized for better working conditions. In the aftermath of the tragedy, Local 25 of the International Ladies Garment Workers' Union (ILGWU) organized a rally against the unsafe working conditions that led to the disaster, while the Women's Trade Union League led the call for an investigation into working conditions.

Family patterns, norms of social interaction, foodways, festivals and holidays, music, dance, and belief systems all underwent change as groups adapted their traditions to a new context, changing practice as a response to new realities, or imbuing traditions with new meanings. Identity also underwent change, particularly across the generations. This new identity found expression in the early twentieth century in the public performance of ethnic identity in American-style civic functions such as parades and picnics. The creation of these traditions led to the emergence of new ethnic symbols outside of traditions inherited from the old country. In some cases, symbols linked ethnic communities to a longer American history. Italian Americans adopted Columbus as an Italian American hero and symbol.[10] Polish Americans celebrated the contributions to the American Revolution of Thaddeus Kosciusko and Casimir Pulaski, who lends his name to many annual Polish American parades. These public displays reflected a sense of ethnic pride that celebrated both an immigrant cultural identity and an emerging national American identity. Thus immigrants transformed themselves into ethnics, as Italians became Italian Americans, Poles became Polish Americans, and so forth.

Americanization and Immigration Restriction

This creation of distinctly ethnic American cultures in the early twentieth century emerged in part as a response to the larger cultural climate of "Americanization," which sought to eliminate ethnic differences through assimilation into the American "melting pot." The melting pot was an industrial metaphor taken from the steel industry: the idea was that the various nationalities would "melt" down into a single American identity. A range of institutions worked to assimilate foreign immigrant populations and inculcate a sense of American "loyalty." The Catholic Church was a powerful agent of Americanization, as was the settlement movement and organizations such as the Daughters of the American Revolution and the Young Women's Christian Association (YWCA). "English only" was promoted as a means to "be American." These attitudes undermined native language and cultural practices among immigrants, promoting a loss of culture and discomfort with ethnicity. This process led to cultural and linguistic loss in second and third generations, relegating the retention of ethnic culture to the private family realm of food and holiday/ritual observances. Nativism was once again an important factor in the development of ethnic identity and experience.

It also affected the demographics of the region. The nationally focused Immigration Restriction League, founded in the late 1800s, politically agitated over the "necessity of further exclusion of elements undesirable for citizenship or injurious to our national character," meaning the "brownish races of Southern Europe." These ideas were increasingly supported by a new scientific racism, represented in eugenics and beliefs about heredity, combined with existing beliefs conflating nation and race. In 1921 Congress passed the National Origins Act, instituting a quota system in which 70 percent of slots were allotted to natives of the United Kingdom, Ireland, and Germany, while strict quotas curtailed immigration from Italy, Greece, Poland, and elsewhere in southern and eastern Europe. Asian immigration remained prohibited, as it had been since 1880. This act was followed by a second act in 1924 that expanded the limitations. Immigration restriction essentially slowed immigration to a virtual standstill, curtailing the growth of Asian, Italian, Greek, and eastern European populations.

POST–WORLD WAR II DIVERSITY

If immigration to the region slowed after World War I, it gained new momentum after World War II, with dramatic effects on regional ethnicity. Changing attitudes toward race, in part an effect of struggles for African American civil rights, combined with a growing postwar American economy, supported an opening up of immigration quotas and legislation. First, World War II liberalized policies toward the Chinese (U.S. allies during the conflict), leading to the settlement of families and the growth of Chinatowns in New York City, Washington, D.C., and Philadelphia. Previously, Asian exclusion legislation had limited large-scale Asian settlement in the Mid-Atlantic to communities of bachelor sojourners, who came east to New Jersey, New York, and southeastern Pennsylvania in the late nineteenth century to work in laundries and food service, and who created small "Chinatowns." After the war Chinese wives joined Chinese American servicemen.

New York City's Chinatown. Courtesy New York State Department of Economic Development.

Families began settling in Chinatowns, which grew into full-fledged ethnic communities/neighborhoods. Often located in "tenderloin" districts, these neighborhoods were impacted by urban renewal in the 1970s and 1980s.

Latino Immigration and Migration

Wartime also brought Latinos to the region through contract work programs. Mexican *braceros* came as wartime labor to work on railroads and in factories in New York and Pennsylvania. Most were repatriated after the war ended. At the same time, Puerto Ricans arrived on work programs that provided labor for agriculture, manufacturing, and domestic service. As a result, Puerto Rican communities formed in New York City, New Jersey, and the Philadelphia area (and to a lesser extent in Washington, D.C.). Of these, by far the largest was and still is in New York City. The 1952 immigration law, which began liberalization of immigration quotas, allowed women to come from Latin America to work as domestics. Cuban exiles came to the United States fleeing the Cuban Revolution and the Castro regime after 1958 and during the early 1960s. Although Latinos settled throughout the Mid-Atlantic, New York City became the cultural center of Latino life in the region. Dominated by Puerto Ricans and infused with a Caribbean sensibility that contrasted with the Chicano culture of other regions, there emerged a distinct "Nuyorican" culture and identity that embraced the diaspora while retaining close ties to life on the island.

Latino immigration and migration continue, making Latinos the fastest-growing ethnic group in the region (currently they represent the fifth largest ethnic group according to the 2000 Census). These communities are not only increasing; they are increasingly diverse as well. Since the 1980s, the region's Latino communities have incorporated Dominicans, Mexicans, Colombians, Peruvians, Venezuelans, Salvadorans, Guatemalans, and others. Central Americans arrived in the 1980s, many as undocumented immigrants (U.S. foreign policy prevented their being formally recognized as refugees), and now, thanks to amnesty programs, have secured citizenship or permanent residency. Large numbers of Central Americans settled in the Washington, D.C., area in the 1980s; Salvadorans are now the largest ethnic group in D.C.'s Maryland suburbs. Dominicans had the largest immigrant population growth in New York City during the 1990s. Mexican migrant labor is increasing in New Jersey, New York, Delaware, and Pennsylvania's agricultural sectors. An estimated 90 percent of the Pennsylvania mushroom industry's labor force was Mexican-born in 1996. The Delmarva peninsula is another destination for migrant Latino workers, where the agriculture and poultry industries employ many. The poultry industry accounts for large numbers of Mexican and Guatemalan workers; over 50 percent of poultry workers in this area are Latino.

Throughout the region, contemporary Latino ethnicity is complicated, multifaceted, and strategic. "Latino" is a term that has emerged only in the context of Spanish-speaking immigration and migration to the United States and has no existence outside of that context. Many Latinos do not identify with the term, which has its origins in communities' cultural and political activism. Nor do they identify with the government-prescribed term "Hispanic," used in many "official" contexts, such as the census. Many choose to highlight their country of origin as Dominicans, Mexicans, Puerto Ricans, or Venezuelans, for instance, each of which is culturally distinct. At the same time, their experience as Spanish-speaking immigrants, and the tendency of the dominant culture to lump them together, leads to an emergent sense of connection and shared identity, expressed as *Latinidad*, or pan-Latino identity.

The visible ethnic presence of Latinos is particularly manifest in cities, where urban *barrios* emerge from the congregation of Latinos in certain neighborhoods. In creating the barrio, Latinos transform the urban landscape and imprint it with their own aesthetics and cultural sensibilities. Businesses and houses may sport Caribbean colors, and storefronts advertise traditional foods, music, and religious artifacts. In Philadelphia, Latinos create murals and community gardens, and build housing projects in a Spanish style, to transform a blighted post-industrial urban landscape. In New York City and Philadelphia, gardens and casitas, or "little houses," bring the countryside of the traditional rural Puerto Rican *jibaro* to the American city. Even rural areas and small towns are being affected; Kennett Square, Pennsylvania, and Vineland, New Jersey, are two examples of smaller communities that have seen a recent influx of large numbers of Mexican migrant laborers. The town of Georgetown, Delaware, has been transformed by Latino immigration, largely poultry workers from Guatemala.[11] These communities work to accommodate and understand newcomers.

Latino festivals such as this one in New York City allow Latinos to transform the urban landscape and imprint it with their own aesthetics and cultural sensibilities. Courtesy New York State Department of Economic Development.

Chinese and Latino communities are only two of the many groups whose presence in the Mid-Atlantic has increased in the second half of the twentieth century as immigration legislation evolved. The 1965 immigration act had perhaps the most dramatic effect, fully eliminating the turn-of-the-century quota system and bringing Asians, Africans, and Latin Americans to the region in large numbers for the first time. As the corporate capital of the world, New York City remains a first destination for many immigrants. The rest of the region has also witnessed major demographic changes along similar lines. These changes have brought new ethnicities, new religions, new identities, and new cultures to the region, as well as complicated notions of race beyond the historic black and white dichotomy.

Asians

South Asians

Of all the new groups to arrive after 1965, South Asians are one of the more dominant in the mid-Atlantic region (especially in New York and New Jersey). In 2000, the U.S. Census recorded over 500,000 South Asians residing in tristate area New York, New Jersey, and Pennsylvania. Some arrived as students in the 1960s and were joined by their families; others have come to work on H-1B visas as technical workers, scientists, computer programmers, and doctors. Unlike previous generations of immigrants, many Indians do not concentrate in major cities or form urban enclaves. Rather, like many new immigrants, they tend to settle directly in suburban areas. Concentrations of Indians in communities such as Iselin and Edison in central New Jersey constitute "Little Indias" where ethnicity is expressed through many media. Ethnic businesses trade in Indian clothing (saris and *salwar kameez*), gold jewelry, religious artifacts, and groceries. These businesses provide vital cultural resources to ever-increasing populations of new immigrants. Ethnicity is maintained and expressed as well through a variety of cultural practices: traditional Indian dance (*bharatnatyam*), music, and dress.

Indian ethnicity is shaped not only by language and culture, but also by significant religious difference from the rest of the mainstream population. Eastern religions such as Hinduism, Islam, Sikhism, and Jainism are important foundations for South Asian life. Creating space for spiritual practice is a priority in Indian communities, whether in the building of a Hindu temple or the creation and maintenance of home altars. Religion thus becomes a central component in perceptions of their ethnic difference by others, as it is for most Asians.

For South Asians, as for many new immigrants, the retention of culture, especially as it is passed down to the second generation, is a primary concern. Parents worry that their children are too Americanized, and seek to inculcate traditional values. In many cases, the differences between the generations result in conflict over issues such as education and careers, dating and marriage, and personal style. "Desis" is a term used to refer to Indian ethnicity, and jokes circulate within the community about "ABCDs," or "American Born Confused Desis." In practice, these second-generation immigrants express a multiple identity shaped by moving back and forth between the American world of school and peers, and the Indian world of home, family, and community. Many spend summers with extended family in India and express the feeling that they are at home neither in the United States nor in India. Some accept an arranged marriage, while others challenge parental authority and choose their own partners. Their cultural practices are deeply hybrid and transnational, embracing American, British, Indian, and other sources. Musical tastes, for example, cross boundaries and genres and span American pop, British bhangra rap, and Bollywood pop music.

Even within the first generation, Indian ethnic identity is complicated, shaped by internal differences inherited from India. These differences include not only traditional caste/class identities, but also ethnic identities that are meaningful in the Indian context, such as Punjabi and Tamil. Each of these groups has their own language and often a specific religious orientation. Once in the United States, these identities become less central, except within the community itself, as immigrants adopt a larger identity as "Indian" in America. For some, especially in the politically active second generation, the identity category "South Asian" has been adopted (versus Indian or Pakistani) as a way of indicating an even broader ethnic identity category. This broader category emphasizes unity that is strategic not only in terms of American ethnic politics, but in the context of Indian/Pakistani conflicts on the subcontinent, conflicts that this generation seeks to transcend. Even then, they often encounter confusion about their identity when Americans conflate Indian with Native American "Indian," or "South Asian" with Southeast Asian.

Other Asian Groups

Other Asian groups to inhabit the Mid-Atlantic since 1965 include Southeast Asians: Vietnamese, Laotian, Cambodian, and Hmong. These communities have formed primarily since the late 1970s, when Southeast Asian refugees were formally resettled in the region. Like other refugees from Africa, Central America, and eastern Europe, these groups fled persecution in their countries of origin, and their experience has been shaped by the involuntary nature of their immigration. Some struggle with residual effects of trauma and the circumstances of arriving with nothing. Communities have grown over the last two decades as first arrivals bring family members over through family reunification programs.

Ethnic identity in these communities is maintained through religion (predominantly Buddhist) and language. In addition, traditional arts play a key role in the maintaining and expression of identity, and in the reconstruction of culture in the wake of persecution or displacement. For example, Cambodian classical dance, an art form that has almost died out in Cambodia, is being revived and taught in Cambodian American communities throughout the region. Hmong women maintain the tradition of *paj ntaub*, or storycloth, a traditional textile composed of elaborate appliqué and embroidery techniques. These colorful cloths visually relate traditional tales and histories, as well as more recent stories of the refugee experience. In another interesting ethnic twist, some Philadelphia area Hmong have found a home near Lancaster, Pennsylvania, where they feel they share a cultural affinity with the Amish. One economic alliance between the two groups has Hmong seamstresses drawing on their traditional skills to make Amish-style quilts for the tourist trade.

Koreans comprise the second largest Asian ethnic group in the region after Chinese. The New York–New Jersey area alone, home to approximately 150,000 Koreans, is the second largest Korean center in the United States, and the Mid-Atlantic is home to almost 30 percent of the Korean population nationally.[12] Pennsylvania and Maryland also have significant Korean communities, the northwest suburbs of Washington, D.C., in particular. Like Asian Indians, Koreans have tended to settle directly in suburban areas as opposed to urban centers. A majority of Korean American families are Christian (Baptist and Presbyterian) although services are held in Korean.

Koreans have had great success in small business ownership. It is estimated that one-third of all Koreans in the United States own their own businesses, and Koreans have the highest rate of business ownership of any group in the United States. There is some evidence that Korean cultural values have helped shape this economic strategy. One tradition that Koreans draw on is *kye*, a type of money lending system within the Korean community in which people join together and contribute a certain amount each month, and share that amount with persons who have the greatest need. This practice provides a ready source of capital to those seeking to start small businesses. Another important Korean American cultural value, *anjông* (establishment, stability, or security), is satisfied by entrepreneurship as opposed to wage labor.[13]

Like many Asians, Korean Americans become conscious of themselves as "Asians" only after immigration to the United States. In many communities across the region, pan-Asian coalitions and alliances are only beginning to emerge, as Asians confront an image of themselves as a "model minority," an image that has prevented the mainstream from addressing issues of discrimination.

African Immigration and Migration

Another group confronting both stereotypes and umbrella identity are Africans, the newest arrivals to the region. Cities such as Washington, D.C., New York City, and Philadelphia (and their suburbs) are now home to ever-increasing numbers of East and West Africans. This influx began after passage of the 1980 Refugee Act, and accelerated throughout the 1990s. Ethiopian/Eritrean communities were formed by resettled refugees in the early 1980s. More recently, refugees from Liberia and Sudan have made their way to the region. West Africans, particularly Nigerians, also comprise a large and growing segment of the population. Like Asian and Latino ethnicity, African ethnic identity is emergent in the context of immigration, as many Africans identify by national origin (Nigerian, Eritrean, or Senegalese, for example) or even by African ethnic group (Yoruba and Efik from Nigeria, Dinka from Sudan, Ga from Ghana, and so forth) as opposed to the umbrella identity of "African." They tend to socialize with members of their own communities and only rarely across pan-African lines.

Africans' ethnic identity is further complex given that many Africans settle in areas where there are large African American communities. Often feeling invisible within these communities, particularly to the outside, they also experience tensions with African Americans that complicate "black" ethnicity. Most do not identify as African American, and mutual misconceptions inform negative interactions between the two communities: Africans may be largely unaware of the historic struggles of African Americans, while African Americans may understand little about the nature of contemporary Africa. Africans share this tension and identity with Afro Caribbean immigrants, who have formed communities in the region, particularly in New York City, where boroughs like Queens are home to concentrations of Guyanese, Haitians, Jamaicans, and Trinidadians.

CONTEMPORARY ETHNICITY: CELEBRATION AND AMBIVALENCE

Contemporary ethnicity in the mid-Atlantic region is complex and continues to change. The 2000 Census revealed that the largest ethnic identifications in the region are African American and German (at over 7 million each), followed by Irish, Italian, and Hispanic/Latino.[14] The region is also home to 2 million Asians. For those who imagine ethnicity primarily in terms of the older European immigrant groups of the past, contemporary demographics represent a surprising new reality. In suburban Maryland, for example, the largest ethnic group is Salvadoran, followed by Chinese, as well as large numbers of immigrants from Korea, India, Germany, Nigeria, and Iran. New York City remains the immigrant city par excellence, where the top countries of immigrant origin in the 1990s were the Dominican Republic, the former Soviet republics, China, Jamaica, Poland, India, and the Philippines.

In the face of such broad diversity, the region has witnessed both a new celebration of ethnicity and renewed nativism and anti-immigrant attitudes. Multiculturalism now characterizes much ethnic expression in the region: cultural celebrations, festivals, and performance of folk arts are all primary means of maintaining and expressing ethnicity. Multiculturalism also manifests itself as a means to celebrate diversity and make social institutions more egalitarian through the embrace or inclusion of different cultural traditions in public representations. Multiculturalism has been made possible largely because of changing attitudes toward ethnicity in general since the 1960s, particularly for the descendants of previous generations of European immigrants. The "ethnic revival" among European ethnic groups who originally immigrated in the previous century stimulated a renewed interest in and exploration of ethnic cultures as second and third generation ethnics sought to rediscover their "roots." Second and third generation Jews express their ethnic identity through "Yiddishkeit," an overall sense of being Jewish, which might include celebrating Jewish holidays, exhibiting ethnic pride, paying attention to Jewish issues, preparing traditional dishes or observing dietary laws, and promoting a revival of interest in the Yiddish language.[15] For African Americans, ethnic revival has meant an attempt to reconstruct cultural roots in Africa, expressed most fully in the philosophy of Afrocentricity. In this case, a reclaimed ethnic identity is asserted in the face of a racist, negative construction of black difference, and the historical erasure of African cultural specificity in the Americas. Now, unlike a century ago, ethnicity often is considered a positive identity choice, an identification that enhances one's sense of self. Ethnic events, like German Oktoberfests, are broadly popular and draw diverse Americans into invented ethnic celebrations. Irish ethnicity has gone mainstream, in the form of St. Patrick's Day, which is seen by many non-Irish as a pretext to "party." Once the focus of derision, the St. Patrick's Day Parade is a major civic event in New York City (as it is in many other cities), while Irish pubs dot many a neighborhood in the cities and towns of the region.

This latter trend points to the commodification and marketing of ethnic culture, particularly as it is tied to local and regional tourism. Tourism feeds commerce in Chinatowns and Amish country, where ethnic traditions are a hot attraction. While this attention undoubtedly brings economic development into some of these communities, it has a dark side as well. Chinatown residents, for example, complain that their communities are seen as a collection of restaurants, as opposed to living neighborhoods filled with family residences, churches, schools, and more. Asian culture in particular has been subject to mainstream consumer interest with fashion's interest in *mehendi* (traditional South Asian henna art), Indian textiles, chinoiserie, and Asian spirituality (Buddhism, yoga). These trends, which trade on a static sense of ethnic culture as "quaint" or "exotic," often efface the complexities of these traditions within ethnic communities themselves.

Irish Americans continue to celebrate their heritage at this New York State Irish festival. Courtesy New York State Department of Economic Development.

Anti-Immigrant Sentiment

Despite interest in consuming difference, the region (as the nation) is also witnessing, once again, increasing discomfort with difference in the form of renewed anti-immigrant sentiment. In part, this reaction has been a backlash against the multiculturalism of the late 1980s and 1990s, the so-called Culture Wars. Contributing to the phenomenon were a broad economic slowdown and restructuring throughout the region. In particular, deindustrialization, fears of cultural balkanization, and race anxiety catalyzed anti-immigrant, antidiversity sentiments that have sometimes exploded into violence. In the 1980s, "Dot-busters" attacked New Jersey's South Asians. In 2002 out-of-work technical workers complained about "curries" dominating the collapsed dot-com field. Since the terrorist attacks of September 11, 2001, legislation such as the Homeland Security Act has significantly slowed immigration to the region. Arab and South Asian Muslims have suffered the most as targets of law enforcement and everyday harassment, and hate crimes against Arabs and Muslims have risen dramatically since 2001.

This anti-immigrant sentiment has fallen hardest on Arab Americans, who had a regional population of about 276,000 in 2000 (70 percent of these in New York and New Jersey). Arabs trace a long history in the region dating back to the late nineteenth century, when immigrants came from a region in Syria (now present-day Lebanon), mostly to work as itinerant peddlers. Many subsequently opened their own businesses and established settled communities in cities and towns across the region (historic Arab American communities in Pennsylvania, for instance, include Philadelphia and Pittsburgh, but also Allentown and Scranton). Predominantly Christian (members of the Maronite Church), they often assimilated or blended into the general white ethnic population. Since the 1960s, the area has been the destination for Palestinians, Syrians, Yemenis, and even some Egyptians. New York City in particular is home to a large community of Yemenis. More recently, the construction of Arab ethnicity has shifted radically. While at the turn of the twentieth century, Arabs were viewed as safely exotic, at the turn of the twenty-first century they became subject to more damaging negative stereotypes and misconceptions. Arab Americans often observe that they are viewed as culturally and religiously homogeneous (seen as Muslim even though the majority is Christian, for example), or that they are targeted as terrorists.

Thus the encounter with negative attitudes continues to shape the development of ethnic identity and experience in the region just as the positive expression of ethnic culture does. Many communities turn to political and cultural advocacy as an antidote to hostility and mistrust. Advocacy and mutual assistance remain values within ethnic and immigrant communities in the region. In addition to local chapters of national organizations, the national headquarters of many ethnic organizations, such as the Arab American Anti-Discrimination Committee, are located in New York City or Washington, D.C. As the region enters a new century of diversity, its residents continue to grapple with issues of racial and ethnic equality, cultural difference, and the ongoing definition of differential local, regional, and national identities.

RESOURCE GUIDE

Printed Sources

Binder, Frederick, and David Reimers. *All the Nations Under Heaven: An Ethnic and Racial History of New York City*. New York: Columbia University Press, 1996.

Bodnar, John E. *The Ethnic Experience in Pennsylvania*. Lewisburg, PA: Bucknell University Press, 1973.

Brueger, Robert J. *Maryland: A Middle Temperament, 1634–1980*. Baltimore: Johns Hopkins University Press and Maryland Historical Society, 1988.

Cary, Francine Curro, ed. *Washington Odyssey: A Multicultural History of the Nation's Capital*. Washington, D.C.: Smithsonian Institution Press, 2003.

Chappelle, Susan Ellery Greene, et al. *Maryland: A History of Its People*. Baltimore: Johns Hopkins University Press, 1986.

Cunningham, Barbara. *The New Jersey Ethnic Experience*. Union City, NJ: Wm. H. Wise, 1977.

Fones-Wolf, Ken. *Transnational West Virginia: Ethnic Communities and Economic Change, 1840–1940*. Morgantown: West Virginia University Press, 2002.

Kimm, Silas Conrad. *The Iroquois: A History of the Six Nations of New York*. Reprint, New York: Fawcett, 1998.

Korrol, Virginia Sanchez. *From Colonia to Community: The History of Puerto Ricans in New York City*. Berkeley: University of California Press, 1992.

Maira, Sunaina Marr. *Desis in the House: Indian American Youth Culture in New York City*. Asian American History and Culture Series. Philadelphia: Temple University Press, 2002.

Merritt, Jane T. *At the Crossroads: Indians and Empires on a Mid-Atlantic Frontier, 1700–1763*. Chapel Hill: University of North Carolina Press, 2003.

Nash, Gary. *Forging Freedom: The Formation of Philadelphia's Black Community, 1720–1840*. Reprint, Cambridge: Harvard University Press, 1991.

Nolt, Steven M. *Foreigners in Their Own Land: Pennsylvania Germans in the Early Republic.* Pennsylvania German History and Culture Series. University Park: Pennsylvania State University Press, 2002.

Pencak, William, Selma Berrol, and Randall Miller, eds. *Immigration to New York.* Philadelphia: Balch Institute Press/New York Historical Society, 1991.

Prasad, Leela, ed. *Live Like the Banyan Tree: Images of the Indian American Experience.* Philadelphia: Balch Institute for Ethnic Studies, 1999.

Schwartz, Sally. *A Mixed Multitude: The Struggle for Toleration in Colonial Pennsylvania.* New York: New York University Press, 1989.

Sharpless, Richard E., and Donald L. Miller. *The Kingdom of Coal: Work, Enterprise, and Ethnic Communities in the Mine Fields.* Easton, PA: Canal History and Technology Press, 1999.

Shaw, Douglas. *Immigration and Ethnicity in New Jersey History.* New Jersey History Series. Trenton: New Jersey Historical Commission, 1994.

Trotter, Joe William Jr., and Eric Ledell Smith, eds. *African Americans in Pennsylvania: Shifting Historical Perspectives.* University Park: Pennsylvania State University Press, 1997.

Whalen, Carmen. *From Puerto Rico to Philadelphia: Puerto Rican Workers and Postwar Economies.* Philadelphia: Temple University Press, 2001.

White, Shane. *Somewhat More Independent: The End of Slavery in New York City, 1770–1810.* Athens: University of Georgia Press, 1995.

Web Sites

An Introduction to West Virginia Ethnic Communities. Online report.
http://www.wvculture.org/arts/ethnic

Building the Gold Mountain: Philadelphia's Chinatown. Online exhibit.
http://www.hsp.org/default.aspx?id=62

ExplorePAhistory.com
http://www.explorepahistory.com/explorepahistory/home.do

First Nation Histories
http://www.tolatsga.org/compacts.html

The German Americans: An Ethnic Experience
http://www.lib.iupui.edu/kade/adams/toc.html

Harlem Renaissance
http://www.nku.edu/%7ediesmanj/harlem.html

Maryland Digital Immigration Library
http://oriole.umd.edu/mddlmddl/791/frameset.html

New York State Archives Legacies Project
http://www.archives.nysed.gov/projects/legacies/index.html

Online histories of Chinese and Latino communities in Albany, Syracuse, Buffalo, Yonkers, and New York City.

On the Lower East Side: Observations of Life in Lower Manhattan at the Turn of the Century
http://www2.arts.gla.ac.uk/www.ctich/eastside/contents.html

Pennsylvania German Folk Art from the Index of American Design National Gallery of Art
http://www.nga.gov/collection/gallery/iadpenn/iadpenn-main1.html

Puerto Rico and the American Dream
http://www.prdream.com/index.html

Award-winning Web site on the history, culture, and politics of Puerto Rico and the Puerto Rican diaspora. Includes film section, an online gallery, discussion boards, historical timelines, and oral histories.

Still Home: The Jews of South Philadelphia
http://nmajh.org/exhibitions/stillhome/

Online exhibit of photographs by Harvey Finkle.

Films

Bought & Sold. Written and directed by Michael Tolajian. 2003 91 mins. 35mm. Coming-of-age story set in the ethnic neighborhoods of Jersey City; explores the funny and touching relationship between a young Puerto Rican man and an immigrant pawnbroker.

From Spikes to Spindles. Christine Choy. 50 mins. Third World Newsreel, 1976. Raw portrait of New York's Chinatown; deals with its history and contemporary struggles against police brutality and real estate developers.

In Search of Africa. Manthia Diawara. 26 mins. Third World Newsreel, 1997. In 1996 the filmmaker and writer Manthia Diawara, now living in New York, returned to Guinea, thirty-two years after he and his family were expelled from the newly liberated country. Diawara expects to be welcomed as an insider, and is shocked to discover that he is not.

Matewan. Directed by John Sayles. Performed by Chris Cooper and Mary McDonald. Columbia Pictures Corporation, 1987. Commercial release. Drama depicting events leading to the Matewan massacre in West Virginia. Includes portrayal of interactions between ethnic groups in the mining camps. Videocassette and DVD.

The Molly Maguires. Directed by Martin Ritts. Performed by Sean Connery and Richard Harris. Paramount Pictures, 1970. Videocassette. Commercial release. Drama portrays labor conflict in the anthracite patch towns of Pennsylvania. Filmed at a reconstructed Eckley miners' village.

The #7 Train: An Immigrant Journey. Hye Jung Park & JT Takagi. 29 mins. Third World Newsreel, 1999. Follows four immigrant passengers on the #7 train through Queens to Manhattan.

Nuyorican Dream. Produced and Directed by Laurie Collyer, 2000. 82 mins. Videocassette. California Newsreel. Follows five years in the life of a New York Puerto Rican family struggling against poverty, drug addiction, and incarceration.

Painted Bride: Henna Art Among Pakistani Women in New York City. Produced by Susan Slymovics and Amanda Dargan. 25 minutes. Queens Council on the Arts, 1990. Videocassette. Ethnographic documentary explores the art of *mehendi* among South Asian immigrant women.

Taxi-vala/Auto-biography. Produced by Vivek Bald. 48 mins. Third World Newsreel, 1994. Videocassette documentary on Indian and Pakistani taxi drivers in New York City.

Recordings

Cuba in Washington. Folkways Records. 40461 12 tracks. 61 minutes. http://www.folkways.si.edu/40461.htm. Performances by Washington-based Cuban groups Afrocuba de Matanzas, Grupo Changui, and others.

Far from the Shamrock Shore: The Story of Irish-American Immigration Through Song. Mick Moloney (CD and book). Crown; book and CD edition, 2002.

Field to Factory—Voices of the Great Migration: Recalling the African American Migration to the Northern Cities. Produced by David Tarnow for Smithsonian. 64 minutes. Smithsonian Folkways 90005. Audio documentary about African Americans who migrated from the rural South to the urban North between 1915 and 1951.

Festivals/Events

Hagerstown Oktoberfest
Downtown Hagerstown, MD
Karen Giffen
Email: kmg@hagerstownmd.org

Two-day celebration commemorates Hagerstown's German heritage and affiliation with its sister city, Wesel, Germany. Claims to be the largest German festival in the mid-Atlantic region.

Kutztown PA-German Festival
P.O. Box 306
Kutztown, PA 19530
Email: david@kutztownfestival.com

The festival is an annual community event, sponsored by the Kutztown University Foundation and Kutztown Fair Association, featuring traditional Pennsylvania Dutch folklife: crafts, entertainment, food, and music. Quilt auction is a special attraction.

National Puerto Rican Day Parade
2804 Third Avenue
Seventh Floor
Bronx, NY 10455
Phone: 718-401-0404
Fax: 718-585-9110

This New York parade began in 1958, became the national parade in 1995, and is held every year on the second Sunday in June.

Polish-American Arts Festival and Pulaski Day Parade
Cheektowaga Town Park
Town Park, 2600 Harlem Road
Cheektowaga, NY 14227

Annual Polish American festival held every July outside Buffalo, New York, home to the largest concentration of Polish Americans in the mid-Atlantic region.

Smithsonian Institution Festival of American Folklife
Center for Folklife and Cultural Heritage
750 9th Street, NW, Suite 4100

Smithsonian Institution
Washington, DC 20560-0953
Phone: 202-275-1150
http://www.folklife.si.edu/cfch/folklife.htm

Annual folk festival on the Mall in Washington, D.C. Initiated in 1967, the festival has become a model of a research-based presentation of contemporary traditions and showcases regional as well as international tradition bearers.

Organizations

American Arab Anti-Discrimination Committee
4201 Connecticut Avenue, Suite 300
Washington, DC 20008
http://www.adc.org/

American Folklife Center
Library of Congress
101 Independence Avenue SE
Room LJ G-49
Thomas Jefferson Building
Washington, DC 20540-4610
http://www.loc.gov/folklife

Asian American Writers Workshop
16 West 32nd Street, Suite 10A
New York, NY 10001
Phone: 212-494-0061
Fax: 212-494-0062
Email: desk@aaww.org
http://www.aaww.org

Established in 1991, the Asian American Writers Workshop is a nonprofit literary arts organization dedicated to the creation, development, publication, and dissemination of Asian American literature.

New York Folklore Society
P.O. Box 764
Schenectady, NY 12301
Phone: 518-346-7008
Fax: 518-346-6617
Email: nyfs@nyfolklore.org
http://www.nyfolklore.org

The New York Folklore Society is a statewide nonprofit organization that offers a wide range of programs and services designed to nurture traditional arts and culture in the communities where they originate, foster the sharing of folk traditions across cultural boundaries, and further cultural equity and cross-cultural understanding.

Philadelphia Folklore Project
1304 Wharton Street
Philadelphia, PA 19147
Phone: 215-468-7871
http://www.folkloreproject.org/index.shtml

The Philadelphia Folklore Project offers exhibitions, concerts, workshops, arts education, and assistance to artists and communities. It conducts ongoing field research into community-based local arts, history, and culture, and preserves a record of Philadelphia's folklife in its archive.

Program for Immigrant Traditional Artists (PITA)
880 Bergen Avenue
Jersey City, NJ 07306
Phone: 201-653-3888 ext. 126
http://www.iinj.org/pITA.htm

This program at the International Institute of New Jersey offers workshops and information on funding and arts programs, and direct technical assistance and social service to provide greater opportunities for immigrant artists to practice and present their work.

Smithsonian Institution
Center for Folklife and Cultural Heritage
750 9th Street, NW, Suite 4100
Smithsonian Institution
Washington, DC 20560-0953
Phone: 202-275-1150
Fax: 202-275-1119
http://www.folklife.si.edu

The Smithsonian undertakes several locally focused ethnographic projects that explore ethnic communities in the Washington, D.C., and mid-Atlantic area (such as African Americans and Latinos).

Museums and Special Collections

Anacostia Museum and Center for African American History and Culture
1901 Fort Place, SE
Washington, DC 20020
Phone: 202-287-2060
http://anacostia.si.edu

Explores American history, society, and creative expression from an African American perspective.

Balch Institute for Ethnic Studies of the Historical Society of Pennsylvania
1300 Locust Street
Philadelphia, PA 19107
Phone: 215-732-6200
http://www.hsp.org

Merged with the Historical Society of Pennsylvania in 2001, the Balch Institute's manuscript and book collections focus on the ethnic and immigrant experience in the United States with special emphasis on the mid-Atlantic region.

Center for Puerto Rican Studies/Centro de Estudios Puertorriqueños, Hunter College
695 Park Avenue, Rm E1429
New York, NY 10021
Phone, Central: 212-772-5688; Library and Archives: 212-772-4197
Fax, Central Main Office: 212-650-3673
http://www.centropr.org

A research center dedicated to the study and interpretation of the Puerto Rican experience in the United States, committed to making its research available and useful to community organizations, public policy makers, and academia. The center is also the world's only repository of archival and library materials dedicated exclusively to the Puerto Rican diaspora.

El Museo Del Barrio
Heckscher Building
1230 Fifth Avenue at 104th Street
New York, NY 10029
Phone: 212-831-7272

Fax: 212-831-7927
Email: info@elmuseo.org
www.elmuseo.org

Founded in 1969, El Museo is New York City's only Latino museum dedicated to Puerto Rican, Caribbean, and Latin American art.

Landis Valley Museum
2002 Landis Valley Museum
2451 Kissel Hill Road
Lancaster, PA 17601
Phone: 717-569-0401
Fax: 717-560-2147
http://www.landisvalleymuseum.org/index.htm

Landis Valley Museum is a nationally significant living history museum that collects, conserves, exhibits, and interprets Pennsylvania German material, culture, history, and heritage from 1740 through 1940.

Lower East Side Tenement Museum
90 Orchard Street
New York, NY 10002
Phone: 212-431-0233
http://www.tenement.org

Offers historical structures, tours, education programs, and archives interpreting the immigrant and migrant experiences of Manhattan's Lower East Side, including an 1863 tenement building at 97 Orchard Street, which was home to successive waves of immigrants.

Museum of Chinese in the Americas
70 Mulberry Street, 2nd Floor
New York, NY 10013
Phone: 212-619-4785
Fax: 212-619-4720
Email: info@moca-NYC.org
http://www.moca-nyc.org/moCA/content.asp

Dedicated to reclaiming, preserving, and interpreting the history and culture of Chinese and their descendants in the Western Hemisphere, with a particular focus on New York City's Chinatown. Formerly the Chinatown History Museum.

National Museum of American Jewish History
Independence Mall East
55 North 5th Street
Philadelphia, PA 19106-2197
Phone: 215-923-3811
Fax: 215-923-0763
Email: nmajh@nmajh.org
http://www.nmajh.org

Presents educational programs and exhibits that preserve, explore, and celebrate the history of Jews in America.

Schomburg Center for Research in Black Culture
New York Public Library
http://www.nypl.org/research/sc/sc.html

The Schomburg Center for Research in Black Culture is a research unit of the New York Public Library devoted to collecting, preserving, and providing access to resources documenting the experiences of peoples of African descent throughout the world, with emphasis on blacks in the Western Hemisphere.

Taller Puertorriqueño
2721 North Fifth Street
Philadelphia, PA 19133
Phone: 215-426-3311
http://www.tallerpr.org

Gallery, bookstore, educational center, and archive devoted to preserving, developing, and promoting Puerto Rican artistic and cultural traditions, as well as promoting a better understanding of other Latin American cultures and common heritage.

FASHION

Emily Workman

Fashion is the mirror of history. It reflects political, social, and economic changes, rather than mere whimsy.

—Louis XIV, 1690

The mid-Atlantic states have played a large part in defining the meaning of fashion in America. During America's formative years the early European settlers and Native Americans of this region traded clothing styles for survival and innovation, making the earliest fashions of the region distinctly hybrid. This hybridity seems to have set a regional precedent and has helped to sustain fashion and its industry as important aspects of American culture. Over time mid-Atlantic fashion has been a political and social catalyst, occupying the forefronts and backgrounds of many historical moments. For these reasons and more, the history of fashion in the region has been an essential thread in the fabric of America.

Although some important trends and developments originated in other mid-Atlantic cities, New York City is and has always been the pulse of fashion in this region. After the American Revolution, Fifth Avenue designers developed a direct connection to Paris that lasted for decades, and as a result European fashion influences still remain. New York designers have contributed to the speedy, ever-shifting nature of trends in the region. Philadelphia and Baltimore have often been close behind New York's fashion trends, and Newark and Philadelphia have long supported the fashion industry through the establishment of retail companies and clothing manufacturers. New York's designers have traditionally dictated the fashion of the mid-Atlantic states, but there are also rich traditions of dress within these states that need to be recognized when understanding the fashion of the area. From the frontier men and women of the colonial era to the African American slaves, dress in the area takes on its own flavors based in utility, protest, religion, and uniformity. The mid-Atlantic region also fostered many reforms through developments in fashion and remains a barometer of trends and values for other parts of America and the world.

NATIVE AMERICANS

As Dutch, English, German, French, Swedish, Scottish, and other settlers explored the land of the mid-Atlantic region they encountered diverse Iroquois and Algonquian tribes. Known as Woodland Indians, these tribes were scattered all over the region, concentrated in parts of western and central New York, much of Pennsylvania, and throughout Maryland and Delaware. These groups shared some similarities in clothing because of alliances and the climate, but features that distinguished tribal identity were important.

The outfits of both Iroquois and Algonquian tribes consisted of a few key garments. Summer dress for men usually included loincloths, buckskin aprons, and blankets or belts over the torso; women wore skirts or petticoats. In winter, deerskin leggings, longer skirts, moccasins, and snowshoes were common with fringed tunics, blankets, and fur-lined cloaks. The tribal variations within these garments were mainly ornamental, or in the materials used to construct them. As colonists took over the region and traded with the Native people, tribal garments were more often constructed from fabrics.

Many Iroquois people lived in the Finger Lakes region of New York, along the Susquehanna River in Pennsylvania, and near Chesapeake Bay. Iroquois clothing was composed of simple basics. An Iroquois might be identified by his belt, which was worn either on the waist or over the shoulder and was decorated with weaving, beadwork, or porcupine quills. Masks, made of braided cornhusks or material from live trees, were an important piece of Iroquois rituals. The Iroquois who lived in the Finger Lakes region decorated pouches and clothing with embroidery or beadwork representing curving lines and figures.

The influence of European settlers brought devastating changes to the Iroquois culture. In the early 1600s Iroquois garments were less often made of skins and more often made of fabrics obtained through trading with or raiding other tribes. The colonists' obsession with furs quickly acerbated European and Iroquois relations as fights broke out over the trade. As demand for beaver fur increased, so did the demand for the Iroquois' land and hunting strategies. The Iroquois defended their beaver hunting ground from the French and other tribes in order to keep the wealth and benefits of owning the land within their own tribe. By the 1660s they were catching tons of beaver to satiate the fur craze. A war erupted between the Iroquois and other area tribes over the Iroquois' monopoly. The Iroquois eventually formu-

Fashion's Influence on Naming the Native Americans

In the eighteenth and early nineteenth centuries, the Tuscarora Indian nation migrated to the mid-Atlantic region from North Carolina and became part of the Iroquois Confederacy. The name *Tuscarora* derives from the Iroquois word for "hemp gatherers." To the region's indigenous peoples, the Tuscaroras were also known as the "shirt-wearing people."

Although the Tuscaroras had fled British rule in North Carolina, the Iroquois nations traditionally sided with the British. A council orator for the Seneca Indians known as Segoyewatha had served as a messenger for British officers during the Revolutionary War. Legend has it that he was given a red coat by the British army in appreciation of his services, and among colonial whites he was known as "Red Jacket."

lated partnerships with the British and French. A culture that had once fought for honor and revenge was now fighting for the purpose of their own economic advancement, and was highly dependent upon European goods.

After the Iroquois made peace with France, their adornments reflected the European influence. In the eighteenth century the Iroquois Oneida tribe wore dresses and shirts stitched from printed fabrics and decorated with ribbons across the upper chest and back. Eventually this decoration became a tradition, but it was a great departure from the tanned skins and beadwork that were once their cultural symbols. In the nineteenth century the curling patterns found in traditional Iroquois decoration resembled floral patterns of a French style, and imported glass beads had largely replaced porcupine quills.

The Algonquian people, living in a similar climate, wore the basic articles that the Iroquois wore, although women's dress was slightly different. The Delaware, or Lenape, women (located in New Jersey, New York, eastern Pennsylvania, and northern Delaware) wore wrap skirts, and the Unami women (located mainly in Lehigh, Pennsylvania) wore skirts below the knee with deerskin blankets tucked into a belt. Some Algonquians might be found wearing snowshoes or moccasins made of mice skin in the winter, and some Unami people wore feathered cloaks. Like the Iroquois, the Algonquians could not avoid conflicts over beaver hunting; the Delaware Indians warred with the Dutch during the mid–seventeenth century. When the Dutch prevailed some Delaware people fled to Pennsylvania, where William Penn assisted them.

There were some very specific distinguishing features of Algonquians. Face painting and tattooing were important elements of their adornment. The Nanticoke men that lived throughout what are now Maryland and Delaware often wore elaborate hairstyles with some parts of the head shaved and other parts grown long. The Piscataway tribe of southern Maryland liked to knot their hair over their left ear, and some men shaved half of their head. These Algonquian tribes found many more ways to dress and distinguish themselves. Popular items for decoration included shells, animal teeth, snake rattles, and birds' wings or claws. Shells worn on necklaces, strings, or belts were often used as wampum, or currency. In many tribes it was a symbol of status to adorn oneself with wampum. As European goods and ideas began to intertwine with the Algonquian culture, cloth, silver pins, and glass beads replaced some traditional adornments. Though similarities between the tribes' dress existed, maintaining distinct identities and appearances was important to the Iroquois and Algonquians, even when homogenizing European influences were present.

European Settlers and Native American Dress Influence

European settlers experienced cultural changes in dress because of their interaction with Native Americans. Traditions and attitudes changed for better or for worse. While the tribal people were educated about new materials from which to fashion garments and decoration, some Europeans learned from Native Americans about how to dress in response to the mid-Atlantic environment and climate. When one ventured off to explore the countryside, he or she would borrow clothing ideas from the Native Americans. For example, the pioneers who settled in West Virginia's Appalachian area had to deal with harsh mountain elements. The men of the pioneer families hunted deer, bear, and foxes, and the skins and furs clothed the family as they did for the Native Americans. Pioneers also grew flax fibers and raised sheep, and pioneer women spun the flax fibers and wool into linen and yarn on their looms. These threads would be used to create linsey-woolsey, a fabric that would be used for clothing, bed covers, and draperies. The fabrics of clothing went a long way, as rags were even salvaged from hand-me-downs to create quilts. Because they had few imported goods the pioneers relied on Native American methods plus their own craftiness for survival.

Like the Native Americans of the region, the settlers were also divided by the diversity of their dress. Within a few generations, this diversity would shift in a movement similar to the way that Native American fashions blended with European ones. Most settlers during the sixteenth and seventeenth century still dressed according to the fashions of their homeland. The industrious Dutch settlers of New York and Delaware offer a great example of this practice. Women commonly carried trinkets and accessories for sewing on a chatelaine, a gold or silver belt, and they also made clothing and linens for their families with looms and spinning wheels, all devices brought with them from Europe. Very concerned with detail, these settlers had a taste for attractive clothing and jewelry that was tempered by their sensibility in dress. A woman might display color, hair ornaments, or quilted or embroidered designs, but her clothes were well adapted to such considerable detail, as she would often take them apart for laundering and mending. If one met a Dutch woman on the street she might have on a short jacket called a "linsey" as well as a skirt that displayed embellished petticoats. New York was already considered a very cosmopolitan port town in 1629. The Dutch community was a workaday, commercial place that fostered the possibility for such styles. One could deduce that the fashion-savvy Dutch colonists were a large reason for the grand trend-setting influence metropolitan New Yorkers would continue to have even into the present.

Colonial Fashion

During the early settling of the mid-Atlantic region, the colonies were a patchwork of fashions from Europe. Pennsylvania and New York were both centers of cultural assortment, with Germans, Dutch, Irish, Swedes, and Scots bringing customs and clothing from their homelands. Things changed almost a century later, as everyday dress began to reflect both the mingling of European styles and the American attitude of utilitarianism, which prompted the early emergence of a distinct brand of American fashion. The beginnings of this shift could be detected across the lands of New York, Delaware, Pennsylvania, and other areas during the seventeenth century when the cavalier style took hold. This fashion came from France in the 1620s, and as many colonies were still following European dress it caught on rapidly. Since Charles I was an exemplar of cavalier style, a loyal population of English in Maryland, New Jersey, and Pennsylvania jumped on the trend, showing the connection between fashion and sociopolitical loyalties. Large sombrerolike hats, embellishments of ruffles on sleeves and boots, and long, curly hair characterized this fashion for men. It was a very gaudy, even feminine style. Fabric differences distinguished class; silk was worn by the wealthy and wool by others. In a wave typical for the region, this fashion caught on like wildfire and involved elite and elaborate looks.

It also involved a sense of reform, another lasting aspect of the region's fashion history. The cavalier style influenced women's dress to become relatively loose fitting and flowing, creating more comfort than usual for the wearer. For example, broad collars called ruffs had always been very stiff along the neckline, and by the 1660s the ruff for both men and women had fallen in soft ruffles along the neckline. The Dutch of New York and Delaware wore a plainer version of the cavalier dress, which is no surprise when taking into account their concern for utility. When compared to British colonists who often ordered fine fabrics from Europe, it took the Dutch some time to move away from traditional homespun fabrics. The fur trade granted great wealth to the Dutch in New York around this time, because they sold the popular furs in the colonies and exported them to Europe to high demand. Due this wealth the Dutch also began purchasing expensive European and Oriental fabrics. This caused the landscape of diversity to shift slightly. It was still present within the region even as reforms and changes were starting the movement toward a defined American style.

No generation of fashion trends in the mid-Atlantic states would be complete without a passing hint of outrageousness; between the late 1600s and early 1700s people in these colonies adopted the European trend of wearing impractical, expensive, powdered wigs which were often stuffed with odd materials such as hay or vegetables. (Imagine the odors these wigs would emit after a week or two!) Even the area's religious groups found it possible to follow some of the less extravagant fashion trends. Most of the religious codes for dress in the mid-Atlantic region were not as stringent as those in New England. This allowed French Protestants and Quakers from Pennsylvania and Jesuits from Maryland to follow the basic fashions of the day, even when uniformity and modesty were among their religious values. Some Pennsylvanians, New Yorkers, Marylanders, and Virginians followed changing English trends, with the exception of older men, who followed traditional dress. This resulted in another kind of diversity of the region; in the seventeenth century a visitor to any of those colonies might see the mingling of fashions of many generations together in one area, as though looking at a living timeline of fashion. In a time when some fashions could last a century, this generational fluidity received much attention from visitors to the country, especially in later centuries.

Distinct Colonial Styles

Eventually, colonists began to develop styles that were more distinct from European influences. By the end of the seventeenth century, New York, Philadelphia, and cities in New England and the South were regularly exchanging commerce, which gave colonists a broader range of fabrics, styles, and accessories from which to choose. This interdependence within the colonies created more possibility than ever for a consistency of American fashion. Those who dared to stray from European fashion standards were sometimes seen as outlandish by European visitors, but such criticism was inconsequential to them; they had started to value more useful, utilitarian clothing to compliment their lifestyle. This brave division from European influences was an important paradigm shift in the history of the country, since it served as the starting point for American ideals that would extend well into the present, beginning with the American Revolution.

The American Revolution left the country with a need for stability. Now that America was not taking imports from England, glamorous fabrics were not as common as they had been. Here the early connections caused by the commerce between colonies developed into a larger regional consistency in fashion because of a politically motivated desire for unification and pride in the new country. Leaders began to model behavior and fashion that portrayed American ideals. George Washington wore the first homespun broadcloth at his inauguration as an example to the country of a genteel demeanor. For about a decade French fashions were primarily sought as standards for American dress in protest against England. Eventually France would become the steadfast source for fashion inspirations in America. Around the turn of the century, "republican simplicity" was paramount in Washington, D.C., and many leaders there did not approve of fashionable dress. In an 1818 commentary Frances Wright noted that women from New York were modestly dressed, a success of republicanism in the new nation.[1]

However, the influence of republican simplicity did not mean that all mid-Atlantic Americans were modest. This was a time when American citizens also strived for gentility for a number of reasons. More genteel immigrants were entering the country, as opposed to the middle-class immigrants who originally populated the country. Americans reinvented themselves through the creation of standards of manners, dress, and cleanliness. Delaware was a great example of an area where genteel citizens settled and built luxurious mansions. In the mid-Atlantic region, one could quickly detect the differences between a genteel citizen and a laborer or country dweller. The genteel dressed in clothing that maintained their posture, and was tucked in and trim. Laborers were easily distinguished by their untucked shirts and unbuttoned vests, which allowed them to move with ease for heavy lifting or working. More specifically, craftsmen wore leather aprons, seamen sported trousers, and serving girls donned crude petticoats and jackets. Local farmers and servants were easy to spot because of their smocks and loose trousers with no stockings. Browns, greens, and grays were usually a sign of homespun fabrics worn by the less wealthy or working class, and the presence of colors, smooth fabric, and shiny buttons or buckles indicated one's raised status. People in the region continued to favor the utility of fashion for laborers, but with the influx of wealthy immigrants and trade came class division. In one sense, gentility gave nonwealthy Americans something proud to strive for, but in another sense it was an early sign of terrible divisions to come. If a laborer or farmer were seen imitating or sporting genteel clothing, he would be mocked for his gracelessness in such a role. This class division portrayed America's conflict between developing positive standards for its citizens that would create pride in the country and the traditional class divisions found in the European countries from which these people came.

American Interest in Gentility

Twenty years after the postrevolutionary period strong styles emerged that were an effect of the American interest in gentility, and republicanism faded. All women wanted to be fashionable, including rural women in places like Buffalo, New York, and log cabins throughout Pennsylvania. Farmers' wives in these areas made homespun fabrics and then traded them in town for fashionable clothing. Some delivered their family's produce to the spas and springs where wealthy people took vacations in order to take note of the latest fashions. Social commentators of the time noticed the excessive attention American women paid to fashion, and publications such as *Godey's Lady's Book* were coveted guidebooks for women of many classes in the region. By 1850, new Easter dresses were worn as if on parade on New York City's Fifth Avenue, a tradition that would be carried out by Americans of different racial and economic backgrounds well into the twentieth century in Atlantic City and elsewhere. The region's resistance to England was not only apparent in the battles that were fought during the revolution, but in the determination of its people to use fashion to define themselves as "American," albeit throughout many distinct, local contexts.

As republicanism gave way to a nation soon earning stability and prosperity, its gains were reflected in the citizens' attitudes. Values of individualism, materialism, status and success encouraged unique and elite fashions. In 1842, New York City women were noted to dress quite differently from rural women because of their adherence to Paris "haute couture," or high fashion. In Washington, D.C., the secretary of state declared in 1853 that the all-male Diplomatic Corps must dress plainly, while their wives were defining a fashion for the elite that was nowhere near plain. Between 1820 and 1842 a number of European travelers documented their reactions to America, often having varied opinions on the fashions they encountered. Frances Trollope traveled through some of the mid-Atlantic states making many judgments of the fashions she encountered. Her analysis was that Philadelphia women were very elegant, neat, and delicate in taste, and essentially models for others in the Union. Trollope highly favored Philadelphians' elegance over gaudy Baltimore fashions and the strange habits she encountered in Washington, D.C., where women dressed improperly for the seasons and wore unstylish wigs. "They never wear muffs or boots, and appear extremely shocked at the sight of comfortable walking shoes and cotton stockings, even when they have to step to their sleighs over ice and snow."[2] Trollope's account shows her high standards and her traditionalism.

While Trollope gave some credit to Philadelphian women, other critics echoed her more scornful commentary. Upon visits to Maryland and New York, one suggested that Americans' manner would benefit from the example of a court, an idea that seemed extremely absurd fifty years after both the American and French Revolutions. In 1834 another criticized women's elaborate bonnets, the wearing of red, and exposure of the legs and feet in hot weather. These European visitors' deeply opinionated reports betray the intensity of their curiosity toward the new nation. Most reports were likely critical of American fashion in order to reiterate the superiority of European fashions over the fledgling country. For a time to come, Paris and London would hold sway over American fashion, but as these accounts have shown, that would not change the fact that Americans had a way of altering those fashions to suit their ideals.

In a nation where people wanted to be self-made like Ben Franklin, new immigrants and lower-class folks in the mid-Atlantic region strived to dress with flair. Servants often copied the dress of their employers, making it hard to distinguish people's wealth. Newspaper typesetters in Washington, D.C., wore some of their nicest dresses while working with messy ink. Some factory workers wore their hoop skirts to work in New York City, and feminist Susan B. Anthony wore fine clothes while teaching. Though some of these jobs offered low wages and poor working conditions, the effort was made to look fashionable even while working. This was not un-

Italian immigrant family at Ellis Island, c. 1910. Courtesy Library of Congress.

usual for women who worked in the clothing industry because their positions gave them fashion ideas and connections, and the possibility of competitive wages. These efforts of the poor demonstrate the value Americans placed on fashion, especially in mid-Atlantic cities, where it was fresh and competitive.

Immigrants have often been a major force in sustaining the heterogeneity of American fashion while also assimilating to its consistency. Like the working American women, even the poorest of immigrants were inspired by their first walk down Broadway to immediately acquire the latest city fashions. The efforts they made to blend in as Americans was remarkable. Because of their enthusiasm, immigrants contributed greatly to the definitions and values that America was working to solidify. Some people thought that immigrants, as well as African Americans, were vulnerable to dressing without the proper social flair because they were overexcited to be a part of the new country. This snap judgment was unfair and showed ignorance of the cultural flavors that immigrants were bringing to fashion in the region. Like the early settlers, immigrants were encountering a diverse number of choices from which they could create a comfortable look. Some immigrants found it easier to assimilate to the diverse American fashions than others, like stylish Irish women who had immigrated alone and had no family to restrict their choice of dress. Jewish immigrants were often noted for their love of extravagant clothing, jewelry, and color. In the early twentieth century, when hats were popular, Yiddish magazines encouraged Jewish women to abandon the conservative fashions from the homeland by wearing hats with gaudy embellishments in the latest style.[3] The *New York Tribune* complimented New York's Lower East Side Jews for their good taste in clothing. It was high praise for an immigrant to be considered fashionable by participating in the changing American trends.

LATE-NINETEENTH- AND EARLY-TWENTIETH-CENTURY FASHION

It is very clear that the mid-Atlantic region has been a hotbed for fashion reform and change. As a region founded and measured by traditional European appearances, some resisted those reforms. Most others supported the formation of unique American values that the region produced, and therefore the historical tendency has been that Americans' choices, no matter how unorthodox or radical, would last. The *New York Times* stated in the early 1920s that "fashion will prevail," and this statement has proven true decade after decade.[4]

One of the earliest and most significant moments of reform came in the late 1800s when a faction of the region's women and doctors began to protest the wearing of the corset. A Brooklyn doctor drew attention to the extreme stress that the corset caused to women's internal organs and bone structure. As people began to understand the negative effects of corset wearing, advocates of alternative underwear and clothing emerged. One of the most famous advocates of the mid-Atlantic region was Amelia Bloomer (1818–1894), who published a temperance paper called *The Lily*, which she used to promote dress reform. At this time a friend of Bloomer's, Elizabeth Smith Miller, created and wore a kind of Turkish pantaloons that she had seen in Europe. This outfit of puffy pants under a knee-length skirt was popular for a time in their home of rural Seneca Falls, New York, and it gained popularity thanks to *The Lily*. Miller's outfit soon came to be known as the "Bloomer" costume because Amelia Bloomer had advocated them so readily.

Around this time similar efforts sprang up to save women from corsets. The hourglass dress, the union suit, and pantaloons became valued pieces of many women's wardrobes, and provided alternatives to wearing tight corsets and heavy dresses. One publication that was supportive of these efforts was *Dress*, the Jenness Miller magazine. This was published between 1887 and 1898 in New York by Annie Jenness Miller, a lecturer who worked all over the mid-Atlantic and New England regions to facilitate dress reform. The magazine offered a means for distributing proreform information as well as ways for women to purchase patterns for the healthy new clothing.

Another faction of reform in New York City was the Rainy Day Club. This ladies group advocated raising skirt hemlines to four inches off the ground as a health measure because wet weather caused ladies' ankles to become soaked from their ground-length skirts. Groups like this one and publications supporting their efforts were met with stark resistance from both men and women in the region who believed strongly in traditional feminine styles. Despite criticism, many reform efforts were successful due to the support of college women, young women, and working women who benefited greatly from the styles.

Around the same time, concerns developed for the poor of the large cities in the mid-Atlantic region. The poor faced extreme difficulties in obtaining clothing that would be presentable in the workplace, or clothes that might help them to move up in society. The New York Society for the Relief of the Industrious Poor opened as a part of the secondhand trade to help these people's health and well-being. Similar organizations sprouted in Philadelphia. The primary sites of help for the poor were the thrift stores that opened in the late 1800s to the early 1900s. They often specialized in offering favorable clothing and suits to the poor for their advancement. The installation of a thrift trade was an important move for the region, and it also showed the levels of class division and class-consciousness therein.

The changes that took place during the late 1800s were quite revolutionary for the time, but they were mere beginnings for the reforms that would take place within the first two decades of the twentieth century. In the mid-Atlantic region, people of all classes, including urban and rural residents, continued to attend to

Fur became a fashion essential in the 1920s. Between 1917 and 1930, many fur farms were established in rural areas across the region to support the fur industry. Courtesy Library of Congress.

and value fashion. Along with clothing, accessories were often noted and argued over. In the 1910s a women's trend for wearing large, feather and hat-pin-bedecked hats gained momentum. Although many considered these hats very pretty, women wore them to excess. They found endless venues for displaying the latest fashion and hat trends, including New York City subways, churches, and theaters, and most notably, Atlantic City's Easter parade. The hat craze prompted priests and men in New York City and New Jersey to beg that the view-blocking distractions be dispensed with in church. The hat craze also got the attention of animal-friendly city folks, due to the wearing of hat feathers. The Audubon Society attacked New York City's hatmakers and even Jews to stop supporting the use of feathers for fashion. This action inspired an anti–steel trap group in Washington, D.C., to take action against fur trappers. Between 1917 and 1930, the number of fur farms increased dramatically across the region to support the fur industry. As the 1920s began, the *New York Times*, always the gauge of fashion, declared fur to be essential in all seasons for people of every economic status, a sentiment that showcased the materialism America valued at this time in history.

Shoes were another issue of debate in the early twentieth century, when fashion and health were sometimes at odds. Many of the region's city dwellers were known to sacrifice comfort for fashion. In light of the unfriendly way that New Yorkers and Philadelphians treated their feet, a manufacturer called Eureka began pushing its arch supports and "ground grippers" in the name of health and safety. Between 1910 and 1920 other shoemakers in the area followed in Eureka's footsteps with low-heeled shoes. Rumblings over shoe reform reached Washington, D.C., when the military had to face the fact that most soldiers' shoes did not fit properly. The military quickly launched a successful effort to furnish troops with good shoes.

Flapper Fashion

Above all of the changes and adjustments in mid-Atlantic fashions, perhaps the most radical was the shift in fashion caused by the flapper generation. The Roaring Twenties, a time of wealth and free spirits in America, produced some of the most shocking fashion changes in U.S. history. Young people began dressing and acting in ways that defied authority and tradition. "Flapper Jane" was the name given to the typical female flapper who wore knee-length short skirts and dresses showing one's arms and back. Clothing styles were straight and lean, and women's cropped hair topped off the boyish look that inflamed conservative-minded people. People wanted to look youthful; athletic clothing and bodies were desired, and young people eschewed symbols of age such as beards and glasses. Men's collars dropped into "soft collars" and American shirts, made of smooth materials that needed no ironing, were unbuttoned to sternums. For men, a great change in fashion was the sweater, which saved them from the discomfort of shirts and jackets. As flappers partook in loose behavior, like drinking and sexual promiscuity, that complemented their loose clothing, religious officials went wild with criticism. Local rabbis and priests spoke of society's sins, including clothing and cosmetics, even going so far as to accuse flappers of setting bad examples for immigrants. The Catholic Church was the loudest critic of the trends in the 1920s, sometimes alienating those who wore such outfits from religious participation.

Longer skirts started to appear again in the late 1920s, but some women loudly protested this return to tradition. A poll taken at New York's Hunter College

The bathing beach policeman measures the distance between a woman's knee and bathing suit, Washington, D.C., 1922. Courtesy Library of Congress.

showed that 70 percent of the girls there were devoted to short skirts. Many cited the freedom and comfort of these skirts, as well as their convenience to city life as reasons for their support. The sentiment of the young had power enough to spread all over the cities, and a famous cry was taken up by Fannie Hurst in support: "Down with the corset and up with the hemline!"[5] It looked like the reforms were here to stay.

The unusual and challenging trends of this time extended beyond the flappers. Around 1925 Ivy Leaguers who spent semesters at Oxford University brought back "Oxford bags," baggy trousers that looked almost like a large skirt when one's legs were together. Golf interests inspired people to sport golf pants and hats on the street. The 1929 stock market crash on Wall Street brought the slogan "chic to be cheap," and women gave up their tomboy look while men's image was still athletic but cleaner. In the 1930s city dwellers of Pittsburgh and New York wore zoot suits like the jazz enthusiasts of the South. Zoot suits were colorful and carefully tailored with a long jacket and baggy pants that tapered at the ankles. City gangsters set their own fashion standards with tasteful, striped, double-breasted suits and felt hats. Jewish immigrants in New York City were said to favor the color trends in suits of the time, and deserve some credit for drawing this trend out in America. The changes incited commentary on the abundance of color in men's clothing, the popularity of men's fine jewelry and watches, and the adoption of clothing that challenged the traditional notions of masculinity and freedom. It wasn't until a decade later that men's clothing permanently took on some of these characteristics without resistance.

From Slavery to Seventh Avenue: African American Fashion, Eighteenth Century to 1930

Although the turn of the twentieth century was a time of radical clothing reforms and some class-consciousness, the mid-Atlantic region was still plagued by racism. Costume was like a stage upon which racism and resistance to it was played out. From the time when slaves were common in Maryland and servants were common in other mid-Atlantic states, African Americans rebelled by either stealing fine clothes from their masters before running away, or by donning the most colorful and elegant clothes handed down to them by their master's family. In defiance, slaves and servants mismatched the fine clothes, scarves, and shoes, dismaying whites because it succeeded in mocking their vanity. This early apprehension of fashion to instigate social reform was continued in the region as African Americans worked to establish citizenship and combat racism.

In the springs and summers of the eighteenth century, New York and New Jersey servants held festivals where a few people who dressed and acted as kings or leaders of the event. These officials would dress in extravagant jewelry, swords, and fancy clothing borrowed from their masters. Their outfits were not worn in the ordinary style, but were creatively pieced together. Between the 1700s and 1800s some groups like the Black Masons held annual parades, which featured their best dress, complete with gold lace and fancy canes. For these Americans, wearing the best fashions of whites was a brave statement for equality that irritated racists in the region. In their study on this time period in American history, Shane and Graham White state, "The struggle over what freedom meant centered on the bodies of African Americans," and that whites detected a "political subtext" in their adornment.[6] This statement is a powerful reflection of the reasons why so much attention was given to the way African Americans looked.

Clothing and accessories were not the only aspects of the African American body that were used to fight for freedom; even hair was an important symbol of struggle. Racist whites often called African Americans' hair "wool," and such hair was devalued in American society by slaveholders. A perfect punishment for slaves who came from an African culture that involved elaborate hair styling, was to demand that a slave style his hair in an unflattering way. For women, this sometimes meant shaving their heads. For those who found a way, hairstyling became a form of resistance. The European-style wigs that were very popular in the mid-Atlantic region during the late eighteenth century were easy for some slaves to copy because of the malleability of their hair. Some slaves brushed their hair into styles imitating the wigs while others attached ponytails with the same notion in mind. Since white hair or light brown hair was stylish at the time for wigs, it was very disconcerting for whites to see black hair being styled in such a way. Generally, the look of African Americans in fine clothing with fine hairstyles presented a bizarre mirror image for racist whites and most often it caused them to respond with anger. Although most of these developments could have been visible in the mid-Atlantic region, particularly in Maryland, they would have been common in most other states as well during the eighteenth century.

Abolition brought more opportunities for African Americans to use fashion to their advantage. Mid-Atlantic cities saw blacks dressed in the latest fashions, like well-dressed whites. One can fairly assume that they did not have much wealth with which to buy such fashions, and this explains why many freed slaves would gather on the street to socialize and display their fashions, instead of finding entertainment, which was unaffordable. In the 1890s, New York City's Seventh Avenue was considered the African Broadway. Decades later this title would move to Harlem. Freed slaves were noticeable on the streets of Pittsburgh, Philadelphia, and New York City, and their flamboyant way of dressing was a matter of pride and freedom after so many years of bondage. Parades led by African American organizations continued in the same manner as they had before abolition, except that celebrations were directed more often toward celebrating emancipation. Starting in 1827, African New Yorkers held these kinds of celebrations every July.

As early as the 1820s, the tradition of the African American ball began in these northern cities. Most balls were held before Easter, and they involved merriment and wearing the best clothes. The parades and balls gave whites added ammunition for ridiculing black people's clothing. Newspapers reported the balls by noting the audacity of African Americans to wear fashionable clothing, and by utilizing patronizing labels for the participants like "dandies and dandizettes." These reports found in the newspaper archives of mid-Atlantic cities are only part of the written material that displays the rampant discrimination of the abolition period. Edward W. Clay's cartoon series "Life in Philadelphia" was a scathing portrait of black behavior. His black caricatures, drawn in fashionable clothing and attempting to speak like whites, became popular in 1830, and encouraged him to develop two more series, including "Life in New York" and "Practical Amalgamation," later in the decade.[7]

Attacks on black appearances continued as the nineteenth century moved on.

Broadway's minstrel shows were created as a response to African American freedom, and such exhibits took every opportunity to mock their appearance. Perhaps the worst reaction to emancipation took place on the streets of New York and Philadelphia, where it was not uncommon for well-dressed blacks to be beaten by a crowd of whites. Even the cities' African American churches, where worshippers arrived in their best clothing on Sundays, were not immune to such attacks. The carriages of whites or bystanders throwing stones often interrupted the Emancipation parades that continued into the century. Some black events even caused violent riots that lasted for days. One brawl that occurred in 1829 in Philadelphia prompted the *Philadelphia Chronicle* to espouse a perfect example of racist sentiment for black appearances: "Sundays, especially, they seem to think themselves above all restraint, and their insolence is intolerable."[8]

Attacks and ridicule would continue, but in direct opposition African Americans continued their Emancipation parades well into the late nineteenth century with a tradition of marching to the Capitol in Washington, D.C. Blacks in mid-Atlantic cities also found some solace at the turn of the century as a market began to grow for African American beauty products. This market allowed blacks more fashion possibilities and job opportunities within the industry, and allowed some to end their employment as servants. Cosmetics were also a symbol for urban black women to show their modernity and independence, and they served as an inspiration to young black women in rural towns and other states. As with most fashion issues, the development of African American cosmetics was a topic of debate. Some saw blacks' use of cosmetics as a statement of freedom in fashion, while other saw it as an imitation of whites that could be easily used against them. But positive developments continued with events like a 1919 African American ball held in Atlantic City. This proud event, which drew an attendance of 15,000, prompted an NAACP writer to note that the black community was beginning to emphasize its own beauty. This shift in focus provided strength as the 1920s approached and blacks continued to challenge supremacist standards. The zoot suits that were popular in that decade were a perfect example of an exaggeration of white elitism by poor blacks. For African American musicians like Dizzy Gillespie and Louis Armstrong, who played in clubs all over New York, Pittsburgh, and other mid-Atlantic cities, zoot suits and tailored suits in general were a way of showing pride in dressing well. Zoot suits, like the fashion balls, Sunday street walks, and beauty pageants, demanded attention and refused the forces that sought to exploit black bodies for purposes of racism and abuse. By the 1930s it was very clear that the region that once welcomed diverse styles was much more concerned with the status that clothing represented. This difference also demonstrates how fashion had become an expression of a more homogenized American identity; thus reformers, African Americans, flappers, and others felt resistance when introducing diversity into dress in the region. Since colonial times fashion had been a visual representation of sociopolitical issues in the mid-Atlantic states.[9]

The Mid-Atlantic Region and the Fashion Business

By 1835, working women no longer had to make all of their own clothing or solicit a dressmaker's services. Ready-made clothing had become a staple industry in the mid-Atlantic region that could mass-produce Paris fashions in multiple sizes

Cab Calloway in a zoot suit in a scene from the Twentieth Century-Fox production *Stormy Weather*. Photofest.

for all women. Dressmakers in the region had hard decisions to make; the influential French still relied on hand sewing for the best fashions, but Americans were taking an interest in ready-made garments. American dressmakers soon found a lack of demand for their services, and those who remained successful were unique. Some took on the title of "Madame," even if they had no French background, to gain the appeal of customers. Most dressmakers would now have to get by on their service to the wealthy.

The Ready-to-Wear Industry

At this time the ready-to-wear industry grew rapidly. Entrepreneurs opened department stores to sell manufactured clothes. Alexander Turney Stewart developed New York City's first department store, Stewart's, in 1846. After years of shopping at specialty stores, people were excited to be able to get everything they needed in one place. Stewart trained salesmen to treat the customers kindly and cater to their individual needs, and provided lots of imported goods for them to choose from. A few of Stewart's impressive business moves included his choice to sell items at fixed prices, rather than selling by bartering as specialty shops did, and to initiate store credits for customers. The first Stewart's building was beautiful, but the second, opened in 1862, was the largest retail store in the world at the time. Made of steel, this building featured marble, glass rotundas, elegant staircases, and open spaces. It was perfect for fashion exhibitions that would attract the attention of potential customers.[10]

Made rich by his investment, Stewart enjoyed the largest home in New York City at the time, and watched many competitors follow his lead. Samuel Lord,

George Taylor, and Arnold Constable soon copied him, as well as John Wanamaker in Philadelphia and Isaac Roberts in Pittsburgh. Most department stores at this time claimed to get the latest fashion tips from Paris, and even put fake French labels on clothes. Lord & Taylor and the Wanamaker stores enjoyed a long success, eventually merging with other companies. By 1854, New York City department stores were so extravagant that they were known as palaces. Around this same time, R. H. Macy was prospering from his department store in the city, partially because he had the business sense to market ready-to-wear clothing under his own label. The May Company, first started in Colorado, ended up moving east in the twentieth century, buying department stores as it grew. Beginning with the purchase of the Bernheim-Leader store in 1927, the May Company bought or merged with at least eight department stores in the mid-Atlantic region through the end of the twentieth century, including Lord & Taylor and Wanamaker's. Although competition and a changing economy have altered the level of success they once experienced, department stores are still an important part of the fashion business in the twenty-first century.

The ready-to-wear industry took New York City by storm. It quickly became a front-running industry in New York, New Jersey, and Pennsylvania. Clearly, an important shift in the way fashion operated in the mid-Atlantic states was under way. Ready-to-wear made fashions that could fit anyone, and it was a way for Fifth Avenue and celebrity fashions to be copied and sold cheaply. Although women were clearly taken by this new possibility to dress well, ready-to-wear helped many people dress for success. Guidebooks explaining how to dress were now able to reasonably give fashion tips on proper work attire and fashions for the middle class. The industry helped American fashion to gain some independence from Paris, and it provided easier access to fashion for the working class and immigrants. With the advent of ready-to-wear, trends could change yearly, or seasonally, never to return to a time when fashions could remain in vogue for a century. The lines between individually tailored clothing and manufactured clothing became indistinct, which contributed to the normalization of styles in the region.

The diversity of mingling ancestral roots and ethnic clothing was still present, but a new dimension of diversity emerged with rapidly changing trends. Unlike the diversity that was so apparent during colonial times, the diversity of trends was directly tied to marketing. With the advent of clothing and trend manufacturing, fashion had taken a dramatic step into the realm of commercialism, and any notions of fashion as a unique expression of identity had shifted to meet this step. The industry was utilized by European manufacturers, which allowed a partnership between Britain and America for sharing sizing systems, and between America and France for obtaining trend information. This was also a first step toward what would become a huge global industry with roots in the mid-Atlantic region.

The ready-to-wear industry based on a network of innovations in fashion manufacturing at the time. In 1864, E. Butterick & Co. established its business on Broadway after the proprietor had invented paper sewing patterns. Beginning with patterns for men and boys' clothes, the company earned great success by making all kinds of fashion, including haute couture, available to everyone through patterns. In 1867 Butterick's first magazine—*Ladies Quarterly of Broadway Fashions*—was introduced, which offered people the chance to browse and order patterns. Nearly ten years later, Butterick's went international, selling patterns in London,

New York fashions for November 1872. Published by E. Butterick & Co. Courtesy Library of Congress.

Paris, Berlin, and Vienna. The legacy of the company continued into the twentieth century, when it established a permanent residence in Manhattan and formed a partnership with *Vogue* magazine. Even during the Great Depression, E. Butterick & Co. was successful because people had to turn to sewing their own clothing again, and in 1945 the company opened a plant in Altoona, Pennsylvania. The partner to such success, of course, was the sewing machine. Newark's Caplan Sewing Machines established its legacy through outfitting workshops in New York and New Jersey with machines when the ready-to-wear industry was in its prime in the 1930s. Caplan is a perfect example of the explosive success enjoyed by the fashion industry in the mid-Atlantic region, which provided opportunities and jobs for residents.

The fashion industry established jobs and wealth for entrepreneurs in New York City in the early part of the nineteenth century, but manufacturing also caused a rash of problems. Immigrants suffered the worst that the fashion industry had to offer because they often worked in the sweatshops that supported ready-to-wear. Living on the crowded East Side, female Jewish immigrants went to work every day in small, unhealthy sweatshops in the garment making center of Seventh Avenue. In 1909, 20,000 of these workers went on strike due to the poor working conditions. Though this event was remarkable, there were still health and safety problems in the industry. The Women's Trade Union and International Ladies Garment Workers Union tried to draw attention to a fire in a Newark, New Jersey, factory that could have been devastating; their cause was not addressed until the Triangle Shirt Waist fire in New York City killed at least 145 workers. Even as

Garment workers parading on May Day, New York City, 1916. Courtesy Library of Congress.

late as 1928 elderly immigrants were still working in shops that made complete-garment method piecing when advances in the industry allowed easier work. Paterson, New Jersey, already established as the "silk city of the world," saw strikes in 1912, 1933, and 1936 due to poor labor conditions. By the 1940s, the industry in New York had established branch factories in New Jersey, Pennsylvania, and upstate New York, already adding to the successful factories in those states, but it had been an unforgiving journey for the early factory workers whose labor this success was built upon. Even into the 1990s the U.S. government has consistently investigated labor law violations in New York and New Jersey factories.

Hairdressing and Jewelry

Other industries related to the fashion business included hairdressing and jewelry. After 1860, the Newark area had become the "fine jewelry capital" of the United States. The prevalence of jewelry in American fashion caused critics like Emily Post to call showiness "un-American," and Fanny Hurst to make anti-Semitic remarks about the "East Side Girl" who enjoyed displaying too much jewelry.[11] These early attacks were not strong enough to take on the jewelry business, which overcame stiff notions of masculinity by winning men's favor in the 1920s, when the wearing of cuff links, fine watches, and other accessories became acceptable.

The hairdressing business in America was already successful in the nineteenth century, and even the earliest hairdressers and hairdressing shops fit the stereotype of a gossip mill. The elite system of "knowing" and affording a good hairdresser was in place throughout the mid-Atlantic cities early on. Hairdressers such as "François," a Washington, D.C., man, took on French names to attract customers. François was famous for sharing juicy rumors with his customers about the European royalty whose hair he had supposedly styled.[12] On New Year's Day, hairdressers in New York City were busy due to female preparations for a Dutch celebration that involved wealthy men's visits to their female acquaintances for food and drinks. Men's barbershops were not immune to gossip, and provided a place of masculine conversation and connection. Some hairdressers even faced the possibility of being suspected of committing lewd acts, for those who served the wealthy in their homes would style female customers' hair in their bedrooms. The lingering Victorian notions of elite circles put a stop to this practice and in some cases prompted the development of separate rooms for hairdressing. The developments in the businesses that accessorized clothing were quite important for setting examples and standards for fashion in the mid-Atlantic region, as were such developments as fashion shows and models.

Models and Fashion Shows

New York City shop owners had young store assistants model for the fashions they sold even before the French began formally using models in the late 1800s. By 1869 the city's dressmakers were holding fall and spring "opening days" to show the latest designs. These were two early developments leading up to the formal modeling and fashion shows that became so vital to the business. By the 1920s fashion shows had advanced enough to become specialized. New York's Hotel Astor hosted a memorable show of fur fashions in 1922, in which the fur upstaged the clothes being shown. Fashion shows had become a great window into teaching Americans to be effective consumers, and some groups in the region even developed formal programs for this purpose.

Atlantic City was a prime location for fashion shows, as it was a popular resort area offering comfort and a beautiful setting. America's first bathing beauty contest took place in Atlantic City in 1921, featuring revealing new trends that excited and offended people across the country. This city was also the site where the first Miss America was chosen during the same year. Four years later, the ceremony for the first Golden Brown National Beauty Contest for African Americans would be held in Atlantic City. Diamond rings, cars, and a trip to this city were the motivating factors for African American women to participate. Sponsored by a cosmetic company, this contest was possibly a way to make a point against the exclusion of African Americans from the Miss America competitions that took place in that same city.

At a time when department stores' regular fashion shows excluded African Americans, they were able to cultivate fashion contests and shows successfully in the 1920s and 1930s. Examples like the Golden Brown contest set a precedent for the 1928 Nelson Girl contest in New York City, and for small local contests, like those held by the *Pittsburgh Courier*. Local fashion shows were a great way to expand the practice, as the New York City Utopia Fashion Show and others of its kind demonstrated in the mid-1930s. African American fashion shows became so popular throughout the region that crowds of thousands were attracted to the events. By this time fashion shows helped the black middle class to distinguish itself from the working class and develop standards for how to dress well. Harlem eventually became a venue known for fashion contests, including the Harlem Drag Balls that represented the homosexual contingent in New York during the 1920s and 1930s. Harlem's Savoy Ballroom was the infamous setting of a bathing suit contest in 1926 that offered an Atlantic City trip as its grand prize and turned into a weekly event of great popularity.[13] Judging from the attendance of such shows in the mid-Atlantic region, it is plain to see that these events were important for the fashion industry and for the many groups trying to succeed in America.

Early Fashion Design in Manhattan

As anyone could imagine, the mid-Atlantic region is a hotbed for fashion design because most of the country's designers have congregated in New York City. Many of these famous designers were responsible for setting major American trends. A brief look at the developments brought forth by designers and others in the field is important to better understanding the political and historical changes and political statements that fashion made the region over time.

Some designers were directly responsible for the achievement of the region's fashion industry. Whether immigrants or Americans, designers or businesspeople, the backgrounds and expertise brought to the fold when laying this foundation all blended to create a strong network for success. Like ingredients of a perfect recipe, none of these people would have contributed as profoundly to fashion without the others. Hattie Carnegie (1889–1956) was a catalyst for the ready-to-wear industry and blazed a path for the upcoming fame of individual designers. An enterprising immigrant, she started small by owning a hat shop in the city and quickly became a clothes designer. Her most valuable entrepreneurial move was to market her own ready-to-wear designs by putting her name on a label. Once she became successful, she opened her own ready-to-wear factory, and attracted a loyal following of hopeful young designers who wanted to work for her. Carnegie's design group was the starting place for three extremely important mid-Atlantic figures in American fashion: Claire McCardell, Normal Norell, and Pauline Trigere. New Yorker Eleanor Lambert (1903–2003), not a designer, also helped by founding the International Best Dressed List in 1940 and the Coty Fashion Critics Awards in 1943. Nicknamed the "Empress of Seventh Avenue," she established fashion weeks during that decade which allowed designers to coordinate their shows and increase business. The establishment of organizations such as the Costume Institute at the Metropolitan Museum of Art in 1937 (something Lambert avidly supported) and the Fashion Institute of Technology in 1944 also indicated the success of the fashion industry in the region at the time.

Claire McCardell (1905–1958) was perhaps the most influential American designer of her time. McCardell developed comfortable, sensible, useful clothing that was immediately popular in her region and across the country. McCardell invented separates, or interchangeable clothes, as well as the "American Look" that was in style after World War II, the monastic and popover dresses, and even leotards. McCardell's styles were simple and wearable, which led manufacturers to hastily copy her clothes. She eventually developed a prosperous business relationship with Lord & Taylor that lasted for years. Her success was an important development for postwar America, as dependence upon French designers was unpopular then. McCardell's fashions were such a staple in American design that she remained popular well into the 1970s.[14]

Norman Norell (1900–1972) was famous for his feminine, classy clothing from the 1940s to the 1970s. Known as "the dean of American fashion designers," he got many ideas from Hattie Carnegie, his employer and advocate. The very slender, snug-fitting, tailored suit popular in the 1950s was one of Norell's trademark styles. A Norell outfit would be fully accessorized with stylish jewelry, a handbag, and a hat. The elegance and sophistication of this look were reflected in his eveningwear as well. Norell enjoyed pairing slim 1920s styles with flashy accents. A

Claire McCardell

Claire McCardell's story is one of invention and innovation. Born in Maryland in 1905 with a unique talent and educated in Paris at Parson's, Claire McCardell would quickly become an American success story. Upon returning to the States from Paris, she gained her footing in New York City and New Jersey while trying to break into the fashion business. She did not flounder for long, and in the 1930s she began working on her trademark fashions. She developed her monastic dress, a simple tentlike garment that could be belted to fit the waist. It marked the first breakthrough as manufacturers quickly replicated her design for their retail stores. McCardell's lack of concern over this fact was unique in the design world; she had once copied Paris trends herself in order to survive on Seventh Avenue. As she traveled to other states and countries on business, she began to design clothing that accommodated her travel. McCardell's clever idea to create separates came from this, as she could pack less but enjoy a variety of clothing combinations for trendy events. This was a major inspiration for McCardell, and she soon began designing these clothes for others. Although manufacturers were first skeptical of this new idea, the charm and practicality of her ideas soon took, and as World War II ended she became the mother of the "American Look."

The American Look, like her separates, was very loose, casual, easy, and elegant. It was made for all day and all occasions. The title came from the fact that McCardell had mixed the styles of pioneer women, children of the nineteenth century, the Wild West, workmen, and even superheroes. The result of this mixture was a reliance on forms like overalls, double stitching, bandanas, tunics, and hoods. She pushed New England cotton mills to make calico again for her elegant clothing. She relied on cotton and jersey and experimented with new fabrics that came along, like Dupont nylon. After the war she began a formal working relationship with Lord & Taylor, and her American Look designs were manufactured in their company's factories.

McCardell's repertoire included many styles as the 1940s drew on. In 1942 her diaper bathing suits were designed for a comfortable fit and quick drying. This same year, her popover housedress, which resembled a popover or muffin around the waist, was fashionable for at least a decade. She developed the leotard in 1943, pairing it with wool jumpers for college women who needed to stay warm during the cold mid-Atlantic winters in their dorms. Ballet shoes complemented almost every McCardell outfit after 1944. Her knickers, hooded sweaters, and tights were designed as winter-wear for play in the region. These fashions reflected a healthy lifestyle, and her models reflected that value by looking natural. This natural look was also seen in the relaxed step of her models, whom she had taught to walk with a slight slouch, hips forward, and hands in deep pockets, a runway walk that is still used today.

By the mid-1940s McCardell was an American fixture, and her work solidified America's independence from Paris fashion. It was unique for a designer to find inspiration in old American looks. World War II had made for some changes in fashion in America. Designers struggled against federal restrictions on yardage, and so fashions of the 1930s and 1940s were very sporty and used less fabric than before. When the war ended and the restrictions were relaxed, McCardell correctly predicted that people would want more traditional fashions, such as fuller skirts, since they had only been able to choose from modest, limited styles for so long. After the war, McCardell produced coats to go with all outfits and all styles. In the 1950s she continued to design with more colors and artistic flair. Her success caused her fashions to gain international notice in this decade, and some of her fashions even revived in the

1970s. McCardell's clothing set a standard for Americans that advocated comfort and durability over status and glamour. In contrast to traditional clothes that made women look feminine and classic like Dior's "new look," a McCardell was simple and powerfully American.

good example of this was a unique dress that began with a tight, black, strapless jersey top and flared into a fuchsia taffeta skirt. Like McCardell, Norell wanted to combine comfort and elegance. Other trademarks of his were the use of sequins, which were the defining feature of his mermaid dresses, and his 1960s tailored wool coat. Norell's fashions may not have been as revolutionary as McCardell's, but they were certainly popular among cosmopolitans into the 1970s. Norell won Coty Awards in 1943 and 1951, and was the first to be inducted into the Coty Hall of Fame. Before his death in 1972, he had started experimenting with the flared sleeves and skirts that would be popular in that decade, but he did not live to see the New York Metropolitan Museum's "Fifty Years of Norell" retrospective that honored his accomplishments.[15]

Pauline Trigere (1909–2002) is a third example of a New York designer who contributed greatly to American fashion. Trigere was born in France and moved to America to start her business in 1942. In 1961 Trigere employed a black model, the first to be hired by a major designer in America. Her styles were simple, elegant, and classic. Early on, she designed suits that paired a bolero or capelike jacket with a tailored skirt. In 1963 Trigere set an unusual precedent by designing underwear to be worn with her clothing. She developed fake diamonds as a price-conscious but elegant accent to her clothing, and in 1967 designed the first rhinestone bra. In the 1970s she reintroduced culottes and also designed a shirt that only had one shoulder, leaving the other bare. She also became a guest teacher at the Fashion Institute of Technology in 1973. Trigere worked into her nineties, even creating accessories for fashion-conscious senior citizens. In 1993 she received the lifetime achievement award from the Council of Fashion Designers of America. Trigere's devotion to fashion, like McCardell's, was more than just a devotion to the elite class. She was committed to innovation and educating others to make positive change through the fashion industry.[16]

These designers paved the way for those who have enjoyed success since the 1950s, like Bonnie Cashin and Bill Blass. Bonnie Cashin (1908–2000) is also a famous name in New York fashion whose work reflects McCardell's. Cashin's groundbreaking ideas were considered "organic," as she created outdoorsy styles with ponchos, flexible pants, sweaters, knits, and woolen or leather outerwear. Anne Klein (1923–1974) was a leader in moving toward casual sportswear and upholding McCardell's wardrobe of separates. She also initiated "junior" clothing, which was marketed to adolescents. This allowed adolescent fashion to move from childlike to an imitation of adult fashion. Bill Blass (1922–) is known for lifting ready-to-wear to high-class clothing. He extended design to household items such as linens, and was one of the first designers to focus on men's fashions. Because of this he won the first 1968 Coty Award for men's fashions. Valentia, who was born Nicholaevna Sanina Schlee in Russia in 1904, immigrated to New York and became well known for her styles that resembled Russian peasant's garments. She designed the apron dress, a hooded cape, headscarves, and wraparound silhouettes. Her designs were adopted by urbanites and celebrities, and traces of her ideas are still apparent in ready-to-wear clothing seen in American fashion shows and stores of the twenty-first century.

THE 1960s

People often debate whether art imitates life or vice versa. This debate is alive and well when it comes to fashion. At some points in the history of the mid-Atlantic region, fashion has not only been an art, but has become interwoven with other art forms. A good example is the importance of fashions during the jazz era, when jazz musicians and enthusiasts sported the zoot suit. Another example of the way in which art and fashion mixed came in 1944 when New York's Museum of Modern Art held an exhibit that questioned the modernity of the era's clothing. Claire McCardell's fashions, as well as many others, were held up against cave people's clothing in an attempt to make a point about the absurd obsession with clothing in America. The exhibit caused Americans to take an objective view of fashion in order to scrutinize it as an artistic and social institution.[17] These regional examples and more highlight the debate over whether the art of fashion imitates life or vice versa.

When it came to the 1960s, however, an even more complicated shift was taking place that involved fashion, art, and rebellion. Prior to this decade, America was experiencing a rebellion in fashion that came from suburban working-class youth. Blue jeans and leather jackets, powerful images of 1950s adolescent gangs, were a direct challenge to conservative, white-collar moral codes and dress. Beatnik fashion, inspired by beatnik poets Jack Kerouac and Allen Ginsberg, was common in Greenwich Village. Opposite the sunny, trim, Doris Day styles of the late 1940s, male beatniks wore dark pants and turtleneck sweaters. Women wore long hair and entirely black dresses, leggings, and dance shoes. In a now materialistic and conformist society, adolescents were struggling to find their identities. The fashion industry had finally perfected clothing that was wrinkle-free, and an interesting response to this was the wearing of blue jeans and leather jackets that molded to the body and showed permanent creases.

The 1960s would see youth wearing clothing that also wrinkled easily, and the hippie generation did not intend to iron out those wrinkles. *POPism: The Warhol Sixties*, an autobiography by Pittsburgh native and artist Andy Warhol (1928–1987), documents the spirit of rebellion that mingled with art and a materialistic America during the 1960s in New York City. The 1960s were a time when using products made of tinfoil and disposing of them was a symbol of wealth and portability. This new American attitude inspired designers like Scaasi, Halston, and Bonnie Cashin to create unusual clothes that reflected consumerism. Another important aspect of this time was the recognition by designers that such a thing as youth fashion existed, as they took fashion ideas from the street and from popular young musicians. Like the effects of the Roaring Twenties, youth fashion was also shocking and avant-garde. It was indissolubly connected to the spirit of social, political, and economic protest that was espoused by America's hippies, beatniks, and pop artists during this time period.

A trend for paper clothing, which hit New York City in the mid-1960s, is a direct reflection of this incentive. Scott Paper Company began the fad with an ad ploy that distributed paper dresses as a joke, but it actually became a fashion trend of the era. Elisa Daggs opened a New York City paper clothes business in 1966. She distributed a wrap mini-dress, caftans, and an A-line tent dress with a petticoat first to Neiman Marcus and eventually to sixty other stores. Between 1965 and 1968, Caroline Little and William Guggenheim III opened a boutique in Manhattan called In Dispensable Disposables; Brooklyn's Abraham & Strauss opened a Waste Paper Boutique; a paper dress ball was held on an ocean liner in the city's harbor; and the local Museum of Contemporary Crafts opened two exhibits called "Made with Paper" and "Body Covering," where the public wore paper slippers and the displays showed space age materials. Bonnie Cashin opened Bonnie Cashin's Paper-Route to Fashion Corporation in 1968, and Tiger Morse opened the Teeny-Weeny shop, dedicated to materials of the future like synthetics and plastic. A Washington, D.C., benefit, attended by Jackie Kennedy, required guests to turn in their designer clothing in exchange for paper dresses. *Time* magazine sent paper dresses to all subscribers. Air India held a paper sari party in New York City to showcase Daggs's work. Like the miniskirts of this period, the paper dress even had a sexual undertone to it, since it was so flimsy and could easily be ripped to reveal a person's body.[18]

Just like Warhol's artistic representation of commercial images on canvas, fashion both worked in partnership with consumerism and mockingly mirrored it. The paper dress was more than just a fad; it was a very notable moment when the mixture of art, entertainment, and fashion symbolized America's materialism of the time. Abraham & Strauss hired Andy Warhol to demonstrate their paint kit by decorating a paper dress while model/singer Nico was wearing it. The dresses were later donated to the Brooklyn Museum. The Museum of Modern Art's OpArt exhibit coupled well with the paper dress craze, and it motivated designers to create OpArt fashions. The paper dress not only was very "Pop," but also was a unique channel through which fashion and art interacted, and life and art were not imitating but intimately speaking through each other.

Though he was not a designer, the account that Warhol provides in *POPism* is unique in that his aesthetic eye gives us a strong understanding of the rapid changes in 1960s New York fashions, including the fashions of entertainers, kids, and designers. He begins in 1963, when he wore black stretch jeans and an Oxford shirt under a college sweater and paint splattered shoes. Girls in the city were wearing shifts and sandals, a folk look that was somehow also hip. Warhol observes that while New York City's girls sported these fashions with Cleopatra eyes and hair, the girls in rural areas and other cities were still wearing 1950s-style cashmere sweaters and tight skirts. In 1964 the preppy look faded and parents tried to look like kids. Brightly colored short dresses were a rage, as were short, teased haircuts, lipstick, and iridescent eye makeup. Women dieted to look thin in the new styles and men began to follow the "mod" style of the Beatles, Rolling Stones, and Kinks rather than the "tough guy" image of the previous decade. The year 1965 in New York brought a departure from the earlier images, with velvet shirts for men, or a Bob Dylan imitation, while girls got into the "Big Baby" look with puffy-sleeved short dresses, tights, and Mary Jane shoes. The sexuality of the era was again evident when some women went without underwear underneath their minidresses or even without clothing under their fur coats. Designers struggled to keep up with the trends, but the manufacturers were worse off. As manufacturers hesitated over fashions that might not "stick," boutiques raked in the profits by selling anything new.

Into the late 1960s, many people had taken cues from hippies, feminists, and civil rights advocates, deciding that it was fashionable to go against the norm, or to refuse conformity. Warhol's travels to San Francisco before this time had led him to conclude that West Coast attitudes toward the Vietnam War were much less cynical than those found on the East Coast. Whereas San Francisco's hippies might have dressed in caftans, secondhand clothes, and love beads early on as a testimony for their cause against war, New York's hippies might have followed the fashions just to be fashionable. San Francisco's hippies had very seriously worked to advocate peace and free speech, but their efforts had significantly deteriorated into drug use by 1967. Symbolically, the Diggers, a philanthropic group based in the famous Haight and Ashbury area, held a funeral for the hippie movement because of this drug use. This happened just around the time that hippie style became an object of consumerism and marketing in other areas of the country like New York. Warhol notes this shift of the late 1960s with the realization that New York City kids were considered fashionable because they had learned to shoplift, a blatant appropriation of nonconformist values. The city's popular boutiques even had a different atmosphere than before, as clerks stayed late into the night relaxing, watching TV, and smoking marijuana. Army/Navy stores became quite popular, as did boutiques like Paraphernalia, which sold cheap clothing such as Barbara Hode's crocheted dresses that would easily fall apart, symbolizing a difference from the well-made clothing that most Americans wore. Paraphernalia expanded to Los Angeles and Washington, D.C., in 1966, leading to the mass-manufacturing of fashions that had once been worn to reflect nonconformist attitudes.

Fashion at this point was very much a race to market shock value, and as a result the exceedingly eccentric fashion of New York City was closed off from the rest of the region and the country. It did not translate into the middle class or into everyday people's wardrobes because it was dangerous and edgy. This kind of inaccessible fashion was encouraged by some of the city's designers. Inspired by street clothes, Arnold Scaasi created outlandish clothes made from aluminum, cellophane, and giant sequins. His work was gritty and challenging, like Warhol's art, but was also expensive couture. Betsey Johnson created clothes that were sold at Paraphernalia, like miniskirts made of shower rings, or do-it-yourself outfits that were disposable. Tiger Morse created couture-type pieces made of silk, satin brocade, and lamé with hand-stitched linings. She designed the shower curtain dress, a light-up dress, and a love/hate dress. Morse also opened a shop on Broadway next to Cheetah Club, where people bought clothes to wear for the evening en route to the club.

The first designer of the time to get beyond this self-serving kind of couture was Halston (1932–) who not only designed Jackie Kennedy's famous pillbox hat, but was one of the most influential designers of the sixties generation. Halston was first a jewelry designer but moved to ready-to-wear fashions in the late sixties. His designs were smooth and streamlined, and he favored soft tie-dye and pale colors. In the next decade he would go on to create flowing caftans, bias cut gowns, and suede shirtdresses that were worn by celebrities to trendy clubs in the city. Halston's fashions were easy and casual, reminiscent of McCardell's, and he was in company with similar designers like Perry Ellis, Geoffrey Beane, and Bill Blass. It was Halston, however, who set the stage for what would be a global obsession with New York brand labels that has lasted beyond the twentieth century.

By 1967 fashion that had built up since the early part of the decade exploded; afros, vinyl electric dresses (with a battery pack), lopsided hemlines, sliver-quilted minidresses, plastic and metal dresses, crocheted skirts and tights, Nehru collars, kneesocks, micro-miniskirts, big hats, high boots, fur, psychedelic prints, 3-D appliqués, striped T-shirts and Levi's, and colored shoes reflected the pop obsession. Men's fashions actually competed in glamour with women's fashions, initiating an interesting reexamination of sex roles through fashion. Sexy clothes, see-through or cut-out types, made it clear that sex was "take it or leave it." In 1967 a Beatles trend came into the city in men's fashions, as they wore the Sgt. Pepper jacket with stovepipe pants. Warhol's account observes the end of the 1960s, and the fashions that began to take young people into the 1970s, like the "Pakistan-Indian-international-jet-set-hippie-look," the embroidered and brocaded clothing, or the velvet-and-satin tunic blouses and pantsuits. Fashions from the city were colorful and outrageous, and with the work of designers like Halston and Blass, they began to catch on in other areas within about a year of their debut. Although Warhol's account is from one perspective, it is a detailed explanation of what would have been seen in the most artistic and fashionable parts of New York City, the nation's fashion capital. Warhol's account provides a tangible record of the fact that the 1960s was a time when art, fashion, sociopolitical issues, and economics were inextricably linked. American fashion at this time in history, almost as a direct result of what was happening in New York City, had reached a very complex point, and was now on its way to becoming a transnational industry that would make waves well beyond the mid-Atlantic region.

MID-ATLANTIC FASHION AND THE TRANSNATIONAL MARKET

The 1960s seemed to open facets of fashion that were previously unthinkable. Designers' attention had shifted from elite, European-inspired clothing to street and youth fashion. The fashion industry went from perfecting wrinkle-free synthetics, streamlined suits, and comfortable middle-class leisurewear to creating fashions inspired by musicians, revolutionaries, and rebellious adolescents. Much to the dismay of the "fashionable," high couture had lost power as the 1970s brought thrift store–inspired fashions that exaggerated elements from the 1920s, 1930s, and 1940s. Glam rockers like the New York Dolls and Lou Reed inspired the glittery, androgynous looks that appeared in the hippest parts of mid-Atlantic cities. Men began wearing longer hair even in mainstream, white-collar circles. Blue jeans, once outlawed in American schools, were now an everyday norm among all classes of people, and were painstakingly marketed and advertised to become a profitable icon of sexuality and leisure. From these years on, fashion in the mid-Atlantic region underwent many changes. The region that once experienced unique forms of diversity and growth through immigration and industry became a player in producing fashion for a transnational market that has had homogenizing effects both locally and globally.

America's fashion capital is much different at the beginning of the twenty-first century than it was in the days when McCardell graced the streets of Seventh Avenue. The early catalyst of this change was the trendy turbulence of the 1960s, but specific responses to that came in the 1970s that included a devotion to marketing fashion to a consumer society interested in the symbolic value of fashion, rather than its utility. In fact, the most well known visual documentation of this shift can be seen retrospectively in the advertisements and fashion illustration or photography of Manhattan-based *Vogue* magazine. Many of the Seventh Avenue designers that started during the 1970s gained popularity as the 1980s and 1990s went on, and are now contributing to the prodigious growth of fashion marketing that has changed the landscape of clothing manufacturing in the mid-Atlantic region and taken New York's brand names to foreign countries.

Betsey Johnson, Donna Karan, and Calvin Klein are among the New York designers who have ushered in this change. Johnson's popularity has grown since the 1970s, and her own line of stores has branched from New York to Europe and Asia, attracting the business of many celebrities. Donna Karan (1948–) and Calvin Klein (1942–) also had their early successes in the 1970s, and their businesses skyrocketed as Wall Street became a center of corporate achievement during the 1980s. Karan, considered the "Queen of Seventh Avenue," and Calvin Klein both created affordable ready-to-wear lines and marketed their urban-inspired clothing through advertising that suggested an attitude or essence of comfort and luxury over material design. Both took in millions in annual revenue and overwhelming success in American and global markets, and this has continued in the twenty-first century.

In a similar manner, Ralph Lauren (1939–) has contributed to the global expansion of New York City fashion with his simple, basic separates that are popular in department stores across America. Lauren considers his work to be an "untrendy, unpackaged individual look," something very different from what designers even in the 1960s were striving for. This change in focus partially reflects the consumer focus on the symbolic value of fashion, but it also reflects a more profound issue. As New York City grows more international by the day, its rich ethnic and cultural diversity has allowed the possibility for unique social conflicts that emerge through fashion. Muslim immigrants, for example, with religious beliefs that dictate particular dress, have found it very difficult to raise their children to honor that code in a trendy, fashion-savvy city. The response from some designers has been to create bland, simple clothing that tends to smooth over differences in appearance and does not take many risks. This has been called the "Gap phenomenon," after a retail store that sells simple but stylish family clothing.

This homogenizing effect has also come from designers who have appropriated and promoted street fashion since the 1960s. Tommy Hilfiger (1951–) is a perfect example of this; he built a successful New York ready-to-wear empire in the 1990s using a blend of street wear inspired by poor urban teenagers and Gap-like family attire. His clothing has been adopted by hip-hop artists and suburban teens, and is a staple for looking cool. Like Klein and Karan, Hilfiger owes his success largely to his business sense and aggressive marketing techniques, which include giving free clothing to celebrities and word-of-mouth advertising in urban ghettos. The clothing produced by Hilfiger and other New York designers is noticeably emblazoned with their labels, a practice that has made their fashions a hot commodity.

It is clear that some of New York's designers have been extremely successful, but they represent only one group that has chosen a particular business strategy. Even though fashion has remained a backbone industry in the mid-Atlantic region for many years, it has had its up and downs. In 1991, a report about the garment district of Seventh Avenue noted, "Except for the tall structures, there's a Third World look about the place. Dingy buildings, filthy streets, shabby men ramming clothes carts on crowded sidewalks, double-parked beat-up vans everywhere." At the end of the twentieth century, the industry in New York, which is known for wholesaling, lost over 100,000 jobs overseas and to other American plants because of consolidation. Security problems and high costs in the Garment Center have also hurt business. In 1993 the Fashion Center Business Improvement District opened in order to evaluate this industry, and has worked since that time to improve business in the city; however, the region is still adversely affected by changes in the industry.

The fashion industry brings in billions of dollars in revenue each year for New York and the surrounding states that house branch factories and businesses. More garment factories operate in the mid-Atlantic states than in any other region in the United States. Many people in the mid-Atlantic region depend on jobs in garment factories; in fact, in 1994 the garment trade was the largest manufacturing industry and possibly the largest employer in New York City. Other manufacturing centers in the mid-Atlantic area include Paterson, Jersey City, Newark, and Philadelphia. Seventh Avenue companies have opened satellite offices in New Jersey that are important contributors to the state's economy. Some of the mid-Atlantic states clearly depend on the success of Seventh Avenue and the Garment Center, but they are now living under the threat of shutdowns and layoffs because of consolidations and a poor economy. In 1994, Philadelphia's Defense Personnel Support Center closed as part of a government downsizing effort, and Woolrich, a well-established Pennsylvania clothing manufacturer, shut down local plants. New Jersey–based Petrie Retail also shut down many of its midwestern stores due to bankruptcy during the late 1990s. Shutdowns like these have come as a result of a poor economy, but also because of competitive, cheap foreign labor and the rise of discount stores. Independent designers and clothing distributors, usually designing high-end expensive clothing, also compete with discount stores like T. J. Maxx and Wal-Mart, thus reducing the amount of variety in the fashion industry and showing how difficult being an entrepreneur in the business can be. A good example of this is the Maryland Manufacturing Company which was founded by an Italian immigrant in 1923 and dissolved in the 1980s because it could not compete with imported clothing. As the twenty-first century begins, designers and clothing manufacturers must have keen business sense to succeed, and this sometimes means sacrificing regional jobs and cultural variety in favor of cheaply made ready-to-wear products that homogenize fashion in the region, the country, and in some cases the world. These issues create serious challenges for those in the fashion business, an industry that has been alive since the 1800s and provided a rich historical flavor to the mid-Atlantic region. Rapidly changing world markets have deeply altered the landscape of this business, and as a result its future in the mid-Atlantic states is difficult to predict.

Besides simply being a facet of the region's economy, fashion has been extremely important in the Mid-Atlantic's social and political formation. The historical diversity of fashion in the region and the development of trends and industry are unique aspects of the mid-Atlantic area. From the early settlers' cultural dress to the artistic clothing of the 1960s, the region's fashion has always represented American values. Mid-Atlantic figures have established distinct American customs such as beauty contests and celebrations, and have used fashion as a medium in expressing political dissidence. A glimpse into the rich history of fashion in this region makes it very clear that "fashion" is not something trivial, but something inextricable from society, something that shapes and reflects a society's complex systems, values, and future.

RESOURCE GUIDE

Printed Sources

"About May; Company History." May Company Web site. June 20, 2003. http://www2 .mayco.com/common/investorhistory.jsp.
"Alternative Spaces: Fashion Shows in Unusual Places." Great American Design. *WWD*, March 27, 1995, 54. Infotrac One File. Reed Lib., Fredonia, N.Y. June 20, 2003.
Anspach, Karlyne. *The Why of Fashion*. Ames: Iowa State University Press, 1967.
"Appearance and Fashion." June 2, 2003. From "Women in America 1820–1842" and *Democracy in America*. Hypertext document. American Studies at University of Virginia Web site. September 6, 2003. http://xroads.virginia.edu/~hyper/detoc/fem/appear .htm.
Baker, Patricia. *Fashions of a Decade: The 1950s*. Ed. Valerie Cumming and Elane Feldman. New York: Facts on File, 1991.
Banner, Lois W. *American Beauty*. New York: Alfred A. Knopf, 1983.
Breward, Christopher. "Fashion Capitals." In *Oxford History of Art: Fashion*. Oxford: Oxford University Press, 2003, 169–216.
Burnham Oliver, Valerie. *Fashion and Costume in American Popular Culture*. Westport, CT: Greenwood Press, 1996.
"Butterick: Our History." 2003. Butterick Company Home page. The McCall Pattern Co. June 12, 2003. http://www.butterick.com/bhc/pages/articles/histpgs/about.html.
Cunningham, Patricia A. "Artistic Dress in America." "Reforming Fashion, 1850–1914; Politics, Health, and Art" online exhibition. The Historic Costume and Textiles Collection, Geraldine Schottenstein Wing, Ohio State University. Department of Consumer and Textile Sciences and College of Human Ecology. September 3, 2003. http://costume.osu.edu/reforming_fashion/artistic_dress.htm.
Cunningham, Patricia A., and Susan Voso Lab, eds. *Dress and Popular Culture*. Bowling Green: Bowling Green State University Popular Press, 1991.
Ewing, Elizabeth. *History of Twentieth Century Fashion*. Totowa, NJ: Barnes and Noble, 1986.
Friedman, Arthur. "Buyers Want Cheaper, Safer SA" *WWD*, January 25, 1995, 8. Infotrac One File. Reed Lib., Fredonia, NY. June 20, 2003.
———. "Industry Praises Words but Wants Action: Giuliani's Fashion Statement." *WWD*, January 24, 1995, 8. Infotrac One File. Reed Lib., Fredonia, NY. June 20, 2003.
Gerard, Eric R. "Garment Center Remains Stable in Good Times and Bad." *Real Estate Weekly*, May 11, 1994, 1. Infotrac One File. Reed Lib., Fredonia, NY. June 20, 2003.
Joselit, Jenna Weissman. *A Perfect Fit; Clothes, Character, and the Promise of America*. New York: Henry Holt, 2001.

Lambert, Eleanor. *World of Fashion: People, Places, Resources*. New York: R. R. Bowker, 1976.

Lee, Sarah Tomerlin, ed. *American Fashion; The Life and Lines of Adrian, Mainbocher, Mc-Cardell, Norell, Trigere*. New York: Quadrangle/New York Times, 1975.

Malinowski, Sharon, and Anna Sheets, eds. *The Gayle Encyclopedia of Native American Tribes*. Vol. 1. Detroit: Gale Research, 1998.

Malone, David. "Amelia Bloomer." August 2, 2003. Women's Rights National Historic Park, Seneca Falls, NY. National Park Service. September 3, 2003. http://www.nps.gov/wori/home.htm.

Warhol, Andy, and Pat Hackett. *POPism: The Warhol '60s*. New York: Harcourt Brace Jovanovich, 1980.

Warwick, Edward, Henry Pitz, and Alexander Wyckoff. *Early American Dress: The Colonial and Revolutionary Periods*. New York: Benjamin Blom, 1965.

White, Shane, and Graham White. *Stylin': African American Expressive Culture from Its Beginning to the Zoot Suit*. Ithaca: Cornell University Press, 1998.

Wilcox, R. Turner. *Five Centuries of American Costume*. New York: Charles Scribner and Sons, 1963.

Wilson, Elizabeth. *Adorned in Dreams; Fashion and Modernity*. Berkley: University of California Press, 1985.

Zina, Sawaya. "Avenue Montaigne It Isn't." *Forbes*, October 28, 1991, 27. Infotrac One File. Reed Lib., Fredonia, NY. June 20, 2003.

Web Sites

Condé Nast Publications. 2003. CondéNet. September 6, 2003.
http://www.condenet.com

Custom Tailors and Designers Association. August 5, 2003.
http://www.ctda.com

Fashion Watch. September 6, 2003.
http://www.fashionwatch.com

New York Public Libraries. June 17, 2003.
http://www.nypl.org

Women's Rights National Historic Park of Seneca Falls, New York. National Parks Service. September 6, 2003.
http://www.nps.gov/wori/wrnhp.html

Events

Costume Society of America's National Symposium
1412 Broadway Suite 2006
New York, NY 10018
http://www.costumesocietyamerica.com

Forum for designers and others to trade ideas and information. The Web site details smaller events happening by region and provides excellent links for fashion information.

Council of Fashion Designers of America Awards
1412 Broadway, Suite 2006
New York, NY 10018
http://www.cfda.com

Held annually.

7th on 6th, New York's Fashion Week
Mercedes-Benz Fashion Week/IMG
22 East 71st Street
New York, NY 10021
http://www.7thonsixth.com

Biannual fashion shows and debuts.

Videos/Films

Calvin Klein: A Stylish Obsession. A&E Television Networks. 2003.
New York: A Documentary Film. Directed by Ric Burns. PBS, 1999. http://www.pbs.org. Public Broadcasting has online programs, videos, and educational resources.

Organizations, Museums, Special Collections

Black Fashion Museum
2700 Vermont Avenue NW
Washington, DC 20001

Comprehensive national collection of fashions, from slavery to present.

Brooklyn Museum of Art
200 Eastern Parkway
Brooklyn, NY 11238
http://www.brooklynmuseum.org

One of America's best collections of nineteenth-century costumes and textiles, and twentieth-century American designers' work.

Costume Institute at the Metropolitan Museum of Art
1000 Fifth Avenue
New York, NY 10028
http://www.metmuseum.org

Known for collections of accessories, American sportswear, and contemporary fashions.

Daughters of the American Revolution Museum
1776 D Street NW
Washington, DC 20006

Houses a preindustrial collection of costumes.

Fashion Institute of Technology and Museum
27th at 7th Avenue
New York, NY 10001
http://www.fitnyc.edu

School and museum with Web information and exhibits of designs and fashion history.

Maryland Historical Society
201 Monument Street
Baltimore, MD 21201
http://www.mdhs.org

Collections include Maryland artifacts and costume.

National Museum of the American Indian
One Bowling Green
New York, NY 10004
http://www.nmai.si.edu

Collections, archives, and film festivals are linked with the Smithsonian Institute.

Senator John Heinz Pittsburgh Regional History Center
1212 Smallman Street
Pittsburgh, PA 15222

Collections include artifacts and costumes from western Pennsylvania.

Textile Museum
2320 S Street NW
Washington, DC 20008
http://www.textilemuseum.org

Historical preserve of the textile industry and production in the region.

Winterthur Museum, Garden, and Library
Winterthur, DE 19735
http://www.winterthur.org

An American country estate with clothing artifacts from local history.

FILM AND THEATER

Thomas S. Hischak

The generalization that the movie industry is concentrated on the West Coast (particularly in Hollywood) while live theater is a product of the East Coast (New York City, in particular) is not as true as it once was. In fact, it was not the case with the origins of both art forms, and each year it becomes less true. New York did not become the center of theater until far into the nineteenth century, while moviemaking did not turn to California until 1910 after it had first prospered on the East Coast. Today many argue that Manhattan is no longer the hub of the American theater and, in the same line of thought, that the film industry has spread far beyond the confines of Hollywood. What is evident, though, is that the mid-Atlantic states played a vital role in the development of both American film and theater.

THE BEGINNINGS OF AMERICAN THEATER

American theater was basically British theater during the colonial era. Not only were the plays English and the few playhouses built in the English style, but most of the actors and their productions were from England, touring the major east coast cities and then returning to the homeland. It was not until the British actor-manager Lewis Hallam (1714–1756) brought his theater troupe to Virginia in 1752 with the intent of staying in the New World did America have anything resembling a native theater company. Hallam's son, Lewis Hallam Jr. (1740–1808), continued his father's plans, founding the American Company and establishing the first permanent theater troupe in the colonies. By the time of the Revolutionary War, the four major cultural centers in America were Boston, New York City, Philadelphia, and Charleston, South Carolina. All had playhouses by the start of the nineteenth century and theater companies moved back and forth among them for their largest audiences. But Boston, the most Puritanical of the four centers, was wary of theatricals and, as Charleston did not continue to grow at the same

What Is Broadway?

Broadway is a street, a district, a form of theater, a union classification, and a state of mind. The street runs the length of Manhattan, continuing north all the way to Albany, New York. As a theater district, it originated in lower Manhattan and gradually moved north as the city expanded. Today the district is on Broadway between 41st Street and 50th Street and on the side streets east and west of the main thoroughfare. A "Broadway play" or "Broadway musical" is that highly polished, highly publicized kind of theater that once meant the finest to be found in America. Contractually, a "Broadway house" is one of some forty theatres designated by the various theatrical unions for a "Broadway contract." The size of the playhouse and its contractual obligations determine which theaters are classified as "Broadway." Finally, Broadway is a state of mind. It conjures up visions of fame and fortune in the theatrical profession. It means the glorious musicals and plays that originated on Broadway and are done all over the country. It is also an illusion since less and less works now originate on Broadway and the famous New York thoroughfare is no longer an accurate representation of the American theater. But the term "Broadway" is still magical and used to sell the glossiest of theater products.

rate as the other three cities, theater was eventually concentrated in Philadelphia and New York. It wasn't until after the Civil War that Manhattan boasted the most playhouses of any city in the Western world (forty-one as opposed to thirty-nine in London and twenty-four in Paris) and became the undisputed center for live theater in America. Not only were plays presented on Broadway but the city became the hub for the dozens of touring productions of those same plays when they were sent out to other cities and rural markets. The development of vaudeville by the end of the century also turned New York into a headquarters for that very lucrative business. Variety houses were everywhere in America, providing cheap entertainment for every sizable town through extensive touring plans called circuits. Some circuits operated out of Chicago and San Francisco but most were channeled through New York and it was the Manhattan vaudeville houses that were considered the crowning jewels of the business, particularly the Palace Theatre in Times Square, which was called the "Valhalla of Vaudeville."

Theater Outside New York City

Although New York would remain the mecca for theater until the 1970s, one cannot dismiss the live theater that flourished in other mid-Atlantic cities. Philadelphia was the first important theater center in the colonies. Considered more cultural than the inconsistent, turbulent, and money-conscious Manhattan, the Quaker City had its factions that opposed theatricals, but enough of the population were theatergoers to allow playhouses to thrive from the middle of the eighteenth century. Philadelphia's Southwark Theatre (also called the South Street Theatre) was the first permanent structure in America built specifically for plays and it produced *The Prince of Parthia* in 1767, the first play written by an American. Three other Philadelphia playhouses had distinguished histories: the Chestnut Theatre (opened in 1793), the Arch Street Theatre (opened in 1828), and the Walnut Street Theatre (which began operation in 1811 and remains today the oldest active theater in the United States). The greatest American and foreign actors performed on their stages and each playhouse made important contributions that were separate and independent of New York theater. The Arch Street was the home of the famous theater company of Mrs. John Drew (1820–1897), the grandmother of Ethel, John, and Lionel Barrymore and an esteemed actor-manager whose productions rivaled the best in Manhattan. From the late 1800s until World War I, the Philadelphia School of Comic Opera presented original musicals that were hits in town and on the road without ever playing in New York, and there was even a school of Philadelphia dramatists who wrote romantic verse dramas that flourished in the city during the first half of the nineteenth century. But stock companies, such as that of Mrs. Drew, disappeared soon after the turn of the twentieth century and Philadelphia was eventually reduced to a tryout town for Broadway plays or a touring stop for productions from New York.

In Maryland, the small city of Annapolis, which called itself the "Athens of America," was the home of theatricals in the early 1700s, long before they were established in nearby Baltimore. It was a frequent stop for the Hallam's American Company and major British actors performed there as well. A playhouse was not built in Baltimore until 1781 but in 1794 the Holliday Street Theatre was erected and served as the most distinguished venue in the city for the next 100 years. ("The Star Spangled Banner" was given its first performance at the Holliday in 1819.) Baltimore native John T. Ford (1829–1894), who built several playhouses in the mid-Atlantic states and the South, ran Ford's

Ford's Theatre and Its Aftermath

Three days after General Lee surrendered to Ulysses S. Grant at Appomattox Courthouse, Abraham Lincoln and his wife Mary attended a performance of *Our American Cousin* at Ford's Theatre. The comedy was a familiar one and Laura Keene (1826?–1873), an actress-manager whose company was highly regarded, played the role of Florence Trenchard, the part she originated in 1858 and had played hundreds of times in various venues. In fact, that evening (April 14, 1865) was advertised as her 1,000th performance of the role. Not long after the play began, the actor John Wilkes Booth entered the President's Box, shot Lincoln in the head, then jumped down to the stage. After shouting *"Sic semper tyrannis!"* Booth ran off through the wings and into an alley where an accomplice on horseback was waiting for him. Lincoln died ten hours later and Booth was burned to death in a fire two weeks after that. The effect the tragic event had on the country, North and South, has been well documented but its effect on theater is less known. Keene and all her company were arrested as accessories to the crime but were eventually released when no connection between them and Booth could be established. All the same, it destroyed Keene's career and made all actors suspect in America. Booth's brother, the renowned tragic actor Edwin Booth, saw his popularity turn to scorn and it took several years before he could perform on stage without shouts of accusation from certain members of the audience. In America, actors were never accepted into proper society and actresses were often deemed to be little more than prostitutes. Yet as the country created its own stage stars, some of the prejudice began to fade. But the assassination of Lincoln by an actor put the profession back several decades. Respectability would not fully arrive until the twentieth century and then it was usually in the more open-minded cities like New York.

Theatre in the city for many years and by the Depression it was the only legit house in town. Baltimore was also an important tryout and touring stop during the twentieth century but it would not produce its own professional theater productions again until the 1960s. Washington, D.C., being a much younger city than the others previously discussed, did not have a strong cultural tradition and the growing metropolis was never considered a very sophisticated town when it came to the arts. Ford converted a Baptist church into a theater in 1861 and called it Ford's Theatre and it was an impressive house that seated 1700 patrons. But its future was cut short four years later when President Lincoln was assassinated there and the building was closed. It was used for various activities and would not re-open as a performance space until 1986. The most successful playhouse in Washington was the National Theatre, first constructed in 1835 and rebuilt after a series of fires. It was a major touring and tryout house in the twentieth century and the closest thing the capital city had to a performing arts facility until the Kennedy Center was built in 1971.

NEW YORK CITY THEATER HISTORY

The first permanent playhouse built in the city was the John Street Theatre in lower Manhattan in 1767. It was modeled after Philadelphia's Southwark Theatre, which in turn had been inspired by the kind of playhouses being built in London at the time. The John Street was the only Manhattan theater for thirty-one years and, when the Park Theatre was erected in 1798, it was demolished. The need for only one theater in the growing town illustrates that New York was behind Philadelphia when it came to the arts. But as the city expanded northward, new theaters were built until an actual district was created. By 1894 there were thirty-nine operating theaters in New York; add to this number the many vaudeville houses, concert halls, and theater restaurants and one sees that the largest city in the country was also becoming the center for many of the arts as well. It was in the first decade of the twentieth century that the Broadway district settled in the Longacre (now Times) Square area where it was not unusual to find a half dozen playhouses on one block and for over 200 plays and musicals to open in one season. The widespread use of electric lights on the theaters' marquees and rooftop signs fostered the expression "the Great White Way," and it was indeed a bright and optimistic place. Most of the Broadway theaters still used today were built during the boom time between 1903 and 1929. The peak of this golden age came during the 1927–1928 season, during which 270 shows opened. The busiest night in the history of Broadway was December 26, 1927, when nine new works premiered. The prosperity of the Roaring Twenties fueled other arts as well, such as the silent film industry, but in New York it was theater that was triumphant. But it was an elitist pastime, to be sure. While the top theater ticket price right after the Civil War was around $1.50 and you could get the best theater seats between 1900 and World War I for $2.00, the average top price was $6.00 by 1925. Of course, there were still tickets that went as low as 35¢ in the second balcony so, in its own way, theater was more accessible then than it is today.

The Depression and the arrival of talking movies put an end to the building of theaters and the glory days of Broadway. The number of productions dropped (from 270 in 1926–1927 to 155 in 1935–1936) and continued to drop until a total of over thirty works on Broadway today is considered healthy. As audiences for live theater dwindled (vaudeville would disappear by the end of the 1930s), some legit playhouses were turned into movie theaters, others became storefronts, and some were demolished. During World War II, the theater in New York gathered some steam from the end of the Depression and the new wartime prosperity. The 1950s are considered a golden age of sorts for the Broadway musical and many of the most revived shows today came from that decade. In the 1970s a few new theaters were built and by the late 1990s some of the playhouses long neglected were restored and returned to live theater.

In the late 1940s, there was enough demand for live theater that "Off Broadway" was born. This alternative to the Great White Way consisted of smaller theaters, usually seating less than 500 patrons, that were spread across Manhattan, many of them in Greenwich Village. There had been a tradition of "little theaters" in New York, such as the Provincetown Playhouse, the Neighborhood Playhouse, and the Washington Square Players, that provided experimental and more challenging fare since the 1910s. But Off Broadway was a popular movement that offered new works, revivals, and smart little musical revues at lower prices and in a less formal setting. Up-and-coming playwrights, such as Arthur Kopit (b. 1937) and Edward Albee (b. 1928), first made their mark Off Broadway, as did many actors, directors, and designers. By 1970 the number of Off-Broadway productions far outnumbered those on Broadway, but with success came higher prices and (many felt) too much conformity in an effort to make money. So in the 1970s, "Off Off Broadway" was formed, though it was more a scattered presence that a unified effort. These productions were often not even presented in theaters but rather in warehouses, churches, storefronts, community centers, and other "found" spaces. Seating was often less than one hundred, budgets were low, production values sparse, and most operated as nonprofit ventures. What was consistent was the tone of Off Off Broadway. The plays and musicals were definitely experimental and often advocated specific causes or philosophies. Many presented only new works and some concentrated on themes or issues, such as antiwar plays, feminist works, gay and lesbian drama, or Hispanic, African American, and Asian points of view. Off Off Broadway was also a potent training ground for playwrights, such as Sam Shepard (b. 1943), whose work was first noticed there. If a production found success, its contract might be rewritten to become an Off-Broadway production without even changing spaces. And there were the occasional Off- and Off-Off-Broadway successes, such as *Hair* (1968), *That Championship Season* (1972), and *A Chorus Line* (1975), that transferred all the way to the Great White Way and found favor.

As the regional theater movement grew across the country, New York had its own version in the number of nonprofit theater companies that had been developing since the 1950s. The most famous was the New York Shakespeare Festival that Joe Papp (1921–1991) founded in 1954 to present free productions of the classics in Central Park during the summer. The organization grew to include a year-round season at the Public Theater and tours that traveled to schools and neighborhoods in the city's other boroughs. Also with a long track record is the Roundabout Theatre, founded in 1965 and situated in various venues over the years until it ended up with houses both on Broadway and off Broadway. While the Public Theatre concentrated on new plays and musicals, the Roundabout was interested in revivals so its offerings were rarely innovative. But both companies brought a quality of theater that rivaled the for-profit offerings. Lincoln Center Theatre, another distinguished nonprofit enterprise, was founded in 1964 and experienced many years of instability artistically and financially until the 1990s, when it finally emerged as one of the city's finest institutions. Other troupes, in Manhattan and Brooklyn, enjoyed popularity and acclaim for a time but the nature of aggressive experimentation in theater usually meant a limited life-span and many memorable companies failed to find the longevity of the previously discussed theaters. One of the more durable was the Circle Repertory Company, an Off-Broadway group that presented several outstanding works during its lifetime of 1969 to 1996. The company was most known for presenting the works of playwright Lanford Wilson (b. 1937), usually directed by Marshall W. Mason (b. 1940) and utilizing the same core of actors season after season. Another influential troupe was the Negro Ensemble Theatre, which between 1967 and 1999 presented potent African American plays and provided a home for outstanding black actors and directors, such as cofounder Douglas Turner Ward (b. 1930).

By the 1980s most of the entries on Broadway did not originate on the Great White Way but instead came from Off Broadway, Off Off Broadway, nonprofit companies, and regional theater. Broadway may well have been the most publicly acclaimed showcase for American theater but little of what it exhibited was homegrown. Even the splashy, spectacular musicals that could not be created in smaller theaters often arrived on Broadway after being developed in London, Toronto, Los Angeles, and elsewhere. Broadway musicals used to try out in major cities while getting ready for New York. By the 1990s these musicals had to be a finished, polished hit before Broadway would even consider taking them in. Perhaps the heart of the American theater was no longer in Manhattan. Maybe no one city could accurately represent the complexity of American theater. If so, then one had to look to the regional theater network.

Regional Theater in the Mid-Atlantic States

When the number of Broadway offerings shrank in the 1930s, the touring business suffered and many major and small American cities saw very little professional theater. Community theaters, which had proliferated since the 1920s, filled the gap and some, such as the Cleveland Play House, the Pasadena Playhouse, and the Pittsburgh Playhouse, developed into semiprofessional "little theaters" that were a mark above the amateur productions seen in schools and community centers. But cities with noteworthy cultural assets felt that professional theater should be part of the landscape and the regional (or resident) theater movement began in the 1950s. These organizations were nonprofit and subsidized by local government and businesses. They hired directors, designers, and actors from New York to guarantee a high level of professionalism. A half dozen or so plays were presented in a season that ran from September to May and each production was assured a month-long run regardless of reviews or box office activity. Actors were hired for the season and, along with the staff, became residents of the theater and the community for the duration. Some companies, such as the American Conservatory Theatre in San Francisco, performed productions in repertory, changing the bill frequently to offer a constant variety of offerings. Because each theater company chose its plays with its region and local patrons in mind, the resident theaters were indeed American in a way that Broadway could never be.

The most noteworthy regional theaters in the mid-Atlantic states include the Arena Stage in Washington, Center Stage in Baltimore, Studio Arena Theatre in Buffalo, McCarter Theatre in Princeton, Geva Theatre in Rochester, Delaware Theatre Company in Wilmington, George Street Playhouse in New Brunswick, New Jersey, Philadelphia Theatre Company, Pittsburgh Public Theatre, Syracuse Stage, Shakespeare Theatre in Washington, and the long-running Walnut Street Theatre in Philadelphia. In addition to many others, the region has a number of professional or semiprofessional summer Shakespeare Festivals, such as the New Jersey Shakespeare Festival in Madison, the Pennsylvania Shakespeare Festival in Allentown, and the aforementioned New York Shakespeare Festival in Manhattan.

Regional theater productions started to outnumber New York City offerings in the 1980s and the pattern has not reversed itself. What has changed direction is the flow of new work. It is more economical to try out new plays and musicals regionally before attempting a Manhattan production, so resident theaters have become a resource for New York City theater, the opposite of the past, when the regions awaited the latest offerings from Manhattan.

By the 1990s funding from both government and industry decreased and most regional theaters were forced to adjust. The expensive repertory system had long since been dropped by all but a few theaters as it was more practical to hire actors for each production rather than a whole season. This meant the "resident" aspect of the theaters was lost. Risky new works were given in small, alternative spaces while popular, small-cast plays in the larger theaters were more financially feasible. Also by the end of the century, the offerings of one regional theater were pretty much like those in another so the individual flavor of the theaters was sometimes missing. Yet the regional theater movement still survives and continues to present much of the most satisfying theater in America.

How the Theater Portrayed New York City

It might be an exaggeration to state that most American plays and musicals are written by New Yorkers about New York for New York audiences but there is more than a little truth in it. So many works over the past 150 years have been set in the Manhattan that one starts to wonder if theater is an urban art form. *The Contrast* (1787), considered to be the first American play to be presented with professional actors, was about the New Yorker Dimple who was such an anglophile that he had to be given his comeuppance by the rugged Jonathan the Yankee. The contrast dealt with citified ways versus rural behavior as much as the difference between British and American behavior and the early comedy set a pattern for many subsequent plays (and later movies). The city was elegant and cultured but also a bit suspect and artificial; the

The Arena Stage in the Nation's Capital

Since Washington had long been considered a cultural vacuum, it is surprising that one of the first and best regional theaters started there and it remains one of the nation's outstanding companies. The Arena Stage was founded in 1950 by a handful of associates from George Washington University, led by Professor Edward Mangum, and gave its first performances in an old movie house in which the seats were arranged "in the round." In 1956 the company moved into a former brewery and retained the arena arrangement. As audiences grew and funds were obtained from government and local companies, the Arena built its modern facility on 6th Street and Maine Avenue in 1961. The primary theater space is a square stage with the audience on all four sides but it includes entrances from beneath the spectators, a sophisticated series of lifts to change the acting area, and a complex lighting system that the unconventional auditorium requires. In 1970 two other spaces were added: a modified thrust stage called the Kreeger and an intimate cabaretlike facility named the Old Vat Room. Starting in the 1960s, the Arena boasted some of the finest American actors among its resident performers and its productions were favorably compared to Broadway. Much of the success of the company was credited to Zelda Fichandler (b. 1924), one of the cofounders and the theater's artistic director until 1991. Under her supervision, the Arena's reputation grew and some of its productions transferred directly to Broadway, most memorably *The Great White Hope* (1967), *Indians* (1969), and *Moonchildren* (1971). Since Fichandler's departure, the company has continued to excel and in 2003 plans were announced for a multimillion-dollar renovation and addition to the performance facility. In many ways the Arena is the model regional theater. It presents a wide variety of productions, from classic revivals to new works; its in-house and outreach programs unite it with the community; and its world-class productions illustrate the diversity and quality of American theater with no ties to Broadway.

Scene from the play *The Great White Hope* (1967) which originally opened at the Arena Stage in Washington, D.C., but soon transferred directly to Broadway. Photofest.

country was honest and noble. Yet most plays were set in the city. A similar kind of contrast can be seen in *A Glance at New York* (1848), in which a country bumpkin arrives in the city and encounters con-men and crooks, only to be saved by the gruff but honest fireman Mose. *Fashion; or Life in New York* (1845), a satire that broke the record for the longest-running play on Broadway, lampooned the ways the social-climbing Mrs. Tiffany puts on airs by speaking bad French and trying to marry her daughter off to a phony count. All three comedies were very popular in New York and in other cities; in fact, *A Glance at New York* was often rewritten for productions in Philadelphia and other large cities, changing the locale in each case but not the jokes. So the New York play was established even before Manhattan became the theater capital.

By the end of the nineteenth century, dramas set in New York were also quite common. The city had become a symbol of the extreme ends of the social spectrum and plays explored the dark, undesirable side of Manhattan whereas comedies had looked mostly at the upper crust. There were many sentimental melodramas on the theme of poverty in the city but a few efforts rose above the cheap theatrics of the genre, such as *Bertha, the Sewing Machine Girl* (1906). Perhaps the best of the early problem dramas was Edward Sheldon's *Salvation Nell* (1908). Nell is a scrub woman in love with a hot-tempered man who beats her. When he is sent to jail for killing a man, she is destitute but, rather than take up prostitution, she joins the Salvation Army and finds the strength to turn both her life around and others' as well. As one critic noted at the time, "The intent is not to entertain us with the disagreeable or to make us acquainted with vice for our amusement." As the American theater slowly matured, so did the New York play.

Eugene O'Neill (1888–1953) is generally considered the greatest of American playwrights and his developing talent mirrored the rise of native drama. O'Neill was very familiar with both ends of the New York spectrum and wrote about each with power and accuracy. Even before he started writing full-length plays, his short dramas captured the urban character. His early one-act *The Dreamy Kid* (1919), for example, focused on an African American youth fleeing from the law after he has murdered a man. The city seems to close in on the boy even as the white authorities surround him. O'Neill concentrated on full-length plays after 1920 and his early drama *Anna Christie* (1921) re-created the grimy waterfront saloons of the city as he dramatized the unlikely romance between a former prostitute and a sailor who believes her to be purity itself. On the other hand, O'Neill used wealthy New Yorkers to convey his ideas in the expressionistic *The Great God Brown* (1926) and the psychological *Strange Interlude* (1928). He would return to a Manhattan setting near the end of his career with the naturalistic *The Iceman Cometh* (1946), an unsentimental look at a group of aimless New Yorkers who cling to their illusions at Harry Hope's bar. When the traveling salesman Hickey prods them into acting on their "pipe dreams," they make an effort to go out and set themselves right. But the real world is too much for them and they soon return to Harry's to find out that Hickey himself is nothing but a lie, having murdered the wife he loved so much. It is one of O'Neill's richest plays and one that makes valiant efforts to capture the many kinds of urban despair. While he cannot be categorized simply as a New York playwright (many of his works are set in New England), O'Neill demonstrated that a play about the city could reach beyond geographic boundaries.

The turbulent 1930s produced many of the best dramas set in New York City. Several of America's finest playwrights were at their peak in the Depression years and many of them wrote about the city they knew best. Elmer Rice (1892–1967) was a native New Yorker who often portrayed his hometown on stage, sometimes expressionistically, as with *The Adding Machine* (1929) and *Dream Girl* (1945), and other times naturalistically, as with *Counsellor-at-Law* (1931) and *Street Scene* (1939). The later is one of the most accomplished of all New York City plays, with its many vibrant characters and acute sense of locale. A block of brownstones has deteriorated into a packed tenement where people of various ethnic backgrounds live in view of their neighbors. The play is more a panorama of city life than a single, straightforward plot. Much happens in the drama—a Jewish boy falls in love with an Irish girl, a Broadway dandy tries to pick up an innocent woman, a jealous husband murders his unfaithful wife—but it is always the neighborhood itself that is the main character and the focus of the piece. A similar effect was achieved in Sidney Kingsley's *Dead End* (1935), which went even further, showing the wealthy in the penthouses above and the struggling classes in the tenements along the river. The naturalistic piece even had construction workers erecting a new building in the wings and street urchins jumping into the river in the orchestra pit. Again there were many vibrant characters and plenty of action (including the gunning down of a racketeer who returns to his old neighborhood to see his mother) but the drama was really about that dead end street.

Not as atmospheric but just as potent were other 1930s plays that grew out of the New York City temperament. Clifford Odets (1906–1963) was one of the era's most controversial playwrights with his left-wing sensibility and disturbing portrayals of desperate New Yorkers. The inflammatory *Waiting for Lefty* (1935) looked at various people in oppressed circumstances, all leading up to a strike of taxi cab drivers. *Awake and Sing!* (1935) was one of the first American plays to look at a Jewish family without comedy or cliché. The struggling Berger household is losing its self-dignity because of the mother's efforts for their survival. In a city full of vitality, the family is suffocating itself and only through a grandfather's suicide can the young hero find the means to break out and live. Another youth sought freedom through a boxing career in *Golden Boy* (1937) and, years later, Odets explored the idea of recapturing lost glory in *The Country Girl* (1950). In each case New York was more than the setting for the play; it was often the antagonist.

Of Broadway's two most prominent dramatic writers of the 1940s and 1950s, Tennessee Williams (1911–1983) and Arthur Miller (b. 1915), the latter used New York as the setting for several of his works. A native of Manhattan, Miller was most interested in the common man and his place in an uncaring society. His masterwork, *Death of a Salesman* (1949), depicts the traveling salesman Willy Loman who peddles his wares in New England but returns home to New York where he never seems to get ahead. His wayward son Biff goes out West to fulfill his dreams but returns to his New York home broken and disillusioned. The city, like Willy himself, encourages one to talk big, be well liked, and grab success by the throat. The fact that it doesn't work is a reflection on New York as well as Willy's American dream. In Miller's view, the city is the perfect setting for tragedy; hopes are dashed

A scene from Arthur Miller's Broadway play *Death of a Salesman*, with Kate Reid, John Malkovich, Stephen Lang, and Dustin Hoffman. Photofest.

there quicker than anywhere else. He returned to New York in several of his later plays, such as the short but evocative *A Memory of Two Mondays* (1955), set in a warehouse where various employees deal with disillusion, *A View from the Bridge* (1955), dealing with illegal Italian immigrants and their relatives in the city, *The Price* (1968), in which two brothers from different social spheres confront each other, and *The American Clock* (1980), which paints a panoramic picture of various New Yorkers during the Depression. There were many contemporaries of Miller who also depicted the city on stage. Two works are of particular interest: Sidney Kingsley (1906–1995), who had written the atmospheric *Dead End* in the 1930s, provided another lucid glimpse into New York life with *Detective Story* (1949), set in the 21st Precinct Police Station. The central story concerned a hard-boiled detective who could not separate personal beliefs from the law but the drama was propelled by the shoplifters, lawyers, burglars, and other citizens whose lives spilled into the station. Years later a similar microcosm was seen in William Alfred's *Hogan's Goat* (1965), which peopled its plot about Brooklyn politics in 1890 with Irish immigrants, civic subordinates, and individuals grasping for public office as a way of proving their self worth. Like some of Miller's New York plays, they depicted a cruel and uncaring city.

This is not to imply that comic playwrights had stopped using the city for their settings. Comedies were rarely set in tenements but instead continued in the traditions of the nineteenth century by satirizing the upper classes. Philip Barry (1896–1949) did it with wit in *Holiday* (1928) and Clare Boothe (Luce) (1903–1987) managed it with venom in *The Women* (1936), to point out two superior examples. The millionaires in *Holiday* are a bit stuffy, take their money for granted, and strive to maintain the status quo. When a young, ambitious stockbroker attempts to upset the system by quitting and enjoying life after he has made his bundle, shock waves result. The wealthy wives in *The Women*, on the other hand, take nothing for granted and money is just a by-product of feminine power. The former comedy is set on conservative Fifth Avenue; the latter takes place mostly on trendy Park Avenue. Both plays are accurately funny as well as strictly New York. George S. Kaufman (1889–1961) and his various collaborators found humor with other levels of New York society: show business types in *The Butter and Egg Man* (1925), *The Royal Family* (1927), and *June Moon* (1929), artists in *Beggar on Horseback* (1924) and *Merrily We Roll Along* (1934), and big business with *The Solid Gold Cadillac* (1953). But arguably Kaufman's best work, *You Can't Take It with You* (1936), written with Moss Hart (1904–1961), may also be his most "New York" play. The middle-class Vanderhof family is eccentric to the point of creating a loving, optimistic world that defies the city that surrounds it. Tax collectors, G-men, and stuffy business types invade the family's territory only to be thwarted by the good-natured Vanderhofs and their happy extended family. The comedy is both affectionate and more than a little anarchic in what it says about conforming to society. The result is a New York play that defies the city and triumphs.

Comedies set in Manhattan were less visible in the 1940s and 1950s but 1961 introduced the American theater's quintessential writer of urban comedy: Neil Simon (b. 1927). A Brooklyn native who began writing for radio and television, Simon made his Broadway debut with *Come Blow Your Horn* (1961) and followed it with three decades of mostly hits that were not only set in New York but were peopled by colorful urban types that were uniquely New York. Sometimes the characters were Jewish, such as the family who makes its fortune manufacturing artificial fruit in *Come Blow Your Horn* or the Depression-era Brooklynites in *Brighton Beach Memoirs* (1983), who are as endearing as they are dysfunctional. But Simon goes beyond ethnic humor and explores all kinds of New Yorkers, from the wisecracking poker players in *The Odd Couple* (1965) to the self-deluding misfits in *The Gingerbread Lady* (1970). Sometimes the city is a romantic valentine, as in *Barefoot in the Park* (1963); other times it is where lovers are forced to evaluate themselves, as with *Chapter Two* (1977). Many of Simon's works edge very close to tragedy but his outlook is basically comic and forgiving. Perhaps the archtypal New York comedy-drama is *The Prisoner of Second Avenue* (1971), in which Simon travels the fine line between jokes and heartbreak. The upper-middle-class couple in the play humorously complain about the ways the city infringes on their sanity but when the problems become major (theft, unemployment, and even paranoia), the comedy takes on an edge and humor becomes their only weapon for dealing with their crumbling lives. Every New Yorker could empathize with *The Prisoner of Second Avenue*, as well as enough others to make the play a hit in other cities. While Simon dominated Broadway comedies for some time, some mention must be made of other comic writers who vividly portrayed New York on stage. Jules Feiffer's *Little Murders* (1967), for example, explored the violence of the city and turned it into a dark farce in which killing is the antidote for those suffering from loss. John Guare (b. 1938) wrote two notable plays about New York, both also dark comedies. *The House of Blue Leaves* (1971) looked at a wacky Queens household where everyone has glorious ambitions: the father wants to be an Oscar-winning songwriter, his AWOL son wants to assassinate the Pope, his mistress wants marriage, and his wife wants her sanity back. No one sees his or her dream fulfilled (in fact, some are dead by the final curtain) but the plucky, never-say-die attitude of the characters is essentially a New York sentiment, pushed here to the extreme. Guare's *Six Degrees of Separation* (1990), on the other hand, deals with a wealthy Manhattan couple who have had their dreams come true yet find how empty their lives are when an intruder, a young African American con-man, briefly disrupts their self-satisfied existence. It is a disturbing comedy that suggests that the lines that separate different levels of New York society are more tenuous than previously thought.

Because the city has been a melting pot for various ethnic and special interest groups since the decade after the Civil War, New York plays have long depicted different races and religions, though not always were they written by members of the group in question. African American characters, for example, had appeared on the New York stage as early as 1769 with *The Padlock* but black playwrights would not become commonplace until the 1960s. While Asian and Hispanic plays have also been in evidence, rarely did they take place in Manhattan. But African American plays often did and the depiction of blacks in the city over the years has provided some exceptional theater. The pioneering Lafayette Players, which flourished in Harlem from 1915 to 1928, presented works written by African Americans and the Negro Theatre, part of the Federal Theatre project in the 1930s, put black actors in both classical and contemporary roles. Two Broadway hits, both written by white authors, attempted to portray a realistic, unsentimental view of African Americans in the city. *Lulu Belle* (1926) concerned a Harlem streetwalker who brings tragedy to the man who loves her, just as the heroine of

Anna Lucasta (1944) is forced to become a prostitute in Brooklyn but is saved by the love of her sweetheart from rural Pennsylvania. The fact that a black female could most capture the attention of white audiences if she was a fallen woman speaks volumes for the racial attitudes of the day. In fact, Lulu was even played by a white actress in blackface. It was not until the era of the civil rights movement that African Americans were depicted with more complexity and honesty on stage. *Dutchman* (1964), a short but powerful drama by Amiri Baraka (b. LeRoi Jones in 1934), best represents this change. A black intellectual is taunted and aroused by a seductive blonde on a Manhattan subway train until the encounter explodes and she kills him. Written by an African American, the play was an angry reaction to the past in which the victim was usually a black female. Two dramas from the late 1960s, also by black playwrights, were also potent pictures of African American life in the city. *No Place to Be Somebody* (1967), by Charles Gordone (1925–1995), was a poetic piece about various white and black patrons of a Manhattan bar whose frustrations are both racial and psychological. It was the first play by an African American to win the Pulitzer Prize and marked a new level for personal and insightful rather than political black drama. *Ceremonies in Dark Old Men* (1969), by Lonnie Elder III (1931–1996), concerned a Harlem family who are torn apart by the desire to make a fortune selling bootleg whiskey. It too avoided stereotypes and presented its issues poetically and honestly. Many African American plays of varying quality followed in the subsequent decades, a good number of them set in New York. A recent example that illustrates the many offspring of these two 1960s dramas is *Topdog/Underdog* (2001), by Suzan-Lori Parks (b. 1963). Two brothers, ironically named Lincoln and Booth, are rivals yet are deeply bound to each other emotionally. Lincoln has a job dressing up as Honest Abe in a Coney Island carnival where patrons get to "shoot" him. By the end of the play, tensions mount and Booth kills his brother for real. The allegorical play moves a long way from the gritty realism of *Ceremonies in Dark Old Men* but continues in a tradition of dramas about African Americans in the city.

While there have been some notable New York feminist plays and works about women—Wendy Wasserstein's *Isn't It Romantic* (1983) and *The Heidi Chronicles* (1988) are outstanding examples—the city's gay culture has been more extensively represented on the stage. Most plays dealing with homosexuals are set in New York, beginning with the groundbreaking *The Boys in the Band* in 1968. While this comedy-drama about a group of gay New Yorkers gathered for a birthday party is now considered to be stereotypic and more sensational than revealing, in its day it was a frank, unapologetic depiction of a culture that had rarely been glimpsed at in a mainstream theater. It was followed by many other gay plays of divergent quality and the somewhat-new genre quickly matured. Terrence McNally (b. 1939) approached the subject as farce in *The Ritz* (1975), a raucous comedy set in a gay steambath, and as tragicomedy in *The Lisbon Traviata* (1985), a dark piece about destructive gay relationships. The epic chronicle *Torch Song Trilogy* (1982), by Harvey Fierstein (b. 1954), was one of the richest (and most successful) works in the genre, following the life and loves of a New York drag queen. With the onset of the AIDS epidemic in the 1980s, many angry or sentimental New York plays were written about how it affected the gay community. But some works rose above the norm and were provocative rather than merely provoking. Larry Kramer's *The Normal Heart* (1985) took an argumentative, political viewpoint while William M.

Hoffman's *As Is* (1985) concentrated on the personal effects of the disease on the victims and those who loved them. Although it was about much more than AIDS and homosexual lifestyle, the two-part *Angels in America* (1993), by Tony Kushner (b. 1958), might be called the definitive New York gay play. Exploring both the institutional and personal aspects of Manhattan's largest subculture, the ambitious work best captured the difficult, complicated, and vibrant tapestry of New York on stage. The social, financial, racial, and political diversity of the city comes alive in *Angels in America*.

The New York Musical

It is estimated that almost half of the Broadway musicals written after 1920 take place in New York City. When the new genre of the musical was first introduced with *The Black Crook* in 1866, the setting was exotic and most of the early musical extravaganzas and later the operettas were set in distant, fanciful places far from the sound of city traffic. But in the Roaring Twenties the location of choice was Manhattan with its nightclubs, penthouses, and restaurants as ideal settings for musical comedy. The popular "Cinderella" musicals, such as *Irene* (1919) and *Sally* (1920), had their heroines sewing in Manhattan tenements or washing dishes in Greenwich Village until they broke into high society and found love and fame. The Gershwin musicals, such as *Lady, Be Good!* (1924) and *Funny Face* (1927), took place on the streets of New York, while Rodgers and Hart's *On Your Toes* (1936) and *I'd Rather Be Right* (1937) used Broadway and Central Park for its romance and comedy. Sometimes the New York of the past was evoked, as in *Dearest Enemy* (1925), set during the Revolutionary War, *Knickerbocker Holiday* (1938), concerning Pieter Stuyvesant's New Amsterdam, or *Up in Central Park* (1945), with Boss Tweed and his cronies in the 1870s. Two of the most celebratory musicals about the city were written by Leonard Bernstein (1918–1990), Betty Comden (b. 1915), and Adolph Green (1915–2003): *On the Town* (1944) saw Manhattan through the eyes of three sailors on twenty-four-hour leave while *Wonderful Town* (1953) took the viewpoint of two sisters from Ohio trying to find success and romance in the scary, exhilarating city. By the 1950s and 1960s, several musicals took a nostalgic or a romanticized view of New York, as with the cockeyed gamblers in *Guys and Dolls* (1950), the starry-eyed couple in *Bells Are Ringing* (1956), the fond portrait of beloved Mayor LaGuardia in *Fiorello!* (1959), the cartoonish world of big corporations in *How to Succeed in Business Without Really Trying* (1961), the sunny view of the gay 1890s with *Hello, Dolly!* (1964), and the rhythmic, contemporary world of *Sweet Charity* (1966). Even protest musicals, such as *Hair* (1968) and *Two Gentlemen of Verona* (1971), used New York locations in order to bring their point to the theater district. Yet sometimes the city was used as a cruel or demanding antagonist in the story, as with the poverty of *A Tree Grows in Brooklyn* (1951), the gang warfare of *West Side Story* (1957), the neurotic tension of the metropolis in *Company* (1970), and the Bohemian squalor of *Rent* (1996). But during the last decades of the century (and into the new one), New York was usually portrayed as a hopeful and carefree place, as witnessed by such musicals as *Annie* (1977), *42nd Street* (1980), *The Producers* (2001), and *Thoroughly Modern Millie* (2002). It looks like the Broadway musical will continue to favor its own city as the setting in which it can best express itself.

Theater in Other Urban Centers

Quite clearly, fewer plays and musicals were set in the other metropolitan areas of the mid-Atlantic states than in New York City. And of the ones that were, only a few captured the temperament of the individual cities. It seems that playwrights often used such cities as Baltimore or Pittsburgh as a setting when they needed a generic urban location outside of Manhattan. But on occasion a city's character shone through and the unique flavor of the location was evident on stage. Washington, D.C., for example, was often pictured as a haven for corrupt or comic politics. The legendary musical satire *Of Thee I Sing!* (1931) was one of the first and best works to portray Washington as the home of slick double-talk, phony campaign platforms, party rivalry, and shenanigans not only in the White House and Congress but in the Supreme Court as well. It was a broad musical comedy that knew how to exaggerate the truth and still be truthful. Three later plays looked at backroom politics with a more serious but still cynical eye. Howard Lindsay and Russel Crouse's *The State of the Union* was a gentle comedy that had a very serious subtext. The Republicans want a certain idealistic industrialist to run for president but it looks like he'll have to compromise most of those ideals in order to win; he finally listens to his conscience and withdraws from the race. Another idealist was the focus of Jerome Lawrence and Robert E. Lee's *The Gang's All Here* (1959). This candidate swallows his pride and trusts the "gang" of politicos who elect him, only to find himself deep in scandal so he commits suicide. Gore Vidal's *The Best Man* (1960) is perhaps the most complex of the Washington plays. He manages to convey the whole political spectrum on stage, from the old school liberals who play at government like gentlemen to the unscrupulous, righteous power-mongers who can only rise by destroying the reputations of others. Vidal's view of Washington is not as bleak as it is unflinching and the tone of the city's major industry vividly comes to life on stage. Not about politicians but just as back-stabbing is Garson Kanin's comedy *Born Yesterday* (1946), in which a corrupt junk-yard mogul comes to Washington to continue his rounds of bribes and payoffs of government officials. He is undone by his seemingly bubble-headed mistress who discovers her power after her sugar daddy tries to educate her. International politics were behind Lillian Hellman's powerful wartime drama *Watch on the Rhine* (1941), in which the struggle for control of Germany is played out in a Washington mansion where a Nazi aristocrat and a German refugee are both guests. Again the District of Columbia location gives the play its impetus. Then there are a few stage works that used the Washington setting arbitrarily, such as the musical fantasy *Damn Yankees* (1955), in which a pact with the devil for baseball fame seems to be funnier in a city where politicians often seem to be selling their souls.

A handful of works set in Philadelphia also manage to put the city's character on stage. Its rich history has generally been neglected, only the musical *1776* (1969), about the ratification and signing of the Declaration of Independence, finding wide popularity. But two comedies of manners were quite successful in presenting pre–World War II Philadelphia life. George Kelly's *The Show-Off* (1924) depicted the middle class with a wry affection, from the caustic mother of the household to her dreamy inventor-son to her bragging, ostentatious son-in-law. Philip Barry's *The Philadelphia Story* (1939), set in the city's suburban Main Line, looked at the upper class with a similar warmth. A spoiled heiress finds her affections divided among her stuffy fiancée with old money, a no-nonsense writer not in her social set, and her knowing ex-husband. It's the kind of society comedy that would not be quite the same if set in New York or any other city with money and that makes it a unique Philadelphia piece. Much later in the century were two accomplished works about the city that concentrated on less lofty families. Albert Innaurato's dark comedy *Gemini* (1977) was about a blue-collar worker in the Italian neighborhood in South Philly and what happens when his son brings two of his WASP friends home from college. The ethnic humor was both hilarious and accurate and the social complications were mixed with sexual ones with farcical results. An opposite temperament was found in August Wilson's penetrating drama *Fences* (1987), set in a black Philadelphia neighborhood in the 1950s. The blue collar worker this time is a garbage truck driver who once was a major baseball player in the Negro Leagues. His bright, athletic son is college material but, unlike the Italian son who mixes with the upper classes, this African American youth is denied a similar future because his father forbids it, knowing the pain of trying to succeed in the white man's world. In both plays there seems to be a fence around the ramshackle Philadelphia neighborhood and to venture outside of it is to court disaster.

Baltimore was considered little more than a good tryout town by New York theater people. How understandable that the city's major depiction on Broadway was as the setting for *Kiss Me, Kate* (1948), a musical about a Broadway show trying out in Baltimore. Many years later the city would be better captured on stage in another musical, *Hairspray* (2002), although it would be a cartoonish, nostalgic look at the town during the early 1960s rather than any attempt at an all-encompassing view of the city. The most noteworthy nonmusical about Baltimore was Lanford Wilson's *The Hot l Baltimore* (1973), an engrossing comedy-drama about the residents and employees of a crumbling downtown hotel. (The title comes from the broken sign with its missing "e.") The once glorious establishment is located near the main train station but when the fortunes of the passenger railroad dwindled so did the hotel, now the home of prostitutes, limited-income residents, and transients. Because the building is meant to represent the deteriorating downtown of all major American cities there is little in the play that is specific to Baltimore. Once again the city was not specifically rendered on stage. The same might be said for Pittsburgh, another mid-Atlantic city that rarely was used as the setting for plays until the 1980s. Even the prolific playwright George S. Kaufman, who was born in the Pennsylvania city, neglected to use it in any of his many comedies and musicals. But a theatrical renaissance of sorts arrived when native August Wilson (b. 1945), an African American poet-turned-playwright, wrote a series of dramas that dealt with black neighborhoods in Pittsburgh. As part of an ambitious ten-play cycle about African Americans during the twentieth century, Wilson set his already-mentioned *Fences* in Philadelphia but most of the other entries were about his home town. *Joe Turner's Come and Gone* (1988) looked at the residents of a Pittsburgh boarding house in the 1910s, *The Piano Lesson* (1990) concerned a Pittsburgh family in the 1930s torn by ghosts from the past, *Seven Guitars* (1996) was the tragic tale of the 1940s set in the city's Hill District, *Two Trains Running* (1992) viewed the residents of a soon-to-be-regentrified neighborhood in the turbulent 1960s, and *Jitney* (2000) was an incisive character study about the employees of a gypsy cab company. By the end of the century Wilson was acclaimed the

American theater's most prolific and awarded African American playwright. How distinctive of him that he did it without setting his plays in New York City.

The Rural Region on Stage

Just as much of the country often forgets that there is more to New York State than the "city," so too the theater has usually neglected the upstate counties and rarely used them for settings in plays, but the exceptions are sometimes interesting and noteworthy. James Fenimore Cooper's popular novel *The Spy*, set in the state's "Leatherstocking" region, became in 1822 the first hit play based on an American novel. An early effort by producer-playwright William Dunlap (1766–1839) called *A Trip to Niagara; or, Travellers in America* (1928) featured panoramic settings of rural New York, climaxing at the Falls, while Richard Penn Smith's *The Triumph at Plattsburg* (1930) was a romantic comedy-drama set upstate during the then-recent War of 1812. Washington Irving's tales set in the Catskill Mountains became *Rip Van Winkle* (1866), one of the most beloved and revived comedies of the nineteenth century. *David Harum* (1900), based on a bestselling book, was a whimsical play about a colorful horse trader and small-town life in the Finger Lakes region. The Catskills were the locale again in 1937 for the comedy *Having Wonderful Time*, which was turned into the Broadway musical *Wish You Were Here* (1952). Another successful musical, *Bloomer Girl* (1944), was about the early days of the Women's Rights Movement in Seneca Falls. So New York State was not totally forgotten.

Unfortunately the same cannot be said for West Virginia and Delaware, which were pretty much dismissed by the stage. Maryland can boast one very popular melodrama, David Belasco's Civil War romance *The Heart of Maryland* (1895), in which a Southern belle called Maryland Calvert helps rescue her sweetheart when the Union army comes upon her Maryland plantation. It was a thrilling piece, climaxing with Maryland climbing the bell tower and hanging on to the huge clapper in order to silence the signal to the troops, but it shed little light on the state itself which remained with the North during the war. Theater saw New Jersey as a suburb of Manhattan and that is how it appeared in the farce *Three Men on a Horse* (1935) and in Thornton Wilder's allegorical *The Skin of Our Teeth* (1942). In the former play a shy greeting-card poet lives a quiet life in Ozone Heights but gets mixed up with big-city horseracing racketeers and his serenity is jolted. In Wilder's expressionistic piece, the hero lives in Excelsior and commutes to the city where he invents things like the wheel and the alphabet. In both plays chaos ensues and the hero ends up in suburban New Jersey, the theater's idea of a happy, unexciting ending. Pennsylvania's diverse regions have been somewhat represented by historical works, such as *Valley Forge* (1934), bucolic pieces, as with the musical *Plain and Fancy* (1955), about the Amish in Pennsylvania Dutch country, and contemporary dramas, most memorably Jason Miller's *That Championship Season* (1972), about small-city politics and disillusions set in the Lackawanna Valley. But these examples aside, the rural mid-Atlantic region has not been a familiar stage setting.

THE AMERICAN MOVIE BUSINESS IN THE EAST

Although the image of Hollywood as the center of American film is still enduring, one must remember that the movie business began in New York and, even after films were manufactured in California, the main money offices were still in the city, as were most of the premieres and the settings for many of the stories. In a way, American movies never left Manhattan.

Nickelodeons proliferated in major cities before 1910 (there were an estimated 10,000 of them in 1908) but in the 1910s one-reelers and then feature films took over and the movie business was a major industry by the 1920s. Since many of the early artists, such as the pioneer D. W. Griffith (1875–1948), came from the theater, Manhattan was the obvious location. The American Mutoscope and Biograph Company was one of the first studios, founded in 1896. Biograph's 14th Street studio made dozens of early shorts and gave Griffith, Mack Sennett (1880–1960), Mary Pickford (1893–1979), and others their start. The studio was well-known enough that one of its stars, Florence Lawrence (1886–1938), was billed as the "Biograph Girl." Other notable New York studios included the New York Picture Company, built in 1909 and the home of the early Charlie Chaplin (1889–1977) shorts and Keystone Kops one-reelers, and the Astoria Studio, started in Queens in 1920. But from the start, movies were not confined to indoor studios and Manhattan street locations were easily available, as were more rural settings in nearby Long Island and New Jersey. In fact, the first "Western," *The Great Train Robbery* (1903), was filmed in the New Jersey countryside. This landmark film is considered the first American movie to have an extended story and, although it only ran about twelve minutes, its tightly constructed plot, location filming with a cast of forty, and innovative camera techniques made it a phenomenon in its day.

By the 1920s filmmakers started to venture further outside of the New York City area. A particularly useful location was upstate New York near Ithaca where cliffs, rivers, forests, and lakes were all readily available. Many early Westerns were shot on the bluffs and the woods passed for jungles in some early Tarzan movies. But the mid-Atlantic states were subject to the contrasting seasons and sunshine could never be guaranteed, so California was soon discovered as a more practical location. It may have been far from the money, distributors, and talent, but it had the ideal climate and the geographical advantages of green valleys, dra-

Hollywood on the East River

In 1920 the Famous Players-Lasky Studio opened in the borough of Queens. The location, just across the river from central Manhattan, was considered ideal, allowing Broadway actors and directors to make movies during the day and return to the theater district to perform at night. Soon called the Astoria Studios after the Queens neighborhood where it was situated, the little factory made over 100 silent films, including all of D. W. Griffith's early works for Paramount. When sound came in, the need for stage actors increased and the studio started making talkies, including two of the earliest movie musicals: the Marx Brothers' vehicles *The Cocoanuts* (1929) and *Animal Crackers* (1930). By the late 1930s all of the major studios were situated in California so the Astoria Studio was used by independent companies until the U. S. Army took over the facility to make training films during World War II. Mostly neglected in the postwar years, the studio started operation again in 1976 and feature films were once again made there. The name was changed to the Kaufman-Astoria Studios (named after George S. Kaufman, the former chairman of the board) and the refurbished facility continues to make movies today. Attached to the studio is the American Museum of the Moving Image, an institution founded in 1988 devoted to the history of American films, television, and video art.

matic mountains, and nearby deserts. While in the east filmmakers shot on the streets of Manhattan for urban stories, Hollywood built its own cityscapes on the back lots. Particularly after sound came in, it was deemed more practical to shoot a movie at the studio where filmmakers controlled all the conditions, from weather to noise to landscapes. It wasn't until the 1950s and 1960s that the studios allowed extensive filming on location. Taking an entire film crew to Spain rather than creating a Moorish castle on the backlot may have been expensive but when widescreen color spectacles were in fashion it was worth the money. Even New York City location shooting started to return in the late 1940s. Film noir movies sometimes got their distinctive look from the real Manhattan cityscape and even musicals, beginning with *On the Town* (1949), were found to be more effective when shot with the real landmarks. By the 1970s the number of movies made in Hollywood dropped low enough that the studios were more often than not looked at as offices and headquarters rather than film factories. It was the end of an era in which the movies came from a single source. Just as the American theater became much more than Broadway, the American film was now much more than Tinsel Town.

NEW YORK CITY ON FILM

Hollywood and the film industry have always had a fascination with New York City. Perhaps it was because so many of the producers, directors, and screenwriters came from there and made movies about what they missed. Perhaps it was all those New York–set plays that were turned into movies. But most likely it was because the city offered a kind of vitality that made a gangster movie, romance, screwball comedy, or musical all the more effective. Early silents used Manhattan in their plots because it was there. How easy to go out on the streets and have the greatest urban scenery imaginable. But even after the industry moved out to California, great pains were taken to re-create New York City in the sound stages and on the studio lots. The diversity of Manhattan made it an ideal setting for every major film genre except the Western. So to try and pinpoint how the city was portrayed in hundreds of films is like trying to describe the American character itself; too many images come to mind. But some major viewpoints should be pointed out, such as the many movies that idealized New York as a place of glamour, romance, and optimism. From the sleek Art Deco penthouses of the 1930s to the trendy Greenwich Village of the 1990s, the city has often been seen through rose-colored glasses and has given moviegoers a fantasy of urban living. The rich may be idle and silly, as in *The Thin Man* films, or conservative and stuffy, as in *Holiday* (1938), but their luxury was unmistakable. A noteworthy example of idealizing the city is the screwball comedy *My Man Godfrey* (1936), in which a wacky family of millionaires take in a tramp as their butler only to find he has more manners and money than they do. The farce shows the upper class as harmlessly lovable children, which Depression audiences liked, but it also idealizes the homeless and finds dignity in the have-nots.

Romance Movies

Romance films set in New York abound and lovers of every class and age have found the city to be an amorous playground. Also there have been a number of optimistic films that illustrate how goodness can conquer the cold cynicism of the big city. *Mr. Deeds Goes to Town* (1936), in which a small-town poet inherits a fortune and goes to New York to do good, is typical of the genre. Mr. Deeds is treated cruelly by the city but his honesty eventually wins out. The movie suggests that the possibility for goodness is stronger in a place where there is so much evil. But for each such optimistic film there are several that take a bleak, pessimistic view of urban living. Because movies can have a documentary-like objectivity, the media was better able to show squalor and decay than the stage or the page. The New York seen in Chaplin's *The Kid* (1920) and *City Lights* (1931) is poetic in its poverty but later a much harsher city was seen in such films as *The Blackboard Jungle* (1955) and *Midnight Cowboy* (1969). One of the most uncompromising examples, *The Pawnbroker* (1965), portrayed the seamy side of New York with a cool, dispassionate eye and the film was a forerunner of the more graphic street dramas to follow. While a movie like *West Side Story* (1961) might romanticize the rivalry within the city, *The Pawnbroker* and its offspring preferred a more gritty viewpoint.

Neighborhood Movies

But New York City is not all penthouses or gutters and many movies have captured the core of the city's character: the neighborhoods. Whether they are ethnic, such as the Irish in *A Tree Grows in Brooklyn* (1945) or the Jews in *The Chosen* (1981), or generational as in *Saturday Night Fever* (1978), the individual character of the neighborhood has propelled many films. From the waterfront dives of *Anna Christie* (1930) to the Manhattan tenements of *Street Scene* (1931) to the multi-ethnic Brooklyn of *Marty* (1955) to the working class Staten Island in *Working Girl* (1988), movies that came closest to depicting the real New York did so by concentrating on the neighborhoods. The colorful characters in *Dead End* (1937) and the subsequent Dead End Kids (1939) films managed to appeal to audiences across the nation and those types became the New York character in their eyes. Even more popular were the gangster movies that heightened these New York characters into deadly but thrilling types. *Lights of New York* (1928), the first all-talking movie, dealt with the mob and sound movies began a love affair with gangsters and cops that has never waned. Early landmark films, such as *The Public Enemy* (1931), set the pattern and it was still going strong decades later in *The French Connection* (1971), *The Godfather* films (1972 and 1974), *Once Upon a Time in America* (1983), and *GoodFellas* (1990).

Show Business Movies

Of the many other genres of New York films, some mention must be made of the show business movie. Backstage comedies and musicals, show business biographies, and unsentimental works about the heartbreak behind the glamour rarely failed to capture the attention of moviegoers. *The Jazz Singer* (1927), the first talkie (though only sections used sound), was a backstage melodrama, as was *The Broadway Melody* (1929), the first musical to use both dialogue and singing throughout. Warner Brothers's *42nd Street* (1933) and the *Gold Diggers* movies presented a musical form of entertainment not possible on a stage yet all of those films were set in New York and culminated in a Broadway show. Even after Hollywood had established itself as the capital of mass entertainment, most show biz films were set in New York. Whether it was cynical, as in *Sweet Smell of Success* (1957) and *All That Jazz* (1979), or sunny, as with *Yankee Doodle Dandy* (1942) and *Funny Girl* (1968), the entertainment business was another part of the city's character captured on screen.

Three New York City Auteurs: Woody Allen, Martin Scorsese, and Spike Lee

Of the many filmmakers who concentrate on New York City, there are three auteurs who write and direct their movies and are perhaps the most distinctive in presenting an individual point of view about the city. Woody Allen (b. 1935) often romanticizes New York yet he seems just as fascinated by the neurotic, restless, and unsettling aspects of the city. Movies such as *Annie Hall* (1977), *Manhattan* (1979), and *Broadway Danny Rose* (1984) are bittersweet pictures of a city where failure is the norm but the effort to find love and/or success is what makes urban life worth living. Allen can be nostalgic about the city's past, as in *Radio Days* (1987) and *Bullets over Broadway* (1994), find romance in the present, as with *Hannah and Her Sisters* (1986) and *Mighty Aphrodite* (1995), or be cynical about moral values, as in *Crimes and Misdemeanors* (1989) and *Celebrity* (1998). But each work is tied so closely to the nuances and quirky behavior of New Yorkers that his films are all of a piece, variations on a theme. Most of his characters are upper middle class or artistic types and are more concerned with analyzing their feeling than struggling to survive, as found in the films of Martin Scorsese (b. 1942). Like Allen, he is a native New Yorker who grew up in a poor ethnic neighborhood and always re-

Scene from *Witness* with Harrison Ford in Amish costume. Photofest.

turned to his hometown for subject matter and locations. But the two men's movies would never be mistaken for each other. Allen's work involves articulate, funny, but unhappy people; Scorsese deals with inarticulate, bitter, and antagonistic New Yorkers. His first major feature, *Mean Streets* (1973), was typical of his work: an autobiographical drama about a restless Italian-American growing up in Little Italy and facing the tough realities of a world that is competitive and uncaring. *Taxi Driver* (1976) is perhaps the archetypal Scorsese movie, with its quietly seething antihero who confronts a decaying, deadly city on its own violent terms. The world that Allen's characters are careful to avoid are the blood and guts of Scorsese's environment. He also has shown a remarkable ability to capture the New York of the past, as with *New York, New York* (1977), *The Age of Innocence* (1993), and *Gangs of New York* (2002), but it is the city that Scorsese experienced firsthand that most comes alive on the screen. The third auteur, and perhaps the finest of the African American moviemakers, is Spike Lee (b. 1957). Born in Atlanta but raised in Brooklyn, Lee's early film efforts were comic, satirizing the behavior of black Americans in *She's Gotta Have It* (1986) and *School Daze* (1988). But with *Do the Right Thing* (1989), an angry outburst of a film about a racial murder in the Howard Beach neighborhood of New York, Lee found his voice. Like much of his subsequent work, it is a bold movie written for black audiences without any concessions to the white box office. Of his subsequent efforts, *Jungle Fever* (1991), *Malcolm X* (1992), *Crooklyn* (1994), and *Clockers* (1995) also were closely tied to the people and places in the city. In each the rhythm of the location (usually scored with a jazz soundtrack) overflows into the story and characters. It is a side of New York that was rarely seen on screen before.

Auteur in Philadelphia: M. Night Shyamalan

Just as Scorcese, Allen, and others have selected New York as the canvas on which to work, so too have some other director-writers chosen other urban centers. The Asian American N. Night Shyamalan (b. 1970) is a recent addition to the auteur directors but in a short time he has created films with a distinctive personal signature as well as an intricate connection to his Philadelphia turf. Born in India but raised in a Philadelphia suburb, Shyamalan wrote and directed his first feature at the age of twenty-two and was a seasoned professional when he made the very successful *The Sixth Sense* (1999). This unique ghost story not only featured many Philadelphia locations but seemed more potent because it took place in a city with a long history. Just as eerie was his *Unbreakable* (2000), which also used Philadelphia and played with flashbacks in a clever way. Shyamalan moved to the nearby countryside for his next two movies: *Signs* (2002), about unexplainable UFO phenomena in Bucks County, and *The Village* (2004), about a small Pennsylvania town that is threatened by spiritual happenings around them. All of the films are uniquely Shyamalan and use Philadelphia and the environs as much more than a backdrop.

THE MID-ATLANTIC REGION ON THE SCREEN

Although fewer movies deal with the region outside of New York City, the diversity of the mid-Atlantic states is represented, for the most part, by various films either set in and/or shot in the other areas. Philadelphia and the state of Pennsylvania were only occasionally seen on screen until the success of *Rocky* (1975) and its sequels revealed the ethnic flavor of the city. The Brian de Palma thrillers *Dressed to Kill* (1980) and *Blow Out* (1981) turned Philadelphia into an urban nightmare and the city was also a cursed place in the futuristic *Twelve Monkeys* (1995) and in the thrillers by M. Night Shyamalan. The comedy *Trading Places* (1983) viewed both the rich and the downtrodden in the City of Brotherly Love, showing both lifestlyes in satirical terms. And the Main Line wealthy of the comic *The Philadelphia Story* (1940) makes an interesting contrast to the similar class level during the AIDS epidemic in the drama *Philadelphia* (1993). Both the city and the Amish countryside were explored in *Witness* (1985) and the rural community was presented much differently than the Quaker sect was in the sentimental old favorite *Friendly Persuasion* (1956). Pennsylvania history was portrayed as a frolic in *1776* (1972) and as a poetic spectacle in *Gettysburg* (1993), but mostly the state was ignored by filmmakers who only portrayed *Pittsburgh* (1942) when the rising steel industry was the background for a steamy romance or re-created the Pennsylvania coal mines for the 1870s labor intrigues in *The Molly Maguires* (1970). A more recent look at rural Pennsylvania was the waggish satire *Bob Roberts* (1992), which followed a fictional presidential candidate through the state's grassroots communities, the small-time reporters lampooning the national press and the locals becoming stand-ins for the uninformed voters across America.

The mostly rural state of West Virginia has slowly become a favorite location for shooting natural settings and a number of recent films even had the story set in the state. *Matewan* (1987), for example, used West Virginia locales in depicting the rise of labor unions in the state's coal mines in the 1930s. Other true stories set (at least partially) in West Virginia include *October Sky* (1999) and *Beautiful Mind* (2002), both about brilliant men whose talents bring them fame and heartbreak. The creepy thriller *The Mothman Prophesies* (2002) is set in a small town in the Appalachian Mountains, letting the isolation of the landlocked state add to the horror. A similar conceit was used in the Maryland woods for the popular, shoe-string-budget thriller *The Blair Witch Project* (1999), but generally the state has only appeared on the screen in Civil War movies. New York State has not fared much better, cities like Buffalo and Rochester mostly forgotten and the countryside used for period pieces such as *Drums Along the Mohawk* (1939), set during the Revolutionary War, *The Farmer Takes a Wife* (1935 and 1953), about life on the Erie Canal in the 1820s, and the various film versions of James Fennimore Cooper's Leather-

Auteurs in Baltimore: Barry Levinson and John Waters

Baltimore has produced two very contrasting auteurs. Barry Levinson (b. 1942) was born in the Maryland city but broke into the movies as a writer in Hollywood. When he finally got his first directing job, he returned to his hometown and made *Diner* (1982), a nostalgic but unsentimental look at some aimless youths in Baltimore in the late 1950s. The film was a low-budget hit so Levinson later returned to the locale for *Tin Men* (1987), about aluminum-siding salesmen with questionable ethics, and *Avalon* (1990), a warm picture of a Jewish family making its start in America. The three movies have been categorized as the Baltimore Trilogy and, although Levinson directed a number of more popular and award-winning films such as *Rain Man* (1988), his hometown movies have a sincerity that the others rarely capture. Levinson's only other project to date that uses Baltimore as its setting was *Liberty Heights* (1999), about racial strife and anti-Semitism in one of the city's neighborhoods.

Also born in Baltimore is the counterculture auteur John Waters (b. 1946) whose cheap, shocking satires enabled him to gradually develop cult status. *Pink Flamingos* (1972), about a Baltimore contest searching for the filthiest person alive, introduced the transvestite star Divine and the high-camp piece was the first of Waters's movies to get a national distribution. His "smell-a-vision" comedy *Polyester* (1981) was also set in Baltimore but it was in Waters's more mainstream effort *Hairspray* (1988) that the city of Baltimore was intregal to the story. A lighthearted romp about the changing sexual and racial mores in the early 1960s, the movie allowed Waters to move out of the counterculture set and into a more conventional career. His view of his hometown in all of these movies is one of affectionate satire of the city, laughing at its quirks and unable to resist its oddball characters.

Set in Baltimore, the movie *Hairspray* is a lighthearted romp about the changing sexual and racial mores in the early 1960s. Photofest.

stocking novels, such as *The Last of the Mohicans* (1920, 1936, and 1992). New Jersey's proximity to Manhattan has allowed several mobster movies to spill across the river and take place in its urban areas, most memorably *On the Waterfront* (1954) in Hoboken. The rest of the state has been represented sporadically. Of the handful of films set in Atlantic City, the most notable is *Atlantic City* (1980), with its antinostalgic and sour reflection on the city in decline. The character comedy *Return of the Secaucus Seven* (1980) also looked back, this time by unsettled young adults recalling their glory days in the radical 1960s. Independent filmmaker Kevin Smith (b. 1970) is a native of suburban New Jersey and has used this setting for a series of provocative "little" features about disoriented youth. His low-budget comedy *Clerks* (1994), set in a New Jersey convenience store, was a raunchy but inspired look at empty lives filled with misadventure. Smith's subsequent features, the disappointing *Mallrats* (1995), set in a suburban mall, and *Chasing Amy* (1997), a bright comedy about comic book artists, completed what Smith referred to his "New Jersey Trilogy." Some of the same characters (and actors) appeared in all three films and the three films paint one of the few cinematic portraits of the state's distinctive suburban character.

As with the theater, Washington, D.C., on screen means politics and government. The disturbing thriller *The Exorcist* (1973) is perhaps the only mainstream hit film set in Washington that has not been about the capital's primary industry. Even the character study *Get on the Bus* (1996), about African American men traveling to the district for a civil rights rally, cannot divorce itself from politics. Washington has sometimes been seen on screen as a corrupt place which can be conquered through the righteous efforts of the common man. *Mr. Smith Goes to Washington* (1939) is the quintessential version of this genre, showing how a humble young senator with strong ideals can topple self-serving power-mongers. Yet the film is thoroughly patriotic in that the government itself is not blamed; the system works and the people can keep it that way. This is a far cry from the wry satire *Wag the Dog* (1997), which shows deceit through every level of the government. Even the provocative *All the President's Men* (1976), a fact-based account of the Watergate coverup, shows that the system eventually corrects itself.

The investigative reporters are modern versions of Mr. Smith, little guys who can change the course of history because they refuse to back down. Films about the various presidents in the White House have also reflected the political climate of each era. When Charleton Heston played Andrew Jackson in *The President's Lady* (1953), the scandal was soft-peddled and the office of the president was upheld; when Anthony Hopkins played *Nixon* (1995), both the man and the office were portrayed as neurotic and pathetic. Fictional presidents have also been presented in various guises, from the sly, foul-mouthed politician in *The Best Man* (1964) to the incompetent stooge in *Dr. Strangelove* (1964) to the romantic hero in *An American President* (1995). Just as Hollywood preferred to criticize government factions rather than the system and the man and not the office, Washington has been depicted on screen as the locale for everything noble and ignoble in American government. The city, with all its monuments and landmarks, is an American icon; films about the city also create images that moviegoers use to picture their own nation.

How successful the American film has been in capturing the the character of the mid-Atlantic states is a matter of perspective. Clichés, generalizations, and even bias abound in the movies set in this region of the country. But, like many exaggerations, there is an element of truth behind it. The diversity of the land, the people, and the culture are such that a movie can only hope to capture one viewpoint or one small aspect of the whole. Only after one has been exposed to a series of various, and even contradicting, images can the full picture begin to emerge.

RESOURCE GUIDE

Printed Sources

Banham, Martin, ed. *The Cambridge Guide to Theatre*. New York: Cambridge University Press, 1992.

Bawden, Liz-Anne. *The Oxford Companion to Film*. New York: Oxford University Press, 1985.

The Best Plays. 82 editions. New York: Dodd, Mead, 1894–1988; New York: Applause Theatre, 1988–1993; New York: Limelight, 1994–2001.

Blum, Daniel. *A Pictorial History of the Silent Screen*. New York: G. P. Putnam's Sons, 1953.

Blum, Daniel, and John Willis. *A Pictorial History of the American Theatre, 1860-1980*. 5th ed. New York: Crown, 1981.

Bordman, Gerald. *American Musical Theatre: A Chronicle*. 3rd ed. New York: Oxford University Press, 2001.

———. *American Theatre: A Chronicle of Comedy and Drama, 1869–1969*. 3 vols. New York: Oxford University Press, 1994–1996.

Bordman, Gerald, and Thomas S. Hischak. *The Oxford Companion to American Theatre*. 3rd ed. New York: Oxford University Press, 2004.

Feuer, Jane. *The Hollywood Musical*. Bloomington: Indiana University Press, 1982.

Green, Stanley. *Broadway Musicals Show by Show*. 5th ed. Milwaukee: Hal Leonard, 1999.

———. *Encyclopedia of Musical Film*. New York: Oxford University Press, 1981.

———. *Encyclopedia of the Musical Theatre*. New York: Dodd, Mead, 1976.

Halliwell, Leslie. *Halliwell's Film Guide*. 7th ed. New York: Harper and Row, 1989.

Henderson, Mary C. *Theater in America*. New York: Harry N. Abrams, 1986.

Hirschhorn, Clive. *The Hollywood Musical*. Rev. 2nd ed. New York: Crown, 1983.

Hischak, Thomas S. *American Theatre: A Chronicle of Comedy and Drama, 1969–2000*. New York: Oxford University Press, 2001.

———. *The Theatregoer's Almanac*. Westport, CT: Greenwood Press, 1997.

Katz, Ephraim. *The Film Encyclopedia*. 3rd ed. New York: Harper-Perennial, 1998.

Konigsberg, Ira. *The Complete Film Dictionary*. 2nd ed. New York: Penguin, 1997.

Maltin, Leonard. *Movie and Video Guide*. 2003 ed. New York: Penguin Putnam, 2002.

Mast, Gerald. *A Short History of the Movies*. Indianapolis: Pegasus, 1971.

Theatre World. 56 editions. New York: Norman McDonald Associate, 1946–1949; New York: Greenberg, 1949–1957; Philadelphia: Chilton, 1957–1964; New York: Crown, 1964–1991; New York: Applause Theatre, 1991–2000.

Wilmeth, Don. B., and Tice Miller, eds. *Cambridge Guide to American Theatre*. New York: Cambridge University Press, 1993.

Web Sites

Artslynx Theatre Resources
www.artslynx.org

Theater support organizations and unions.

Box Office Magazine
www.boxoff.com

Monthly trade publication online.

Broadway.Com
www.broadway.com

Articles, news, and reviews on contemporary theater.

Film Comment
www.filmlinc.com./fcm/online

Bimonthly publication by Film Society of Lincoln Center online.

Playbill on Line
www.playbill.com

Articles and news regarding contemporary Broadway and regional theater.

Theatre History Online
www.theatrehistory.com

Texts, archives, and resources.

Organizations, Museums, Special Collections

American Academy of Motion Picture Arts and Sciences
8949 Wilshire Blvd.
Beverly Hills, CA 90211
www.oscars.org

American Film Institute
1180 Avenue of the Americas
New York, NY 10036
www.afionline.org

American Museum of the Moving Image
35th Ave. at 36th St.
Astoria, NY 11106
www.ammi.org

Curtis Theatre Collections
University of Pittsburgh
Pittsburgh, PA 15213
www.library.pitt.edu

George Eastman House International Museum of Photography and Film
900 East Ave.
Rochester, NY 14607
www.eastman.org

Film Society of Lincoln Center
70 Lincoln Center Plaza
New York, NY 10023
www.filmlinc.com

Museum of Modern Art
11 West 53rd St.
New York, NY 10019
www.moma.org

Museum of the City of New York
1220 Fifth Ave.
New York, NY 10029
www.mcny.org

New York Public Library for the Performing Arts
40 Lincoln Center Plaza
New York, NY 10023
www.nypl.org

Shubert Archive
234 W. 44th St.
New York, NY 10036
www.shubertarchive.org

Theatre Collection of the Free Library of Philadelphia
1901 Vine St.
Philadelphia, PA 19103
www.library.phila.gov

Theatre Communications Group (TCG)
520 Eighth Ave.
New York, NY 10018
www.tcg.org

Theatre Development Fund (TDF)
1501 Broadway
New York, NY 10036
www.tdf.org

Selected Regional Film Festivals

Atlantic City Film Festival
2921 Atlantic Ave.
Atlantic City, NJ 08401
www.atlanticcityfilmfestival.com

Brooklyn International Film Festival
200 Eastern Parkway
Brooklyn, NY 11238
www.brooklynfilmfestival.org

DC Independent Film Festival (DCIFF)
2950 Van Ness St. NW
Washington, DC 20008
www.dciff.org

Garden State Film Festival
1000 Ocean Ave.
Asbury Park, NJ 07712
www.gsff.org

Ithaca Film Festival (IFEST)
1201 N. Tioga St.
Ithaca, NY 14850
www.ithacafilmfest.com

Maryland Film Festival
107 E. Read St.
Baltimore, MD 21202
www.mdfilmfest.com

New Jersey Jewish Film Festival
760 Northfield Rd.
W. Orange, NJ 07052
www.njjff.org

New York Animation Film Festival
22 E. 12th St.
New York, NY 10001
www.nyaf.org

New York Film Festival
70 Lincoln Center Plaza
New York, NY 10023
www.filmlinc.com

Pennsylvania Film Festival
321 Spruce St.
Scranton, PA 18503
www.pafilmfest.com

Philadelphia Festival of World Cinema
234 Market St.
Philadelphia, PA 19106
www.phillyfests.com

Rochester International Film Festival
900 East Ave.
Rochester, NY 14607
www.rochesterfilmfest.org

Syracuse International Film and Video Festival
262 S. Salina St.
Syracuse, NY 13201
www.syracusefilmandvideofest.com

Washington DC International Film Festival (Film FestDC)
P.O. Box 21396
Washington, DC 20009
www.filmfestdc.org

West Virginia International Film Festival
P.O. Box 2165
Charleston, WV 25328
www.wviff.org

Wilmington International Film Festival
800 N. French St.
Wilmington, DE 19801
www.wilmingtonfilmfest.com

FOLKLORE

Michael Lovaglio

Some Maryland residents never eavesdrop on cattle on Christmas Eve, because the last person who did slipped and fatally hit his head while snooping. In New Jersey, visitors to Ringwood Manor are cautioned not to travel to the estate at night or else the ghosts of dead soldiers who fought in the Revolutionary War will haunt them. Delaware is known as the Blue Hen State because of a citizen who brought two blue hen fighting cocks with him to the Revolutionary War. The mid-Atlantic region is full of these and similar tales. They reflect the beliefs of early European settlers, who in many cases found the landscape of the New World to be alien and threatening; they reveal how historical events become re-presented in larger-than-life stories; they show how, even after centuries of living in the same region, one's homeland can still evoke feelings of mystery, excitement, and insecurity; and, perhaps more than anything else, they indicate the richness and power of the region's "folk" and their traditions. The following collection highlights the long history of mid-Atlantic folktales.

NATIVE AMERICAN FOLKLORE

The Algonquin

The first Indians to welcome the Dutch, English, and French were the Algonquin, who were also the first to fight the Europeans after being victimized by their insatiable appetite for land. Living in bands of 100 to 300 members, the Algonquin divided into hunting groups of up to 25 family members settling predominantly in Quebec, Canada, and were at one time the largest of the North American Indian groups. As a result of their numbers the Algonquin made significant impressions on both the cultures and languages of other tribes, often through marriage. One such nation is the Blackfoot, who are believed to have settled in the Northern Plains as well as in New York State along the Hudson River. Their lodges were mostly built from bent saplings and birch bark, housing husband, wife, unmarried daughters, and sons and their families as well. The Algonquin primarily hunted buffalo, deer, moose, and other animals during the winter months. The rest of the year was spent fishing and gathering fruits, nuts, and roots. The Algonquin would use snowshoes and toboggans during the winter months to travel, and use canoes of birch bark during the spring, summer, and fall. Spiritually, the Algonquin believed in a very powerful god they referred to as the Great Spirit. They believed the ancestral spirits of animals, plants, and nature greatly affected their lives. Specific men and women (referred to as shamans) were used in order to communicate with this spiritual world. Today there are approximately 4,000 Algonquin, who reside mostly in eastern and southwestern Quebec.

Two Algonquin tales resemble an Iroquois origin tale very similar to the biblical tale of Cain and Abel. A woman from the sky gives birth to two sons, but dies after having complications with the second. The first was known as Sprout/Plant Boy and the second Flint. These two men represent two Native American traditions of survival. Sprout/Plant Boy represents the agricultural tradition and Flint represents the hunting tradition. The following two tales of the Algonquin Indians are examples of possible origins for both.

The Origin of the Buffalo Hunter's Dance

As an alternative to hunting, the Algonquin would drive buffalo over cliffs as a means to slaughter many in order to feed large tribes during the winter months. However, this method was not always successful, for in some cases the buffalo would not move, and could therefore not be driven off the cliff. The Buffalo Hunter's Dance stems from this particular context. It tells of how a daughter from one of the houses got up to gather water for her family one morning and spoke to the buffalo. To her surprise the buffalo spoke back.

She said, "If only you would come over here, I would marry one of you." At that moment, not one, but all the buffalo that were grazing in the nearby field came over. The eldest buffalo approached the girl and said, "Come with me. I have kept my end of the bargain, now you are to be my wife." The girl had no choice but to go with the buffalo and keep her promise. Immediately following the girl's departure her family wakes to find no sign of her. Her father sees buffalo tracks in the dirt and concludes that the buffalo have taken her. So he sets out to find his daughter.

After searching for a while the father stops to rest. He sees a magpie and asks if it has seen his daughter. Now, at the time magpies were thought to have magical powers, so when the father addressed the bird, it was reasonable to expect a reply. The magpie said that it had seen a girl with the buffalo traveling just across the plains. Too exhausted to travel any further, the father asks the magpie if it would tell his daughter that her father is coming. The magpie finds the girl among sleeping buffalo and gives her the message. The magpie also awakens the girl's buffalo husband, who is unaware of the magpie's visit and asks his wife to fetch some water from the nearby stream.

At the stream the girl meets her father, who tries to take her home. In fear of what her buffalo husband might do if he sees the girl's father, she refuses to go home with her father and tells him to leave. The girl hurries back to where the buffalo were resting and finds her suspicious buffalo husband waiting for her. Even though the girl returns willingly, the buffalo smells the scent of her father nearby. He has the buffalo find the girl's father and when they do the buffalo trample him to death, beating his body so powerfully that all that is left is ground into dust.

The girl falls to the ground where her father was trampled and begins to sob. Puzzled, her buffalo husband asks why she only cries for her father, but not when the buffalo are driven over the cliff to their deaths. Feeling remorseful, the buffalo tells the girl that if she is able to bring her father back to life, then he will let both of them go. The girl asks the magpie (who had all along watched as the previous events unfolded) to find a remaining piece of her father regardless of how small it may be, which it does, and the girl sings a revivifying song that heals him. The buffalo is amazed by the power of the song and teaches the girl a buffalo dance that should be danced while the song is played. If, after a slaughter, the Indians sang and danced to gratify the buffalo for their sacrifice, the celebration would have the power to bring the buffalo back to life. In the wake of this story the slaughter of the buffalo becomes a sacred act, and the song and dance ritual is conducted out of respect for not only the buffalo, but also the spiritual bond now shared by the Indian and the buffalo.

The Origin of Maize

Even though the Algonquin Indians relied heavily on the hunt as their principal source of nutrition, maize was their chief crop. The following story is about a boy who experiences a vision after worrying about how his family will survive once they can no longer rely on hunting; for he is still too young to hunt game and his father is growing old, no longer able to hunt as efficiently as before. The boy has a vision of a young man with green plumes on his head who challenges him to a wrestling match. The boy's antagonist wins, returning frequently to wrestle him, only to leave victorious. The last time the young man visits he tells the boy that he must kill and bury him. Not only must the boy do this but he must also care for the site where the young man is to be buried. The boy does what has been asked, and after some time corn begins to grow where the young man has been buried (or, in other words, planted). After the child's vision he realizes that his family will no longer need to worry, for the land will provide them with all they need.

The Iroquois

From east to west in the mid-Atlantic region, the Iroquois Indians formed a federation of tribes that once occupied most of upper New York State. The tribes included the Mohawk, Oneida, Onondaga, Cayuga, Tuscarora, and Seneca. The Huron, Erie, Neutrals, Susquehanna, and (down in the lower Appalachians) the Cherokee all spoke the language of the Iroquois. The Iroquois referred to themselves as the "Ongwanonhsion," which translates to *we longhouse builders*. The federation (formed in the early 1600s) was referred to as the Six Nations and soon developed into the most influential North American Indian organization. When the Iroquois die, a small hole is engraved in the tomb, which allows for the soul to travel at its leisure.

The Rejection of the Suitors

This Iroquois folklore story begins with a mother and daughter living alone in a wigwam at the outskirts of their village. Because the girl is far prettier than any of her potential suitors she refuses every one of them. This upsets her mother, who is annoyed that her daughter holds herself in such high regard above those who are not as beautiful as she. The girl's vanity plays a pivotal role in the adventure she is about to embark on. If it were not for her vanity, if the girl were not mortally flawed, she would not have had her adventure, and her story would never have found a voice.

One afternoon while the girl and her mother are out collecting wood far from the village, the sky grows dark. The mother assumes this unexplained darkness to be that of a magician and thinks it would be best to make a small wigwam from some tree bark and set up camp rather than risk the journey home. Later that evening, while her mother is asleep, a man equally handsome as the girl comes to call on her. The girl asks for her mother's approval, which she gives only after meeting him. They are married and the girl ventures off with her new husband to his home.

After two full days and nights with one another the girl's husband tells her that he must go out to hunt, yet immediately after he leaves the girl hears a strange sound outside. Later that evening, when her husband is still out hunting, the girl hears the same strange sound. A large serpent enters the lodge, puts its head on the girl's lap, and asks her to pick the lice from it. She agrees to do so and when she is finished, the serpent exits the lodge. Her husband then enters and asks his wife if she was afraid of him when he entered as the serpent. The girl replies that she was not afraid, thinking that any other reply would upset her husband. The following morning after her husband leaves to hunt, the girl goes out to collect firewood. She finds several large serpents basking on the rocks near their home. Reminded of her husband's transformation the previous night, the girl decides that she no longer wants to stay and on this third day, without warning, she flees.

Escaping into the woods, the girl meets an old man called a "Thunderer." The Thunderer is an important figure in this folk tale. It is his "mission to keep the earth and everything in it in good order for the benefit of the human race. If there were a drought, it would be his duty to bring rain; if there were serpents or other noxious creatures, a Thunderer would be commissioned to destroy them. In short, the Thunderer does away with everything injurious to mankind."[1] In this particular tale the Thunderer tells the girl that she has married one of seven evil magician brothers whose hearts are no longer in their bodies, but beating under the bed where she and her husband sleep back at the lodge. The Thunderer explains that the brothers believed that their hearts were their most vital and weakest assets. If not for their hearts, they would not be able to survive. Therefore, if they were attacked while hunting, their lives would be in no imminent danger because their hearts were safely secured at the lodge. The displacing of hearts for safety is a classic shamanic motif. In this case, the Thunderer instructs the girl to run back to the lodge while her husband and his seven brothers are out hunting and destroy the hearts if she wishes to be freed from them "for all eternity."

The girl races back to the lodge to find the bag of hearts under the bed just as the Thunderer had said they would be. By this time her husband is nearing home and sees his wife leaving with the bag of still-beating hearts. He chases after her, demanding that she stop. Seconds before her magician husband seizes her, the Thunderer grabs the girl. Here the tale takes a confusing turn, describing the Thunderer pulling the girl out of water. Safe but confused, the girl asks the Thunderer what she was doing in water, as she had no recollection of ever falling in a river or pond. The Thunderer explains that once the girl agreed to marry the magician, she had consciously removed herself from the realm of the rational and transcended into the sphere of the unconscious; thus "being under water" signifies how the girl was trapped in an unconscious realm, and kept from that which she rationally understood.

The adventure the girl experiences tells the tale of a person seeking a husband for reasons of physical attraction, rather than more substantive reasons. Because the girl chose to value life on a superficial level, the magician was easily able to seduce her. Even though it appeared that she was living with him willingly, the girl was still a prisoner, unable to leave without first planning an escape. The reality of her capture was unclear to the girl's naked eye—in other words, her conscious self. All the while her unconscious self was struggling to breathe, suffocating within the altered state manufactured by her magician husband. It was not a coincidence that the girl ran into the Thunderer in the thick of the woods (far enough away from the magician that his hold over his wife was weakened), for it is the Thunderer's responsibility not just to restore the balance, but to protect the girl, the Iroquois, and all of humanity from evil.

The Seneca

The Seneca Indians once populated an area from the Genesee River to Canandaigua Lake in western New York. The Seneca name is O-non-dowa-gah, which means "people of the great hill," referring to a hill near Canandaigua Lake where the tribe originated, according to Seneca legend. The Seneca were called the "keepers of the western door" because the land they occupied made up the westernmost part of the Iroquois territory. The Seneca villages were typically built on hills near a river, with a tall wooden stake fence surrounding the village to protect it from attack. These villages included 30 to 150 large rectangular houses called "longhouses," which sheltered both immediate and extended families.

The Storytelling Customs of the Seneca

The storytelling customs of the Seneca were similar to those of other Iroquois tribes. Each community had their own storytellers who had been taught the specifics of tradition and legend, which were often believed to have mysterious origins. The wood fairies, otherwise referred to as "the little people" (djoge'o), would not allow any fables, myth-tales, or ancient adventure stories to be told during the summer months according to ancient traditions. The djoge'o would masquerade through settlements under the guise of an insect or a bird making sure no storytellers were ignoring the rule. Punishment for telling such stories often resulted in injury or death; bees would sting the storyteller's lips or tongue, forbidding speech for a specified period of time, or a snake would make his way into the storyteller's bed and strangle them as they slept.

There are many reasons why such stories were not permitted to be told in the summer months, as well as why the consequences for doing so were so severe. The first concerned the need to make certain that no animals would hear outrageous tales of man's superiority over them. Second, the djoge'o were concerned that if animals were to hear these Indian tales they would become enthralled with the life of men and abandon their role in nature, disrupting the order of things. Further, listening to such stories in the summer months made men, the trees, plants, and animals lazy. It was believed that "all the world stops work when a good story is told and afterward forgets its wonted duty in marveling. Thus the modern Iroquois, following the old time custom, reserves his tales of adventures, myth and fable for winter when the year's work is over and all nature slumbers."[2]

The storyteller was referred to as "Hage'ota," and his stories were called "ganondas'hago." It was customary for the storyteller's guests to bring him small gifts such as tobacco and jewelry. When the storyteller would tell the story, it was called "e sege'ode," and the gift given to him in return was called "dagwa'niatcis."

The storyteller would announce his telling of a story by saying "I' 'newa 'engege'ode, Hau' 'nio' 'djadao 'dii us!" And during the story, the listeners would often respond by saying "he'" throughout. Falling asleep while a story was being told was rude. And if the listeners did not respond to the storyteller by saying "he'" it was a sign that they were not listening, which was considered the fault of the storyteller. Thus it was necessary that a compelling and great story be handed over by a compassionate storyteller, an example offered with this next folktale.

The "Outsider" in Seneca Folk Stories

The issue of "outsideness," or of not belonging, is an important characteristic of Senecan folk stories. Such an issue signifies, no doubt, phenomena common to our current moment in American history, which continues to display signs of an uneasy relationship to immigration issues. But considering the fact that present-day American identity arises out of a diverse immigrant settler society (peoples, we need to remember, that all originated from cultures that were *outside* the landscape that came to be known as the Mid-Atlantic) that was placed overtop the remains of an expansive native presence, examining a tale of outsideness from an original constituency that now has limited power means also that this tale carries a rare regional significance. A particular Senecan story of outsideness concerns a young man by the name of Gaqka (which means "Crow"), whose parents had suddenly died, leaving him without a home. His uncles did not want to be bothered caring for the child, so he lived alone in the woods, feeding off birds and squirrels. His clothes were torn and dirty and he lived in a hut made of weak branches. Whenever the villagers saw the child they would make fun of him, holding their noses as they passed by, and calling him the "Filth-Covered-One." This setting emphasizes the extent to which Gaqka lacked the kind of communal companionship that would enable him to establish an identity in terms of his community or cultural accomplishments. His character expresses a fear common to folktales: the individual that will never amount to anything, and remain nothing more than a "filthy outsider."

The story takes a turn when, on one particular evening, Gaqka discovers a magical canoe that takes him on a ride through the air and above the stars and the moon. Paddling south, Gaqka eventually makes a new home atop a cliff overlooking a river. The first evening Gaqka spends on top of the cliff he hears a voice call out to him, saying, "Give me some tobacco." Gaqka looks but cannot see anyone, so he asks the voice why he should give it tobacco. Again, the voice says, "Give me some tobacco." After this second request Gaqka throws some tobacco over the cliff. The voice then replies, "Now, I will tell you a story." Gaqka comes to the conclusion that it is in fact the cliff speaking to him, and at the end of the story, the cliff tells Gaqka that if he will throw tobacco over the cliff nightly it will tell him a set of stories—on the condition that Gaqka not fall asleep during the storytelling.

It is curiously in the wake of this storytelling that the character of Gaqka begins to establish himself as a member of a community. After several nights of listening to the stories, Gaqka stumbles across a village while out hunting during the day. He makes many friends among the villagers, who teach him the hunting activities that are necessary for him to become a member of a community. In the wake of the villagers' hospitality, Gaqka takes them to the cliff in the evenings to hear stories. The cliff does not mind the extra company, but will only speak when Gaqka is present.

Gaqka becomes so much an accepted figure that he eventually marries into the community, bringing his wife to live with him on the cliff. The story takes a revealing turn when Gaqka's wife discovers that the cliff's voice is the spirit of her dead grandfather. She tells Gaqka that she will make a pouch and leave it at the edge of the cliff. Each time the cliff tells them a story, they leave a trophy inside the pouch. The following spring when the pouch is full of trophies and Gaqka has learned all of the spirit's tales, Gaqka and his wife journey north—to the land where he was hostilely treated as a child. Because of this Gaqka is hesitant to leave, but his wife assures him that he is a new man, dressed in fine clothing and healed of all old wounds. When Gaqka returns home he tells the villagers that he was the child they had treated as an outcast. But once he begins telling stories the villagers no longer taunt him. The story ends triumphantly for Gaqka; he and his wife grow old in the same village that had once turned him away, where he became one of the most respected men.

In this tale Gaqka becomes the man remembered by the Senecan as their first storyteller. The tale carries additional significance, for storytelling lies at the heart of how cultures establish themselves and their traditions. Stories generate a sense of identity, which is then handed down to subsequent generations. The remarkable idea that stands at the heart of this noteworthy story is that the formation of a cultural heritage—which in the present is based more often than not on combative notions of identity, on a dynamic of "us" against "them," "our" heritage and traditions against the traditions of those strange and unwanted "others" that lie on the outside—originates in the very breakdown of the barriers that separate inside from outside, innate from exterior. The "origin" here involves no claims to cultural supremacy, but rather entails a lesson concerning a relation to the unknown and the manifestly different. The starting point of cultural narration is an embrace of the unknown as a source of great energy and creativity, and not an element of reality to fear and conquer.

Origin of Seneca Medicine

This story concerns the need to understand and respect sacred spaces, which are fundamental to the Seneca, in addition to other Native American tribes and cultures. Like many folktales, the story is situated in the past. It begins, "Over two hundred years ago a man went hunting alone in the woods." There he hears distant singing and the beating of drums. He follows the noise to what appears at one time to have been a populated campground, though he now sees no one there. Situated in the center of the campground is a hill with three ears of corn and a squash vine with three small squashes. He investigates the area further, but finds no one. The next evening he awakes to find a man staring at him. The man accuses him, "Beware! I have come for you. What you saw the previous evening [referring to the deserted campground] was sacred and now you will die." The hunter notices that his accuser is not the only one watching him. The others suggest that they pardon the man's ignorance and teach him their secrets.

The hunter is then taken to a place are people were singing and dancing in crowds. Their movement appears ritualistic, and the hunter asks, "Why are these people singing and dancing in such a way that I have never seen before?" Rather than explain their rituals to the hunter, a member of the tribe chooses to show him instead. Heating a stick, he stabs it through the hunter's cheek. While the hunter is still in shock and before he can experience the full measure of his pain, the man applies medicine to demonstrate how quickly the hunter's wound will heal. He does the same to the hunter's leg, while the rest of the tribe sings what the hunter soon learns is their "medicine song."

After the tribe teaches the hunter about their medicines and instructs him on how to apply them, each member of the tribe transforms into a variety of animals. Before the hunter can question the tribe about these transformations, they flee into the woods.

The tribe tells the hunter to take one stalk of dry corn and pound it till it is very fine. They instruct him to do the same with the squash, telling him how much vegetable to use for a dose and to apply it with water running upstream, never down. These prescriptions are used by the hunter "over the next hundred" years, giving the medicines the additional weight of historical custom.

The Sure Revenge

This revenge tale concerns a matter of contestation between the Seneca Indians and the Illinois Indians. The tale—a "captivity narrative" of sorts—begins "centuries ago" with a description of the Illinois Indians, who attacked a tribe of Seneca Indians who had settled on the banks of Lake Erie. The Seneca Indians are presented as being caught off guard, but as also fighting well. Even so, the Illinois are too many and slaughter all but a few of the Seneca Indians. Among the few survivors are a mother and her son, who are taken prisoner by the Illinois.

The evening after the first day's travels, the Illinois men stop to make camp. They start a fire, sit, and sing songs of the Illinois. They ask the child to sing with them. In Seneca the boy replies that he cannot sing with them, not being familiar with their language. He says that he will, however, sing on his own. The men are pleased, but the boy chooses not to sing the Illinois' tribal song; he chooses a song associated with the Seneca tribe. Knowing that the Illinois men cannot understand him, the boy sings a song of resistance in which he states that he will never forget what these men had done to his people. He sings that he will never forget that they had taken his mother away from her family, and that if he were fortunate enough to live, he would scalp each and every one of the Illinois men.

After the third day of traveling with the Illinois, the boy's mother became sick with exhaustion and could no longer walk. She told her son never to forget that he was a Seneca Indian. She also told him to escape back to the Seneca and tell them how cruelly the Illinois had treated them. At a certain moment in their traveling, when she can continue no further, the Illinois men kill her. Before her death, her son swears that he will never forget who he is and vows that he will someday avenge her death.

At this point in the narrative we are to see how the Illinois had not only taken the child away from all his former cultural connections, but also destroyed that which was crucial to his identity. The taking away of cultural identity pushes the character of the boy into a different arena that calls for a different formation of his identity. No longer sustaining any human bonds, the boy was now able to take on the role of the "imposter." He would "become" an Illinois, while also never forgetting those he was spiritually connected to. His outward dress and appearance changes, but he remains a Seneca within. In his new subjectivity of imposter, the boy remembers his heritage. But he also plans his revenge not only to obtain justice, but to take back his stolen identity.

When the Illinois return to their village with the child, a council is held regard to his fate. It is decided that the

A Seneca Legend of Hi-nu and Niagara

In the Seneca heritage, Niagara Falls was the site at which the God of Cloud and Rain, Hi-nu, intervened in mortal affairs and saved the lives of a young Senecan woman and her village. Similar to the Algonquin story in which a girl embarks on an adventure because she rejects all but one of her suitors, this Senecan legend begins with a girl fleeing her one and only suitor and ends with her becoming an instrument in saving the lives of her village.

In a moment of desperation a beautiful young Indian woman, whose marriage was being arranged by her family with an elderly suitor, chose to canoe down the treacherous waters of Niagara River rather than marry her old and hideous lover. Moments before the young woman was about to crash and drown, the God of Cloud and Rain, Hi-nu swept out of the sky and rescued her from death. Hi-nu had seen the girl wrestling with the roaring Niagara from his cave, which rests along the water's shore. The great being could not stand to witness the destruction of this beautiful youth, so he rescued her without hesitation and offered her lodging for the next few weeks. Also, it was not uncommon for a god to intervene and offer aid on behalf of those in distress in Senecan folklore.

Being a god, Hi-nu was very knowledgeable about the ways of the world, and he explained why there was so much death and sickness within the young woman's village. He told her that her village's troubles were not the result of nature, but of a large snake living underground, beneath the village. The snake would purposefully poison the village's water supply so that he could feed off the dead with little risk of being discovered.

Hi-nu would not let the young woman leave his lodging until her suitor had died and she could safely travel home to warn her village of the snake. Before she could return, her tribe left and traveled closer to the waters of Niagara. For a while the sickness ceased, but the snake eventually followed and caught up with the villagers. Before it could prey on the people again, Hi-nu intervened and threw large bolts of lightning at the snake. To both Hi-nu and the villagers' surprise, the snake would not die and continued its journey toward the new village. Hi-nu then fired lightning bolt after lightning bolt until the snake finally died. The people then rolled the dead snake's body into the Niagara River in order to be rid of it for good. Because the snake was so large it became wedged in between the rocks. There it stayed until the water eventually rose over its body. The weight of the dead monster pressed on the rocks, leaving a U-shaped waterfall, which eventually came to be Niagara Falls.

boy will have to prove not only his potential strength as a man, but his value as an Illinois. If he is unable to do so, then he will be executed the following morning as a Seneca. While the Illinois are in council deciding his fate, the child has a vision. In his vision, the boy is warned of the Illinois' plans. As in "The Origin of Maize"—where the son's idea to grow food to help his family when they can no longer hunt is inspired by a vision—the hero is helped in some way by the "mystical."

The Illinois test the boy by submitting him to a warrior's trial. The boy is made to stand in fire until his feet are severely blistered. Then the blisters are cut open and filled with tiny rocks. The child is then made to run a race barefoot. The boy knows that if he runs far enough, proving his worth, the Illinois will let him live. When he thinks he cannot run because the pain is unbearable, he begins to think about his mother and the Seneca. This gives him strength and makes him forget about the pain. The boy succeeds in passing the test, yet it is decided that he will still be sentenced to death as a result of his age and because of the strength of the Seneca blood running through him. A majority of the tribe's elders believed that if the child ever held onto his heritage he would be able to tell the Illinois's enemies where their village was.

In the narrative we see the boy brought as fully as possible into the Illinois culture. When the day comes for the boy to be killed, an elder chief emerges from the woods and tells the tribe to spare the child's life, for he thinks that the boy will make a fine warrior under his tutelage. The tribe adheres to the chief's request and over the next few years the child learns the ways of the Illinois and is trained as a warrior. The elder trains the boy so well that he lives to be the "most promising warrior" in the village. He is renamed Ga-geh-djo-wa.

Now Ga-geh-djo-wa, the boy is firmly established in the alien culture as an accomplished hunter. Moreover, he eventually marries the chief's daughter. It is at this point that the imbrication—as total as possible—of the boy into the culture prepares the stage for the tale's focus: the confrontation between identity construction and the threat to one's cultural heritage. The time arises when the Illinois decide to attack the Seneca again. In the tale we are told that Ga-geh-djo-wa desperately wants to take part in the hunt. He convinces the tribe that he will make an excellent scout because he still knows better than anyone the area of the Seneca land. The Illinois agree. But when Ga-geh-djo-wa leaves to scout out the area, he returns to his Seneca tribe to warn them about the Illinois tribe's plans. He tells the story of the kidnapping of himself and his mother, of her death, and the events that led to his "passing" as a member of the Illinois tribe. Because of this, the Seneca are prepared for the attack. Before the Illinois can strike, the Seneca ambush them. The story ends with this resolution of revenge. Its significance lies in the attention it pays to the preservation of tradition. The narrative is not one that addresses the potential for "hybridity"; it is not about cultural exchange, or the fluidity of identity. For, the story suggests, there *are* lines to be drawn in the interaction between cultures. The construction of identity from context, the narratives seems to be arguing, does not mean that one should submit to the prioritization (or in this case, erasure) of one cultural context over another. Such violations, in fact, are met with equal violent acts of retribution.

The Legend of Penn's Cave

Many Native American folktales were preserved by non-native whites of European descent. Such preservation no doubt had an effect on the ways in which tales were re-presented as they shifted contexts when being handed down through different historical eras. One important nonnative folk preservationist was Henry W. Shoemaker, who was known as Pennsylvania's first state folklorist.

The best-known folktale preserved by Shoemaker is "The Legend of Penn's Cave." The story takes place in Penn's Woods, located in central Pennsylvania, considered the "heart" and "highlands" of the state—"a storied place with countless small towns, ethnic varieties, and legends at every turn."[3] Set at the turn of the twentieth century, the story concentrates on a young Frenchman named Malachi Boyer, a drifter who often spent his time traveling through the woods of Sunbury, where Bellefonte is now located in Lancaster, Pennsylvania. Rural folklore of Bellefonte describes Malachi as a short and stocky man, whose handsome features (namely, his black hair and eyes) never went unnoticed by the local women. Though Malachi befriended many Indians, one particular encounter, with Chief O-ko-cho and his seven sons, one spring along the shores of Spring Creek resulted in his death.

Malachi would often eat and trade with the chief and his tribe, spending most of his time among them, leaving only at night during religious ceremonies. But after Malachi falls in love with the chief's daughter, he is no longer welcome among the tribe. The chief orders his sons to capture Malachi. They take him to a remote cave and keep him prisoner. Malachi tries a number of times to fight his way through, but eventually gives in. His character, though beaten, continues to express a sense of traditional nobility and anger by refusing to give his captors the "satisfaction of watching him die." He therefore descends into the depths of the cave and soon after dies from hunger. The brothers eventually find him, and sink the body into a green limestone pool inside the cave. Like many folktales of this sort, the narrative does not end with the death of the unfortunate hero, but ends with an "echo"—both literally and figuratively. The ending is addressed to the audience in the present: "Still to this day those who have heard this folktale and visit the cave on summer nights can hear the echo of Malachi's voice crying for his lost love 'Nita-nee,' 'Nita-nee.'" In this sense, the present-day audience is given "evidence" of the story's validity in the literal echo of Malachi's cry. But the story also continues figuratively in the sense of not coming to a traditional and final conclusion: the story's main character maintains his presence *in* the present, thus making the entire narrative itself forever "echo" for future generations. In this sense, the tale does not end, but continues to express its central dilemma—the sense of a loss that will never be filled.

COLONIAL FOLKLORE

Colonial folklore begins with the first European settlers of the mid-Atlantic region. These settlers brought with them a collection of stories and beliefs that took on new forms as they adapted to what was, to the European mind, a strange and sometimes hostile world. Hazardous creatures, for instance, became entities endowed with mystical powers. Snakes especially held a peculiar fascination for travelers in the "New World." One story tells of a New Jersey farmer who, in the midst of removing a haystack, became transfixed by the eyes of a rattlesnake. Unable to move for hours, he was released from the snake's hold by his wife, who was able to distract the gaze of the snake away from her husband.

The following early colonial story has a similar pattern. It tells of a young Albany woman who was traveling through the woods with her African American servant when

> a Black Snake being disturbed by its amours, ran under her petticoats, and twisted around her waist, so that she fell backwards in a swoon . . . The negro came up to her, and . . . lifted up her cloaths . . . found the snake wound about her body as close as possible; the negro was not able to tear it away, and therefore cut it, and the girl came to herself again; but she conceived so great an aversion to the negro, that she could not bear the sight of him afterwards, and died of a consumption.[4]

Laden with sexual overtones, this tale in particular reveals the extent to which European settlers found not only the land to be threatening, but other races as well. The woman believes that she cannot trust her African American servant, and feels violated by his close proximity. The tale indicates the degree to which an ideological view of the non-European as sexually promiscuous and aggressive (the snake disappears as a threat, but its phallic presence carries over when the African American servant lifts the white woman's clothes) colors the colonial mind.

The figure of the snake was not only connected with the sexual assault of women. One story tells of a poor colonial planter from Maryland who had become ill and extremely emaciated from a "lingering distemper." When English doctors failed to cure his illness, he turned to an Indian friend named Jack. Jack placed a defanged rattlesnake tightly around the man's chest. Through the night the snake twitched violently. The snake's twitches eventually grew weaker, and by morning it was dead. The planter's illness disappeared, having been transferred to the snake throughout the course of the evening.[5] In addition to its characterization of the snake as a curative entity, this tale also reveals how colonial folklore gradually became a mix of both Native American and European traditions.

Colonial folklore would eventually become associated with the founding fathers of the United States as the mid-

The Devil in the New World

Names found today in the Hudson Valley carry folkloric traditions from the region's colonial days. One tradition holds that Danskammer, a plateau near Newburgh, New York, on the west bank of the Hudson River, was named by the crew of Dutch explorer Henry Hudson. As they sailed by the region on the *Half Moon*, Hudson's men were struck by the spectacle of American Indians painted in bright colors and dancing around a fire, and the sailors dubbed the area Duyvells' Dans Kamer, or "Devil's Dance Chamber."

Traveling southward, we find another location with a name of demonic origin, Spuyten Duyvil. While many people mistakenly think the name is a translation of "Spitting Devil," it actually refers to a legend about Anthony Van Corlaer, a trumpeter for the Dutch garrison at New Amsterdam. Van Corlaer attempted to warn the surrounding villages of a British invasion, but a raging storm drowned out the sound of his trumpet. Undaunted, Van Corlaer pledged to swim across the river and warn the villagers "*en spuyt den Duyvil*" (in spite of the Devil). But a monstrous devilfish dragged Van Corlaer to his death, and British forces took over New Amsterdam (now called New York).

Atlantic region and the other original thirteen colonies grew into a nation separate from England and other European countries. Perhaps the best-known tale is that of George Washington.

At the age of six, so the story goes, George Washington was given the gift of a hatchet, which he applied to anything on which he could get his hands. However, one afternoon, while slicing his way through his mother's pea sticks in the garden, George accidentally chopped into his father's cherry tree, causing it to fall. The following morning, his father found his tree cut in two and asked George if he knew how it fell. "I cannot tell a lie, Pa," George supposedly responded. "I did cut it with my hatchet." His father is said to reply, "Glad am I, George, that you killed my tree; for you have paid me for it a thousand fold." In light of this stark honesty, the accident of cutting the tree is turned into a purposeful event of the highest kind: "Such an act of heroism in my son is more worth than a thousand trees," adds George's father. It is in this manner that George learns the value of truth, and that there will never be any honor in telling a lie.

In *The Life of Washington*, published in 1809, Mason Locke Weems argues the case that the country's first president's "appreciation for truth" developed at an early age after accidentally chopping down his father's cherry tree. Moreover, the narrative offers more than simply a fable about the need to accept responsibility in order to learn the value of truth. The fable also suggests that on the day Augustine Washington lost his beloved cherry tree, he gained a son whose newfound appreciation for truth would forever change the face of the nation to come.

Washington Irving

Washington Irving (1783–1859) was an accomplished author who was a literary success in the United States and Europe as well. His best-known works are "The Legend of Sleepy Hollow," which details a schoolmaster's encounter with a headless horseman, and "Rip Van Winkle," which tells the story of a man who sleeps for twenty years and awakes to find that the life he once led is no more. Both have been scripted into children's cartoons, and continue to be widely popular: Paramount Pictures released *The Legend of Sleepy Hollow* in the fall of 1999, grossing over $100 million domestically—proving a sustaining American appetite for traditionalist folklore.

Whether he intended to or not, Washington Irving chose to create a new genre of literature rather than follow the literary path of his contemporaries, such as Cooper, Hawthorne, and Melville. This had a profound effect on the direction of American literature. Manipulating traditional folklore with rural reality, Irving inspired a dialogue among his peers and followers for years to come. Irving's excessive concentration on the detail of rural New York's landscapes and its inhabitants has been both praised and condemned by his critics. His contemporaries carped at Irving's intricate attention to detail, questioning whether it was by choice or merely intended to make up for a lack of creativity. For example, fellow author and lawyer Horace Binney Wallace suggested that Irving's "constant following of the minutiae of a scene to turn them into picturesque effect—this constant subordination of reflective action to outward appearance—damps and feebles the intellectual power."[6] Irving was also condemned for never publishing a traditional text, the supposed reason being that he did not have what it took to write anything of that caliber. In response to these allegations Irving replied, "It is comparatively easy to tell a story to any size when you have once the scheme and the characters in your mind."[7] Irving's scheme was to re-create a comfortable reality for his readers. His description of the "everyman" and his rural town was so accurate that it felt like the reader's very own. Once his readers identified with Irving's protagonist and his environment, they were hooked. For if the consequences of the story's lore could touch a town so similar to the reader's very own, what was preventing them from touching the reader themselves? Such was—and is—the power of his folklore.

Irving's brilliant storytelling through folklore not only tore through the readers' spine "at the midnight hour," but touched upon political sensitivities as well. In "Rip Van Winkle," which Irving adapted from a German folktale, the protagonist falls into a deep sleep for years. And when he awakes, it is not into the arms of his King, but under the blanket of a new democracy. Even though the old man awakes in the very place he fell asleep, he still wakes into a different nation. The reason Irving's protagonist finds himself in this position is because he was running away from his wife and the chores she was imposing on him. He was running away from responsibility. Jenifer S. Banks (an editor of Irving's *Letters*) wrote, "Irving's tale connects the image of woman with the birth of America as a nation and with the theme of growing up. As the voice of duty and obligation, she most clearly exemplifies Irving's imaginative use of women as a focus of those elements in society he wished to escape."[8] Irving himself even wrote that "Rip Van Winkle is perhaps the first registering of disillusionment with America as idea and fact."[9] Irving's extreme characterization of the "everyman" (more specifically the rural American everyman) may be why, after taking a closer look at both Ichabod Crane (from "The Legend of Sleepy Hollow") and Rip Van Winkle, one sees that these men not only have the same fantasies, but a similar lust for the simple pleasures of rural life, such as afternoon naps and a nice drink of ale.

"The Legend of Sleepy Hollow" is set in a glen along the Hudson River valley within the quiet confines of Tarrytown, New York. The townspeople are descendants of Dutch settlers who built the town and developed its community. The main character, Ichabod Crane, a schoolmaster, is the only one living in the town not of Dutch descent. Crane, it was said, traveled from Connecticut to take on the responsibility of headmaster. His cultural marginality is further emphasized by his build: he stretches nearly seven feet tall, and his appetite is larger than that of most families combined. Even "worse," his head is always stuck in a book. Reading and eating, in fact, are how Ichabod spends most of his time when not playing the role of disciplinarian in the schoolhouse, or rehearsing with the local church choir. All this changes when he lays eyes on Katrina Van Tassel.

Katrina is described as being "the prettiest girl in the town." And her father— "Old Baltus Van Tassel"—is one of the wealthiest farmers in the county. Katrina is thus a prize for a man of Ichabod's caliber, and the schoolmaster recognizes this. As such, the competition for Katrina's hand in marriage is severe. Even so, the only man that poses a challenge to Ichabod in the story is Brom Van Brunt, who is known as "Brom Bones" (the name given to him by his cohorts, the Sleepy Hollow Boys). Brom, described as a large man (as "thick as a tree stump"), is playful and well liked in the town. Even so, his "chiseled features" are assumed to be impenetrable, thus making him appear intimidating to Ichabod.

In the development of the story, Baltus Van Tassel throws a party for the entire town. Ichabod attends and dances with Katrina before consuming in great amounts the hoard of food set out for the partiers' consumption. After the evening's dancing stops and patrons are filling their plates, Old Baltus requests that his guests tell ghost stories. The story that holds everyone's attention is, of course, the tale of the headless horseman. This "story-within-the-story" details the unfortunate events of a German Hessian soldier fighting in the war against England. It was said that a cannonball had knocked his head clean off, and that he rides in search of his head through the night on a black stallion, haunting the trail back into town and terrorizing travelers. The horseman's power is limited to the trail leading into town: once a traveler crosses the bridge into town, the horseman will not follow. Thus the tale places emphasis on the town/country opposition, characterizing the limit beyond town culture, the woods, as being a site of peril. The headless horseman is of the woods; his powers are limited to the woods, thus making the town a place of safety and civilized security.

In the midst of this narrative, Brom claims that he challenged the headless horseman to a ride one evening, and just before the Hessian could attack, Brom crossed the bridge, rendering the Hessian powerless to harm him. The story has the greatest effect on Ichabod, who is characterized as overly paranoid or superstitious. After the dance, while riding his horse Gunpowder back into town, Ichabod encounters the headless horseman. In a clearing, when the moon is shining at its most brilliant, Ichabod sees the horseman with his head missing, and, resting in one hand, a pumpkin. Frightened, Ichabod makes a dash for the bridge, but the headless horseman launches his pumpkin at the schoolmaster, knocking him from his horse. Nothing is found of Ichabod the next morning except his hat. He is never again seen in the town of Sleepy Hollow. The story thus ends without resolving the mystery it presents. Suggestions are made as to the disappearance of Ichabod (such as moving to

The Story of Rip Van Winkle

The story of Rip Van Winkle is set in the Catskill Mountains along the Hudson River. Van Winkle's forefathers were among the many Dutch settlers who scattered and built communities all along the Hudson River in New York State. The tale characterizes Rip as being widely known in the town as a kind and generous person. But it also describes him as being incredibly lazy. One of the paradoxes of his character is that he constantly attends to other people's needs (hence the portrayal of Rip as generous), but that he rarely adheres to the demands of his wife (called Dame Van Winkle). His wife grows angry and is depicted as "storming through the town" each time Van Winkle fails to return or do his family duties.

The well-known "nap" that Van Winkle takes occurs after he drinks heavily from a keg of liquor offered to him by a large hairy man that he meets out hunting one afternoon. Van Winkle drinks too much from the keg, suggesting that he is the kind of man that overindulges, and consequently falls asleep for twenty years. When he awakes on what he assumes to be "the next morning," he discovers his gun rusted and his beard grown a foot longer. Fearing the wrath of his wife for being out all night, he quickly makes his way home. Once back in, he meets people that he does not recognize. A man speaking to a crowd in the street asks him what his political views were, whether he was a Federalist or a Democrat. Obviously confused, Van Winkle replies that he was loyal to the King, King George. When he returns to his former and now abandoned residence, he finds the painting of King George replaced by a painting of George Washington. Exiting his house, he finds himself confronted by a gathering crowd. In the crowd he discovers his daughter and son, who inform him that his wife died several years ago. Full of sorrow, he grieves for the loss of his wife, but is thankful that he is reunited with the remains of his family. The narrative concludes with Van Winkle continuing his habits, though now with his son, of taking long afternoon naps under the trees. He ends his days by telling his narrative of slumber to the town's children.

Scene from the movie *Sleepy Hollow* with Johnny Depp as Ichabod Crane. Photofest.

New York City to run for the Senate). Nonetheless, the characters Brom and Ka-trina are married, and the whereabouts of Ichabod, and whether or not he is alive or dead, are left unsolved. However, the story expresses a general consensus on the part of the townspeople, who all believe in the truth of the headless horseman, and the dangers of the forest territory that lies beyond the road of the rational world.

The tale contains other factors as well. As William L. Hedges wrote in 1965, "'The Legend of Sleepy Hollow,' like 'Rip Van Winkle,' is a story about a home and a way of settling down. Ichabod Crane is a solitary interloper in foreign ter-rain, a half-starved bachelor with no permanent home who boards around the neighborhood, spending a week at a time with one family and then going onto the next. . . . He is not a fighter but a dreamer."[10] Hedges further explains, "The story suggests that a large imagination may be only a means of camouflaging narrow ca-pacities. Too much dreaming, even of the great American dream, appears to in-duce impotence."[11]

The traditional American dream is intended to motivate Americans to work hard; for when you work hard enough your dream just might become reality. Under this platform the American "everyman" has struggled in order to achieve his dreams, all the while adding to the collective American trust. At least this is how the American dream was presented, and as such, interpreted. Instead, Irving offered two tales of men whose initiative was to dream, yet not prosper through hard work and initiative. Hard work and initiative were seen through the process of dreaming itself. Therein lay all of the work, the entire process for Rip Van Win-kle and Ichabod Crane. Rip Van Winkle dreamt his life away, thus living his Amer-ican dream at the cost of losing a majority of his life. And while Ichabod did not literally nap his life away, his daydreams of inheriting a wealthy life by marriage into the Van Tassel family (whether figurative or not) cost him his head. After all, it is suggested that he who donned the black cloak of the headless horseman was none other than Brom Bones, Ichabod's rival in winning the heart of Katrina Van Tassel. Whether Brom actually sliced away at Ichabod's head Irving does not reveal. The reader is left with two possible conclusions—either Ichabod was murdered as a result of taking advantage of the American dream's premise, or the horseman literally "scared the dreaming out of him," so to speak, leaving the schoolmaster to abandon his previous head in search of a more practical one. It is suggested that such a head would fulfill the intended collective ideals of the American dream.

At the conclusion of "The Legend of Sleepy Hollow," Irving suggests that his protagonist abandoned the dreary town to take a seat in the Senate, a role similar to Irving's as a U.S. diplomat. And Rip Van Winkle spent his remaining years lying in the sun, surrounded by only those who loved and adored him. It is said that Washington Irving had done the same, which leads this reader to believe that each of these tales is autobiographical, each referencing a chapter in Irving's life. Regardless of the extent to which Irving's stories were, or were not, autobiographical, his tales offer the kind of exploration of American ideals that the culture continues to find valuable.

FOLK HEROES AND LEGENDS

Johnny Appleseed

Born on September 26, 1779, in Leominster, Massachusetts, to Elizabeth and Nathaniel Chapman, John Chapman was otherwise known as the Apple Tree Man or "Johnny Appleseed." Tradition has it that Chapman planted more apple trees in forty-nine years that produce more apples than most people can eat in their lifetime. The orchards Chapman planted in Indiana, Kentucky, Pennsylvania, New York, and Ohio over 200 years ago still bear fruit today.

Little is known of Chapman's childhood other than the fact that he was well educated, and by the time he was twenty-five he had become a nurseryman planting trees in western New York and Pennsylvania. In the 1790s Chapman worked as a Bible missionary along the banks of the Potomac in eastern Virginia (though this information was given only by Chapman told through stories later in his life). His passion was apple seeds, which he picked from local cider mills. In the early 1800s many people were settling in the Northwest Territory (Ohio, Michigan, Indiana, and Illinois). Chapman took it upon himself to begin planting orchards so that when families settled, they would have food waiting for them. The price of an apple tree was only a few pennies, and when settlers could not muster up the change, Chapman would take their word to pay him back at a later date or trade for used clothing. If a customer were ever in need Chapman would charge nothing at all. Thus Chapman was presented as having a high business ethic that extended beyond the boundaries of capitalist accumulation.

Chapman's physical makeup was also depicted in the historical record. He was described as having a skeletal frame, with clothing draping off him. He was said to walk barefoot (though this was not uncommon at the time and in the region).

Born in 1779, John Chapman was otherwise known as the Apple Tree Man or "Johnny Appleseed." Courtesy of Library of Congress.

Many claim that he often traveled wearing a kettle on his head as a hat, though it is more likely that he traveled with one tied to his pack. Yet despite his appearance, accounts that he was never short of cash suggest that Chapman was not exactly poor. Neither was he extremely wealthy. Moreover, Chapman seemed to be suspicious of state economic structures; rather than relying on a bank Chapman apparently buried his money in different areas along the frontier. In addition, his kind and likable presence led to erroneous tales about him being able to heal animals with his bare hands or make friends with dangerous animals such as wolves and bears.

Each fall Chapman would travel back to western Pennsylvania to collect seeds from the cider mills. He often traveled alone, making friends along the way when the opportunity arose. Chapman was depicted as having friendly relations with Native Americans, for they both shared a love for the land. Many tribes were said to hold Chapman in high regard, impressed with his appreciation for all life. Chapman also found companionship with wildlife, and with one animal in particular. In the legend, Chapman is said to have come across a large black wolf that was caught in a trap. Chapman removed the steel trap from the wolf's leg and bandaged its wound. He stayed with the wolf until it could walk again, and when the wound finally healed Chapman bade the animal farewell, but the wolf followed him. In this fashion Chapman acquired the wolf as a constant associate: wherever Chapman traveled, the wolf was by his side.

John Chapman died of pneumonia near Fort Wayne, Indiana, at the home of friend William Worth in 1842, though other dates have also been documented. It is said that this was the only time he had ever fallen ill. Once when asked why he had no fear, Chapman's supposed reply was that he "lived in harmony with all people" and that "he could not be harmed" as long as he lived according to "the law of love."

John Henry

John Henry was born into slavery between the years 1840 and 1850. It is not certain where exactly Henry was born, but it is possible that his mother was a slave on the Henry plantation of Winchester, Virginia. His saga is an introduction into the struggle African Americans faced shortly after the Civil War. Aside from being black and southern, Henry, like most other men in his position, would soon be competing for work against machines—confronting the new age of industrialization. Even though the industrial revolution would not happen for another half a century, tools like the steam drill were being manufactured and replacing men who worked for the railroad companies.

Henry was still a child when the Civil War began, and when the war ended he traveled north to West Virginia, where he found men working on the railroad. Folklore describes Henry as a likable but overly confident man. When he asked the foreman for a job, for instance, Henry claimed that he was born to work on the railroad. The foreman dismissed him as nothing more than a braggart. Determined to please his future boss, Henry asked a man by the name of Li'l Willie (who has been written into folklore as Henry's sidekick) to hold a stake while he drove it into the ground with only three swings. And with those three swings of a hammer the legend of John Henry began: what typically took two men a good fifteen minutes to do, Henry did in three seconds. Needing no further convincing, the foreman hired Henry immediately.

While working for the Chesapeake Railroad, Henry met his fiancée, Pollie Ann, who like many others heard of the living legend's strength and came to see him in action. Like most steel drivers of his day Henry soon found himself working for the C&O (Connecticut and Ohio) Railroad Company because of the higher wages they paid. The C&O was eager to run track over as much of frontier America as possible. The line Henry was worked on at the time of his death was a developing route from Washington, D.C., to Cincinnati, in an attempt to link the shipping lanes of the Chesapeake Bay to the Ohio Valley. Henry was probably employed under Captain W. R. Johnson, who was a conductor for the C&O and worked at the Big Bend Tunnel the same time as he.

Henry's entire identity rested on the fact that no man or machine was more powerful than his somewhat superhuman capacities. The moment he became the most powerful man within earshot was the moment Henry was no longer Irving's American "everyman," but an inspiration to every workingman. This was most important to the growing industry, for Henry came to espouse the kind of subjectivity to which all men were supposed to aspire: working harder than the machine industry itself. So when Henry was presented with the challenge of matching the productivity of a steam drill, he had no choice but to accept the duel. Not only his identity, but also his life's ambition was at stake. Maybe it was a salesman who presented the idea to Henry, or the C&O conductor, W. R. Johnson; regardless, he accepted a challenge to race through the Big Bend.

There is no documentation of how long the race lasted, when it began or ended. Some say thirty-five minutes, others two days. The more popular folktales time it from sunrise to sundown. In the tale, Henry rips through the mountain with two hammers, though he is at first no match for the drill. Refusing to give up, Henry pounds away. Eventually, the drill dulls, and has to be replaced. During this time

John Henry: The Steel-Driving Man

This ballad of John Henry was first published in sheet music form by the Blankenship Broadside Company, and cost a nickel per copy.

John Henry was a railroad man
He worked from six till five,
"Raise 'em up hollow and let 'em drop down,
I'll beat you to the bottom or die."

John Henry said to his captain:
"You are nothing but a common man.
Before this steam drill shall beat me down,
I'll die with my hammer in my hand."

John Henry said to the Sinkers:
"You must listen to my call,
Before this steam drill shall beat me down,
I'll jar these mountains till the fall."

John Henry's captain said to him:
"I believe these mountains are caving in."
John Henry said to the captain:
"That's my hammer you hear in the wind."

John Henry he said to his captain:
"Your money is getting mighty slim,
When I hammer through this old mountain,
Oh captain will you walk in?"

John Henry's captain came to him
With fifty dollars in his hand,
He laid his hand on his shoulder and said,
"This belongs to a steel driving man."

John Henry was hammering on the right side,
The big steam drill on the left,
Before that steam drill could beat him down,
He's hammered his fool self to death.

They carried John Henry to the mountains,
From his shoulder his hammer would ring.
She caught on fire by a little blue blaze
I believe these old mountains are caving in.

John Henry was lying on his death bed,
He turned over on his side,
And these were the last words John Henry said,
"Bring me a cool drink of water before I die."

John Henry had a little woman,
Her name was Pollie Ann,
He hugged and kissed her just before he died,
Saying, "Pollie do the very best you can."

> John Henry's woman heard he was dead,
> She could not rest on her bed,
> She got up at midnight, caught that No. 4 train,
> "I am going where John Henry fell dead."
>
> They carried John Henry to that new burying ground
> His wife all dressed in blue.
> She laid her hand on John Henry's cold face,
> "John Henry I've been true to you"[12]

Henry is able to catch up. By sunrise Henry had beaten the drill by four feet. But he had worked so hard that it cost him his life.

John Henry did not merely inspire steel-driving men in life, but his story has lived on through song. Workers would sing the ode of John Henry, keeping the folk hero's spirit alive and their spirits up while driving steel. Over the years John Henry's ballad has changed depending on the region in which it is sung, though the original can still be found. The irony of this tale can be found in the cost levied from humanity by the rise of machines. Henry is seen as a hero—as the person who shows industry that human labor can beat out the labor of machines. Though in "keeping up the spirits" of laborers who live and die under the rule of industrialization, this supposed "triumph" of humanity has the effect of keeping humanity chained to the socioeconomic structure that rules its existence.

Joe Magarac

The folktale of Joe Magarac (Muhgu-rutz) originates in Pittsburgh, Pennsylvania—in the Monongahela Valley area known as Hunkietown (from "Hungarian," because the town's population was comprised mostly of immigrant Hungarian steelworkers). Many suggest that the legend of Magarac was nothing more than a joke played on a local reporter who had no idea that Magarac meant "jackass" in Croatian. Others claim that the legend should read as an inspirational story of hope, arguing that Magarac is to steelworkers what Paul Bunyan is to lumberjacks and woodsmen. Still others see the story as an example of the connection of tall tales to the desire of men and women to achieve perfection, as the writer George Carver argued. Tall tales are thus many times characterized by larger than life heroes, heroes with whom readers identify in their attempts to evolve and cultivate competitive and redoubtable skills in the long course of life.

Magarac was a folk hero made of steel who represented the Hungarian steelworkers of western Pennsylvania, although the Irish, whose ancestors also worked the same steel mills years earlier, claimed that Magarac was not Hungarian, but Irish and named Joseph Patrick McGarrick. This question of Magarac's ethnicity marks him as one of the most treasured and most powerful immigrant folk heroes of the Mid-Atlantic. Whether he was Irish or Hungarian, the seven-foot-tall titan was able, according to the tale, to twist iron ingots with his hands, mix white-hot steel, and shape train rails by merely squeezing them between his fingers. Legend has it that Magarac was born on an ore mountain in the Old Country, yet his fable has spread far across the Mid-Atlantic. A statue of Magarac, which once stood at the Manchester Bridge, can now be seen at the Allegheny Center Mall in Pennsylvania.

In the November 1931 issue of *Scribner's* magazine, Owen Francis published "The Saga of Joe Magarac: Steelman," which was the first time the general public read of the man of steel. Benjamin Botkin retold Francis's tall tale in *A Treasury of American Folklore* and reworked it again in 1950 in the popular *Standard Dictionary of Folklore, Mythology and Legend*. These three versions of the Magarac myth describe the giant as a workhorse whose only desire was to work day and night, asking nothing in return but to be fed.

According to the legend, Magarac came to Hunkietown the night Steve Mestrovich (commonly referred to as Big Steve) was to give his daughter's hand in marriage to the "strongest man in the county." The contest to reveal the strongest man involved lifting dolly bars; the first was 350 pounds, the second 500 pounds, and the third 1000 pounds. In Hunkietown power and respect were often judged by strength, especially among the steelworkers. Using this rationale, Big Steve thought that only the strongest man would be able to protect his daughter Mary. His daughter was not against this ritual, for she was already in love with the person already assumed to be the strongest man in Hunkietown, Pete Pussick.

The competition was severe, and included a local named Eli Stanoski in addition to dozens of men from along the Monongahela River as far away as Johnstown. Pete, Eli, and one of the men from Johnstown were able to lift the 500-pound bars, but one could move the 1,000-pound one. After another man from Johnstown failed to lift the 1,000-pound bar, the crowd laughed. In a fit of anger he dared any man to come and lift the bar. Magarac, standing at the back of the crowd, accepted the challenge. This introduction of Magarac helped the legend survive for many years as a true story. Persons who lived in or around the rural Hunkietown would find value in the tale because it focused around the lives of fellow Hunkietowners, men and women whom they had either met themselves or someone related to them.

When Magarac accepted the challenge, the crowd fell silent. The townspeople had "never seen a man of steel before" and were suspicious of his intentions. Even though Magarac assumed a towering presence, his disposition was friendly. His back was judged "as broad as an automobile" and his wrists were said to be "as round as a man's waist." The man from Johnstown struck Magarac for laughing at him, but before he could get another punch in, the jovial Magarac picked him up in one hand and made a figure eight out of the 1,000-pound dolly with the other. Even though Magarac won the contest, he did not accept the offer to wed Mary. Instead he suggested that Pete and Mary wed due to their young love for one another. This addition to the Magarac tale offers not only a human side to the Magarac character, but also an understanding of love even though he had no interest in such things. Magarac's only interests were work and food, which the people of Hunkietown were more than happy to offer.

Working at the Braddock mill during the day and the Homestead mill in the evenings, Magarac stopped working only to eat—five meals a day in all. Many versions of the legend claim that Magarac would eat just about anything offered to him; others suggest that he ate only stuffed cabbage. There are also stories about how Magarac died. Many claim that he dove into boiling steel, sacrificing himself to make stronger steel for the steel workers. Others do not even mention his death, which makes Magarac one of few folk heroes who were not beaten or destroyed by the system they were working in or fighting against. Magarac was a protector. Even though he was working for the steel industry, his primary purpose was to protect the steel-driving men. Living legend claims that he still roams the Pittsburgh steel mills and construction sites protecting its workers. As with the "echo" in the legend of Penn's Cave, there have been many stories of near-fatal accidents avoided by a mysterious giant no one has seen before who arrives at the zero hour and saves the day. Regardless of how Magarac's story ends, his folktale continues to have an impact.

GHOSTLORE

Typically, ghosts appearing within folktales are described as creatures yet to have gone to "the next plane of existence." They are those whose work is not yet finished on this earth, remaining until their purpose has been fulfilled. Many are characterized as the victims of murder. In this sense, these tales carry the intention of retribution "here on earth," for the ghosts remain until the identity of their assailant has been uncovered. They linger between this world and the next until their wrong has been corrected. For example, in the folktale "The Wife of Usher's Well," three dead sons visit their mother in the night. These were ghosts of the woman's sons who had taken on the appearances of their former selves in order to comfort their mother in her time of grief. Only when they leave does the woman realize that they were in fact the ghosts of her sons and not the physical persons. At one time or another the ghost stories that follow were reported as fact. Patrick W. Gainer traveled to the rural southern Appalachians of West Virginia and documented the following lore.

Hitchhiker Narratives

Gainer heard the following story of the hitchhiking ghost in 1955 from Doris Lilly, a student at West Virginia University, who heard it from the victim's family.

Late one evening on Highway 33 a man, driving alone, picked up a hitch-hiker, who he saw standing on the side of a bridge waving her hands in the air. She asked if he could give her a ride back home to Elkins, West Virginia. Because the man was already heading that way he agreed and offered her a seat beside him. The girl was very relieved, for she told the driver that her parents would be worried and that she had trouble with her car. When arriving at the girl's home, the man went around opening her door, but when he did there was nobody there. Confused, the man walked up to the house and knocked on the door assuming the girl had run inside. A middle-aged woman answered and the man explained that he had just given her daughter a ride, and was curious if she had run into the house. The woman told the stranger that he had picked up her daughter's ghost. The girl was killed in a car accident on Highway 33 two years ago and has haunted the road ever since.[13]

The story of the hitchhiker/prophet has been retold in just about every region of America. Typically, pedestrians in rural areas pick up the hitchhiker. When the stories are retold the hitchhiker is often described as an angel or a holy person (if they predict the future) or as a loved one who recently passed on (if the hitchhiker shares an intimate moment with the driver). Regardless, these cautionary tales have led many drivers to think twice about picking up strangers.

Another ghost tale concerns a Maryland man by the name of Jack, who appears in the woods at night as a wandering ghost holding his lantern—or what is known as a jack-o'-lantern. Instead of focusing on the appearance of the spirit and what he might do to people traveling through the woods today, the tale relates the origin of Jack and his lantern, and serves as a moral lesson to those who think they can cheat death and lead an immoral life without fearing the potential of punishment in the afterlife. The story is purported to having taken place sometime around the turn of the twentieth century.

The story opens with Jack—who is known for his excessive drinking, and for treating his wife and children poorly—confronting the devil. Having had too much whiskey one particular evening, he finds himself on the verge of dying. Facing death, Jack sees the devil, who comes to claim him. The devil forces Jack to follow him along a trail. Along the way Jack and the devil pass a grog shop. Jack asks the devil if he would like to stop for a drink. The devil answers that he would, but that he has no change. Jack tricks the devil into changing himself into a dime, but instead of taking the coin into the bar, Jack puts it in a purse that is hidden in his pocket. The purse is in the shape of a cross, and because of this the devil cannot escape and change himself back into his original form. The devil pleads to be let out, and Jack agrees only after making the devil promise that he will not come to take him to Hell for at least another twelve months. Jack has it in mind that he will "find religion" in the course of the coming year so that he will not end up in Hell. But then Jack decides that six out of the twelve months will be enough time to repent, and returns to his life of drinking. After those six months are up, he decides that a *month* will be enough time to repent, and thus continues to drink. He changes his mind in a similar fashion several times, until the last day of the twelve-month respite is up and the devil comes for him again.

Once more the two set out, and once more Jack tricks the devil. He convinces the devil to climb a tree in order to get an apple, and before the devil can climb back down, Jack carves a cross at the base of the tree. This time, Jack gets the devil to agree to *never* come back to take him to Hell, at which point Jack erases the cross and the devil disappears. Years later when Jack dies he knows that he will not be taken to Hell, so he tries to get into Heaven. However, the angel at the gate refuses him entry. Jack then tries to enter through the gate of Hell, but the devil turns him away as well. Left alone in the darkness at the gates of Hell, Jack pleads with the devil for some light so that he may find his way back. The devil throws him a chunk of burning coals from out of the fires of Hell, which Jack turns into a lantern. For the reminder of his existence, Jack is forced to wander with his lantern, unable to be part of either this world or the afterlife.[14]

Ghost tales such as the ones discussed above abound in the mid-Atlantic region. They belong more to local legends than to real folklore. Stories such as these have more to do with enticing someone over a late-night campfire to accept a dare, or to spend the night in a purportedly haunted region of the forest (or a haunted house). In some cases ghost tales stem from particular historical events that took place in a specific region, such as the many ghost tales surrounding the area of Gettysburg, Pennsylvania, the site of one of the Civil War's major battles. Frequently, these kinds of tales arise out of the commercialism of local tourist industries, offering travelers the chance to go on "ghost walks" and "ghost tours." All in all, ghost tales reflect the continuing fascination with the Unknown and the mystery of the "afterlife."

CONCLUSION

Folklore not only represents the creativity of particular peoples and their regions, but also reflects the continuing fascination with things unknown. It also reveals the endurance of humanity's concern for establishing and maintaining a moral existence. In this sense, folktales speak not of facts, but of these larger cultural considerations. In the realm of folklore, it does not matter whether or not George Washington chopped down his father's cherry tree. What matters is that a child learned the value of honesty. Likewise, that a historian cannot locate for us the physical proof that John Henry lived does not mean that the tale carries no significance in the present world. The tales discussed throughout this chapter thus have value precisely in that they give us an indication of how various peoples inhabiting the region came to terms with their environment. They reveal the richness of the region's landscape and, more important, the creativity, diversity, and vitality of its citizens.

RESOURCE GUIDE

Printed Sources

Aderman, Ralph M. *Critical Essays on Washington Irving*. Boston: G.K. Hall, 1990.

Bascom, William. "The Forms of Folklore." *Journal of American Folklore* 78 (1865): 3–20.

Bronner, Simon J. *Popularizing Pennsylvania: Henry W. Shoemaker and the Progressive Uses of Folklore and History*. University Park: Pennsylvania State University Press, 1996.

Courland, Harold, ed. *A Treasury of Afro-American Folklore: The Oral Literature, Traditions, Recollections, Legends, Tales, Songs, Religious Beliefs, Customs, Sayings, and Humor of Peoples of African American Descent in the Americas*. New York: Marlowe, 1996.

Cox, Marian Roalfe. *An Introduction to Folk-lore*. Detroit, MI: Singing Trees Press, 1968.

Gainer, Patrick W. *Witches, Ghosts, and Signs: Folklore of the Southern Appalachians*. Grantsville: Seneca Books, 1975.

Hedges, William. *Washington Irving: An American Study, 1802–1832*. Baltimore, MD: Johns Hopkins University Press, 1965.

Hurston, Zora Neale. *Folklore, Memoirs, and Other Writings*. New York: Library of America, 1995.

Irving, Washington. *The Legend of Sleepy Hollow*. New York: Library of Congress, 1966.

———. *Rip Van Winkle*. New York: Library of Congress, 1966.

Johnson, John B. *Tracking Down a Negro Legend*. Philadelphia: James Crissy, 1832.

Leeming, David, ed. *Myths, Legends, and Folktales of America: An Anthology*. New York: Oxford University Press, 1999.

Marshall, John. *The Life of George Washington, Commander in Chief of the Armed Forces*. Philadelphia: James Crissy, 1832.

Parker, Arthur C. *Seneca Myth and Folk Tales*. Lincoln: University of Nebraska Press, 1989.

Peck, Catherine, ed. *A Treasury of North American Folktales*. New York: W. W. Norton, 1998.

Reutter, Clifford J. "The Puzzle of a Pittsburgh Steeler: Joe Magarac's Ethnic Identity." *Western Pennsylvania Historical Magazine* 63, no. 1 (1980).

Smith, E. A. *Myths of the Iroquois*. New York: Smithsonian Institute—Bureau of Ethnology, 1994.

Stouteneburg, Adrien. *American Tall Tales*. New York: Viking Press, 1966.

Weems, M. L. *The Life of George Washington*. Philadelphia: J. B. Lippincott, 1860.

Williams, Brett. *John Henry: A Bio-Bibliography*. Westport, CT: Greenwood Press, 1983.

Web Sites

Folklore and History of Maryland

http://funkmasterj.tripod.com/mdf.htm#mdf (accessed March 2, 2004)

Includes Maryland's cultural institutes and organizations, as well as the cultural organizations of its neighboring states.

Native American Lore Index Page

http://www.ilhawaii.net/~stony/loreindx.html (accessed January 10, 2004)

Includes several Native American folktales such as "The Origin of the Hunter's Buffalo Dance."

Native Language of the Americas: Algonquin (Algonkin, Anishnabe, Anishinabe, Anishnabeg)

http://www.native-languages.org/algonquin.htm (accessed January 10, 2004)

Also includes Algonquin History and Cultural links.

Events

New York Folklore Society Annual Conference

http://www.nyfolklore.org/progs/conf2003.html

Held in the fall of each year to celebrate folklore in New York State.

Organizations

American Folklore Society
Timothy Lloyd, AFS Executive Director
Mershon Center, Ohio State University
1501 Neil Avenue
Columbus, OH 43201-2602
Phone: 614-292-3375
Fax: 614-292-2407
Email: lloyd.100@osu.edu

New York Folklore Society
P.O. Box 764
Schenectady, NY 12301
Phone: 518-346-7008
Fax: 518-346-6617
Email: nyfs@nyfolklore.org

Virginia Folklore Society
Nancy Martin-Perdue, President and Editor
Charlottesville, VA
Email: np8h@virginia.edu

FOOD

*Robert F. Moss,
with Caffilene Allen*

Unlike some parts of the United States—such as New England and the South—the mid-Atlantic region does not have a single predominant style that defines its food culture in the popular imagination. A variety of distinct foodways can be found in the region, such as Chesapeake Bay cooking, Pennsylvania Dutch cooking, and Italian American cooking, each of which has its own characteristic ingredients, cooking techniques, and signature dishes. Diverse as they are, these food cultures do share common traits. Mid-Atlantic dishes tend to be simple, hearty creations based on the natural products of the region—most notably seafood, poultry, fruits, and vegetables. These products show the influence of the area's seashores, bays, and rivers as well as the fertile soil and mild climate that characterize the Mid-Atlantic's environment. The food culture also reflects the region's rich, varied history, in which successive waves of immigrants came to the region, adopted the new ingredients they found there, and adapted them to their own traditional ways of cooking and eating. Many of these foods, such as bagels, hot dogs, and pizza, crossed over from being specialties of immigrant neighborhoods and became staples of the general diet not only of the Mid-Atlantic but also of the United States as a whole. Over time, industrialization and improved transportation have dampened the distinctiveness of the region's cooking, as mass-produced food products and imported produce have increasingly dominated the local diets. But classic mid-Atlantic cooking can still be found in remarkable variety. From the mountains of West Virginia to the shores of Chesapeake Bay to the streets of New York City, these dishes define the food culture of the Mid-Atlantic.

NATIVE AMERICAN AND COLONIAL COOKING

The story of food in the Mid-Atlantic begins with the dozens of Native American tribes that originally populated the region. The primary mid-Atlantic tribes—the Delaware and Powhatan along the Chesapeake coast and the Mohawk, Cayuga,

Oneida, Onondaga, and Seneca in New York and Pennsylvania—shared similar foodways. Their societies were largely agricultural, depending upon cultivated crops for most of their diet, supplemented by fish and game. Typically, more than half of a Native American's calories would come from what the Iroquois called the "three sisters": corn, beans, and squash. These three staples were grown together using an interplanting method that allowed each of the crops to support the others. First, corn kernels were planted in shallow holes in the ground and allowed to germinate. As the seedlings grew, the Native American women (for it was women and children who performed most of the crop-raising duties) would add soil around them, building mounds that would eventually be a foot high and two feet across. About two or three weeks after the corn was sown, beans would be planted in the hills, where they contributed nitrogen to the soil and helped the corn grow. The corn stalks, in turn, served as climbing poles for the beans. Between the corn and bean mounds the women would plant squash or pumpkins, and these plants' broad leaves would shade the cultivated ground, helping to preserve moisture in the soil and inhibit weeds.

The three sisters were supplemented by other cultivated plants such as sumpweed, maygrass, and sunflowers—whose seeds and roots (now known as Jerusalem artichokes) could be eaten—as well as wild nuts and berries. Along the Great Lakes, wild rice was available and incorporated by the tribes as a supplement to corn and beans, and maple sugar was tapped from trees and used as a sweetener. The primary food-related role of Native American men was hunting and fishing. Deer was the most common game hunted in the mid-Atlantic region, and dried or smoked venison was one of the primary sources of protein in the native diet. Other game included bear, rabbit, moose, and passenger pigeons. Fishing was also an important part of Native American foodways, with bass, walleye, sturgeon, and trout being abundant in the region's many rivers and streams. Crabs, mussels, and clams were available along Chesapeake Bay and in other coastal areas.

The most common Native American dishes were soups and stews made from corn, beans, and squash, which were typically cooked over a fire in a single pot and eaten from a common vessel, usually with the fingers. Corn was dried and ground into meal to be used in porridges or baked on hot rocks into a coarse bread, and green ears of corn were roasted in hot ashes. When it was available, fresh game or fish would be roasted over an open fire, but for most of the year meat was available only in a preserved form—usually dried or smoked—and so was often included in the stew pot along with corn and beans.

The foodways of the mid-Atlantic tribes defined not only what Native Americans ate but also the structure of their lives. The first major activity of the year occurred during March, the spawning season for the region's fish. Native Americans would leave their villages, where they had been sheltered during the coldest part of winter, and break up into fishing camps of 100 to 200 people. Positioning themselves along streams and rivers, the members of the camps constructed traps from wooden poles driven down into the bed of the waterway, forming triangular enclosures to catch the spawning fish. The catch was cleaned, then smoked over fires to be preserved for the upcoming months. The fishing camps broke up around the first of April, and the tribes returned with their stores of fish to their villages. From late spring until early fall, the women would devote themselves to the planting and tending of corn, beans, and squash, while men would embark on periodic hunting trips for deer, rabbit, and squirrel. In October, once the crops were harvested and put away for winter, the main deer-hunting season would begin. Women and children would beat the brush with sticks, herding the deer toward archers concealed in the woods. After they were killed, the deer would be cleaned, their skins preserved, and the meat smoked. By November the tribes would return to their villages to prepare for the upcoming winter, and the cycle would begin again.

It was this Native American food culture that the first European settlers found when they arrived in the mid-Atlantic region in the 1600s, and they quickly adopted many of the foods and cooking techniques as their own. The settlers came from different parts of Europe, but predominant among them in the early years were the Swedes, who settled in Delaware; the Dutch, who settled in New Amsterdam (later New York); the Scotch-Irish, who settled in West Virginia; and the English, who settled first on the shores of Maryland and then throughout the region. Later, Germans—better known as the Pennsylvania Dutch—settled in Pennsylvania, Italians settled in New York and Maryland, and a range of other ethnic and religious groups, including Jews, Quakers, Shakers, and the Amish, settled throughout other parts of the mid-Atlantic area.

Because of the nearby sea and its bounty, the fertile farmland, and the plentiful game in the surrounding mountains, the mid-Atlantic colonists generally had a more than ample food supply. Fish, oysters, clams, terrapins, wild turkey, bear and deer meat, hams, and bacon were common fare when they were in season, as were fruits such as peaches, strawberries, and cranberries. The Europeans adopted the cultivation of corn from their native neighbors, and it quickly became the staple grain in the colonial diet. Ground into cornmeal, it was the primary ingredient used for bread, wheat flour being scarce and expensive. Cane sugar—which had to be imported from the West Indies—was fairly rare due to its high price, but honey was readily attainable since there was plenty of land for beehives, and it was often the sweetener of choice. Preparation and storage of food during colonial times were difficult, however, and like the Native Americans, the European settlers had a diet that was very much controlled by the seasons.

The English colonists brought with them their own methods of food preparation and adapted them to local ingredients. Boiling was the dominant English cooking mode, as can be seen in early mid-Atlantic recipes. Staple items include boiled dumplings and puddings made from cornmeal or wheat flour and flavored with eggs, milk, or apples. Boiling was used to preserve food as well. Cream cheese, for example, was made by heating cream or milk over low heat and then allowing it to stand for several weeks so that it would lose its moisture and become semisolid. Apples would be preserved similarly, with the fruit mashed to a pulp and simmered until partially dried, then seasoned with sugar and spices. While a little further south in Virginia smoking was the standard way of preserving meats, in Maryland and Pennsylvania drying was more common. Dried beef, which would last several years, was a staple of the diet and was used to flavor puddings and dumplings when fresh meat was not available.

In colonial Maryland, tobacco was the primary cash crop, but over time more and more farmers began to plant wheat, and by the time of the American Revolution the colony had become a major source of wheat flour. The first record of a wheat shipment from Baltimore shows that in 1758 John Stevenson bought a thousand bushels of wheat and shipped them from that port. That shipment sold quickly, and others began to follow suit. Large quantities of wheat and flour were soon being shipped from the colony, and wheat replaced corn as the chief food export crop.

Transporting food was a particular challenge in a day when there were no railroads, no paved roads, and no refrigeration. Movement via water was the main mode of shipping, but vessels became infested with rodents, and food supplies rotted because of poor storage or other conditions. These problems began to be addressed as early as the mid-1700s by new road-building projects. The Great Eastern Road (now called Route 1) was built to link Philadelphia to Baltimore, and the Frederick Road, completed in 1769, connected western Maryland to the eastern port of Baltimore. Still, there was no road connecting the western mid-Atlantic farmlands in Maryland, West Virginia, and Pennsylvania to the Chesapeake Bay area until 1818, when the Old National Road (now known as U.S. Route 40) was completed. Envisioned by George Washington and laid out by Thomas Jefferson in 1806, the road started at Cumberland, Maryland, and stretched westward to Wheeling, West Virginia, on the Ohio River. At its Maryland terminus, it connected with the existing eastern turnpikes and allowed traffic to flow freely toward the eastern shores of the Mid-Atlantic.

These roads were supplemented by a new series of canals that were built in the early part of the nineteenth century. Perhaps the most important of these was the Erie Canal, completed in 1825, which linked the Great Lakes with the Hudson River and made New York City a marketing outlet for the farmlands of New York State. The Chesapeake and Delaware Canal (1829) connected the Delaware Bay with the Chesapeake, and the Delaware and Raritan Canal (1834) in New Jersey connected the two rivers of the same name. Both provided a cheaper, faster way to bring produce from the country to the cities where it could be sold. The influence of these canals lasted only a few years before they were replaced by a second transportation revolution: the rise of railroads. The Camden and Amboy Railroad (1830) linked New York City and Philadelphia. The Philadelphia, Wilmington, and Baltimore Railroad (1838) provided the first through rail service among those cities. The completion of the Baltimore and Ohio Railroad to Wheeling, Ohio, in 1852 gave midwestern grain producers ready access to the markets of eastern cities, both ensuring the decline of mid-Atlantic grain producers and enhancing Baltimore's stature as a major flour milling and exporting center.

These transportation improvements laid the groundwork for the transformation of the region's cookery that would occur over the course of the nineteenth century. The region's rich natural resources and the rise of industrialization gave birth to thriving food industries, such as Hershey's Chocolate in Pennsylvania, Campbell's Soups in New Jersey, and McCormick's Spices in Maryland. The new wealth of the industrialist class helped launch a culture of fine dining in the restaurants and hotels of the Mid-Atlantic's cities, a movement led by Delmonico's in New York City, the first formal restaurant in the United States. At the same time, millions of new immigrants came to the mid-Atlantic states, forming a rich variety of ethnic communities with distinctive styles of cooking and eating. The food culture of today's mid-Atlantic region is built on this foundation from the preceding eras.

ENVIRONMENTAL INFLUENCES ON MID-ATLANTIC FOOD

The food culture of the Mid-Atlantic is strongly influenced by the region's environment, and the foremost aspect of this environment is the presence of water. New Jersey, New York, Pennsylvania, Delaware, and Maryland all share at least one shore with either Chesapeake Bay or the Atlantic Ocean. Fishing has long been a mainstay of the Mid-Atlantic's economy, and seafood is a central feature of the region's cooking.

Seafood

To mid-Atlantic natives, a clam is not just a clam. It can be a cherrystone, little-neck, or surf (all varieties of hard-shell clams), or a manninose, a soft-shell clam with a thin shell and elongated body. These are as many clam recipes and there are types of clams. They are eaten raw or steamed "on the half-shell," with an accompaniment of butter or lemon juice; breaded and fried as clam strips; and steamed and tossed in pasta. Although clam chowder is often associated with New England, it has been a signature dish for the entire Eastern Seaboard since colonial days. Clam chowder is a hearty stew with a base of whole or chopped clams cooked with onions, salt pork, and potatoes. In most recipes, cream is used to give richness and body. Manhattan clam chowder, a variety created in New York City in the mid–nineteenth century, is unique in that it substitutes tomatoes for cream. This deviation has been roundly decried among New England–style chowder lovers (in 1939 a Maine legislator introduced a bill forbidding the use of tomatoes in chowder), but it is strongly defended by its partisans in and around New York.

Like clams, crabs are known by a variety of names to mid-Atlantic residents. They can be soft shell or hard shell. A young female crab is a sook, while a male crab is a jimmie. Jimmies can be identified by the inverted T-shape on their undersides, and they are best used for steaming. Sooks are more often sent to picking plants, where their meat is prepared to be canned and sold. Chesapeake Bay produces the majority of blue crabs sold in this country and is the source of the famous Maryland soft-shelled crabs. Blue crab season runs from May through early October, and fishermen use many methods to catch the crab. The two most popular ways are trotlines and crabpots. The first are long lines (sometimes measuring over 1,000 feet) that are baited at different places, laid on the water bottom, and held down by weights at both ends. The crabber uses a boat to move up and down the line, pulling it up from the bottom and using a net to catch the crabs that were holding onto the bait before they can swim away. Crabpots are baited wire-mesh traps set up so that crabs can easily swim into them but can't swim back out.

Different grades of crabmeat are used for different types of cooking and recipes.

Early Manhattan Clam Chowder Recipe

The following recipe for Manhattan-style clam chowder was collected by Pierre Blot in his *Hand-Book of Practical Cookery* (1867):

Put in a *pot* . . . some small slices of fat salt pork, enough to line the bottom of it; on that, a layer of potatoes, cut into small pieces; on the potatoes, a layer of chopped onions; on onions, a layer of tomatoes, in slices, or canned tomatoes; on the latter a layer of clams, whole or chopped (they are generally chopped), then a layer of crackers.

Then repeat the process . . . till the pot is nearly full. Every layer is seasoned with salt and pepper. Other spices are sometimes added according to taste; such as thyme, cloves, bayleaves, and tarragon.

When the whole is in, cover with water, set on a slow fire, and when nearly done, stir gently, finish cooking, and serve.[1]

Jumbo lump is the top of the line, consisting of large pieces of crab with no shell or cartilage. Backfin meat is taken from the backfin of the crab and has large pieces of lump but also some broken body meat and perhaps a small amount of shell. Backfin is often used for the Chesapeake area's famous crabcakes. "Special meat" is taken from the entire body of the crab and includes a little bit of jumbo lump, but it can contain quite a bit of cartilage and shell, which must be removed before it can be used in cooking. Special crabmeat is often used for soups. Like lump, claw meat comes in large pieces, but it contains more moisture and therefore has a different texture and generally is the least expensive type of crabmeat.

The crab cake is perhaps the dish most closely associated with Chesapeake Bay cooking. Each area has its own local version of the dish, and many families closely guard their prized recipes. All crab cakes share the same basic ingredients: crabmeat, bindings, and seasoning. Any type of crabmeat can be used, although jumbo lump and backfin are considered the highest quality. The bindings hold the meat together into a cakelike shape, and they vary greatly from recipe to recipe. Eggs, mayonnaise, and cream are common, along with fillers such as bread crumbs, cracker crumbs, or milk-soaked bread. Crab cakes are typically highly seasoned with flavorings such as lemon juice, mustard, parsley, horseradish, and hot sauce. Once the meat, binding, and seasonings are mixed together, they are formed into patties, then fried, sautéd, or broiled in butter and/or olive oil. There are as many way of serving crab cakes as there are recipes for preparing them: on a bed of grits, atop salad greens, in small patties as a cocktail hors d'oeuvre, or on a bun as a crab cake sandwich.

The social gatherings in any region are frequently shaped by local foods. New England has its clambakes, South Carolina its oyster roasts, and Texas its beef barbecues. One of the most prominent food-based events in the Mid-Atlantic is the "crab feast," which features bushel baskets of steamed blue crabs. The crabs are coated in pungent spices and placed on a rack in specially designed crab pots, in which they are steamed above boiling beer, vinegar, or a mixture of the two liquids. The cooked crabs are dumped onto newspaper-covered picnic tables, where diners crack the shells open with mallets and pick out the tender meat. More than just dinners, crab feasts are occasions for families and communities to gather together for fun, relaxation, and celebration, and they are a characteristic part of mid-Atlantic life.

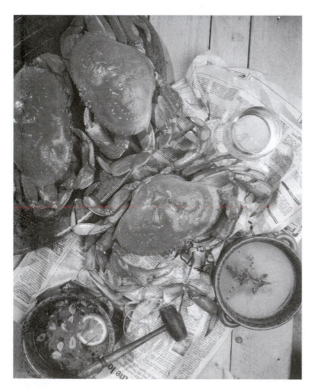

In the "crab feast," cooked crabs are dumped onto newspaper-covered picnic tables where diners crack the shells open with mallets and pick out the tender meat. © Getty Images/PhotoDisc.

In addition to crab cakes and crab feasts, the mid-Atlantic is known for a third type of crab delicacy: the soft-shelled crab. Blue crabs normally have a hard exterior, but they shed their shells as they grow, a process known as "molting" that occurs several times in their three-year life span. Once they shed their shells, they can be harvested as soft-shelled crabs. The unusual feature of soft-shelled crab dishes is that, apart from the very front part of the head, the crabs are served and eaten whole. One of the most popular preparations is to bread and deep-fry the crabs, then serve them as a sandwich, the crispy legs of the crab hanging out from the edges of the soft white roll. Soft-shells can also be sautéd, blackened, or broiled. Chesapeake Bay alone accounts for 90 percent of the soft-shelled crab production in the United States.

Crab is not the only shellfish for which the region is famous. Equally well known is the oyster, which can be found in the harbors and bays along the entire coastline of the Mid-Atlantic. Perhaps more than any other type of seafood, the flavor and character of an oyster are strongly determined by the location where it grows. An oyster is a filter feeder, so it absorbs the salts and nutrients (and pollutants, as well) from the water in which it lives, and these have a strong effect on the color and flavor of the oyster's flesh. For this reason, oysters are usually identified not by their biological species but by the location where they were harvested, and the Mid-Atlantic boasts some of the most flavorful and popular varieties in the country. Maryland natives are particularly proud of their Tangier and Chincoteague oysters, which contain a high salt content that makes them particularly appetizing eaten raw on the half shell. Oysters are also plentiful in New York's harbors and sounds, and Long Island's bluepoint, box, and Duck Island varieties are popular at upscale oyster bars.

The harvesting and eating of oysters has a long history in the Mid-Atlantic. Oyster houses (also called oyster cellars, oyster bars, and oyster saloons) were among the first public restaurants in the country, serving cheap raw or steamed oysters and plentiful alcoholic beverages. These were plain establishments, with rough tables and floors covered with sawdust to absorb dropped shells and other detritus. By the 1850s New York City's Canal Street was dotted with oyster cellars, and diners could have all they could eat for only six cents. With the coming of the railroads, the oyster craze spread westward, and New York City became the capital of "barreled oysters," which would be packed in barrels with salt and shipped on trains to satisfy the palates of midwestern diners. By 1880 the average American was eating over 600 oysters per year. The enormous demand for the shellfish resulted in the Chesapeake oyster wars, in which many watermen were killed over territorial fishing rights. The industry reached its peak around the turn of the twentieth century, employing some 20,000 Chesapeake residents and 2,000 "skipjacks"—the sail-powered oystering workboats.

Oyster Packing in Colonial New York

As soon as the oysters are caught, their shells are opened and the fish washed clean; some water is then poured into a pot, the oysters are put into it, and they are boiled for a while; the pot is then taken off the fire again and the oysters taken out and put upon a dish till they are almost dry. Then some nutmeg, allspice and black pepper are added, and as much vinegar as is thought sufficient to give a sourish taste. All this is mixed with half the liquor in which oysters are boiled, and put over the fire again. While boiling great care should be taken to skim off the thick scum. At last the whole pickling liquid is poured into a glass or earthen vessel, the oysters are put into it, and the vessel is well stopped to keep out the air. In this manner, oysters will keep for years, and may be sent to the most distant parts of the world.[2]

Today, only a small number of oysters are harvested in the region, compared to the booming oyster industry in the 1800s. By the 1960s, oystering in the region had fallen into serious decline as a result of overfishing, diminishing bay grasses that filter the water, and parasites that preyed on oysters. Recent conservation efforts have reversed those trends, however, and the mid-Atlantic oyster population is beginning to be revitalized. The unique regional varieties are enjoyed today not only in local oyster bars but, thanks to a thriving oyster shipping industry, at restaurants throughout the country, where they appear as specialty items on raw bar menus.

Apart from some minor modern improvements, the two primary methods used to harvest oysters today—dredging and tonging—are the same as those used by watermen in the nineteenth century. In the first, a large metal dredge is thrown from one of the skipjacks and dragged along the oyster bed, capturing hundreds of oysters and depositing them on the floor of the boat. The crew picks over them, sorts them according to size, and throws back those that are too small or broken. Tonging involves a waterman's lowering a forty-pound set of tongs onto the oyster bed and then closing the blades around a haul of oysters. He then pulls it back onto the boat, where the crew sorts and categorizes them.

River Roadways

While the sea leaves its imprint on the major portion of the mid-Atlantic area, powerful rivers also contribute to excellent food production in the area, not so much by providing food directly as by providing a transportation system for delivering food and an irrigation source for crops grown in the area. The Potomac River supports Washington, D.C.'s wharf markets; the Severn, Patapsco, Pocomoke, Wicomico, Wye, Chester, Elk, and Susquehanna rivers wind their way through various parts of Maryland; and the Shenandoah River provides nourishment to the rich farmlands of West Virginia. The Hudson River valley is home to some of New York's most fertile agricultural land, and its waterway, feeding into the harbor of New York City, has long been an important transportation corridor through which crops were shipped from farm to market.

Any land adjacent to water forms its own personality derived from that water, and mid-Atlantic shorelines are no exception. The beach is an obvious manifestation of this, but seaside regions generally have large wetland areas, as is the case along Maryland's Eastern Shore. Within these wetlands are many types of ducks and other waterfowl, deer, and other types of wildlife that often end up on mid-Atlantic tables, dressed in various ways, especially during hunting seasons. These wetlands produced one of the specialties of nineteenth-century mid-Atlantic cuisine: the diamondback terrapin. This small turtle has a shell measuring five to seven inches across and decorated with diamond-shaped marks that are actually growth rings. Although diamondback terrapins can be found in brackish semisaltwater marshes all along the Atlantic and Gulf coasts, the wetlands of the upper Chesapeake Bay were long renowned for producing the finest examples of the species. During the eighteenth and nineteenth centuries, terrapin meat was considered a great delicacy, and it was the chief ingredient in terrapin soup, a staple of formal Victorian dinners. This simple, elegant soup consisted of boiled terrapin meat in its own broth, flavored by sherry and spices and thickened with the yolks of hard-boiled eggs. The popularity of terrapin dishes decimated the turtle population by the early twentieth century, and now the diamondback terrapin is a protected species and its famous soup an artifact of the past.

Climatic Factors

As important as the ocean, rivers, and wetlands are to the cooking of the Mid-Atlantic, they are but one of the environmental factors that have shaped the region's food culture. Also influential has been the climate and topography of the region. Most parts of the Mid-Atlantic have a mild climate, with average temperatures of around 35 degrees Fahrenheit in the winter and 75 degrees in the summer, a range ideal for farms and orchards. The mild weather results in a long growing season—as much as 200 days in nonmountainous areas. This climate—when combined with the rich soil of the many river valleys—has made the Mid-Atlantic a productive agricultural area. In the early part of the nineteenth century, New York's Genesee, Hudson, and Mohawk valleys were a national center of wheat production; after the Civil War, when wheat growing shifted to the midwestern states, New York farmers turned to fruit, vegetable, and dairy farming. The latter is the most important agricultural activity today, with milk, butter, and cheese accounting for more than half the state's farm income. Apples, grapes, cherries, and pears are the primary products of New York's many orchards. New Jersey's nickname, "The Garden State," reflects the state's important role as a producer of fresh

New Jersey's nickname, "The Garden State," reflects the state's important role as a producer of grapes and other fresh fruits. Photo by George Semple. Courtesy New Jersey Commerce & Economic Growth Commission.

fruits and vegetables (many of them grown in greenhouses) that supply the large markets of New York City and Philadelphia. New Jersey is also a leading producer of cranberries and blueberries.

To the south in Maryland and Delaware, the poultry industry dominates farming. Chicken production is concentrated on the eastern shore of the Delmarva peninsula, with "broilers"—young chickens raised for meat—being the most important product. Led by the Perdue poultry empire, Maryland and Delaware's farmers produce more than 500 million broilers a year. Chicken and eggs, naturally, are important features of mid-Atlantic cuisine, and the state of Maryland is renowned for its fried chicken. In the classic recipe, chicken pieces are soaked overnight in buttermilk and spices, then breaded with seasoned flour and fried in lard or oil until golden brown. The finished chicken is traditionally served with a cream gravy made from the drippings in the frying pan. Recipes such as this, based upon fresh produce of local farms, form the core of classic mid-Atlantic cooking.

ETHNIC AND RELIGIOUS INFLUENCES ON MID-ATLANTIC FOOD

Just as the environment helps determine the foods that are characteristic of a particular area, so does the ethnic and religious mix of the local population. New immigrants bring to a region the tastes, ingredients, and cooking techniques of their native cultures and, by adapting them to the ingredients available in their new home, help expand and diversify the foodways of the region. This is especially true for the Mid-Atlantic. Ellis Island in New York was the largest gateway for immigrants to the United States, processing thousands of new arrivals each year, and for many years the port of Baltimore was the next busiest point of entry. Many of the immigrants who arrived through mid-Atlantic ports moved on to other parts of the country, but millions remained near their point of arrival, forming thriving ethnic communities that eventually merged into and helped shape the culture of the entire region.

Pennsylvania Dutch Cooking

One of the earliest groups of European settlers in the Mid-Atlantic were the Pennsylvania Dutch, who created a type of ethnic cuisine unique to the region. In the early eighteenth century, thousands of German-speaking immigrants settled in eastern and central Pennsylvania. Since the German word for German is *Deutsch*, these immigrants became known as the Pennsylvania Dutch. Though they shared a common tongue, the Pennsylvania Dutch primarily came from four different parts of Europe: the German state of Swabia, the Pfalz, Switzerland, and Alsace, a German-speaking province of France. The original immigrant settlements were concentrated in a thirty-county region in Pennsylvania (known today as "Dutch Country"), though their descendants would spread outward beyond the state's borders to Maryland, Virginia, West Virginia, and the Midwest.

A subset of the Pennsylvania Dutch are the Amish, a religious-based community that is an offshoot of the Mennonite faith. Although Amish now live in some twenty states, their core community, known as the Old Order Amish, numbers some 18,000 members and is based in Lancaster County, Pennsylvania, where they cluster around towns named Intercourse (named for the intersection of two roads) and Bird-in-Hand. The Amish faith emphasizes humility, simplicity, and separation from the modern world. The most visible manifestation of these beliefs is the community's resistance to (but not complete rejection of) modern technology. The Amish, for example, use horses and buggies instead of automobiles, and they have no electricity in their homes. Traditionally, Amish communities have been farm-based, with each family raising most of its own food. Their meals are typically prepared from scratch, being cooked on wood or kerosene stoves. The Amish community is changing slowly and is beginning to adopt modern products such as packaged pastry mixes and factory-produced cheeses. But because they have resisted such changes longer than most Americans, the Amish have earned a reputation for their old-style cooking, their fine canned fruits and vegetables, and the cheese, yogurt, and ice cream made from their own herds of milk cows—the best of Pennsylvania Dutch foodways.

Pennsylvania Dutch cookery is often characterized as "plain and plenty," and it reflects traditional German and Swiss flavors and techniques adapted to mid-Atlantic ingredients. Many of the standard recipes are one-pot dishes, hearty concoctions that use long, slow cooking to transform inexpensive ingredients into rich, complex flavors. Classic examples include *boova shenkel* ("boys legs"), a rich beef stew with half-moon shaped potato dumplings; *schnitz und knepp*, a stew of smoked ham and dried apples topped with steamed dumplings; and *rivel* soup, a meat-based broth containing rice-shaped bits of dumpling. The economy of these one-pot dishes is reflected in other Pennsylvania Dutch specialties, such as scrapple, a dish that originated as a way to use every available part of a pig. The name refers to the scrap meat that is removed from the boiled bones and heads of a newly butchered hog, which is mixed with livers, hearts, and kidneys and thickened with cornmeal into a sausagelike loaf. Scrapple is usually sliced and pan-fried until golden brown, and it is a classic part of the Pennsylvania Dutch breakfast.

Though one-pot dishes such as *boova shenkel* and *rivel* soup are not well known outside the region, other Pennsylvania Dutch recipes have spread into the wider American food culture. Apple butter, a thick spread made from apples, cider, and brown sugar, can be purchased on supermarket shelves throughout the country. Lebanon bologna, a reddish smoked beef sausage named for Lebanon, Pennsylvania, is a common sandwich ingredient. Funnel cakes are created by swirling batter through a funnel into hot oil, resulting in a squiggly, donutlike pastry. Though they originated among the Pennsylvania Dutch, the powdered sugar-topped treats are staples of country fairs not only in the Mid-Atlantic but in the Midwest and the South as well.

There are many options available for today's visitors who wish to sample Pennsylvania Dutch cooking. Dutch Country is home to many historic inns, bed-and-breakfasts, and restaurants where one can enjoy traditional dishes made with fresh local ingredients. An increasing number of farms offer guests the opportunity to learn about traditional agriculture in a hands-on fashion, from helping plant and harvest corn to trying their hand at milking dairy cows. The Amish are known for their excellent farmers' markets, where local producers sell fruits and vegetables, eggs and cheese, baked goods and pastries, and meat products. Most Amish farmers stick close to home to sell their goods, but some travel outside the area to larger venues like the Central Market and Reading Market in Philadelphia and the Penn-

Funnel cakes, like those shown here at the Kutztown Festival in Pennsylvania, are created by swirling batter through a funnel into hot oil, resulting in a squiggly, donut-like pastry. Though they originated among the Pennsylvania Dutch, the powdered-sugar–topped treats are staples of country fairs throughout the Mid-Atlantic. Courtesy Kutztown Festival.

sylvania Dutch Farmer's Market in Annapolis, Maryland. These markets sell wares such as sausages and pickles, homemade jams, fudge, cakes, pies, and soft pretzels along with distinctive Amish specialties like sweet bologna, scrapple, *schnitzel* (dried apple), and shoofly pie. This last dish—also called "pie cake," "Granger pie," and "molasses cake"—has a crumbly layer of brown sugar, flour, cinnamon, and butter spread over a bed of molasses and baked in a pie shell. The "shoofly" name was taken from a brand of molasses, and though called a pie it is actually served as a breakfast cake along with plenty of hot coffee.

Jewish American Cookery in the Mid-Atlantic

Another important ethnic influence on the cookery of the Mid-Atlantic has been that of Jewish immigrants. Jews have been present in the region since at least 1654, when twenty-three Sephardic Jews arrived in New Amsterdam from Brazil, and the Jewish population grew steadily during the colonial period. The diet of early Jewish settlers was not much different from that of other Americans, being largely seasonal and based on corn, beans, and fish. The main differentiator was the adherence to Jewish dietary laws, which define detailed rules for determining which foods are *kosher*, a Yiddish word derived from the Hebrew for "proper." These laws direct both the types of foods eaten and the ways in which they are prepared. To be kosher, an animal must have a cloven hoof and chew its cud (making beef kosher, but not pork), and fish must have scales and fins (so salmon can be eaten but oysters cannot). In addition, strict rules govern the slaughter of animals, defining a set of rituals that must be performed to produce kosher meat. Meat and milk products may not be eaten together, and separate dishes and utensils must be used to cook meat and dairy dishes. For early American Jews, kosher laws meant primarily that they had to slaughter their own meat, avoid pork, and fry foods in olive oil rather than animal lard—a method that became popular among non-Jews as "Jewish-style" frying.

American Jewish cooking began to take on a more distinctive character during the mid–nineteenth century, when some 200,000 German Jews immigrated to the United States, many settling in the mid-Atlantic region. These immigrants brought with them kosher versions of German staples, such as beef sausages, sauerkraut, and chicken soups, along with a sophisticated culture of baking that included a wide variety of *kuchen* (coffee cakes), breads, and tortes. Between 1880 and 1920, a third wave of immigration brought more than 2.5 million new Jewish Americans, with the majority arriving from eastern European countries. These newcomers created large immigrant neighborhoods in mid-Atlantic cities—especially on the Lower East Side in New York City and in South Philadelphia—and it was out of these communities that traditional Jewish American cookery emerged.

This cookery is a blend of cultures from Germany, Russia, and other eastern European countries modified to reflect kosher laws and the foods available in America. Because pork—the staple meat for so many other mid-Atlantic residents—is not kosher, beef has been the primary meat in Jewish American cooking. Brisket—a large cut from the front quarters of a steer—was an economical choice for poorer immigrant families and has therefore become a popular centerpiece in Jewish meals. The beef is braised in a small amount of liquid, the slow cooking tenderizing the meat and imparting rich flavors. Because of the size of the cuts, leftover brisket can be ground and used as the filling for knishes (a stuffed pastry) or kreplach (a meat-filled dumpling). The stock or gravy from the brisket can be used as the base for a variety of soups. Beef is also widely used in sausages and preserved meats, reflecting the German descent of many Jewish immigrants. One classic examples is liverwurst, a smooth smoked sausage made from chopped liver seasoned with onions, pistachios, and other spices. Pastrami, a sandwich staple, is made from corned beef that has been dried, rubbed with coarse pepper and other spices, smoked, and then steamed.

The long tradition of baking in the Jewish American community is reflected in its many distinctive breads and cakes. The best known of these, the bagel, is a round yeast bun with a hole in the middle. Its name derives from the Yiddish *beygel*, which comes in turn from the German word *beugel*, meaning a round loaf of bread. Traditional bagels are shaped by hand, boiled, and then baked. Because of the size of its Jewish American communities, New York has long been considered the home of the bagel, along with traditional toppings such as lox (smoked salmon), cream cheese, and sliced onions. Over the past fifty years, the bagel has evolved from an ethnic specialty to a part of the mainstream American diet, available on the shelves and in the freezers of supermarkets across the country. In the process, the bagel has become a light, fluffy industrial food product that bears little resemblances to the chewy original (writer Calvin Trillin calls such imitations "round bread"). Bagels can now be purchased in a variety of flavors ranging from the fairly traditional onion and poppy seed to dessertlike varieties additions such as blueberries and raisins.

The bagel is by no means the only Jewish American bread. Bialy—a doughy, chewy loaf made from wheat flour, salt, yeast, and water—can be found in traditional Jewish delis throughout the Mid-Atlantic. The dough is shaped into a loaf with an indentation in the middle, then sprinkled with chopped onions or poppy seeds before being baked. Challah, a holiday bread, is made from braided white yeast dough with eggs and poppyseeds. Matzoh is an unleavened, crackerlike bread eaten during the Passover holiday, when the use of leavening is forbidden. Crushed matzoh (also called matzoh meal) is also used year-round to make matzoh balls, a classic addition to traditional Jewish chicken soup.

An important institution in Jewish American food culture is the delicatessen. The word—now often shortened to simply "deli"—derives from the German for "delicacies," and it refers to a grocery store that sells cooked meats and other prepared foods. Originally, New York's delicatessens were run primarily by non-Jewish Germans and Alsatians, but large numbers of newly immigrated Jews entered the grocery business in the late nineteenth century, making the delicatessen a characteristic feature of Jewish American life. By the turn of the century the typical deli was a combination grocery store and restaurant, with a counter and a few stools where patrons could eat meals on the premises. Their kosher fare included smoked beef, pastrami, liverwurst, frankfurters, potato knishes, rye bread, mustard, and pickles. As the diet of American Jews evolved, so did the delicatessen, adding newer specialties such as bagels, bialys, potato salad, and cheesecake. And as the second- and third-generations of immigrant families moved out of lower Manhattan and South Philadelphia into middle-class suburbs, the deli moved with them. Today, restaurants calling themselves delis can be found in every state of the Union, offering a wide range of sandwiches, some of them (such as pastrami on rye) representative of classic kosher fare and others (club sandwiches with ham, turkey, and roast beef) decidedly not.

Italian American Cooking in the Mid-Atlantic

The large wave of Jewish immigration to the Mid-Atlantic was paralleled by a surge of immigrants from Italy. Between 1890 and 1910, more that 5 million Italian immigrants arrived on American shores, the great majority of whom passed through Ellis Island and settled in East Coast cities. By 1920 more Italians lived in New York than lived in the city of Florence. As with other ethnic groups, the eating habits of first and second generation of Italian immigrants remained close to their European roots. In Italian neighborhoods throughout the Mid-Atlantic, grocery stores stocked foodstuffs imported from the Old Country, such as canned tomatoes, bottled anchovies, and boxes of macaroni (a term that at the time was used in the generic sense of "pasta" rather than referring to a particular type of noodle). Local grocers learned to make mozzarella cheese from cow's milk rather than the traditional buffalo milk; butchers made salami and sausages from local meats; and zinfandel grapes from California were widely used for homemade wine. These adaptations of traditional tastes to New World ingredients helped create a new and distinct type of cuisine: Italian American cooking.

Most Italian immigrants came from the impoverished southern agricultural regions of Italy, and their food culture centered on home cooking, not restaurant dining. The immigrant neighborhoods of mid-Atlantic cities, however, proved fertile breeding grounds for a new type of business: the Italian American restaurant. These restaurants started around the turn of the century as small family businesses catering to fellow immigrants. Unlike French restaurants in the United States, which modeled themselves closely on an existing European tradition, Italian American restaurants in the early twentieth century were something of their own genre. Their dishes were based primarily on family food, though in considerably larger portions and with a much greater emphasis on meats and sausage. Foods that were reserved for festival days in the Old Country became daily fare: steaks, chops, veal, and swordfish. Red sauce–based pasta dishes such as lasagna and ravioli were staples of the menu, as were rich desserts such as zabaglione, cannoli, and cheesecake—the latter a wholly American invention.

During the 1920s, Italian restaurants flourished in East Coast cities, expanding from mom-and-pop storefronts to large banquet-hall operations. By the 1930s, "Italian" was well established as an American restaurant theme, though its cooking rarely was given the respect accorded French cuisine (even though the kitchen staffs of most of mid-Atlantic French restaurants were dominated by Italian immigrants) and few nonimmigrant families tried making Italian dishes at home. Mid-twentieth-century Italian restaurants were constrained by the clichéd decor and cuisines expected by middle-class American diners: red-checked tablecloths and wicker-basket Chianti bottles, menus dominated by spaghetti and meatballs with heavy red sauce. This would begin to change in the 1960s, when a new American interest in "gourmet" dining led to the opening of so-called Northern Italian restaurants, whose cream sauces and tableside service had no more precedent in native Italian cooking than the red-sauce palaces of the decades before. It was not until the 1980s and 1990s that American chefs became interested in the native cooking of Italy, a rich tradition that varies greatly from one region to another and has long been a part of the home cooking of the Italian American immigrant communities in this country.

As in Pennsylvania Dutch and Jewish American cookery, many of the classic Italian American recipes show the use of common, basic ingredients to create hearty fare, a reflection of the impoverished roots of so many immigrants to this country. Italian cooking is characterized by simple dishes made with fresh, seasonal ingredients. Staples such as olive oil, anchovies, capers, and garlic provide bold, distinctive flavors, as do the many fine cheeses, which range from mild cow's milk varieties such as Asiago and bel paese to sharper and more pungent types such as gorgonzola and pecorino romano. The two most popular Italian cheeses in the United States are mozzarella and parmigiano-reggiano (often called simply parmesan). Although the market is dominated by tasteless industrial versions that bear little resemblance to their Italian counterparts, authentic fresh mozzarella and creamy, aged parmigiano-reggiano are still widely available in mid-Atlantic supermarkets and are an indispensable part of Italian American cooking.

Grains form an important base for this style of cooking. Risotto—rice cooked in broth to a creamy consistency and flavored with cheeses, pesto, and/or vegetables—and polenta—cornmeal cooked in water to a similarly creamy texture—are two classic preparations. But more than any other, the food most closely associated with Italian American cooking is pasta. Pasta itself is nothing more than a simple dough of flour and water (and sometimes egg), but it can be shaped into a seemingly endless array of noodles, tubes, and shells. There are two main categories: *pasta fresca* (fresh pasta made from soft wheat flour) and *pasta secco* (dried pasta made from hard durum wheat, or semolina). The latter has the greatest variety of shapes, ranging from long, thin noodles of differing widths (spaghetti, linguine, vermicelli, fettuccini) to spirals (rotini) and tubes (manicotti, penne, macaroni, rigatoni).

Although in Italy pasta is regularly served as a separate course prior to the main part of the meal, in the United States it is more frequently the main course. Pasta dishes consisting of noodles, meat, and cheese topped with a thick tomato sauce have become the most popular features of Italian American cooking. Such dishes include spaghetti with meat sauce and lasagne, a baked dish with layers of pasta, meat sauce, and cheeses such as ricotta, mozzarella, and parmegianno-reggiano. Ravioli—packets of thin pasta filled with a combination of meat, cheese, and/or vegetables—have long been staples of Italian American restaurants, typically being filled with ground meats and topped with lots of mozzarella and tomato sauce. But not all Italian American pasta dishes are heavy and covered with tomato sauce. In the past two decades cooks have used ravioli in a wide range of dishes, filling the pasta with everything from spinach to lobster and topping them wide a range of rich, flavorful sauces. Many traditional Italian pasta preparations are simple and light, such as spaghetti carbonara (tossed with pancetta bacon, egg, and parmegianno-reggiano) and spaghetti aglio e olio (tossed with garlic, olive oil, and sometimes chile peppers). Pasta alla primavera (fettuccini tossed with fresh vegetables such as zucchini, broccoli, and peas and a heavy cream and cheese sauce) and fettuccini alfredro (fettuccini with heavy cream, butter, and parmesan cheese) are two distinctly American creations.

Italian American cooking has long been associated with New York City, whose neighborhoods offer everything from small pizzerias and family *ristoranti* to theme park–like banquet halls and expensive upscale restaurants. But Italian American cooking can be found throughout the Mid-Atlantic. Baltimore's Little Italy, for example, is famed for its many excellent restaurants. This section extends north to Pratt Street, east to Eden Street, west over Route 83 to Jones Falls, and south to the Inner Harbor. Northern, Tuscan, central, southern, and Sicilian cuisine are available at one or more of the twenty restaurants in the area. For those who want to taste a little of everything but don't have time to sit down at each restaurant and sample its fare, Little Italy sponsors a Taste of Italy food festival each September that highlights the broad range of dishes and ingredients that make up Italian cuisine. Other food events include the feast of St. Anthony in June, which is held around St. Leo the Great, a historic church built in 1880 that survived the Great Fire of 1904. Legend holds that the fire, which destroyed much of Baltimore but stopped just outside the boundaries of Little Italy, did so because residents prayed hard to St. Anthony that their neighborhood be saved. It is through these community festivals, the restaurants the neighborhoods support, and—

Chef in Marconi's Restaurant on Mulberry Street, New York City, preparing two Italian sausage sandwiches, New Year's Eve, 1942. Courtesy Library of Congress.

most important—the home cooking of Italian American families that this style of mid-Atlantic food is maintained.

FOOD INDUSTRIES IN THE MID-ATLANTIC REGION

During the nineteenth century, as successive waves of immigrants were transforming the food culture of the Mid-Atlantic, another force also had a profound influence in shaping how the people of the region cooked and ate: the rise of industrial food processing and distribution. Although all parts of the United States would be affected by these changes, the Mid-Atlantic played a central role in the process. In part because it was a major center of vegetable production in the nineteenth century and in part because its large metropolitan areas provided a ready industrial base, the Mid-Atlantic was the birthplace of some of the first and largest American industrial food processors.

One of these major processors was the Campbell Soup Company, which was founded in 1869 in Camden, New Jersey, by fruit merchant Joseph Campbell and icebox manufacturer Abraham Anderson. The company was originally named the Joseph A. Campbell Preserve Company and produced a line of canned tomatoes, vegetables, jellies, and condiments. In 1897, John T. Dorrance, then a chemist for the company, invented the product that would make the company a global giant: condensed soup. By removing most of the water from its prepared soups, the company was able to lower the cost of packaging, shipping, and storing, allowing it to sell a ten-ounce can of condensed soup for ten cents that, when reconstituted by the consumer, was equivalent to a thirty-two-ounce, can that sold for thirty cents. Campbell's did not rely on its price advantage alone. It was a pioneer of advertising in the food industry, launching widespread magazine promotions around the turn of the twentieth century and being the first company to advertise on the sides of New York City streetcars. In time, the company phased out its lines of jams, jellies, and condiments and made soups the focus of its business, renaming itself the Campbell Soup Company in 1923. Over the decades that followed, the company purchased a succession of smaller producers, creating an international food conglomerate with a stable of brands that include Franco-American canned pastas, V8 vegetable juices, Swanson's frozen dinners, and Pepperidge Farm baked goods. Today, Campbell's—still based in Camden, New Jersey—sells over 3 billion cans of soup a year and brings in over $6 billion in revenue from its worldwide operations.

Another major mid-Atlantic food producer, the H.J. Heinz Company, was founded in the same year as Campbell's, 1869, and it, too, would grow over the next century to be a multinational food giant. Based in Pittsburgh, Pennsylvania, its initial product was grated horseradish sold in clear glass jars, and Heinz soon added pickles, sauerkraut, and vinegar to its line. In 1875 the company introduced tomato ketchup, the product that would soon become its most popular brand. That was followed by a range of condiments and vegetables, including red and green pepper sauce, mustard, olives, baked beans, and pickled onions. In 1896 the company adopted the slogan "57 Varieties" to characterize its products, though by then it was actually selling more than sixty different items. Like Campbell's, Heinz began advertising its products heavily in the early twentieth century, which helped the company grow into a worldwide food producer. The company today remains

H. J. Heinz Company factory, Pittsburgh, Pennsylvania, 1869. Courtesy H. J. Heinz Company.

best known for its ketchup, "57 Sauce," and other condiments, which help it generate more than $2.5 billion in sales.

The influence of industrial food packagers like Campbell's and Heinz on the cooking of the Mid-Atlantic (and the rest of America) has been dramatic. On the one hand, the preservation of food in cans was a great convenience, making it possible for consumers to purchase vegetables and fruits when they were out of season and, because they could be shipped safely across the country, making available a variety of novel products. But canned goods soon became something more than a substitute for unavailable seasonal produce or an occasional exotic novelty. Instead, during the late nineteenth and early twentieth century they increasingly replaced fresh fruits and vegetables altogether in the diets of many Americans, including residents of the Mid-Atlantic. The Campbell Soup Company, in addition, used its large advertising budget to produce a flood of cookbooks and meal planners that promoted its canned soups (particularly thick white varieties such as cream of mushroom) as the base for recipes. The company estimates today that its soups are used in one out of every ten meals cooked in American homes. Despite their roots in the Mid-Atlantic, the products of the major food producers such as Campbell's and Heinz do not reflect the distinctive dishes of the mid-Atlantic region. Marketed and sold in every part of the county, such industrial food products are one of the strong forces that largely erased regional differences in the American diet during the twentieth century.

Hershey's Chocolate

One of the most famous mid-Atlantic food businesses—and one that has had a major impact on the food industry worldwide—is Hershey Chocolate. Its founder, Milton Hershey (1857–1945), was born in Lancaster, Pennsylvania, to Mennonite parents. He left school after the fourth grade and later became an apprentice at Royer's Ice Cream Parlor and Garden, where he learned the confectionary trade. Following this apprenticeship, Hershey opened two different candy manufacturing businesses that ended in bankruptcy, and he traveled in the West working with other candy makers to further learn the business. He finally succeeded with his third venture, the Lancaster Caramel Company, in his Pennsylvania hometown. Although his primary product was initially caramel, Hershey became fascinated with chocolate-making after he visited the World Exposition in Chicago in 1893 and purchased some of the German chocolate-making machinery he saw on display there. He had the equipment shipped back to Pennsylvania, where he began experimenting with recipes for making milk chocolate—the product that would eventually make his name famous worldwide.

The earliest recorded sale for Hershey Chocolate is dated April 17, 1895. Within six years, the Hershey Chocolate Company reported sales of $622,000 a year. In 1903 land was set aside in Derry Church, Pennsylvania, to build not just a chocolate factory but an entire industrial town, including a hotel, bank, post office, and general store along with workers' homes, transportation, and medical facilities. In 1906 the name of the community was changed to Hershey, and a year later Hershey Park—an entertainment retreat for the company's employees—officially opened. In 1909 Hershey and his wife, Catherine, established the Hershey Industrial School, where orphaned boys (and later girls) were guaranteed not only room and board but also eventual employment in one of the many thriving Hershey ventures. Many of the school's students went on to become executives within the Hershey Corporation.

One of Hershey's most important contributions to the candy-making process was the introduction of mechanical assembly. In 1921 his factory began using a mechanical wrapping machine for chocolate "kisses," which previously had been wrapped by hand. Another major change was the mass-production of milk chocolate. Most of the machinery necessary for this mass-production was either developed or adapted in one of the Hershey factories.

Today, the town of Hershey, Pennsylvania, still thrives and remains a major tourist destination in the area. Visitors can tour the chocolate factory, relax in a chocolate "mud" bath in a fancy day spa, or visit the gardens, the zoo, or one of the many other attractions in the Hershey theme park.

FOOD DISTRIBUTION SYSTEMS

At the same time that the rise of industrial food packaging changed what the residents of the Mid-Atlantic ate, a series of changes beginning in the late nineteenth century had a profound effect on the way they acquired the food for their tables. At the end of the Civil War, the diet of typical mid-Atlantic residents was largely based on meat and produce raised within a few hundred miles of their homes. Though industry was in the process of overtaking farming as the leading source of jobs, many families still raised their own food on farms and in garden plots. In cities, residents purchased food from local shops, from peddlers who came door-to-door, and at produce markets where food was sold directly by the farmers who raised it. Small grocery stores, bakeries, butcher shops, and dry goods merchants could be found on almost every neighborhood corner. These businesses stocked a relatively limited variety of goods (since they served only a few blocks' worth of customers), extended credit readily, and often delivered to customers' homes. These small retailers usually had only a single shop, and they were supplied by a network of wholesalers who acquired meat, produce, and dry goods from regional producers. Over the course of the next hundred years, these arrangements would change dramatically.

While the Piggly-Wiggly in the South is generally considered to be the first chain of self-service grocery stores in the country, the mid-Atlantic region can lay claim to being the birthplace of one of the largest and most successful grocery chains. In 1861 tea and spice merchants George Huntington Hartford and George Gilman opened a store in New York City on the corner of Broadway and Grand Street. Initially, they sold only tea and coffee, but over time they gradually expanded their stock to cover a wide range of grocery and dry goods items. In 1870 they renamed their company the Great Atlantic & Pacific Tea Company, in honor of the transcontinental railroad. During their early days of operation, Huntington and Hartford used peddlers in horse-drawn wagons to sell their wares along 5,000 routes throughout the nation, but before long it was their retail stores that became their primary outlets. By 1876 the A&P had more than 100 stores, making it the nation's first major grocery chain. By 1930 it was dominating the supermarket business.

At first, chain grocery outlets such as A&P did not look significantly different from their independent competition, being stores of similar size stocking the same types of merchandise. The chains had two advantages over the traditional single-outlet grocer, however. First, they adopted a "cash-and-carry" business model under which they no longer extended credit accounts to customers and eliminated home delivery of purchases, both of which reduced operating costs. In addition, the chain stores gained from economies of scale. Because they were purchasing for dozens of stores at a time rather than just a single outlet, the chains were able to negotiate lower prices from their suppliers and, as their size grew, were able to eliminate the wholesaler altogether. This allowed the chains to sell retail goods for a significantly lower price than the independent grocer could. Independents tried a range of counterattacks, from promoting their superior customer service to attempting to prosecute the chains through the courts for anticompetitive behavior, but they were largely unsuccessful. By the 1920s, chain groceries had firmly established themselves in the market. In the 1930s, they further consolidated their position by increasing the size of the stores and the number of products carried—creating the first supermarkets, the model for grocery shopping that dominates the market to this day.

In 1974 A&P's corporate headquarters relocated to Montvale, New Jersey, where it is still located today. During the next several years, the chain continued to expand, acquiring several smaller competing chains such as Kohl's, Dominion, Waldbaum's, and Shopwell-Food Emporium. Today, the chain has an annual sales volume of over $10 billion from 680 stores, most of them in the mid-Atlantic region. It is by no means the only major grocer in the region, though. Giant Food Inc., which dominates the Baltimore and Washington, D.C., market, has 190 outlets in the area. Giant Food Stores, a separate chain based in Carlisle, Pennsylvania, has 110 stores, primarily in Pennsylvania, where they compete with the 160 stores of Sunbury-based Weis Markets. Safeway, a California-based grocery empire, recently purchased Genuardi Family Markets, giving it a major foothold in the mid-Atlantic region. A large number of smaller chains and independent supermarkets can be found throughout the region as well. All told, these supermarkets account for more than 90 percent of all retail sales of fresh produce and grocery items in the Mid-Atlantic.

The food sold in these stores comes from a broad network of producers and suppliers. The primary model for food distribution in the region (as in the nation as a whole) involves producers, food brokers, wholesalers, and retailers. Food producers (including farmers, industrial food processors, and food factories) sell their goods through brokers, who provide sales and order servicing functions. Wholesalers buy their products through the brokers and handle the storage, shipping, and delivery of the food to the smaller grocery chains and independent supermarkets. The larger grocery chains operate their own warehouses and buy directly from food brokers. Supported by the growth of an inexpensive long-distance transportation network and multinational food producing conglomerates, this food distribution system is now of not only national but international reach. A 1997 U.S. Department of Agriculture study of the Jessup Terminal Market in Jessup, Maryland, which supplies the D.C. metro area, found that the biggest producing states represented (in terms of poundage) were California (29 percent), Florida (14 percent), and Washington (14 percent). Products from the mid-Atlantic region accounted for just 5 percent of the total produce available.[3] One hundred and fifty years earlier, most produce in such a market would have come from within a hundred-mile radius. The average shipping distance for all crops at the Jessup Terminal Market was 1,685 miles.

Wholesale and Farmers' Markets

Despite the predominance of supermarkets and the national food distribution network, they are not the only sources of food available to mid-Atlantic residents. The region's plentiful seafood, for example, is available fresh in wholesale markets in the larger cities and at smaller retail outlets up and down the Atlantic coast. One of the most notable of these is New York City's Fulton Fish Market, the oldest and largest wholesale fish market in the United States. Located in the South Street Seaport just south of the Brooklyn Bridge, the market comes alive around midnight, when hundreds of refrigerated trucks from all over the United States and Canada line up to unload. Most of the market's sixty wholesalers open around 3:30 A.M., and the peak selling hours are between 4:00 A.M. and 7:00 A.M., when the stalls are filled with retail fishmongers and restaurateurs seeking the top quality and lowest priced fresh fish for their establishments. By 9:00 A.M., the unsold fish has been refrigerated for the next day and the stalls have been hosed down and closed for the day. Total sales at the Fulton Fish Market have fallen in recent decades, as the major supermarket chains began buying directly from fishing fleets and shippers and airline deregulation allowed imported seafood to be flown directly to Baltimore and Philadelphia. But the market is still active and thriving thanks to the huge market of restaurants and fishmongers in New York City who insist upon high-quality fresh seafood.

New York City's Fulton Fish Market is the oldest and largest wholesale fish market in the United States. Courtesy New York State Department of Economic Development.

The Fulton Fish Market may be the most famous seafood market in the Mid-Atlantic, but it is hardly the only one. Mention the D.C. Wharf Market to tourists in the nation's capital, and you're likely to get a blank stare. Although it's only a few minutes away from the Tidal Basin and the Washington Monument, most visitors are not aware of the market that covers an entire D.C. block between 11th and 12th Streets in the southwest part of the city. Locals, however, speak of the wharf market to each other as casually as they would discuss a mutual friend. During summer, when crab feasts are common in Maryland backyards, the wharf is packed with locals seeking the best deal on live or steamed crabs. In the months hospitable to oysters, locals try the same approach and haggle for the freshest varieties.

The earliest recorded sale at the D.C. Wharf Market occurred in 1794. At first, seafood and produce was brought in by slow-moving small boats. In time, these were replaced by refrigerated trucks and massive steel barges that help transport quantities of seafood that could not have been imagined in the early days. The wharf spawned not only a method of food distribution but also a way of life for many people. The Gangplank Marina and the Capital Yacht Club have space for some 400 boats, many of them houseboats that are year-round homes. Watermen from the Chesapeake area and other workers sleep in cabins built atop the barges until it is time for them to return to their central work location in company vans that bring relief crews. Today, the thriving market boasts 600 different types of seafood available each day.

Mid-Atlantic cooks seeking fresh fruits and vegetables to go along with their seafood have plenty of alternatives to their local supermarket. At large farmers'

Mid-Atlantic Train Station Dining

Railroads have long played an important role in the food distribution systems in the United States, revolutionizing the transport of food. A related—and more glamorous—way of getting food to consumers was through the restaurants and other food outlets that developed at the grand mid-Atlantic train stations during the late nineteenth century.

Union Station is a popular name for train stations around the country, but the Union Station in Washington, D.C., stands out for several reasons. Designed by architect Daniel Burnham, it is one of the finest examples of Beaux Arts architecture in the country, and at the time it was built in 1908 it was the largest train station in the world, occupying some 200 acres with seventy-five miles of track. Since it is among the most visited destinations in the nation's capital, with more than 25 million visitors per year, Union Station has become a popular spot for restaurateurs, who have opened establishments throughout the two levels of the station. The food court alone offers more than forty dining spots. In addition to these casual outlets, the station hosts several sit-down restaurants. America, one of the most popular, features menu items representing every state and offers spectacular views of the nation's capital. Perhaps the most upscale restaurant in the station is B. Smith's, named after its owner, Barbara Smith, a fashion mogul famous for her cookbooks and her television show, *B. Smith's with Style*. Located in what was once Union Station's presidential suite, B. Smith's features an eclectic mix of Cajun, Creole, and southern cuisine. One of the more popular dishes at B. Smith's is an item called the Swamp Thing, a plate of seafood served on a bed of greens and covered with a mustard-based sauce. Desserts such as coconut cake, red velvet cake, and sweet potato pecan pie have also made the restaurant popular.

Like Union Station, the Reading Terminal in Philadelphia boasts dozens of restaurants and lunch stands, featuring everything from hoagies to Philly steaks to Atlantic oysters to sushi. What is most distinctive about the station, however, is its indoor food market, which dates back to the opening of the Reading Terminal in 1892, when two nearby markets were consolidated under the train shed of the new terminal. Today the market is home to close to a hundred food vendors. From Wednesday through Saturday Amish merchants offer a variety of Pennsylvania Dutch foods, especially baked goods such as shoofly pie and blackberry turnovers. The variety of local foods at the Reading Terminal Market make it one of the best places to sample the distinctive cuisine of Philadelphia and the surrounding region.

While restaurants abound at New York City's Grand Central Station, perhaps the most famous is the Grand Central Oyster Bar, which has been in operation since 1913. This is no ordinary food-court restaurant. Its glazed white tile ceiling, columns, ship's wheel lighting fixtures, countertop eating area, and twenty-three-seat Oyster Bar cover 27,000 square feet. A daily handwritten menu offers seventy-five or more seafood dishes, which will be served to an average of 1,800 diners every day. This menu includes scallops, mackerel, grouper, sea bass, and a variety of dishes featuring clams, shrimp, lobsters, and mussels. Much of the seafood comes from the mid-Atlantic area, including Long Island and Maryland's Chesapeake Bay. Oysters are served in almost every way imaginable—fried, baked, and stewed—but the most popular way to eat them is raw at the Oyster Bar, which features more than twenty-five different varieties, including extra large Belons from Maine, Glidden Pints, sweet Pacific varieties, and Wellfleets. The in-house bake shop churns out more than 3,000 biscuits and more than fourteen desserts daily, including cheesecake and key lime pie. More than 400,000 customers each year consume over 1.7 million pounds of fresh seafood, making it one of the most popular restaurants in New York City.

With more than 25 million visitors per year, Washington, D.C.'s Union Station has become a popular spot for restaurateurs. Courtesy of the Washington, D.C., Convention & Tourism Corporation.

markets (like the Reading Terminal Market in Philadelphia) and at countless roadside stands in the countryside, consumers can buy fresh, local produce directly from the farmers who grew it. In the larger cities, green markets, fruit stands, and neighborhood farmers' markets are becoming increasingly popular, fueled in part by the recent organic farming movement and a renewed demand among consumers for better, fresher produce.

Mid-Atlantic Restaurants

Perhaps more than any other region, the Mid-Atlantic is famous for its restaurants. New York City is widely regarded as a world capital of fine dining, and Philadelphia, Pittsburgh, and Baltimore have earned places in the spotlight for their many extraordinary restaurants. Dining opportunities in the Washington, D.C., area range from dinners at the White House (for selected guests only, of course) to the many cafeterias built for quick service and basic food for congressional representatives, government workers, and the many tourists who visit the District of Columbia each year. As a world capital, the city is a melting pot of international cuisines, with hundreds of restaurants featuring varieties of ethnic cooking from every continent.

Restaurant dining is not limited to the region's major cities. New York state boasts many extraordinary dining experiences, especially in the Hudson Valley area. The New Jersey shore offers both whimsical boardwalk fare and seaside restaurants fine enough to once host the likes of the Vanderbilts and others who made their fortunes in the early 1900s. The Eastern Shore of Maryland is renowned for its seafood restaurants, which range from humble crab shacks to upscale bistros. Further west the blue mountains and green trees of West Virginia's Shenandoah Valley shelter rustic restaurants in state parks and elegant dining at resorts such as Coolfont in Berkeley Springs and the Greenbrier in White Sulphur Springs, which was voted the best resort in the world in 2002.

Lobster feast on Long Island, New York. Courtesy New York State Department of Economic Development.

Delmonico's

The Mid-Atlantic's reputation as a restaurant capital is not a recent development. In fact, the region can lay claim to being the birthplace of American fine dining, for it was the home of Delmonico's, the most prestigious restaurant in the United States during the nineteenth century. Giovanni Del-Monico, a former sea captain from the Swiss village of Mariengo, and his brother, Peitro, an expert candymaker and pastry chef, moved to New York City and, in 1827, invested their combined savings of about $20,000 in a small café and pastry shop on Williams Street, simplifying the name to read just "Delmonico and Brother." The pastry shop had half a dozen pine tables with chairs to match and a counter that held cakes and other pastries. Serving these pastries along with coffee, candy, and wine, the shop attracted mostly fellow Europeans. Three years later, the brothers opened Restaurant Francais next door to their café. This was the forerunner of the famous Delmonico's and is considered to be America's first restaurant.

Delmonico's featured new types of food cooked by French chefs, but its real novelty was that it offered a menu. Previously, customers at an inn or tavern paid a set price for their food, and everyone was served the same meal at the same time of day. Often, customers did not know what food they were paying for until it appeared in front of them. Delmonico's was modeled on European restaurants, especially those in Paris. Unlike taverns and cafés, which were usually part of a larger lodging establishment, customers could enter Delmonico's at any time while it was open and order food from a list of individually priced dishes.

These innovations, combined with the high quality of Delmonico's food, led to rapid success for Restaurant Francais, and the brothers soon expanded their operations. To ensure a steady supply of fresh vegetables, they purchased a 220-acre farm on Long Island, where they grew their own produce. The famous name Delmonico's was formally attached to the restaurant for the first time in August 1837, when the brothers erected a three-story building adorned with marble pillars imported from Pompeii. Public dining areas were located on the first and second

Annual banquet of the Sons of the Revolution at Delmonico's, 1906. Courtesy Library of Congress.

floors, while private dining rooms and the kitchen were on the third. The restaurant's cellar held more than 16,000 bottles of French wine. In 1856 the Delmonicos added a second location on Chambers Street, which became the most fashionable place to dine for the New York social set, and six years later Lorenzo Delmonico converted a mansion in Union Square into another luxury restaurant. A fourth restaurant, on Broad Street, was opened in 1865.

In 1876 the Delmonicos moved their Union Square restaurant further north, to a location near Madison Square, an area booming with new residences, theaters, and hotels. This Delmonico's was the grandest of all, rising five stories high and occupying the entire south side of 26th Street between Fifth Avenue and Broadway. The windows overlooked a lawn that served as a foreground for the trees and flower beds of Madison Square. On the first floor of the restaurant, silver chandeliers hung from a frescoed ceiling, mirrors lined each wall, and the furniture was all mahogany. The second floor housed a ballroom, decorated in red and gold, and four private dining rooms, each decorated in a different color of satin. More dining rooms and a banquet hall, each decorated in different colors and styles, were on the third floor, and living quarters for a few single men and restaurant employees, as well as storage rooms and laundry, could be found on the top two floors.

In its heyday, Delmonico's introduced many new foodstuffs to the restaurant scene, including the "alligator pear," which we today know as an avocado. The restaurant was also the birthplace of many dishes that are now a classic part of the American culinary scene. These include lobster Newburg (lobster meat served in a sherry cream sauce), eggs Benedict (toasted English muffins topped with grilled ham, poached eggs, and hollandaise sauce), and chicken à la king (creamed chicken and vegetables in puff pastry shells). The restaurant's most famous dessert, Baked Alaska, was created to celebrate the American purchase of the Russian territory in

1867 and featured an ice cream core surrounded by whipped cream that was toasted to a light brown crust in a hot oven. The restaurant's name was affixed to the Delmonico steak and Delmonico potatoes, both of which were copied by restaurateurs across the country. Although their popularity would be eclipsed by new European-inspired styles during the renaissance of American restaurants in the 1980s and 1990s, for more than a century Delmonico's signature dishes formed the foundation of fine dining in the United States.

World War I signaled the end of an era for Delmonico's. In 1917 the flagship restaurant on William Street, which had been in continuous operation since 1830, closed. The last remaining Delmonico's was sold to restaurateur Edward Robins in 1919 on the day that Prohibition went into effect. The outlawing of alcoholic beverages was a disaster for a French restaurant, especially one operating on such a grand scale as Delmonico's. The new owner had to do away with the extensive wine cellar and could not use any wine in cooking, which severely restricted the dishes that could be served. Wealthy patrons turned away from restaurant dining and began entertaining in their homes, where they had access to their own wine cellars. Delmonico's responded, in turn, by trying to supply the alcohol desired by the customers, but in 1921 it was raided by "dry agents," who arrested employees for serving vodka and gin. On May 31, 1923, a final dinner was held at the last Delmonico's Restaurant. The great French restaurant, once noted for its fine wines, featured only mineral water in its final hours.

City Tavern (Philadelphia)

While the glory days of Delmonico's in New York are long gone, the City Tavern, first established in Philadelphia in 1772, lives on, its history closely interwoven with that of the Revolutionary War and of the city of Philadelphia. The tavern was built by a handful of wealthy Philadelphians who wanted an establishment that reflected the high status of the city during the early days of the country. The tavern originally had three floors with lodging rooms, several large club rooms, a bar, and a coffee room, complete with British and American newspapers. It was a success from the start. Various benevolent and social organizations, such as the St. George's Society and the Friendly Sons of St. Patrick, made it their home. Its rooms hosted high-society balls, and city business was routinely concluded in the coffee room. The tavern, however, is most important for the role it played during the American Revolution. In 1774 some of Pennsylvania's leading citizens held a meeting at the tavern to determine their colony's response to what were seen as outrageous and intolerable political acts by Great Britain. A few months later, the First Continental Congress arrived at the tavern, thrusting it into the midst of the current events of the day. From that time until the close of the century, the tavern hosted, at various times, the foremost leaders of the day, including George Washington and Thomas Jefferson.

After the success and excitement surrounding the Revolutionary War, the City Tavern fell into decline. During the first half of the nineteenth century, its building was adapted for other purposes, serving as a home for a merchants' exchange. In 1834 it was partially destroyed by fire, and it was finally demolished in 1854 in what appeared to be the end of a historic institution. One newspaper of the day predicted that in a generation or two the tavern would not be remembered by anyone except a few curious historians, and for almost a half century that prediction seemed correct. Then, in 1948, Congress commissioned a historically accurate reconstruction of the tavern. That task was completed in 1976, in time for the nation's bicentennial celebration.

The reconstructed City Tavern is a landmark not just of political history but of food history as well. It is a fully operational restaurant today with a menu designed to reflect traditional eighteenth-century fare. Among its offerings are sweet potato biscuits (a favorite of Thomas Jefferson) and Martha Washington–style colonial turkey pot pie, which contains turkey, mushrooms, English peas, red potatoes, and a sherry cream sauce, all baked in a pewter casserole dish and served with fried oysters and egg noodles. Seafood dishes include "giant cornmeal fried oysters," Tavern lobster pie (lobster tail, shrimp, mushrooms, shallots, and sherry cream sauce), "Chesapeake-style" crab cakes, and a paillard of salmon, which is marinated in a citrus solution and then pan-seared. The tavern also does a booming take-out dessert and bakery business. Each day baked goods such as Sally Lunn bread, anadama bread, sweet potato biscuits, and different types of dessert are offered for sale, all of which offer visitors a taste of Philadelphia's culinary past.

The Automat

Delmonico's and its mid-Atlantic competitors helped change the food culture of upper- and middle-class Americans during the nineteenth century, shifting social entertaining away from the home and toward dining out at restaurants. By the turn of the twentieth century, other mid-Atlantic establishments had a similar effect on the dining habits of working- and middle-class Americans. One such venture was the Horn & Hardart Automat chain, established by Joseph Horn and Frank Hardart in Philadelphia in 1902 and in Manhattan in 1912. At their peak, Automats catered to more than 800,000 people each year, making it the largest restaurant chain in the world at the time.

Lunch at the Automat, New York City, c. 1960.

The Automat slogan, "Less Work for Mother," shows that the restaurants were targeting not just travelers and unmarried workers (as boardinghouses and taverns had a century before) but also families, providing a substitute for home-cooked meals. The Horn & Hardart restaurants were huge chrome-and-glass rectangular halls, adorned with beautifully ornate mirrors and marble. While hot foods were served buffet-style from steam tables, Horn & Hardart is best remembered for its vending operations. Customers received change from "nickel-throwers"—women in glass booths who gave the change needed to purchase food. Rather than ordering from a menu, diners chose from a wide selection of dishes that were displayed in small compartments behind glass doors. Patrons would put nickels in a slot, open the window, and remove the item they wanted.

Except for the nickel-throwers, the Horn & Hardart restaurants might appear to a visitor to be completely automated. Behind the scenes, however, the automats required a large staff of workers to operate. As soon as a customer removed a food item from one of the vending compartments, a person behind the machine replaced it with an identical item. At the end of the day, Horn & Hardart staff members removed all the packaged food from the machines and the hot food from the steam tables. The restaurant had a strict policy that no food could remain in the outlets overnight, and each evening truckers delivered surplus food to "day-old" shops, where it was sold at a discount. The Horn & Hardart operation was highly centralized and emphasized standardized food quality and presentation. Each manager had a book that precisely described how each of the 400 food items had to be handled and precisely where each item on the buffet table had to be located. It even stated how many times each day an employee had to wipe the tables.

In addition to its coin-operated distribution system, the Horn & Hardarts are remembered for pioneering the concept of an excellent cup of affordable coffee. Their coffee became so renowned for its excellence that Irving Berlin celebrated it in a song titled "Let's Have Another Cup of Coffee," which eventually became the theme song for Horn & Hardart. Horn & Hardart introduced the first fresh-drip brewed coffee to Philadelphia and New York. Before then—at working-class restaurants, at least—coffee was prepared by boiling it for long periods of time. Broken eggshells were sometimes mixed with the coffee grounds in hopes of making the drink more palatable. Under the coffee-making system devised by Horn & Hardart, employees brewed coffee that could stay in the container for no more than twenty minutes. After twenty minutes, what remained was discarded and a fresh batch was made.

In its heyday, the Horn & Hardart had about 180 locations throughout Philadelphia and New York. Eventually, however, the outlets had a more and more difficult time competing with newer types of fast-food outlets such as McDonald's and White Castle, which had lower labor and food costs. In the 1970s, Horn & Hardart replaced most of its restaurants with Burger King franchises. In 1991 the last Automat, located in New York City, closed. Today a row of vending machines taken from that restaurant is featured in the Smithsonian Institution, an artifact from a lost era of American cultural history.

Mid-Atlantic Contributions to American Popular Eating

The dining establishments of the mid-Atlantic region helped shape not just where ordinary Americans ate dinner but also the food they ate. Beginning in the nineteenth century, cities such as New York, Philadelphia, and Baltimore produced many new dishes that would become a standard part of the diet not just of the region but of America as a whole. Like so much of mid-Atlantic culture, these new foods often originated from immigrants' adapting the traditional cooking of their homeland to their new environment in the United States. As their popularity grew, these foods were adopted by industrial food producers and transformed into mass-produced commodities. As a result, they have a mixed legacy in the food culture of the Mid-Atlantic. On the one hand, they mark some of the region's most significant contributions to the nation's cuisine, defining what it means to eat like an American; on the other hand, they have become part of the wave of standardized, mass-marketed foodstuffs that to a large extent have erased distinctive regional cookery over the past century and a half.

Cheesesteaks

One such contribution is Philadelphia's own sandwich specialty: the cheesesteak. As its name suggests, the cheesesteak is a sandwich made from fresh beef, which is fried in grease on a grill and chopped into bits as it cooks. The steak is combined with cheese and other toppings such as onions and pepper and served on a soft roll. This mid-Atlantic delicacy was first created in the 1930s at Pat's King of Steaks on Passyunk Avenue in South Philadelphia. Originally, Pat's topped the meat with pizza sauce (a variation known today as the pizza steak), but the cheese-only variety won out as the standard. Geno's, another famous cheesesteak vendor, opened directly across Passyunk Avenue in 1966, and the two restaurants now compete twenty-four hours a day, seven days a week along with other popular outlets such as Jim's in West Philadelphia. The city's natives are divided over which restaurant serves the best cheesesteak, and each vendor has its own variations on the sandwich. Pat's uses sliced rib eye cow meat, while Geno's sells only rib eye steer, and Jim uses top round. Many Philadelphians insist on provolone cheese for their steaks, while others are partial to American or Cheese Whiz (which was introduced at Pat's in the 1950s because it melts faster). Most vendors now offer all three types of cheese and let their customers choose. The cheesesteak has spread out from its birthplace and can now be found (in name, at least) in restaurants and sandwich shops in all fifty states, but—as any Philadelphian will attest—the true Philly cheesesteak can still be had only in the mid-Atlantic city that gave it its name.

Hot Dogs

The hot dog, initially known as the frankfurter, was introduced around the turn of the century. There are many competing claims for the originator of the hot dog. Some maintain it was created by Charles Feltman, who operated a popular German beer garden on New York's Coney Island and began serving small boiled sausages inside a soft roll. Others give the credit to Harry Magely Stevens, the director of catering at the New York City Polo Grounds. The derivation of the word "hot dog" is equally uncertain, but popular legend attributes it to a drawing by T. A. (Tad) Dorgan, a sports cartoonist, which showed a dachshund wedged between two slices of bread. Culinary historians consider this derivation to be a myth, as no copy of this cartoon has been found and German Americans had been referring to small sausages as dogs since the middle of the nineteenth Century. Whatever its origin, though, the "hot dog" nickname stuck, much to the chagrin of Coney Island vendors, who feared it would make customers question the quality of their sausage ingredients. One such vendor was Nathan Handwerker, a former employee at Feltman's, who opened his own concession stand in 1916. The business prospered when Handwerker dropped the price of his dogs from ten cents to just a nickel, and Nathan's Famous eventually grew into a New York hot dog empire, with a chain of stands throughout the city and a brand of sausages sold in grocery stores nationwide. From its roots in the Mid-Atlantic, the hot dog has become an iconic part of the food culture of the United States, and it can be found at ballparks, beaches, and amusement parks throughout the country.

Pizza

Pizza is another classic American dish that originated among the immigrant communities of the Mid-Atlantic. In the 1890s, Italian bakers and grocers in New York City installed coal-fired ovens in their shops and began selling traditional Neapolitan tomato and mozzarella pies. As business grew, the shopkeepers added tables and chairs, and by the 1920s the pizzeria was an established part of Italian neighborhoods not just in New York but in cities throughout the region. The first pizzas had handmade bread crusts topped with fresh tomatoes, garlic, and—often, but not always—fresh handmade mozzarella. Anchovies, olives, mushrooms, and sausage were sometimes added as toppings. Before World War II, pizza (along with spaghetti) was still considered an ethnic food, found only in immigrant neighborhoods and seldom eaten by non–Italian Americans.

Beginning in the 1950s, pizza entered the mainstream American diet. At the same time, its character began to change from a handmade specialty food to a mass-produced product. Many of these changes were initiated when New York City pizzerias began serving pizza by the slice, which quickly became one of the city's most popular lunch items. To support the increased demand, restaurant owners sought ways to increase the speed of production. Coal ovens were gradually replaced by gas-fired models, which could bake more pies at once, and pizzerias began prebaking their products. The crust changed, too, becoming softer and thinner, in part to suit the American preference for soft white bread and in part from the creation of hand-tossed crust, which became something of a show in pizzerias during the 1960s. The quality of ingredients declined as well, particularly when commercially made mozzarella replaced the original fresh, handmade variety. New toppings, such as pepperoni, onions, and peppers, were added to the pies and soon became standard features of pizzeria menus. Today, pizza is largely a mass-produced commodity, with sales dominated by national chains that feature home-delivery service. But old-style pizza can still be found in independent pizzerias throughout the Mid-Atlantic, some even using the old coal-fired ovens that once gave the pies their distinctively crispy crust.

CONCLUSION

Over the past 500 years, the food culture of the Mid-Atlantic has undergone a radical transformation. From the indigenous cooking of the Native American tribes to organic green markets and hot dog stands, food has closely mirrored the history and people of the region. In many respects, the standardization of convenience foods, fast-food restaurants, and other mass-produced commodities has damped the distinctiveness of the mid-Atlantic food culture, making the diet of its residents little different from that of any other Americans. The unique dishes and flavors of the region are not wholly lost, however. They can be found at the crab feasts on the shores of Chesapeake Bay, in the wholesome homemade goods at

Amish farmers' markets, and in the cheesesteak stands in downtown Philadelphia. And most of all, they can still be found in kitchens of homes throughout the region, where fried chicken, homemade chicken soup, and lasagna are still made from scratch and enjoyed by entire families. It is this cooking—simple, hearty, and rooted in a broad range of diverse traditions—that is the Mid-Atlantic's most important contribution to the food culture of the United States.

RESOURCE GUIDE

Printed Sources

The American Heritage Cookbook. New York: American Heritage Press, 1969.

Better Homes and Gardens Heritage Cook Book. New York: Meredith Corporation, 1975.

Brenner, Joel Glenn. *The Emperors of Chocolate: Inside the Secret World of Hershey and Mars.* New York: Broadway Books, 1999.

Camp, Charles. *American Foodways: What, When, Why, and How We Eat in America.* Little Rock, AR: August House, 1989.

Diehl, Lorraine, and Marianne Hardart. *The Automat: The History, Recipes, and Allure of Horn and Hardart's Masterpiece.* New York: Clarkson Potter, 2002.

Hess, John L., and Karen Hess. *The Taste of America.* 1972. Reprint, Champaign: University of Illinois Press, 2000.

Mariani, John, and Galina Mariani. *The Italian American Cookbook.* Boston: Harvard Common, 2000.

Nathan, Joan. *Jewish Cooking in America.* Expanded ed. New York: Knopf, 1998.

O'Neill, Molly. *New York Cookbook.* New York: Workman, 1992.

Shields, John. *Chesapeake Bay Cooking.* New York: Broadway Books, 1998. Companion cookbook to the Public Television series.

Slomon, Evelyne. *The Pizza Book.* New York: New York Times, 1984.

Weaver, William Woys. *Pennsylvania Dutch Country Cooking.* New York: Abbeville Press, 1993.

Web Sites

Authentic Berks County Recipes: Pennsylvania Dutch Cooking
http://berksweb.com/pam/recipe.html

Chesapeake Bay: Our History, Our Future. Online exhibit.
http://www.mariner.org/chesapeakebay/home..html

From Farm to Table: Making the Connection in the Mid-Atlantic Food System
http://www.clagettfarm.org/Introduction.html

Jewish Cooking
http://www.jewfaq.org/food.htm
Includes descriptions of and recipes for classic Jewish American dishes.

Overview of the Retail Grocery Market in the Mid-Atlantic United States.
http://atn-riae.agr.ca/us/e2316.htm

Pat's King of Steaks. Company Web Site
http://www.patskingofsteaks.com
Includes history of the cheesesteak.

Festivals and Events

Chatsworth Cranberry Festival
Chatsworth, NJ
http://www.cranfest.org.

A celebration of the New Jersey cranberry harvest.

Crab Days
Chesapeake Bay Maritime Museum
Mills Street
P.O. Box 636
St. Michaels, MD 21663
Phone: 410-745-2916
http://www.cbmm.org

An annual summer event featuring crabbing and crab picking demonstrations, crab races, and lots of steamed crab.

Kutztown Festival: Pennsylvania Dutch Folklife and Fun
Kutztown Fairgrounds
Kutztown, PA
http://www.kutztownfestival.com/index.shtml

This midsummer festival includes family-style feasts, ox roasts, pies, pastries, and other Pennsylvania Dutch specialties.

Naples Grape Festival
P.O. Box 70
Naples, NY 14512
http://www.naplesvalleyny.com/grapefestivalpage.htm

A harvest celebration that features all varieties of grape products including wine, jellies, cookies, and the famous grape pies.

National Hard Crab Derby and Fair
Crisfield Chamber of Commerce
906 W. Main Street
Crisfield, MD 21817
http://www.crisfieldchamber.com/crabderby.htm

Held each Labor Day since 1947, it features crab races, crab cooking contests, crab picking contests, and a giant crab feast.

New Cumberland Apple Festival
New Cumberland, PA
http://www.newcumberlandpa.com/applefes.cfm

A festival that celebrates the apple harvest with homemade foods, music, and an apple pie baking contest.

Taste of Baltimore
Camden Yards
Baltimore, MD
Phone: 410-494-1066 ext. 347
http://www.tasteofbaltimore.com

This August event provides a sampling of classic Baltimore cuisine from local vendors, with everything from traditional Baltimore crab cakes to pizza from Little Italy.

Taste of D.C.
Pennsylvania Avenue between 7th & 14th Streets
Washington, DC
Phone: 202-789-7002
http://www.washington.org/taste

Held annually in Washington, D.C., on Columbus Day weekend, this event is one of the largest food and music festivals on the East Coast and draws up to 1 million visitors, who sample diverse dishes from the city's many international restaurants.

LANGUAGE

Rebecca Roeder

A myriad of social, linguistic, and geographical factors have conspired during the last four centuries to forge the pattern of dialects found in the United States today. Throughout the history of this process, no region has been more influential than the mid-Atlantic area, here defined as the states of New York, Pennsylvania, New Jersey, Delaware, Maryland, and West Virginia, and the District of Columbia. Beginning with the establishment in this region of the original thirteen British colonies, the United States has seen waves of immigrants pour through the portals of the East Coast to mingle with both each other and those who were already there. As languages, dialects, and other cultural practices came into contact with one another, changes began to occur, and a new, American culture emerged. And as people moved westward and southward, they left new and dynamic forms of language in their wake. Natural boundaries, such as rivers and mountains, and resistance from indigenous peoples affected the paths that settlers chose when moving across the country. Amazingly, however, the migration routes used by the first European settlers mapped out the major dialect boundaries that still hold true today. Then, as cities sprang up, these urban areas became hotbeds of language contact and leaders in linguistic change.

The impact made by the first settlers on the dialects that eventually emerged was profound and enduring. In fact, it is quite often the case that the first settlers to an area lay the foundation for the future linguistic pattern of that area, even if the founding group is small. In his book titled *The Cultural Geography of the United States*, Wilbur Zelinsky formalized this phenomenon as the doctrine of First Effective Settlement. In addition, each individual group of European settlers to North America initially remained more connected to its European homeland than to neighboring towns in colonial America. Transportation between settlements was not good and often unsafe, and communication was difficult because the settlers in one town usually emigrated from a different European land than the settlers in another town. Because of this isolation from other settlements, quite distinctive dialects arose in the first stages of settlement. Each of these dialects continued to evolve, both from within—for it is the nature of any language to constantly change—and from without, as speakers came into contact with external influences, such as the arrival of new immigrants.

Before Europeans arrived, however, the Americas were occupied by a diverse group of native inhabitants. This chapter begins with a brief summary of the Native American people and languages that were present in the mid-Atlantic region before the arrival of Europeans. Following this is a section dedicated to mainstream Anglo varieties of American English. The main reason for separating discussion of Anglo varieties from other varieties of American English is that the histories of other varieties (e.g., Latino American dialects, African American Vernacular English dialects, and Native American English dialects, to name a few) are connected to quite different cultural backgrounds and patterns of immigration and migration. For example, European migration was largely from east to west; Central and South American immigration and migration has primarily fanned out from the southwest; Cuban immigration and Puerto Rican migration has spread from the southeast; and African American movement has historically been south to north. Given these patterns, colonialization of the Eastern Seaboard was especially crucial to the formation of Anglo American English dialects. In large cities, however, the Anglo population is decreasing, now accounting for less than 50 percent of the total population. Whereas large cities have traditionally been epicenters of language innovation and change in the United States, changing demographics will no doubt have ramifications on urban dialects and the focal areas of change. African American Vernacular English, in particular, is now a primarily urban dialect, and is discussed at some length near the end of this chapter.

The chapter begins with a broad overview of the three major dialect regions that now exist in the United States (North, South, and Midland), followed by a summary of the roles played by New York City, Philadelphia, and Pittsburgh in the formation of distinctive eastern dialects. Two unique nonstandard dialects located in geographically isolated regions are discussed: the speech of natives of Smith Island, Maryland, in Chesapeake Bay, and the Appalachian Mountain dialect of West Virginia. The final section looks at three ethnic language varieties that exist in the mid-Atlantic region—African American vernacular English, Pennsylvania German, and Chicano English. Here we see that the cultural history of the United States has given rise to a diverse and fascinating range of dialects of American English, many of which began on the mid-Atlantic coast in the seventeenth century.

NATIVE AMERICAN INFLUENCES

The European settlers that came to the New World during the seventeenth century inevitably came into contact with the indigenous peoples of North America. Initially, much of the interaction was friendly, but the Native American tribes were soon overpowered and conquered. Consequently, the influence that their several thousand languages have had on English is minimal. Historically, the language of the conquerors dominates and affects the language of the conquered, rather than the other way around, and this situation was no exception. So, although only a small number of words were adopted into English from Native American languages, many words were adopted into the native languages from the languages spoken by the colonizers—primarily French, English, and Dutch in the mid-Atlantic region. A similar phenomenon occurred during the Norman Conquest, from roughly C.E. 800 to 1200 C.E., when the Vikings occupied and conquered the British Isles. This is why so many of the most basic words we use in English today—such as *bread* and *hand*—are of Old Norse origin instead of Celtic origin.

Eastern Algonquian

The first Native Americans that the Europeans encountered were the Eastern Algonquians. The Eastern Algonquians lived all along the Atlantic coast in North America—from the Maritime provinces in Canada down to South Carolina—or in areas that were only slightly inland. In the mid-Atlantic region, the territories they occupied included what are now the states of Delaware and New Jersey, most of Maryland, extreme eastern Pennsylvania, and southeastern New York State. Much of this area was inhabited by the Delaware, an Eastern Algonquian tribe whose major languages were Unami and Munsee. These two languages were spoken throughout present-day New Jersey, northern Delaware, eastern Pennsylvania, and southeastern New York State (including western Long Island). Interestingly, the tribes now included under the umbrella of Delaware were not grouped together under one name until after they had left the area and moved westward. Although culturally and linguistically similar to each other, they were never unified as one group politically. Other Eastern Algonquian languages spoken in the mid-Atlantic area were Nanticoke (Chesapeake Bay area) and Mahican (upper Hudson River valley). As was the case among all Native American language families of North America, many Eastern Algonquian languages were lost completely during the eighteenth, nineteenth, and twentieth centuries, including both Mahican and Nanticoke. Of those that remain, only one, Micmac (spoken in the Canadian Maritime provinces of New Brunswick and Nova Scotia), has more than 1,000 native speakers left, and most have fewer than 50. Although tribal membership may reflect numbers much higher than this, the vast majority of Native Americans in the United States today do not speak their tribal language fluently. For this reason, and especially because many of these cultures are based on oral tradition and have no written language, great efforts are being made to document and record these languages before they disappear.

According to extensive work done by the scholar Charles Cutler, about half of all the loan words into English from Native North American languages came from Algonquian languages. Eastern Algonquian languages are part of a larger group of Algonquian languages that were spoken by tribes throughout the continent. But a large percentage of the borrowings came from the Eastern Algonquians, as they were the first to be encountered by the Europeans. Furthermore, most of these borrowings occurred early on, before the mid–eighteenth century. There are several reasons for this, but the most significant may be that the decimation and westward migration of Native Americans occurred rapidly, due to a combination of war and disease.

Most of the words that were adopted into English from Native American languages are words for things that did not exist in the places from which the settlers came—primarily plants, animals, cultural items, and place names. Table 1 lists some of the loan words that are discussed in Charles Cutler's *O Brave New Words!*

Table 1. Loan Words into American English from Eastern Algonquian Languages

English Word	Indigenous Word	Original Language	Date	Explorer
Animals				
moose	*mos*	E. Abenaki	1605	James Rosier
raccoon	*aroughcun*	VA Algonquian	1608	John Smith
opossum	*aposoum*	VA Algonquian	1610	*
terrapin	*torope*	VA Algonquian	1613	Alexander Whitaker
skunk	*squnck*	Massachusett	1634	William Wood
Plants and Food				
hominy	*uskatahomen*	VA Algonquian	1612	John Smith
hickory	*pocohiquara*	VA Algonquian	1612	John Smith
squash	*askutasquash*	Narragansett	1643	Roger Williams
pecan	*paccan*	VA Algonquian	1612	William Strachey
Cultural Items				
sagamore	*sakama*	E. Abenaki	1605	James Rosier
wampumpeag	*wampompeag*	Massachusett	1627	William Bradford
papoose	*papoos*	Narragansett	1634	William Wood
tomahawk	*tamahaac*	VA Algonquian	1605	James Rosier
powwow	*powwaw*	Narragansett	1605	James Rosier
Place Names				
Roanoke	*rawranoke*	VA Algonquian	1624	John Smith
Manhattan	*menahanwi*	Proto-Algonquian	*	unattested
Massachusetts	*Massachussett*	Massachusett	*	*
Tammany	*Tamanend*	Delaware	*	*

Note: An asterisk (*) signifies that the earliest date or explorer is unknown.

The second column shows the original word from which the English word was derived; the third column shows the language from which the word came; and the fourth column gives the date of the first known written example of that word in English. The last column indicates the explorer given credit for first documenting the word. Four early explorers in particular—James Rosier, William Strachey, Roger Williams, and John Smith—kept detailed records of the new words they encountered during their journeys. Probably, at least some of these words were in use by explorers and settlers long before any single traveler translated them into English and wrote them down. An interesting example of the difficulties that Europeans encountered in trying to pronounce and spell Native American words comes from the writings of John Smith in Virginia in the early seventeenth century. He was the first to document the word *raccoon*, but he spelled it several different ways, including *rahaugcum* and *raugroughcum*. Although the spelling system was not yet standardized in English, this variety may also reflect difficulty in understanding the Virginia Algonquian sounds. In addition to the problems that historians encounter in determining exactly when a word came into American English from a Native American language, it is often nearly impossible to know a word's linguistic origins, as documentation of such information was not widespread during colonial times. Furthermore, settlers often did not know the name of the tribe with which they were interacting.

As can be seen in the table above, five American English words for animals that come from Eastern Algonquian languages are *moose, raccoon, opossum, terrapin*, and *skunk*. Some plant and food names that come from Eastern Algonquian languages are *hominy, hickory, squash*, and *pecan*. The original meanings of the words are equally interesting. For example, the word *squash* originally comes from a word meaning "that which is eaten raw," and *moose* refers to the fact that this animal strips the bark and lower branches off a tree when eating.

Many borrowed words that refer to cultural and religious practices or objects have been lost over time. Several examples of cultural words that were in use by early settlers are *sagamore*, "a chief" and *wampumpeag* (later shortened to *peag* or *wampum*) "band of shell beads." The word *wampum* literally meant "white string," and these strings of beads were often used as currency by the Eastern Algonquian tribes. They were so common that they came to be accepted as valid currency by many European fur traders.

Three Eastern Algonquian cultural words that have been preserved to the present day are *papoose*, "an infant or very young child," *powwow*, "a meeting or gathering" (although its original meaning was "medicine man"), and *tomahawk*, "a light ax."

Despite the fact that European colonialization nearly wiped out Native American languages, many indigenous place names have endured that were adopted by the settlers for areas and natural formations that had no European name. Among those that come from Eastern Algonquian languages are *Roanoke, Manhattan*, and *Massachusetts*. *Roanoke* was the first colonial place name with Native American origins. It was coined in 1624 by John Smith and comes from a Virginia Algonquian word meaning "wampum." Another interesting name, derived from a Delaware language, is *Tammany*, as in the corrupt political machine of New York City called *Tammany Hall*. This name originally came from a diplomatic seventeenth-century Delaware chief named *Tamanend*.

Iroquois

Early settlers to the mid-Atlantic region encountered both Iroquoian and Eastern Algonquian tribal communities. The area of the mid-Atlantic region inhabited by the Iroquois was west of that occupied by the Eastern Algonquians. Their territories composed of what is now New York State (west of the Hudson River valley), part of northern Maryland, and central and northwestern Pennsylvania. Among the Iroquoian languages spoken in this area were the languages of the Iroquois confederacy, known as the Five Nations—Mohawk, Oneida, Onondaga, Cayuga, and Seneca. A sixth Iroquois language, Susquehannock, was spoken further south, along the Susquehanna River in Pennsylvania and into northern Maryland. Linguistic evidence indicates that this area was occupied by the Iroquois for over 4,000 years before the arrival of the Europeans.

Not as many animal, plant, or cultural words have been documented as having been adopted into English from Iroquoian languages as from Eastern Algonquian languages, but there are many American place names that come from Iroquois. The name *Niagara* comes from *Ongiaahra*, meaning "an overwhelming flood," which was the name of an Iroquois town. *Ohio* and *Saratoga* also come from Iroquois languages.

AMERICAN ENGLISH DIALECT REGIONS

The United States has had several major periods of immigration during its history, but, as mentioned above, the earliest colonists, who were primarily English and Dutch, were the most crucial to the establishment of American English dialect boundaries. The largest number of Dutch lived in the Hudson Valley region and lent many very basic words to American English. Table 2, compiled from *American Talk* by J. L. Dillard, gives a list of colonial Dutch words that were borrowed into American English.

The number of words for food, basic cultural terms, and place names indicates the degree of interaction that took place between the English and Dutch settlers throughout the seventeenth and early eighteenth centuries. The fact that the Dutch arrived to the Hudson Valley region before the English gave them an advantage in terms of place names. Even the naming of New York itself, which was originally called Nieuw Amsterdam, was no doubt influenced by the previous Dutch name. Eventually, however, the Dutch were outnumbered by the English and culturally assimilated, along with the Swedes and Finns.

The English settlers to the mid-Atlantic area were mostly from the southern and midland counties of England and spoke a wide range of dialects. After 1720, Scots-Irish and Palatine Germans began to arrive in the Philadelphia area and

Table 2. Loan Words into American English from Dutch

English Word	Dutch Word	Dutch Meaning
Food		
cookie	*koekje*	little cake
cruller	*krulle, krul*	curl; also a crooked piece of pastry
hot cake	*heetekoek*	pancake
pit	*pit*	cherry, peach, or plum pit
waffle	*wafel*	waffle
Cultural Items		
Santa Claus	*Sinter Klaas*	St. Nicholas
how come?	*hoekom*	why?
poppycock (to mean "Nonsense!")	*papekak*	soft dung
boss	*baas*	boss
stoop	*stoep*	a small porch with seats or benches
Place Names		
Broadway	*Bredeweg*	wide road
Brooklyn	*Breuckelen*	marshland
Harlem	*Nieuw Haarlem*	from a place name in the Netherlands

The earliest colonists, who were primarily English and Dutch, were the most crucial to the establishment of American English dialect boundaries. Courtesy Library of Congress.

spread west into Pennsylvania and south into Maryland, Virginia, and the Carolinas, bringing with them new forms of language and cultural practices. Language diversity was an inherent part of life in colonial America. Native Americans of different tribes, English of various dialects, Dutch, Germans, and Scots-Irish all mingled. When the first census was taken in 1790, only half of the population of the original thirteen colonies was English. Out of the melange of tongues emerged the seedlings of American English. By the time more Germans and the Irish began to immigrate in huge numbers during the 1830s and 1840s, the dialects of the coastal cities in the East were already well established.

In 1949, linguist Hans Kurath mapped out three main dialect regions in the eastern United States based on where certain words were used or not used. He labeled these three major regions North, Midland, and South. Kurath's boundaries were based only on lexical differences. For example, there is a major boundary between North and Midland that runs across northern New Jersey and Pennsylvania. It was generally only people south of this region who said *right smart*, for example, indicating the existence of a northern dialect area where people did not use this phrase. People in the North said *pail*, whereas further south they said *bucket*. As it turned out, many words seemed to cut off along this same North-Midland line. Later researchers noted that pronunciation differences exist that fall out along this line, as well. For example, the North has historically preserved a distinction between the *w* sounds of words such as *which* and *witch*. In the North, the *h* in words such as *which* is still pronounced by some, although it appears that the distinction is rapidly being lost. Other pairs of words in which this difference can be seen are *whale/wail*, *whine/wine*, and *where/wear*.

Similarly, it seems to be mostly in the region designated as South that people merge the vowels of words such as *pin* and *pen*, so that both sound like *pin*. In terms of vocabulary, Kurath noted that southerners said *low* for "moo" and *lightwood* for "kindling." Grammar differences exist, as well. For example, in the South, speakers use what are called double modals, constructions such as *might could* and *might oughta*, whereas these seem very strange to Midland and Northern speakers.

There has been some disagreement over how best to describe and label what Kurath calls the Midland dialect region, most notably by Craig Carver and Lawrence Davis and Charles Houck. However, the boundaries themselves have withstood close scrutiny over the past fifty years and do not seem to have moved much, having been further supported by evidence based on both pronunciation and grammar. The mid-Atlantic states are spread out over all three dialect regions, with most states straddling one of these regional boundaries. Of the six states under discussion here only New York and West Virginia are completely within one major dialect area—North and Midland, respectively. In addition to these major boundaries, there are also many minor dialect boundaries within each region. The areas share significant characteristics but also differ from each other. According to Kurath's research, in the eastern United States, the North includes six subdivisions, the Midland has seven dialect areas, and the South has five. Just like the larger regions, these subdivisions reflect geographical and migratory patterns. In addition, however, they were shaped by religious, ethnic, and economic differences to a greater degree than the more general areas. With some deviations due to geography and industry, these three dialect regions move straight west to the Mississippi River, beyond which they mingle a great deal with each other and with previously unencountered languages and dialects. The main cultural centers and dialect regions of the eastern United States, summarized below, were formed long before any cohesive western Anglo dialects began to emerge.

New York

The state of New York is in the North dialect region. Within this, the state can be divided into the following three general dialects: New York City, Hudson Valley, and Upstate New York. As discussed above, the Hudson Valley area was originally settled by the Dutch, and the current dialect has been influenced by both the Dutch and metropolitan New York City. Very little research has been done, however, on the unique qualities of this dialect in its current state. West of the Hudson Valley is Upstate New York, which is currently undergoing an interesting pronunciation shift called the Northern Cities Chain Shift (NCCS). This change affects vowel pronunciation and is occurring in large cities throughout the North, including Syracuse, Rochester, and Buffalo in the state of New York, as well as Cleveland, Chicago, and Detroit farther west. Interestingly, however, this change is not taking place in the eastern cities of Albany or New York City, even though all of New York State is considered to be in the North dialect region.

In the first stages of this vowel shift, words such as *bag* and *laugh* begin to sound to non-NCCS speakers like *beg* and *lef*. Also, words such as *hot* and *sock* begin to sound closer to *hat* and *sack*. In later stages, the vowel in words such as *bed* can begin to sound like the vowel in *bud*, and the vowel in words such as *caught* can sound like the vowel in *cot*. What is happening is that the vowels are moving and pushing each other out into a new place. It is an intriguing example of language change in motion. Evidence shows that young, urban, middle-class women tend to be the first to be affected by the NCCS. It is often the case that young, urban women are the leaders in language change.

Pennsylvania and New Jersey

Northern Pennsylvania and northern New Jersey are both a part of the North linguistically. Most of the northern edge of Pennsylvania is in the Upstate New York dialect region and the rest is in the Hudson Valley region. The northeastern corner of New Jersey is included in the New York City dialect area. Below this, in the Midland area, the southeastern tip of Pennsylvania and the southern half of New Jersey are a part of the Delaware Valley (Philadelphia) dialect region, originally settled by Quakers from the southeast of England. The rest of Pennsylvania is basically divided into two parts. The Susquehanna Valley, where many Pennsylvania Germans still live today, was first settled by immigrants from the Palatine region of Germany. They moved westward from the Philadelphia area to develop their own community and continue their agricultural lifestyle. This dialect is discussed under the section on ethnic variation. West of this are the Allegheny Mountains, beyond which lies Pittsburgh. Western Pennsylvania was settled by the Scots-Irish, who primarily came from Ulster in Northern Ireland.

Maryland and Delaware

Both Delaware and Maryland straddle the major dialect boundary between Midland and South. Northern Delaware and northeastern Maryland are in the Philadelphia dialect area (Midland region). Southern Delaware is part of Kurath's Delmarva dialect area, which consists of the lower part of the peninsula between the Chesapeake Bay and the Atlantic Ocean. Its name is a blend of the three states that share parts of the peninsula—Delaware, Maryland, and Virginia. The dialect of this area has historically been somewhat different from that of the rest of Maryland because of its geographical isolation, although little, if any, reliable current research exists on the dialect as it is today.

The rest of Maryland is split roughly into three dialect regions. The area in northern Maryland that is near the Susquehanna Valley is Pennsylvania German. Migrants from Pennsylvania during the eighteenth century and immigrants from Germany during the nineteenth century kept the German culture and language strong there. The area in the northwest corner of Maryland has Appalachian speech. Finally, the southern region west of Chesapeake Bay is influenced by Virginia Piedmont Southern. One very distinctive feature of southern speech is vowel monophthongization before voiced consonants. For example, a word such as *time* is pronounced as *tom* in the South, but *taym* in the Midland and North. Where the vowel in *taym* has two parts to it, the vowel in *tom* only has one. Two lexical differences that Kurath found that distinguished Virginia Piedmont Southern from the South Midlands dialect just to the west were the words for *turtle* and *peanut*—in the Virginia Piedmont they were *terrapin* and *goober*, respectively, and in the South Midland area they were *cooter* and *peanut*. The words *goober* and *cooter* both have West African origins and reflect the small but enduring influence of West

African languages on the speech of the southern plantation regions, some of which spread into the South Midlands.

Baltimore, the largest city in Maryland, is in Kurath's southern dialect region, but it is actually a transitional area between South and Midland, in general, and between southeast and northwest, within Maryland. Baltimore speech has also been heavily influenced by German. According to Bonnie Greatman in her 1970 dissertation titled *A Dialect Atlas of Maryland*, by 1900, 85 percent of the substantial German population of Maryland lived in or near Baltimore. An ethnic German community existed in Baltimore well into the twentieth century that was quite separate from the Pennsylvania German group further north and west.

Baltimore's population in 2000 was 64.3 percent black and 31.6 percent white. As a slave state before the Civil War and a border state during the war, Maryland has always had a high percentage of African Americans. During the nineteenth century, both slaves and free blacks could be found in the city, making it a volatile place to live. Largely due to its cultural history, of all the cities discussed in this section, Baltimore is still the most southern in its speech characteristics.

West Virginia

West Virginia is in Kurath's South Midland region but has many southern features in its dialects. Although there are several large cities, including Charleston and Clarksburg, much of the state is still rural and characterized by Appalachian speech. Because of its mountainous terrain, this area was not heavily settled until the second half of the eighteenth century, and not many settlers went to West Virginia from Maryland until the nineteenth century, when the B&O Railroad reached the Cumberland Gap.

Washington, D.C.

Washington, D.C., is in Kurath's South linguistically. Similar to Baltimore, it is an area of transition between North and South, culturally. Its population in 2000 was 60 percent black, 30.8 percent white, and nearly 8 percent Latino. Unlike Baltimore, however, Washington has a very transient middle class, meaning that many people who live in Washington do not stay long and are not originally from the East Coast. Very little research has been done on the speech of native residents of D.C., so not much is known about the features that distinguish their speech from the speech of Virginia and Maryland residents. There are many speakers of African American English in the city's black population, as well as a growing Latino population.

LANGUAGE AND IDENTITY: CITY TALK

How do features of a dialect spread to new areas? According to the *cascade model* of dialect diffusion, new speech characteristics tend to appear first in large cities, where people from many different backgrounds interact. The biggest cities, which serve as centers of culture and communication, then begin to transfer these innovations to nearby mid-size cities. Each feature, in turn, then filters out from the mid-size cities to smaller cities and towns, until finally the rural areas are affected. In this way, dialects spread feature by feature instead of all at once.

This is, of course, an idealized model, and many other factors are involved in the spread of speech characteristics, including social class, gender, and geography. Many changes begin in the "upwardly mobile" upper working class and lower middle class and then spread to other social classes from there. In addition, much research has shown that young adult women tend to be the leaders of linguistic change. Putting the features mentioned so far together would indicate that young, urban, upper-working-class and lower-middle-class women are the most likely to introduce new elements that endure into a dialect. This, in fact, does seem to be the case in many instances although there are also many exceptions. Many people may think of teenagers as the main innovators of new words and ways of speaking. However, these forms tend to be age-related and usually soon disappear from a person's speech.

The social and cultural factors that influence how and when dialect features spread are complex. In addition to the factors mentioned above, there is often resistance to change in the form of *covert prestige*. Covert prestige occurs, for example, among rural communities such as the Pennsylvania Germans, who feel their lifestyle being challenged by the growing boundaries of neighboring cities. Covert prestige also occurs in inner-city ethnic groups, such as African Americans, who wish to preserve their cultural identity. Feelings such as these can cause people to resist assimilation and conversion to more standard dialects.

Geographical factors also play a role in dialect diffusion. Areas that are easily accessible to large cities, such as the area between Baltimore and Washington, D.C., may adopt changes quickly. However, remote areas—such as the Delmarva Peninsula of the Chesapeake Bay area, or the Appalachian region in West Virginia—may not adopt features of nearby dialects for quite a long time, due to the presence of physical obstacles such as mountains or bodies of water.

Two big cities, in particular, have played a crucial role historically in the development of the dialects now spoken in the mid-Atlantic region of the East Coast—New York and Philadelphia. Pittsburgh served as a gateway to the West and inland South. A brief history of each of these cities, and a summary of some of the more distinctive speech characteristics to be found in each, is given in this section. As mentioned in the introduction to this chapter, the dialects to be discussed here are representative of mainstream, middle-class speech. Other varieties are discussed in other sections of the chapter.

New York City and Northeastern New Jersey

After being settled by the Dutch as Nieuw Amsterdam in 1625, the Hudson Valley region and the island of Manhattan were seized in 1664 by the English, who renamed the area New York. Even then, as pointed out by Ann Sen in her article titled "English in the Big Apple: Historical Backgrounds of New York City Speech," the population was far from ethnically homogeneous, being made up of Dutch, French-speaking Walloons, European Jews, and black slaves. One hundred and fifty years later, this mix included Irish, Germans, Scots, and many New Englanders, with millions of new immigrants yet to come. New York has been a city of immigrants and cultural diversity throughout its history, and by 1900 its population was two-thirds foreign born. The influence of these many languages has certainly contributed to the vocabulary of New York City, and American English, in general. In addition, many ethnic enclaves formed in the city that have their own speech varieties. The history of mainstream New York speech, however, seems to have been largely unaffected by this linguistic diversity, and has its roots in British English.

Economically, New York City was very tied to England before the American Revolution, and many of the colonists who lived there were British Loyalists. The British occupied the city for seven years during the war, and this may have contributed to the features of London speech that have been preserved in New York City speech. For example, postvocalic *r*-lessness—the loss of *r* at the end of a syllable, after a vowel, in words such as *car*, *park*, and *Saturday*—was a feature of British speech that was not adopted by the other mid-Atlantic colonies but was picked up by New Yorkers. In the eighteenth century, *r*-less speech was a sign of high social status, but today this characteristic is stigmatized and is fading out of the dialect. In a famous study done in the 1960s by linguist William Labov, he showed that the loss of *r* was more common in the speech of all New Yorkers when they were speaking casually instead of formally. In addition, the higher the socioeconomic status of a speaker, the less often he or she dropped *r*. In other words, *r*-lessness was very common in the speech of lower-working-class people (although it still varied according to speech style), but it was fairly uncommon in the speech of upper-middle-class speakers. This trend has continued, and these results are consistent with the idea that New York speakers are trying to get rid of this speech characteristic because it has become socially undesirable.

Now New York City is the largest city in the United States, with a population of 8,008,278, according to the 2000 U.S. Census. In fact, the population increased by 9.4 percent between 1990 and 2000, and it is the only city examined in this chapter that grew during this period. The demographics are a bit different now than they were 300 years ago, but whites still make up less than 50 percent of the population which, in 2000, was 44.7 percent white, 26.6 percent black, and 27 percent Latino/a. New York continues to have a distinctive Anglo American accent, however, that is easily recognizable to most Americans. In addition to *r*-lessness, other pronunciation features are listed below:

Pronunciation Features of the New York City Dialect

1. Pronunciation of *th* as *d* or *t*
   Examples: *dis*, "this," and *wit*, "with"
2. A change of the vowels in words such as *hat* and *bear* toward the vowel in *beer*. When put together with *r*-dropping this means that words such as *bad*, *bared*, and *beard* could all sound the same (something like *bee-ad*) in the speech of someone who has fully shifted pronunciation.
3. A change of the bolded *a* sound in words such as *father*, *chocolate*, and *pajamas* toward the *aw* sound in words such as *law* and *coffee*.
4. A movement of the *aw* sound in words such as *coffee*, *off*, *lost*, *song*, *talk*, and *caught* toward a *u* sound, as in *lure*.
5. Before a *u* sound, the *h* sound becomes a *y* sound.
   Examples: *yuge*, "huge," and *yumid*, "humid"

There are also some words and phrases that are unique to New Yorkers. As is the case in any big city, many of these terms refer to local places or things and so only really have meaning to people who are familiar with New York. For example, *DUMBO* is an acronym for "Down Under Manhattan Bridge Overpass" and refers to an artists' community near Brooklyn. And due to the fact that New York's subway trains have small straps hanging from the ceiling for passengers who cannot find a seat, subway riders are commonly referred to as *straphangers*. But other terms refer to things that are not quite so local. A few examples are given below.

New York Word	Standard English Word
hero	submarine sandwich
egg cream	a drink made of seltzer water, milk, and chocolate sauce
potsy	hopscotch
pie wagon	police patrol wagon; paddy wagon
schlepp	to lug, or to haul (Yiddish)
chutzpah	impudence, guts (Yiddish)

These last two, from Yiddish, are now used widely outside of New York, but their source was the large eastern European Jewish population of New York City. Another well-known phrase, *I need this like a hole in the head*, is also apparently a direct translation from Yiddish.

Philadelphia, Northern Delaware, and Southern New Jersey

Philadelphia, in eastern Pennsylvania, is the fifth largest city in the United States, with a population of 1,517,550, according to the 2000 census. This is down 4.3 percent from 1990 and reflects a common trend of movement away from the city to the suburbs, combined with loss of industry and jobs. Philadelphia's population has actually been in decline since the 1970s. During colonial times, however, Philadelphia was the largest and most dynamic city in the colonies, serving as the main port of entry for new immigrants throughout the eighteenth century. It was the seat of the nation's capital from 1790 to 1799 and continued to be the center of American cultural and intellectual life until 1800. In fact, by 1776, the only English-speaking city in the world that was larger was London. Because of its long-term status as an important metropolitan area, Philadelphia has had an enormous impact on the surrounding regions in terms of language. The Philadelphia dialect area includes the suburbs of Philadelphia, southern New Jersey, the northeastern tip of Maryland, and most of Delaware. Furthermore, because of its status during the eighteenth century as both a hub for trade and commerce and as the point of entry for so many immigrants before they moved westward, Philadelphia had perhaps the greatest influence of any mid-Atlantic city on the establishment, and early growth, of American English dialects.

Philadelphia was actually one of the last major coastal cities on the Atlantic to be established, and it was not founded until 1682, although the earliest European settlers, who were Dutch and Swedish, came to the area in fairly small numbers earlier in the seventeenth century. In 1681, King Charles II granted what is now the state of Pennsylvania to William Penn, whose ultimate goal was for the area to be a religious refuge for the English Quakers. In 1682, Penn also acquired the deed to what is now Delaware from the Duke of York. Quakers flocked to Philadelphia in large numbers between 1681 and 1700, and following the doctrine of First Effective Settlement mentioned earlier, they established it as an English-speaking city. But Penn's policy of religious tolerance and his belief in the potential wealth of Pennsylvania attracted many other western Europeans, as well—English, Welsh, Scots-Irish, German, Dutch, and Swedish—and the city became ethnically and religiously diverse early on. Some new arrivals, such as the Palatine Germans and some Scots-Irish, continued westward into Pennsylvania, but many others settled in Philadelphia and its environs. All of these groups left their mark on the language and culture of the growing metropolis. Despite the fact that they soon became a minority of Philadelphia's population, the Quakers continued to control policy and legislature for over a century.

Of all the early immigrant groups other than the Quakers, the Germans and Scots-Irish made the greatest impression on the dialect. As pointed out by Kurath, Salvucci, and others, it is very difficult to find out the exact history of a word or speech characteristic, but some examples are given below of current features of the Philadelphia dialect that may well have come from specific immigrant languages and dialects. It is important to point out, also, that there are very few features that are used in only one dialect of American English, although any given combination of features may uniquely characterize that dialect. Consequently, most of the features discussed here can also be found in other dialects.

Features of the Philadelphia Dialect Possibly from Immigrant Languages and Dialects

1. *r*-fulness. By the seventeenth century, many dialects from the south of England, including London, were dropping the *r* at the end of a syllable, after a vowel (as in the words *father* and *artist*). Although speakers (especially the elite) in eastern New England, Tidewater Virginia, and New York City adopted this speech trait, most of the mid-Atlantic colonies, including Philadelphia, retained an *r*-pronouncing dialect. This may have been partly in protest against the British and partly because many of the early settlers, including the Scots-Irish, the Germans, and people from northern England, had *r*-ful speech and had no reason to change.

2. positive *anymore*. It is common in most American English dialects to use the adverb *anymore* in a negative sense. In other words, it is used to talk about something that used to be true but is no longer true, as in *I don't smoke anymore*. But in the Philadelphia dialect, as in the north of Ireland, *anymore* can also be used in a positive sense, to talk about something that was not true at some time in the past but is true now. An example of this usage can be seen in the sentence *Cars are so expensive anymore*.

3. *with* used alone. The preposition *with* can appear without an object in certain cases, as in *Do you want to come with?* This construction is found in German as well, and was probably first introduced into Philadelphia speech by German immigrants.

4. The word *smearcase*, "cottage cheese," comes from German *schmierkase*.

5. The word *cruller*, a type of twisted doughnut, comes from Dutch *krul* or *krulle*, "curl."

Below are some other features of the Philadelphia accent that make it distinctive, although their history is not certain. Most of the features mentioned both here and in the section on Pittsburgh are taken from work done on Pennsylvania speech by Claudio Salvucci.

Pronunciation Features of the Philadelphia Dialect

1. The *o* sound in Philadelphia is one of its most distinctive features. In his book *A Grammar of the Philadelphia Dialect*, Claudio Salvucci writes the *o* as two sounds, "eh-oo." This is the sound used in words such as *hope, coat, row*. It sounds like a regular Standard English (SE) *o* before *l*, however, (e.g., *coal, bowl*). One more interesting fact about the sound *o* in Philadelphia speech is that it is often changed to an *a* sound at the end of a word, as in *mehda*, "meadow," and *tomorra*, "tomorrow."

2. The *e* sound of SE *pet* and *merry*, becomes the *u* sound of *fur* before an *r*.
   Examples: *murry* for "merry" and *vurry* for "very"
   furry for both "furry" and "ferry"

3. Before *l*, the *i* sound of SE *fit* and *sick*, becomes the *u* sound of *full*. So, *fill* and *full* sound the same in Philadelphia.

4. The *a* sound of SE *hot* and *father* is pronounced as an *oo* sound in the words *water* (sounds like "wooder") and *quarter* (sounds like "quooder"). According to Salvucci, these are the only two words in which this happens.

5. The vowel sound in the three words *mad, bad,* and *glad* is said differently than the vowel sound in all other words ending in *-ad*, such as *sad, fad, dad*, etcetera

6. As in New York City speech, *h* becomes *y* before a *u* sound.
   Examples: *yuge*, "huge" and *yuman*, "human"

7. The *t* sound is often changed to an *n* after another *n*.
   Example: "winter" sounds like *winner*

Philadelphia Words

The list below shows a few words that are common in the Philadelphia area but unusual in many other places. Some of them, such as *pavement*, are even unusual outside of Philadelphia proper.

Philadelphia Word	Standard English Word
hoagie	submarine sandwich
jimmies	sprinkles (for ice cream)
pavement	sidewalk
pole cat	skunk
spicket	water faucet
youse, ya's	you (plural)

One feature that is common to the dialects of both Philadelphia and New York City but is often looked down upon is the transformation of the *th* sound into a *d* at the beginning of words, as in *dem*, "them," *dis*, "this," and *dos*, "those." In most, if not all, varieties of American English, *th* is pronounced as *d* sometimes, or dropped completely (e.g., *'em* for "them"). It just happens to be a standard feature of some dialects. Since this characteristic is regarded as incorrect by the larger society, New Yorkers and Philadelphians often attempt to change this aspect of their speech. Speech is hard to change, however, because usually people do not consciously think about how they are going to pronounce something. They just say it. People learn the dialect they are surrounded with as children, and their pronunciation reflects environment, not intelligence.

Some features that, in standard dialects, show up only in casual or rapid speech are not looked down upon. For example, using a contraction, such as *wasn't* or *can't*, is not a formal way to talk, but it is completely acceptable in all informal standard dialects. The reason any given feature is stigmatized is related to the hearer's attitude about the person speaking, not any inherently defective quality of the sound itself. There is nothing about a *d* that makes it worse than a *th* sound. But when it is said in certain places, or by certain people, hearers may attach preconceived social beliefs to it. In accordance with this tendency, stigmatized variants also tend to be the variants used by groups that have less power in the society at large. Accordingly, minority speech and working-class speech are usually seen as less prestigious than middle-class or upper-class speech, because they are not the variety used in education and government, for example. The popular judgment made about a speech characteristic is random, depending completely on social mores. For example, *r*-dropping is seen as wrong in New York City but is highly valued in both the upper-class Brahmin dialect of Boston and the standard British English of London.

The Philadelphia dialect has many other features that contribute to its uniqueness, and it continues to change, as with any language variety. One change that is going on right now has to do with the way people say the *a* sound in words like *planet*, *camera*, and *algebra*. It is conditioned by the following sound and is becoming different from the way Philadelphians say the *a* sound in words such as *hat* and *black*. This is a change that does not seem to be caused by the speech of an outside group but is, instead, internally motivated. New immigrants continue to influence Philadelphia speech, however, ensuring that it will be a distinctive and colorful dialect of American English for many years to come.

Pittsburgh and Western Pennsylvania

Pittsburgh is the focal point of a distinctive dialect, nicknamed *Pittsburghese* by local residents, which encompasses most of western Pennsylvania. One reason this dialect has many characteristics that are quite different from the rest of the East Coast is that the Pittsburgh area is separated from the rest of Pennsylvania and the East Coast by the Allegheny Mountains. Therefore, speech norms outside the region did not generally affect local speech until fairly recently, when pop culture began invading via television and radio. The immigrants who had the greatest influence on the formation of this dialect were the Scots-Irish, who began settling in this area as early as 1730, despite the barrier presented by the mountains. Their ancestors had fled Scotland to Ulster, in Northern Ireland, during the beginning of the seventeenth century to escape persecution and discrimination by the English. Their speech was not heavily influenced by Irish, but was a somewhat archaic form of Scots English (SE).

One pronunciation feature of the Pittsburgh dialect that is common in various forms throughout the southern United States is called *monophthongization*. This simply means that a word that would be pronounced with two vowel sounds in

SE (like *out* as "ah-oot") is pronounced with one vowel sound in this dialect (*out* as "aht"). This happens in the Pittsburgh dialect with several vowels. One is the *ow* sound mentioned above. Another is the long *i* sound, when it comes before *l* and *r*. So, the word *fire* is pronounced "fah-yer" in SE, but "fahr" in Pittsburghese; and *pile* is pronounced "pah-yel" in SE, but "pahl" in Pittsburghese. Other unique pronunciation features of the Pittsburgh dialect include the following:

Pronunciation Features of the Pittsburgh Dialect

1. A merger of the vowel sounds in *cot* and *caught*, so that both words are pronounced the same way, with a vowel that is somewhere between the two. Although western Pennsylvania is the only area in the Mid-Atlantic that shows this feature, it is also found in western New England, the western United States, and Canada.

2. Change of the *ee* sound when it comes before an *l*. So, for example, *peel* and *pill* both sound like *pill*. Other examples are *feel* and *fill*, which would both be pronounced like *fill*, and *steel* and *still*, which would both be pronounced *still* (as in the Pittsburgh *Stillers*).

3. Changing *-ash* to *-orsh*, as in *worsh* for "wash" and *squorsh* for "squash."

4. Pronouncing *greasy* as *greazy*, with a *z*. This pronunciation is found throughout the South.

The House Needs Painted

One of Pittsburgh's very distinctive grammatical traits that has endured is the *needs* + past participle construction. Where Standard English speakers would say, for example, *The car needs **to be** washed*, a speaker of the Pittsburgh dialect might say *The car needs washed*, leaving out the *to be*. As with many features that come from Scots-Irish, this feature is also common west and south of Pennsylvania, in central and south-central parts of the Midwest.

Below is a list of some words that probably come from Scots-Irish:

Pittsburgh Word	Standard English Word
diamond	town square
nebby	nosy
redd up	to clean up
slippy	slippery
yinz (or you'uns)	you (plural)

By way of the Pennsylvania Germans, they also brought positive *anymore* (e.g., *It rains a lot anymore*) and words such as *sauerkraut* and *hex* to Pittsburgh.

Pittsburgh Words

Below is a list of some more western Pennsylvania words:

Pittsburgh Word	Standard English Word
ground squirrel	chipmunk
gumband	rubberband
onion snow	a light spring snow
redlight	a traffic light
spicket	water faucet
telepole	telephone pole

There are also some words in the Pittsburgh dialect which are associated with a specific company or brand name. Two words that were coined by the owner of a Pittsburgh-based dairy store chain named Isaly's are *chipped ham* (1933) for "thinly sliced ham" and *Klondike* (1929) for "ice cream bar." The *Clark bar* was invented by Pittsburgh's D. L. Clark Company in 1886.

ISOLATED REGIONS

In remote areas, dialects tend to diverge from the mainstream because contact with mainstream speakers is limited. In this section, two language varieties that exist in isolated places are introduced—Appalachian English and the dialect spoken on Smith Island, Maryland.

Appalachian English

Although the Appalachian Mountains extend from Maine to Alabama, the area typically known as Appalachia is much smaller. West Virginia is right in the center of Appalachia, with of the surrounding states also included—Ohio, Kentucky, Tennessee, North Carolina, Virginia, Maryland, and sometimes others. This area was not settled to any great extent until the second half of the eighteenth century, when many Scots-Irish and Pennsylvania Germans journeyed south and west from Pennsylvania. Settlers also came from the east, from Maryland and Virginia, and in this way Midland and southern influences intermingled in the dialects that developed there.

As in any culturally and socially complex area, there is dialect variation within Appalachia. The most nonstandard, or vernacular, forms are usually found in the speech of older rural people, of lower socioeconomic status, who have lived in the area their entire lives and have not received much education. All these factors contribute to their isolation from standard speech habits, which come from middle- to upper-class norms, are distributed through education, and emanate from large cities. The examples given here are most commonly found in this type of speaker and rely heavily on the extensive research done on the speech of this region by linguist Walt Wolfram. This variety will be referred to as Appalachian English (AE).

Because of the mountainous terrain, many of the towns in West Virginia have been fairly isolated and remote since their beginnings. In addition, most of the people who first came to live in West Virginia were poor and so did not travel much, adding to their isolation. Insular areas frequently develop their own unique dialects, and variants known as *relic forms* are often found. These are forms that used to be common in the speech of the ancestors of the current speakers but have since been lost outside of that isolated community. For example, the words *it* and *ain't* used to have an *h* at the beginning—*hit* and *hain't*, respectively—and they are still said this way by some speakers of AE. Another relic form that persists in AE is called *intrusive t*, which occurs when a *t* sound is added at the end of a word that does not usually have a *t* at the end. This form is only found in a few words—such as *oncet*, *twicet*, *acrosst*, and *clifft*. Again, however, these forms are not random inventions, but instead survivors from an earlier variety of British English. A third relic form is the addition of *-n* to possessive pronouns (e.g., *hisn*, "his," and *yourn*, "your").

One of the most well known characteristics of AE is *a*-prefixing, in which the prefix *a*- is added on to a verb or adverb. This feature also has its roots in an earlier dialect of English, with the *a*- prefix originally being derived from the preposition *on*. When combined with the process of changing *-ing* to *-in'* on verbs, which is common in nearly all dialects of American English, sentences such as the following are produced:

1. The baby was *a-cryin'*.
2. That man started *a-talkin'* and wouldn't stop.

Just like *-in'*, however, *a*-prefixing is not allowed on nouns or adjectives. For example, the sentences below are incorrect:

1. I like *a-fishin'*.
2. The book was *a-borin'*.

In addition, there are rules about what type of letter the following word must start with, and where the stress needs to be on that word, for *a*-prefixing to be acceptable. Although this feature has been encountered in other dialects of American English, it is most common in AE. Below are several characteristics that AE shares with many other vernacular dialects. The dialects that share this feature are mentioned in parentheses.

Features That AE Shares with Other Vernacular Dialects of American English

1. Double negation (most dialects of American English). This means that the negative is marked on the sentence more than once.
   a. *Nobody didn't* understand the problem.
   b. *Didn't nobody* understand the problem.
2. Deletion of *-ly* in adverbs (many southern dialects).
   a. I come from West Virginia *original*.
   b. He likes meat *awful* well.
3. Changing *th* sound to *f* (African American Vernacular English).
   a. It was my *birfday* yesterday.
   b. He went *wifout* me.
4. positive *anymore* (many dialects of American English). As mentioned in the section on the Philadelphia dialect, most speakers of American English can use the adverb *anymore* to talk about something that used to be true but is no longer true, as in *He doesn't write letters anymore*. But *anymore* can also be used in a positive sense in some dialects, to talk about something that was not true at some time in the past but is true now.
   a. She's a good friend *anymore*.
   b. That plant is more dead than alive *anymore*.
5. No plural on nouns of weight and measurement (many southern dialects).
   a. I need three *pound* of sugar and two *gallon* of milk.
   b. He walked ten *mile* in three *hour*.

Appalachian English is a unique and historic variety of American English, but one that is severely stigmatized. It is important to keep in mind that all dialects are logical and rule-governed. Stereotypes about language are perpetuated by beliefs about the speakers of that language or dialect, not by any inherent weakness in the variety of the language that is spoken by those people. Linguistic prejudice reflects social prejudice.

Smith Island, Maryland

Located off the southern coast of Maryland in Chesapeake Bay, Smith Island (which is actually a small group of islands) has been an isolated enclave for over 300 years. It was first settled by the British in the late seventeenth century. Even today, it is only possible to reach the island from the mainland by boat and is advertised to tourists as the only inhabited island in Chesapeake Bay that cannot be reached by a bridge. Tourism is not the main industry of this tiny community, however. Traditionally, islanders have made a living from crabbing and oystering in the bay, but pollution has drastically reduced the quantity of marine life in Chesapeake Bay within the past few decades. Recently, residents have begun to move away in search of work. In addition, the island is sinking and may need to be completely abandoned within the next fifty years. Fifty years ago, the population was nearly 700, but now it is barely half that size. The sociolinguist Natalie Schilling-Estes, who does work on dialect death, has studied the speech of Smith Islanders and has written an article based on research collected by her and others in 1983 and 1993–1995. Much of the information presented in this section comes from this article.

Most of the features of this dialect are shared by other dialects in the United States. One feature that this dialect shares with Appalachia and southern speech is the use of double modals. A double modal is simply a combination of two modal verbs (e.g., *might, can, will, should, could, would*). For example, the sentence *I might could go now* uses a double modal. Other features that Smith Island and Appalachia share are listed below:

Features of Smith Island Speech That Are Shared with Appalachia

1. *a*-prefixing (also the South).
   Example: *I was a-laughin'*.
2. Intrusive *t* word-finally.
   Examples: *clifft, acrosst*
3. No plural on nouns of weight and measurement (also the South).
   b. She's lived there seventeen *year*.
   b. He walked two *mile* in the snow.

Here are several more features, most of which are discussed elsewhere in the chapter, that Smith Island shares with other dialects. The dialects that share this feature are mentioned in parentheses.

Features of Smith Island Speech That Are Shared with Other U.S. Dialects

1. The merger of the vowel in *cot* and *caught* (western Pennsylvania, western New England, western United States, and Canada).

2. *r*-lessness after vowels at the end of a syllable (New York City, eastern New England, and the South).
3. Existential *it*. This means using *it* instead of *there* in sentences like *There is no wind*. Smith Islanders would say *It is no wind* (the South and African American Vernacular English).

One feature that may be unique to this dialect is the pronunciation of *g* in words such as *singing* and *hung up*. Another rare feature used there is adding *-some* to the end of an adjective to mean "sort of, or somewhat," as in *It's not that late. It's late-some*. Smith Islanders also use some unusual words, as exemplified in the following list:

Smith Island Word	Definition
kofer	warped
hide and switch	hide and seek
edge of dark	twilight
proging	collecting arrowheads
gut	stream

There are also many different maritime words; for example, there are at least nine different words for a crab that are dependent on what stage of the molting process it is in.

Although this colorful dialect is headed quickly for extinction, it is an important piece of the cultural history of this area. Interestingly, the dialect seems to be getting stronger and more exaggerated in the few remaining speakers, instead of weaker. As Schilling-Estes points out, this may be because of an increased sense of solidarity among those who are left.

LANGUAGE AND IDENTITY: ETHNIC VARIATION

In addition to dialects that are nonstandard for reasons of geographic isolation, there are also many dialects of American English that are nonstandard for other reasons, such as ethnic identity. In this section, two ethnic dialects that are spoken by large numbers of people in the mid-Atlantic region are discussed—African American Vernacular English and Pennsylvania German.

African American Vernacular English

African Americans make up a substantial percentage of the population in each of the five largest cities in the mid-Atlantic region—U.S. census numbers for 2000 show Baltimore (64.3 percent), Washington, D.C. (60 percent), Philadelphia (43.2 percent), Pittsburgh (27.1 percent), and New York City (26.6 percent). Many, if not most, African Americans are bidialectal in African American Vernacular English (AAVE) and some form of Standard English (SE). AAVE can be considered an ethnic speech variety, because it is based on the identity of a *culturally constructed group*. Describing a group as culturally constructed means that membership in it is not based on anything biological, but on a set of ideas about what it means to be a member of that group. In other words, a person does not have to be black to speak AAVE—there are nonblacks who speak it as a native variety—and not all black people speak AAVE. Also, it is only used in certain situations, not all the time, since most of its speakers also speak some form of SE. Speaking AAVE signifies membership in the group, which is true of most ethnic varieties, but AAVE is unique for several reasons.

For one thing, most immigrants have come to the United States voluntarily, whereas black people originally came from Africa involuntarily. The social history of slavery is inextricably intertwined with the language, and since its beginnings, AAVE has been as much about making sense of life as a black American as it has been about speaking English. For example, as pointed out by the linguist Geneva Smitherman, secrecy was a necessary part of survival for slaves. The tradition of talking in a code that was not understandable to the slave masters may, in part, lie behind the AAVE characteristic of using words to mean the opposite of what they mean in mainstream culture. Common examples are *bad* to mean "good," *stupid* to mean "excellent," and *dope* to mean "very good, superb."

Another characteristic that distinguishes AAVE from other ethnic varieties is that African Americans have been a part of American culture as long as Europeans. Because they have not historically been a part of the power group, however, they have had to carve out a unique identity, and language has been a part of that. This is illustrated by the struggle that has gone on over the last few decades to find an appropriate name for the English spoken by this group. During the 1960s and 1970s, *Black English* was the term most often used by scholars, but many found this problematic because the English spoken in the Caribbean, or Africa, for example, could then also be called *Black English*. In 1973, the term *Ebonics* (a blend of *ebony* and *phonics*) was introduced by the psychologist Robert Williams as a means of indicating the cultural independence of the black community from mainstream America. Other terms used to describe this variety since 1970 are as follows: *Negro Dialect, Substandard Negro English, Nonstandard Negro English, Afro-American English, Vernacular Black English*. All of these are problematic in one way or another. Even the term used here, *African American Vernacular English*, is not completely accurate, because many speakers of this variety consider themselves to be Americans, not African Americans. Furthermore, the term *vernacular* is often looked down on as substandard. So, the search goes on for a term that is appropriate to the dialect.

One interesting characteristic of AAVE is the fact that the numerous varieties of AAVE in the United States have many more similarities than differences. This is not the case for mainstream varieties of English. Although the term *Standard English* can be used to denote the written variety that is taught in schools and used in government, spoken standards vary by region. Since the vast majority of AAVE speakers migrated to northern areas from the South, however, it is perhaps not too surprising to find homogeneity in varieties of AAVE all over the country.

AAVE is now primarily an urban dialect, and the de facto segregation to be found in large U.S. cities creates an environment in which speakers of AAVE and speakers of mainstream dialects often do not interact much. This may be one reason why AAVE speakers are not assimilating to local dialects.

Anglicist Versus Creolist Hypotheses

With this brief introduction as background, the history of AAVE should be examined. There are two major hypotheses about the origins of AAVE—the Anglicist hypothesis and the Creolist hypothesis.

A *pidgin* is a form of communication that people who speak different languages must use. Pidgins are not full languages; they are simplified codes that are created to just get enough information across to communicate and are often used in trade, for example. A *creole* grows out of a pidgin and is a full language that can be learned by children as their native language. The root of the Anglicist versus Creolist debate lies in determining whether the Africans who were brought to the colonies as slaves during the seventeenth, eighteenth, and nineteenth centuries went through a period of *pidginization* (creating a pidgin) and then *creolization* (developing a creole out of the pidgin) or not.

The Anglicists believe that the slaves learned English fairly quickly and soon lost most aspects of their native languages. The Creolists believe that the slaves combined African languages, English, and other European languages to make a pidgin. Then, as contact with native African languages was lost in the New World situation, a creole developed, which changed slowly over time—in a process called *decreolization*—so that speakers gradually began speaking a dialect closer to the Standard English of their region.

There is very little documentation on how slaves actually talked, because nearly all of them were illiterate, and not much value was placed on their speech by Anglo society. So it is difficult to conclusively solve this debate. Even so, each side presents many pieces of evidence in support of their view. For example, an Anglicist might make the point that, since over 80 percent of slaves were part of households that had fewer than four slaves, conditions were not such that a creole could have developed. The development of a creole requires the extended interaction of a large number of people. A Creolist may retort by giving examples of features that are found in AAVE that are also found in most creoles of the world. One such feature is called *copula absence*. The copula is any form of the verb *to be*, and its absence would be exemplified in a sentence such as *She ready* (for Standard English "She is ready"). Regardless of the answer to the question of origin, however, it is fascinating to note that AAVE continues to be an internally cohesive dialect, and is perhaps more different from mainstream varieties than it was a hundred years ago. This point will be returned to below.

Features of AAVE

As mentioned with relation to the other dialects discussed in this chapter, it is rare for any given feature to be unique to one dialect. It is, instead, the combination of features that are present in a dialect, and the degree to which each is used, that make it different from others. AAVE, for example, has many features that are also found in various dialects of the South. Copula absence is one of them. Several more, relating only to pronunciation or "accent," adapted from a list compiled by Guy Bailey and Erik Thomas, are listed on the following page.

Features That AAVE Shares with Southern Dialects

1. Loss of *r* after consonants and in unstressed syllables. This is slightly different from the loss of *r* found in the mainstream New York dialect.
   Examples: *thow,* "throw," *pofesa,* "professor"
2. Turning *th* into *f* or *v.*
   Examples: *baf,* "bath," *bavs,* "baths"
3. Merging the vowels in words such as *pen* and *pin,* so that they both sound the same. Other examples are *hem* and *him,* also *send* and *sinned.*
4. Changing the stress on a word to the first syllable.
   Examples: ***police, Detroit***

There are a few features present in AAVE that have not yet been found in any other dialect of American English, but linguists do not agree on the full list of these unique features. Based on work done by the sociolinguists Walt Wolfram and Ralph Fasold, however, four are given below about which there seems to be some consensus of opinion:

Features Unique to AAVE

1. The use of habitual *be.* This form indicates something that happens on a regular basis.
   Example: *Sometimes my ears be itching.*
2. Possessive *-s* absence.
   Examples: *Mary dog,* "Mary's dog"
   boy shoe, "boy's shoe"
3. Present tense, third person *-s* absence.
   Examples: *He write,* "He writes"
   She see, "She sees"
4. Substitution of *k* for *t* in *str* clusters.
   Examples: *skreet,* "street," *skream,* "stream"

There are many other features of AAVE that distinguish it from SE. Some are unique to AAVE, but most are shared by other informal, or vernacular, dialects. All of these characteristics have rules that govern their use, however, and most of these features can also be found in other languages. For example, multiple negation (e.g., *He **didn't** do **nothing** wrong*), a stigmatized feature that is often associated with AAVE, is actually found to some extent in most informal varieties of American English, and it is fairly common in the languages of the world. For example, both French and Spanish mark negation more than once within a clause. The fact that such features are shared with standard languages around the world makes it clear that AAVE (as well as other nonstandard varieties) is grammatically different from SE, not deviant from it.

Convergence Versus Divergence

A final issue that is often addressed in discussions of AAVE has to do with whether the dialect is becoming more or less like Anglo vernacular dialects in the United States. Although it would seem to make sense that AAVE has become more similar to white dialects since the end of the Civil War, evidence has recently come to light that this may not be so. Research done in the 1980s by William Labov in Philadelphia suggests that, at least in that city, the speech of African Americans is moving in a different direction from the speech of local Anglos, meaning that the two varieties are diverging from each other. Walt Wolfram conjectures that this may be because a sense of cultural pride and a desire for ethnic solidarity is prompting working-class inner-city black people, the most predominant users of AAVE, to distance themselves from mainstream society, linguistically and otherwise. It is not yet clear whether the divergence is due to rapid changes in AAVE or to the fact that African Americans are not participating in the major dialect changes occurring in Anglo speech. It is probably a combination of both, with the latter explanation accounting for more of the movement. Either way, AAVE is becoming more distinctive.

Vocabulary

During colonial times, the West African languages of the slaves contributed a few words to English, such as *gumbo*, *banjo*, *zombie*, and *voodoo*. Today, AAVE is having an impact on the vocabulary of mainstream varieties of American English through, for example, the medium of hip-hop and the language of the hip-hop generation. For instance, words such as *def*, *down*, *fly*, *homey*, and *phat* and phrases such as *Word up!* and *in like Flin* have largely been appropriated into mainstream speech. This trend is often not well received by the African American community, however, and, as pointed out by the linguist Geneva Smitherman, a word or phrase that *crosses over* into mainstream speech is usually quickly abandoned by black culture.

Pennsylvania German

Just as the dialects of Appalachia and Smith Island have grown in quite different directions from neighboring dialects because the speakers are geographically isolated, the language of the German enclaves in America inevitably diverged from the language of their homeland due partially to lack of contact with Germany. Although most Germans who came to America moved to big cities such as Philadelphia and Baltimore and assimilated to American life and the English language within a few generations, the Pennsylvania Germans have succeeded in preserving their own culture and language for several centuries. This success may be partially due to their numbers. By the time of the 1790 census, nearly one-third of the population of Pennsylvania was German.

Most of the settlers to the Pennsylvania German area of south central and southeastern Pennsylvania came from the Rhine Palatinate region of what is now Germany and could understand each other's dialects. Some also came from Switzerland and Alsace (now a part of France), but the unified language that developed was basically a dialect of Palatine German. One of the most interesting problems faced by language researchers and Pennsylvania German authors was that no standardized orthography of this language variety existed until the 1950s, so that spelling varied greatly. In addition, it was not clear to scholars how the various dialect islands of German that existed throughout the United States and Canada should be categorized. According to Silke van Ness in her 1990 book on Pennsylvania Ger-

Table 3. Borrowings into Pennsylvania German English from Pennsylvania German

PA English Word	PA German meaning	Example sentence
fossnock	type of doughnut eaten the day before Lent begins	
all	all gone	The bread is **all**
heap	haystack	
till	by the time	**Till I** get there, the game will be over
schmutz	to kiss; to caress	
what for	what kind of	I know **what for** a car you have
rutchie	a hill for sledding	
sneaky	finicky about food	I'm kind of **sneaky** when it comes to meat.

man in West Virginia, it is now the consensus opinion that all North American varieties of German that resulted from migration out of Pennsylvania should be categorized as dialects of Pennsylvania German.

Although Pennsylvania Germans maintained their language for many generations, the community eventually became bilingual. Now many Pennsylvania Germans, especially the younger people, are basically monolingual English speakers. Their English, however, shows strong Pennsylvania German influences. Table 3 gives a list of words that appear in the English of Pennsylvania Germans. The examples are adapted from Shields, Wolfram and Schilling-Estes, and *The Dictionary of American Regional English*.

One pronunciation feature of Pennsylvania German English that comes from German is a process known as *word-final devoicing*, in which, for example, *d* becomes *t* and *g* becomes *k* at the end of a word (e.g., *bat* for "bad" and *rak* for "rag").

Although the German language, in general, has contributed many words to American English, and Pennsylvania German continued to influence the English of eastern Pennsylvania well into the twentieth century, evidence of Pennsylvania German in mainstream southeastern Pennsylvania dialects now appears to be very limited.

Chicano English

The U.S. Census Bureau gives the Latino population of the United States as roughly 23 million, or 12.5 percent of the total population, as of the year 2000. These numbers are not broken down by nation of origin, however. In the mid-Atlantic states, as well as the nation at large, immigrants from Mexico make up the largest group of people from Central America, South America, or the Caribbean. Many people have also moved to this region from the Dominican Republic, Guatemala, and the Commonwealth of Puerto Rico, among others. Very little research has been done yet on varieties of English spoken by people from any of these areas. Most of the research that has been done has focused on the speech of Mexican Americans in the southwestern United States. Some Mexican Americans, or Chicanos, are bilingual Spanish and English speakers, although many speak only English and come from families that have lived in the United States for several generations. As with the African American population, many Chicanos speak varieties of Standard English. Identity and environment play an important role in language use, however, and many also speak a variety referred to as Chicano English (CE). CE shows definite Spanish influence, but it should not be confused with Spanglish, which is the label often given to the English spoken by people who are native Spanish speakers and are not yet fluent in English. CE is a full-fledged dialect of American English, guided by rules and spoken as a first language.

One of the most distinctive features of CE, a feature that reflects Spanish influence, is its stress and intonation (rhythm and melody). Stress is often put on a syllable or word that would not be stressed in other dialects. Some examples of stress patterns given by Carmen Fought in her study of CE in Los Angeles are given below:

1. *Thanksgiving Day* (stress is on the second syllable)
2. *Some girls don't think what they're gonna **go** through* (stress is on **go**)

With respect to intonation, the rise and fall of the voice is a feature that is often caricatured in imitations of Mexican American speech. Another feature common to CE that is present in Spanish but is also present in many nonstandard American English dialects is double negation, as in the following sentence from an article by Timothy Frazer on CE in the midwestern United States: *He don't hardly hang around with Italians no more*.

As with African American English, there are many varieties of CE, but there are also some features that are common to most varieties. In addition, people speak varying degrees of CE in that their speech seems to reflect Spanish influence less if they grew up around fewer Spanish speakers (whether they themselves are Spanish speakers or not). In addition, African American English seems to have had some influence on CE, although early documentation of CE is so sparse that it is hard to know its origins for sure. The intonational uniqueness of CE seems to be the most persistent feature, appearing in speakers whose speech is otherwise standardized.

CONCLUSION

Written language differs significantly from spoken language in many ways. The written word can be saved, copied, distributed in original form, and standardized. Because of this, the rules one finds in grammar books and language texts are easier to uphold in written language. Spoken language changes more quickly because it is fluid and cannot be taken back, perused, and revised. In addition, although vocabulary differences show up clearly in written language, pronunciation differences do not. For example, how does one pronounce the word *inchoate*? Even common words such as *crayon* and *tomato* can be read aloud in more than one way.

Before the printing press was introduced into England in 1476 by William Caxton, English had no written standard whatsoever. And every shire had its own spoken dialect. Since most people were illiterate and did not travel far from home, and most legal documentation was in Latin or French, this had not yet presented much of a problem. But the printing press made it possible to reach a large audience. Therefore, some form of standardization in written English became necessary. Interestingly, however, even though London English was soon chosen to be the standard written form, continued variation in spoken dialects was not viewed negatively until over 200 years later. During the eighteenth century, the Age of Reason, a small group of intellectuals, including the dictionary makers Samuel Johnson and Noah Webster, set their minds on imposing rules on spoken language. It was felt that language change equaled language decay.

The legacy of these eighteenth-century scholars endures to the present day, but in actuality a standardized spoken language is no more natural than a standardized written language. It serves a purpose and must be mastered by those who will use it well, but it is a contrived form of communication. It is in the nature of language, as an element of life, to change and grow. The most dramatic difference between spoken and written language lies in the fact that any normal human being will learn how to speak, while reading and writing must be carefully taught and diligently practiced. For this reason, although a somewhat universal written English is conceivable, a universal spoken English is not. The standard Englishes of Kenya, Australia, India, and the United States are quite different because they start from different places. The same can be said about the English considered standard in New York City versus that considered standard in Washington, D.C. People learn to speak before they learn to tie their shoes. Try as we might, variation cannot be erased from language and reflects the rich history and culture of humanity.

RESOURCE GUIDE

Printed Sources

Bailey, Guy, and Erik Thomas. "Some Aspects of African-American Vernacular English Phonology." In Mufwene et al., *African-American English*, 85–109.

Barry, Anita. *English Grammar: Language as Human Behavior*. Upper Saddle River, NJ: Prentice Hall, 2002.

Carver, Craig M. *American Regional Dialects: A Word Geography*. Ann Arbor: University of Michigan Press, 1987.

Cutler, Charles. *O Brave New Words! Native American Loanwords in Current English*. Norman: University of Oklahoma Press, 1994.

Davis, Lawrence, and Charles Houck. "Is There a Midland Dialect Area?—Again." *American Speech* 67, no. 1 (1992): 61–70.

Dillard, J. L. *American Talk: Where Our Words Came From*. New York: Random House, 1976.

Fought, Carmen. *Chicano English in Context*. New York: Palgrave Macmillan, 2003.

Frazer, Timothy C. "Chicano English and Spanish Interference in the Midwestern United States." *American Speech* 71, no. 1 (1996): 72–85.

Goddard, Ives. "Eastern Algonquian Languages." In Trigger, *Handbook*, 15: 70–77.

Greatman, Bonnie. *A Dialect Atlas of Maryland*. Ph.D. diss., New York University, 1970.

Hall, Joan Houston, chief ed. *The Dictionary of American Regional English*. Vol. 4. Cambridge: Belknap, 2002.

Kurath, Hans. *A Word Geography of the Eastern United States*. Ann Arbor: University of Michigan Press, 1949.

Labov, William. *Principles of Linguistic Change: Internal Factors*. Cambridge: Blackwell, 1994.

———. *Principles of Linguistic Change: Social Factors*. Cambridge: Blackwell, 2001.

———. *Sociolinguistic Patterns*. Philadelphia: University of Pennsylvania Press, 1972.

Lebofsky, Dennis. *The Lexicon of the Philadelphia Metropolitan Area*. Ph.D. diss., Princeton University, 1970.

Lounsbury, Floyd. "Iroquoian Languages." In Trigger, *Handbook*, 15: 334–343.

McDavid, Raven. "The Urbanization of American English." *Philologica Pragensia* 18, no. 4 (1975): 228–238.

McElhinny, Bonnie. "More on the Third Dialect of English: Linguistic Constraints on the Use of Three Phonological Variables in Pittsburgh." *Language Variation and Change* 11 (1999): 171–195.

Mencken, H. L. *The American Language*. 4th ed. New York: Knopf, 1963.

Mithun, Marianne. *The Languages of Native North America*. Cambridge: Cambridge University Press, 1999.

Mufwene, Salikoko, eds. *African-American English: Structure, History, and Use*. New York: Routledge, 1998.

Reed, Carroll. *Dialects of American English*. Cleveland, OH: World Publishing, 1967.

Rickford, John. "The Creole Origins of African-American Vernacular English: Evidence from Copula Absence." In Mufwene et al., *African-American English*, 154–200.

Salvucci, Claudio. *A Dictionary of Pennsylvanianisms*. Bucks County, PA: Evolution Press, 1997.

———. *A Grammar of the Philadelphia Dialect*. Bucks County, PA: Evolution Press, 1995.

Schilling-Estes, Natalie. "Accommodation Versus Concentration: Dialect Death in Two Post-Insular Island Communities." *American Speech* 72, no. 1 (1997): 12–32.

Scott, Charles. "American English 'Short A' Revisited: A Phonological Puzzle." *American Speech* 77, no. 4 (2002): 358–369.

Sen, Ann. "English in the Big Apple: Historical Backgrounds of New York City Speech." *English Journal* 68, no. 8 (1979): 52–55.

Shields, Kenneth, Jr. "Germanisms in Pennsylvania English: An Update." *American Speech* 60, no. 3 (1985): 228–237.

———. "A Note on the Greasy/Greazy Isogloss in East-Central Pennsylvania." *American Speech* 64, no. 3 (1989): 280–284.

Shuy, Roger. *Discovering American Dialects*. Champaign, IL: National Council of Teachers of English, 1967.

Smitherman, Geneva. "Word from the Hood: The Lexicon of African-American Vernacular English." In Mufwene et al., *African-American English*, 203–225.

Suro, Roberto. *Strangers Among Us: Latino Lives in a Changing America*. New York: Random House, 1998.

Trigger, Bruce, ed. *Handbook of North American Indians*. Vol. 15. Washington, DC: Smithsonian Institution, 1978.

van Ness, Silke. *Changes in an Obsolescing Language: Pennsylvania German in West Virginia*. Tubingen: Narr, 1990.

Wolfram, Walt, and Donna Christian. *Appalachian Speech*. Washington, DC: Center for Applied Linguistics, 1976.

Wolfram, Walt, and Natalie Schilling-Estes. *American English*. Oxford: Blackwell, 1998.

Zelinsky, Wilbur. *The Cultural Geography of the United States*. Rev. ed. Englewood Cliffs, NJ: Prentice Hall, 1992.

Web Sites

Kretzschmar, William, Jr. *Linguistic Atlas of the Middle and South Atlantic States (LAMSAS)*. 1998. Linguistic Atlas project, University of Georgia Special Collections. October 29, 2003.
http://us.english.uga.edu/lamsas

Labov, William, Sharon Ash, and Charles Boberg. *A National Map of the Regional Dialects of American English*. 1997. TELSUR project, Department of Linguistics, University of Pennsylvania. October 24, 2003.
http://www.ling.upenn.edu/phono_atlas

Salvucci, Claudio. *The American Dialect Homepage*. Evolution Publishing Company. October 24, 2003.
http://www.evolpub.com/Americandialects/AmDialhome.html

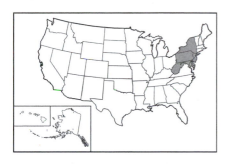

LITERATURE

Russell Leo

Literature from the mid-Atlantic region of the United States is hardly a homogeneous body of work. It is, rather, a highly diverse archive that reveals, upon close analysis, an incredible number of unique and often divergent perspectives—each carrying different origins, languages, and notions of regional identity. This survey explores the polyphony of mid-Atlantic voices, tracing the development of specific regional literary cultures from early modern writing to the emergent literatures of the twenty-first century. An investigation of the archive of mid-Atlantic writing reveals regional participation in literary periods and movements that are, perhaps, too often conceived in general terms without local significance. From John Leacock's political representations of the American Revolution to meditations on race by such writers as John Woolman, Lydia Marie Child, and Jupiter Hammon, to the work of such influential and celebrated novelists as Herman Melville, James Fenimore Cooper, Edith Wharton, Richard Wright, and John Barth, mid-Atlantic writers speak directly from the region in shaping our understanding of literary concepts and categories. The vast majority of the labels attached to mid-Atlantic writers or writing—newspaper verse, sentimental poetry, realism, or modernism, for instance—are not strictly regional terms. Nevertheless, a careful analysis of regional participation in literary movements and genres yields a richer understanding of the material as well as of the diverse cultural inheritance of the mid-Atlantic states.

NATIVE AMERICAN LITERATURE

Works of literature are artifacts in the sense that they reveal important historical and cultural information from specific areas. They register common ideas and concepts as well as conflicting emotions and anxious situations. The earliest literary account of the mid-Atlantic region, known as the Wallum Olum—the Red Record of the Lenni Lenape, the Delaware Indians—is such an artifact. The Red Record is no mere historical text tracing the migration and development of the Lenni Lenape; it is an epic poem, depicted physically through the use of characters or hieroglyphs. It tells the story of the coming of a devastating flood, accounting for the creation of the world as well as its corruption, with the introduction of evil to the new world of men. The Red Record is also a catalog of "sachems" (a chronicle of leaders and people) that begins immediately after the flood with the migration from Asia across the Bering Strait and well into the mid-Atlantic region of what is now the United States, and ends with the coming of the European colonists to the Delaware River in the first quarter of the seventeenth century. The Red Record, in fact, ends by pointing to a different voice, with a description of the colonists and a question regarding their identity: "For at that time / From north and south, / The white people came. / Friendly people, / In great ships; / Who are they?"[1] Thus we see that from its early period, the mid-Atlantic literary archive bears witness to the multiple and often conflicting cultures that gave shape to the region.

The Red Record is a literary achievement for several reasons. To begin, we may classify it as literature insofar as it is a written record—the cultural, political, and spiritual history of a group of people rendered in writing. To quote David McCutchen, a recent translator and editor of the work, "Purely oral traditions tend to break down over long periods of time. As generations go by, the vagaries of memory begin to add up and facts begin to disappear. Yet by a systematic effort of memory, assisted by written symbols, the essentials of history can be preserved, despite the passing generations."[2] The Red Record is the earliest written account of a people indigenous to North America; it is, indeed, the inaugural document in a literary archive specific to the mid-Atlantic region. But what the physical history of the Red Record tells us is as informative as the work itself. After the coming of European colonists in the early seventeenth century, the Delaware Indians were systematically displaced and driven westward—from the Delaware River valley through Pennsylvania and Ohio, and eventually to Indiana. The work first passed from indigenous to European hands in the early nineteenth century when the wooden records depicting the symbols of the Wallum Olum were used as payment for the services of a physician after sickness devastated a displaced Delaware village in Indiana. The Red Record soon came into the possession of Constantine Rafinesque (1780s–1840s), who began decoding and translating the work in Philadelphia in 1826. With access to the Moravian Archives, the records of the United Brethren that contained dictionaries and translation guides to the Delaware language, Rafinesque was able to produce a fairly accurate translation in 1833. While more accurate—and, indeed, literary—translations have been produced since the early nineteenth century, the Rafinesque Manuscript is significant because of the material that is attached to it. Called the "Fragment," the added material is written in English with Delaware names, apparently compiled and translated by an untraceable source named John Burns. Nevertheless, it offers readers a glimpse into the written history of the Delawares after the coming of the Europeans. Rafinesque's "Fragment" begins as follows:

On the History of the Linapis since abt 1600, when the *Wallamolum* closes. Translated from the Linapi—By John Burns

1. Halas, Halas! We know now who they are, these Wapsinis (White men) who then came out of the Sea to rob us of our land; starving wretches! with smiles they came, but soon became Snakes or foes.[3]

EARLY COLONIAL NARRATIVES

The Red Record, the first work in a literary archive specific to the mid-Atlantic region, records the initial violent encounter between the Lenni Lenape and the Europeans in its unsettling conclusion. Early colonial narratives written by Europeans in the New World record various other perspectives in this complex literary history. The reasons for such writing vary, as do the languages and cultures informing such texts. Many early colonial narratives were written in French, specifically from the regions in New York that were once part of New France, or Louisiana. In his "Letter to King Louis XIV" from the *Description of Louisiana, Recently Discovered Southwest of New France, By Order of His Majesty*, Father Louis Hennepin (1626–1701?) depicts the region of Upstate New York as well as the Iroquois who inhabited it. His is not only an anthropological survey of the region but also a captivity narrative—a genre that often functions as a record of the trials of a particular figure while held as a captive among strange inhabitants in a foreign land; in this case, Hennepin's text represents the hardships he faced among the Indians after attempting to convert them to Christianity. It would be misleading to think that Hennepin's narrative merely reflects a dry diplomatic engagement of the purely political order or a record of his failed conversion attempts. Rather, the *Description* renders such natural landmarks as Niagara Falls in a language both exotic and fantastic.

The captivity narrative was a popular genre during the seventeenth century; in this case, Hennepin narrates his courage and fortitude among the Indians, records their seemingly strange, pagan habits, and speculates upon such anthropological concerns as their origins, customs, and manners. Hennepin is interested in their conversion to Catholicism; what is more interesting to modern readers is the fact that the Dutch and the English are listed among the impediments to this desired conversion.

Evident, then, in Hennepin's narrative is a concern for other European settlements outside and opposed to New France. By interrogating such moments of conflict and anxiety in the text one might reveal the extent to which the regional archive as we know it is the product of struggles for power, whereby certain narratives dominate over others. Certainly the French were not the only Europeans writing back from the New World. There is a considerable archive of writings from the mid-Atlantic region in Dutch. Travel narratives and accounts of encounters with indigenous inhabitants include such works as Emanuel Van Meteren's *On Hudson's Voyage* (1610) and *The Representation of New Netherland* (1650), Cornelis Van Tienhoven's *Answer to the Representation of New Netherland* (1650), and Johannes de Laet's (1582–1649) *New World, or Description of West-India* (1625). These are narrative accounts exchanged between representatives of the trading company from the margins of the new territory to its colonial center, indicative of a systematic communications network between agents at home in Europe and abroad. These accounts include geographical details, translation guides, precise locations (i.e., latitude and longitude), and local customs and habits. The print history of *New World*, however, hints at a popularity and possible interest in the narrative beyond company business: Laet's text was first published in Dutch in 1625, again in a revised edition in 1630, in Latin in 1633, and in French in 1640.

Many of the Dutch texts not related to business are of a religious nature. Reverend Johannes Megapolensis Jr.'s *A Short Account of the Mohawk Indians* (1644), like Hennepin's French account, gives anthropological details on the Mohawks with reference to their opposition to the Dutch Christians. Additionally, there exist several poetic representations of New Netherland. Jacob Steendam (1616–?) was an East India Company employee who moved to New Netherland in the early 1650s. Steendam held an important place in the literary archive specific to the mid-Atlantic states: the title page of an 1861 collection of his poems names him "First Poet in New Netherland."[4] Henricus Selyns (1636–1701) is another important Dutch poet writing from New Amsterdam, employing classical and biblical references to make sense of his New Amsterdam experience.

Representing the German experience in North America, Francis Daniel Pastorius (1651–1719/1720) followed William Penn to what is now Pennsylvania in 1683. His *Circumstantial Geographical Description of Pennsylvania* (1700) is as much a private meditation as it is a geographical or ethnographic survey. The preface reveals a certain autobiographical devotion: "So the thought came to me that it might be better that I should expound for the good of the newly-discovered American peoples in Pennsylvania that knowledge given me by the grace of the highest Giver and Father of Light, and should thus make them participants in the true knowledge of the Holy Trinity, and the true Christianity."[5] Pastorius is also responsible for, among other works, *A New Primmer* (1698)—an anxious text dealing specifically with issues of naming, translation, and literacy. Writes Pastorius: "*Reading* makes a full Man, *Writing* an exact man, saith *Francis Bacon*; and *Francis D. P.* doing the Will of God, Happy Men and Women."[6]

Narratives of Maryland are, perhaps, the first from the region to be written in English and come to us from a variety of sources. The anonymous 1635 document *A Relation of Maryland* combines the genre of promotional literature with a narrative of the founding of the colony, complete with a description of the landscape, a catalog of useful or desirable commodities, and stories of Indian encounters. Pamphlets, written in Maryland and published in London, were used for political as well as promotional purposes. George Alsop (1636?–1673?) immigrated to Maryland as an indentured servant in 1658. While there, he maintained detailed correspondence with his contacts in England. Upon his return (after the Restoration of Charles II in the early 1660s), Alsop compiled these letters into a book, *A Character of the Province of Maryland* (1666). The work contains many of the generic characteristics specific to promotional literature and travel narratives. These genres of writing feature catalogs of commodities and detailed descriptions of the natural landscape of the New World from experiential perspectives, and were used to generate interest in the New World, to promote immigration or speculation, and to entertain and inform the European reader. Alsop's narrative also includes a rather lively and witty personal commentary on his observations and experiences as well as selections of verse spread throughout. The third chapter, for instance— "The necessariness of Servitude proved, with the common usage of Servants in Mary-Land, together with their Priviledges"—reveals an argument for servitude based on Alsop's own tenure as an indentured servant: "Why should there be such an exclusive Obstacle in the minds and unreasonable dispositions of many people, against the limited time of convenient and necessary Servitude, when it is a thing so requisite, that the best of Kingdoms would be unhing'd from their quiet and well setled Government without it."[7] There is also ample evidence of Alsop's ribald sense of humor. In the opening poem, "The Author to his Book," Alsop writes to the possibility that his work might be misinterpreted, or fall into the hands of an ignorant reader: "Say he should miss thee, and some ign'rant Asse / Should find thee out, as he along doth pass, / It were all one, he'd look into thy Tayle, / To see if thou wert Feminine or Male."[8]

Another work in English, *A Short Description of Pennsilvania* (1692), was written by Richard Frame (unknown) and printed in Philadelphia. The full title of the work gives us as readers insight into the reasons behind Frame's composition: *A Short Description of Pennsilvania: or, A Relation What Things Are Known, Enjoyed, and Like to Be Discovered in the Said Province. [Presen(?)] tted as a Token of Good Will* [to the People(?)] *of England*."[9] The text is directed at an English audience, and conveys in verse precisely from the potential benefits of Pennsylvania. Of no little interest in this poem is Frame's citation of "A Paper Mill Near German-Town," which the editor Albert Cook Myers has identified as the first paper mill in America.[10] This reference points to a development in print technology in the New World, a detail intimately related to the literary archive specific to the mid-Atlantic region as well as to literacy in America in general.

THE EIGHTEENTH CENTURY

The mid-Atlantic eighteenth century is marked by a number of narratives in English—by both native-born "Americans" and new colonists and emigrants from England. Of the latter sort are both Ebenezer Cooke (1667–1732) and Richard Lewis (1700?–1734). Cooke's works include *The Maryland Muse* (1731) and the popular work *The Sot-Weed Factor* (1708). According to editors Jehlen and Warner, *The Sot-Weed Factor* appealed "to a London audience that wanted both descriptions of the colonies and a cosmopolitan sense that greater civility lies at home, [where] the poem burlesques the primitive culture of the colonial sots, while supplying local color through Indian words and informative footnotes."[11] Cooke's depiction of the inhabitants of America ranges from humorous to satirical to brutal: "These *Sot-weed* Planters Crowd the Shoar, / In Hue as tawny as a moor: / Figures so strange, no God design'd, / To be a part of Humane Kind: / But wanton Nature, void of Rest, / Moulded the brittle Clay in Jest."[12] Richard Lewis, likely an immigrant to Maryland from Wales, published many works, including the *Congratulatory Verses* (1732). His work is primarily described as pastoral; "A Journey from Patapsko to Annapolis, April 4, 1730," for instance, was published in the London *Weekly Register* on January 1, 1732. This is a pastoral work in which Lewis describes his travels through various American landscapes—from the enclosed plantation along the rural road through forests and clearings, remarking upon the flora and the fauna as well as the effect these things have upon his senses.

The works of another important author from the region, Thomas Godfrey (1736–1763), include *The Court of Fancy* (1762), the blank verse tragedy *The Prince of Parthia* (first performed in 1767, after his death), and the compendium *Juvenile Poems on Various Subjects, with the Prince of Parthia: A Tragedy* (1765), published by Nathaniel Evans (1742–1767). Evans, himself a native of Philadelphia, wrote "Ode to the Memory of Mr. Thomas Godfrey," a dedication to his friend and fellow poet. Evans's own poems were published after his death from tuberculosis in 1767 by Provost William Smith of the College of Philadelphia in a volume titled *Poems on Several Occasions* (1772).

Elizabeth Ashbridge's (1713–1755) autobiography accounts for her journey to America from England, her travels in the mid-Atlantic region, and her conversion to the Quaker religion in Pennsylvania. Published posthumously in 1774, *Some Account of the Fore-Part of the Life of Elizabeth Ashbridge, . . . Wrote by Herself,* allows us access to her thoughts and experiences rendered as prose. Her autobiography is indeed indebted to the conversion narrative genre, recounting the many trials leading up to her eventual salvation through her duty to God. Another Quaker author, John Woolman (1720–1772), born in what was then called West Jersey (now New Jersey), is best known for his *Journal* (published in 1774), an intimate and private account of his life and piety. He is also known for his *Considerations on the Keeping of Negroes* (1754), in which he considers the institution of slavery from the perspective of "the liberal distribution of favors from heaven"—with the understanding that black and white people "are of one blood" and "of the same species" and that the present state of relations between the races should be cause for reflection rather than celebration.[13] According to Woolman:

> We allow them to be of the same species with ourselves; the odds is we are in a higher situation and enjoy greater favours than they. And when it is thus that our Heavenly Father endoweth some of his children with distinguished gifts, they are intended for good ends. But if those thus gifted are thereby lifted above their brethren, not considering themselves as debtors to the weak nor behaving themselves as faithful stewards, none who judge impartially can suppose them free from ingratitude. When a people dwell under the liberal distribution of favours from heaven, it behooves them carefully to inspect their ways and consider the purposes for which those favours were bestowed, lest through forgetfulness of God and misusing his gifts they incur his heavy displeasure, whose judgements are just and equal, who exalteth and humbleth to the dust as he seeth meet.[14]

An influential argument for the abolition of slavery, Woolman's statement forces slave owners to come to terms with their role and to reconsider how and to what end they—as Christians—keep human beings in bondage. His works are important not only for their emotional content but also for their use of generic forms such as sermons and rather intimate journal entries to render the political dimension of eighteenth-century life.

The American Revolution

The American Revolution was an event that had no little effect on the writing scene. Matters pertaining to the Revolution were rendered in poetry and prose and published in newspapers, magazines, pamphlets, and books. "Broadsides" or "broadsheets," another important print medium, made their first appearance very soon after the development in print technology that changed European culture in 1450. This medium was brought to the New World and became very prominent in American print culture. First used to print official documents and statements, "all the familiar types of broadside imprint [later] made their appearance: news stories, admonitions based upon disaster, marching songs, and, much more sparingly, romantic ballads."[15] The broadside in American literature is thus associated with the popular perspective, and an immediate one at that, given the relative quickness and ease with which information could be printed and circulated. While many broadsides were printed featuring literature inspired by the French and Indian Wars, editor Ola Elizabeth Winslow notes that

> [a]s early as 1765, popular balladry began to serve a new cause—"Liberty, Property and No Stamps." In the next ten years more verse was printed in broadside than during any preceding decade in American history, and yet these many issues were representative neither in amount nor in quality of the verse written during the period of the Revolution. The chief reason was that the newspapers, by this time numerous in all the colonies, had greatly limited the broadside market. All of them were hospitable to verse, especially that of a political nature, and with their weekly and biweekly issues, they offered the poet almost as immediate a hearing as the penny sheet.[16]

Broadsides

Nevertheless, broadsides remained an important medium for the circulation of writing. Thus far, this survey of the literatures of the mid-Atlantic region has been organized in terms of authority, or according to the identity of the writer of the work. It is important to note, however, the variety of written material published anonymously: "Given the absence of copyright laws, editors were free to pirate materials from whatever publications came to hand or to print verses sent to them by readers."[17] This notion of authority is an important feature of literature written and published during the period. Quaker writer Deborah Norris Logan (1761–1839), for instance, published verse anonymously after 1815 in the *National Gazette*. The *Heath Anthology of American Literature* reprints many Patriot and Loyalist verses and ballads that were popular during the time leading to and during the Revolutionary War, works that were often published anonymously or under a pseudonym. Ballads and verses would have been printed as broadsides as well as in newspapers. Francis Hopkinson (1737–1791), from Philadelphia, wrote "Battle of the Kegs" (1778), a satirical work inspired by the British occupation of Philadelphia and their confusion regarding a number of kegs seen floating in the Delaware River. Set in the water by Americans, the kegs startled the British troops, who suspected that they were something on the order of mines. The kegs were fired upon, hence the subject of Hopkinson's satire. "Battle of the Kegs" was first printed in the *Pennsylvania Packet* on March 4, 1778, and then later reprinted as a broadside.

Mid-Atlantic Writers in the Eighteenth Century

A survey of specific writers from the mid-Atlantic region during the second half of the eighteenth century also reveals the profound effect the Revolution had on literature and writing in general. A Quaker writer, Milcah Martha Moore (1740–1829), had her compilation of poetry—*Miscellanies, Moral, and Instructive* (1787)—published in London, Dublin, and the United States. In addition to writing patriotic verse, Moore herself participated in an active community of Pennsylvania poets, circulating verses among such writers as Susanna Wright (1697–1784), Deborah Norris Logan, Elizabeth Graeme Fergusson (1737–1801), and Anna Young Smith (1756–1780). According to the *Heath Anthology*, Elizabeth Graeme Fergusson "was among the best-known of the middle-colony poets of the eighteenth century"; this acclaim came from her correspondence with notable figures of the day as well as "her reputation as a leading salon hostess during the years prior to the Revolution."[18] Among her best-known poems are "On a Beautiful Damask Rose, Emblematical of Love and Wedlock" and "On the Mind's Being Engrossed by One Subject"; both appeared in the *Columbian Magazine* in 1789, published in the May and June issues, respectively. Elizabeth Graeme Fergusson encouraged her niece, Anna Young Smith, to write. Her poem "An Elegy to the Memory of the American Volunteers, Who Fell in the Engagement Between the Massachusetts-Bay Militia, and the British Troops, April 19, 1775" conveys her grief as it pertains directly to the events of the American Revolution:

> Our future fate is wrapt in darkest gloom
> And threat'ning clouds, from which their souls are freed;
> Ere the big tempest burst they press the tomb;
> Not doom'd to see their much-lov'd country bleed.[19]

Annis Boudinot Stockton (1736–1801) often published her works anonymously, under the pseudonym "Emelia," or under her initials, A. S. Stockton was a New Jersey poet who, like her friend Elizabeth Graeme Fergusson, was involved in the literary salon culture of her day. In her introduction to a collected volume of Stockton's works, editor Carla Mulford notes another important distinctive feature regarding the terms of publication during the eighteenth century: "Much of the writing of this time, unless it was then published, has been available only in manuscript form. That is, even though the writers were known to one another and passed manuscripts among themselves—thus receiving a public notice *like* publication—their writings have not been passed down through the common notice that literary scholars have traditionally paid to works published as books, pamphlets, or broadsides."[20] Mulford goes on to note that this distinction is increasingly important when we consider women's writing during the eighteenth century, as women's works were more likely to be exchanged in manuscript form. Nevertheless, whereas Stockton's own statement regarding the transmission of her poetry in manuscript form—"Only for the Eye of a Friend"—is evidence of this particular form of circulation, many of her works were published in magazines, including the *Columbian Magazine* and the *Christian's, Scholar's, and Farmer's Magazine*. Stockton's own elite social status informs her understanding of the social function of literature and the arts: "What emerged in the eighteenth century . . . was a highly public and social poetry, a poetry that appealed to and personified abstract qualities and expressed the general, the typical, the ideal." This is evident in her poem "The Vision"—"*written and inscribed to* General WASHINGTON, *a short time after the surrender of* York-Town" and dated "*New Jersey, May 1789*."[21] Published in the *Gazette of the United States* on May 16, 1789, this patriotic poem personifies abstract and ideal categories of law and justice in the figure of the "Chief" or "Hero," Washington:

When lo! HIMSELF, the CHIEF rever'd,
In native elegance appear'd,
And all things smiled around
Adorn'd with every pleasing art,
Enthron'd the Sov'reign of each heart,
I saw the HERO crown'd.[22]

Annis Boudinot Stockton, who herself had frequent correspondence with Washington, is important not only as a figure of the elite literary salon culture of the eighteenth century but also for the way she rendered the new United States as poetry.

Ann Eliza Bleecker (1752–1783), born in New York City, wrote poetry representing the Revolution from a different perspective from that of Stockton, the elite salon hostess. Bleecker, who moved from New York City to a frontier settlement in Upstate New York called Tomhanik, saw the effects of the American Revolution from the rural mid-Atlantic viewpoint. Her poem "Written in the Retreat from Burgoyne" (dated October 29, 1777), for instance, describes the sorrowful experience of fleeing her home in the wake of destruction—which included the death of her daughter, Abella—at the hands of British troops under the leadership of John Burgoyne. Her poetry is described as "sentimental" and "melancholic," attributes that critics ascribe not only to the experience of war but also to her loneliness upon leaving the fast-paced city for an isolated existence at the edge of the wilderness. While Bleecker never actually "published" anything in her lifetime, the majority of her work circulated among her friends and family in letters. Her work was published conventionally after her death (by her daughter, Margarette Faugères), appearing in the *New York Magazine* in 1790 and 1791 and then in book form as *The Posthumous Works of Ann Eliza Bleecker* (1793). The latter volume included her poetry as well as her novel *The History of Maria Kittle*, a fictional captivity narrative written toward the end of her life.[23]

Philip Freneau (1752–1832), a close friend of James Madison (1731–1836), was born in New York. His poems, very popular during his day, were printed and reprinted in a number of influential papers in the region. Given the absence of copyright laws and the sheer number of newspapers in which Freneau was published, compiling his complete works has posed a problem to contemporary scholars. Indeed, attributing questionable poems to Freneau is something of a literary science, as seen in Judith

The First Well-Known African American Writer

Jupiter Hammon (1711–1790?/1806?) wrote literature dealing with the Revolutionary War as well as with slavery and other social issues, particularly race. Born a slave on Long Island in New York, Hammon is arguably the first well-known published black writer in America. Among his most famous works are *Evening Thought: Salvation by Christ, with Penitential Cries* (published as a broadside in 1760), *The Kind and Dutiful Servant* (1790), and the *Address to the Negroe: In the State of New York* (printed in 1787 in New York and Philadelphia and again in New York in 1806). Jupiter Hammon is also known for his verse letter to poet Phillis Wheatley and for his sermons, especially for the way in which he identified the slave with Christ. In *A Winter Piece: Being a Serious Exhortation, with a Call to the Unconverted: and a Short Contemplation on the Death of Jesus Christ* (1782), Hammon addresses the issue of his status as a black writer in a literary culture dominated by white masters. He argues that he has the authority to address and to teach his fellow slaves, as the supposed authorities have neglected and failed to do so. Hammon's works speak to and from the black perspective very deliberately.

R. Hiltner's *The Newspaper Verse of Philip Freneau*. Freneau himself was well known for his patriotic verses. Among his most famous works are *The British Prison Ship* (1781), written while the British held Freneau captive in 1780, *American Liberty* (1775), and *A Poem on the Rising Glory of America* (written with friend Hugh Henry Brackenridge [1748–1816] in 1771 and published in 1772). Freneau also wrote *The Village Merchant: A Poem to Which Is Added the Country Printer* (1794), *A Journey from Philadelphia to New-York, by Way of Burlington and South-Amboy, by Robert Slender, Stocking Weaver* (1787), and *Letters on Various Interesting and Important Subjects, Many of Which Have Appeared in the Aurora* (1799). He was associated with newspapers such as the *Freeman's Journal* in Philadelphia and served as editor of the *National Gazette* from 1790 to 1793. The extent to which newspapers were important literary mediums can not be stressed enough. The most well-known contemporary defenses of the Constitution—arguments for its ratification and such, which we refer to in hindsight as the *Federalist Papers*—were written by Alexander Hamilton (1757–1804), James Madison, and John Jay (1745–1829) under the collective pseudonym "Publius" and "appeared first in New York newspapers between October 1787 and May 1788. New York was a crucial state in the ratification contest" and so the appearance of these essays and the choice of this medium for circulation were crucial to the future of the emerging nation.[24] Freneau's involvement as both a writer of newspaper verse and as a newspaper editor is indicative of his status as a political authority. Freneau's work, however, is not limited to the writing of the Republic; he was also acclaimed for his ability to render nature as literature.

Hugh Henry Brackenridge wrote an important American novel, *Modern Chivalry* (first published in 1792, but revised and updated until 1815). Brackenridge, who moved from Scotland to Pennsylvania as a child, was "a Princeton classmate of Freneau and James Madison" as well as "chaplain in Washington's army."[25] While also known for his dramas based on the American Revolution, it is his novel that has consistently earned him the most acclaim. According to critic Edward Wagenknecht, *Modern Chivalry* "is the closest American approach to the picaresque novels of Europe . . . [and it] gives a vivid picture of backwoods America and the eighteenth-century frontier, and nearly every American institution gets a thorough going-over."[26]

John Leacock (1729–1802), a member of the radical "Sons of Liberty" in Philadelphia, is largely regarded as having been a propagandist for the American Revolution. Leacock wrote *The First Book of the American Chronicles of the Times* (1774–1775) in the manner of the Old Testament. It is parodic, using Old Testament names for real-life figures of the Revolution (i.e., Obadiah as John Hancock, Mordecai the Benjamite as Benjamin Franklin), and was first published in pamphlet form. Leacock is also known for his play *The Fall of British Tyranny* (1776), a tragicomedy that portrays the struggle between the ever-virtuous Americans and the villainous British, foes of republicanism. Critics have made note of Leacock's employment of Native American themes and imagery in his propagandist work; Carla Mulford argues that such instances in Leacock's writing "represent the emerging impulses of white Americans to identify themselves with the Native American population in order to propagandize republicanism as a peculiarly American right."[27] According to Mulford, these impulses were especially useful in their capacity to appeal across class strata in America; indeed, Leacock's formidable ability as a propagandist derives precisely from this range of appeal.

Benjamin Franklin (1706–1790)—one of the most famous (and, perhaps, infamous) Americans of his day and after—was actually born in Boston, where he spent his early life as a printer's apprentice. His earliest published works, known as the "Silence Dogood" papers (1722), were published in his brother's newspaper, the *New England Courant*. At the age of seventeen, Franklin left his family abruptly, reaching New York first and then heading to Philadelphia. It was here that he not only earned a reputation as a printer but also honed his skills as a writer, publishing his most popular and influential works. The publication of the first *Poor Richard: An Almanack* in 1732/33 inaugurated a series of texts written under the pseudonym Richard Saunders; witty as well as informative, Franklin's periodicals became the most popular almanacs in the region and throughout the colonies. His catalog of work is formidable. Franklin wrote pamphlets for political or public purposes, including *A Proposal for Promoting Useful Knowledge* (1743), *Proposals Relating to the Education of Youth in Pennsilvania* (1749), *Plain Truth* (1747), and *A Narrative of the Late Massacres* (1764); these works display his ability as a rhetorician, alternating between reasonable and passionate voices, as well as a journalist. Franklin also wrote more personal or philosophical pieces, such as "Advice to a Friend on Choosing a Mistress" (1745), *The Way to Wealth* (1757), and *The Morals of Chess* (1779). His greatest literary achievement, however, is his *Autobiography*—a text that Franklin worked on periodically after 1771 and that ultimately remained unfinished upon his death. Franklin's autobiography is a complex work in which the author refashions his own life according to certain virtuous principles, including a strong work ethic, achievement of mastery through practice and experience (as seen in the section above dealing specifically with language), and an attention to morality. Perhaps the most famous section of the autobiography is Franklin's treatment of the virtues and their precepts, where the author meticulously defines, orders, and charts the catalog of virtues and his fidelity to them. Franklin's autobiography is, in many ways, an attempt to define and to achieve the perfect character: "I enter'd upon the Execution of this Plan for Self Examination, and continu'd it with occasional Intermissions for some time. I was surpris'd to find myself so much fuller of Faults than I had imagined, but I had the Satisfaction of seeing them diminish."[28]

Franklin's impact on literature during the period also extends to his circle of correspondents and political allies, including Thomas Paine (1737–1809). Paine, a native Englishman, only lived in America for thirteen years. His influence on the country during this period, however, was quite remarkable. Paine arrived in Philadelphia in 1774 after meeting Franklin in London; this important reference—coupled with his abilities as a writer, rhetorician, and radical—earned him a position as editor of the *Pennsylvania Magazine*. In 1776, Paine published his popular pamphlet arguing for American Independence—*Common Sense*. Later in 1776, Paine published the *Crisis Papers* in the *Pennsylvania Journal*, installments of which continued until 1783. The *Crisis Papers* were intended to support the American cause during the most trying of times, reminding the colonists that "Tyranny, like hell, is not easily conquered," and assuring them that "God Almighty will not give up a people to military destruction, or leave them unsupportedly to perish, who have so earnestly and so repeatedly sought to avoid the calamities of war, by every decent method which wisdom could invent."[29] According to critic Sharon M. Harris, "Paine's literary accomplishments earned him a controversial, salaried position from Congress that enabled him to continue writing propaganda to serve the colonial forces."[30]

Like Paine, J. Hector St. John de Crèvecoeur (1735–1813) was, in many respects, a foreign voice in American literature. Crèvecoeur was born in France and spent time in both England and Canada before landing in New York harbor in 1759. He became a naturalized citizen of New York in 1765. His *Letters from an American Farmer* was first published in English in 1781. A conversational work which collects fictional letters from the persona of James, the Quaker farmer, to the "enlightened European," it touches upon such topics as the definition of the American, the description of the landscape, life at the frontier, and the balance of life in the new Republic. Crèvecoeur writes, as James, "Good and evil, I see, are to be found in all societies, and it is in vain to seek for any spot where those ingredients are not mixed." *Letters from an American Farmer* celebrates a certain kind of freedom—of thought and of action—that critic Albert E. Stone reads as having specific literary implications. According to Stone, "*Letters from an American Farmer* has been one embryo from which, figuratively speaking, a succession of significant American works has developed. The fictional characters that Crèvecoeur drew have had many avatars. James, the American Farmer, is the precursor of the sensitive, naïve individual alienated eventually from the community and longing . . . to head for the western territories."[31]

THE NINETEENTH CENTURY: A NATIONAL LITERATURE

Many of the writers during the revolutionary period were actively engaged in representing the new republic, in attempting to come to terms with what it meant to be an American or what an ideal America might look like in print. In this specific survey, this was an America from the mid-Atlantic perspective. Certainly this activity, this attempt to render the nation in writing—whether to glorify it or to call attention to its existing faults or potential failures—continued after the War for Independence had ended. In terms literature, this break with England precipitated a need for American authors to prove themselves as capable and even ingenious; "the self-conscious clamor for a national literature arose as much from the desire to impress England as to escape her influence, so that until the English reviewers had spoken one had no way of knowing how well a native writer had done his work."[32] Charles Brockden Brown (1771–1810) achieved acclaim in America and in Europe for his novels. Born in Philadelphia and trained as a lawyer, Brown is known for the synthesis of European Gothic literature and an American landscape. He began his career writing essays and poetry, publishing his collection of essays—*The Rhapsodist*—in the *Columbian Magazine* in 1789. What followed was quite remarkable:

> Writing at what must have been a high degree of intensity, he completed and published in four years all of the work for which he is remembered today: *Wieland* [*Or, the Transformation. An American Tale*] in 1798; *Ormond*, the first part of *Arthur Mervyn*, and *Edgar Huntly* in 1799; [*Memoirs of*] *Stephen*

Calvert, published serially in the *Monthly Magazine and American Review* in 1799 and 1800; the second part of *Arthur Mervyn* in 1800; and *Clara Howard* and *Jane Talbot* in 1801.[33]

After this period of productivity, Brown engaged in political pamphleteering, writing on such subjects as foreign commerce and expansion into new territories. He also began to publish the *American Register, or General Repository of History, Politics, and Science* in 1807, representative of his shifting interests. Nevertheless, it is his career as a novelist that earned Brown his reputation. *Edgar Huntly*, for instance, is notable for its representation of Native Americans as well as for its elaborate plot device, sleepwalking—both of which seemed unusual and supernatural to contemporary readers. *Wieland; or, the Transformation: An American Tale* deals with madness and murder. His works, however, were not only weird fictions. Brown was associated with the Friendly Club, a radical group of intellectuals interested in feminist reform (among other things), after moving to New York in 1796. His representations of sexuality and gender, in works such as *Alcuin* and *Ormond*, reflect not only his ability as a novelist to challenge the boundaries of acceptable literature but also his radical political tendencies.

While Charles Brockden Brown represented the Native American as a sort of supernatural figure—the subject of the Gothic—Henry Rowe Schoolcraft (1793–1864) sought a different literary representation of Native America. His compilation of Native American tales and myths, *Algic Researches*, was first published in 1839. It is a literary achievement as much as an anthropological work, reflecting Schoolcraft's knowledge of Native American languages as well as his attempt to render in writing a long-standing oral tradition. Moreover, his is an attempt to come to terms with a literary past that predates European colonization of the Americas—specifically the introduction of English to the continent. This indigenous literary past seemed to authorize a new American literature, a national literature that stood to inherit the language and history of their predecessors. This compilation, however, poses a problem insofar as it collects Schoolcraft's own translations and interpretations of indigenous works; one must not forget that this is a very specific interpretation of Native America, and one in a distinctly European language.

James Fenimore Cooper

While Charles Brockden Brown had received critical praise in England for his writing, James Fenimore Cooper (1789–1851) became one of the world's most popular novelists as well as the first American to earn a living simply by writing novels. Cooper was born in Burlington, New Jersey, but moved with his family to New York at a very young age. His father, William Cooper, was a real estate speculator and developer who founded the frontier estate of Cooperstown. Cooper lived a rural existence at the edge of the wilderness, a setting that conflicted with his former life of manners and urbanity in New Jersey. Moreover, it was here in Cooperstown that Cooper came into contact with Native Americans from the region, experiences which would prove a basis for his most successful novels. Before writing, however, Cooper attended Yale—from which he was expelled in 1805—and served in the navy. His decision to become a novelist was preceded by a period of failure and debt. His first novels—*Precaution* (1820) and *The Spy* (1821), both published anonymously—were well received, but critics (both then and now) seem to agree that neither work is particularly innovative. Indeed, both works illustrate Cooper's dependence on English modes of narration and novel conventions, borrowed traits that did nothing to bolster a national literary identity. *The Pioneers* (1823), Cooper's third novel and the first in a series of *Leather-Stocking* novels in which Natty Bumppo appears, was more successful: "by noon of the first day [it] sold 3500 copies, an amazing figure. In accordance with publishing devices of the time, it had been preceded by an extract in newspapers."[34] Four other *Leather-Stocking* books followed: *The Last of the Mohicans* (1826), *The Prairie* (1827), *The Pathfinder* (1840), and *The Deerslayer* (1841). Fenimore's fiction is indebted to the experience of the frontier, relying on a romantic view of the movement of Americans into the wilderness and a rustic, idealistic portrayal of the Native American, the dispossessed noble savage. The earlier works are meditations on the progress of man and nation, on self-sufficiency as well as freedom, and on the relationship between the individual and a larger, structured society. They also render the American military tradition as fiction, representing the French and Indian War. *The Last of the Mohicans*, in particular, uses this historical backdrop to build suspense; the scientific and social climate of the period influences this work as well, where the fear of what Native Americans might do to captured white women in the novel fuels its suspense. The latter two novels, written at a later stage of his career, reflect Cooper's critical attitude toward the United States. The wilderness in these novels is classical in the sense that it is serene, romanticizing what had once been untouched and pristine before government policies interrupted it. Nevertheless, Cooper's works are difficult to read ideologically because of their complexity; Native Americans, for instance, are at once represented as savage and noble, as necessarily subject to the laws of a new regime and as standing before or beyond this law.

Cooper also wrote several works of sea fiction, including *The Pilot* (1823), *The Red Rover* (1827), and *The Water-Witch* (1830), and political novels such

Illustration from James Fenimore Cooper's *The Last of the Mohicans*, c. 1910. Courtesy Library of Congress.

as *The Bravo* (1831) and *The Headsman* (1833). He also wrote works of nonfiction; *Notions of the Americans* (1828), for instance, speaks to the young nation's emerging social attributes as well as to its foundational principles, and his *History of the Navy of the United States of America* (1839) seeks to offer the reader an educational account of an important military institution. Toward the end of his life, Cooper became increasingly dissatisfied with the political climate of his day, the literary culture of the United States, and the role of literature in general. His works centered more and more around such problems as greed and alienation; *The Crater* (1847) reveals the extent to which this pessimism and disillusionment permeated his writing. Cooper's travel books, written during a period spent abroad, give the author leave to comment on politics and what he saw as the greatest evils of his day: a concept like " 'free trade' . . . [for instance] is a pretentious humbug that hides the unrestrained operation of greed—the cheating of a poor Indian by an unscrupulous trader or of a helpless traveler in a foreign land by a cab driver; a government that wants men to be truly free will regulate conduct that needs regulation." Such an opinion reflects his feelings on government and property as well as his own experiences with "the tyranny of the press"—"the vices, capricious interests, the pecuniary cupidity of the commercial class whose members controlled it."[35] His last works, *The Oak Openings* (1848) and *The Sea Lions* (1849), are organized around experiences of religious conversion; Cooper himself took an interest in the Bible and became Episcopalian in 1851, just before he died.

Washington Irving

Washington Irving (1783–1859) was born in New York City and trained as an attorney. The practice was not for him, however, and after a two-year tenure as the editor of the *Analectic Magazine* (1812–1814) and an experience as a militia officer in the War of 1812, Irving turned to writing. During his earliest years as a writer, Irving was involved in the New York literary scene, also known as the "Knickerbocker" scene. According to James T. Callow, "Between 1807 and 1825 New York City became the literary capital of America. Since even Philadelphia and Boston, the former cultural centers, yielded to their Dutch neighbor, whose writers, magazines, and publishing houses exceeded all others in number and prestige, New York's literary preeminence was an indisputable fact. . . . *Salmagundi*, a collection of witty prose from the pens of Washington Irving, William Irving, and James Kirke Paulding, appeared in 1807; and certainly the decade to which it belonged marks the beginning of an unusual productivity among the 'Knickerbockers,' a name later given to almost any author working in New York."[36] Irving was thus part of a larger movement that included Gulian Crommelin Verplanck (1786–1870)—the political satirist, editor, and Shakespeare scholar—and the poet William Cullen Bryant (1794–1878). During this period in New York writers and artists worked together, forming social groups and forums for discussion and collaborating in a variety of literary journals and magazines, including the aforementioned *Salmagundi*, the *New York Review and Atheneum Magazine* (1825–1826), the *New York Mirror* (1823–1842), the *Knickerbocker* (1833–1865), the *Literary World* (1847–1853), and the *Columbian Lady's and Gentleman's Magazine* (1844–1849). This is a literary culture that Irving was not only immersed in, but was an integral part of; Irving himself was rather prolific. His fictional works include *A His-*

Portrait of Washington Irving. Courtesy Library of Congress.

tory of New York (1809, under the pseudonym "Diedrich Knickerbocker"), *The Sketch Book of Geoffrey Crayon, Gent.* (1819–1820), which features such famous tales as "The Legend of Sleepy Hollow" and "Rip Van Winkle," and *Tales of a Traveller* (1824), a rather unsuccessful collection of short stories. Perceiving this failure, Irving then turned to writing works of nonfiction and histories, such as his *History of the Life and Voyages of Christopher Columbus* (1828), and the travel narrative *A Tour of the Prairies* (1835). Irving eventually wrote other works of fiction, such as *The Alhambra* (1832)—a collection of stories and essays influenced by his time in Spain (as was his history of Columbus)—but his later period is marked by an attention to writing histories and biographies. The *Life of George Washington* (published in five volumes between 1855 and 1859) was his last work. Irving is remembered not only for the way in which his fiction, with all of its humor and mythic properties, influenced later American authors such as Poe or Hawthorne, but also as a short-story writer in his own right; his satirical sketches and charming tales informed by folk traditions, both European and American, answer the call to a national literature.

The American Renaissance in Writing

Critics refer to the middle of the nineteenth century as the American Renaissance, that period which marks the emergence of a national spirit or consciousness in American writing. Such notable authors as Nathaniel Hawthorne (1804–1864), Edgar Allan Poe (1809–1849), Herman Melville (1819–1891), and Walt Whitman (1819–1892) are usually employed to characterize this spirit—the latter three having spent considerable time writing in the mid-Atlantic states. The events of the nineteenth century, however, would demand that this developing national literature attend to social and political crises, such as the Civil War, slavery, and the women's rights movement. Frederick Douglass (1818–1895) was born a slave in Maryland. During his early years, he worked in the Auld family house in Baltimore, where he taught himself to read and write. At the age of sixteen, however, Douglass was moved to the fields, where he experienced the true horrors of slavery firsthand, a cruel management which precipitated his escape in 1838. After living in both New York City and New

Bedford, Massachusetts (where he became acquainted with the abolitionist newspaper the *Liberator*), Douglass moved to Rochester, New York, in 1847. He began to publish his own newspaper there, the *North Star*, as well as participate in abolitionist and women's rights demonstrations and conventions (he attended the first women's rights convention in Seneca Falls in 1848). His political speeches and writings, including "What to the Slave Is the Fourth of July?"—a speech delivered in Rochester on July 5, 1852—reveal his mastery of rhetoric and his control of English. His most famous work, however, is his *Narrative of the Life of Frederick Douglass, an American Slave, Written by Himself* (1845), an uncompromising denunciation of slavery as well as a gripping and realistic portrayal of racial hatred.

Like Douglass, Harriet Ann Jacobs (1813–1897) was born a slave, but in North Carolina. Caught between an unwanted lover—her master, Dr. James Norcom—and a white neighbor, Samuel Tredwell Sawyer, by whom she gave birth to two children, Jacobs decided to run away in order to insure her family's freedom. This, however, was hardly

Portrait of Frederick Douglass. Courtesy Library of Congress.

easy, and Jacobs spent almost seven years hiding in the attic of her grandmother's house waiting to flee, as she wanted to stay close to her children, whom Sawyer allowed her grandmother to raise. Jacobs eventually escaped to New York in 1842. By 1849, she was reunited with both her son and her daughter in Rochester, New York. While there, she ran "the local Anti-Slavery Reading Room . . . [and] became part of a circle of anti-slavery feminists."[37] Her involvement in politics carried over into her writing; *Incidents in the Life of a Slave Girl, Written by Herself* was published in 1861 with a preface by activist and writer Lydia Marie Child (1802–1880), whose own work, *Hobomok: A Tale of Early Times* (1824), was scandalous for its representation of racial intermarriage or "miscegenation" as a viable alternative to an unjust racial politics of purity. *Incidents* draws from her life experiences, and, according to critic Jean Fagan Yellin, "is unique among slave narratives for its double thrust: it is at once the first-person tale of a heroic mother who rescues her children from slavery, and the first person confession of a 'fallen woman'" because of her unwanted sexual encounters.[38] Despite this alternating voice, *Incidents in the Life of a Slave Girl* is direct in its attack against slavery and in its establishment of Jacobs as a notable abolitionist writer and activist.

Lydia Marie Child was criticized in such magazines as *Ladies' Magazine*, the

American Monthly Magazine, the *North American Review*, and the *American Monthly Review* for her work *Hobomok*. This, however, only served her cause, for each review publicized her political convictions in identifying precisely what they found offensive about the work—women's rights, justice for the dispossessed Native Americans, and racial equality. In addition to antiracist fiction, Child wrote historical novels and surveys, such as *The History of the Condition of Women, in Various Ages and Nations* (1835). Child also paid close attention to literacy as a political category: "In 1865 with her own funds she had printed and circulated especially among blacks, *The Freedman's Book*, a collection of essays, biographical sketches, and poems by and about black people. It was designed, in the tradition of Child's commitment to 'art for truth's sake,' as a literacy text and to promote the ideas of votes for blacks and black pride."[39] She also wrote books offering domestic advice—*The Frugal Housewife* (1829) and *The Mother's Book* (1831)—and political fiction for children, to say nothing of her nonfictional letters, articles, and essays. Child founded and edited a children's magazine, *Juvenile Miscellany* (1826–1834), and also served as editor of the *National Anti-Slavery Standard* beginning in 1841. Child moved from Massachusetts to New York City to serve as editor of the latter publication, a vantage point from which she published her influential weekly "Letters from New York," addressing such topics as poverty and crime in addition to her other political passions. Among her other works of political fiction are the feminist "The Kansas Emigrants" and her exploration of sexuality and aesthetics, "The Rival Mechanisms," both of which were collected in *Autumnal Leaves: Tales and Sketches in Prose and Rhyme* (1857).

While Lydia Marie Child published many articles and was often featured in newspapers and literary magazines, Fanny Fern, or Sara Payson Parton (1811–1872), was the first American woman newspaper columnist in the sense that her column was regular and her position was salaried. In September 1852 Fern began writing articles for the *New York Musical World and Times* that were billed specifically under the heading "Fanny Fern's Column." By 1855, she was making one hundred dollars a week writing a regular column for the *New York Ledger*. It was after this favorable development that Fern moved to New York City and continued to write and publish actively. In terms of social issues, Fern was concerned with children's rights as well as more adult issues such as suicide and crime. She published novels—*Ruth Hall* (1855) and *Rose Clark* (1856)—and children's books as well as numerous collections of articles, columns, essays, and stories, including *Fresh Leaves* (1857), *Ginger Snaps* (1870), and *Caper Sauce: A Volume of Chit-Chat About Men, Women, and Things* (1872).

Elizabeth Cady Stanton (1815–1902), from Johnstown, New York, was another nineteenth-century activist whose contributions to the literary archive of the region include works for women's rights and against slavery. Her *Eighty Years and More: Reminiscences, 1815–1897* (1898) is an intimate record of her political struggle, offering a literary alternative to her speeches and letters. She also published *The Woman's Bible* in 1895 and 1898, an ambitious attempt to offer in print an interpretation of the work that challenged the often-quoted "justifications" for the subordinate status of women to men.

While not native to the region, such monumental writers as Edgar Allan Poe, Herman Melville, and Walt Whitman spent considerable time writing in the mid-Atlantic states; these are those figures who are, perhaps, most widely recognized as American Renaissance authors. During his first residency in New York—from 1837 until 1839—Poe wrote *The Narrative of Arthur Gordon Pym* (1837) and earned money as a freelance writer. He moved to Philadelphia in 1839, serving first as assistant editor of *Burton's Gentleman's Magazine* and then later working for *Graham's Magazine*, where he wrote important reviews. It was also during this period in Philadelphia, between 1839 and 1844, that Poe wrote some of his most enduring fictions, many of which were collected and published as his successful *Tales of the Grotesque and Arabesque*: "Ligeia," "The Fall of the House of Usher," "The Tell-Tale Heart," "Eleonora," "The Pit and the Pendulum," "The Masque of the Red Death," and "The Gold Bug."[40] Returning to New York in 1844, Poe embarked on another creative run in his career, composing "The Raven" (which appeared in the New York *Evening Mirror*) as well as serving as the editor of the *Broadway Journal*. Poe was also connected to Baltimore; not only did he publish many of his stories there, but he died in Baltimore in 1849, arriving in the city "for reasons unknown."[41]

Melville was born in New York in 1819 but spent his formative years (from 1841 to 1844) as a sailor. After the traumatic events of 1832, during which his father lost all of the family's money, Melville was forced to leave New York City. For the next few years he moved between Massachusetts and Albany, where he worked as a store clerk, a teacher, and a farmhand. In 1839 Melville earned a place aboard a ship sailing to England and back. This was a relatively brief journey, but after an interior trip along the Mississippi River, Melville left in 1841 aboard a whaling vessel. He would not return to the United States until 1844; it was during this time that he would draw most of his material as a writer. His early works, for instance, were instances of sea fiction informed by his experiences; while they are not autobiographical, they are suspenseful and exciting while at the same time realistic. *Typee: A Peep at Polynesian Life* (1846) and *Omoo: A Narrative of Adventures in the South Seas* (1847) were early successes, recounting in fiction his having left the whaling business abruptly in 1842 by jumping overboard and escaping to the island. In both novels, Melville developed a critical voice as well as an authoritative one, using his enduring and exciting fiction to engage the reader in a social or political statement. His novels—which also include *Redburn* (1849), *White Jacket; or, The World in a Man-of-War* (1850), *Pierre; or, The Ambiguities* (1852), *The Confidence-Man: His Masquerade* (1857), *Israel Potter: His Fifty Years in Exile* (1855), and of course *Moby-Dick; or, The Whale* (1851)—all reveal a critical voice, one that calls into question philosophical issues such as metaphysics and truth, textual issues such as the composition and direction of a narrative, and social and political issues—from colonialism to capitalism to race to sovereignty. Indeed, Melville's texts challenge Americanism in general, and invite a more diverse understanding of American identity and history. He also wrote *The Piazza Tales* (1856), a collection of short stories, many of which had appeared in magazines such as *Putnam's* and *Harper's*. This volume include "Bartleby" as well as "The Encantadas," ten sketches of life in the Galapagos Islands. His short stories and novels, although important, did not all meet with commercial success, and Melville experienced years of psychological crisis. This culminated in 1863, during the Civil War, when Melville moved back to New York City. There he would spend the rest of his life. During this time he wrote the verse works *Battle-Pieces and Aspects of the War* (1866) and *Clarel: A Poem and Pilgrimage in the Holy Land* (1876) as well as the collections

John Marr and Other Sailors (1888) and *Timolean Etc.* (1891). Melville died in relative obscurity, forgotten by readers and critics; he had failed to reclaim the popularity of his early works. However, Melville's critical voice as well as his phenomenal talent prompted his rediscovery, and it is indeed hard to imagine an American canon today without Herman Melville.

Walt Whitman went to New Jersey in 1873 and spent the rest of his life there. It was during these last years in Camden that he published a volume of prose and poetry in honor of the American centennial in 1876 and published the final edition of *Leaves of Grass* in 1881. He also wrote a companion to his poems in prose called *Specimen Days* (1882). Critics note that it is during this last period of his life, in New Jersey, that Whitman turned toward a more religious perspective in his writing.

In terms of political writing, Henry Adams (1838–1918), best known for *The Education of Henry Adams* (1907), worked in Washington after the Civil War in an effort to promote reform. His tenure in the mid-Atlantic region was brief, however, as his essays and letters failed to curb the tide of corruption in American politics and this disturbing fact forced him back into an academic career at Harvard.

Although Henry James (1843–1916) was born in New York, he spent most of his life abroad and eventually settled in England, where he became naturalized. Nevertheless, much of James's work—both fiction and nonfiction—is inspired by his experiences in America. Early in his career, James published works in American literary magazines such as the *Continental Magazine* and *North American Review* before traveling through Europe. Narratives from his travels, such as *The American Scene* (1906), contrasted the setting in Europe with the slums of New York City; the novels *Daisy Miller* (1878) and *The American* (1877) render the American character as one that is unable to negotiate foreign cultures and situations. James wrote and published prolifically in American literary mediums throughout his life, as many of his works were serialized and letters and reviews were more than common.

JOURNALISM IN THE REGION: NEWSPAPERS AND PROSE

During the nineteenth century writers practiced a realist style which demanded of "art and literature [a] fidelity to nature or to real life and to accurate representation without idealization of the most typical views, details, and surroundings of the subject. Realism rejects imaginative idealization in favor of a close observation of outward appearances." Naturalism "was the basis of a late 19th- and early 20th-century aesthetic movement that, in literature, extended the tradition of realism, aiming at an even more faithful, unselective representation of reality, presented without moral judgment. Naturalism differed from realism in its assumption of scientific determinism, which led naturalistic authors to emphasize the accidental, physiological nature of their characters rather than their moral or rational qualities."[42] Naturalism—the transformation of realism as such—is often thought of with reference to journalism, as a style which developed in tandem with a particular type of reporting. Stephen Crane (1871–1900) was born in Newark, New Jersey, but made his first real appearance as a newspaper reporter in 1891, where he earned a reputation for covering stories about police corruption and for his newspaper sketches of slums and urban life, in New York City. At this time, the role of the newspaper and national literacy were intimately connected:

> After the Civil War the newspaper and book publishing industries both grew dramatically. The consolidation of the publishing industry in New York and a variety of technological innovations—such as typesetting machines, faster presses, and wood-pulp paper—enabled publishers to produce books more quickly and less expensively. Improvements in transportation and communication, such as the vast expansions of the railroad and the telegraph, united regional markets into a single national market. A rapidly growing population, increases in literacy, a shortened work week, a rise in real income—all these factors combined to increase the size of the book-buying public.[43]

This was the print culture Crane was immersed in. Crane published many stories in such places as the *New York Tribune*, the *New York World*, and the *Buffalo Commercial*. His career as a novelist began in New York City as well when he wrote *Maggie: A Girl of the Streets* (1893). His most famous work, *The Red Badge of Courage*, was serialized in 1894 and then published as a book in 1895. His other works include *The Black Riders and Other Lines* (1895), *George's Mother* (1896), *The Third Violet* (1897), and *War Is Kind* (1899). Crane, the journalist, considered himself a realist and sought to render life in writing without any romantic glosses or exaggerations; he was influenced by, and in turn had a profound effect on, realist writing in America, as a novelist, journalist, and professional writer in general.

The developments in print culture and technology during the second half of the nineteenth century, as well as the consolidation of the publishing industry in New York, had a profound effect on the mid-Atlantic region. In terms of journalism, the realist/naturalist trend continued—especially in its capacity to facilitate a professional literary social activism. Representing journalism in and from the region, Jacob August Riis (1849–1914) worked in New York City as a reporter for the *New York Tribune* and the *New York Evening Sun* between 1878 and 1899. During this time, Riis earned a reputation as a "muckraker" and as a social and political activist, using his talent as a writer and his daily forum to send a moral message to the public about life among the poor. Himself an immigrant from Denmark (arriving in 1870) who had experienced some aspects of tenement life, Riis's works include *The Children of the Poor* (1892), *Out of Mulberry Street: Stories of Tenement Life in New York City* (1898), and the classic *How the Other Half Lives: Studies Among the Tenements of New York* (1890). The issues in Riis's books include child labor and abuse, the terrible living conditions of the urban tenements, abuse of the immigrant, moral reform, American identity, and the corruption of the law. He also wrote an autobiography, *The Making of an American* (1901), as well as several works on Christmas.

Journalism has not only borne upon the aesthetics and subject matter of novels; periodical print culture—journals, newspapers, and magazines—has maintained a strong influence in the region since the eighteenth century. Early newspapers, such as the *New-York Mercury*, the *Pennsylvania Mercury*, and the *Maryland Gazette*—as well as numerous different periodicals operating at one time or another under the name the *New-York Gazette*—established a precedent in the region for "mass communication with the printed page."[44] During the nineteenth century, newspaper production and distribution reached new heights, especially in New York. James Gordon Bennett (1795–1872), a Scottish immigrant, worked for the *Enquirer* and his first newspaper, the *Pennsylvanian*, in Philadelphia before founding the successful New York *Herald* in 1835. Bennett expanded newspaper coverage to include "much more local news . . . improved the paper's foreign coverage, [and] he introduced a column of 'Theatrical Chit-Chat,'" all attempts to make the *Herald* stand apart from other newspapers.[45] Bennett was also known for his aggressive reporting, what was later termed "muckraking." Horace Greeley's (1811–1872) *Tribune*, another successful and influential newspaper, was founded in 1841. Bennett and Greeley transformed newspaper journalism as well as the audience and distribution for such writing. In many cases, such communication networks were also used to distribute subversive information, the news as carried by dissenting voices. For instance, newspapers played a key role in the debates regarding race and slavery; during the nineteenth century, "the hub of Black journalism . . . was New York." Frederick Douglass's *North Star* "attacked slavery, advocated universal emancipation, and called for the moral and intellectual improvement of the race." Elsewhere in the region, John H. Murphy and Dr. Carl Murphy began publishing the *Afro-American* in Baltimore in 1892; the paper dealt with controversial political issues.[46] Having ushered in a new era of newspaper publishing, Bennett and Greeley were followed by such figures as Henry J. Raymond (1820–1869) at the *New York Times*, Edwin Lawrence Godkin (1831–1902) at the *Nation* and the *New York Evening Post*, and Charles A. Dana (1819–1897) at the helm of the *New York Sun*. The next generation of publishers, near the turn of the nineteenth century and into the first few decades of the twentieth, defined a certain type of journalistic sensationalism, giving rise to the phrase "yellow journalism." Joseph Pulitzer's (1847–1911) New York *World*—which he purchased in 1883—and William Randolph Hearst's (1863–1951) *New York Journal* were such publications, and were in fierce competition. The popularity and influence of Pulitzer's and Hearst's newspapers are reflected in the circulation figures as well as in the extent to which the print and marketing innovations they implemented are now considered standard to the genre—from comic strips to serial political cartoons to the striking titles and typography at the heads of columns.

Nevertheless, the death of figures such as Pulitzer and Hearst brought a strange armistice to the competitive market of the early twentieth century. As Turner notes in the epilogue to *When Giants Ruled: The Story of Park Row, New York's Great Newspaper Street*:

> The *Sun* was sold in January 1950 to Scripps-Howard's *World-Telegram*. The *Herald Tribune*, *Journal-American*, and *World-Telegram and Sun*, all losing millions, announced plans in 1966 to merge into a single new company, publishing the *Herald-Tribune* in the morning, *The World Journal* in the afternoon, and the *World Journal Tribune* on Sunday. A strike over the issue of severance pay for almost three thousand employees prevented the printing on April 25, the day before publication. But this time, unlike the blackout of 1962–63, other papers continued to publish. Agreements were worked out with all the unions, and the first edition of the *World Journal Tribune* was published on September 12. The new paper, after losing more than $5 million, ended publication less than eight months later.[47]

Turner articulates not only the end of a regional competition, but a move toward conglomeration and foreign/transnational ownership of such properties as the *New York Times*. For instance, "Australian and British press tycoon Rupert Murdoch purchased the *Post* in late 1976 from liberal-minded Dorothy Schiff and turned it into a sensational newspaper. Murdoch lost millions of dollars before selling the daily to a New York real estate developer, Peter Kalikow, and then repurchased it five years later."[48]

Despite the trend to conglomeration, the latter half of the twentieth century was not without its regional figureheads. Katharine Graham (1917–2001) became publisher of the Washington Post Company—including the *Washington Post* and *Newsweek*—in 1963, "and by harsh, efficient management built it into a news vehicle that is economically and journalistically dominant in the capital of the United States."[49] Under Graham, the *Washington Post* publicized such documents and events as the Pentagon Papers and the Watergate affair. Graham, who won a Pulitzer Prize for her autobiography *Personal History* (1997), thus became one of the most influential figures in journalism and politics, in and outside of the mid-Atlantic states.

In addition to newspapers and a certain journalistic style of writing, literary magazines have shaped the medium and the audience for fiction and prose. We have seen the degree to which many authors submitted their works to periodicals for publication prior to—or even instead of—publishing novels. Literary magazines published in the mid-Atlantic region during the twentieth century and to the present include such notable titles as *Harper's Magazine* (founded in New York in 1850) and *Vanity Fair*.

The New Yorker

Perhaps no other literary magazine has had as profound an effect on writing as *The New Yorker*. Founded in 1925 by Harold Ross (1892–1951), *The New Yorker* developed into the premiere magazine for showcasing creative writing, as well as both a cultural and a regional institution. The success of *The New Yorker* has launched the careers of writers such as John Cheever (1912–1982). Cheever is best known for his short stories, critical response to which "has run the gamut from its rejection as merely a successful execution of 'the *New Yorker* Story,' thought by some critics to be a formulaic and trivial manifestation of fiction, to attempts to delineate the particular achievement of his stories, especially as they combine disparate modes of storytelling."[50] Nevertheless, Cheever (neither a native of New York or of the mid-Atlantic region) is often mentioned with reference to the popular literary magazine, itself a regional character. While many of his works were first published through such venues, and particularly *The New Yorker*, collections of his stories include such titles as *The Way Some People Live: A Book of Stories* (1943), *The Enormous Radio and Other Stories* (1953), *The Housebreaker of Shady Hill and Other Stories* (1958), *Some People, Places, and Things that Will Not Appear in My Next Novel* (1961), and *The Day the Pig Fell into the Well* (1978). Cheever's novels include *The Wapshot Chronicle* (1957), *The Wapshot Scandal* (1964), *Bullet Park* (1969), and *Falconer* (1977). Kay Boyle (1902–1992), the author of such works as *Fifty Stories* (1980) and *Plagued by the Nightingale* (1931), is also known for her *New Yorker* connection, as well as a successful writing career which took shape in (among other places) New York.

Joseph Mitchell (1908–1996) was a major figure in the history of journalism in New York, indeed one of the single most important proponents of literary journalism over the last century, who also is closely associated with *The New Yorker*. After moving to New York from North Carolina, he began his career writing short fiction and sports reporting, but he spent most of the 1930s writing at the *World Telegram*. In the late 1930s, Mitchell moved to *The New Yorker*; his books *McSorley's Wonderful Saloon* (1943), *Old Mr. Flood* (1948), and *The Bottom of the Harbor* (1959) are collections of stories written for the publication. *Up in the Old Hotel* (1992) is regarded as exemplary with respect to Mitchell's writing style and subject matter. Today, *The New Yorker*, in addition to its reviews, poetry, cartoons, and investigative journalism, publishes the fiction of a culturally diverse group of writers from young and upcoming to older and acclaimed.

Another important journalist is Jimmy Breslin (1930–), who is known for his personal and accessible style of reporting. Writing for the *New York Herald Tribune*, the *New York Times*, and *New York Newsday*, Breslin pioneered a style called the New Journalism—an approach to writing that blended prosaic aspects of the fictional novel with true stories and events. His books include a number of collections as well as a work about Watergate, *How the Good Guys Finally Won: Notes from an Impeachment Summer* (1975), and a biography, *Damon Runyon: A Life* (1991). Norman Mailer (1923–), born in New Jersey and raised in New York, wrote such notable books as *The Naked and the Dead* (1949), *Why Are We in Vietnam?* (1967), and *The Prisoner of Sex* (1971). He is also the author of a biography of Marilyn Monroe (1973) and a gripping meditation on the death penalty, *The Executioner's Song* (1979). *The Armies of the Night: History as a Novel, the Novel as History* (1968) deals specifically with the 1967 March on the Pentagon; in his work Mailer blurs the line between fact and fiction, writing journalistic or historical subject matter in insightful and beautiful prose.

Pennsylvania native Rachel Carson's (1907–1964) *Silent Spring* (1962) is a book that, like Jacob Riis's work, uses a journalistic approach to literature in order to send a social and political message. In this case, Carson's is also a scientific message; *Silent Spring* deals specifically with the harmful effects of DDT and other chemical pesticides. Carson was not trained as a journalist, however, but rather as a writer of short stories—which began appearing in such magazines as *St. Nicholas* in 1918—and as a scientist, having attended graduate school for zoology at Johns Hopkins University (until she was forced to leave because of financial and personal reasons in 1934). After leaving Johns Hopkins, Carson lived in both Maryland and Washington, D.C., working for the United States Bureau of Fisheries. This influenced her career as a writer, as she wrote several books about marine life that contain both beautiful prose and scientific information, including *Under the Sea-Wind: A Naturalist's Picture of Ocean Life* (1941), *The Sea Around Us* (1951), and *The Living Ocean* (1963). Many of her books were bestsellers, a testament to her writing, but what marks her career is an attention to nature and humans' relation to it. Carson's is an activism rendered as literature.

THE TWENTIETH CENTURY TO THE PRESENT

Returning to the realm of novels, Edith Wharton (1862–1937), a close friend of Henry James, published such famous books as *The House of Mirth* (1905), *Ethan Frome* (1911), and *The Age of Innocence* (1920), as well as numerous other novels, short stories, poems, articles, and works of criticism. She began her career writing poetry in New York that saw publication in magazines such as the *Atlantic, Scribner's,* and *Harper's*. Soon after marrying in 1885, Wharton moved to Massachusetts and proceeded to travel to Europe as often as possible. She spent the majority of her life in France, and was eventually buried there. Nevertheless, New York and New York society tended to be the subject of her work, including *The Age of Innocence*, which won the Pulitzer Prize in 1921.

Maryland native Dashiell Hammett (1894–1961) wrote several novels, including *Red Harvest* (1929), *The Glass Key* (1931), and *The Thin Man* (1934). However, his greatest literary achievement—or at least his most popular—is *The Maltese Falcon* (1930). Hammett is also the author of a number of short stories, most of which were edited by Ellery Queen and were published in anthologies. The success of *The Maltese Falcon* lies in Hammett's rendering of the detective as a sort of rough antihero, as an emotionally elusive figure who leaves the reader in suspense. Drawing on the author's experience as a detective, Hammett's novels were also compelling for their realism.

The Harlem Renaissance

The Harlem Renaissance, perhaps "the most significant event in African American literature and culture in the twentieth century . . . was a self-conscious movement. That is, writers and poets who participated in the movement were aware that they were involved in a literary movement and assumed at least partial responsibility for defining the parameters and aesthetics of the movement; black scholars and intellectuals were also aware of the Harlem Renaissance (even if they railed against it) and attempted to define the movement in terms of literature and the political and social implications of that literature."[51] The Harlem Renaissance included in its artistic, social, and political scope a variety of genres of writing—from poetry to essays to prose fiction. Some of the writers associated with the movement were Nella Larsen (1893–1963),

Portrait of Edith Wharton. Courtesy Library of Congress.

known for her novels *Quicksand* (1928) and *Passing* (1929); Alain Locke (1886–1954), who wrote and edited critical and sociopolitical works such as *The Negro in America* (1933) and *The New Negro: An Interpretation* (1925); Langston Hughes (1902–1967), the famous poet, novelist, and writer of short stories whose works include *The Weary Blues* (1926), *Dear Lovely Death* (1931), *The Dream Keeper and Other Poems* (1932), and *Not Without Laughter* (1930); and poet and author of children's literature Countee Cullen (1903–1946), whose works include *The Ballad of the Brown Girl: An Old Ballad Retold* (1927) and *Color* (1925). These authors, as well as others, participated in a cultural and aesthetic movement that both celebrated blackness on its own terms—and, really, worked to define and to explore those terms—and introduced said culture to white America, if not the world. Equally notable is the effect that the Harlem Renaissance had on future black writers, particularly in the mid-Atlantic states, how the conversation that the former writers sought to make audible enabled future readings of race and its relationship to personal and national identity. Ralph Ellison (1914–1994), who wrote *Invisible Man* (1952) and *Shadow and Act* (1964) a generation later, also spent much of his career writing in New York. His investigations of race reveal not only a particular attention to identity but the influence of the Harlem Renaissance writers as well. Richard Wright (1908–1960) is perhaps best known for *Uncle Tom's Children: Four Novellas* (1938), *Native Son* (1940), and *Black Boy: A Record of Childhood and Youth* (1945). While Wright did write much of his work in Chicago and, later, in Paris, his active involvement in the Communist Party (beginning in 1937) led him from Chicago to a mid-Atlantic landscape in 1937—specifically, to Harlem. Wright's work reveals a political commitment as well as an investigation of the relationship between race and politics, an investigation that, we might assume, drew in part from his experience in New York. Indeed, "James Baldwin, who began his writing career as Wright's protege, called *Native Son* 'the most powerful and celebrated statement we have yet had of what it means to be a Negro in America.'" James Baldwin (1924–1987), the author of *Go Tell It on the Mountain* (1953), *Another Country* (1962), *Tell Me How Long the Train's Been Gone* (1968), and *Harlem Quartet* (1987), was born in New York City. In addition to the aforementioned novels, Baldwin wrote plays, such as *The Welcome Table* (1987), and essays, including *Notes of a Native Son* (1955) and *Black Anti-Semitism and Jewish Racism* (1969). His reading of racism and identity is remarkeable for his ability to explore "the psychological implications of racism for both the oppressed and the oppressor."[52]

Modernism

The mid-Atlantic states are not without modernist representatives. Modernism, defined as a "movement of the early-to-mid-20th century that represented a self-conscious break with traditional forms and subject matter and a search for a distinctly contemporary mode of expression," shaped the literary landscape of the period.[53] In terms of poetry, H. D. (Hilda Doolittle) (1886–1961) was born and raised in Pennsylvania; however, she spent the majority of her life in Europe with such other notable writers as Ezra Pound and T. S. Eliot. H. D.'s modernism drew from such sources as psychoanalysis and the cinema—medical and media developments, respectively, which were particular to her time. Her works include collections of verse as well as other forms of poetry, such as her 1925 *Collected Poems*, and *Sea Garden* (1916) as well as an epic—*Helen in Egypt* (1961)—and essays, her most famous being her *Tribute to Freud* (1956). Her poetry is influential in its experimentation with genre, language, and consciousness or voice; moreover, H. D. wrote literature that reflected on modernism and the twentieth century—leaving us with a distinct impression of what the early twentieth century, with its wars, technological developments, and crises might have looked like from America and from abroad. Wallace Stevens (1879–1955), another important American poet from Pennsylvania, worked as a lawyer, a reporter for the *New York Tribune* (where he published regularly), and an insurance agent after moving to New York City. During his lifetime, he wrote in between jobs; he was never a professional poet in the truest sense of the term but, nevertheless, is remembered as one of the defining poet voices of the twentieth century. His works include collections of poetry—

Harmonium (1923; revised 1931), *Ideas of Order* (1935), *The Man with the Blue Guitar, and Other Poems* (1937), *Transport to Summer* (1947), *The Auroras of Autumn* (1950), and *The Collected Poems of Wallace Stevens* (1954)—as well as collections of essays and nonfiction texts, such as *The Necessary Angel: Essays on Reality and the Imagination* and *Three Academic Pieces: The Realm of Resemblance, Someone Puts a Pineapple Together, Of Ideal Time and Choice* (1947).

Mid-Atlantic Poets

A list of poets from the mid-Atlantic states also includes such major figures as William Carlos Williams (1883–1963), e. e. cummings (1894–1962), and Allen Ginsberg (1926–1997), individuals who shaped not only the writing in their respective periods and schools but literature in general. William Carlos Williams, born in Rutherford, New Jersey, is best known for his poetry, including works such as *The Temper* (1913), *Al Que Quiere!* (1917), *Kora in Hell: Improvisations* (1920), *Sour Grapes* (1921), *The Cod Head* (1932), *An Early Martyr and Other Poems* (1935), *The Complete Collected Poems of William Carlos Williams, 1906–1938* (1938), and *The Wedge* (1944). In addition, Williams wrote critical essays which commented on history and tradition in relation to criticism; early works like *In the American Grain* (1925) and *The Great American Novel* (1923) reveal a poet calling into question the concept of identity (national and literary) and radically critiquing aesthetic "puritanism." It is difficult to situate Williams's engagement with the American tradition as well as his rethinking the work of poetry, but while terms such as "modernist" or "modernism" may or may not be adequate to describe his style or achievement, it is certain that Williams had an influence on later writers.

e. e. cummings was born in Cambridge, Massachusetts, and educated at Harvard. However, cummings's exceptional literary career took place primarily between Paris and New York City. He published his first book of poetry, *Tulips and Chimneys* (1923), while writing for *Vanity Fair*. In addition, most of his first play, *Him* (1927), was written in New York. cummings is also known for

Poet Allen Ginsberg, Timothy Leary, and Ralph Metzner at the Village Theater, New York City, c. 1965–1970. Courtesy Library of Congress.

such books as *XLI Poems* (1925) and *The Enormous Room* (1922), and like H. D. and Wallace Stevens, is often associated with modernism.

Allen Ginsberg, born in Newark, New Jersey, was one of the key figures of "Beat poetry." Ginsberg's *Howl and Other Poems* (1956) became infamous when it was declared obscene and thus became the subject of controversy. Nevertheless, the style of poetry as well as the subject matter characterized a certain political aesthetic and existentialism—as well as a particular type of activism—which informed countercultural activity during the 1950s and 1960s. According to biographer Thomas F. Merrill, "To be beat in the fifties was to feel the bored fatigue of the soldier required to perform endless, meaningless tasks that have no purpose," as well as to search "incessantly" for a reality "within" the individual rather than what society dictates as real and to do so with "a freestyle religiosity."[54] In addition to *Howl*, Ginsberg's body of work includes *Kaddish and Other Poems, 1958–1960* (1961), *Planet News* (1968), *The Fall of America: Poems of These States, 1965–1971* (1973), and *White Shroud* (1986), as well as numerous other titles.

Poet Elizabeth Bishop (1911–1979) spent part of her career writing in New York, specifically from 1935 to 1938. Her works include *North and South* (1946) and *Questions of Travel* (1965). Bishop is also known for her friendship with fellow poet Marianne Moore (1887–1972), herself born and raised in Pennsylvania. In 1918, the modernist poet and Pulitzer Prize winner moved to New York City, where she wrote and served as editor (after 1925) of the literary journal *The Dial*. Moore's list of works includes *Pangolin, and Other Verse: Five Poems* (1936), *What Are Years and Other Poems* (1941), *Collected Poems* (1951), and *Tell Me, Tell Me: Granite, Steel, and Other Topics* (1966).

Playwright and poet Amiri Baraka (1934–   , known as LeRoi Jones until 1967)—from Newark, New Jersey—began his career writing poetry inspired by the work of the "Beats." Later works, however, were influenced by more radical politics informed by the civil rights movement and black nationalism. Eventually, Baraka came to renounce black nationalism and embrace the politics of Third World socialism. His works include *Preface to a Twenty Volume Suicide Note* (1961), *Dutchman [and] The Slave: A Fable* (1964), *The System of Dante's Hell* (1965), *Black Magic: Sabotage; Target Study; Black Art; Collected Poetry,*

Portrait of Marianne Moore. Courtesy Library of Congress, Prints & Photographs Division, Carl Van Vechten Collection, LC-USZ62-42513-DLC.

1961–1967 (1969), *It's Nation Time* (1970), *Afrikan Revolution: A Poem* (1973), *Hard Facts: Excerpts, People's War, 1975* (1975), and *The Motion of History and Other Plays* (1978). Baraka is also the author of several critical or historical works, such as *Blues People: Negro Music in White America* (1963).

Mid-Atlantic Dramatists

Notable dramatists from the region include Arthur Miller (1915–) and Neil Simon (1927–). Born in New York City, Miller won the Pulitzer Prize in 1949 (among other awards); his most famous works include *Death of a Salesman* (1949), *The Crucible* (1953), *After the Fall* (1964), and *The Misfits* (1961). Miller was asked to appear before the House Un-American Activities Committee in 1956 after writing such inflammatory works as *The Crucible* and his adaptation of Ibsen's *Enemy of the People* in 1950—works that criticized the mania and fear sweeping America regarding the spread of communism. Miller is also the author of an autobiography—*Timebends: A Life* (1987)—as well as works of criticism, short stories, travel narratives, and plays. Simon, from the Bronx, New York, wrote such plays as *The Odd Couple* (1965), *Brighton Beach Memoirs* (1982), *Biloxi Blues* (1984), and *Rumors* (1988), in addition to numerous screenplays (many of them adaptations of his stage plays) and unpublished plays. Many of his works depict life in and around New York, representing culture there while at the same time shaping it.

Writer/activist Amiri Baraka (aka Leroi Jones) influenced the American literary and political landscape. Photofest.

Jewish American Writers

While not necessarily modernist novelists, many Jewish American authors and intellectuals have written of the modern occasion—from immigration in the twentieth century to World War II—in order to investigate concepts of identity, both American and regional. Bernard Malamud (1914–1986) wrote such works as *A New Life* (1961), *The Fixer* (1966), *The Tenants* (1971), *Dublin's Lives* (1979), and *God's Grace* (1982). He is also the author of several short stories. Malamud grew up in New York, the son of Russian Jewish immigrants, perhaps his most famous works are *The Natural* (1952), a baseball novel modeled after an Arthurian romance, and

The Assistant (1957). Herman Wouk (1915–), also of Russian Jewish parents, wrote *The Caine Mutiny: A Novel of World War II* (1951), for which he won a Pulitzer Prize in 1952. Wouk is also the author of numerous other novels—including *The Winds of War* (1971), and its sequel, *War and Remembrance* (1978), and *Inside, Outside* (1985)—as well as several plays. Similarly, Cynthia Ozick's (1928–) genealogy reads as such: "a native New Yorker whose Russian Jewish immigrant parents encountered American life for the first time on the Lower East Side of Manhattan." According to biographer Lawrence S. Friedman, Ozick, "like Bernard Malamud . . . writes most frequently about Jews in contemporary New York," a characteristic which does indeed define, in part, her fiction.[55] Ozick's works include *Trust* (1966), *The Pagan Rabbi, and Other Stories* (1971), *Bloodshed and Three Novellas* (1976), *Levitation: Five Fictions* (1982), *The Messiah of Stockholm* (1987), and *The Shawl* (1989).

Philip Roth (1933–), a prolific contemporary author from Newark, New Jersey, received the Pulitzer Prize for fiction for his novel *American Pastoral* (1997). His work is often read with reference to the novels of other Jewish American authors, such as Malamud and Saul Bellow. The author of over twenty books—a career spanning forty years—Roth has written such titles as *Goodbye, Columbus, and Five Short Stories* (1959), *Letting Go* (1962), *Portnoy's Complaint* (1969), *The Great American Novel* (1973), *The Ghost Writer* (1979), *The Counterlife* (1986), *Operation Shylock: A Confession* (1993), *Sabbath's Theater* (1995), *I Married a Communist* (1998), *The Human Stain* (2000), and *The Dying Animal* (2001).

In terms of the evaluation of literature and its intersection with philosophy and aesthetics, Susan Sontag (1933–), born in New York, wrote *Against Interpretation, and Other Essays* (1966) and *Styles of Radical Will* (1969)—two important works of criticism that dealt with aesthetic theory and modes of reading. Sontag has also written novels—such as *In America* (2000)—as well as short stories and essays.

Other Mid-Atlantic Fiction Writers

Returning to novels and short stories, Albany, New York native William Kennedy (1928–) draws from the charm of his birthplace in such works as *O Albany! An Urban Tapestry* (1983), *Billy Phelan's Greatest Game* (1978), and *Legs* (1975). Best known for his Pulitzer Prize–winning *Ironweed* (1983), Kennedy also cowrote the script for the film *The Cotton Club* (1986) with Francis Coppola and Mario Puzo. Joyce Carol Oates (1938–) is best known for her many novels and short stories, including *By the North Gate* (1963), *Upon the Sweeping Flood and Other Stories* (1966), *Haunted: Tales of the Grotesque* (1994), *Fox Fire* (1993), *The Goddess and Other Women* (1974), *The Assassins: A Book of Hours* (1975), and *Angel of Light* (1981). The prolific writer was born in Lockport, New York, and is also responsible for dramatic works and several works of criticism. John O'Hara (1905–1970), "one of the most popular, prolific, and financially successful authors in the United States" during the 1950s and 1960s,[56] wrote such novels as *Pal Joey* (1940), *A Rage to Live* (1949), *From the Terrace* (1958), *Elizabeth Appleton* (1963), *The Lockwood Concern* (1966), and *The Instrument* (1967). O'Hara also wrote short stories, collected in such volumes as *The Doctor's Son, and Other Stories* (1935), *Hellbox* (1947), and *49 Stories* (1962).

Mary Lee Settle (1918–) was born in Charleston, West Virginia, but began her writing career in New York City in the late 1930s. Settle worked at *Harper's* before she began writing fiction. Her most famous and popular works are the five novels comprising her *Beulah Quintet*: *O Beulah Land* (1956), *Know Nothing* (1960), *Prisons* (1973), *The Scapegoat* (1980), and *The Killing Ground* (1982). These novels deal with the development of a West Virginia family from the founding of the settlement to the present, against the backdrop of American history. Settle is also the author of several other novels, stories, and works of nonfiction.

Contemporary authors from the region also include the prolific John Updike (1932–), from Reading, Pennsylvania, the author of numerous novels, essays, short stories, and works of poetry. Updike is best known for his Rabbit series, including *Rabbit, Run* (1960), *Rabit Redux* (1971), *Rabbit Is Rich* (1981), and *Rabbit at Rest* (1990). Gore Vidal (1925–), from New York City, is the author of many novels treating subjects from history, including *Julian* (1964), *Lincoln* (1984), and *The Smithsonian Institution* (1998). Vidal also wrote several mystery stories in the 1950s under the pseudonym Edgar Box, as well as dramatic works, short stories and essays. Reclusive writer J. D. Salinger (1919–) was born in New York City and has spent much of his life writing in New York. Salinger is the author of the immensely popular books *The Catcher in the Rye* (1951), *Nine Stories* (1953), and *Franny and Zooey* (1961), the latter work collecting two short stories that originally appeared in the *New Yorker*—works that helped to define the American canon in the latter half of the twentieth century. Richard Price (1949–) writes in a manner that recalls fellow New York native Hubert Selby Jr. (1928–) as well as expatriate Henry Miller (1891–1980), particularly in Price's first book, *The Wanderers* (1974), described as a "grittily realistic portrayal of gang life in the Bronx."[57] His other works include *Bloodbrothers* (1976), *Ladies' Man* (1978), *The Break* (1983), *Clockers* (1992), *Freedomland* (1998), and *Samaritan* (2003). Selby is himself the author of *Last Exit to Brooklyn* (1964), *The Room* (1971), *The Demon* (1976), and *Requiem for a Dream* (1979). Miller, best known for his books *Tropic of Cancer* (1934) and *Tropic of Capricorn* (1939), often reflected on his childhood in New York, particularly in his short story "The 54th Ward," from *Black Spring* (1936).

Oscar Hijuelos (1951–), author of such novels as *The Fourteen Sisters of Emilio Montez O'Brien* (1993), *Mr. Ives' Christmas* (1995), and *Empress of the Splendid Season* (1999), was born in New York City. Hijuelos's second novel—*The Mambo Kings Play Songs of Love* (1989)—is set in Spanish Harlem in the 1950s and earned him a Pulitzer Prize in 1990. In it he also investigates Latino culture in New York. E. L. Doctorow (1931–), a native of New York City, is the author of *Billy Bathgate* (1989), *The Book of Daniel* (1971), and *City of God* (2000), among other books. Much of his fiction takes history as its object, rewriting it in order to call into question notions of historical inheritance and the claim to truth based on tradition; *Ragtime* (1975) portrays historical figures as characters and by doing so interrogates the line separating politics from fiction.

Don DeLillo (1936–) wrote *Americana* (1971), *The Names* (1982), *Libra* (1988), *Mao II* (1991), *Underworld* (1997) and *The Body Artist: A Novel* (2001), among other novels, short stories, and plays. His most famous novel, *White Noise* (1985), is representative of his work insofar as it challenges the consumer capitalism of contemporary America. John Barth (1930–), from Maryland, wrote, among other novels, *The Floating Opera* (1956), *The End of the Road* (1958), *Giles, Goat-Boy; or,*

The Revised New Syllabus (1966), *Chimera* (1972), *The Tidewater Tales* (1987), *The Last Voyage of Somebody the Sailor* (1991), and *Coming Soon!!! A Narrative* (2001). He is also the author of several collections of short stories, including *Lost in the Funhouse: Fiction for Print, Tape, Live Voice* (1968), and works of nonfiction. Barth's 1960 book *The Sot-Weed Factor* revisits the mid-Atlantic states' literary archive insofar as it is based on Ebenezer Cooke's eighteenth-century verse of the same name. Not only an exercise in inhabiting a period style, Barth's *Sot-Weed Factor* is notable for its humor and its authorial voice.

Writers like Barth and DeLillo, Hijuelos and Doctorow are regarded as ushering in a new era of innovative fiction. Their works that draw from cultural patterns in the mid-Atlantic states comment on their regional inheritances and allow them to participate in that same regional culture—a participation that often means revisiting the historical archive. Where such authors revise the traditions they invoke, we again read the extent to which the literary archive of the mid-Atlantic states is hardly a homogeneous body of work. It is a highly diverse archive that reveals, upon close analysis, an incredible number of different voices—each carrying different origins, languages, and perspectives. Theirs is a literary investigation that traces this regional diversity from the past to our present.

RESOURCE GUIDE

Printed Sources

Axelrod, Alan. *Charles Brockden Brown: An American Tale*. Austin: University of Texas Press, 1983.

Bleyer, Willard Grosvenor. *Main Currents in the History of American Journalism*. Boston: Houghton Mifflin, 1927.

Callow, James T. *Kindred Spirits: Kinckerbocker Writers and American Artists, 1807–1855*. Chapel Hill: University of North Carolina Press, 1967.

Castillo, Susan, and Ivy Schweitzer. *The Literatures of Colonial America: An Anthology*. Cambridge, MA: Blackwell, 2001.

Colvert, James B. *Stephen Crane*. San Diego: Harcourt Brace Jovanovich, 1984.

Cooper, James Fenimore. *The Pioneers*. New York: Penguin Classics, 1988.

Copeland, David A. *Colonial American Newspapers: Character and Content*. Newark: University of Delaware Press, 1997.

Crèvecoeur, J. Hector St. John de. *Letters from an American Farmer and Sketches of Eighteenth-Century America*. New York: Penguin Classics, 1986

Crow, Charles, Ed. *A Companion to the Regional Literatures of America*. Malden, MA: Blackwell, 2003.

Davis, Deborah. *Katharine the Great: Katharine Graham and Her Washington Post Empire*. New York: Sheridan Square Press, 1979.

Dekker, George, and John P. McWilliams, eds. *Fenimore Cooper: The Critical Heritage*. London: Routledge and Kegan Paul, 1973.

Douglas, George H. *The Golden Age of the Newspaper*. Westport, CT: Greenwood, 1999.

Franklin, Benjamin. *The Autobiography and Other Writings*. New York: Penguin Classics, 1986.

French, Warren. *J. D. Salinger*. Twayne's United States Authors Series. Boston: Twayne, 1963.

Friedman, Lawrence S. *Understanding Cynthia Ozick*. Columbia: University of South Carolina Press, 1991.

Grossman, James. *James Fenimore Cooper*. Stanford: Stanford University Press, 1949.

Hall, Clayton Coleman, ed. *Narratives of Early Maryland, 1633–1684*. New York: Charles Scribner's Sons, 1910.

Hiltner, Judith R. *The Newspaper Verse of Philip Freneau: An Edition and Bibliographic Survey*. Troy, NY: Whitston, 1986.

Irving, Washington. *Irving's Sketch Book*. ed. Mary E. Litchfield. Boston: Ginn, 1904.

Irving, Washington. *Stories of the Hudson*. Harrison, NY: Harbor Hill, 1984.

Jameson, J. Franklin, ed. *Narratives of New Netherland, 1609–1664*. New York: Charles Scribner's Sons, 1909.

Jehlen, Myra, and Michael Warner, eds. *The English Literatures of America, 1500–1800*. New York: Routledge, 1997.

Jones, Peter. *A Reader's Guide to Fifty American Poets*. London: Heinemann, 1980.

July, Robert W. *The Essential New Yorker: Gulian Crommelin Verplanck*. Durham: Duke University Press, 1951.

Kennedy, J. Gerald, ed. *A Historical Guide to Edgar Allan Poe*. Oxford: Oxford University Press, 2001.

Kennedy, Richard S. *Dreams in the Mirror: A Biography of E. E. Cummings*. New York: Liveright, 1980.

Kessler, Lauren. *The Dissident Press*. Beverly Hills: Sage, 1984.

Kramer, Victor A., ed. *The Harlem Renaissance Re-examined*. New York: AMS Press, 1997.

Lauter, Paul, gen. ed. *The Heath Anthology of American Literature*. 3rd ed. Boston: Houghton Mifflin, 1998.

McCutchen, David, trans. *The Red Record: The Wallum Olum*. New York: Avery, 1993.

Mankowitz, Wolf. *The Extraordinary Mr. Poe*. New York: Summit Books, 1978.

Merrill, Thomas F. *Allen Ginsberg*. Twayne's United States Authors Series. Boston: Twayne, 1988.

Molesworth, Charles. *Marianne Moore: A Literary Life*. New York: Atheneum, 1990.

Mulford, Carla. *Only for the Eye of a Friend: The Poems of Annis Boudinot Stockton*. Charlottesville: University Press of Virginia, 1995.

Myers, Albert Cook, ed. *Narratives of Early Pennsylvania, West New Jersey, and Delaware, 1630–1707*. New York: Charles Scribner's Sons, 1912.

Myerson, Joel, ed. *Antebellum Writers in New York and the South*. Dictionary of Literary Biography 3. Detroit: Gale, 1979.

Pastorius, Francis Daniel. *A New Primmer*. New York, 1698. From the original, now on deposit in Friends House, London. Boston: Massachusetts Historical Society, 1939.

Poe, Edgar Allan. *The Fall of the House of Usher and Other Writings*. New York: Penguin Classics, 1986.

Reilly, Edward C. *William Kennedy*. Twayne's United States Authors Series. ed. Frank Day. Boston: Twayne, 1991.

Ringe, Donald A. *Charles Brockden Brown: Revised Edition*. Twayne's United States Authors Series. ed. Pattie Cowell. Boston: Twayne, 1991.

Robertson, Michael. *Stephen Crane, Journalism, and the Making of Modern American Literature*. New York: Columbia University Press, 1997.

Schoolcraft, Henry Rowe. *Algic Researchers: North American Indian Folktales and Legends*. Mineola, NY: Dover, 1999.

Spanier, Sandra Whipple. *Kay Boyle: Artist and Activist*. Carbondale: Southern Illinois University Press, 1986.

Steendam, Jacob. *A Memoir of the First Poet in New Netherland: With His Poems Descriptive of the Colony*. The Hague: Brothers Giunta D'Albani, 1861.

Travisano, Thomas J. *Elizabeth Bishop: Her Artistic Development*. Charlottesville: University Press of Virginia, 1988.

Turner, Hy B. *When Giants Ruled: The Story of Park Row, New York's Great Newspaper Street.* New York: Fordham University Press, 1999.

Wagenknecht, Edward. *Cavalcade of the American Novel.* New York: Henry Holt, 1952.

Walcutt, Charles Child. *American Literary Naturalism, A Divided Stream.* Minneapolis: University of Minnesota Press, 1956.

Waldeland, Lynne. *John Cheever.* Twayne's United States Authors Series. Boston: Twayne, 1979.

Webb, Constance. *Richard Wright: A Biography.* New York: G. P. Putnam's Sons, 1968.

Whittemore, Reed. *William Carlos Williams: Poet from Jersey.* Boston: Houghton Mifflin, 1975.

Winslow, Ola Elizabeth. *American Broadside Verse.* New Haven: Yale University Press, 1930.

Witalec, Janet, proj. ed. *The Harlem Renaissance: A Gale Critical Companion.* 3 vols. Detroit: Gale, 2003.

Wintz, Cary D., ed. *Remembering the Harlem Renaissance.* New York: Garland, 1996.

Zott, Lynn M. *The Beat Generation: A Gale Critical Companion.* 3 vols. Detroit: Gale, 2003.

Web Sites

Contemporary Authors Online. Gale Literary Databases. Gale Group, 2003. *Literature Resource Center.* Accessed August 1, 2004.
http://galenet.galegroup.com/servlet/GLD/

Harper's Weekly Online Archive
http://www.harpweek.com

Literature Resource Center Online. Gale Group, 2004. Accessed August 1, 2004.
http://galenet.galegroup.com/servlet/LitRC

Maryland at a Glance: Literature. *Maryland State Archives*, July 12, 2004. Accessed August 1, 2004.
http://www.mdarchives.state.md.us/msa/mdmanual/01glance/html/lit.html

Merriam-Webster's Encyclopedia of Literature. Merriam-Webster, 1995. *Literature Resource Center.* Accessed August 1, 2004.
http://galenet.galegroup.com/servlet/LitRC

Moore, Phyllis Wilson, consultant. "MountainLit." Bridgeport, WV: Bridgeport Library, 2001. Accessed August 1, 2004.
http://www.mountainlit.com

New Yorker Online
http://www.newyorker.com

Literary Festivals and Book Fairs

New York Is Book Country
http://www.nyisbookcountry.com

Ohio River Festival of Books
http://www.ohioriverbooks.org

Small Press Book Fair
http://smallpress.org/events/bookfair/default.asp

West Virginia Book Festival
http://www.wvhumanities.org/bookfest/bookfest.htm

Literary Organizations and Sites

Charles Brockden Brown Society
http://cbbsociety.babson.edu

James Fenimore Cooper House, Burlington, NJ
http://08016.com/cooperhouse.html

James Fenimore Cooper Society
http://external.oneonta.edu/cooper/

Stephen Crane Society
http://guweb2.gonzaga.edu/faculty/campbell/crane

Frederick Douglass Museum and Cultural Center, Rochester, NY
http://www.ggw.org/freenet/f/fdm

Fenimore Art Museum, Cooperstown, NY
http://www.fenimoreartmuseum.org

Graeme Park (Elizabeth Graeme Fergusson), Horsham, PA
http://www.ushistory.org/graeme/index.htm

Langston Hughes Society
http://www.langstonhughessociety.org/pages/582859/index.htm

Henry James Society
http://mockingbird.creighton.edu/english/jsociety.htm

Arthur Miller Society
http://www.ibiblio.org/miller

NY State Lit Tree
http://www.nyslittree.org

Edgar Allan Poe Society of Baltimore
http://www.eapoe.org

Wallace Stevens Journal
http://www.wallacestevens.com

Edith Wharton Society
http://guweb2.gonzaga.edu/faculty/campbell/wharton

MUSIC

Christine M. Battista

One might initially think that music is important solely for its entertainment value, but music has played a central role in the development of the mid-Atlantic region throughout history, and in a variety of ways. Music is significant to the Mid-Atlantic for aesthetic, cultural, political, racial, and even economic reasons. Music has been used as a tool for freedom, as a way of expressing and celebrating heritage, as a method of communication, as an instrument that helps in the revival of values, and even as a powerful form of resistance. For early Native Americans of the Mid-Atlantic, music, in addition to being a form of amusement, expressed a tribe's spiritual beliefs and was indispensable to the continuation of its cultural values and identity. For the early German Pietists of Pennsylvania, musical instruments were a way of establishing a regional identity in opposition to the Puritans, who eschewed the use of musical instruments on religious grounds. For African Americans of the early twentieth century, who were instrumental in the founding of new musical forms such as ragtime and jazz, music was a means of empowerment in a world governed by severe racial inequalities. And for a contemporary folk musician such as Ani DiFranco, music, among many things, is a way to creatively criticize traditional gender roles and a means to speak out against the kind of economic oppression that has hit not only sections of her hometown of Buffalo, New York, but elsewhere as well in the mid-Atlantic region. Music, therefore, is an essential medium of creative expression that unites many areas of human production.

NATIVE AMERICAN MUSIC AND DANCE

Access to native musical compositions depends on the work of non-native scholars. In New York, Theodore Baker (1851–1934) compiled together the very first collection of Native American music. He did fieldwork in the summer of 1880, where he gathered Iroquois harvest songs in Western New York as well as some songs from several tribes in Pennsylvania. Two of the earliest tribes in Pennsylvania were known as the Iroquois and Delaware. Much of their energy was devoted to a respect and praise for Earth, which they creatively integrated into forms of song and dance. Before colonization occurred and cultural, ethnic, religious, and social borders were constructed, the Native Americans were able to more freely express themselves through music. Considering these individuals were not influenced by domineering European ideologies and constructed boundaries, their music was graceful, unpretentious, and spiritual.

The Native Americans settled in the Americas more than 15,000 years ago. Beginning in the late fifteenth century, and continuing up into the twentieth Century, European colonization slowly, then more intensely, forced Native Americans from their homelands, and eventually confined them to reservations. Fortunately, they were able to hold onto their distinctive cultural identity. A significantly crucial and remarkable component of these tribes' identity preservation was their concerted effort to continue their expression of cultural heritage through music and dance.

Customarily, each tribe was divided specifically according to region, and music was instrumental in the creation of each tribe. Some of the earliest Native Americans on the East Coast of the United States were known as the Eastern Woodlands Tribe. They lived everywhere from the Atlantic Ocean to the Mississippi River, as well as from New Brunswick down to the Gulf of Mexico. The tribes primarily exclusive to the mid-Atlantic region were known as the Northeast Tribe, and included the Haudenosaunee—Iroquois, Wabanaki, and Delaware. These particular tribes placed heavy emphasis on drums, flutes, and whistles.

However, many Native American tribes placed most of their emphasis on vocals. These vocals were not in lyrical form, but instead were a rich and spirited form of expression illustrated through powerful tones and pitches. Vocals took precedence over instruments because mid-Atlantic Native Americans used music as a primary source of communication. Instruments, however, were not totally absent, and in some cases were an integral component, serving as a complement to vocalization. Europeans have notably described Native American music as short and without much harmony. Aesthetics, however, arise from local contexts. Mid-Atlantic Indians focused primarily on praising the land by emphasizing rich emotional tonal shifts and boldly energetic sounds. Dance rituals were especially prominent, and they expressed their devotion and loyalty to their culture through powwows. The powwow was an artistic and spiritual ceremony that represented a tribe's beliefs, and was often performed in honor of family members.

EARLY EUROPEAN MUSIC IN THE MID-ATLANTIC

The earliest formal composition of music was linked directly to the colonization of English settlers. From the landing of the Pilgrims to the beginning of musical performance such as operas, music had begun to flourish at a rapid pace. Early music of Puritan colonizers was highly religious in character. The form of music that came with the colonists was generally "hymnal." Though generally known for their influence in the New England area, the Puritans also influenced music in the Mid-Atlantic. Some of the earliest colonists in the Mid-Atlantic included the Swedes at Fort Christian (now Wilmington, Delaware), who arrived in 1638; and the German Mennonites in Pennsylvania, who arrived in 1683. Because of its German inhabitants, who brought with them an extensive history of musical development, Pennsylvania became one of the earliest musical centers. The first "American" composer, Jonathan Kelpius, was thus German. He came from the mid-Atlantic region and led a group of settlers known as Pietists. This particular group was one of the first to leave a musical record. They came to Pennsylvania in 1694, and sang songs, hymns, and anthems. Unlike the Puritans in the North, they did not reject the use of instruments (many Puritans at that time believed that instruments were tied to the devil). In 1705 Kelpius put together a ten-piece collection of sacred music called *"The Lamenting Voice of the Hidden Love."*[1]

Regardless of the efforts made by the early German Mennonites, music was not unanimously welcomed early on in the Pennsylvania region. In fact, any form of musical expression in Philadelphia before the middle of the eighteenth century was considerably looked down upon. In 1716 a group of Quakers known as the Yearly Meeting of the Friends were strictly advised to guard against taking part in any type of music or dance. In fact, a desire for new forms of music in Philadelphia led to a long struggle against these chaste Quaker traditions and strict regulations. Music was first accepted in churches, and Christ Church, founded in 1695 in Philadelphia, was one of the first churches in Pennsylvania to have music. In 1728, the church authorities purchased an organ, which would prove to be an immensely fruitful beginning for sacred music. In 1782, one of the first church orchestras was established and music became an integral component of the Catholic mass. Dancing assemblies also began to form around the middle of the eighteenth century; most were made up of members of the Church of England (and mainly men).

CLASS DIVISION

In addition to the struggles against certain religious codes of conduct, music was also subject to the strict class divide that existed between the elite and the working class. This class divide was so significant that it helped to establish a kind of schism within the realm of music itself, creating the two categories that came to be known as art music and folk music. Each type of music was characteristic and reflective of the class itself.

During the 1720s, this divide came to shift the nature of music itself. No longer strictly sacred and religious, music began to take on the persona of a mirror. It was clearly beginning to reflect the developing traditions and standards within varying social groups. As the mid-Atlantic society began to evolve, music came to carry heavy political undertones, especially during the Civil War era. Transformed into a social tool, music began to be used for social gatherings and political rallies. The invention of the printing press during the second half of the nineteenth century, which meant the availability of cheaper, mass-produced texts, helped music become an important resource for politically active groups that wanted to address the uneven class divide. As with the Native American tribes that created and performed music for sacred, historical, and tribal customs, social classes and politically active groups found music to be more than an exclusively aesthetic medium.

THE DEVELOPMENT OF ART MUSIC

Art music was generally a product of and for the elite and wealthy. Some of the earliest examples of art music were in the forms of keyboard, parlor, and ensemble music. Concert life began in the 1730s in large wealthy urban areas such as Philadelphia. However, because it was expensive to attend these events, crowds were limited to those with substantial amounts of money. There was a clear divide between the common folk and the elite at musical gatherings. Boxes were intended for the wealthy, the pit for the working class.

As New York developed culturally in the early eighteenth century, concert music became an established phenomenon. The city's public concert life may have begun as early as 1736, thanks to Charles Theodore Pachelbel (1690–1750). A major turning point in the musical life of the city was also heavily influenced by William Tuckey (1708–1750). Tuckey organized many concerts and balls, and even built some choirs at local churches. Outdoor concerts were becoming popular, as well as many pre-war musical extravaganzas (this was the era before the American Revolutionary War). The city flourished at the war's end, filling with over 33,000 Loyalists. This heightened the city's theater and musical life.[2] On April 18, 1796, the piece "The Archers or Mountaineers of Switzerland" was presented at the John Street Theatre in New York City. The music was written by Benjamin Carr, who arranged popular airs such as "Yankee Doodle."

EARLY ART MUSIC COMPOSERS AND INSTRUMENT INVENTORS

James Lyon (1735–1794) was one of America's first outstanding art music composers. Born in Newark, New Jersey, in May 1760, he published a collection of psalm and hymn tunes titled *Urania*. This was one of the first collections of this type of music, and was in heavy circulation for many years after its creation. During the next quarter century, many of Lyon's pieces appeared widely in American tune book collections.[3]

Another well-known early composer was Francis Hopkinson. Born in Philadelphia on September 21, 1737, he eventually moved to New Jersey. Hopkinson was one of the signers of the Declaration of Independence. During the Revolutionary War, he wrote many influential prose and satirical works in support of patriotism. His best-known work was "Battle of the Kegs" (1778), in which he mocked the British.

Composing musical pieces went hand in hand with the production of musical instruments. Two of the earliest inventors of music instruments born in the mid-Atlantic region were James Sylvanus McLean and John Isaac Hawkins. McLean had the earliest known patent for the piano. Unfortunately, on December 15, 1836, a fire in the patent office in Washington, D.C., destroyed many documents, many of which contained specifics of McLean's detailed invention. The second inventor, John Isaac Hawkins, reportedly had two patents of another early form of the piano, which included a simple drawing of an iron frame. This frame was to be used within the piano to help keep it in tune.[4]

The fabrication of instruments was not the only form of construction brought on by the rise of music in the Mid-Atlantic. As music became more popular, buildings needed to be constructed where performances could be held. Baltimore, Maryland, had many interesting and captivating early places for musical entertainment. The Baltimore Symphony Orchestra, first organized in 1915, was the first symphony in the country to be supported by municipal funds. It was legally established in 1916 with a tax grant of $6,000. By 1952, it was running steadily with twenty-week sessions of music throughout the course of the year.

Among other early developments was the Baltimore Civic Opera Company (renamed the Baltimore Opera Company in 1970), which featured many standard popular operas at the time. The current company began officially in 1949, but dates back as far as 1927 when Eugene Martinet founded his Martinet School of Opera, which performed at the Maryland Casualty Auditorium in Baltimore. The school grew into the Baltimore Civic Opera Company, and featured local talent such as John Charles Thomas, Robert Weeded, Helen Stokes, Letitia Schenk Bernhardt, Phyllis Frankel, and Bette Hankin. This earlier company ceased to exist after Martinet's death in 1947. When it was revived by supporters two years later, the company turned to the great diva Rosa Ponselle for its artistic director. There was also the Hilltop Musical Company, which was dedicated to rare and unusual music, and specialized in chamber operas of both the past and present era. Places such as the Academy of the Holy Names were built for private music instruction. And the well-known Peabody Conservatory in Baltimore is the oldest major music conservatory in the nation. Places such as these offered programs that enhanced students' abilities in the piano, organ, and violin, and provided both private and group instruction.[5]

Unlike Baltimore, not much scholarly consideration has been given to the history of music in Washington, D.C., perhaps because there was little musical activity in this area until the 1900s. Glenn Dillard Gunn describes Washington as basically a ghost town until modern achievements: "Until 1925 when Elizabeth Sprague Coolidge established her foundation in the Library of Congress, Washington, musically speaking, was what is known in the trade as a 'tank town.' "[6] The Coolidge Foundation changed musical life in Washington. Under its sponsorship, major chamber music organizations were formed, and many concerts were offered for free in the Coolidge Auditorium. In 1931, Hans Kindler came to Washington and organized the National Symphony, which would later be directed by Howard Mitchell. And in 1937, Gertrude Clarke Whittall created a second musical foundation in the Library of Congress. Until this was built, musical life was limited to the activities of a place known as the Friday Morning Music Club. Eventually, the Phillips Gallery of Art was constructed and served as a place where local talent could gather and show off their musical abilities. Washington's first prestigious music schools designed for serious music students included the Toutorsky Music Studios, the Washington Musical Institute, and the Modern School of Music.

One notable early symphonic ensemble was the Balalaika Symphonic Orchestra. Directed by Alexander Kutin, the symphony specialized in using modern woodwinds, brass, and percussion. As indicated by the name, the orchestra used two main instruments: the balalaika and the dombra. These instruments date back to the ninth century, and were repopularized in the fifteenth century. This twentieth-century orchestra aimed at being as authentic as the original balalaika orchestra in the fifteenth century. (The balalaika was a Russian stringed instrument, developed from the dombra. It had a triangular shape with three strings and movable frets.)

MUSIC ON THE MOVE: THE NINETEENTH-CENTURY TRAVELING ORCHESTRA

During the nineteenth century, art music became increasingly popular. It was not only an art form, but also a recreational activity. Most centers for music, however, were located in large cities. Therefore, the public literally had to travel if it wanted to enjoy musical performances. The Theodore Thomas Orchestra would change this.

In the 1870s and 1880s, the orchestra took to traveling. Thomas (1835–1905) a violin virtuoso, traveled with a full orchestra which included anywhere from forty to sixty musicians at a given time. In fifty-one days between September 29 and November 18, the orchestra gave forty-eight concerts, stopping at Troy, Syracuse, Rochester, and Buffalo, New York; Pittsburgh, Harrisburg, and Philadelphia, Pennsylvania; Washington, D.C.; and Newark, New Jersey. In 1874, the traveling musicians expanded their tour to include West Virginia; Erie, Albany, and Poughkeepsie, New York; Baltimore, Maryland; Hudson, Jersey City, Paterson, Meriden, and Hoboken, New Jersey; and Norristown, Scranton, and Wilkes Barre, Pennsylvania. Art music, in other words, was becoming increasingly decentralized. The constant movement of this orchestra encouraged and stimulated musical activities in cities all over the country. Among this group, one of the most ambitious traveling opera companies was the American Opera Company, which was created by Jeanette Thurber in New York in 1885.

Despite the alternative successes described above, most support for the arts was generated by the wealthy during this era. It was relatively impossible for independent practices to exist, and free concerts were difficult to come by, as the musicians relied on the income generated by their audiences. A major step, however, in public contribution occurred in 1914, when the city of Baltimore put up $8,000 to help establish a symphony orchestra.

ART MUSIC IN THE TWENTIETH CENTURY

Arguably the best-known American composers of the mid-Atlantic region, George Gershwin (1898–1937) and Aaron Copland (1900–1990) were both born in Brooklyn, New York. They each came from nonmusical families, and were children of immigrant Russian Jewish parents. Gershwin trained and worked with the school of music that developed in Tin Pan Alley. (Tin Pan Alley was the name given to the publishing business that hired composers and lyricists on a permanent basis to create popular songs. Before this business emerged, however, Tin Pan Alley was a nickname given to an actual street—West 28th between Broadway and Sixth Avenue in Manhattan—where many popular music publishers had their offices. Eventually, this became the generic term for all publishers of popular American sheet music, regardless of geographic location.) Copland, however, studied abroad, engaging in a more formal training in Paris. Even though both incorporated an American flavor in their musical compositions that had an international feel, in formal ways the two composers were very different. Gershwin preferred to write more popular forms of art music, while Copland worked almost exclusively within the realm of classical art music.

Gershwin was taught and became interested in the forms of American vernacular music, and sought forms of concert hall music. Copland also sought out styles of American vernacular. Both composers were highly active in New York, and composed a number of piano concertos. The style and timbre of jazz bands from the 1920s greatly affected and influenced many works of the two composers, namely Gershwin's *Rhapsody in Blue* (1924) and Copland's *Music for the Theatre* (1925).

When Gershwin's career first got started, he was approached to write a concerto. (He did not even know what a concerto was at the time!) Though he was popular, he was not well respected by critics. However, he would prove all of his critics wrong after he began to establish a reputation as a composer who could combine an eclectic mix of elements into his music. He became immersed in the popular music business, working up to his masterpiece, *Porgy and Bess*. This musical meshed popular song and musical theater as well as his extended concert works. In this sense, most of Gershwin's concert music was concerned with the synthesis of many diverse elements. While Gershwin presented more of an eclectic assortment

Portrait of George Gershwin. Courtesy Library of Congress, Prints & Photographs Division, Carl Van Vechten Collection, LC- USZ62-42534.

within his music, Copland investigated American art music from the position of a formally trained classical musician. Many of his pieces during the twentieth century were both eloquent and artistic, capturing a sense of the nation, both past and present. In addition to *Billy the Kid* and *Rodéo*, one of his most famous works was the ballet *Appalachian Spring* (1943–1944).

The twentieth century is also known for producing a number of major orchestras in the Mid-Atlantic such as the Baltimore Symphony, the New York Philharmonic, and the Philadelphia Orchestra. Each of these has come to take a preeminent place among the world's most important orchestras. The Baltimore Symphony, first organized in 1916, is known internationally, but still maintains close ties to the Baltimore and Maryland areas through local educational and community outreach programs. The New York Philharmonic is the oldest symphony orchestra in the United States, and one of the oldest in the world. It was founded in 1842 and has been in continuous operation, playing a leading role in the production of classical music for two-thirds of the nation's history. In addition, the Philharmonic is one of the most active orchestras in the nation, performing some 180 concerts a year. Throughout its history, the New York Philharmonic has had a number of world-famous conductors: Leonard Bernstein, Pierre Boulez, Zubin

Leonard Bernstein

One of the world's most famous conductors and composers, Leonard Bernstein (1918–1990) had a long and distinguished career. Born in Lawrence, Massachusetts, he attended Harvard University and the Curtis Institute of Music in Philadelphia, studying piano and conducting. His first permanent conducting post came in 1943, when he was appointed assistant conductor of the New York Philharmonic, eventually becoming the Philharmonic's musical director in 1958. From 1958 to 1969 he led more concerts with the Philharmonic than any previous conductor. Bernstein made over 400 musical recordings, more than half of them with the Philharmonic. He was an advocate of American composers, and counted Aaron Copland as one of his closest friends. In addition to his work on musicals, Bernstein composed a number of classical compositions, including Symphony #1, "Jeremiah," Symphony #2, "The Age of Anxiety," Symphony #3, "Kaddish" (dedicated to the memory of John F. Kennedy); two operas, *Trouble in Tahiti* and *A Quiet Place*; a "Serenade" for violin, strings, and percussion; a song cycle for six singers and orchestra entitled "Songfest"; the "Chichester Psalms" for choir, boy soprano, and orchestra; the musicals *Candide* (in collaboration with Richard Wilbur and Lillian Hellman), *On the Town* (in collaboration with Betty Comden and Adolph Green), and the landmark *West Side Story*, which was also made into an Academy Award–winning film.

Mehta, and Arturo Toscanini, to name a few. The Philharmonic's current director is Lorin Maazel, who became musical director in 2002.

The region is known for its internationally renowned orchestral directors as well. Conductors such as Leonard Bernstein and Eugene Ormandy became giants in the world of classical music. Ormandy served as musical director of the Philadelphia Orchestra from 1938 until 1980. Under his direction, the orchestra became known for its romantic "Philadelphia Sound." Well known for having an infallible ear and an extraordinary musical memory, Ormandy rarely conducted with a score. His conducting technique was influenced by his training as a violinist: "his frequent gesture of the bent left arm, bent fingers shaking, emulating the violinist's vibrato, was a familiar sight to musicians and audiences alike."[7] Born in Budapest in 1899, Ormandy came to New York City in 1921. For the next decade and a half, he would guest conduct for orchestras in the United States and Europe. In the spring of 1936 he became the co-conductor of the Philadelphia Orchestra, sharing the podium with the great Leopold Stokowski.

GROWTH OF SECULAR AND POPULAR MUSIC

Secular music became increasingly popular from the colonial period on. Philadelphia was a burgeoning secular music site in the 1700s, and theater life within this region began to grow at a rapid pace. The increasing popularity of secular music was, of course, heavily opposed by the Quakers. However, in April 1754, a group called "a Company of Comedians" from London obtained permission to present twenty-four performances of plays. They later became known as the Old American Company. The group was versatile as its members tripled, expanding to include not only actors, but also singers and dancers. The company's popularity grew swiftly along the East Coast. Philadelphia and Baltimore became important sites for their performances until they eventually settled in New York City.

Philadelphia was the largest cultural capital of the American colonies. Public theater began in the city around 1749. Because dancing was an act that marked heavy defiance of the Quakers, public dancing and singing became extremely popular among non-Quaker citizens. Around 1756, many musical developments occurred: open public concerts, the appearance of music stores, and organized concerts. Theatrical troupes were incredibly popular in the larger cities of Annapolis and Baltimore, which had much to do with the musical life within Maryland. Musical expression could be practiced more freely within this state because it was not under Quaker or Puritan rule. In fact, secular music edged out most sacred music. Though small towns were the focus of cultural life, they did not support the musical arts to the extent of the cities did. One of the earliest forums of secular music, known as the Tuesday Club (1745–1756), was located in Annapolis. The club performed songs, odes, and minuets, and their motto was "Fiddlers, Fools, Farces." Public music performances were becoming increasingly popular.[8]

EARLY WOMEN'S MOVEMENTS

Musical composition and the conducting of great orchestras were dominated in general by men. A few notable women, however, were important figures in the Mid-Atlantic. Women also began creating musical societies that eventually became highly competitive and prestigious. Amy Fay, for instance, was the president of the Women's Philharmonic Society of New York from 1903 to 1923. Laura Langford, director of the Seidl Society of New York, provided summer concerts at Brighton Beach. During this era women of the upper classes were always required to be escorted by men in public. To address this problem, Langford arranged musical events in such a way that women could travel for free as a group. In the summer of 1889, the Seidl Society sponsored trips for working girls, children, and orphans to Coney Island and the concerts held there, free of charge. In 1890, Langford organized Wagner concerts at the Brooklyn Academy of Music. Her struggle enabled her to become one of the first Americans to help offer art music to the general public. Langford believed music should be appreciated and enjoyed by all, regardless of gendered social constructs and the boundaries they created.

Musical ability was considered an impressive and highly respected accomplishment for women in the nineteenth century. In 1885 Jeanette Thurber convinced the internationally known musical composer Antonín Dvořák to come for a two-year residency. His presence would become an important step in the evolution of American music. In addition to Langford, other women had an effect on loosening the hold men had on the music industry. Harriet Gibbs Marshall was one of the first women to establish musical societies (she founded the Washington, D.C., Conservatory of Music in 1903), as was Mary Louis Curtis Bok (who established the Curtis Institution in Philadelphia in 1924).

Massive Music Festivals

Large music festivals began to grow in popularity during the early nineteenth century as well. Multiday events—which included orchestras with hundreds of players and choral ensembles with thousands of members—became common. These festivals eventually made their way to New York. Two major contributors to these events were Walter Damrosch and Theodore Thomas. The two were in heavy competition with one another. Damrosch founded the Oratorio Society of New York in 1873, as well as the New York Symphony Society in 1878. In 1881, he launched the first of these massive music galas. Not long after, Thomas began a festival in Philadelphia called the Philadelphia Centennial Festival. Damrosch and Thomas even went so far as to have dueling music fests. Even though the events were highly competitive, the battles were healthy and fruitful, as they drew massive crowds, helping musical culture blossom.[9]

NEW YORK CITY: A MUSICAL PLAYGROUND

The North's urban centers during the 1800s were very prosperous. As a result, its cities would dominate all phases of music in decades to come. Cities were the spaces in which much was happening, especially in terms of musical progression. New York City in particular has played remarkable role in the evolution of music, not only within the mid-Atlantic region, but in the United States as a whole. The city was a place of incredible ethnic diversity and was home to many famous firsts. Musical theaters began to flourish, for instance, in New York City during the 1700s. The first opera known to be performed in the mid-Atlantic states, *The Beggars' Opera* (1728), debuted in New York City on December 3, 1750.

The New York Philharmonic Society, established in 1842, was the first permanent musical organization in the region and in the United States. A founding member of the Philharmonic was a German pianist named Henry Christian Timm. George Frederick Bristow (1825–1898) was also involved in the creation of the Philharmonic Society, and one of his most important contributions was his involvement with a meeting in 1842 to discuss symphony life in New York. The ultimate decision of this meeting would lead to the creation of the Philharmonic Society of New York.

Opera began to grow swiftly along with the building of the Philharmonic. The Orleans Theatre (1827–1833) was central to the creation and evolution of opera in the mid-Atlantic states. (It is important to note that at this time most operas were European in origin.) The tour of the Orleans Theatre brought opera to the cities of Baltimore, Philadelphia, and New York City.

In 1900, the Philadelphia Orchestra, one of the first in the region, encouraged the construction of other great music halls. One such hall was built in New York City to house the Russian Symphony Orchestra (1903). The music of this orchestra was remarkably interesting and offbeat. It brought a taste of the exotic Russian nationalists' music to New York, thereby challenging the dominant German sound of the Philharmonic. Around 1906, in addition to the creation of these musical centers, two of the very first and most important opera houses were built: the Metropolitan and Oscar Hammerstein's Manhattan Opera House.

During this great musical boom, people became more interested in understanding not only the construction of musical pieces, but also the art and craft of the performance. Hence this marked the birth of musical education in schools in New York. In 1885, one of the first musical conservatories was built in New York, the National Conservatory of Music.

Virtuosos and Early Musical Developments

Around the 1840s, virtuoso instrumentalists began arriving in the United States. Instrumentalists of all kinds, who had performed extensively in Europe before arriving in the United States, began creating a concert circuit along the East Coast. It was during this era as well that Americans were introduced to itinerant European chamber ensembles. One of the most influential chamber groups was the Germania Musical Society, which arrived in 1848. The ensemble had a significant impact, especially outside of New York City. It consisted of thirty-two members, including Hungarian composer and conductor Joseph Gungl.

Opera companies were beginning to boom as well during this period. One notable company was the Havana Opera Company, which played and performed in Pittsburgh as well as many other East Coast cities. Between the 1840s and 1850s, the popularity of opera increased significantly. By the early 1850s, there were enough Italian singers living in New York to form Italian opera companies. One of the most important visiting orchestras of the mid-1850s was the ensemble of French conductor Louis Antoine Jullien. He arrived in New York City in 1853 with twenty-seven instrumentalists. His concerts consisted of dances, overtures, and symphonies. He was known for being rather flamboyant, and was often criticized for being far too gimmicky. However, his influence on American culture was profound.

In 1825, the first Italian opera performance was given in New York City with the arrival of the Garcia Company. The group managed the Park Theatre, where the troupe performed for almost a year. Manuel Garcia (1775–1832), born in Seville, headed the company. He first became known throughout Spain as a tenor and a composer of comic operas. In 1808, he appeared for the first time in Italian opera. Eventually, Garcia and his company would make the trek to the United States, and would become the earliest Italian opera company to establish itself in America. This was the first in a series of original-language opera companies, and would essentially set the standards for opera. Clinging to their ethnic roots, the Italians were able to preserve their heritage by performing operas in their own language. Music thus enabled Italians to establish a substantive cultural identity in the region. Around the 1830s, however, the emergence of English opera would provide a good deal of competition for the Italians.

New York's dominance as America's entertainment capital was well established by the mid-nineteenth century. Musical events were beginning to headline and dominate the city's life. *The Black Crook*, for example, was considered a precursor to the American musical. It was produced in 1866 in Niblo's Garden, which was the best-appointed theater in New York during this era. After the popularity of minstrelsy, the vernacular musical stage began to evolve. It would mark the beginning of a more sophisticated type of entertainment that would attract a large audience.

A more playful kind of music was beginning to emerge with performances such as the ballet-pantomime of the 1830s and 1840s. Moving from a more distinguished and eloquent dance, this was the first to include ballet mixed with gymnastics, farces, and other comic pantomimes. This type of entertainment was first performed mainly by the Ravel family, and started a trend. The ballet-pantomime was symbolic of an attempt to appeal to a broad range of tastes.

The burlesque, a humorous and satirical parody of well-known plays or stories, was also beginning to rise in popularity. One of the first was a burlesque of Shakespeare's *Hamlet*, which was presented in 1828. This indicated a shift in American entertainment, and would essentially mark the beginning of the American comedy.

Vaudeville and Tin Pan Alley

Vaudeville was a form of popular entertainment inspired by earlier minstrel shows, which combined an array of singers, dancers, and comedians. One of the earliest and best known contributors to this phase of entertainment was Tony Pastor. His era of glory was during the 1880s, and he was often referred to as the Father of Vaudeville. Since vaudeville shows were affordable, they were considered entertainment for the common folk. Many shows included acrobats, juggling, clowns, magicians, comedians, impersonators, and singers. In addition to these comedic routines, it was not uncommon to see ragtime and popular music of the time included in the venues as well. By the 1920s, vaudeville was becoming popular in Hollywood.

Vaudeville was certainly making its impact in New York City as well, with 28th Street being an early stomping ground for many musicians. An array of musical instruments and sounds could be heard rattling and rumbling around 28th Street, affectionately nicknamed Tin Pan Alley (a phrase coined by the writer Monroe H. Rosenfeld). In addition, clusters of music publishing houses were beginning to pop up on 28th Street, close to the William Morris booking agency. As vaudeville increased in popularity, it was soon covered in music journals. The *New York Clipper* was one of the first vaudeville and popular music journals.

Early African American Music

One of the earliest forms of African American music was celebrated in a festival known as Pinkster Day, which took place in New York City in the mid–eighteenth century. During this time, slaves in the northern states were achieving more freedom than they had previously known. Taking any possible chance they could with their still limited freedom, they were able to release their energies and celebrate their heritage through this festival. The celebration included banjos and various types of drums from West and Central Africa. In New York City, the African Grove Theater—a center for performances such as tragedies, ballets, and operas—was created.

In the nineteenth century, black music and social activity centered primarily around the church. Secular theater music became far more popular, and Philadelphia essentially became a center for the concert world. An important secular musical society developed in Philadelphia at this time, known as the Philadelphia Musical Fund Society. Leopold Meignen, from France, was its conductor.

The year 1898 was an important one for the production of African American musical shows. These productions proved remarkably successful on Broadway, and opened the door for a plethora of shows in the following years. With a title that would never be used today, *A Trip to Coontown* was the first full-length musical written and performed by blacks on Broadway. This show was written and produced in New York City in 1898 by entertainer and playwright Robert Cole (1863–1911). Two important musicals that followed were *The Creole Show* (1889) and *Black America* (1895), and were said to be an indirect offspring of black minstrelsy. A notable star performer was Ernest Hogan, who had come from black minstrelsy. His most famous performance was in *Clorindy, the Origin of the Cake-Walk*, which was created by Will Marion Cook. This essentially opened the doors for black musicians on Broadway. The first wave of African American musicals would swiftly follow with *In Dahomey* (1902), *In Abyssinia* (1906), and *In Bandana Land* (1908).[10]

Musicals and Dance

Musicals in New York City had a great period of achievement in the thirty years that began with *Show Boat* (1927) and ended with *West Side Story* (1957). Broadway audiences of the early 1940s mostly wanted escape-from-reality forms of entertainment. Such productions as Irving Berlin's *Louisiana Purchase* (1940) and *This Is the Army* (1940); Cole Porter's *Panama Hattie* (1940) with Ethel Merman, *Let's Face It* (1941) with Eve Arden and Danny Kaye, and *Something for the Boys* (1943) all fit the bill. Berlin's longest running hit was *Annie Get Your Gun* (1946). The best-known musical of the 1940s was Rodgers and Hammerstein's *Oklahoma!* (1943), which ushered in an era of less slapstick and more serious musical dramas. That same year Hammerstein had transformed Bizet's opera *Carmen* into *Carmen Jones* (1943)—the longest running black musical of the 1940s. Cole Porter made a comeback in 1948 with *Kiss Me Kate*, which saw over 1,000 performances. Burton Lane and E. Y. Harburg's *Finian's Rainbow* (1947) is the story of an Irishman who stole a pot of gold from a leprechaun. David Wayne, the actor who played the leprechaun, became the first person in a musical to receive the Theater Wing's Antoinette Perry Award, now known as the Tony. The 1950s saw such musicals as George Forrest and Robert Wright's *Kismet* (1953), which included musical themes adapted from Alexander Borodin's *Prince Igor*; Frank Loesser's *Guys and Dolls* (1950), *The Most Happy Fella* (1956), and *How to Succeed in Business Without Really Trying* (1961); and Rodgers and Hammerstein's *The King and I* (1951), *Me and Juliet* (1953), *Flower Drum Song* (1958, was directed by Gene Kelly), and the giant *The Sound of Music* (1959), which had a run of 1,443 performances.

Stephen Sondheim (b. March 22, 1930, in New York City) grew up in Pennsylvania, where he met Oscar Hammerstein II. While Hammerstein was working on the musical *Oklahoma!* he became intrigued with musical theater and became a lyricist for both *West Side Story* (1957) and *Gypsy* (1959), which were directed by Jerome Robbins. His first score as a composer-lyricist, for the comedy *A Funny Thing Happened on the Way to the Forum* (1962), earned him success. Other musicals he was responsible for composing include *Anyone Can Whistle* (1964), *A Little Night Music* (1973), and the more recent *Assassins* (1990). Other successful musicals include *Oklahoma!* (1943), directed by Rouben Mamoulian; *The Music Man* (1957), directed, by Morton Da Costa and choreographed by Onna White; *Camelot* (1960) and *Fiddler on the Roof* (1964), directed and choreographed by Jerome Robbins; *Mame* (1966), directed by Gene Saks; *Man of La Mancha* (1965) and *Les Miserables* (currently play-

Twyla Tharp

Arguably one of the most famous American choreographers, Twyla Tharp earned her reputation early on as a student at Barnard College in New York City. She studied at the American Ballet Theater School with legends Martha Graham, Merce Cunningham, Paul Taylor, and Erick Hawkins. From that point forward, she devoted much of her energy to dance. In 1965, she began her own dance company, known simply as Twyla Tharp Dance. Her style was characterized as avant-garde, and pushed the limits of dance. Her pieces had an edge to them that added a humorous yet dynamically unpredictable flavor, and she often combined ballet techniques with common movements such as running and walking. In 1980, her first work, *When We Were Very Young*, went to Broadway, and was followed the next year by *The Catherine Wheel* (1981). In 1985, she choreographed *Singin' in the Rain*, and finally received her first Tony Award in 2003 for *Movin Out*. She also contributed her talents as a choreographer in the films *Hair* (1978), *Ragtime* (1980), *Amadeus* (1984), and *White Nights* (1985).

Scene from the Broadway musical *West Side Story*. Photofest.

ing), directed by Trevor Nunn and John Caird; *Cats* (1982–2000), the longest-running Broadway show; *A Chorus Line* (1975), which was directed and choreographed by Michael Bennett; and *Chicago* (originally choreographed by Bob Fosse), which also became a successful film hit.

Bob Fosse (1927–1987), one of the most famous American choreographers, was responsible for directing and choreographing some of Broadway's biggest hits, including *Sweet Charity* (1969), *Pippin* (1972), *Chicago* (1972), and *Dancin'* (1978), which finished with a total of eight Tony Awards. He also was quite successful in the film industry, as he choreographed *My Sister Eileen* (1955), *The Pajama Game* (1957), and *Damn Yankees* (1958). Other musicals he choreographed included *How to Succeed in Business Without Really Trying* (1961), *Liza* (1974), and *The American Dance Machine* (1978).

Musicals also came to be associated with movies once techniques for adding sound to films were developed in the 1920s. Although the majority of these films were made in Hollywood, the first film musical was made in the mid-Atlantic. *Don Juan*, a film with operatic music, made its debut in New York in 1926. Two of the first Broadway singers and actors from New York to make the transfer to Hollywood were Al Jolson and Fanny Brice. The famous pop vocalist Eddie Fisher, born in Philadelphia, would later go on to recall the style of both Al Jolson and Tin Pan Alley in hits such as "Any Time" and "Tell Me Why" (both 1952).

EARLY IMMIGRATION AND MUSIC

Musical influences of other countries were essentially the bread and butter of American music. American music would not be what it is today without the conglomeration of Eastern and European influence. Around the turn of the nineteenth century, the United States experienced a population explosion, mainly due to serious political and economic problems in various parts of Europe. At the same time, public transportation was developing. During the 1820s and 1830s, all the major cities in the northern and eastern states were connected by paved roads. The Erie Canal was built in 1825, marking a step forward in water transportation. Steamships provided service between Liverpool and New York City, allowing large amounts of people to move between continents. The cities of Baltimore, New York, and Philadelphia, especially were becoming heavily populated.

The increase in population in these areas provided much cultural diversity. This created a great mix of musical activity, especially in theaters and halls. During the 1820s and 1830s, performing organizations began to appear. In New York City, the Sacred Music Society (1823) and the New York Choral Society (1824) were formed. Philadelphia was also a major cultural center, housing the Musical Fund Society (1820) and the *Mannerchör* and *Junge Mannerchör* ("Mannerchör" meaning "men's singing society"). The Irish and Germans in particular were important contributors to the development of early music in the Mid-Atlantic.

Irish Influence

The Irish were often musically talented, bringing their own distinct melodies and tunes with them to the United States. They were responsible for the opening of many cultural musical centers, such as the Celtic Hall in New York City, which was built by Patrick Fitzpatrick, a Uillean piper from Ireland. The "Stage Irish"— group of well-known Irish musicians—were a group of men involved in the New York theater. These talented individuals brought an expanse of cultural breadth with them, incorporating their unique style and customs into New York stage and music halls. Many Americans, however, found the influence of immigrants to be rather intrusive and resented against what were considered to be "foreigners." The Stage Irish, for example, were not admiringly noted for their talent, but were thought to be burly, boisterous, and loud. Nonetheless, the Irish successfully carried on with their traditions.

During the 1920s and 1930s, hundreds of traditional instrumental recordings were made of Irish music and musicians. Paddy Killoran, born in Ballymote, Ireland, was one of the first to establish a hearty Irish center in the United States. During his stay in New York City, he not only ran a successful bar in the Bronx, but also founded one of the very first Irish orchestras, known as the Pride of Erin. Another notable Irish musician was Michael Coleman. Coleman came to New York City in 1914 and earned a reputation as one of the finest Irish fiddlers of his time. During his career, he recorded more than eighty sides for several record companies.

German Influence

The German musical style was very conservative. Highly inclusive and protective about their style, the Germans shied away from modern music. Their aim was to keep the sounds of their homeland as authentic and pure as possible in the context of their new American homeland.

The Germans had a significant influence on American music, especially within the mid-Atlantic region. During the 1850s, Germans came to dominate the American musical scene. Pennsylvania in particular was a significant area for German settlers, and it was here that they formed highly influential Anabaptist communities known as the Moravians. The Mannerchöre singing societies contributed to the distinction between art and folk music, which was a profoundly remarkable breakthrough during this era. In fact, through their music, the Germans were among the first to break down the barrier between the classes.

The range of music extended anywhere from German folk songs to works of early art music composers. Philadelphia and New York City were two very important sites for Mannerchöre art music concerts. Some of the earliest and largest men's German singing societies were the Mannerchör in Philadelphia (1835) as well as the Liederkanz, which existed in both Baltimore (1836) and New York City (1847). By 1850, these societies had become very popular in Charleston, Buffalo, and Pittsburgh as well. Sangerfest Halls were the first permanent singing halls to be built for the Mannerchöre. These structures were built in the late nineteenth and early twentieth centuries, and two of the most elaborate halls were in Baltimore and Philadelphia. The Philadelphia Hall is not only the most recent, but the grandest. Built in 1912, it holds over 19,000 people. In addition to the overwhelming growth in the popularity of secular music, many sacred music societies began to promote European choral music as well.

The Germans' heavy musical influence was not strictly centralized, as they had a significant influence in other parts of the Mid-Atlantic, New York City being one of the major areas. Carl Bergmann (1821–1876), the director of the Mannergesangverein Arion, was an important figure in the establishment of German musical life in New York. Soon after settling in the city, Bergmann went on to play cello in the Mason-Thomas chamber ensemble, and conducted the Philharmonic Society from 1855 to 1876. Theodore Eisfeld (1816–1882), American-born, worked exclusively with Bergmann, and became one of the most influential American conductors during the first half of the century. He was not only a composer and co-conductor with Bergmann of the Philharmonic Society, but also contributed his talents by being an active member in the society. The Philharmonic Symphony Society of New York (modern-day New York Philharmonic Orchestra) was founded in 1842 by Ureli C. Hill (American), Henry C. Timm (German), Anthony Reiff (German), and Charles Edward Horn (English). By 1855, fifty-three of the orchestra's sixty-seven musicians were German, performing mainly works by Beethoven, Mendelssohn, Mozart, and Haydn.

Caribbean Influence

The first Puerto Ricans began arriving in New York in the early 1900s. Since their arrival, New York City has been internationally recognized as *the* center of contemporary Latin and West Indian music. Latin themes, in fact, became so well known that they were even evident in vaudeville and popular music of the 1920s. Trinidadian calypsonian Wilmoth Houdini and Cuban instrumentalist Alberto Socarras were on stage in many early New York theater performances. In 1930, Don Azpiazu's Havana Casino Orchestra brought authentic Cuban music to Broadway. In the late 1930s, New York–based Afro-Cuban musicians Machito and Mario

Bauza intricately wove a mix of mambo and Latin percussion with African American big band jazz and swing.

Caribbean music brought with it a number of dance styles as well, styles that are still popular among the Caribbean population in New York City. Perhaps the best known is the salsa, a dance based on a blending of Cuban dance music and African American jazz. It became the primary expression among New York's Puerto Rican population (also known as Nuyorican) during the 1960s and 1970s. The soca is a mix of Trinidadian calypso and African American soul which appeared in Brooklyn during the 1980s. Finally, the Haitian dance called the kompa and the Dominican merengue are favored in New York's club scene. Both dances are upbeat, electric, horn-driven ensembles.

Scandinavian Influence

The Finnish tenor Hannes Saari directed the Finnish Choirs in New York City, and many of the songs he recorded came directly from Finland. William E. Stein was a pianist from New York who composed many operettas for Finnish American organizations. The earliest Finnish folk musician to record commercially was Erik Kivi. On August 9, 1929, he entered Victor Studios in New York City, a landmark moment that led to many other ethnic recordings. Companies such as the Scandinavian Music House (a major source of Scandinavian recordings) in Brooklyn's Scandinavian section and Harry Pace's Black Swan company in New York City (one of the first ethnic companies to specialize in the production of records for the black market) were instrumental in spreading ethnic compositions.

Jewish Influence

Another significantly immigrant group in New York was the Jewish community. Many Jewish immigrants came from eastern Europe, where Yiddish was their exclusive language. There was a flourishing Yiddish theater in New York, which was an integral component in the conservation of this ethnic group's cultural heritage. The unifying characteristic that brought together their many styles of music (both secular and sacred) was known as the *krecht*, which was a wailing, sobbing sound (this distinguished Jewish music from other ethnic music at the time). In the face of early-twentieth-century impoverishment, the music business was one of the few places that Jewish citizens could find work. They quickly caught on to the music of ragtime and began integrating this style into their own. Some early famous Jewish musicians include Tin Pan Alley founders Irving Berlin, George Gershwin, and Harold Arlen.

Polish Influence

The Polish American music tradition has been around since the late 1800s, beginning with the Poles who migrated to America between 1860 and 1920. The Polka Belt, an area enriched with Polish ethnicity and music, ran north to Buffalo, New York, east to Newark, New Jersey, south to the Pennsylvania border, and west. The polka was derived from military practices and eventually developed into a dance in both regional and national forms in central and eastern Europe. This high-energy

Italian American Pop Singers

Italian Americans were some of the first to break into the music industry. Performers from the mid-Atlantic region include singer Dion DiMucci (b. 1939), Dean Martin (1917–1995), and Frank Sinatra (1915–1998). DiMucci, better known as Dion, grew up in the Bronx. Early in his career, he formed the quartet known as Dion and the Belmonts. In 1958, they recorded their first hit, "I Wonder Why," and the following year earned even more of a reputation with their top-ten hit, "A Teenager in Love." In 1961, Dion chose to pursue a solo career that had more of a rock and roll feel. Some of his solo hits include "Runaround Sue," "The Wanderer," and "Donna the Prima Donna."

Actor and singer Dean Martin (born Dino Paul Crocetti) was famous for more than his music. He began singing in nightclubs at the age of seventeen, and after his quick rise to success, officially changed his name to Dean Martin in 1940. In 1947, Martin teamed up with Jerry Lewis to perform many successful comedic routines. They went on to make sixteen films together between 1949 and 1956, until their eventual split. Martin pursued a successful solo career which included songs such as "That's Amore," "When You're Smiling," and "Oh Marie." He also acted in films and was famous for his involvement with the "Rat Pack," which also included Frank Sinatra, Sammy Davis Jr., Joey Bishop, and Peter Lawford.

Frank Sinatra, born in Hoboken, New Jersey, is considered by many the greatest male singer of the twentieth century. In 1939, Henry James, who recruited him to sing for his swing band, discovered Sinatra. He eventually became the lead singer of the Tommy Dorsey Orchestra (1940–1942), and recorded over ninety songs with this ensemble. He ran his own radio show until he was fired in 1949. Sinatra's career began to look up, however, when he made the move to Hollywood and starred in the film *From Here to Eternity* (1953), which earned him an Academy Award for best supporting actor. He is famous for songs such as "New York, New York," and his performances with the "Rat Pack" both on stage and on screen.

dance eventually made its way to the United States and became part of American folk music. Dana Records, which was housed in New York, was intimately linked with polka music. It had considerable success with the Polish bands of Gene Wisniewski, Frank Wojnarowski, and Walt Solek. New York City–based Orkiestra Witkpwskiego was one of the earliest Polish orchestras responsible for the eastern-style polka—an orchestral big-band sound. Big Walt Solek (b. 1911), who sang songs such as "Who Stole the Kiszka" and "My Girlfriend Julida," carried on the traditional eastern style in his music. Bud Hudenksi and the Corsairs from Pittsburgh as well as the G-Notes and the Krew Brothers from Buffalo perfected the eastern style in the 1960s. There was a major shift in the polka style in the East, however, as the more bluesy rock and roll Chicago style made its way through the Buffalo circuit in the 1960s. In fact, by 1975, 90 percent of the polkas heard in the greater Buffalo area were in Chicago style.

The eastern side of Buffalo was home to a large Polish community, and the region has been the site of many polka music festivals and gatherings. Famous polka bands such as the Dynatones, the G-Notes, the Jumping Jacks, Big Steve and the Bellares, the Hi-Notes, and the Polecats originated in the Buffalo region. By the mid-1970s, polka rose in popularity with the aid of organizations such as the Polka Boosters Club, the Eddie Blazonczyk and the Versatones Fan Club, and the Happy Richie and the Royalaires Fan Club. Though Buffalo is one of the most popular sites for polka music in the region, this music is in high demand in other areas as well, with bands such as the Treltones in Pittsburgh, and Jimmy Sturr of New York City.

AMERICAN REBELLION MUSIC

In addition to the diversity of ethnic musicians and small businesses, which added variety to the German-dominated sounds of music of the nineteenth century, many American-born musicians rebelled against the German hold on music. Ureli Corelli Hill organized the first chamber music series in New York. This series worked to establish a non-German musical revolution, teaming up with the increasingly Germanic Sacred Music Society.

Two types of American musicians who worked outside the German sphere were singers (who predominantly studied under the Italians) and virtuosos. Clara Louis Kellogg (1842–1854), for example, was American-born and had a thirty-two-year career in New York, heavily influencing the impact of opera performance in this area. Kellogg was one of the many Americans who worked against foreign-dominated music through rival performances. This could be seen as healthy competition, enriching and broadening the ethnic colors and tastes of music. At the same time, however, such competition easily shifted to become an early form of American ethnocentrism.

Such were the contradictions in the move to develop a "pure American" style (which was, in many respects, responsible for the growth and development of much of the music in the region, and the country). There was a bitter divide between what was considered to be "American" music and what wasn't. Jerome Hopkins (1836–1898) was one musician among many who was interested in furthering the "authentic feel" of American music. In 1856, he helped establish the New York American Music Association. Charles Hommans (1800–1862) was a composer in Philadelphia who was also highly supportive of this venture. George Bristow (1825–1898) and William Henry Fry (1813–1864) were two of the most productive native-born composers of orchestral music during the 1850s. Both were against German domination within the musical sphere, and sought to create sounds that were distinct. Bristow, Brooklyn-born, was a violinist in the Philharmonic Society as well as a director of the Mendelssohn and New York Harmonic societies. He was also highly influential as a music teacher in the New York public school system. Eventually, Bristow would go on to write three operas and four symphonies, among other orchestral and chamber music pieces. Fry, born in Philadelphia, was a composer, lecturer, and music critic in both Philadelphia and New York, and also worked for the *Tribune*. Fry spent much of his time on operatic and symphonic works and was one of the first composers to put English words to Italian melodies. The first half of the nineteenth century was therefore a key historical moment in the development of American culture. The growing middle class, industrialization, virtuosos, and the competition among German Romanticism, American nationalism, and ethnic pluralism provided for great diversity in shaping early American music.

As music made its way into the twentieth century, it became more eclectic and diverse, incorporating new patterns. Music continued to mirror shifting social patterns, reflecting historical changes. The music industry began to flourish in the years after World War II. The development of tape recording made it possible to preserve music, and eventually led to the development of radio. In this sense, New York was no longer the musical center it was in the 1920s.[11]

In the 1920s, three new and important institutions were built for music: the Eastman School of Music, in Rochester, New York (1921); the Juilliard School of Music, in New York City (1923); and the Curtis Institute, in Philadelphia, Pennsylvania (1924). These music centers provided training for many prospective composers and musicians. The fact that schools for music were erected clearly reflects the increasing importance of music.

In the 1930s and early 1940s, America's economy took a serious hit as a result of the Great Depression. Unfortunately, music took a hit as well. Nevertheless, during this economic slump many musicians were able to express their critical outlook on the sociopolitical and economic inequalities that marked this era. American symphonies and operas continue, and American ballet was born. Russian Nicolas Nabokov composed one of the first ballets in America. Known as *Union Pacific*, it was first presented in Philadelphia in 1934. Reflecting the economic and political climate, many Broadway shows were responsive to and critical of the condition of the nation. For example, Harold Rome's *Pins and Needles* (1937) and Marc Blitzstein's *The Cradle Will Rock* (1937) were harsh renditions of the state of the nation, both satirizing political figures. In this sense, music continued to be a tool of communication and a form of resistance.

FROM MINSTRELSY TO RAGTIME

During the nineteenth century, one of the most popular forms of theatrical music was performed in New York. It was known as minstrelsy, and African American culture was its source material. This period was an important one for the of growth of an African American middle class. William Henry Lane (1825–1852), known as "Master Juba," was the only black entertainer to tour with early major minstrel groups. His fame took off when he began as a dancer in the Five Points district of New York City. Elizabeth Taylor Greenfield (1824–1876) was one of the first black prima donnas—women musicians who were pursuing careers in European art music. Greenfield was born a slave in Mississippi, but she was adopted by Quakers and raised in Philadelphia. After her education in Europe, she returned to the United States to tour frequently, establishing herself as an artist. She eventually went on to organize and direct an opera troupe in Philadelphia.

Ragtime was an offspring of minstrelsy. Its heyday began in the late 1890s. Ragtime was originally a piano style invented and developed by black musicians, and its roots are found in the 1880s in New York. The eastern ragtime scene was far different from the styles of ragtime present in other regions of the country. The musicians of the East were far more concerned with variety as opposed to the rigid formality found elsewhere. When we refer to the *ragtime era*, we think of a moment in time that reflected the pepping up of American society through music. In other words, it was a literal quickening of the American pace that was reflected in changing musical styles during this era. The intense pace of ragtime dancing had an effect on dance styles that would develop in the future. The dance craze, which began at the beginning of World War I (the era that included the creation of dances such as the polka), saw faster two-step dances such as the foxtrot, turkey trot, and bunny hug.

James P. Johnson was one of the most notable ragtime artists of the era. Born in Brunswick, New Jersey, Johnson blended ragtime with a taste of the blues, and was directly influenced by Scott Joplin. His earliest and most famous pieces were the "Caprice Rag" (1914) and "Daintiness Rag" (1916). Eubie Blake is another notable of this era. He was born in the red-light district of Baltimore, and in 1899 composed his most famous piece, the "Charleston Rag."

An important forerunner of jazz in New York was known as orchestral ragtime. From the late 1890s until the end of World War I, black orchestras at stage shows played this music. In the early 1900s, New York's Black Bohemia furnished the syncopated dance orchestra. James Reese Europe (1881–1919), who also was founder of the famous Clef Club, gave many of these concerts from 1905 to 1910.

As early as 1898, ragtime was being incorporated into Broadway shows, through the 1910s, thousands of songs were published in the name and style of ragtime. These particular ragtime songs told a variety of stories and catered to a vast array of audiences. Around 1910, a group of pianists in New York City created an extension of ragtime known as stride, which was a virtuoso style with a quick tempo.

Scott Joplin was one of the premiere ragtime composers of his day. His most popular work was known as the "Maple Leaf Rag," which would eventually become a jazz standard. Joplin had a major impact on many important figures to come, including, mid-Atlantic native Joseph Lamb. His earliest compositions reflected those of Joplin. As a white man, Lamb was actually considered to be a racial minority within the ragtime genre. He spent most of his life in New Jersey and New York, but it wasn't until he reached New York City that he began to earn a name for himself, eventually becoming known as one of the greatest ragtime classicists.

Jazz

The migration of African Americans from the rural South to the urban North began in the 1890s. By the 1920s, New York had a large black population and was a thriving center for black musical theater, providing many opportunities for musical enrichment. James Reese Europe was a key figure who helped bring jazz and dance music into the cultural mainstream. He moved from Washington, D.C., to New York to advance his music career. In 1910, Europe established the Clef Club, which created a union for black musicians in New York. This exclusive club provided a newly professional climate for black musicians, allowing them to get the best jobs in hotels, ballrooms, and restaurants.

Jazz bands began touring in the 1900s and worked their way around the country. Eventually, some would settle in New York City and create a center for this increasingly popular musical genre. King Oliver, a famous jazz musician who once employed Louis Armstrong, carried his gig to New York. Another notable first in jazz was the group known as the Original Dixieland Jazz Band. Unlike most jazz musicians, the group was white. This five-member band was one of the first to bring the Jazz Age to New York, transporting the sound all the way from its birthplace, New Orleans. They opened a café in January 1917, and by March the following year had made their first recording.

Jazz eventually came to be mixed with other styles of music. Unique stylistic devices were also emerging within jazz itself. The solo piano style (*stride*, for example, which was otherwise known as "Harlem") began to develop in New York. It was an attractive loud, rhythmic style, which would catch on and become a staple of early jazz. This distinctive way of playing was created by James P. Johnson (1894–1955). "Rhapsody in Blue," by Gershwin, was one of the most successful jazz pieces of the early period. Paul Whiteman's Orchestra began to make its recordings during this era as well. Whiteman (1890–1967) was of the first to mix his dance arrangements with jazz.

In 1921, recording companies became hip to the up and coming market of music performed by black musicians. The audience was anxious to hear more, and artists were bustling with new and innovative forms of jazz. Among these artists, black female singers much as Bessie Smith, Clara Smith, Trixie Smith, Ethel Waters, Alberta Hunter, and Ida Cox were on the rise to fame and popularity. Bessie Smith (1894–1937) was representative of black women performers during this era. She exuded a powerful, tough persona common among female blues singers during this time. Smith would later become known as the "Empress of the Blues."

Early Swing

Swing music emerged in relation to jazz. The difference, however, is that swing music was more upbeat, and designed for dancing. Many notables musicians were responsible for the popularity of swing. One was Fletcher Henderson (1897–1952), who came to New York from Atlanta to pursue a career in the music business. By 1923, he had become a piano accompanist to many singers, including Bessie Smith. He was at the center of the blues craze during this time, and his band was celebrated for rising above the stereotypes that clung to much African American music. Benny Goodman (1909–1986) was another important figure in the rise of swing music. In the 1920s he was a part of the Ben Pollack Band, a white band that appealed to the young college crowd, and was both an influence on and inspiration for white swing bands of the 1930s.

Edward Kennedy "Duke" Ellington (1899–1976) first made his mark in New York as leader of the band named the Washingtons. Ellington played a wide variety of styles, making it his goal to sound much like Henderson. His fame began to rise once he began performing at the Cotton Club in 1927. Shows at the club included scenes that appealed to the white audiences' desire for a sexually charged and forbidden atmosphere, which was linked exclusively to black culture. Ellington composed many original pieces that complemented the dances at this club. By 1930, both Henderon and Ellington stood out as leaders of the emerging swing style.[12]

A musician who spent a good deal of his time playing around on 52nd Street was Charlie Parker (1920–1955). Parker settled in New York in 1944, teaming up with Dizzy Gillespie. The two created a powerful sound that would map the course for much of the New York jazz scene. Dizzy helped reintegrate the Spanish tinge or Latin rhythms into jazz, and in 1945 formed a big band to bring bop concert to this era. In 1947, the group added Chano Pozo (1915–1968), a Cuban drummer working in New

Duke Ellington directing his band from the piano at the Hurricane Cabaret, New York City, 1943. Courtesy Library of Congress.

York. This eclectic mix began a trend of bongos, congas, and Latin rhythms in jazz and orchestras of the day.

One of the important early women jazz musicians was Billie Holiday (1915–1959). Holiday began recording under Benny Goodman, quickly assimilating the style of Louis Armstrong. By 1938, her musical career was on the rise as she teamed up with tenor saxophonist Lester Young. Notably, Holiday was part of an important and emerging small group involved in a new music activity that was happening on New York's 52nd Street. Eventually, this bustling activity would stimulate the beginning of an era known as bebop.

Big Bands, Swing, and Bebop

In the wake of World War II, jazz band members were beginning to cluster in some of America's major urban centers. After the war years, big bands and new ensembles began experimenting, as they were growing tired of traditional forms of music. Music was becoming commercial, and musicians were interested in taking a more artistic approach. To be more specific, they wanted to integrate the musical scene of 52nd Street and to reawaken an interest in an incorporation of modern western art music.

In the 1940s, Claude Thornhill (1909–1965) formed the Thornhill Band. Gil Evans (1912–1988) arranged bebop concerts for them. The band consisted of a cross-section of 52nd Street members and was headed by trumpet player Miles Davis, who was backed by John Carisi (1922–1992) and Gerry Mulligan (1927–1996). In the late 1940s, Evans's apartment near 52nd Street became a conservatory for many young musicians and writers. This band, known as the Birth of Cool, did not become popular until the early 1950s.

The 1950s were a musical turning point. Essentially, jazz was beginning to become more "Americanized." In this regard, it was losing some of its original flavor, and many African American musicians sought to reclaim their music by integrating some of the original characteristic sounds of the genre. The jazz of the 1950s consisted of hard bop, cool bop, funky, third stream, modal, and free. This diversity reflected both the ethnic and geographic influences within jazz. Cool jazz was essentially becoming the popularized form of this genre. As it began to lose its authenticity, young black musicians felt bound to reclaim its original sound by rebelling against this change in tone.

Hard Bop

One of the outstanding and essential characteristics of African American jazz was the strong beat. Many hard bop styles were shaped by drummers Kenny Clarke, Max Roach, and Art Blakey. Because of the emphasis on drumbeats, complex rhythms were being worked into jazz. In conjunction with this new spin on jazz, rhythm and blues began to develop (starting in the 1940s), much to the dismay of many young black jazz musicians. R & B offered a far more subdued and bluesy feel to this type of music. Horace Silver, born in 1929, combined R & B with Latin music into bebop. He brought this fresh approach to New York in the 1950s. Silver worked with artists such as Miles Davis and Art Blakey, and worked to introduce a funky feel, which was a mix between popular music and jazz.

One key musician to compose during this diverse period was Miles Davis (1926–1990), an established leader and stylist in the jazz community. By 1945, he was dabbling with hard bop (playing with pianist Horace Silver). By the 1950s he was exploring hard bop, and had a successful quintet of players. In 1956, Davis was working with Columbia Records, participating in a third stream brass choir. Davis's ensemble would evolve throughout his career, eventually moving toward a more modal style. This was the closest form at the time to freestyle jazz.

Another important musician was John Coltrane (1926–1967). Coltrane moved to Philadelphia in 1943, eventually becoming acquainted with Davis in New York around 1955. However, Coltrane was battling a heavy heroin addiction that seriously affected his musical performance. Coltrane was eventually able to overcome his addiction, and in 1958 rejoined Davis. By the 1960s, he would leap from a side artist to a highly influential lead artist, which would affect many other jazz bands.

While much of the musical development of the twentieth century occurred in New York City, its effects were felt throughout the region. Newark, New Jersey, for instance, was one of *the* happening nightlife spots from 1925 to 1950. The Orpheum, built in 1872 and reconstructed in 1910, was an important stop on the African American theater circuit. It was shabby and a bit run-down in comparison to other downtown theaters. Even so, it was known as a showplace for the black community, and held some of the most elite and popular black acts at the time, including Bojangles, Butterbeans and Susie, and the legendary Bessie Smith. Wilton Crawley was one of the most popular performers at the Orpheum, and was lovingly known for being able to make his clarinet "talk like a chicken."

Though not a giant in terms of famous musicians or events, Delaware became a diverse center for musical activity in the twentieth century. Wilmington, for example, supports a symphony orchestra as well as a professional theater. Many community theater groups are found in Newark and Dover, and the Grand Opera House in Wilmington is a popular site as well. Delaware has one of its biggest music festivals at the Schwartz Center for the Arts, which works to bring artists from all over the country to perform. Delaware has an incredible folk following as well, with organizations such as the Delaware Friends of Folk, a nonprofit organization that works to promote the popularity of folk music in the state. The group sponsors the Delmarva Folk Festival. Other large and popular musical centers in the state include the Delaware Valley Philharmonic Orchestra, the Delaware Symphony Orchestra, the Newark Symphony Orchestra, and the Delaware's Children Theater in Wilmington.

FOLK MUSIC

Secular music had its counterpart in folk music. Not designed for the elite world of orchestral halls and theater spaces, folk music was more informal than art music. Generally speaking, folk music did not necessarily have consistent vocals or rhythm. It was more of a pastime for people to escape the rigors of everyday life. Characteristic of folk music were free-flowing ballads, dance tunes, and work songs. Because of the heavy class divide, the working class was generally unable to attend formal musical performances. Since many of the events were pricey, for the most part only wealthy individuals were able to enjoy this form of music. These influences informed the how folk music came to be an expression of those who were oppressed by society. Folk music became a means of escape from the overtly repressive class system governing workers' lives.

During the late nineteenth and early twentieth centuries, folk music in the New Jersey area began to shift to a more sacred context as religious life became more pronounced. As Jewish immigrants began to settle in many East Coast cities, the Yiddish theater music establishment flourished. Presbyterianism, however, was the religion most widely practiced, and because of the generally conservative nature of the religion at the time, the use of musical instruments was prohibited.[13] One of the most important, yet perhaps least recognized facts, is that much folk music was directly influenced by African Americans. West Virginia's first settlers brought slaves with them, and in an attempt to escape their tumultuous lives, slaves often looked to the arts. This historical context made West Virginia something of a center for folk music. African Americans spent much of their time singing and hymning tunes in an effort to engage in something more than the immediate confines of the system of slavery. Eventually, their hymns would catch on as a form of music. Many African Americans played the fiddle and various other string instruments. As a result, the fiddle became one of the primary instruments involved in folk music.

To this day West Virginia remains one of the largest centers for folk music in the United States. Much of the music reflected local customs, and was richly painted with emotion. The folk music of the area, and the manner in which it expanded to other realms of artistic expression, was faithful to cultural values and identity. For instance, with folk music comes a great amount of dancing—often reflective of local cultural customs. In the late eighteenth and early nineteenth cen-

To this day West Virginia remains one of the largest centers for folk music in the United States. This Appalachian string band performs at a summer music festival. Photo by David Fattaleh. Courtesy West Virginia Tourism.

turies, the German influence on folk music was heavy, which can be heard in many folk tunes in West Virginia and Pennsylvania. The Pennsylvania Germans (the Pennsylvania Dutch) were among the first to develop folk music in the state. In May 1935, George Korson mounted the first annual Pennsylvania Folk Festivalin Allentown. Many of the songs were performed by Pennsylvanian Germans, and the event itself would be one of the first festivals to be recorded for a major record company.

The fiddle was the instrument of choice for all of West Virginian folk music. Specific areas in West Virginia with strong fiddling traditions include Webster, Pocahontas, Clay, Calhoun, and Braxton. Lewis Johnson "Uncle Jack" McElwain (1856–1938) was known as one of the greatest fiddlers of his time, and led the genre by creating and performing numerous tunes which were reflective of his time. McElwain would eventually become an important model for later folk music.

Folk Music in the Early Twentieth Century

Early-twentieth-century folk music within the mid-Atlantic states consisted primarily of English folk song repertories. For the most part, such songs have taken as their subject maritime occupations in this area. In addition, an important urban folk song movement developed around the end of the twentieth century, focusing on the importation of the southern rural folk song tradition to the North. This movement eventually found a home in Greenwich Village. A musician known as Leadbelly (Huddie Ledbetter, 1885–1949) was an important figure in the movement. One of his best-known songs was "Bourgeois Blues." An important folk club in the village was The Bitter End, which served as a springboard for folk musicians throughout the 1960s. Peter, Paul, and Mary made their debut at The Bitter End in 1961.

During the 1930s and 1940s in New York, there was a great degree of social revolution. Pete Seeger (b. 1919) assembled a group known as the Almanac Singers. His ideas, energy, and dedication led protesting folk song movements throughout the 1940s. The principal causes espoused by the Almanac Singers were opposition to the war and supporting unions. Their main goal was to bring people together in support of peace. Woody Guthrie would eventually join the group, also in support of peace.[14]

Ani DiFranco

Arguably the best-known politically active folk singer/songwriter of the present era is Ani DiFranco (1970–). Born in Buffalo, New York, she has devoted most of her musical energies to fighting social repression. Commenting upon notions of the personal and the political in her music, DiFranco has said: "Since political edifices are purporting to dictate me, whether I can or cannot have an abortion, what drugs I can or cannot ingest, where on this earth I can and cannot go, and who on this earth I can love (just to name a few things), then it seems obvious to me that the personal is political. . . . Conversely, once you understand yourself to be connected to other living things, and the earth beneath your feet, you respond to the oppression of people and the destruction of the environment by governments by taking it personally. . . . The personal and the political are of one realm; to separate them is artificial."[15]

Her music is rarely heard on the radio, as she chooses to not become commercialized, and instead promotes her music through live concerts and tours. She sells her albums through her independently-owned record company, Righteous Babe Records, which is located in Buffalo, and continues to successfully produce many albums, averaging one or two a year. Her albums include her first, self-titled work *Ani Difranco* (1990), followed by among others, *Out of Range* (1994), *Dilate* (1996), her first live album, *Living in Clip* (1997), *Up Up Up Up Up Up* (1999), *Evolve* (2003), and *Educated Guess* (2003).

The Rock and Roll Era

Bob Dylan was one of the many to begin this movement. Arriving in New York in the fall of 1960, he began singing folk songs in Greenwich Village, which was a popular youth hangout. His penetrating social commentary took a stand against big business, the military, and politicians. Dylan inspired many founders of rock and roll. His albums include *Desire* (1976), *Slow Train Coming* (1979), *Dylan* (1973), *Empire Burlesque* (1985), *Time out of Mind* (1997), and *Love and Theft* (2001). Among his many famous songs are "All Along the Watchtower," "Hurricane," "Everything Is Broken," "Like a Rolling Stone," "Mr. Bojangles," and "Mr. Tambourine Man."

Frankie Avalon

Born on September 18, 1940, in Philadelphia, Frankie Avalon was an important part of the sound that emerged in the Philadelphia region during the late 1950s and early 1960s. He began playing music professionally around the age of thirteen when he formed a band in Atlantic City, New Jersey. He quickly became a local celebrity and soon went on to perform on Paul Whiteman's television show in Philadelphia. He eventually made his way to nationally broadcast television shows, such as *The Jackie Gleason Show*. His first records were released in 1957, and one of his biggest hits came out the following year, titled "Dede Dinah." Avalon pursued a successful acting career as well, starring in the motion picture *Disc Jockey Jamboree*. His other films include *Guns of the Timberland* and *The Carpetbaggers*.

The Rascals were another powerful voice in the movement of peaceful resistance. The white group from New York created a mix of gospel and southern soul to create antiracist lyrics. One of their most popular singles was "People Got to Be Free" (1968), a social commentary about repressive political constructions.

In the late 1960s, one of the most quintessential pop groups to emerge was the Mamas and the Papas. Cass Elliot (Ellen Naomi Cohen), known as "Mama," was born in Baltimore on September 19, 1941. She developed her musical interests when she was young, and chose to rebel against her parents' wishes that she attend a prestigious women's music college when she graduated from high school. She moved to New York City and became involved in the folk scene. In Greenwich Village, she joined a group known as the Big Three, and continued singing folk music until she formed with the Mamas and the Papas. Their first album, released in 1966, was called *If You Can Believe Your Eyes and Ears*. The first single to be released from it was "California Dreamin," followed later by their hit "Monday, Monday." After the group separated, she achieved success as a soloist, but died suddenly in a London hotel room of a heart attack in 1974.

Around the middle of the twentieth century, commercially mediated working-class and rural musical forms disrupted the dominance of Tin Pan Alley music. Genre categories were hardening, segregating artists as well as audiences along racial lines. Rock and roll was originally created by black Americans (the rhythms of rock and roll could be heard as early as the late 1920s in certain country blues recordings), but was taken over by white artists and white businessmen who established control the industry. Thus, rock and roll was not solely a form of music; it was an ideological construct that coincided with social claims to power. Because of commercialism, many rock musicians fought against the power of big business, which imposed homogenizing musical genre categories across the board, categories more useful to the music industry than to the artists. The 1960s especially were a time when rock artists began to speak out through music.

Woodstock

Woodstock was a three-day, peace-promoting musical extravaganza held in Bethel, New York, August 15–17, 1969. The event was intended to promote peace through art and expression. Over 500,000 people attended the event. The highly diverse crowd, included everyone from anti-war protestors to antigovernment advocates to human rights activists. Each came to proclaim and celebrate "Three Days of Peace and Music" (the slogan of Woodstock). The event exemplified the nonviolent, antiwar sentiment that was running through the country. The event cost over $2.4 million and was sponsored by John Roberts, Joel Rosenman, Artie Kornfeld, and Michael Lang.

Among some of the famous musicians who played were Crosby, Stills, & Nash (& Young), Santana, Sweetwater, Creedence Clearwater Revival, Jefferson Airplane, The Who, Grateful Dead, Jimi Hendrix, Janis Joplin, and Joe Cocker. Because of this gathering, many social barriers were torn down, resulting in a remarkably successful and important moment in rock and roll. The first anniversary of Woodstock was held in 1994, and it would again be revisited in 1999 in Rome, New York.

Also during the 1970s, disc jockeys became popular as music performers. Disc jockeys developed innovative ways of creating music by mixing and cutting on turntables. This was the beginning of the era of disco, which attracted a large part of the populace to dance clubs and bars. Different dance crazes had hit the nation before disco, made manifest, for instance, in the astoundingly popular TV show *American Bandstand* (which originated in Philadelphia). But disco was a much larger phenomenon. In the 1970s clubs called discotheques popped up everywhere. Among the most famous was New York's Peppermint Lounge, along with its house band, Joey Dee and the Starliters. The group would go on to perform their hit (which was dedicated to the lounge), "Peppermint Twist." Other dances that were popularly performed in addition to the twist included the pony, the mashed potatoes, and the monkey.

Hip-Hop and Rap Music

During the late 1950s through the 1960s, many Puerto Ricans and African Americans collaborated musically, mainly due to the facts of racial exclusion. Hip-hop was born out of this fusion. Early street-based bands such as the Harptones, Vocaleers, and Frankie Lymon and the Teenagers combined black and Latin members. The music was essentially African American rock and roll with subtle mambo beats. The Latin influence craze was prevalent during the late 1960s, and was marked by musicians Pete Rodriguez, Joe Cuba, and Joe Bataan.

Rap first began in the Bronx during the mid-1970s when African American poets added musical beats to their spoken words. Street sounds, drum beats, and many other forms of instrumental music were used as accompaniment. J. Saddler was the first to take rap to a more advanced level when he learned to mix music from two turntables. Rap was the subject of much controversy because it was used as a vehicle for many underprivileged African Americans to speak out against political repression, impoverished living conditions, violence, and many other daunting issues with which they were faced. Despite the harsh criticisms, rap sprouted at a rapid pace all along the East Coast including New York City, Washington, D.C., and Philadelphia. When the Sugar Hill Gang wrote "Rapper's Delight" in 1979, rap caught on nationally. Shortly thereafter, two early forms of rap music emerged: Old School and New School. Old School (1979–1984) was the first genre in rap music and shaped the very nature of its style. Important artists from this genre include Kool DJ Herc, Grandmaster Flash and the Furious Five, Afrika Bambaataa,

Kool Moe D, and the Fantastic Freaks. The very sound of rap music changed with the beginning of New School in 1984. From here on out, rap became incredibly innovative and complex with artists such as Public Enemy, LL Cool J, and Rakim. It was essentially blues-derived and infused with African American traditions. Its quintessential components included the combination of improvisation, alternation, and tongue-twisting lyricism. One of the earliest Puerto Rican rappers was Rubie Dee, who was also one of the first musicians to rap in Spanish. Tomas Robles ("TNT") was another important cultural icon of Puerto Rican rap. He was one of many who used rap as a vehicle to affirm his history, language, and culture under the repressive conditions of exclusion and discrimination. He is known as a hard-core street-wise lyricist with a strong sense of history entwined with poetics.[16]

As with ragtime, jazz, and swing, the new era of hip-hop and rap also brought with it a new style of dance. Break dancing eventually came along with the evolution of hip-hop. Many joined in this freestyle upbeat style of expression. One of the earliest contributors was the Puerto Rican group Rock Steady Crew, which eventually became one of the most accomplished break dance groups of the 1980s.

Hip-hop originated within the ghettoes of New York City. It began with the first Disc Jockey, Kool Herc, who later integrated rapping into the style as well. Other early hip-hop artists include Grand Wizard Theodore and Grandmaster Flash, who invented two of the quintessential components in hip-hop today: scratching and the backspin. Run-DMC was the first major hip-hop artist to get a break on MTV. It was more than just a style of music, however—it was a culture, a way of life. The earliest aspects of hip-hop include graffiti, break dancing, and block parties. Started by Taki 183, the art of graffiti became incredibly popular among the black and Latino communities in the streets of New York.

The New York Punk Scene

Punk music began in the 1970s as a direct rebellion against increasing corporatization. Punk rock originated in New York City, and three of the earliest groups were the Velvet Underground, the Stooges, and the New York Dolls. Much punk music was characteristically rough-edged and anticommercial, with a focus on topics such as sexual deviancy, drug addiction, violence, and social alienation. The New York Dolls, for example, rejected traditionally instituted male gender norms, and performed many of their concerts in fishnet stockings, bright red lipstick, feather boas, and army boots. The popularity of the punk scene picked up speed during the mid-1970s and began to infiltrate the club scene. In fact, one of the first clubs to collectively center this punk craze was a converted music club called CBGB & OMFUG (Country, Bluegrass, Blues & Other Music for Urban Gourmandizers), which was located in Manhattan. Patti Smith (b. 1946), a New York–based poet and singer, was the first rock musician to regularly perform at this club. Shortly thereafter, the club grew immensely popular, and it was not uncommon to see groups such as Television, Blondie, and the Voidoids perform there. The first authentic punk band was the Ramones, formed in 1974 in New York City. The Ramones began to perform consistently at the CBGB in 1975, and after signing a record deal with Sire Records (an independent label), they became increasingly well known. The Talking Heads, formed in 1974, first appeared at CBGB's in 1975 as the opening act for the Ramones. The band's style reflected

The Ramones, punk rock pioneers from New York City. Photofest.

their interest in minimalism—which emphasizes the combinations of a limited number of elements (such as colors, sounds, and words). This musical approach was becoming increasingly popular in the New York art music scene of the 1960s and 1970s, and the Talking Heads helped merge minimalism into the alternative rock scene. Composers such as Steve Reich, Terry Riley, and Philip Glass were also known for making this style popular.

D.C. Hardcore

This style of music began in 1976 and picked up speed with the punk movement in Washington, D.C., during the 1980s. Creative, loud, fast, energetic, and politically charged, hardcore was one of the most popular music scenes to emerge in D.C. Some of the earliest bands, such as Minor Threat and The Faith, became incredibly political and merged with many activist organizations. Hardcore also brought its activism to bear against the monopolization of its music. Dischord Records, an independent record label, was created in an attempt to fight the widespread corporatization of music by major record companies. The scene began with bands such as White Boy, Teen Idles, the Untouchables, and Rites of Spring, and continued with—Fugazi and Good Charlotte. Hardcore expanded along the East Coast and served as a springboard for later musical styles, such as emo and grunge.

Avant-Garde Music

From the late 1970s until the early 1990s, avant-garde music (which, significantly, was not categorized as such by those who performed it) began to develop in underground New York City. Laurie Anderson (b. 1947), who was part of the emerging New York avant-garde scene, began thinking about developing her musical career further when she met composer Philip Glass. The lyrics were anything but mainstream, and they often included powerful social commentary. During the late 1980s, artists such as Anderson were using less music and more political commentary in their performances.

Rhys Chatham was another artist who challenged mainstream music. He was one of the first to experiment with rock aesthetics and classical music. Born in Manhattan in 1952, he developed an interest in minimalism. He combined the two elements and created his own style. Chatham was the first musical director of the Kitchen in New York City. He was in charge of the musical programming between 1971–1973 and 1977–1980. He challenged the classical world of music by creating this new fusion of music, and his most notable works were written for massive ensembles of 100 electric guitars, and include "An Angel Moves Too Fast to See" (1989), "Warehouse of Saints, Songs for Spies" (1991), and "Music for Tauromaquila" (1992–1993).

John Zorn (b. 1953) began the free improvisation movement, otherwise known as New York Noise. This style dominated music in New York and other large cities from 1983–1990, and is still highly active today. The downtown improvisation scene of the 1980s prided itself on the difficulty of the music. Zorn, known as the downtown postmodernist, took music cuts from a vast array of musical genres including European avant-garde, bluegrass, bebop, Beethoven, heavy metal, TV commercials, Indian ragas, and

Bruce Springsteen and the E Street Band

Bruce Springsteen (1949–) is often credited with putting New Jersey on the rock and roll map. Springsteen arose from the Jersey Shore musical scene that also yielded such artists as Billy Chinnock and Southside Johnny and the Asbury Jukes. Beginning with his first albums, *Greetings from Asbury Park, N.J.* (1973) and *The Wild, the Innocent, and the E Street Shuffle* (1974), Springsteen and his band recorded folk-inspired rock songs full of youthful romance and rock mythology, often set in New Jersey locales. His breakthrough album, *Born to Run* (1975), set the tone for 1970s American rock and roll with its combination of revved-up rock and poetic sensibilities. New Jersey once considered making the title song its state song.

Springsteen often sings about Freehold, New Jersey, his hometown, in his music. "My Hometown," from the album *Born in the USA* (1984), is a song mainly about Main Street, a place in his town in which he spent most of his youth. In "Born to Run," he sings about his two-story home next door to Ducky Slattery's Sinclair station on South Street, as well as the school he attended as a youth, St. Rose of Lima. Many of his songs are dedicated to the working-class neighborhood in New Jersey where he grew up. In 2002, he released *The Rising*, an album largely inspired by the September 11, 2001, terrorist attacks.

Bruce Springsteen. Photofest.

Activism in the 1980s and 1990s

During the 1980s and 1990s, a new type of musical activism broke loose in direct response to AIDS and HIV. William Parker (1943–1993) was responsible for one of the first gatherings to bring together artists and composers in response to the oppression many AIDS victims were suffering. He asked composers to write a three- to five-minute song that would serve as a musical panel. The premiere of this ground-breaking event occurred in Alice Tully Hall, in New York City, on June 4, 1992. The songbook that resulted was one of the most important compilations of music to come from artists and composers against AIDS.

Many of the pieces addressing the AIDS situation were in the form of testimonials. They were filled with anger directed not at the disease, but toward those who stigmatized AIDS victims. Many of the works were aimed at government bureaucracies, social services, the slow-moving search for a cure, and a society that was generally uncaring. The music also responded to problems of marginalization, ignorance, and systems of power that denigrated those with this disease.

In regard to this activism, the Broadway musical *Rent* (1996) was created by Jonathan Larson to open the public's eyes to the AIDS pandemic. Movements such as these were intended to speak out against social, political, religious, and medical responses of people in positions of power who were neglecting not only those afflicted with the disease, but anyone who came to be associated with the epidemic: "gay men, ethnic and racial minorities, lower social classes, the impoverished, women, and other so-called social eyesores."[17]

thrash. In 1974, he assembled a group of musicians who began writing pieces, and in 1986, his breakthrough to the public came in a recording called *The Big Gundown*. A good example of his work is shown "Cat o' Nine Tails" (1988). This piece was composed for a string quartet and consisted of sixty movements, which included quotations from other string quartets, cartoon elements, tangos, waltzes, classical cadences, and noise.[18]

CONCLUSION

Music has played a tremendous role in the lives of many since the beginnings of human interaction in the mid-Atlantic region. From the first Delaware and Iroquois Indians to the early German and Irish settlers, from the African Americans of the early twentieth century to the more recent Cuban influence, music in the Mid-Atlantic has been influenced by a rich mix of diverse peoples and traditions. The music of each of these distinct cultures and races contributed extensively and underwent transformations that occurred locally in the Mid-Atlantic: the movement from minstrelsy to ragtime and the rise of big bands; the founding of the region's first Irish orchestra by Paddy Killoran in New York City; the bringing of Cuban music to Broadway by Don Azpiazu and his Havana Casino Orchestra; the establishment of the "Philadelphia Sound" by Eugene Ormandy and the Philadelphia Orchestra; the documentation of a New Jersey working-class background in the songs of Bruce Springsteen, to mention a few examples. In addition, musicians in the Mid-Atlantic have also fought against the homogenization and corporatization of music, as in the case of the independent recordings of ethnic musicians in the early twentieth century, and the folk musicians such as Ani Difranco who keep this tradition alive by establishing and maintaining independent recording labels in the late twentieth and early twenty-first centuries. Music in the Mid-Atlantic thus arises in reaction to historical processes, and more often than not, it empowers regional artists to transcend the economic, political, racial, and cultural limitations imposed on their artistic creativity. From classical to folk to jazz to rock, music in the Mid-Atlantic has been an indissoluble part of the region's distinct creativity and history.

RESOURCE GUIDE

Printed Sources

Ahlquist, Karen. *Democracy at the Opera: Music, Theater, and Culture in New York City: 1815–60*. Champaign: University of Illinois Press, 1997.

Allen, Ray, and Wilcken, Lois, eds. *Island Sounds in the Global City: Caribbean Popular Music and Identity in New York City*. New York: New York Folklore Society and Institute for Studies in American Music, Brooklyn College, 1998.

Beebe, Richard. *Rock Over the Edge*. Durham: Duke, 2002.

Daulhaus, Carl. *Foundations of Music History*. New York: University of Cambridge, 1997.

Gann, Kyle. *American Music in the Twentieth Century*. New York: Schirmer, 1997.

Goepp, Philip H., ed. *Annals of Music in Philadelphia and History of the Musical Fund Society*. New York: Da Capo, 1973.

Goodman, Henry. *The New Country*. New York: Syracuse, 2001.

Grushkin, Paul. *The Art of Rock*. New York: Abbeville, 1987.

Heintz, James R. *Perspectives on American Music Since 1950*. New York: Garland, 1999.

Idelsohn, Abraham Z. *Jewish Music: Its Historical Development*. New York: Dover, 1992.

Jablonski, Edward. *The Encyclopedia of American Music*. New York: Doubleday, 1981.

Kaufman, Charles H. *The Music of the Eighteenth Century New Jersey*. Newark: New Jersey Historical Commission, 1975.

Keil, Charles, and Angeliki V. Keil. *Polka Happiness*. Philadelphia: Temple University Press, 1992.

Kingman, Daniel. *American Music: A Panorama*. New York: Schirmer, 1979.

Kukla, Barbara, J. *Swing City: Newark Nightlife, 1925–50*. Piscataway, NJ: Rutgers University Press, 2002.

LeBlanc, Michael L. *Contemporary Musicians: Profiles of the People in Music* Detroit: Gale, 1991.

Marsh, Dave. *Born to Run: The Bruce Springsteen Story*. New York: Doubleday, 1979.

Merriam, Alan P. *Anthropology of Music*. Chicago: Northwestern University Press, 1964.

Milnes, Gerald. *Play of a Fiddle: Traditional Music, Dance, and Folklore in West Virginia*. Lexington: University Press of Kentucky, 1999.

Nettl, Bruno. *Comparative Musicology and Anthropology of Music: Essays on the History of Ethnomusicology*. Chicago: University of Chicago Press, 1991.

Nicholls, David. *The Cambridge History of American Music*. New York: Cambridge University Press, 1999.

Rohrer, Gertrude Martine. *Music and Musicians of Pennsylvania*. New York: Kennikat, 1970.

Spaeth, Sigmund, and William J. Perlman, eds. *Music and Dance in the Southeastern States*. New York: Alectra, 1952.

Sportswood, Richard. *Ethnic Recordings in America: A Neglected Heritage*. Washington, DC: Library of Congress, 1982

Starr, Larry, and Christopher Waterman. *American Popular Music*. New York: Oxford, 2003.

Wilson, Earl. *Sinatra*. New York: Macmillan, 1976.

Web Sites

Ani Difranco's record company home page
http://www.righteousbabe.com

Bob Fosse biography
http://www.nodanw.com/biographies/bob_fosse.htm

Davey D's Hip Hop Corner
http://www.daveyd.com/blackculturelet2.htm

Music in Delaware
http://www.delaware.info/2Music.htm

Rap
http://www.katharinen.ingolstadt.de/projekte/lurz/rap1.htm

Tiber, Elliot. *How Woodstock Happened*. Times Herald-Record, 1994.
http://www.woodstock69.com

Tin Pan Alley
http://www.kcmetro.cc.us/pennvalley/biology/lewis/crosby/tinpan.htm

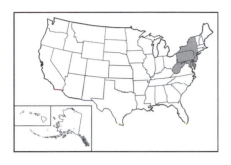

RELIGION

Jeremy Bonner

The mid-Atlantic colonies began their existence as laboratories for religious pluralism. Despite being positioned between the Congregationalist establishment in New England and the Church of England dominance found farther south in Virginia, North Carolina, South Carolina, and Georgia, the authorities in the Middle Colonies had stability and settlement as their principal objectives and chose to allow considerable local initiative in religious practice, particularly in Pennsylvania. The region's inhabitants largely embraced the American Revolution and applied the rhetoric of liberty not only to their political situation but to their religious denominations, seeking greater acceptance for personal spirituality and a lessened reliance on theological nuance. In the years after the Revolutionary War, upstate New York and western Pennsylvania helped incubate the national spiritual rebirth known as the Second Great Awakening. It was here that some of the strongest forces for moral reform, most notably the abolitionist movement, found their home in the years preceding the Civil War.

The Mid-Atlantic did not long remain a Protestant bastion, however. Its rapid urbanization and industrialization served as a magnet for immigrant Catholics and Jews seeking greater economic opportunity and political refuge. This influx quickly transformed the region's cities during the late nineteenth century, turning whole neighborhoods into ethnic and religious enclaves. Many of these newcomers had a much less well-defined "American" religiosity than their Protestant neighbors and continued to adhere to traditions and practices brought from abroad. Beginning in the 1910s, they were increasingly supplemented by waves of black Protestants fleeing poverty in the South and seeking a new life in the urban North. The mainline Protestant denominations responded to these successive influxes by the development of a new theology known as the Social Gospel, which called for a greater emphasis on alleviating the social problems of industrialism. Under the leadership of such men as Richard Ely and Walter Rauschenbusch, they forged a network of "institutional churches" in all the major denominations that sought to minister to the working-class communities around them.

With the end of widespread immigration in the mid-1920s, Catholics and Jews both began to abandon the ties that had previously linked them to the religion and culture of their countries of origin and fashioned doctrinal stands that took account of their status as Americans. By 1930 the Mid-Atlantic had become one of the most heavily Catholic regions in the United States and the church had finally shed its feelings of social inferiority. In 1928 American Catholics made a new incursion into the public sphere with the presidential candidacy of Al Smith of New York. The Mid-Atlantic thus began to demonstrate, once again, the sort of religious pluralism that had prevailed during colonial days, although it was increasingly accompanied by a rising tide of secularism that threatened to make religious identity in urban areas more a marker of ethnic than spiritual identity. Today, most major denominations are experiencing a loss of membership and income and a declining comprehension of religious practices and traditions by their members. Yet the churches remain an important instrument of social cohesion, whether in the declining coalfields of West Virginia or the black ghettos of Newark and Harlem, and in New York City one still can find a modern example of the old-fashioned enclave in the Hasidic Jews of Williamsburg.

IROQUOIS PRACTICES

The earliest forms of religion in the mid-Atlantic region were those practiced by the Northern Iroquois of the New York region and the Delaware tribes of Maryland and Delaware, whose rituals largely reflected those of the Iroquois. Iroquois theology acknowledged both a creator spirit and an array of minor deities. Religious festivals were held at the commencement of the planting season, at the ripening of the first fruits, and at harvest time, and included a report on the condition of the village, thanksgiving prayers, dancing, and feasting. On occasion, a special bowling game, symbolizing the struggle of the creator spirit with the forces of darkness, was also played. The most important religious festival was the midwinter rite held in late January, which marked the start of the new year and was an occasion not only for songs and prayers of thanksgiving but also for the interpretation of dreams, on which the Iroquois placed great spiritual significance, by members of a medicine society known as the Chanters for the Dead. Other medicine societies included the masked False-faces, who were charged with healing the sick, and the Husk-faces, who represented spirits with knowledge of hunting and agriculture. Although most major life events were not surrounded by ritual, the Iroquois had a great fear of death and ghosts, and their death rituals were most elaborate, with mourning and the burying of a dead person's possessions with his corpse, followed by a ten-day feast. The Iroquois enjoyed a highly developed political system, but the wars of the eighteenth century destroyed the Iroquois Confederacy, and its religious life was but a shadow of its former self by 1789.

COLONIAL RELIGION, 1600–1776

Christianity in the mid-Atlantic region began with the Dutch settlement of New Amsterdam (1626–1664), where the local authorities followed the practice of the mother country in permitting the existence of dissenting sects but denying them the right of public worship. The Dutch Reformed Church in the Netherlands had to approve any minister sent to the colony, and all colonists were obliged to pay tithes to support such ministers. After the transfer of the colony to English control, it became clear that a great diversity of religious belief prevailed there. A new code was drawn up for New York that provided liberty of conscience and omitted a religious test for public office, but required all towns to build a "public church," the denomination to be determined by majority vote. Ministers were required to show proof of ordination from Protestant England or a country ruled by a prince of the Reformed faith, but religious minorities were given the freedom to profess their faith and worship publicly.

Some of these gains were reversed in 1688, when religious tests for public office were introduced and Catholic worship was made illegal. Five years later, a short-lived attempt to establish the Church of England in New York (1693–1708) was launched, but this applied only to the city of New York and the counties of New York, Richmond, Queens, and Westchester. Most of the local vestries doggedly resisted efforts to force them to levy taxes to support an Anglican clergyman, most notably the Presbyterians of Jamaica parish in Queens in 1703 and 1704. After 1709, the pressure was relaxed and New York Anglicans were less inclined to be confrontational, but renewed controversy surfaced over plans to organize King's College and the issue of whether it would be controlled by the Anglican minority. This proved to be a wedge issue for non-Anglicans, especially Presbyterians, who also opposed the idea of an Anglican bishop for the colonies. In 1769 Presbyterians and Baptists founded the Society of Dissenters to combat establishment tendencies and English policy generally. At the time of the American Revolution, New Yorkers were divided over whether to give Roman Catholics full toleration, something opposed by John Jay, but ultimately Catholics were not penalized and all ministers were prohibited from holding civil or military office.

Pennsylvania and the Great Awakening

If New York represented an imperfect form of establishment, Pennsylvania was the creation of a Quaker—William Penn—who deliberately marketed his colony to religious sectarians in England, France, and Germany. Pennsylvania's first royal charter contained the requirement that no preacher approved by the bishop of London and who had been requested by at least twenty settlers could be denied residence, but the right to independence of religious belief was secured to all laymen. Office-holding was initially restricted to those who affirmed the authority of the Old and New Testaments and the divinity of Christ. After 1705 it was restricted to Protestants, but Catholics were left free to worship, own land, and vote. Such a tolerant environment proved attractive to both sects and established denominations. At least twenty-four groups came into being in the colony, the first being the Church of the Brethren. The first Lutheran church was erected on Tinicum Island in 1654, and the first American presbytery was established in Philadelphia in 1706. In 1742 Henry M. Muhlenberg arrived in Pennsylvania and within six years had organized the Ministerium of North America—the first Lutheran synod in the New World.

Pennsylvania was also a center of the Great Awakening that began in the 1720s,

Illustration of a Quaker meeting. Courtesy Library of Congress.

whose message of evangelical renewal and cooperation between the denominations played well in the colony. One of the most effective spokesman for this revival—the Anglican clergyman George Whitefield—made Philadelphia a base for his operations. Whitefield's activities contributed greatly to the establishment of colleges in New York (Columbia), New Jersey (Princeton and Rutgers), and Pennsylvania (Dickinson and the University of Philadelphia). In 1735, moreover, the Moravians arrived in North America and quickly established a major settlement at Bethlehem and Nazareth in Pennsylvania, which soon became the Northern Province of the Moravian Church in America. Its founding principle, "In essentials, unity; in non-essentials, liberty; in all things, love," reflected an emphasis on heart religion and a relationship with Christ and a ministry to those neglected by other Christian groups that spoke to Pennsylvanian religious sensibilities.

In 1776 a constitutional convention dominated by Presbyterians sought to enshrine Penn's ideals in law. Under the leadership of Judge George Bryan, author of "A Declaration of the Rights and of the Inhabitants of the Commonwealth or State of Pennsylvania," the notion of liberty of religious conscience was retained, although the right of election to the legislature was restricted to those who professed belief in God and in the divine inspiration of the Scriptures. Overall, it represented one of the most liberal constitutions drafted among the thirteen colonies and was liberalized further when it was revised in 1790 and eligibility for election to the legislature was made dependent on belief in the being of God (thus opening it to non-Christians).

New Jersey, largely unsettled before 1664, had neither the Dutch precedents for establishment nor the principled commitment of Penn toward toleration. In colonial New Jersey, it has been argued, "the goal was to keep the divisive issues of religion out of the public arena."[1] Until 1676, governors and proprietors were flexible in permitting religious diversity in order to attract settlers, though they also implemented the New York practice of selecting an official town church by majority vote. Eastern New Jersey, settled by New England Congregationalists, proved more dictatorial that Quaker-dominated West Jersey. Newark's residents restricted the franchise to church members and discouraged others from settling there. Between 1676 and 1702, Congregationalists and Quakers united in the drive to ban profanation of the Sabbath, penalize disturbing a minister conducting a service, and outlaw blasphemy and profanity, but diverged on the issues of the franchise and holding public office. In East Jersey, Catholics were barred from participation in 1698, while West Jersey required only a belief in the Trinity and the divine inspiration of Scripture. In 1702 the colony passed to the Crown, but despite the desire to establish the Church of England, few new laws were passed and attempts to restrict Quaker participation in government proved abortive. Indeed, a bill against denying Christ's divinity or the Trinity or spreading atheistical books was defeated in the legislature in 1721.

ANTEBELLUM REVIVAL, 1776–1865

The American Revolution transformed the churches in the Mid-Atlantic, none more so than those of the Anglican community, which, unlike that of Virginia, embraced the cause of England. Many clergy consequently went into exile and the Anglican-established College of Philadelphia and King's College, New York, were reorganized in 1779 and 1784, respectively, to make them nonsectarian. The great beneficiaries of the new political climate were the Methodist and Baptist churches, which maintained that the spiritual impulses of the ordinary believer were worthy of respect and that clergy should no longer be viewed as a privileged religious order. Evangelists, especially on the frontier, turned to the camp meeting, where people were encouraged directly to embrace the process of conversion and where religious emotionalism was given precedence over rational discussion of theological minutiae.

Older Protestant groups like the Congregationalists and Presbyterians,

Presbyterian Church in Rensselaerville, New York; built in 1845. Courtesy New York State Department of Economic Development.

which had supported the Revolution but continued to resist the democratic climate, found themselves outpaced. In western Pennsylvania, former Presbyterian Alexander Campbell launched a crusade for a Christianity that abandoned social distinctions and learned theology in favor of the right of all Christians to read and understand the Bible for themselves. In 1830 his movement coalesced into the Disciples of Christ, which had become the fifth largest Protestant denomination in the United States by 1860. The spirit of religious liberty embodied in Campbell's *Christian Baptist* emphasized a complete rejection of the idea of church government. Ultimately, the Presbyterians learned from the practices of the newer bodies. Their leading voice was Charles Grandison Finney, a New York lawyer ordained in 1824, who led revivals in western New York from 1825 to 1830. Refusing formal ministerial training, Finney used Methodist techniques of preaching and encouraged female participation, and in 1835 he came out against the Calvinist orthodoxy of the Old School Presbyterians.

The Methodist and Baptist Churches

Methodists and Baptists spent the first half of the nineteenth century trying to find a balance between enthusiasm and order. Methodist leader Francis Asbury encouraged the laity to participate in the process of evangelization and formally instituted the practice of itinerant ministry. By 1828 the Methodists claimed 2,500 itinerant preachers and Asbury himself annually covered 5,000 miles over a thirty-year period. Later Methodist leaders like Nathan Bangs, a preacher in New York's St. Lawrence Valley after 1801, had reservations about Methodist "enthusiasm" and tried to inculcate a more orderly approach to worship and church life. Similar tensions racked the efforts of American Baptists to create a national denomination after the General Missionary Convention of 1814, which was dominated by cosmopolitan pastors like William Staughton of Philadelphia's First Baptist Church. In 1822 these leaders helped establish Columbia College in Washington, D.C. (later George Washington University), but many ordinary Baptists viewed such institutionalization with disquiet, and Baptist groups opposed to centrally organized missionary work soon came into being in New York and Pennsylvania.

One important feature of the postrevolutionary setting was the greater willingness of Methodist and Baptist churches in the Mid-Atlantic to accept African Americans as full members. Emotional religion and the openness of the Methodists to licensing black preachers both drew many African Americans to the church, but some African Americans repudiated the paternalistic attitudes of white church leaders. In 1787 Richard Allen, a licensed Methodist preacher, led a group of African members out of St. George's Methodist Episcopal Church in Philadelphia to protest their exclusion from the life of the church and formed Bethel African Methodist Episcopal Church. Nine years later a similar secession under Peter Williams took place at John Street Methodist Episcopal Church in New York City, which led to the establishment of Zion Church. Both retained links with the white Methodist Episcopal Church until 1816, when a group of churches formed the African Methodist Episcopal Church headed by Richard Allen (today based in Tennessee). In 1820 the church's decision to send unsolicited missionaries to Philadelphia led to the establishment of the African Methodist Episcopal Zion Church (today based in North Carolina). By contrast, the Union Church of Africans, established in Wilmington, Delaware, in 1813, was the first church in the United States to be originally organized by and wholly under the control of black people. Its successor body, the African Union First Colored Methodist Protestant Church, is still based in Delaware.

Protestant Sect Formation

Popular religion also gave birth to more esoteric sects, particularly in that section of western New York known as the "Burned-Over District." It was here, in Palmyra, New York, that the Mormon prophet Joseph Smith received his famous visions that offered a new revelation that Christianity in America had fallen into apostasy and now spoke with a divided voice. Employing Old Testament images of cultural desolation and impending divine wrath, Smith gave voice to an "American" religious creed that condemned the rich, the proud, and the learned. The 1830s also witnessed the activism of William Miller, a member of Low Hampton Baptist Church, who caused a stir by issuing warnings to local ministers that the world would come to an end on October 22, 1844. Between 1831 and 1839, Miller delivered 800 sermons and acquired an extensive following in central and western New York. When his prophecy failed to be realized, however, Miller was expelled from his church, and his followers remained scattered until eventually coming together in 1863 under Ellen White to form the Seventh Day Adventist Church.

While Protestantism was undergoing its emotional upheaval, the cities of the Mid-Atlantic were experiencing the first wave of what would soon become a new religious majority—Roman Catholicism. The few prerevolutionary Catholic communities had been comparatively small and confined to states like Maryland and had also been ethnically homogeneous. Such a situation did not survive the opening of America to widespread foreign immigration. As early as 1785, German Catholics in Philadelphia had sought and been granted a "national" parish—Holy Trinity—that catered to their ethnic religious traditions. A similar state of affairs prevailed in Rochester, New York, where St. Joseph's Church was dedicated in 1837, while Philadelphia's St. Mary Magdalene de Pazzi (1852) was the first Italian Catholic parish in the United States. An increasing source of tension between lay Catholics and the clerical hierarchy during this period was the system of lay trusteeship that had governed the incorporation of Catholic churches before 1800. The legal requirement for a lay majority on boards of trustees led to conflicts with bishops from the 1830s onward over the appointment of certain parish priests. In the extreme case of St. Louis Church, Buffalo, New York, dissenting parishioners appealed to the nativist and anti-Catholic Know Nothing Party to pass the Church Property Act of 1855, upholding their authority vis-à-vis the bishop. Such a state of affairs tended to weaken the authority of the parish priest and accentuate the power of the Irish-dominated episcopate, which ultimately refused to authorize the establishment of any new parish unless its title was vested in the bishop's name. This internal politicking took place in the context of the rise of anti-Catholic groups like the Know Nothings over such issues as Bible reading in the public schools—which Catholics resisted because it involved the use of Protestant translations—and the creation of a parochial school system. Anti-Catholic riots swept America's larger cities in 1844 and again, ten years later, in Newark, New Jersey, and Brooklyn.

Religious tensions were not confined to anti-Catholic violence, however. The climate of opinion cultivated by the Second Great Awakening favored the application of evangelical morality to existing social problems. In upstate New York, in particular, many local churches became swayed by the ideology of "perfectionism," or the notion that individual spiritual rebirth necessarily involved the purification of the earthly sphere. Many found the unwillingness of their mother churches to commit themselves on vital questions of the day to be untenable, and a large number separated themselves from direct Presbyterian or Methodist oversight. Such men and women formed the shock troops for campaigns in favor of temperance and against slavery and threw themselves into politics in support of the Liberty and Free Soil parties that upheld the abolitionist cause. By the time the Civil War intervened formally to split the major Protestant denominations, many congregations in the mid-Atlantic region had long since gone their own way.

THE ERA OF IMMIGRATION, 1865–1950

The Roman Catholic Church

During the second half of the nineteenth century, the pace of foreign immigration only accelerated, and by 1880 the Roman Catholic Church had become the largest single denomination in the mid-Atlantic region. Irish migrants headed for metropolitan centers like New York and Philadelphia, while German Catholics settled in the smaller cities of the interior like Rochester and Pittsburgh. The new visibility of the Catholic population demanded the creation of an ecclesiastical infrastructure to support it, while the dominant influence of Irishmen among the clerical establishment led to the emergence of separatist "national parishes" that served ethnic communities. In 1880 this was most evident in the western fringe. The proportion of national parishes was 22 percent in Pittsburgh, 20 percent in Harrisburg, and 18 percent in Buffalo, but only 12 percent in New York City. Between 1880 and 1930, moreover, 30 percent of the new parishes established were national parishes. A critical element in the new infrastructure was the development of a parochial school system. While the schools used the curriculum from the public system, they added catechetical instruction and Bible history and served as instruments of Catholic socialization. By 1880 New York had 209 schools and 76,392 pupils, Pennsylvania had 169 schools and 44,217 pupils, and New Jersey had 80 schools and 22,503 pupils. Only 30 percent of parishes throughout the Northeast maintained schools, however, and only one-fifth of Catholic pupils were enrolled in them, not least because the Irish exerted great influence over the public school system in New York City.[2]

A new emphasis on priestly authority became necessary in the late nineteenth century, particularly as churches became dependent on organized fundraising— bazaars, lotteries, and lecture series—for their maintenance. An organized devotional life also put demands on the ordained ministry. Most parishes in the 1880s had three to five Masses every Sunday, as well as sung Vespers and monthly recitation of the Rosary, and hour-long homilies were the rule. Long hours were also devoted to the sacrament of Confession, despite the fact that many received Communion only at Easter. This grueling schedule was increasingly supplemented by devotions to the Virgin Mary as well as novenas and retreats. The Forty Hour

Public Adoration of the Blessed Sacrament first appeared in the United States in 1853 in Philadelphia and was introduced in New York in 1865. The Redemptorist Order increasingly took a leaf out of the Protestant book by organizing parish missions—revival meetings in all but name—that included Confession and Benediction. Within the parish setting, a variety of organizations came into being, both sacramental and pastoral. The former included such groups as Sodalities of the Blessed Virgin Mary (for women) and Societies of the Holy Name of Jesus (for men). In 1872 the Catholic Total Abstinence Union was formed, reflecting trends long evident in mainline Protestantism. Most parishes also boasted sickness and death benefit societies, building and loan associations (to help low-income Catholics obtain credit), and Reading Room societies. For those laymen who wished to become involved in welfare or youth work, there was membership in the Society of St. Vincent de Paul.

By the mid-1880s an increasingly large number of Catholic immigrants hailed from central Europe. Slovaks, Croats, and Slovenes settled in western Pennsylvania, while Italians and Poles largely migrated to New York. Such cultures helped spur the development of aggressively nationalist parishes, especially among the Poles, whose first church was St. Laurentius Church in Philadelphia. Many Polish parishes were racked by disputes over lay authority, which gave rise to a number of independent schismatic parishes in Buffalo in the early 1890s. Then, in 1896, a group of parishioners seceded from Sacred Heart Church, Scranton, Pennsylvania, to organize St. Stanislaus Church and called as priest Father Francis Hodur, who was excommunicated two years later for calling for his parish to have the right to administer its own property and a say in clerical appointments. In 1904 the Polish National Catholic Church (which still exists, though with declining membership) was organized from a cluster of Buffalo and Scranton parishes, and Father Hodur was consecrated a bishop by the Old Catholics in 1907.

Similar clashes took place in Slovak parishes whose parishioners resented the appointment of Hungarian priests, whom they associated with Magyarization in their mother country. In 1909 parishioners at St. Michael's Church, Homestead, who had failed to get a parish priest removed, organized St. Anne's Independent Slovak Catholic Church. In contrast, Italian parishes reflected the more village-centered culture of southern Italy than the nationalism of central Europe. Often, priests faced more indifference than conflict—especially from men—although many parishes gloried in their local saints and benevolent societies. The first Spanish national parish—Our Lady of Guadalupe—was organized in New York City in 1902, followed by Our Lady of the Miraculous Medal in Philadelphia in 1912.

Eastern Orthodox Churches

The early twentieth century also witnessed the arrival of a substantial number of Eastern Orthodox immigrants in the mid-Atlantic region. Oldest of all is the Orthodox Church in America (OCA), which began as a Russian mission to Alaska in 1794 and in 1905 was organized into an archdiocese based in New York. The OCA's Greek counterpart is the Greek Orthodox Archdiocese of North and South America, also based in New York. Formed in 1918, the archdiocese has about the same number of members as the OCA, and its current leader, Archbishop Iakovos, has been a pioneer of ecumenical dialogue. Smaller Eastern Orthodox bodies include the Antiochian Orthodox Christian Archdiocese of North America (which began as a Syrian mission in 1895 and whose Archimandrite Raphael Hawaweeny was the first Orthodox bishop consecrated in the United States), the Armenian Church of America, and the Ukrainian Orthodox Church of the United States.

Protestant Churches

While Catholicism grew stronger in the immediate aftermath of the Civil War, the reforming zeal that had animated the northern Protestant churches in the 1850s suffered a temporary setback. Until the late 1870s, they tended to express general approval about national progress and eschewed engagement in the problems of industrial society. Their churches' confidence in the continued improvement of American social conditions was severely dampened by the industrial unrest that swept the Northeast in 1877, 1886, and 1890–1894. An early voice of warning came from the Protestant Episcopal Church, including Bishop Henry Potter of New York, who frequently preached on the perils of wealth and indifference to social need. As early as 1870, St. Mark's Church in Philadelphia launched a workingmen's club, an initiative that became a model for other churches, and four years later the Episcopal Church Congress—a body dedicated to discussion of social problems—held its inaugural meeting in New York.

As the 1880s wore on, a new Protestant ideology emerged that sought to challenge secular socialism with a Christian alternative that would appeal to a largely unchurched working-class population. Richard Ely, a professor at Johns Hopkins University in Baltimore and a founder of the American Economic Association, asserted in 1886 both that Christian ethics should animate the labor movement and that workingmen should not be treated as commodities. His new formulation upheld the principles of arbitration of industrial disputes and mutual aid associations for unemployment relief and insurance purposes. Ely's book *The Social Aspects of Christianity* (1889) proved very influential in persuading mainstream Protestant leaders that the failure to deal with social regeneration represented an imperfect practice of the Gospel message. Once again, the Episcopal Church took the lead with the formation in 1887 of the Church Association for the Advancement of the Interests of Labor, which intervened in several New York labor disputes and helped begin the observance of Labor Sunday. At St. George's Episcopal Church, New York, William Rainsford helped launch the institutional church movement, which sought to give parishes the physical resources to minister to the working-class population. A subsequent initiative was the settlement house—modeled on the English Toynbee Hall—which included such examples as Kingsley Hall in Pittsburgh and Union Settlement Association in New York.

After 1900 the intellectual leadership of the Social Gospel passed to Walter Rauschenbusch, a Baptist minister from Rochester, New York, whose *Christianity and the Social Crisis* (1907) embodied the centrality of the realization of the Kingdom of God—an immanent God whose indwelling depended upon human solidarity. Rauschenbusch wrote in favor of such concepts as social justice, collective property rights, industrial democracy, and cooperation. Within all the major Protestant denominations an active Social Gospel element now emerged, whether in the form of the Presbyterian Charles Stelzle, who founded the Labor Temple on New York's East Side in 1910; the Episcopal Joint Commission on Social Service, established in 1911; or the Methodist General Conference of 1908, which articulated the "Social Creed of Methodism." That same year, the major Protestant denominations came together in Philadelphia to establish the Federal Council of Churches.

As the churches entered the 1910s, they found the optimism of the previous decade in significant decline. The Social Gospel soon fell prey to the conservatism of the 1920s, while most of the Protestant churches were forced to grapple with the implications of the debate over fundamentalism. In the case of the Presbyterians, this ultimately took the form of a full-scale secession led by Princeton Theological Seminary theologian J. Gresham Machen in 1932, which produced the Orthodox Presbyterian Church, now based in Pennsylvania, and the even more fundamentalist Bible Presbyterian Church, now based in New Jersey. The Roman Catholic Church, by contrast, having weathered its own internal crises, had begun to express a willingness to be involved in secular politics. In 1919 it had drafted a program for social reconstruction, and Father John Ryan of the Catholic University of America proved an able spokesman for social Catholicism during the 1920s. With the onset of the Great Depression and the emergence of an alliance between the Democratic Party and the labor movement, Catholicism took the lead in pushing forward the reforms of Franklin Roosevelt's New Deal, aided and abetted by priests like Ryan and Father Charles Owen Rice of Pittsburgh. By the close of World War II, the association of mid-Atlantic Catholicism with New Deal Democratic politics was complete.

Jews in the Mid-Atlantic Region

Of all the non-Christian communities that have settled in the Mid-Atlantic, it is the Jews who represent the largest community. Not only is the Jewish regional percentage higher than anywhere else (10.3 percent), but almost 45 percent of the nation's Jews reside in the mid-Atlantic states.[3] The distribution is uneven, with most Jews residing in New York (15.6 percent), Maryland (9.1 percent), and New Jersey (9.1 percent). In the District of Columbia, Jews account for a respectable 6.8 percent, but in Pennsylvania and Delaware, they represent only 4.5 percent and 3.1 percent of the churchgoing population, respectively, and in West Virginia, a statistically insignificant 0.3 percent. Such a distribution reflects the preference of Jewish immigrants for an urban environment. During the nineteenth century, East European Jews settled in New York City, Baltimore, Newark, and to a lesser extent Philadelphia—settings far removed from the *shtetl*s of Poland and Russia. Although most Jews today reside in the suburbs, they remain an overwhelmingly urban religious culture.

Although there were some Jews in the New World before 1800, it was not until the 1830s that the first wave of immigrants appeared. Early nineteenth-century Jewish migrants were largely composed of educated, upwardly mobile Jews from Germany. Most embarked upon successful careers in commerce and organized synagogues that espoused the rationalism of the Jewish Reform tradition. Such an approach coincidentally served to make these German Jews less culturally distinctive and more susceptible to assimilation into American society. The Jewish community was transformed in the 1880s, however, when waves of Polish and Russian Jews began to arrive, fleeing a resurgence of Russian anti-Semitism. These newcomers lacked either the intellectual or financial resources of their German precursors and were completely resistant to the forces of the Enlightenment on their religious culture. The Orthodoxy they espoused prescribed a complete separation from mainstream American life, and they had little in common with their assimilated coreligionists.

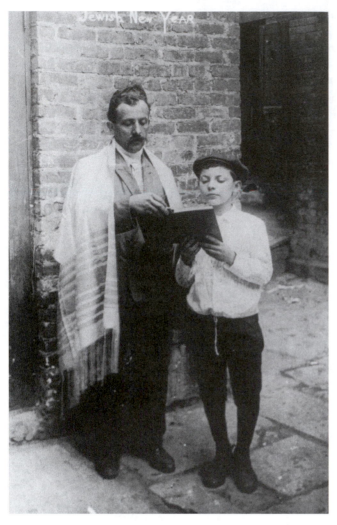

Rabbi and boy, Jewish New Year, 1907, New York City. Courtesy Library of Congress.

Within the Orthodox tradition—which represented the overwhelming majority of Jews until the 1930s—the notion of the Jews as a "chosen people" meant that conversion was always a rare event. Central to the life of the observant Jew is the proper observance of *Shabbos*—the Sabbath—which requires that no physical labor be performed from sundown on Friday to sundown on Saturday. It is no accident that familial rituals take the place of what would be regular church attendance in a Christian household, especially for women, since Jewish spirituality is rooted in the family. Within the synagogue, which is segregated by gender in Orthodox communities, prayer services are held regularly, provided that a quorum of ten male members are present. A combination of readings from the Torah (the Old Testament) and recited prayers is accompanied by homilies from the rabbi. Devout Jews will cover their heads and wear phylacteries (small boxes containing Hebrew texts on vellum) while praying. Attendance at synagogue will certainly occur during the Days of Awe—Rosh Hashanah, the two-day holiday that marks the start of the ten-day period when God decides the fate of all creation, and Yom Kippur, the day of fasting and prayer commonly known as the Day of Atonement. Orthodox Jews will periodically participate in the *mikvah*, a ritual bath performed in special bathhouses, and will only eat *kosher* foods, approved by their rabbis as having been slaughtered in the prescribed fashion.

Such a description of religious practice conceals the variations within the different strands of American Jewry. The Reform tradition grew out of the experience of the Jewish Enlightenment in Europe and was fostered in America by Rabbi Isaac Meyer Wise, who founded the Union of American Hebrew Congregations in 1875 and the Central Conference of American Rabbis in 1889. Under the influence of Wise, Reform Jews developed an American Judaism that repudiated many of the classical injunctions of the Old Testament as peculiar to the times in which the text had been written, and adopted an English liturgy in place of Hebrew. As a Philadelphia Orthodox girl remarked: "When we . . . saw the people at K. I. [Keneseth Israel], and the imposing building, we felt the line of demarcation. They were different Jews. Reform. We thought that meant almost Christian."[4] In 1887 a countervailing Conservative movement headed by Rabbi Solomon Schecter emerged, which organized the Jewish Theological Seminary Association to oppose the efforts of Reform. While accepting certain innovations—the use of English, nonsegregation of the sexes, and secular education—Conservative Jews repudiated the wholesale Americanization of Jewish cultural practices. In 1913 they established the United Synagogue of Conservative Judaism to set standards for congregational practice.

The Orthodox community in America is represented by the Rabbinical Council of America. They also operate several distinguished educational institutions including New York's Yeshiva University and Baltimore's Ner Israel Rabbinical College. The most prominent face of Orthodoxy today is the Hassidic community of Brooklyn. In neighborhoods like Crown Heights they have erected an enclosed world of synagogues, schools, and kosher shops. The Hassidim represent a singular strand of Orthodoxy, which places a high value on community and is animated by a much stronger sense of the value of mysticism and emotional religion than is generally found in Jewish spirituality. The Lubavitcher branch of Hassidim has been engaged in aggressive campaigning to bring Jews who have become separated from their religious roots back to their spiritual heritage, another practice not commonly found in Judaism. By virtue of their dominance of particular localities, the Hassidim, though not generally involved in secular politics, have learned how to be effective in persuading city politicians to block measures—such as public housing projects—that might damage community stability.

Few other Jewish communities have proved as self-contained as the Hassidim, particularly as they have moved out into the suburbs of New York and New Jersey. The pattern of religious education in New York in the early 1960s testifies to how the Orthodox advantage diminished with displacement. The Orthodox had 60 percent of school enrollment in the city but only 12 percent in the suburbs, while the Conservatives had 21 percent in the city and 39 percent in the suburbs, and Reform had only 11 percent in the city but 45 percent in the suburbs.[5] Although interest in religion generally revived during the 1950s, the religious commitment of Jews born after 1930 could not withstand the cultural traumas of the 1960s. In New York and Philadelphia, many Jews have ceased any religious practice except perhaps on high holidays, and in politics have come to identify themselves with cultural issues that their Orthodox counterparts consistently shun. This is not to say that more conservative Jewish communities could not become involved with progressive causes. Congregation Bnai Abraham—a liberal Conservative congregation in New Jersey—was headed for a time by Rabbi Joachim Prinz, who helped organize a popular community forum that showcased speakers on civil rights and accompanied Dr. Martin Luther King to Washington in 1963.

Muslims

There has been a marked rise in other religious groups since the 1950s. Perhaps the most dramatic increase has occurred among American Muslims, who erected their first mosque in New York in 1952. In 1992 there were 329 Muslim centers and mosques in the region, with 171 in New York and 59 in New Jersey. The best served communities were Brooklyn (37), New York (25), Philadelphia (21), Newark (13), and Baltimore (10). There has been considerable growth in Washington, D.C., and New York in the past twenty years, which has prompted a greater focus on education, marriage within the faith, and religious observances, although there has also been some adaptation to the American setting. In Paterson, New Jersey, Friday noon prayers are actually held on Sunday. The Muslim community also boasts national organizations like the Council on American-Islamic Relations, based in New York, which is the voice of Sunni Islam in America, and provides funding to communities for the erection of mosques and schools, and the D.C.-based American Muslim Council, founded in 1990, which seeks to represent all branches of Islam, combat discrimination, and serve all Muslim communities. Consideration should also be given to non-Arab Muslim groups, such as the First Muslim Mosque of Pittsburgh, chartered in 1945, which was the first mosque organized by indigenous Muslims in the United States.[6]

Eastern Religions

Eastern religions also play a role in the Mid-Atlantic, although their adherents tend to be of a higher social status than most American Muslims. A variety of Buddhist groups operate in the region, including the Soka Gokkai International in Maryland, the Zen Mountain Monastery in New York's Catskills, and the Namgal Monastery Institute of Buddhist Studies in Ithaca, New York, which has served as the American headquarters of the Dalai Lama since 1992, but there is no large indigenous Buddhist tradition. By contrast, the high-tech industries of the Northeast have attracted many skilled workers from the Indian subcontinent since the

Zen Mountain Monastery in New York's Catskill Mountains. Courtesy Zen Mountain Monastery Archives.

1960s, laying the basis for a significant body of Hindu residents and the erection of Hindu temples in New York, New Jersey, and Maryland. Despite the rise of an aggressively militant Hinduism in India, there has been far less nationalism associated with the practice of Hinduism in America than is associated with some Muslim groups. Moreover, the architecture of American temples has been obliged to reflect much more the diversity of the Indian community in America, with multiple shrines to different regional gods, the separation of sacred space from kitchens and classrooms (instead of the integration), and the practice of festivals solely within temple grounds rather than the local neighborhood. Unlike India, where temples tend to be sponsored by governments or wealthy individuals, the American temples have elected boards of trustees.

MODERN-DAY RELIGIONS ADHESION

The mid-Atlantic region is a stronghold of Roman Catholicism, with more than half of its residents belonging to that denomination in 2000.[7] While a quarter of the rest are Jews, the Protestant presence is split between the even distribution of United Methodists and local clusters of Lutherans, Presbyterians, and Southern Baptists. Participation in any church organization is surprisingly high for an urban region. In New York (65.7 percent), the District of Columbia (61.7 percent), Pennsylvania (61.4 percent), and New Jersey (61.3 percent), participation compares with parts of the Deep South. In Maryland and Delaware, by contrast, the respective rates are only 48.3 percent and 46.0 percent, while isolated West Virginia has the lowest figure, 41.4 percent.

The basic pattern is the same in New York and New Jersey, with the main difference being the Jewish share standing at 15.6 percent in New York and only 9.1 percent in New Jersey, and the Catholic hold being correspondingly stronger in New Jersey (67.4 percent) than in New York (61.6 percent). The figures for the leading Protestant groups—Black Baptists (4.2 percent in New York and 4.8 percent in New Jersey) and United Methodists (3.9 percent in New York and 3.5 percent in New Jersey)—reveal a similar pattern of distribution, as does the Presbyterian (1.7 percent in New York and 2.9 percent in New Jersey) and Episcopal (2.0 percent in New York and 2.2 percent in New Jersey) presence. There is also the Protestant Reformed Dutch Church. Founded in 1628 in New Amsterdam (later New York), the Reformed Dutch Church ministered to the Dutch community in North America, although it cut its ties to the mother church in the Netherlands after the American Revolution. Active in mission work in China, India, and Africa from the 1790s onward, the church expanded with the arrival of new Dutch immigrants during the 1840s. In 1857, however, it experienced schism as several congregations left to form the Christian Reformed Church. Today, there are only about 100,000 members of the Reformed Church in America in the mid-Atlantic region (the Christian Reformed Church accounts for fewer than 10,000), with 32,691 members in New Jersey and 68,261 in New York. There is little variation at the county level. In New York, Catholics constitute a majority in forty-five counties and pluralities in another fourteen, while Methodists have pluralities in the remaining three. The centers of Catholic strength include seven counties in the north, two counties in the west around Buffalo, the state capital of Albany, and six counties in the New York city area (including the Bronx and Richmond).

In New Jersey, the Catholic strength is even more overwhelming, with majorities in twenty and a plurality in Salem County.

By contrast, Pennsylvania is not nearly so overwhelmingly a Catholic state (50.4 percent) nor are its Jews as numerous (4.5 percent). Methodists are more influential (9.9 percent), as are the Presbyterians (5.3 percent), while the Black Baptists are slightly less numerous (3.0 percent) and the Episcopalians about the same (1.9 percent). What truly distinguishes Pennsylvania, however, is the strength of the Evangelical Lutheran Church in America, which claims 9.4 percent of the churchgoing population in a state that was once the heartland of the Lutheran Church. Interestingly, the state also lays claim to a comparatively high share of members of the United Church of Christ, whose 3.9 percent is one of their best showings outside New England. Catholics have majorities in eighteen counties and pluralities in another twenty-nine, while the Methodists have pluralities in fifteen and the Evangelical Lutheran Church in America has pluralities in five. The centers of Catholic strength include the Wilkes-Barre and Scranton corridor (five counties in the northeast), greater Philadelphia (four counties in the southeast), and greater Pittsburgh (seven counties in the southwest), while the Methodist counties are mainly in a thinly settled north-south corridor through the center of the state.

Although the District of Columbia enjoys a participation rate comparable to that of the urban states, it is truly a unique entity, not least for its black majority. Roughly a third of churchgoers are Black Baptists (27.5 percent) and others are members of the African Methodist Episcopal Zion Church (10.6 percent). Roman Catholics are at a comparatively low level of 20.7 percent, while the Jewish congregations stand at 6.8 percent. Other influential groups are the American Baptists (9.0 percent), United Methodists (4.9 percent), Southern Baptist Convention (4.7 percent), Episcopalians (4.3 percent), and Presbyterians (2.6 percent). Maryland and Delaware belong to the same border zone as the District of Columbia, but lack the same minority population, and their profiles are fairly similar. Maryland is 36.0 percent Catholic, and 13.4 percent Methodist, and 11.3 percent Black Baptist, while Delaware is 38.0 percent Catholic, 19.9 percent Methodist, and 12.0 percent Black Baptist. The great discrepancy comes with their Jewish residents, who represent 9.1 percent of churchgoers in Maryland but only 3.1 percent in Delaware. As for the rest, the Presbyterians achieve 5.0 percent in Delaware and 2.0 percent in Maryland, the Episcopalians achieve 4.3 percent in Delaware and 3.6 percent in Maryland, and the Evangelical Lutheran Church in America achieve, 2.2 percent in Delaware and 4.6 percent in Maryland. Only Maryland has significant numbers of Southern Baptists, with 5.7 percent compared to Delaware's 1.9 percent. In Delaware, Newcastle County (where most of the state's residents live) has a Catholic plurality, while the other two counties have Methodist pluralities. In Maryland, the denominations also divide control, with Methodists having majorities in two counties and pluralities in eleven and Catholics having majorities in two and pluralities in nine. Methodist strength is found on the Eastern Shore and in western Maryland, while Catholic strength is found in Baltimore, Anne Arundel, and Montgomery Counties and extreme southern Maryland.

If the District of Columbia is racially distinctive, West Virginia is also set apart in the mid-Atlantic region. Landlocked and with low religious participation, it is a separate religious culture, the only community where Catholics run third (14.6

percent), behind the American Baptists (17.8 percent) and the Methodists (24.6 percent). The Southern Baptists are at their strongest, but still claim only 5.8 percent, while the Presbyterians have 5.1 percent and the Black Baptists only 2.4 percent. West Virginia also boasts some high totals for fundamentalist Protestant groups. The Church of the Nazarene has 3.5 percent, the Church of Christ has 3.4 percent, and the Church of God (Cleveland) has 2.7 percent. Although the Methodists are strongest, it is the American Baptists who have greater territorial dominance, with majorities in three counties and pluralities in twenty-four, compared to the majorities in three counties and pluralities in seventeen enjoyed by the Methodists. Baptists dominate the south, including around the state capital of Charleston, while Methodists are strong in the north and east. Catholics have a majority in one county and pluralities in another three, all adjacent to southwestern Pennsylvania, while the Southern Baptist Convention has pluralities in two southern counties and the Church of the Brethren and the Free-Will Baptists each have a plurality in one.

The Catholic presence in the Mid-Atlantic is surely one of the most striking aspects of contemporary American life. A church of immigrants a century ago, today it once again claims immigrants among its most loyal followers, but now from Central and South America (particularly Puerto Rico). The rate of growth in the middle-class white population, however, has stabilized and is even in decline in some areas, reflecting greater acceptance of birth control among lay Catholics than in the past. Suburban churches have grown dramatically since the 1950s but are not as community-centered as in past generations. Conservative Catholics place much of the blame for this on the liturgical reforms implemented by the Second Vatican Council (1962–1965), arguing that the mystery of the Mass has been lost. Nevertheless, the Catholic Church remains the leading proponent of the sacramental life, including Baptism, frequent reception of the Eucharist, Confession and Unction, veneration of the saints, especially the Virgin Mary, and an all-male celibate priesthood. There are twenty-five dioceses in the region, including eight each in New York and Pennsylvania and five in New Jersey. There is also a sizable educational establishment of sixty-two colleges and universities (some of which have eschewed their specifically Catholic identity in order to receive state funding), including the universities of Duquesne, Scranton, and Villanova in Pennsylvania, Fordham in New York, and Georgetown and the Catholic University of America in Washington, D.C.

The parish continues to be an essential unit of Catholic identity, but today most parishes provide specialist services based on the geographical community they serve, rather than incubating a particular ethnic group. Since Vatican II, there has been considerable growth in lay participation, with parish staffs now more likely to include permanent deacons and members of the laity. There has also been a rise in the number of parish councils intended to help set priorities and act as a clearinghouse for parish organizations, but these bodies do not have ultimate authority over the conduct of church policy. For some, the shift to celebrations of the Mass in the vernacular and the introduction of more contemporary music have proved a great disappointment, and attachment to traditionalist bodies like the Society of Pius X has risen. One of the most dramatic illustrations of this was the purported vision of the Virgin Mary to Veronica Lueken in the late 1960s and early 1970s outside St. Robert Bellarmine Church in Bayside, New York City. The messages Lueken conveyed included denunciations of abortion, immodest dress, and Freemasonry, along with the Vatican II innovation of receiving the Communion wafer in the hand and charismatic Catholicism. Despite the lack of official church recognition, she retains many followers across North America. By the early 1970s, it was clear that there had been a considerable increase in the number of people leaving the church compared to the 1950s, and attendance at Mass was also down, trends that persist to the present day.

The largest Protestant voice in the Mid-Atlantic is provided by the United Methodist Church, the product of the 1939 reunion of the northern and southern branches of American Methodism. Methodism was historically distinguished by its espousal of Arminianism—the belief that Christ died for all, not just for the elect, and that man is a free moral agent with the ability to choose or reject God. In America it also acquired a strong inclination toward pietism—an emphasis on the devotional life of the laity and private study of the Bible. Today it affirms the sufficiency of the Bible for salvation and recognizes the sacraments of Baptism and the Lord's Supper. Nevertheless, it also takes very seriously its obligation to pursue ecumenical dialogue, seeing the core of Wesleyan doctrine a part of a common Christian heritage. To this end, New York Methodists helped organize Kingston, New York's, Church of Christ Uniting in 1962.

The advent of the Social Gospel in the early twentieth century transformed the Methodists and gave them a new sense of social mission. In western New York, local Methodists established a Children's Home in Binghamton in 1918; during the 1950s the Children's Home began to treat child abuse and childhood mental illness. Another institutional initiative was the United Methodist Homes—homes for the aged launched in northeastern Pennsylvania and western New York during the 1950s. In 1996 one of these homes became the first collaborative project jointly undertaken by the United Methodists and the Roman Catholic Church. In 2001 the New York Wyoming Conference cared for 1,000 residents and employed around 1,300 staff. It also operated a high school—Wyoming Seminary—with a high enrollment from thirteen states and twenty-three countries. The church is organized around district and annual conferences, which form a hierarchy of authority, with the quadrennial general conference being the church's highest legislative and policymaking body. There are twelve annual conferences in the Mid-Atlantic, including five in New York and three in Pennsylvania. There are also two Methodist seminaries—Wesley Seminary in Washington, D.C., and Drew University Theological School in New Jersey—and eleven colleges and universities with Methodist antecedents, including American University in Washington, D.C., Drew University in New Jersey, and Syracuse University in New York.

Although there is a significant African American presence in the mid-Atlantic region and both the African Methodist Episcopal Church and African Methodist Episcopal Zion Church were organized in Philadelphia and New York City, respectively, few of the major black denominations are based in the region. Since these bodies do not have consistent methods of calculating numbers, it is impossible to know their geographic distribution accurately, but the Great Migration from the South in the early twentieth century brought many African Americans to the urban North. Although black Baptists, Pentecostals, and Methodists are theologically distinctive, they also have certain theological commonalities, including a strong sense of God's immanence and direct connection with the sufferings of humanity. While personal sin is deplored, a much higher condemnation is accorded communal sin than by conservative white Protestants. The availability of the Holy Spirit to all believers is generally acknowledged but is particularly emphasized by the Pentecostal Church of God in Christ. In recent years, the black Methodist churches have become more open to female ministers—Vashti McKenzie Murphy became the first female AME bishop in 2000—but the Baptists and Pentecostals remain more conservative on this issue. Structurally, the Methodist churches are more hierarchically organized than their Baptist and Pentecostal counterparts, which operate more on the principle of voluntary association.

A striking phenomenon of the twentieth century has been the emergence of Pentecostal sects, which have traditionally been viewed as movements of the "dispossessed." (Pentecostalism from its earliest beginnings has been seen as the religion of poor farmers and agricultural workers deprived of most of the fruits of their labor or even forced off their land by mechanization.) In the Mid-Atlantic, most of these bodies are heavily African American. Two of the oldest are the Church of Our Lord Jesus Christ of the Apostolic Faith in New York and the United House of Prayer for All People on the Rock of the Apostolic Faith in Washington, D.C. The former was founded in 1919 by Robert Lawson and has planted churches in Jamaica, Antigua, the Virgin Islands, and Trinidad. The United House of Prayer (founded in 1927) was the initiative of Bishop C. M. ("Sweet Daddy") Grace, who came to nationwide attention during the Great Depression. Over the next thirty-three years, Grace erected over one hundred Houses of Prayer, fed the poor, and held integrated services throughout the South, with a message devoted to nondenominational establishment and maintenance of the Apostolic Faith. After his death in 1960, the movement took up the cause of affordable housing, with the erection of the McCullough Canaanland Apartments, the McCullough Paradise Gardens, and the McCullough Haven, all on Washington, D.C.'s Seventh Street. The House of Prayer continues to devote itself to the erection of multifamily housing, daycare centers, commercial malls, and housing for senior citizens, all without either private mortgages or federal or local government assistance.

A younger Pentecostal group that drew on House of Prayer's methods is the District of Columbia–based Bible Way Church of Our Lord Jesus Christ World Wide, a non-Trinitarian Apostolic Pentecostal denomination founded by Smallwood E. Williams (1907–1991) in 1957. Williams sought to develop a social service/social justice ethic for Pentecostal responses to social problems, articulated in his *Significant Sermons* (1970). He sponsored a supermarket and housing complex near his church and also became involved in city politics, an unusually activist approach for a black Pentecostal. While Williams addressed one aspect of social justice, John L. Meares focused on another—interracial dialogue. In 1955 Meares came to Washington for a revival as a white minister in the predominantly white Church of God but stayed to organize the Washington Revival Center and a radio show, *Revival Time*. His success in attracting a largely African American audience irked his superiors in the Church of God, and Meares left the denomination in 1956 to lead the National Evangelistic Center. Despite the conflicts of the 1960s, Meares held his organization together and in 1975 opened Evangel Temple (which moved to Maryland in 1991). The denomination—known today as International Evangelical Church—now focuses on Africa, where most of its member congregations are located, and on Pentecostal ecumenism. Meares helped organize the

International Communion of Charismatic Churches in 1982 and the annual Inner-City Pastors' Conference in 1984.

The other large grouping present in the Mid-Atlantic is that of the Lutherans of Pennsylvania (and, to a lesser extent, other mid-Atlantic states), who claim descent from the first extensive and enduring Lutheran community in North America. Largely of German origin, these Lutherans belonged first to the United Lutheran Church in America, which existed from 1918 to 1962, and then to its successor, the Lutheran Church in America (LCA). Lutherans in the mid-Atlantic region have always been more open to the mainstreaming of American Lutheranism. They placed less reliance on the Augsburg Confession—the creedal statement of Lutheranism drafted in 1530, which laid particular stress on grace and rejected any righteousness based on human works and merits. They were also unusually open to "unionism," or cooperation with other Lutheran and even other Protestant denominations, even in matters of worship.

The LCA played a leading role in the intradenominational National Lutheran Council and participated in the National Council of Churches and the World Council of Churches. An Inter-Lutheran Commission on Worship, formed in 1966, helped foster ties even with the antiunionist Lutheran Church-Missouri Synod and the Roman Catholic Church. In the late 1960s, the LCA reached altar and pulpit fellowship with the midwestern American Lutheran Church (ALC) and then began to move toward merger with the ALC and a group of Missouri Synod secessionists. In 1980 the district synods of the LCA voted 87 percent in favor of merger compared with 64 percent for the ALC. The new body—the Evangelical Lutheran Church in America—which came into being in 1982 and was only fully merged in 1988, was an even more hierarchical body than the LCA and stressed justification by faith and the sacraments of Baptism and the Eucharist. Today there are thirteen Evangelical Lutheran Church in America regional synods, seven of them in Pennsylvania and two in New York. The church maintains seminaries in Philadelphia and Gettysburg, Pennsylvania (the latter being one of the most significant in American Lutheran history), and operates five colleges, four of them in Pennsylvania.

SOCIAL LIFE AND ACTIVITIES

During the 1950s, Catholic devotionalism stood at an all-time high. Catholics regularly attended Mass and Confession, said the Rosary, and took part in novenas (a special nine-day devotion). Within ten years the reforms of Vatican II had swept away much of the old parish life, and indeed many of the fixtures that had decorated the old churches, particularly statues, in order to refocus attention on the meaning of the Mass. The shift from simple devotion to comprehension was not as dramatic a transformation as it appeared at the time, but spoke to the new educated middle-class Catholics who increasingly formed the suburban constituency of the Church. Some shifts antedated Vatican II, most notably the couples ministries, Cana and Pre-Cana. The director of the Family Life Program in New York remarked of them, "Family life was not only a mission of the church *to* and for the family, but it was a movement *by* Church families for the Church and for the nation."[8] This focus on the family remains a key aspect of parish life in large suburban churches to this day.

The abandonment of the Latin Mass, the modification of the disciplines of fasting and abstinence, and the reworking of the church calendar to emphasize the church year rather than the festivals of specific saints inevitably destroyed what remained of the old ethnic Catholicism. The Second Vatican Council also laid great stress on the fact that the *charism* was a property of all believers, not just the ordained ministry, a fact of which educated lay Catholics have taken full advantage. Given the current shortage of priestly vocations, there has been a marked rise in the number of permanent deacons (often older men) as well as greater involvement by women in a variety of church functions. There is a much greater emphasis on parish education, including the Confraternity of Christian Doctrine (for children) and the Rite of Christian Initiation for Adults. Lay ministry has also grown in scope, with services to church youth, the sick, and the dying, such as the Emmaus Grief Ministry. Laymen now serve on parish councils, giving them a sense of involvement in decisionmaking, though their impact varies from parish to parish. One of the great success stories has been the *cursillo* movement, which aims to assist spiritual growth among the laity and has been adopted by a number of Protestant denominations. Another lay-led initiative was the Catholic Charismatic movement that began at Duquesne University in the late 1960s and reaped a considerable harvest during the 1970s. At the same time, commitment to key tenets of Catholicism among many educated Catholics, particularly in the matter of birth control, has waned and mixed marriages have increased significantly.

The church has had to deal with a different set of issues in approaching the Hispanic population. As early as the 1950s, New York priests were sent to Puerto Rico to learn Spanish and Cardinal Francis Spellman began the tradition of an annual parade in New York City on the Feast of San Juan Baptista (June 24). Most of the Puerto Rican parishes favor a much more traditional style of devotion, albeit with Spanish music as an accompaniment, than many priests assigned to such parishes expect. The church also has to deal with the issue of African American parishes that are often starved of funds and poorly led. In 1989 the Archdiocese of Washington obtained an unfortunate degree of publicity when George Stallings, a former priest at St. Teresa of Avila Catholic Church in Washington, D.C., and a critic of its lack of action against racism, was excommunicated following his creation of the Imani Temple as a schismatic parish.

From 1900 onward, Methodist worship increasingly came to be seen as intended to promote peace and social justice rather than effecting conversion. In response to the changes made under Vatican II, Methodists underwent their own period of liturgical innovation and adopted the Roman Catholic liturgical year. New York Methodists also followed a national trend by acquiring a campsite that could also serve as a retreat and conference center in 1947, which acquired a very positive reputation, not least because many attendees experienced a call to ministry there. Despite these developments, the rural parts of the Methodist Church continued to suffer erosion. The Wyoming Conference fell from 86,818 members in 1955 to 67,675 in 1999 and the mother church of regional Methodism—Centenary Church, Binghamton—was forced to merge with another struggling congregation.

The return of young African Americans, especially those with professional qualifications, to the churches of their parents has been one of the great success stories of the 1990s. Worship is central to the spiritual life in most African American churches. Music—both spirituals and gospel—affirms that human beings are made in the image of a personal God who shares in their suffering. Choirs like that of the Church of God in Christ's Washington Temple also have an evangelistic function by recording albums that serve to attract newcomers from all over New York. The pastoral sermon is another essential element that allows the speaker to relate the message of Scripture to the facts of everyday life, while the giving of personal testimonies, vocal prayers, and altar calls all enable the congregation to participate in the worship experience. Churches have learned to adjust to a younger generation by relaxing dress codes, using everyday images in sermons, and seeking to inculcate a renewed appreciation of worship, prayer, and faith as well as an understanding of African heritage. Bethel AME Church in Baltimore provides adult mentors for male adolescents to train them in proper conduct, while Metropolitan Baptist Church in Washington, D.C., provides after-school tutoring and Allen AME Church in New York started a church school in 1986, which blended religion and culture with a traditional educational curriculum. Congregations have increasingly been forced to deal with the effects of drugs, violence, and AIDS in their communities. The Harlem Congregations for Community Improvement Corporation was launched in 1985 to provide AIDS information and support, and the Black Church Week of Prayer for Healing of AIDS began four years later.

Lutheran church life was significantly reshaped after World War II, beginning with a new service book and hymnal in 1958. Many Lutherans felt an absence of evangelical fervor, as witnessed in the request of the Eastern Pennsylvania Synod to the 1964 LCA convention to study the nature and mission of the congregation. Beginning in 1967, the church experienced a decrease in numbers as people moved out of the Northeast. Church auxiliary units for men and children withered on the vine, leaving only Lutheran Church Women as an effective force in such areas as literacy, welfare reform, and race relations. In 1969 Parish Life Development was implemented in twenty-four congregations in central Pennsylvania and Maryland, combining small pastor-led institutes that mapped out a congregation's needs and a mission statement, and larger workshops that trained parishioners in decision-making, problem-solving, and communication skills. So successful was this program that it was later implemented churchwide. As in other denominations, new liturgies were also tested during the 1960s and a lectionary adopted that reflected the festivals of the church year. In another effort to revitalize congregations, "pastor evangelists" from successful congregations were sent out to pass on their skills to others. The Word and Witness program was implemented to teach ordinary Lutherans how to evangelize, and social ministry teams were developed in many parishes. Since the merger that created the ELCA, mid-Atlantic Lutherans continue to be influential in parts of rural Pennsylvania but are a minor force in most other sections of the region.

THE CHURCHES AND THE WIDER WORLD

With the election of John F. Kennedy in 1960, many Catholics believed that they had finally achieved political acceptance. The strength of the Catholic vote in the mid-Atlantic states testified to the enduring impact of the New Deal realignment on political behavior. At that moment of success, however, many church leaders realized that they could no longer rely on their members to vote in a "Catholic" fashion, in the way that the Legion of Decency had commanded Catholic loyalty in its efforts to block unsuitable motion pictures or that anticommunist Catholicism had been dominant during the 1950s. Increasingly, Catholic priests and nuns repudiated the chain of command to participate in civil rights and anti-war protests, while rank-and-file Catholics were heard to utter sentiments that were far from patriotic, a measure of how secure they now felt in the new pluralistic America. The 1967 attempt to remove Father Charles Curran at the Catholic University of America because some of his statements on contraception seemed at odds with the Vatican's position proved abortive, as the idea of academic freedom even in doctrinal matters took increasing hold in the Catholic university system. On the ground level, it became clear that declining Catholic neighborhoods in New York and Philadelphia no longer commanded the respect of city leaders that they had a generation before. Nevertheless, the Archdiocese of New York was able to put together coalitions in the 1970s and 1980s to oppose gay rights and abortion legislation. Increasingly, many politicians who claim to be Catholics do not hold to the church's teaching in their legislative behavior, something that brings the contrast between religious and "ethnic" Catholicism into sharp relief.

While there is no question that Methodism has a very liberal constituency, this has not translated into direct action in most of the Mid-Atlantic. It has, however, been very vocal internally on women's rights and homosexuality. Ruth Underwood became the first ministerial member of the Wyoming Conference in 1957, and the proportion of women ministers rose from 8.2 percent in 1990 to 20.0 percent in 2000. In 1988 delegates to the Wyoming Conference declared it a "reconciling conference," or one offering homosexuals full participation in congregational and sacramental life, though in 1990 they revoked that designation in order to avoid controversy. Two congregations continued to designate themselves as "reconciling," however, and a local clergyman served on the national Reconciling Ministries Network.

The black churches have always been committed to engagement in the world at large. The tradition of ministerial involvement in politics began with Adam Clayton Powell, pastor of New York City's Abyssinia Baptist Church, a U.S. congressman from Harlem from 1944 to 1969, who helped shape national social policy during the 1960s as chairman of the House Education and Labor Committee. A second generation of leaders rode to power on the tails of the civil rights struggles of the 1950s and 1960s. One product of those times is the Washington, D.C.–based Progressive National Baptist Convention (PNBC), formed in 1961 over a leadership dispute within the National Baptist Convention of the United States. The PNBC represented those most supportive of Martin Luther King, who joined the secession, and today has 2,000 churches and 2.5 million members (compared to the 7 million in the National Baptist Convention of the United States). Other politicians included Walter Fauntroy, a PNBC minister, who served as the District of Columbia's delegate in Congress (1971–1991), and Floyd Flake of New York's Allen AME Church was a congressman from Queens (1987–1997).

Ministers like Flake perceived the need for black churches to foster a positive economic culture. Allen AME Church purchased a run-down business district and transformed it into a thriving commercial center. Today the church has a $24 million budget and employs 825 employees (one of the largest employers in the Borough of Queens), while Bridge Street AME in Bedford-Stuyvesant offers low-interest loans to entrepreneurs who wish to start small businesses. In Baltimore, Montel Hill, Chief Executive Officer of H&R Consulting, worked with church leaders to introduce insurance and retirement plans to their congregations. The Baptist churches also established the Minority Enterprise Financial Acquisitions Corporation, which provided assistance for building low-cost housing. The East Brooklyn Congregations launched the Nehemiah Homes project in the early 1980s, which built housing and pressured the local government to clean up neighborhoods, and later began to erect healthcare facilities.

From its inception, the Lutheran Church in America took Lutheranism in a new direction toward greater political involvement under the direction of the Board of the Social Ministry. After 1,000 Lutherans participated in the 1963 civil rights demonstrations in Washington, D.C., the LCA's 1964 convention passed a statement of race relations supporting social justice and civil rights legislation. In 1966 it endorsed the abolition of capital punishment, the War on Poverty, and the right of conscientious objection to military service on nonreligious grounds. In 1970 a statement on marriage and the family controversially accepted divorce, family planning, and abortion. On foreign policy, the church increasingly favored more of a role for the United Nations and also began to embrace the idea of applying social criteria to church investments. While it refused to accept extreme forms of black nationalism, the LCA allocated $2 million to urban civic programs such as migrant ministries, daycare, college opportunity grants, urban leadership, and non-profit housing. It sought to encourage recruitment of minorities and establishment of minority congregations in a largely white denomination. It also took steps in favor of women's rights by refusing to meet in states that failed to ratify the Equal Rights Amendment.

RELIGION AND THE CITY

Mid-Atlantic culture has for at least a century and a half been defined by its cities.[9] Above all are the five boroughs of New York City. Church participation here ranges from 63.7 percent in Queens County (below the statewide average of 65.7 percent) to a high of 79.0 percent in Richmond. Roman Catholics constitute a plurality in New York County (49.7 percent) and a narrow majority in Kings County (52.4 percent), and have clear majorities in Queens County (58.9 percent), Bronx County (70.7 percent), and Richmond County (79.0 percent). Jews are at their weakest in Richmond (10.4 percent) and Bronx (10.6 percent), but represent around a quarter of churchgoers in New York (24.1 percent), Queens (25.8 percent), and Kings (27.2 percent). Black Baptists are well above the statewide average of 4.2 percent, but are at their strongest in Bronx and Kings (both 8.5 percent), with 6.7 percent in Queens, 5.4 percent in New York, and only 2.1 percent in Richmond. Few other groups have a significant presence except in New York itself, where the American Methodist Episcopal Zion Church has 7.0 percent, the American Baptists, United States, have 2.6 percent, and the Episcopal Church have 2.1 percent, and in Kings, where the American Baptists, United States, have 4.0 percent.

Further south lies the region's second city, Philadelphia, which bears more comparison with New York City than with the state of Pennsylvania as a whole. While its 58.8 participation rate is 2.6 points below the statewide average, its 57.6 percent Catholic share is 7.2 points above the statewide average. Its 11.7 percent black Baptist population is higher than that of any other urban community except Baltimore, while its 11.4 percent Jewish share is among the highest in the region. Other groups with significant representation are the Episcopalians (2.6 percent), United Methodists (2.5 percent), American Baptists (2.4 percent), and the Evangelical Lutheran Church in America (2.4 percent).

Other coastal cities also reflect the strong Catholic and Jewish presence. In Essex County, New Jersey (Newark), and Hudson County, New Jersey (Jersey City), participation rates are well above the statewide average of 61.3 percent, at 67.1 percent and 69.6 percent, respectively. Jersey City is overwhelmingly Catholic, with 84.3 Roman Catholics, 4.9 percent Black Baptists, and 4.1 percent Jews. Newark is distinctly lower, with 59.0 percent Catholics, 14.6 percent Jews, and 10.4 percent Black Baptists, while minor groups include American Baptists (3.2 percent), Presbyterians (2.5 percent), Episcopalians (2.1 percent), and African Methodist Episcopal Zion (2.0 percent). Baltimore (the city and county together) has a participation rate of 49.3 percent. Its Catholic share of 36.5 percent is one of the lowest for the cities of the region, while Black Baptists constitute 15.4 percent and Jews constitute 13.4 percent. Methodists are the largest white denomination (9.6 percent), followed by the ELCA (4.9 percent). Minor groups include the Episcopal Church (3.6 percent), the Southern Baptist Convention (3.1 percent), the American Baptists (2.0 percent), and the Presbyterians (2.0 percent).

In the interior of Pennsylvania and New York are two types of city: the ethnic Catholic and the religiously diverse. Participation in the former is high, with 73.5 percent for Lackawanna County, Pennsylvania (Scranton), 75.8 percent for Allegheny County, Pennsylvania (Pittsburgh), and 79.4 percent for Erie County, New York (Buffalo). Roman Catholics account for 68.7 percent of churchgoers in Pittsburgh, 74.5 percent in Buffalo, and a high of 78.0 percent in Scranton. In Scranton, only two other groups break 2 percent, with the Methodists at 8.3 percent and the Presbyterians at 3.0 percent. Pittsburgh and Buffalo are slightly more cosmopolitan. Among Pittsburgh Protestants, the Presbyterians achieve 7.4 percent, the Methodists achieve 5.4 percent, and the ELCA achieve 3.7 percent, while the Black Baptists have 3.4 percent and the Jews have 2.6 percent. In Buffalo, the spread is rather more even, with the Black Baptists, Methodists, and the ELCA all at 2.9 percent, the Jews at 2.4 percent, and the Presbyterians at 2.2 percent. Compare all this with the situation in Dauphin County, Pennsylvania (Harrisburg), and Monroe County, New York (Rochester), where participation rates are only 55.5 percent and 53.5 percent, respectively. Catholics are strong in Rochester (61.2 percent) but constitute less than one-third of churchgoers in Harrisburg (28.3 percent). In Harrisburg there are two strong Protestant groups, the Methodists (18.9 percent) and the ELCA (15.2 percent). Black Baptists are at 6.4 percent, the Presbyterians at 4.9 percent, the United Church of Christ at 4.7 percent, the Church of God–General Convention at 2.2 percent, and the Jews at 2.0 percent. As in Buffalo, there is a more even distribution of non-Catholic believers in Rochester. The Presbyterians (4.7 percent), the Black Baptists (4.6 percent), the Jews (4.3 percent), the American Baptists (4.2 percent), and the Methodists (4.1 percent) are all clustered together, while minor groups include the ELCA (3.2 percent), the Episcopal Church (2.7 percent), and the Lutheran Church–Missouri Synod (2.2 percent).

As the urban churches entered the 1950s, they faced a very changed environment from the beginning of the century. In the run-down Fells Point area of Baltimore, distinguished by overcrowding and an absence of high schools and playgrounds, two Methodist churches—Broadway and East Baltimore—came together in 1952. Both opened their doors to the local community at least six days a week, with six choirs, five Scout groups, religious education, crafts, and sports, into all of which the teachers sought to introduce a religious component and give participants a sense of spiritual uplift. Staff from both churches worked together, while the two pastors divided their efforts, with one overseeing the church programs and providing adult counseling and the other visiting unchurched Protestants in the area and acting as the chaplain for the local unit of Goodwill Industries. Such cooperation had its limits, however. Union services were poorly attended and church members showed little enthusiasm for pulpit exchange, while potential church leaders continued to be lost to the suburbs.

Nazarene Congregational Church in Brooklyn took a different approach in 1961 when a group of parishioners resolved to adopt a functional identity based on their willingness to commit to Christ, ranging from Apostles (who pledged to form the core of a new lay ministry) to Neighbors (who wished to explore the implications before making a full commitment). They agreed to meet for weekly Bible study (with a focus on Paul's Epistle to the Ephesians) to assess the role of Christian urbanites toward both church and city. In order to deepen the direct experience of God in their lives, they accepted the need to develop deeper relationships with those around them and repair those that had been broken, through witnessing, community organizing, and youth ministry. City parishes, they concluded, needed to accept the fact of an enduring urban crisis and develop a theology for their members that allowed them to take advantage of that fact. Christian urbanites had to be willing to participate fully in the development of a city's structure and be willing, if they lived in the suburbs, to have membership in both an urban church where they worked and a suburban church where they lived.

In addition to fostering the spirit of mission, urban churches increasingly employed novel methods of evangelization. In 1974 Albany's First Reformed Church became the first church in the United States to conduct drive-in worship in a downtown business district, initially with a makeshift platform but later with a designed outdoor worship center and public address system. The simple half-hour service included a Scripture reading, prayers, music, and a fifteen-minute address, with visitors asked to honk their horns in place of spoken responses. Pastor William Cameron publicized his services on the radio, in newspapers, and on billboards, seeing it as one means of reaching the unchurched and those who, for one reason or another, were unsettled by formal church services. Although it attracted only around thirty-five cars, some of those who attended proved very faithful and drove up to fifteen miles in order to be present.

In addition to parish initiatives, transdenominational bodies like Metropolitan Associates of Philadelphia (MAP) became increasingly popular in the 1950s. MAP—the brainchild of Dr. Jitsuo Morikawa—consisted of a group of sixty men (most laity). MAP was devoted to helping business, governmental, and social organizations with which its members were involved find their God-given role. It had the support of the National Council of Churches and the American Baptists, Episcopalians, Lutherans, and the United Church of Christ. Organized into seven sector groups—politics and government; business and industry; physical development; social organizations; art and education; health; and communications media—the lay associates met twice a month and participated in "issue workshops" on matters of citywide interest. In 1967 MAP maintained special task forces on antipoverty activities, improvement of housing in the Ludlow ghetto of North Philadelphia, and the study of industrial hiring practices as they related to minorities. Declared Robert McLean III, a marketing expert, Yale graduate, active Episcopalian, and MAP lay associate: "If we really believe God is the Lord of history, then he must affect the changes going on through human decisions. MAP is an attempt to take secular life more seriously and to see its religious base, a way to be responsible about God's action in history."[10]

The great urban issue of the 1960s, of course, was racial integration. Some urban churches moved relatively swiftly, as was the case with St. John's Lutheran Church in the Bronx. As early as 1931, when three African American children seeking a Sunday School were received amicably, the church began to welcome blacks into its ranks, although whites remained a majority. Pastor Alfred Schroder was president of the Lutheran Interracial Mission, and St. John's was one of the first churches where the Lutheran Interracial Service helped organize intercultural activities that could form a basis for home missions and evangelism. The church also made use of the services of a member of a black Lutheran Church–Missouri Synod parish who could approach the African American community and bring in children for weekday religious education. The shift toward an interracial congregation was deliberate and focused on children, with only five white families leaving over the issue, but it spoke to the heavily unchurched black population in this part of the Bronx.

A more controversial undertaking was launched in Rochester, New York, after a race riot swept through the city in July 1964. The city's black population had grown from 7,800 in 1950 to 35,000 in 1964, but many were unskilled workers who were unable to get jobs in high-tech industries like Eastman-Kodak and had been confined to poor-quality housing in Rochester. The black Rochester Ministers Conference therefore turned to Chicago's radical priest, Saul Alinsky, and his program of empowering the powerless by means of community organizations built on the basis of self-interest. Such a program evoked criticism in the wider Rochester community, but many white churches did agree to contribute to the costs of FIGHT (Freedom, Integrity, God, Honor, Tomorrow), although the Lutheran Church in America was divided on the issue. FIGHT was headed by Franklyn Florence, pastor of the Reynolds Street Church of Christ and a close friend of Malcolm X, and it quickly adopted a militant stance, barring whites from membership and confronting Eastman-Kodak, a paternalistic company that had nevertheless had a good record of hiring and training blacks for specialist jobs. By 1968 the support of white churches had fallen considerably, although the Catholic bishop Fulton Sheen later appointed a Vicar for Urban Ministry who had been a member of the (white) Friends of FIGHT. The general goodwill among the churches that had prevailed in the immediate aftermath of the riots was nevertheless rendered much less effective by the insistence of militants in FIGHT on obtaining a victory without compromise.

Integration was but one part of the equation, since many black churches existed as second-class citizens within the mainstream denominations. Such was the case when Father Edward Miller came to St. Bernadine's Catholic Church in 1975, a declining black parish in inner-city Baltimore. Miller sensed the lack of parish identity and sought to ameliorate this by steeping himself in the black experience, visiting black churches in order to understand their worship style. Beginning with liturgical reform, Miller hired a Baptist minister of music, trained him in Catholic liturgical practices, and supported the establishment of a gospel choir. In his homiletical style, Miller sought to develop the assigned Scripture passage to address the lives of parishioners and argued that worshippers should be free to express themselves, give testimony, or respond to an altar call within the framework of the Mass. Only a liturgy that spoke to the concerns of parishioners, he insisted, could prompt both evangelization and service to the wider community. The church staff needed to set an example that the congregation would emulate, and families needed to be reminded of their duty to evangelize. Miller helped raise the profile of St. Bernadine's with an aggressive publicity campaign, including buttons, mugs, and rented billboards. The church choir also performed throughout the city, attracting a positive response. The results became clear when, for three years in a row, St Bernadine's led the Archdiocese of Baltimore in converts, many of them relatives and friends of parishioners.

Even today, some Catholic churches continue to project their mission onto the needs of the wider community. One example is the Good Friday procession that has been conducted from St. Brigid's Church on New York's Lower East Side since 1967, which represents a mixture of public prayer and political critique. A Spanish parish, St. Brigid's became a testing ground for socially conscious clergy who designated various points of community concern—such as a health clinic that provided abortions, a street corner where drugs were sold, a deteriorating public school and a park associated with vice—as places where the stations of the Cross would be recited. Parish youths were invited to perform some of the stations as contemporary social dramas relating to drugs and racial tensions. The church also sponsored block parties, opened the rectory to troubled teenagers, introduced the Spanish Mass, and created a Spanish devotional society, Los Caballeros de Santa Brigida. It is important to note, however, that much of the more aggressively political posturing has come from non-Spanish priests, and many of the church's lay members remain divided over the advisability of mixing politics and faith so strongly.

CONCLUSION

There is a sense in which the Mid-Atlantic has, in religious terms, come full circle since the 1850s. As immigration transformed the region, the pluralist tradition that had characterized the early republic was replaced by a confrontation between the declining Protestant denominations and the emerging Catholic hegemony. Early Catholicism was a largely defensive religious culture that was more concerned with building its own institutions than with seeking to take control of the levers of power. The idea of a unified Catholic culture could not be realized until a majority of Catholics had grown up in America. After 1920, however, the national Catholic Church began to take notice of some of the principles of social justice with which the Protestant churches had experimented at the turn of the century. The coming of the New Deal brought down many of the ethnic institutions that had underpinned Catholic life, even as Catholic laborers became more involved in the labor movement.

The impact of the civil rights revolution coincided with the dramatic changes in the nature of Catholic life brought about by Vatican II. Acceptance of the Catholic Church by the wider community was ironically accomplished by a diminution in the status of the hierarchy amongst many lay Catholics and a consequent weakening of Catholic influence on public policy. For many, the fact that the Mid-Atlantic was a Catholic region seemed to matter less than in the days when Catholicism was a largely introspective spiritual body. The changes that have taken place within the Methodist and Lutheran communities speak to the wider problem facing mainstream Protestantism in the Mid-Atlantic and in the United States generally—the absence of an obvious religious culture that nurtures those who participate in it. Only the black churches seem to have found a formula that elevates community and engages in social renewal, but still appreciates that material well-being is a means, not an end; yet black culture is a comparatively small part of the whole, and it still has to grapple with some of the most severe social problems of any of the Christian churches. Religious pluralism certainly exists in the Mid-Atlantic today, yet it is only vaguely comparable with that of the early nineteenth century. There has been no revival to match the Second Great Awakening, not even the unified sense of urgency that produced the Social Gospel. Religion has increasingly been privatized, and its access to the public square is increasingly hedged about by restrictions imposed by secularly minded bureaucrats.

RESOURCE GUIDE

Printed Sources

Casino, Joseph J. "From Sanctuary to Involvement: A History of the Catholic Parish in the Northeast." In Jay P. Dolan, ed., *The American Catholic Parish: A History from 1850 to the Present*, Vol. 1. Mahwah, NJ: Paulist Press, 1987, 7–116.

Collins, John J. *Native American Religions: A Geographical Survey*. Lewiston, NY: Edwin Mellen Press, 1991.

Crist, Robert G. *Penn's Example to the Nations: Three Hundred Years of the Holy Experiment*. Harrisburg: Pennsylvania Council of Churches, 1987.

Cross, Whitney R. *The Burned-Over District: The Social and Intellectual History of Enthusiastic Religion in Western New York, 1800–1850*. New York: Octagon Press, 1950.

Dolan, Jay P. *The American Catholic Experience: A History from Colonial Times to the Present*. Garden City, NY: Doubleday, 1985.

Ellison, Elaine K., and Elaine M. Jaffe. *Voices from Marshall Street: Jewish Life in a Philadelphia Neighborhood, 1920–1960*. Philadelphia: Camino Book, 1994.

Gilbert, W. Kent. *Commitment to Unity: A History of the Lutheran Church in America*. Philadelphia: Fortress Press, 1988.

Harris, Lis. *Holy Days: The World of a Hasidic Family*. New York: Summit Books, 1985.

Hatch, Nathan O. *The Democratization of American Christianity*. New Haven, CT: Yale University Press, 1989.

Helmreich, William B. *The Enduring Community: The Jews of Newark and MetroWest*. New Brunswick, NJ: Transaction, 1999.

Hopkins, Charles H. *The Rise of the Social Gospel in American Protestantism*. New Haven, CT: Yale University Press, 1940.

Jacobsen, Douglas G. *An Unprov'd Experiment: Religious Pluralism in Colonial New Jersey*. Brooklyn, NY: Carlson, 1991.

Lederhendler, El. *New York Jews and the Decline of Urban Ethnicity, 1950–1970*. Syracuse, NY: Syracuse University Press, 2001.

Melton, J. Gordon. *Encyclopedia of American Religions*. 6th ed. Detroit: Gale Research, 1999.

Pinn, Anthony B. *The Black Church in the Post–Civil Rights Era*. Maryknoll, NY: Orbis Books, 2002.

Pratt, John W. *Religion, Politics, and Diversity: The Church-State Theme in New York History*. Ithaca, NY: Cornell University Press, 1967.

Waghorne, Joanne P. "The Hindu Gods in a Split-Level World: The Sri Siva-Vishnu Temple in Suburban Washington DC." In Robert A. Orsi, ed., *Gods of the City: Religion and the American Urban Landscape*. Bloomington: Indiana University Press, 1999, 103–130.

Web Sites

The Catholic University of America
http://www.cua.edu

Council on American-Islamic Relations
http://www.cair.com

Greater New York Council of Reform Synagogues
http://uahc.org/gnycrs

Lutheran Theological Seminary at Gettysburg
http://www.ltsg.edu

Polish National Catholic Church
http://www.pncc.org

Roman Catholic Archdiocese of Newark
http://www.rcan.org

Festivals

Feast of Our Lady of Mount Carmel
Shrine Church of Our Lady of Mount Carmel
North 8th and Havemeyer Streets
Brooklyn, NY 11211
Phone: 718-384-0223
http://www.olmcfeast.com
Held July 9–July 20.

Organizations

Center for Jewish History
15 West 16th Street
New York, NY 10011
Phone: 212-294-8301
http://www.cjh.org

Moravian Museum of Bethlehem
66 West Church Street
Bethlehem, PA 18018
Phone: 610-867-0173
http://www.moravianmuseum.org

Old Stone Presbyterian Church
200 Church Street
Lewisburg, WV 24901
Phone: 304-645-2676
http://www.oldstone.us

Old Swede's Church
1108 Adams Street
Wilmington, DE 19801
Phone: 302-652-5629
http://www.oldswedes.org

St. Anne's Episcopal Church
199 Duke of Gloucester Street
Church Circle
Annapolis, MD 21401
Phone: 410-267-9333
http://www.stannes-annapolis.org

Washington National Cathedral
Massachusetts and Wisconsin Avenues NW
Washington, DC 20016
Phone: 202-537-6200
http://www.cathedral.org/cathedral

Zen Mountain Monastery
Route 28
Mount Tremper, NY 12457
Phone: 845-688-2228
http://www.zen-mtn.org/zmm/zmmhome/index.html

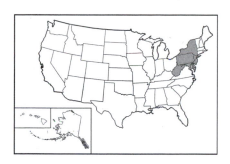

SPORTS AND RECREATION

Geoffrey Griffin

Many popular American sports were born in the mid-Atlantic region. Furthermore, in the Mid-Atlantic American sports could be found at their most pure before they became commercialized as their popularity increased beyond the region. When sports such as baseball and football got their start in the Mid-Atlantic, they were played by people who were simply looking for an enjoyable way to pass the time, with no idea that people and companies would one day make huge sums of money from their "games."

Today we are used to stadiums named after large corporations where multi-millionaire athletes perform on a global stage as a result of big money television contracts. After the games players and coaches hold press conferences in front of backdrops that prominently feature the name of one of the team's corporate sponsors for TV cameras to pick up. It may seem hard to imagine a time or place when the games were not commercialized.

It should come as no surprise that the mid-Atlantic region would be the cradle of American sports when one considers that native peoples were conducting athletic contests in the area before there even was an America. The Iroquois confederation of tribes in upper New York State was playing the sport of lacrosse before the arrival of European immigrants. The game was considered a gift from "The Creator" and was an important part of their culture and religion. Rituals and ceremonies were often held before and after games that were played to resolve conflicts, heal the sick, and develop strong men.

After the Europeans settled in America, they began developing their own games, including bat and ball games brought along from England. These were gradually changed and expanded upon until a group of young men in New York City put together a game known as "baseball" in the mid–nineteenth century. Not long after baseball was born, two New Jersey universities, Rutgers and Princeton, played the first game of college football in 1869 as that sport gradually evolved from soccer and rugby.

The involvement of the mid-Atlantic region in the creation of American sports is not just part of history. The area continues to be a place where new sports are growing in the twenty-first century. Playground basketball, often called "street-ball," grew phenomenally in the late 1990s and the early twenty-first century. Certain outdoor courts and players from the Mid-Atlantic are considered to be the heart of the sport.

The Mid-Atlantic has been a place where many courageous women took their place on the field, court, or diamond and asserted their own right to participate in what had been a male dominated area of life. In particular, a young woman in New Jersey in the 1970s was willing to go to court to gain an opportunity to play Little League baseball with boys. The timing of her battle coincided with the passage of a federal law requiring that high schools and colleges give girls and women equal opportunities to play sports, and the landscape of athletics was drastically changed.

Youth sports have also played an important role in the history of sports in the Mid-Atlantic. Little League baseball was created in Williamsport, Pennsylvania, in 1938 and 2.5 million children worldwide continue to participate in the program today. Baseball is just one of the many sports that young people in the mid-Atlantic region take part in at the beginning of the twenty-first century. The area is particularly well known for its high school lacrosse teams and Pennsylvania high school football is referred to as the "Cradle of Quarterbacks."

The mid-Atlantic region also offers a wide variety of outdoor recreational activities. Outdoors enthusiasts can climb mountains, raft rivers, walk on sandy beaches, ski, or fish without ever leaving the mid-Atlantic area.

NATIVE AMERICAN SPORT

Long before the American sports of baseball, football, and basketball were born, Indian tribes were playing the first sport of the North American Continent—lacrosse. Those early games might involve up to 1,000 players per side playing on fields that could be 15 miles long in games that lasted days and were even sometimes used to resolve conflicts between tribes. Besides lacrosse, Native Americans engaged in a variety of sports to help train young people in skills needed to survive or to develop strength and endurance.

Lacrosse was popular with many tribes in North America. There were three versions of the game—Southeastern, Great Lakes, and Iroquois. The Iroquois federation (Mohawk, Oneida, Onandaga, Cayuga, and Seneca) from the area of upper New York State had a special passion for the game. The Iroquois, also known as the "Five Nations," played a version of the game that gave rise to modern lacrosse. They would later become the "Six Nations" in 1722 when the Tuscarora Indians joined the league of tribes.

The Iroquois believed lacrosse was a gift from "The Creator" and it played an important role in their culture. There were often rituals and ceremonies before and after games which were sometimes played to aid in the healing of the sick. Games were open to all members of the tribe, regardless of status.

The lacrosse sticks used by the Iroquois were saplings bent into a hook at one end. The netting portion was laced with leather thongs. The earliest balls were made of wood and later of deerskin or baked clay. Players would carry the ball in the netting portion of their sticks and either run with the ball or pass it to team-mates as they tried to advance down the field and put the ball in the other team's goal. The other team would try to get the ball by intercepting passes or using their own crosses to knock the ball out of the opponent's crosse.

French Catholic missionaries noticed the game in the 1600s and called it lacrosse because the sticks resembled a bishop's crosier. French Canadians learned the game from the Mohawks around 1750. In the nineteenth century, European immigrants began taking up the game, with the mid-Atlantic region playing a prominent role. New York University formed the first college team in the United States in 1877. Two years later, eleven college teams formed the National Lacrosse Association, with most of the teams being from the New York area.

While lacrosse was becoming more popular among white Americans in late-nineteenth-century America, the game was declining among Indian tribes. Some historians feel that this was because of the United States government's policy of trying to get native peoples to leave their Indian culture behind and become assimilated into American culture. The irony was that while the government was trying to get the Indians to become more "American," American culture was becoming more "Indian" by taking up the sport of lacrosse.

While lacrosse has been embraced by a wide variety of American people, it is important not to forget the Iroquois who started it all. They are still playing the game. The "Iroquois Nationals" team, organized in 1983, regularly takes part in the World Games and at international tournaments. The Iroquois are considered an autonomous nation, just like Australia, the United States, or England. The team is the first all-Indian sports team to be recognized as a national team by other countries. The team has its own passports, flag and anthem.

Baltimore is the home of the Lacrosse Museum and Hall of Fame, created in 1957. The vast majority of those who have been inducted played for mid-Atlantic region college programs that have dominated NCAA competition in the sport. For instance, the ten inductees from the 2004 class all have connections to the mid-Atlantic area. Seven of the ten were selected for their involvement in college programs in the Mid-Atlantic. The ten inductees are Jane Barbieri, Dick Edell, Rosalia Gioia, Jackie Hufnell, Barb Jordan, Peter Kohn, Sal LoCascio, Dave Pietramala, Ruth "Stevie" Stevenson, and Mike Thearle.

While lacrosse is a major contribution that native peoples have made to American sports, it should be noted that it is certainly not their only contribution. There have been many great American Indian athletes, coaches, and teams in a variety of sports. For example, Charles "Chief" Bender, the son of a Chippewa mother and a German father, pitched for the Philadelphia Athletics when they won the World Series in 1910, 1911, and 1913. He compiled a career record of 212–127 and an earned run average of 2.46. He threw a no-hitter in 1912.

The Carlisle Indian Industrial School in Carlisle, Pennsylvania, developed a great football program during its existence from 1879 through 1918. Jim Thorpe, voted the greatest athlete of the first half of the twentieth century, was a first-team All-American while playing for the school in 1911 and 1912. He went on to play professional baseball, win two Olympic Gold Medals, and help found the National Football League. Glenn S. "Pop" Warner, one of the most famous football coaches of all time, coached at Carlisle from 1899 through 1912. Even though Carlisle didn't have a home field to play on and had to face all of its opponents on their home fields, the team still built a winning tradition. Carlisle was ranked fifth in the nation in 1906 and in 1911 posted a record of 11–1.

Many Carlisle athletes are honored in the American Indian Athletic Hall of Fame which opened in 1972. The Hall is located on the campus of Haskell Indian Nations University in Lawrence, Kansas.

A RIVER RUNS THROUGH IT—ROWING

While Native Americans were the first to play sports in the mid-Atlantic region, when European settlers arrived they began holding athletic contests as well. Hunting, fishing, and other forms of outdoor recreation were the first sporting events taken up by Eurpoean settlers. However, rowing was the first sport that was actually "organized" in terms of starting clubs, holding official events, and providing opportunities for people to make money.

The rivers of the Mid-Atlantic were often used for travel, and many men made their living by rowing people across or along rivers as the taxis of the day. Oarsmen such as the New York Whitehaulers began having races to prove to themselves and their customers who could row the fastest. They would also row against visiting crews from ships anchored in New York harbor. The first known organized race occurred on the Hudson River in New York City in 1758.

Rowing clubs began forming in the early 1800s, and these groups began holding "regattas," or series of races, on the rivers of the Mid-Atlantic. The Knickerbocker Club was the first U.S. rowing club, formed in 1823. The oldest surviving club is the Bachelor's Barge Club, formed in Philadelphia in 1853. A group of nine Philadelphia rowing clubs that rowed on the city's Schuylkill River united in 1858 to form the "Schuylkill Navy," the oldest amateur athletic governing body in the United States.

As rowing grew as a sport, some of the best in the sport began to make a living at it. Races for prize money drew tens of thousands of spectators and the winner of such races could often make a thousand dollars or more for winning a race, a significant amount of money in the nineteenth century. Until it was eclipsed by baseball, football, and horse racing in the 1890s, professional rowing was the most popular sport in America.

While professional rowing races have faded in popularity, rowing at the college, high (prep) school, and club levels continues to be popular, with the mid-Atlantic and New England areas leading the way.

Rowing became the first organized college sport in 1852 when a group of schools formed the Rowing Association of American Colleges. That organization was followed by the Intercollegiate Rowing Association, formed in 1895 by mid-Atlantic schools Columbia, Cornell, and Penn. National Championship races have mainly been held in Poughkeepsie and Syracuse, New York, and now on the Cooper River in Camden, New Jersey. The largest collegiate regatta is the Dad Vail Regatta, held on the Schuylkill each May.

The tradition of high school rowing teams was created in large part by prep schools of the Mid-Atlantic, and later joined by public schools such as Virginia's Washington and Lee, the first public school to join in rowing against the private schools. Today thousands of high school students participate on rowing teams. The biggest high school regatta is Stotesbury, held on the Schuylkill since 1927. In 2003, 4,000 athletes from 142 high schools rowed 665 boats at Stotesbury.

Rowing clubs continue to be an important part of the sport, just as they were in the 1800s. Club teams can still take part in events such as the Thomas Eakins Head of the Schuylkill Regatta, first held in 1874, or the Crab Feast Regatta in Washington, D.C., or events held on the Christina River in Wilmington, Delaware.

Rowing became an Olympic sport in 1900. The first team to win gold in the eight-man event was a United States squad composed entirely of rowers from the Vespers Club in Philadelphia. Olympic rowers continue to train on the Schuylkill today.

HOME OF THE NATIONAL PASTIME—BASEBALL

The mid-Atlantic region is central to the history and development of baseball—America's national pastime. Baseball was born in Manhattan and grew in popularity in the large cities of the mid-Atlantic region. The first organized game was played in Hoboken, New Jersey. The first players' association held its first convention in Philadelphia. While baseball spread through the nation as a uniting force and became a way for immigrant groups to assimilate into American culture, the sport still had a shameful policy of excluding African Americans, who responded by forming their own teams and leagues. That chapter in baseball history would come to an end in Brooklyn in 1947. Today, the small town of Cooperstown, New York, is where the sport's history is preserved and displayed in the Baseball Hall of Fame. From the game's beginnings to the present day, the mid-Atlantic region has played a prominent role in baseball.

Championship baseball game at the Elysian Fields, Hoboken, New Jersey, c. 1866. Courtesy Library of Congress.

Birthplace of Baseball

Organized team sports as we have come to know them did not begin to appear on the American scene until the mid–nineteenth century, coinciding with the rise of large cities in the mid-Atlantic region. The development of urban areas such as New York City, Philadelphia, Baltimore, and Washington, D.C., meant that for the first time a large population was contained in a small geographic area in the United States. This was one of the conditions necessary for baseball players to create teams and leagues and to also find people to come watch the games.

By 1850, New York City had 500,000 residents and Philadelphia had 300,000. The numbers would only grow from there. America's urban population more than doubled between 1880 and 1900 from 14 million to 30 million. By 1890, there were 2 million people living in New York City and Brooklyn and 1 million in Philadelphia, while Baltimore and Washington, D.C., had 500,000 each. As America moved from the country to the city, there were worries that urban dwellers were not getting enough exercise and fresh air. Therefore, public officials encouraged vigorous outdoor games that could help develop strong citizens of the young nation.

Consider the words of religious leader James Cardinal Gibbons in 1896 as he stated the importance of baseball to the general public: "Let me say that I favor Base Ball as an amusement for the greatest pleasure-loving people in the world. . . . It is a healthy sport, and since the people of the country generally demand some sporting event for their amusement, I should single this out as the one best to be patronized and heartily approve of it as a popular pastime."[1]

There are references to games involving bats and balls as far back as the 1700s, and Americans regularly played British games such as cricket and rounders. There are also early-nineteenth-century references to similar games call "base," "cat," and "trap-ball." What these various Old World games had in common was the use of some sort of stick to hit a ball, with the goal being for the hitter to advance to a location on the field of play. The citizens of the New World took these games and their rules and adapted them to create their own sports.

"Town ball" was one such game. There were no foul lines or set fielding positions, and the form of getting batters out was by throwing the ball at them. Some historians have suggested that baseball eventually won out over cricket, which enjoyed some popularity in the early nineteenth century, because baseball was a uniquely American creation whereas cricket was English.

Baseball as we might recognize it today first appeared in 1845, when Alexander Cartwright and a group of men formed the Knickerbocker Base Ball Club in Manhattan. The Knickerbockers created a diamond with foul lines and put in a rule that gave three strikes to a batter, but changes would continue to occur for many years before the rules of modern baseball were set. The Knickerbockers took part in the first known organized baseball game, a 23–1 loss to the New York Base Ball Club on June 19, 1846, at Elysian Fields in Hoboken, New Jersey.

Early Mid-Atlantic Teams

Class distinctions were important in sports at that time (some would argue they still are today), and the Knickerbockers were a group of "gentlemen." The team wore blue trousers, white shirts and straw hats. Formal dinners followed their games against the Gothams, Harlems, Putnams, Excelsiors, and Eagles—all teams from the mid-Atlantic region. As upper-class gentlemen, the Knickerbockers and their early opponents emphasized the importance of participating in leisure activity rather than "common" matters such as winning and losing. As members of the upper class, the Knickerbockers had no need to prove themselves to their peers. To care too much about victory would only appear vulgar to those they associated with.

However, working-class players would soon begin forming their own ball clubs. The year 1855 saw the birth of the Eckford Club of Brooklyn, made up of shipwrights and mechanics, and the Newark (New Jersey) Mechanics Club. Working-class teams were known to begin games as early 5 A.M. so as not to interfere with the employment of players. These teams may have been looking for something different in the game.

The baseball field was a rare place in nineteenth-century society where class, wealth, and lineage did not matter. A working-class man could be the equal of an upper-class gentleman in the meritocracy between the foul lines.

As the *Newark Call* newspaper pointed out in 1887: "If anywhere in the world the social barriers are broken down it is on the ball field. There are many men of low birth and poor breeding are the idols of the rich and cultured; the best man is he who plays best. Even men of churlish disposition and coarse hues are tolerated on the field."[2]

A working class team might take more interest in winning and losing than the Knickerbockers had previously shown because the players were anxious to prove themselves to the rest of society. Immigrant groups in particular saw the game as a way to demonstrate how "American" they had become.

In their book *Diamonds in the Rough*, Joel Zoss and John Bowman note: "The WASP code of gamesmanship throughout the nineteenth century called for a somewhat cavalier attitude toward winning. This would eventually be pushed aside by the image of the 'hungry' immigrant, anxious to claw his way up the ladder of financial independence if not social acceptance."[3]

Once the working-class teams appeared on the scene, teams like the Knickerbockers lost their apparent disdain for worrying about winning and losing. What was a way they could defeat the working class teams? They had more money, so why not hire the best players to play for them? The Knickerbockers did just that, hiring Henry Wright as the first professional baseball player in 1856.

This was an important development in the history of baseball and in the history of sports in general. Baseball set a pattern that will be seen in other American sports. The sport starts as a game that people play for fun in their spare time, becomes more competitive, and finally turns into a way to make money as the stakes for winning and losing are raised even higher. Even activities as apparently innocent as skateboarding and surfing have been turned into corporate sponsored professional sports that seek television exposure. However, it should also be noted that the way a particular sport gains exposure and grows in popularity is precisely through following this pattern. Furthermore, if someone is talented at a sport and enjoys doing it, why shouldn't they have the opportunity to make a living at it?

Throughout history, going back to the ancient Greeks and Romans, people have always managed to make sports into something more than just a leisure activity. However, baseball in the late nineteenth century was particularly ripe for commercial exploitation because the society that surrounded it in the large cities of the Mid-Atlantic was sufficiently built up in terms of population and had sufficient free time and disposable income.

One reason baseball teams could afford to start paying players was because they were able to gather crowds who were willing to pay to watch the best players. In 1858, 2,000 fans in Long Island paid fifty cents each (a not inconsiderable sum at the time) to attend a game, and an 1859 game between the Excelsiors and Atlantics, both of Brooklyn, drew a paying crowd of 15,000.

Once the Knickerbockers had hired a player, other teams followed suit, and the issue soon became prominent in the emerging sport. When the National Association of Base Ball Players held its first convention in Philadelphia in 1867, one of the issues the leagues and players needed to address was who was a professional and who wasn't. Some teams might pay to employ a player or two, something not always known to their opponents. However, things were cleared up when a group of Ohio businessmen created the first all professional team, the Cincinnati Red Stockings, in 1869.

The Red Stockings went on a sixty-five-game barnstorming tour in 1869. Though their profit came to just $1.39 for that first season, investors still recognized that there was a future in the business of baseball. By the 1871 season, nine other professional teams had been created. They got together to form the National Association of Professional Baseball Players, and there was now a section of the game devoted to making money.

Black Baseball in the Region

The mid-Atlantic region has played a major role in the history of African Americans in baseball. The area was home to the first black teams and first black professional player as well as some of the greatest teams in the Negro Leagues. African Americans got involved in the game soon after its creation and began to put together their own teams and leagues. The first known game between African American teams occurred in 1867 as the Excelsiors of Philadelphia played games against the Monitors and Uniques of Brooklyn. The first black professional player was John W. "Bud" Fowler, who was paid to play for a team in New Castle, Pennsylvania, in 1872. The first African American team composed completely of professional players was the Cuban Giants of Long Island, who first took the field in 1885.

African American players and teams began to experience discrimination as soon as they attempted to join white teams and leagues. As early as 1867, the National Association of Ball Players issued a statement arguing that racial integration would lead to a "division of feelings" and cause "injury."[4] The issue came to a head in the Mid-Atlantic on July 14, 1887, when the National League arrived in Newark, New Jersey, to play the local International League team in an exhibition game. Newark had scheduled African American George Stovey as the starting pitcher that day, but Chicago player "Cap" Anson said he would not play with a black player on the field. Anson, whose nickname was "The Grand Old Man of Baseball," was the most prominent baseball player of the nineteenth century, and his views carried great weight among game officials. Later that day, the International League made an official announcement that African Americans would no longer be allowed to play in the league.

Despite the ban, black players created their own teams and leagues. The first league to last for any significant time was the Negro National League, begun in 1920 by Andrew "Rube" Foster. Other regional Negro Leagues developed later, with the mid-Atlantic region playing an important role. The Pittsburgh Crawfords and the Homestead Grays are considered to be two of the greatest teams in the history of the Negro Leagues.

The Courage of Jackie Robinson

Major League Baseball observed a "gentlemen's" agreement on not allowing African Americans for nearly the first half of the twentieth century. However, one baseball executive, Brooklyn Dodgers president Branch Rickey, was determined to bring about change. He knew that he would need someone who was both a talented baseball player and a courageous human being who could deal with the racism he would face as the first black in the game. Rickey found these qualities in one remarkable individual—Jackie Robinson.

On April 15, 1947, Robinson made history by starting at first base in the Dodgers' season opener, a 5–3 win over the Boston Braves. Despite all of the challenges Robinson, need that season, he hit .297, tied for the team lead in home runs with 12, led the team with 125 runs scored, and led the National League with 28 stolen bases. Fans thrilled to Robinson's base stealing abilities, especially when he stole home. The Dodgers drew a record 1.8 million fans that season as Robinson helped them win the National League pennant. He was also voted the Rookie of the Year.

The importance of Jackie Robinson's accomplishments in 1947 can hardly be overstated, both in regard to his impact on baseball and to race relations in America. Baseball was still the unquestioned number one sport in the country at that time, and Robinson was the biggest story in the game. His success opened the game up to other black players and helped to prepare the way for the civil rights movement that would emerge in the 1950s and 1960s.

African American Dodger pitcher Don Newcombe said: "We were paying our dues long before the civil rights marches. Martin Luther King told me in my home one night, 'You'll never

Jackie Robinson wearing his Dodgers uniform during batting practice at Ebbets Field, New York City, April 1947. Courtesy Library of Congress.

know what you and Jackie and Roy (Campanella) do to make it possible to do my job.'"[5]

Baseball Rivalries

The most intense mid-Atlantic rivalries may have occurred just in one city in one sport. New York City at one time had three of Major League Baseball's sixteen teams; the Giants and the Brooklyn Dodgers in the National League, and the Yankees in the American League. Anytime the Yankees met the Giants or Dodgers in the World Series it would be dubbed a "subway series" and New Yorkers would defend their loyalty to their given team. There were six subway series between 1921 and 1941, but the real golden era came during a ten-year stretch from 1947 through 1956, when there were seven subway series. However, the Giants and Dodgers left for the West Coast soon thereafter. Nevertheless, New York got another National League team, the Mets, who met up with the Yankees for a subway series in 2000.

National Baseball Hall of Fame

The mid-Atlantic region is where baseball preserves its history at the National Baseball Hall of Fame in Cooperstown, New York. The hall features various historical exhibits and artifacts from baseball history and is open to the public. The hall is also where plaques for 256 Hall of Fame inductees, most of them players, are displayed. The Hall of Fame Weekend is held in late July for new inductees.

FOOTBALL

Like baseball, football was born and grew up in the mid-Atlantic region before eventually becoming a huge money-making machine as America's most popular spectator sport. Before there were college football bowl games that made seven-figure payouts, there were young men in the mid-Atlantic region in the nineteenth century who were playing a dangerous free-for-all takeoff on soccer and rugby with no pads or passing. Before the National Football League became king of American pro sports, in 1892 the Allegheny Athletic Association of Pennsylvania paid William Pudge Heffelfinger $500 to play for them in their big game against the Pittsburgh Athletic Club. He proved to be worth the price as he scooped up a fumble and ran 35 yards for the game's only score as Allegheny won 4–0.

Unlike baseball, in which professional teams became popular almost from the start among a wide variety of fans, football started out as a college sport. Professional football struggled for many years and did not become popular until decades after the college game had been established. The development of football was also different from baseball in that football was a sport that the public generally watched, whereas baseball was a sport they generally people played.

The first known college football game occurred on November 8, 1869, when Princeton played Rutgers in New Brunswick, New Jersey. There were twenty-five men on each side who were allowed to advance the ball by either kicking or punching it. Teams scored one point by putting the ball between a pair of posts. Many other colleges soon took up some form of the game, but it was Princeton, Columbia (in New York City), Harvard, and Yale that would be the main schools to help college football grow quickly in its early years. When Princeton and Yale played for the first time in 1878, the game drew an audience of 4,000. When the two schools played just ten years later, they drew a crowd of 40,000.

A group of football playing colleges formed the Intercollegiate Football Association in 1876, started using an oval ball, set the field at 140 by 70 yards, decided to play two forty-two-minute halves per game, and chose Thanksgiving Day for their championship game. In the 1880s they moved that championship game to the Polo Grounds in the Harlem section of New York City and started drawing large crowds. In 1893, a huge throng followed a Thanksgiving Day parade up 5th Avenue in Manhattan to the Polo Grounds, where 40,000 fans paid as much as $15 for a ticket to watch Princeton beat Yale 6–0.

Putting on a big spectacle also required that college football programs be able to make money, and even back in the nineteenth century commentators were complaining (as they still are in the twenty-first century) that college football was the tail wagging the academic dog.

For example, in 1893 Caspar Whitney complained in *Harper's Weekly* about "[t]he exhibition of our college boys, sons of gentlemen, resorting to the intrigues of unprincipled professionals."[6] James A. Leroy wrote in 1900: "Victory has come to mean advertising, full treasuries, improved athletic fields, expert coaches and the satisfying howl of approval from an ever-growing bleacher crowd. Faculty control is a myth."[7]

A Dangerous Game

Football spread from the mid-Atlantic and New England regions throughout the country in the late nineteenth century. By 1896 it was estimated that 5,000 high school and college games were played on Thanksgiving Day. However, there was one problem that threatened to derail the popularity of the game—injuries and even death. Football is, of course, an inherently rough sport, but around 1900, the rules, style of play, and lack of protective equipment all combined to make the game quite dangerous.

For example, in 1884 Princeton first tried the "*V*" formation, where a group of blockers would form a *V* around of the player running with the ball to keep him protected. The strategy would later become known as the "flying wedge." Teams would back up 20 yards behind the line of scrimmage, form their wedge, and then get a running start toward the line. They would be going full speed when they met up with the defense.

Adding to the problem was that teams played two games a week, Wednesday and Saturday, and players could only be replaced if they were injured. Helmets were invented in 1896, but many players refused to wear them, feeling that it made one appear weak in front of opponents. The rules of the time also allowed players to help their teammates who were carrying the ball by pushing them ahead through defenders. Halfbacks even had handles sewed into the backs and shoulders of their jerseys so that teammates could pick them up and throw them over the crunch at the line of scrimmage. Further, the forward pass had not yet been legalized, meaning that there was often a tangled pile of bodies in the middle of the field.

In 1904 there were twenty-one football deaths, and the number jumped to

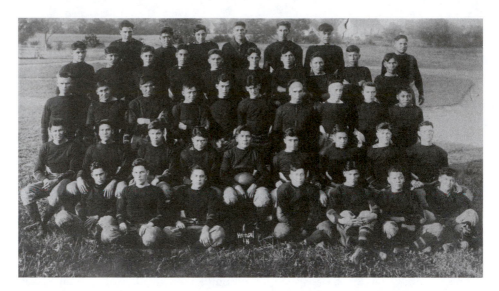

Carlisle School football squad, November 1914. Courtesy Library of Congress.

twenty-three in 1905. There was a public outcry and some were calling for an end to football. However, football had the nation's number one fan in Washington, D.C., willing to help out. President Theodore Roosevelt was a fan of the "manly sport" and felt that athletics were an important part of the college experience. Roosevelt wanted football to continue in the colleges, but he also knew there would have to be changes to make the game safer. In 1905 he summoned football leaders from Princeton, Harvard, and Yale to the White House and told them to make reforms or face abolition.

In December of that same year, Henry M. McCracken, the chancellor of New York University, called a meeting in New York City to address possible reforms. Approximately seventy schools attended, some of which wanted to banish football from their campuses. That first meeting would lead to the development in 1910 of the National Collegiate Athletic Association, the body that now governs college athletics.

Although promises were made at the White House and at the New York City meetings, it would take a few years for reforms to kick in. The first was to legalize the forward pass in 1906. It would take a few years before teams would begin to pass regularly. Once they did, it meant that players were more spread out around the field, thus helping to reduce the injuries and even fatalities that had previously plagued the game. Passing was facilitated by gradually changing the ball, which was made smaller so that it was easier to grip and throw.

Paid to Play

Football followed the same pattern as baseball in becoming professional, but it took much longer for football to establish a viable professional league. Pro football lagged behind baseball and college football in terms of popularity. The pro game at that time was seen as less legitimate than the college version, and it was felt that even the best pro teams would be no match for the top college squads of the day.

Different professional football associations were formed in the early years of the twentieth century, but never worked out until August 20, 1920, when a group of men gathered in the Jordan and Hupmobile Automobile Showroom in Canton, Ohio, to form the American Professional Football Conference—which two years later would come to be known as the National Football League (NFL). However, it would still be decades before the NFL would achieve popularity on par with college football, much less baseball.

Rivalries between mid-Atlantic teams are intense. Two of the most important games that made the NFL an American institution took place between New York and Baltimore teams. In 1958 Johnny Unitas led the Baltimore Colts to a 23–17 overtime victory over the New York Giants in the NFL championship game. The game was significant because it was televised widely and showed a large audience just how exciting football on TV could be as Unitas led the Colts on a last-minute game-tying drive.

In 1969, the New York Jets of the upstart American Football League met the established Colts of the National Football League in Super Bowl III. The Colts were heavy favorites, but the Jets' quarterback, Joe Namath, nevertheless guaranteed a New York victory. Players today make "guarantees" all the time, but when Namath made his, such a move was almost unheard of and had never been made on such a large stage. Namath and his long-haired teammates represented a younger league and a younger generation and delivered a shocking 16–7 upset win over Baltimore. This helped bring the two leagues together into the NFL as we know it today and made the Super Bowl into the annual hype-fest it has become.

TAKING BASKETBALL TO THE STREETS

Besides being an area that has made vital contributions to the history of American sports, the mid-Atlantic region continues to be a place where sports are developed before being exported to the rest of the world. As discussed in earlier, the mid-Atlantic region has played a defining role in the history of America's most popular sports.

One sport that has quickly grown to prominence in the twenty-first century is outdoor playground basketball, also known as "streetball." The street game is an exciting mix of hoops and showmanship that is as much about entertainment as sport. It has attracted the attention and participation of filmmakers, rap artists, clothing designers, and video game makers.

While other sports reach the public by having their games televised during a season in which a champion is crowned, the gospel of streetball is spread through videotapes that focus on show-stopping trick dribbling and dunks rather than scores of games. Streetball is not so much about wins and losses as it is about guys with nicknames like "Hot Sauce" and "Half Man-Half Amazing" putting on a show with crowd-pleasing moves such as the "Twisted Blister" or "Flintstone Shuffle."

A playground in the Harlem section of New York City became legendary for hosting games where the best players, including National Basketball Association (NBA) stars, gathered to test their game against the toughest competition. Streetball developed a national audience when a Pennsylvania-based athletic shoe company (AND1) started marketing videotapes of a young point guard from the Queens borough of New York City (Rafer Alston) who could do amazing tricks with the ball.

The Rucker

Rucker Park, at the corner of 155th Street and Frederick Douglass Boulevard, is considered to be the center of the streetball universe. One documentary referred to the place as "hallowed ground." Rucker Park is named after Holcombe Rucker, who began organizing outdoor basketball tournaments in Harlem and Manhattan in 1946.

Rucker organized his playground tournaments because he wanted to give young men an alternative to the drugs and violence found on the streets. During his lifetime Rucker helped hundreds of young men to get college scholarships as he worked from 5 A.M. to 10 P.M. every day. Rucker died in 1965 at the age of thirty-eight of cancer, but his name and vision live on at the park named after him, where tournaments are still played. The park opened in 1956 as P.S. 156 Playground, before being named Holcombe Rucker Park in 1974. Over the years it has simply come to be known as "the Rucker."

Many of the greatest players in basketball history have performed at the Rucker and other streetball tournaments over the years. The list includes some of the most famous players from the National Basketball Association, such as Julius "Dr. J" Erving, Kareem Abdul-Jabbar, and Wilt Chamberlain. However, there is also a list of players who never became famous in the NBA, but whose streetball exploits are nonetheless still remembered. For example, there's Joe "The Destroyer" Hammond, who allegedly scored 50 points *in one half* against Dr. J (he denies it) in a Rucker League game in 1970. Or Earl "The Goat" Manigault, who could reportedly dunk a ball, grab it in midair, and dunk it again.

FEMALE PIONEERS IN SPORTS

Throughout the history of American sports, many female sports pioneers have come from the mid-Atlantic region. One of the first known athletic events in America involving women as competitors took place in Hempstead Plains, Long Island, New York, in 1780 when a horse race was held for women riders. It is believed that the first sport that men and women played together in America was croquet. In 1864 the Park Place Croquet Club in Brooklyn had twenty-five members of both genders. Just one year after that, Vassar College opened in New York, which included a "School of Physical Training." The Laurel Baseball Club was formed at the college the next year, and other women's teams would soon follow, such as the Dolly Vardens, an African American pro team from Philadelphia. Women would continue be involved in baseball with the appearance of "Bloomer Girls" teams in the 1890s. Squads such as the Philadelphia Bobbies, New York Bloomer Girls, or Baltimore Black Sox Colored Girls would go on barnstorming tours to various cities.

While women enjoyed baseball in the late nineteenth century, they were also involved in a variety of individual sports. The Harlem River was the site for women's rowing races in 1871, and a mile-long swim race in 1873, when Delilah Goboess beat nine other women to win first prize, a silk dress. Also popular in the 1870s were walking matches known as "pedestrians." In 1876 Mary Marshall beat Peter Van Ness in a series of three matches held in New York City. Golf was also a popular sport for women, and ladies' golf tournaments are known to have been held in 1894 in Morristown, New Jersey, and in 1895 at the Meadow Brook Club in Hempstead, New York.

A school in Pennsylvania was an important site for the development of two women's sports. An English woman named Constance M.K. Applebee first introduced the sport of field hockey to America in 1901. While visiting Harvard for a seminar she set up a field and showed those present how the game worked. In 1904 she came to Bryn Mawr School in Pennsylvania and proceeded to get the sport going there. She was the president when the American Field Hockey Association was founded and she also created the first field hockey camp in the United States when she opened the Tegawitha Hockey Camp in Mount Pocono, Pennsylvania, in 1923.

Bryn Mawr was also the place where Rosabelle Sinclair helped to popularize the sport of lacrosse for women. As mentioned earlier, lacrosse was played by the Iroquois and other American Indian tribes before being picked up by white European immigrants in the late nineteenth century. Sinclair introduced the sport to the school in 1926. Sinclair would later become the first woman inducted into the Lacrosse Hall of Fame, also in Baltimore, in 1993.

1915 Vassar College field hockey team. Courtesy Library of Congress.

Title IX

While women played many sports in the twentieth century, they were clearly second-class citizens when compared with the opportunities available to men. In 1972, Congress passed, and President Richard M. Nixon signed Title IX of the Civil Rights Act of 1964, which prohibits discrimination on the basis of gender at institutions that receive funding from the federal government. Since most high schools and colleges receive federal funding, they are required by law to offer females the same athletic opportunities that are available to males.

Another significant development in women's access to sports occurred around this same time in New Jersey. In 1972, Maria Pepe of Hoboken, where the first official baseball game had been played back in 1846, filed suit against Little League Baseball, Inc., for the right to be able to play Little League Baseball just like the boys. A court ruled in her favor in 1974, opening the door for girls to take part in the national pastime. While girls can now play baseball, the vast majority of female athletes play fast-pitch softball. Little League Baseball now runs softball programs for girls.

Title IX and Little League sports for girls have had a positive effect for women participating in sports. A study by the Feminist Majority Foundation estimated that there were 817,073 girls involved in high school sports in 1972, a number that rose to 1,997,489 in 1993. However, there are arguments that women still have a long way to go before achieving equality. An investigation by the *Pittsburgh Tribune-Review* in 2003[8] found that in 129 western Pennsylvania and Pittsburgh city high schools, two of three athletes were male and sixty-nine cents out of every dollar spent on sports went to boys' teams.

SPORTS FOR CHILDREN AND TEENS

The mid-Atlantic region is the place where organized youth sports were invented. At the high school level, western Pennsylvania is known nationwide for its football teams, while schools from Maryland and New York dominate prep lacrosse.

Baseball on a Smaller Scale

In 1938, Carl E. Stotz gathered a group of children together in Williamsport, Pennsylvania, to play baseball. One year later Stotz and the Bebble brothers, George and Bert, founded Little League Baseball with three teams sponsored by local businesses—Lycoming Dairy, Lundy Lumber, and Jumbo Pretzel. From there the program grew to the point where in 2001 over 2.5 million boys and girls competed in the program in over 7,000 leagues in over 100 countries worldwide.

Little League has followed the same course as the adult version of baseball. Little League began holding its own annual World Series in Williamsport. Now a high-stakes competition, it picked up corporate sponsors as early as 1949 and today has a television contract.

A 2003 report in the *Miami Herald* stated that today, "Little League is seen as quaint and outdated."[9] Top youth players in the twenty-first century usually play on "travel teams" that have no geographic restrictions (which Little League does) on who can play on a team. Players and their families spend significant time and money to compete year-round and travel (sometimes cross-country) to tournaments. This group sees Little League as a program for those who aren't really serious about the sport.

The Cradle of Quarterbacks

Western Pennsylvania has been called the "Cradle of Quarterbacks" because of the football talent that has been produced in the area. Hall of Fame quarterbacks such as Johnny Unitas, Joe Namath, Joe Montana, Dan Marino, George Blanda, and Jim Kelly all hail from the area. There are twenty-five Pennsylvania natives in the Pro Football Hall of Fame—more than from any other state.

Those famous players learned the game while playing high school football in western Pennsylvania. The area continues to have some of the best programs in the nation. In 2002, *USA Today* marked the twentieth year of its "Super 25" high school football poll, in which schools from Pennsylvania have figured prominently over the years. The *USA Today* poll looks at a possible 22,000 schools in thirty-nine states and Washington, D.C. Over a twenty-year period 292 different teams had been ranked in the Super 25, thirty-six of them from Pennsylvania. The only state with more teams ranked was much more populous California with forty-seven. Pennsylvania had more teams ranked than states that are typically thought of as football hot-beds, such as Texas, Florida, and Ohio. One Pennsylvania school, Doylestown Central Bucks West, was ranked no less than eight times between 1985 and 2000, finishing in the top 10 seven of those times.

Pennsylvania also produced more than its fair share of number one teams at the end of the season that could claim a mythical national championship. Berwick, a town of under 11,000, was declared the top team in the land three times, more than any other school, in 1983, 1992, and 1995. The school's program, under the direction of coach George Curry, had also produced thirteen quarterbacks at NCAA Division I college programs. North Hills High School from Pittsburgh was also the number one team in America at the end of the 1987 season, giving Pennsylvania four national champions over twenty years, again more than any other state except California, which had five.

The Home of Lacrosse

As mentioned earlier, the Iroquois tribe in New York was one of the Native American groups that played lacrosse for hundreds of years, and the sport continued to be a popular sport in the mid-Atlantic region among whites from the nineteenth century forward. The game continues to be popular at the high school level in the Mid-Atlantic, particularly in New York and Maryland.

Crowds of 5,000 are not unknown for high school lacrosse games in either of those states, where one can regularly find lacrosse nets in driveways along with basketball hoops. In the April 25, 2003, edition of the LAXPower national coaches' poll for high school lacrosse teams, every one of the top ten schools was from either New York or Maryland despite the continuing growth of the sport across the country. In a later poll in June that same year, twenty-nine of the top fifty teams in the nation came from either New York or Maryland.

Stickball and Stoopball

While children in the mid-Atlantic region in the twenty-first century have a variety of organized leagues and other sporting activities to keep them busy, there was a time when all kids needed to get a game going was a rubber ball, a broom handle, a few friends, and the street.

The large urban areas of the Mid-Atlantic sometimes left children with nowhere to play but the street, and they took advantage of it, creating a variety of games that they could play with their friends in front of their apartments and houses. The most famous of these were stickball and stoopball.

Stickball was much like baseball in that a ball was pitched and hit and a runner tried to get around the bases while the ball was being fielded. The ball was a small pink rubber ball made by the Spalding company, but called a "Spaldeen" in the New York accent. The bat was a broom handle with tape around it. The field was the street and bases could be whatever was handy. Home plate was usually a manhole cover, while first base might be a car, second might be another manhole cover, and third might be a tree or a trashcan depending on the street. While Willie Mays was playing for the New York Giants and lived in the Bronx, he was said to sometimes play stickball in the streets with the kids and was known as a "four-sewer man" because he could hit the ball the length of four manhole covers in the street.

Stickball is believed to have started in New York City. Between the 1880s and the 1920s the city swelled with immigrants. Many of them were anxious to learn the game of baseball so that they could become more fully "American." However, time, money, and access to space did not always afford them the opportunity to play baseball, so they developed a cheaper version that could be played right where they lived.

Stickball could be played by any number of children, but if there were only two or three kids around, they could play stoopball, a game that also used a Spaldeen. One of the players would try to bounce the ball at an angle off either the curb or the front stoop of a house or apartment building. The other player or players would try to catch the ball. There are endless variations on the game, but generally if the bouncer could bounce the ball far enough or get it by other players he would get a certain number of points. If another player caught the ball on the fly it would be his or her turn to be the bouncer.

Street games such as stickball and stoopball had their best days in the 1940s and 1950s and began to fade at the end of the 1970s due to increased traffic in the city, the arrival of video games, and parents not feeling that their children were safe out on the streets anymore. However, stickball is enjoying a comeback among adults who played the game as children. The adults in turn are trying to teach the game to a new generation.

Perhaps the most well known adult stickball league is the New York Emperors Stickball League, which was founded in 1985 and holds a Memorial Day tournament in the Bronx every year. Games are played at Stickball Boulevard, which was recently renamed Steve Mercado Boulevard after the former league president, a firefighter who died in the September 11, 2001, terrorist attacks.

OFF TO COLLEGE

Athletes who enjoyed the youth and high school sports opportunities offered in the Mid-Atlantic have also been able to find top competition in the area's many colleges and universities as well.

Princeton dominated early on in college football, winning or sharing thirteen national titles in the nineteenth century and four more in the early twentieth century. Penn also did well in the early years, winning or sharing four national titles between 1895 and 1908. Another Ivy League school, Cornell, won championships in 1921 and 1922.

In college football the rivalry between two military academies, Army (in West Point, New York) and Navy (in Annapolis, Maryland), has been called the purest rivalry in America and has featured many important games over the years.[10] What is particularly notable about the annual game between the two service academies is that afterwards they gather together to sing the school songs of both teams, as students from both colleges must learn to work together to defend America.

Army took its first national title in 1914 and then won championships again during 1944 and 1945. Between 1944 and 1946 Army was involved in four games between the number one and number two teams in the Associated Press rankings against either Navy or Notre Dame.

Pittsburgh has won two national titles, although very far apart. One came in 1918, while the next came in 1976. Penn State has enjoyed great success for nearly four decades under head coach Joe Paterno. The Nittany Lions won national championships in 1982 and 1986, and Paterno had three other teams that finished the season undefeated but were not named national champion. Paterno and Florida State's Bobby Bowden have more coaching wins than anyone else in the history of NCAA Division I-A coaching.

In several college sports, mid-Atlantic schools have had a chance to develop rivalries because they are always battling each other for national championships. In college rowing, four mid-Atlantic schools (Columbia, Cornell, Penn, and Syracuse) won all of the national titles between 1895 and 1916. In men's college lacrosse, mid-Atlantic schools won twenty-eight of thirty-two possible titles between 1971 and 2003, led by Syracuse with eight, Johns Hopkins with seven, and Princeton with six. In NCAA women's lacrosse, Maryland won seven straight titles between 1995 and 2001, but those titles were bookended by Princeton championships in 1994 and 2002 as well as 2003.

In some college sports, rivalries have not been an issue because one school from the Mid-Atlantic has so thoroughly dominated the sport. Villanova won six consecutive titles in women's cross country from 1989 through 1994. Penn State won eight titles in men's and women's fencing during the eleven years between 1990 and 2000. Old Dominion racked up eight women's field hockey championships between 1982 and 1999. Finally, West Virginia won thirteen national titles in men's and women's rifle shooting during the twentieth century. This included winning ten out of eleven years between 1988 and 1998.

The Mid-Atlantic, and in particular New York City, was the center of college basketball in the 1950s before a gambling scandal hurt many of the programs in that area. In 1951, City College of New York (CCNY) won both the NCAA and National Invitational Tournament (NIT) titles. Both events were held at Madison

Square Garden, where most of the important college basketball games were held at the time. Philadelphia's LaSalle won the NIT in 1952 and the NCAA in 1954. The Final Four for the 1953 NIT was all Mid-Atlantic. The event was won by Seton Hall of New Jersey, while New York schools St. John's and Manhattan took second and fourth, respectively, and a Duquesne team out of Pittsburgh took third.

The Mid-Atlantic returned to prominence in the 1980s when the Big East Conference, containing several schools from the region, became the most formidable league in the nation. Between 1982 and 1989, the Big East in men's basketball had seven different teams in the Final Four, five of them making it to the championship game. The most dominating year for the league came in 1985 when three of the Final Four, Villanova, Georgetown, and St. John's of New York City, were Big East squads. Villanova won the title that year, knocking off a Georgetown team which had won the national title the year before. Although mid-Atlantic teams have not been as dominant since then, the Big East it is still one of the premiere conferences in the land. Syracuse has enjoyed particular success, making the national championship game in 1996 and winning the title outright in 2003.

As of the year 2000, over sixty colleges and universities in the mid-Atlantic region fielded NCAA Division, I basketball teams.

ON THE LINKS—GOLF

> In the history of American field sports there can be found no outdoor pastime that developed and attained such popularity in such a relatively short period of time as the game of golf.
> —*New York Times*, 1895

Golf first hit American shores in the late 1800s and quickly became so popular that it surpassed even baseball in terms of participation. It is estimated that by 1915 there were between 2.5 and 3.5 million golfers playing some 600 courses in the United States.

The game was quickly taken up by women as well as men. The first women's tournament was held in 1894 in Morristown, New Jersey, and the first women's golfing organization, the Women's Golf Association of Philadelphia, was formed in 1897.

In the twenty-first century, there are

Today, there are millions of golfers playing thousands of courses in the mid-Atlantic region. Courtesy New York State Department of Economic Development.

millions of golfers playing thousands of courses in the mid-Atlantic region alone. For example, the New Jersey State Golf Association has over 100,000 members even though joining the organization requires that a golfer first register with a local club, pay a fee, and play enough rounds to establish a handicap. Therefore, those 100,000 members probably represent just a small percentage of people who regularly play golf.

The Mid-Atlantic provides a wide variety of courses, including courses that tie in with the area's history. For example, the Augustine course in Virginia is named for the land's former owner, Augustine Washington, father of George.

The Mid-Atlantic also has its share of unique courses such as the Caverns, near Old Dominion. The first hole is believed to be the only one in the world where a golfer has to avoid a cavern opening. The good news is that is no penalty stroke for those who have a ball fall in the cavern.

Some of the top courses in the country can be also be found in the Mid-Atlantic. In 2002 the U.S. Open was held at the Bethpage State Park Black Course in Farmingdale, New York, the first time the event was held on a public course. The Shinnecock Hills Golf Course in Southampton, New York, was the site of the 2004 U.S. Open.

HOCKEY

While ice hockey unquestionably has strong ties to Canada, the mid-Atlantic region has helped the sport to grow in the United States from the National Hockey League (NHL), to college, to high school, to little league, and club teams.

The New York Rangers were one of the original six teams in the NHL that still survives today. Since the Rangers joined the league in 1926, several other mid-Atlantic teams have come along and experienced great success. The New York Islanders won four straight Stanley Cups between 1980 and 1983, while the New Jersey Devils won three championships between 1995 and 2003. Other mid-Atlantic teams include the Philadelphia Flyers (Cup winners in 1974 and 1975), the Pittsburgh Penguins (Cup winners in 1991 and 1992), the Buffalo Sabres, and the Washington Capitals. Of the thirty teams in the NHL in 2004, seven are located in the mid-Atlantic region. The entire five-team Atlantic Division is composed of mid-Atlantic teams.

The best success in NCAA hockey by a mid-Atlantic team was enjoyed by the Cornell teams of the late 1960s and early 1970s. Cornell made it to the "Frozen Four" four times over a five-year period, taking third in 1968, second in 1969, and then winning the national title in 1970. Cornell also placed second in 1972. Goalie Ken Dryden played for the school from 1967 through 1969 before going on to become one of the greatest goalies in the history of the NHL.

Over the years the Mid-Atlantic has developed, and continues to have, strong programs at the high school and little league levels. There are also many adults in the area who enjoy playing hockey at the club level. It should also be noted that perhaps the greatest moment in American hockey history occurred in Lake Placid, New York, in 1980 when the U.S. Olympic team shocked the world by defeating the Soviet Union and winning the gold medal.

THE OUTDOORS AND THE CITY: RECREATION IN THE MID-ATLANTIC

> Removed from the dust and hurry-scurry of terra firma, our position enables us to survey several shows and the employments of busy life.... We are near enough to the metropolis to hear its noises subdued into a musical monotone.
> —Genio C. Scott on boat fishing near New York City in 1888.[11]

The mid-Atlantic region has a long tradition of being a place where people enjoy recreation in the outdoors. Whether in areas specifically set aside as natural preserves, or even in the large cities of the Mid-Atlantic, the people of the region have participated in outdoor activities. They have a wide variety of settings in which to commune with nature—from beaches to mountains and everything in between.

Of course, the first naturalists in the Mid-Atlantic were the Indian tribes that had lived in the area long before the arrival of European settlers. After the white immigrants settled and began to build urban areas, the perception of the outdoors began to change. One didn't have to go out into the outdoors just to find food to survive. The outdoors could instead be a place of recreation where people could go to relieve the stresses of living in an urban environment that was no longer connected with nature.

Personal journals from the early 1700s refer to shooting and fishing parties on Long Island and hunting parties for "entertainment" purposes in Virginia.[12] Later in the eighteenth century, Virginia gentlemen such as George Washington and Thomas Jefferson were known to enjoy hunting for sport and recreation. Various

Outdoors enthusiasts raft the New River in West Virginia. Photo by David Fattaleh. Courtesy West Virginia Tourism.

groups began to form their own hunting and fishing clubs and even set aside areas devoted to those sports. The people of the Mid-Atlantic even began creating their own equipment for outdoor activities. The "New York" reel was a new type of fishing reel made of brass and silver that was developed in the mid-nineteenth century. Reels had previously been handmade by one person, but now they began to be produced in factories in New York City, Newark, and Philadelphia.

Outdoor recreation was encouraged because it was seen as a way for both men and women to reconnect with nature and get a break from city life that was often viewed as unhealthy.

As Genio C. Scott observed in 1888, "Many ladies of New York and its suburbs are experts at casting a fly for trout or a bait for bass; and in my opinion, they lend one of the principal charms of ruralizing."[13] Note that Scott didn't just fish in rural areas, but in and around New York City, a practice that continues into the twenty-first century. Inhabitants of the nation's capital also sought recreation close to the city. Proximity to Washington, D.C., was why President Herbert Hoover used what would become Shenandoah National Park as "Camp Hoover" during the summers. It was within 100 miles of Washington, D.C., it had a trout stream, and the altitude was high enough to discourage mosquitoes.

The 196,295 acres that compose Shenandoah Park were designated a national park on December 26, 1935. Shenandoah was unusual as a national park in that the government had to acquire 3,850 privately owned tracts of land and move 465 families who had made a living farming, grazing, livestock and logging. Today the 2 million visitors a year to Shenandoah can engage in a variety of activities, including motoring along Skyline Drive, a 105-mile road that runs parallel to the Appalachian Trail and overlooks the Shenandoah Valley. The park also has peaks, a seventy-foot waterfall, and a grove of giant hemlocks that are hundreds of years old. Such diversity in outdoor activities within Shenandoah Park is typical of the wide variety of settings available for recreation in the mid-Atlantic region.

The outdoor enthusiast in the Mid-Atlantic has many choices: see the famous waterfalls in Niagara Reservation State Park in New York; ski at Allegany State Park in New York; go rafting in the gorge of Ohiopyle State Park in Pennsylvania; go birdwatching in Presque Isle State Park in Pennsylvania; watch seals and dolphins while visiting Island Beach State Park in New Jersey; go surf fishing at Cape Henlopen State Park in Delaware; ride the bike trails of Patapsco Valley State Park in Maryland; see

Plenty of Snow

The only place in the world to host two Winter Olympics is Lake Placid, New York, where the world gathered in 1932 and 1980. The area has many natural advantages that make it ideal for a wide variety of winter sports, including Whiteface Mountain, which has the largest vertical drop (3,216 feet) east of the Mississippi.

Upstate New York is also an excellent place for cross country skiing, whether in the Catskills not far from New York City, the Hudson River valley farther north, or way up in the Adirondacks. Other states in the region also offer excellent skiing opportunities. Pennsylvania alone has twenty-three ski resorts, many of them not far from major cities such as Philadelphia, Pittsburgh, Washington, D.C., and Baltimore.

There are many different ways for residents of the Mid-Atlantic to become involved in skiing and related winter activities. For example, the 600-member Delaware Valley Ski Club, headquartered in Cherry Hill, New Jersey, offers not only a variety of ski activities for its members during the winter, but sporting events throughout the entire year. In Pennsylvania, a snow pass program allows fourth graders to ski up to sixty-four days at twenty-one different resorts for just $10.

Surf fishing at Island Beach. Photo by George Semple. Courtesy New Jersey Commerce & Economic Growth Commission.

where Captain John Smith landed in 1607 at First Landing/Seashore State Park in Virginia; hike to the highest plateau east of the Rockies in Canaan Valley Resort State Park in West Virginia; hunt for crabs and clams at Holts Landing State Park in Delaware; camp on some of the nearly 40,000 forest acres of Green Ridge State Forest in Delaware; stay in cabins by the inlets of the Chesapeake Bay at Janes Island State Park in Maryland; enjoy winter sports at Elk Neck State Park in Maryland; see seventeen-mile-long Gennessee River Gorge, known as "The Grand Canyon of the East," at Letchworth State Park in New York; see the "Black Forest" of Cook Forest in Pennsylvania; hike over 10,000 acres of Appalachian highlands in Watoga State Park in West Virginia; visit a nineteenth-century ghost town in Allaire State Park in New Jersey; or see wild horses at Assateague State Park in Maryland.

RESOURCE GUIDE

Printed Sources

Anderson, Bill. *Fishing the Rivers of the Mid-Atlantic*. Centreville, MD: Tidewater Publishers, 1991.

Farra, Ron, and Johanna Farra. *Winter Trails New York: The Best Cross Country and Snowshoe Trails*. Guilford, CT: Globe Pequot, 2000.

Lewis, Cynthia, Thomas J. Lewis, and Sheila Buff. *Best Hikes with Children in the Catskills and Hudson River Valley*. Seattle: Mountaineers Books, 2002.

Lomax, Michael E. "The African American Experience in Professional Football." *Journal of Social History* 33 (1999).

Nemec, David, and Saul Wisnia. *100 Years of Baseball*. Lincolnwood, IL: Publications International, 2002.

Peterson, Robert. *Only the Ball was White: A History of Legendary Black Players and All-Black Professional Teams*. Oxford: Oxford University Press, 1970.

Reisler, Jim. *Babe Ruth Slept Here: The Baseball Landmarks of New York City*. South Bend, IN: Diamond Communications, 1998.

Schwartz, Steve. *Sports New York: Where to Play, Learn and Watch in and Around the Big Apple*. New York: City and Company, 1998.

Slam Presents Streetball. Special collector's issue of *Slam* magazine, no. 30 (summer 2003). Contains a variety of articles on the history and development of streetball as well as profiles of players past and present.

Umphlett, Wiley Lee. *Creating the Big Game: John W. Heisman and the Invention of American Football.* Westport, CT: Greenwood Press, 1992.

Web Sites

http://www.baseballhalloffame.org

Official site of the National Baseball Hall of Fame.

http://www.insidehoops.com

Reports on the Entertainers Basketball Classic at Rucker Park and has an interactive chat room.

http://www.littleleaguebaseball.org

Official site of Little League Baseball.

http://www.nascsports.org

Native American Sports Council home page.

http://www.northnet.org/stlawrenceaauw/sports.htm

Information on milestones in women's sports history.

http://www.rowersworld.com

Contains information about rowing events, training, etcetera.

http://www.streetplay.com

Has information about various street games such as stickball and stoopball.

http://www.uslacrosse.org

U.S. Lacrosse home page.

Organizations

Lacrosse Museum and Hall of Fame
113 W. University Parkway
Baltimore, MD 21210
Phone: 410-235-6882

National Baseball Hall of Fame
25 Main Street
Cooperstown, NY 13326
Phone: 888-Hall-of-Fame

Women's Sports Foundation
Eisenhower Park
East Meadow, NY 11554
Phone: 800-227-3988
http://www.omenssportsfoundation.org

Films

And 1: The Mix Tape Series. A series of films from different years about the "Mix Tape Tours" put on by the And 1 shoe and apparel company. Ventura Distribution. Further information can be found at http://www.and1.com.

Baseball. A series of nine two-hour documentaries on the history of baseball directed by Ken Burns. PBS, 1994.

The Jackie Robinson Story. Directed by Alfred E. Green. MGM/UA. 1950. A film biography of Jackie Robinson starring Jackie Robinson playing himself.

A League of Their Own. Directed by Penny Marshall. Columbia/Tristar Pictures, 1992. A fictionalized story of the All-American Girls Professional Baseball League starring Geena Davis, Tom Hanks, and Madonna.

NFL Films: Inside the Vault, vols. 1–3. NFL Films–Warner Home Video, 2003. These three volumes cover the early years of NFL Films, beginning with the 1962 NFL championship game, and continuing through 1970.

On Hallowed Ground: Streetball Champions of Rucker Park. Turner Network Television, 2000. Documentary on the history of playground basketball at Rucker Park.

Events

The Entertainers Basketball Classic at Holcombe Rucker Park
Corner of 155th Street and Frederick Douglass Boulevard
2861 8th Ave.
New York, NY 10039
Phone: 212-862-2323

Games held for nine-week period between June and August, Monday through Thursday nights at 8 P.M.

Hall of Fame Weekend. Held in Cooperstown, New York, in late July to induct newly elected members of the Hall of Fame. Note: There may be years when there are no new members voted in.

Little League Baseball World Series. Held in Williamsport, Pennsylvania, in August every year. Features teams of eleven- to twelve-year-olds from around the world.

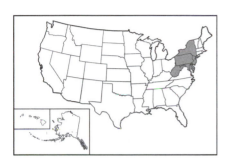

TIMELINE

35 Million Years Ago	Chesapeake Bay is formed in part by a meteor.
26,000–8,000 B.C.E.	Sometime during this period the descendants of Asian peoples cross the Bering Straits.
10,000–7000 B.C.E.	Paleoindian America. The Laurentide Ice Sheet covers most of Canada.
6500–3200 B.C.E.	Heavy sedimentation builds up along the valley floors, increasing the amount of arable land.
1000–500 B.C.E.	Inhabitants of the mid-Atlantic area cultivate crops, make pottery, develop the bow and arrow, and trade food.
900–1500 C.E.	Development of a common system of agriculture; a shared body of ideas and beliefs unifies the settlements from the Gulf coast to the Great Lakes.
1492 C.E.	Columbus lands in the Bahama Islands.
1497–1498	John Cabot sails to New England and along the coast of the Mid-Atlantic as far south as South Carolina. This exploration becomes the base for England's claim to North America.
1524	Giovanni da Verrazano, commissioned by Francis I of France, sails up North American coast from North Carolina to Newfoundland. This voyage becomes the base for France's claim to North America.
1534	Jacques Cartier explores Gulf of St. Lawrence; takes possession of region for King of France.
1536	John Calvin publishes *The Institutes*, which becomes a fundamental text for colonial protestant theology.

1563	John Foxe publishes *The Book of Martyrs* in London, a fundamental text for Puritans of the seventeenth century.
1584	Walter Raleigh sends expedition to America. Island of Roanoke founded. Queen Elizabeth names new land Virginia.
	Richard Hakluyt presents *Discourses on Western Planting* to the Queen, which encourages colonial development in America and offers a complete plan for settlement.
1585	John White's *American Indians at Play*—first drawing of Indians, showing participation in lacrosse, archery, foot racing, and pitching of balls at target on top of high tree.
1587	Virginia Dare born—first white child of English parents born in North America. Manteo, the first Indian convert to Protestant Christianity, baptized into the Church of England. Manteo is named Lord of Roanoke by Sir Walter Raleigh.
1600	Indian population in what would become United States about 1 million.
1607	Ships from the London Company arrive in Chesapeake Bay.
	Captain John Smith journeys up Chickahominy River to trade with Algonquians. He is captured by Indians and his life is saved by Pocahontas.
1608	John Smith's *A True Relation of Such Occurrences and Accidents of Noate as Hath Hapned in Virginia Since the First Planting of That Colony* published in London. Considered to be the first American book.
	Map of Chesapeake Bay and its rivers made and sent to England.
1609	Raising of corn learned from Indians.
	Henry Hudson explores what will subsequently be named the Hudson River as far as present-day Albany.
1612	Captain John Smith's *A Map of Virginia* published in London.
	Cultivation of tobacco begun by John Rolfe in Virginia.
1613	Hendrick Christianson and Adriaen Block establish Dutch fur-trading post on Manhattan Island.
1614	System of private holdings begins in Virginia.
1619	First African slaves brought to Virginia, beginning slavery in the English colonies.
1620	Henry Ainsworth's *Psalm Book* brought to America by Plymouth Pilgrims. Thought to be the first music book,

414

it was considered the best collection of its kind, and brought together English, French, and Swiss psalters.

1624 First permanent settlers from Holland arrive at Manhattan Island. Fort Nassau, opposite present-day Philadelphia, founded.

1626 Peter Minuit purchases Manhattan Island from Indians for twenty-four dollars.

1632 Lord Baltimore granted Maryland by royal charter; the area is carved out of original grant to Virginia.

1634 First Roman Catholic church built in St. Mary's City, Maryland. Catholic Church gains permanent foothold in America when the *Ark* and the *Dove* arrive in Maryland with colonists selected by Cecilius Calvert, second Lord Baltimore.

1636 Lord Baltimore's *Conditions for Plantations;* formation of 1,000-acre manors in Maryland.

1638 American log cabin introduced by Swedish settlers in Delaware.

1639 Governor's Castle built in St. Mary's, Maryland, becoming the largest building erected in the English colonies.

c. 1640 Margaret Brent, first woman barrister in America, works for Cecilius Calvert, Lord Proprietor of Maryland.

1643 New York City's population already "cosmopolitan" with twenty different nationalities and sects living on Manhattan Island, speaking eighteen languages.

1647 Earliest painting of New York made by an unknown artist. It includes the first representation of a striped flag, with four stripes symbolizing the confederacy of four colonies: Plymouth, New Haven, Connecticut, and Massachusetts.

1656 First structure in present-day Syracuse, New York, built by Jesuit priest.

1657 First reference to golf in America, when a complaint is issued by the sheriff of Fort Orange (Albany, New York) against three men for playing "kolven" (an early form of golf) on a Sunday.

c. 1660 Pinkster Day celebration among Africans in Fort Orange (Albany), with Congo dances accompanied by African rhythms and airs.

1664 Slavery Act in Maryland—lifelong servitude for black slaves. Similar acts passed in New Jersey and New York. These acts are not passed in Delaware and Pennsylvania.

1666 George Alsop's *A Character of the Province of Maryland* published.

	Construction begins on First Presbyterian Church in Elizabeth, New Jersey.
1668	First sports trophy presented to winner of horse race at Newmarket Course, Hempstead Plains, Long Island.
1670	First printed account of New York City published: *A Brief Description of New York* by Daniel Denton.
1675	Religious toleration and commercial activity increase New York City's cosmopolitanism; population includes English, Jews, Africans, Indians, Madagascan pirates, and French Huguenots.
1677	First large group of Quakers from England settle in West Jersey and found the city of Burlington. First charter guaranteeing separation of church and state framed by William Penn at Burlington.
1681	The land of roughly present-day Pennsylvania granted to William Penn, a Quaker.
1690	German settlers establish first American paper mill in Pennsylvania.
1694	Quaker Meeting House in Flushing, New York, built—oldest religious building on Long Island.
1700	Approximately 275,000 inhabitants in the colonies, with about 5,000 living in New York City.
1714	Robert Hunter's (from New York) *Androboros*—first play published in the colonies.
1728	Various newspapers founded in Philadelphia, New York, and Annapolis.
1723	Opposition in Philadelphia to interracial marriage leads to a petition in the colonial assembly.
1725	Slave population in the colonies at 75,000.
1726	Riot of the city's poor breaks out in downtown Philadelphia.
1727	Benjamin Franklin forms the Leather Apron Club, later called the Junto. The club opposes slavery. The Junto grows into the American Philosophical Society in 1743.
1728	One of the first church organs installed in Christ Church, Philadelphia.
1729	First permanent colonial Hebrew congregation formed in New York City.
	First serial appears in an American newspaper, Daniel Defoe's *Religious Courtship*, in the *Pennsylvania Gazette*.
1730	Baltimore, Maryland, settled. It operates as an important seaport for the grain and tobacco lands around Chesapeake Bay.

1731	First circulating library in the world, the Library Company of Philadelphia, is founded by Benjamin Franklin.
1732	First stagecoach line established, between Burlington and Amboy, New Jersey.
	The Fish House Club of Philadelphia formed–the oldest sporting organization of North America.
1741	First symphony orchestra in America formed in Bethlehem, Pennsylvania.
1754–1763	The French and Indian War (in Europe the Seven Years' War, 1756–1763).
1761	Earliest known American cookbook published in New York City—*The Complete Housewife; or, Accomplished Gentlewoman's Companion; Being a Collection of Several Hundred of the most Approved Receipts in Cookery, Pastry, etc.*
1763	The Moravians of Pennsylvania publish a collection of hymns in the Delaware Indian language.
1765	Stamp Act riot in New York City.
1766	St. Paul's Chapel built—oldest surviving church in Manhattan. First permanent theater in America—Southwark Theater—erected in Philadelphia.
1769	Anthracite coal used for the first time in Wilkes-Barre, Pennsylvania.
1765–1775	Period of popularity and fashion of horse racing in Maryland.
1775–1783	American Revolution.
1776	The Declaration of Independence published for the first time in the *Pennsylvania Evening Post*. Congress resolves that the words "United States" should replace "United Colonies."
1781	Bank of North America established by Congress.
	Articles of Confederation ratified by Maryland.
1782	First complete English Bible published in the United States in Philadelphia.
	J. Hector St. John de Crèvecoeur publishes *Letters from an American Farmer* in London (first published in Philadelphia in 1793).
1783	Noah Webster publishes *The American Speller*.
	Pennsylvania Evening Post begins publication in Philadelphia—the first daily newspaper in the United States.
1786	First recorded strike in the United States by printers takes place in Philadelphia.

	Federal Indian Act passed; establishes reservations north and south of the Ohio River.
1787	Isaac T. Hopper establishes what will become known as the Underground Railroad, a system designed to help fugitive slaves escape to the North.
	Delaware ratifies the Constitution on December 7 and becomes the first state.
	Pennsylvania ratifies the Constitution on December 12 and becomes the second state.
	New Jersey ratifies the Constitution on December 18 and becomes the third state.
1788	Maryland ratifies the Constitution on April 28 and becomes the seventh state.
	Virginia (which includes what will become West Virginia) ratifies the Constitution on June 25 and becomes the tenth state.
	New York ratifies the Constitution on July 26 and becomes the eleventh state.
1789	Federalist Party formed.
	First session of U.S. Congress convened.
	George Washington inaugurated as first president of the United States.
	The "first American novel" published—William Hill Brown's *The Power of Sympathy; or The Triumph of Nature*.
1790	Philadelphia becomes the nation's capital.
1792	Cornerstone of the Capitol laid. Work begins on the White House.
1793	New York City's first daily newspaper founded—*American Minerva*.
1797	First centralized water supply distribution system goes into operation in Philadelphia, drawing water from Schuykill River.
1808	New York Academy of Fine Arts founded.
1809	Publication of Washington Irving's *History of New York*.
1817	Construction of Erie Canal begins in New York.
	Benjamin Latrobe, influential in the Greek Revival movement, sees his building, the Second Bank of the United States, completed in Philadelphia.
1826	America's first railway steam locomotive tested in Hoboken, New Jersey.
1828	Play of Washington Irving's *Rip Van Winkle* first performed in Albany, New York.

First recorded factory worker strike at a textile plant in Paterson, New Jersey.

1829	Chesapeake and Delaware Canal formally opened.
1830	"Primitivism" popular in folk paintings of the period.

President Andrew Jackson signs the Indian Removal Act, which calls for resettlement of all Indians east of the Mississippi River.

1832   Mrs. Frances Trollope's *Domestic Manners of Americans* published.

1834   Antiabolition riots break out at an antislavery society in New York City.

1837   House of Representatives passes Slavery Resolution which asserts that slaves do not have the right of petition given to U.S. citizens by the Constitution.

Thomas Cole finishes romantic rural masterpiece *In the Catskills*.

1839   The antislavery Liberty Party holds its first national convention at Warsaw, New York.

The Olympic Theater reopens in New York City, specializing in the production of burlettas (light comic operas).

1840   James Fenimore Cooper's *The Pathfinder* published. Edgar Allan Poe's *Tales of the Grotesque and Arabesque* published in Philadelphia. *The Beacon*, leading antireligious magazine, begins publication in New York City. Growing poverty in New York City sees organization of more than thirty relief agencies in the city. First international cricket match between New York team and Toronto club. Ten-hour workday established by executive order for all federal employees—a longtime goal of U.S. labor.

1841   Cooper's *The Deerslayer* published.

1843   First minstrel troupe formed in New York City. First matinee offered at Mitchell's Olympic Theater in New York City.

1845   Industrial Congress of the United States, an early labor organization, is organized in New York City. Poe's *Tales* published in New York City. Rules for baseball are drawn up, and the first baseball club, the Knickerbockers, is formed.

1846   Grace Church is constructed in New York City and is an important early example of Gothic Revival architecture. The first recorded baseball game takes place at Elysian Field in Hoboken, New Jersey.

1847	Smithsonian Institution formally dedicated in Washington, D.C.
1848	Associated Press organized. New York grants property rights to women equal to those of men.
	Lucretia Mott and Elizabeth Cady Stanton call the women's convention at Seneca Falls.
1849	Amelia Bloomer begins publication of *Lily*, which dealt with woman's suffrage, marriage laws, and education, and was to have a major influence on American society.
1850	The homeless are seen as a new class of people, with 18,456 persons sheltered in 8,141 cellars in New York City.
1851	The *New York Daily Times* begins publication; it changes its name to the *New York Times* in 1857. Herman Melville's *Moby Dick* published. Karl Marx's "Revolution and Counter-Revolution" makes its first appearance in print in the New York *Tribune*. The Erie Railroad, the longest railroad to date, opens; the route is 483 miles long, and runs between Piermont, New York, and Dunkirk, New York.
1852	First Jewish hospital in the United States incorporated in New York City. Named Jews' Hospital, it will later be called Mt. Sinai Hospital.
1853	Crystal Palace Exhibition of the Industry of All Nations is held in New York City.
1855	Melville's *Israel Potter: His Fifty Years of Exile* is published.
1856	George F. Bristow's *Second Symphony in D Minor* performed by the New York Philharmonic Society—one of the few orchestral works by a native-born composer performed during the nineteenth century.
1857	The Studio Building constructed in New York City by Richard Morris Hunt, who this same year helped found the American Institute of Architects.
1858	Work begun on St. Patrick's Cathedral in New York City; designed by James Renwick, and an example of Gothic Revival.
1859	International cricket match takes place in Hoboken, New Jersey, between an English and a U.S. team.
1861–1865	American Civil War.
1861	The first casualties of the Civil War occur in Baltimore, Maryland.
1862	Stewart's, the largest retail store in the world, is built in New York City; it is eight stories high and employs 2,000 people.

1863	West Virginia becomes the thirty-fifth state. The Battle of Gettysburg occurs July 1–3. Abraham Lincoln delivers the Gettysburg Address on November 19.
1864	Racetrack built in Saratoga, New York; it holds the first organized meets in the United States.
1867	Augustin Daly's *Under the Gaslight* opens in New York City.
1869	The first elevated ("el") railroad completed in New York City.
1870	Pimlico racetrack built in Baltimore, Maryland. The first boardwalk in United States is completed in Atlantic City, New Jersey.
1871	James McNeill Whistler exhibits the painting popularly known as *Whistler's Mother* at the Pennsylvania Academy of Fine Arts. Henry James makes a trip to Niagara Falls and records in a travel essay a scathing picture of commercialism choking the beauty of the Falls. Grand Central Station opens in New York City.
1874	The Chautauqua movement founded on the shores of Lake Chautauqua, New York.
1877	Thomas Eakins's painting *William Rush Carving the Allegorical Figure of the Schuylkill River* spotlights American provincialism.
1879	Henry James's *Daisy Miller* published. Gilbert and Sullivan open *H.M.S. Pinafore* in New York City's Bowery Theater.
1880	Participation of women in sports increases; activities include tennis, archery, croquet, riding, cycling, swimming, boat racing, fencing, bowling, and skating. Sarah Bernhardt makes her American debut in Alexandre Dumas's *La Dame aux Camélias* in New York City.
1881	The first electric power plant in the world is constructed in New York City. The city also sees the completion of all of the major elevated railroads. Coney Island becomes a famous place for recreation.
1882	William Dean Howells's *A Modern Instance* published. Handball becomes known as a sport in the United States with the construction of a court and school in Brooklyn, New York. The New York *Morning Journal* begins publication. Known for its sensationalist journalism, it will be sold to William Randolph Hearst in 1895 and renamed the New York *Journal*.
1884	Mark Twain's *Huckleberry Finn* published. Greyhound racing is introduced in Philadelphia, Pennsylvania.

1886	*Cosmopolitan* magazine founded in Rochester, New York. The tuxedo makes its first recorded appearance at the annual Autumn Ball of the Tuxedo Club, Tuxedo, New York.
1887	The first golf club, called the Foxbury Golf Club, is formed in Foxbury, Pennsylvania. Racetrack betting becomes legal in New York.
1888	Edward Bellamy's *Looking Backward* published. Several scholarly organizations founded, such as the Geological Society of America, the American Folklore Society, the American Mathematical Society, and the National Statistical Association.
1889	The first two volumes of Henry Adams's *The History of the United States* published. Edward MacDowell performs his *Second Piano Concerto* in New York City.
1891	Carnegie Hall opens in New York City, with Tchaikovsky conducting an evening of his works. The first international six-day bicycle race is held at Madison Square Garden.
1892	The final edition of Walt Whitman's *Leaves of Grass* published. The American Fine Arts Society formed. Dvořak's *New World Symphony* premieres in New York City.
1893	First recorded intercollegiate relay race held in Philadelphia. Edison Laboratories in West Orange, New Jersey, finishes construction of a pioneer film studio called the Black Maria. Publication of Stephen Crane's *Maggie, a Girl of the Streets*.
1894	Publication of Mark Twain's *The Tragedy of Pudd'nhead Wilson*.
1895	Publication of Crane's *The Red Badge of Courage*. Hydroelectric power generators go into operation at Niagara Falls, New York. American Bowling Congress formed in New York City.
1896	First moving pictures shown at Koster and Bial's Music Hall in New York City. Publication of James's *The Spoils of Poynton* and *What Maisie Knew*.
1898	Publication of James's *The Turn of the Screw*. *Cyrano de Bergerac* opens at the Garden Theater in New York City.
1900	Publication of Theodore Dreiser's *Sister Carrie*.
1901	President Roosevelt dines with Booker T. Washington, causing an uproar of racism in the United States.
1902	The successful musical *Floradora* closes in New York City after 547 performances. Coal miners' strike in Pennsylvania.

1905	Publication of Edith Wharton's *The House of Mirth*.
1906	The plays of George Bernard Shaw at the height of their popularity in New York City, with *Caeser and Cleopatra*, *Arms and the Man*, *Man and Superman*, *John Bull's Other Island*, and *Mrs. Warren's Profession* all being performed that season. Oscar Hammerstein opens his second Manhattan Opera Company in New York City. Oscar S. Straus of New York becomes the first Jew to be appointed to a presidential cabinet.
1907	The first *Ziegfeld Follies*. Adams's *The Education of Henry Adams* printed privately and distributed to friends of the author.
1908	President Roosevelt names the National Commission for the Conservation of Natural Resources.
1909	Founding of the National Association for the Advancement of Colored People. The first animated motion picture, *Gertie the Dinosaur*, made by Winsor McCay, cartoonist for the New York *American*.
1910	Publication of Ezra Pound's *The Spirit of Romance*. Farm population continues to decline, with 32,077,000 farm inhabitants in 1910; 30,529,000 in 1930; 25,058,000 in 1950. Taylorization becomes a staple of American industrialism and the management of labor in factories. First performance of Victor Herbert's *Naughty Marietta* in Syracuse, New York.
1913	Construction of Woolworth Building in New York City, then tallest in the world at 792 feet.
1914–1918	World War I.
1915	First transcontinental telephone call by Alexander Graham Bell in New York City to Dr. Thomas A. Watson in San Francisco. The experimental Neighborhood Playhouse opens in New York City.
1916	Philadelphia Symphony Orchestra premieres Mahler's *Eighth Symphony*.
1917	Catskill Aqueduct dedicated; under construction for twelve years, it cost $177 million and was cut through solid rock. A total of 4,842,139 motor vehicles were registered in the United States. The Original Dixieland Jass Band opens at Reisenweber's Restaurant in New York City.
1920	Publication of Edith Wharton's *The Age of Innocence*. Opening of Eugene O'Neill's *Beyond the Horizon* at Morosco Theater in New York City, and *The Emperor Jones* at Neighborhood Playhouse.

1922	Supreme Court declares Nineteenth Amendment, which provides for women's suffrage. Opening at New York City's Apollo Theater of D. W. Griffith's *Orphans of the Storm*, starring Lillian and Dorothy Gish. American opening of Luigi Pirandello's *Six Characters in Search of an Author* at New York City's Princess Theater.
1924	Opening of O'Neill's *All God's Chillun Got Wings*, starring Paul Robeson.
1925	Publication of Theodore Dreiser's *An American Tragedy* and F. Scott Fitzgerald's *The Great Gatsby*. Premiere of Aaron Copland's *Symphony for Organ and Orchestra* by the New York Symphony. Opening of *The Cocoanuts* at the Lyric Theater in New York City, starring the Marx Brothers.
1926	Schools in White Plains, New York, grant recess for school children one hour each week for religious instruction. First known talking picture, *Don Juan*, featuring John Barrymore, shown at Warner Theater in New York City.
1927	Premiere of George Antheil's *Ballet Mécanique* at Carnegie Hall in New York City. First successful demonstration of television takes place in New York City. Opening of Holland Tunnel, the first underwater motor vehicle tunnel in the United States.
1928	First program of scheduled television broadcasts begun by station WGY in Schenectady, New York. First exhibition of color motion pictures in United States by George Eastman in Rochester, New York.
1930	Publication of Dashiell Hammett's *The Maltese Falcon*. Inauguration at the Eastman School of Music in Rochester of the Annual Festival of American Music. One out of every 4.9 Americans owns an automobile.
1931	Opening of O'Neill's six-hour-long play *Mourning Becomes Electra* at Guild Theater in New York City. Empire State Building opened to the public.
1932	Franklin D. Roosevelt from New York introduces the term "New Deal" in his speech accepting the Democratic nomination for president.
1934	Publication of Fitzgerald's *Tender Is the Night* and Hammett's *The Thin Man*. Opening of the musical comedy *Anything Goes* at Alvin Theater in New York City.
1935	The Works Progress Administration (WPA) instituted. Opening of George Gershwin's *Porgy and Bess* at the Alvin Theater.
1936	Founding of Federal Theater Project under the WPA.

1937	Construction of Harlem River Houses, one of the first public housing projects, in New York City. Upholding of minimum wage law for women by U.S. Supreme Court in *West Coast Hotel v. Parrish*. U.S. Supreme Court upholds Social Security Act of 1935.
1938	Staging of Orson Welles's radio play *The War of the Worlds*.
1939	Premiere of Charles Ives's *Second Piano Sonata* at New York City's Town Hall.
1941–1945	World War II.
1942	Orson Welles's *Citizen Kane* named best film of 1941 by New York Film Critics. Premiere of Copland's ballet *Rodeo*. Premiere of Thornton Wilder's *The Skin of Our Teeth* at New York City's Plymouth Theater.
1944	Premiere of Walter Piston's *Second Symphony* in Washington, D.C. Premiere of Copland's ballet *Appalachian Spring* by Martha Graham in Washington, D.C.
1945	Frank Lloyd Wright displays his model for the Guggenheim Museum in New York City.
1949	Arthur Miller's *Death of a Salesman* opens at Morosco Theater.
1950	Benny Goodman and the NBC Radio Orchestra premiere Copland's *Clarinet Concerto*.
1951	First section of New Jersey Turnpike opened. Publication of J. D. Salinger's *The Catcher in the Rye*.
1954	Premiere of Roy Harris's *Symphonic Fantasy* by Pittsburgh Symphony. Premiere of T. S. Eliot's *The Confidential Clerk* at Morosco Theater. Premiere of Copland's *The Tender Land* at New York's City Center.
1956	Opening of New York Coliseum. Publication of John Barth's first novel, *The Floating Opera*.
1957	Opening of William Inge's *The Dark at the Top of the Stairs* at New York City's Music Box.
1958	Leonard Bernstein directs the New York Philharmonic Orchestra and begins to play more works by American composers.
1959	Opening of Jay Thompson's musical comedy *Once Upon a Mattress* at New York City's Phoenix Theater. Opening of Arthur Laurents, Julie Stein, and Stephen Soundheim's *Gypsy* at Broadway Theater.
1959–1975	The Vietnam War. Although involved in the war for many years, the United States first sends troops in 1965.
1960	Opening of Gore Vidal's *The Best Man* at Morosco Theater. Publication of John Barth's *The Sot-Weed Factor*.

1961	Opening of Eugene Ionesco's *The Rhinoceros* at Longacre Theater in New York City. Harold Pinter's *The Caretaker* opens at the Lyceum Theater. Publication of Joseph Heller's *Catch-22*. The National Council of Churches at their meeting in Syracuse, New York, endorse birth control as a means of family limitation.
1962	Supreme Court rules New York State law permitting recitation of official prayer in public schools unconstitutional. The first International Jazz Festival takes place in Washington, D.C. New York City's Lincoln Center for the Performing Arts opens. *My Fair Lady*, the longest-running Broadway musical, with 2,717 performances, closes.
1963	An estimated 200,000 people engage in the Freedom March on Washington, D.C.; Dr. Martin Luther King is among the speakers. Demonstrations in New York City seek to increase hiring of minority workers; there are more than 700 arrests. The Guggenheim Museum holds the first large-scale exhibition of pop art. Publication of Thomas Pynchon's first novel, *V.*
1964	A race riot breaks out in Harlem, New York City, after a black youth is shot by an off-duty police officer. *Fiddler on the Roof* opens at the Imperial Theater in New York City.
1965	Malcolm X assassinated at the Audubon Ballroom in Washington Heights, New York City. Nationwide antiwar demonstrations take place. White House holds Festival of Arts and Humanities; the poet Robert Lowell refuses to attend because of his distrust of U.S. foreign policy.
1966	Antiwar demonstration in Washington, D.C. Ten thousand picket the White House; 63,000 voters' pledges displayed at the Washington Monument to vote only for antiwar candidates. Demonstrations against the war also occur on the anniversary of the bombing of Hiroshima. Publication of Thomas Pynchon's *The Crying of Lot 49*.
1967	100,000–400,000 antiwar protestors demonstrate in New York City, marching from Central Park to UN Headquarters. U.S. Supreme Court rules unconstitutional state laws forbidding interracial marriages. Race riot in Newark, New Jersey, leaves 26 dead and 1,300 injured. Opening of Tom Stoppard's *Rosencrantz and Guildenstern Are Dead* at Alvin Theater. New York premiere of James Rado's *Hair*. Opening of Harold Pinter's *The Homecoming* at the Music Box Theater.
1968	President Johnson signs the 1968 Civil Rights Act.

1969	Woodstock festival takes place near Woodstock, New York, with an estimated attendance of 400,000.
1970	Earth Day observed across the country. President Nixon signs the National Air Quality Control Act. *Hello, Dolly!* closes, beating out *My Fair Lady* as longest running musical, with 2,844 performances.
1971	At an antiwar protest in Washington, D.C., scores of Vietnam veterans return their medals and military decorations on the steps of the Capitol. National Women's Political Caucus takes place in Washington, D.C., addressing equal representation of women in the nation's political system. Kennedy Center for the Performing Arts opens. Publication of E. L. Doctorow's *The Book of Daniel*. Publication of Don DeLillo's first novel, *Americana*.
1972	Gloria Steinem launches *Ms.* magazine. The Newport Jazz Festival takes place in New York City. Pocono International Raceway opens at Long Pond. Publication of John Gardner's *The Sunlight Dialogues*.
1973	Publication of Thomas Pynchon's *Gravity's Rainbow*. John Barth's *Chimera* wins the National Book Award.
1974	Pynchon's *Gravity's Rainbow* wins National Book Award. Opening at Broadway Theater of Leonard Bernstein's *Candide*. Mikhail Baryshnikov makes his U.S. debut with the American Ballet Theater in New York City. Charles Ives Festival observed in New York City.
1975	New York and New Jersey vote down state equal rights amendments. Publication of E. L. Doctorow's *Ragtime*. First International Women's Art Festival held in New York City. Beverly Sills debuts at the Metropolitan Opera.
1976	Revivals of *Porgy and Bess*, *My Fair Lady*, *Guys and Dolls*, and *Fiddler on the Roof*. Opening of Ntozake Shange's play *For Colored Girls Who Have Considered Suicide/When the Rainbow Is Enuf* in New York City. Premiere of Twyla Tharp's *Push Comes to Shove* at the American Ballet Theater in New York City. Premiere performance of Alvin Ailey's *Pas de "Duke"*—a ballet honoring Duke Ellington—in New York City. Premiere of Philip Glass's *Einstein on the Beach* at the Metropolitan Opera House. Reverend Sun Myung Moon holds "God Bless America" rally in Washington, D.C. Publication of John Gardner's *October Light*.
1977	Opening of David Mamet's *American Buffalo* at New York City's Ethel Barrymore Theater. Opening of David Rabe's antiwar play *The Basic Training of Pavlo Hummel* at

New York City's Longacre Theater. Gardner's *October Light* wins the National Book Critics Circle Award.

1978   The American Indian Movement (AIM) organizes the longest walk ever taken, 2,700 miles from Alcatraz Island, California, to the steps of the Capitol in Washington, D.C. President Carter declares the Love Canal area of Niagara Falls, New York, an environmental disaster area; the area had been used as a toxic waste dump from 1947 to 1952. First black woman pilot, from Baltimore, Maryland, begins working for Texas International Airlines. Woody Allen's *Annie Hall* wins Academy Award for best picture. Opening of Richard Maltby's *Ain't Misbehavin'*, celebrating songs of Fats Waller, at Longacre Theater.

1979   Publication of John Barth's *Letters*. Opening of Andrew Lloyd Weber's *Evita*.

1980   President Carter orders evacuation of 710 families from Love Canal area in Niagara Falls. Winter Olympic Games are held in Lake Placid, New York. John Lennon shot and killed outside his apartment building in New York City. Publication of Toni Morrison's *Tar Baby*.

1982   Publication of Gardner's *Mickelsson's Ghosts*. Opening of David Edgar and Stephen Oliver's *The Life and Adventures of Nicholas Nickleby*, an eight-and-a-half-hour play based on Charles Dickens's novel. The Supreme Court upholds the constitutionality of religious services held in campus buildings by student organizations.

1983   Opening of Neil Simon's *Brighton Beach Memoirs* at the Alvin Theater. *A Chorus Line* becomes the longest-running show, with 3,389 performances.

1985   Publication of DeLillo's *White Noise*; it wins the National Book Award.

1986   The Supreme Court upholds affirmative action programs in a case involving a New York City labor union.

1987   Publication of John Barth's *The Tidewater Tales: A Novel* and Toni Morrison's *Beloved*, which wins the 1998 Pulitzer Prize for Fiction. William Bolcom composes *12 New Etudes for Piano*. John Conigliaro composes the opera *A Figaro for Antonia*.

1988   Love Canal in Niagara Falls, New York, declared safe to live in. Publication of Don DeLillo's *Libra*.

1989   Supreme Court continues to support constitutional right to abortion, but encourages states to set limits; Pennsylvania becomes the first state to restrict abortions since the Supreme Court decision *Roe v. Wade*. David N. Dinkins becomes the first African American mayor elected in New York City.

1990	Publication of Thomas Pynchon's *Vineland*. Congress passes clean air legislation. *A Chorus Line* closes after 6,104 performances.
1992	Supreme Court upholds part of Pennsylvania law that imposes strict limits on a woman's right to abortion. Production of Philip Glass's opera *The Voyage*, which commemorates Christopher Columbus.
1993	Janet Reno becomes first woman U.S. Attorney General. President Clinton signs order repealing ban on abortion counseling at U.S.-funded clinics. Toni Morrison wins Nobel Prize for Literature. Tony Kushner's *Angels in America: Millennium Approaches* wins the Pulitzer Prize for Drama.
1994	Twenty-fifth anniversary of Woodstock celebrated at Saugerties, New York; some 350,000 attend. Kushner's *Angels in America: Perestroika* opens.
1995	Luois Farrakhan organizes "Million Man March" in Washington, D.C.
1996	The musical *Rent* opens in New York City.
1997	Publication of Thomas Pynchon's *Mason and Dixon* and Don DeLillo's *Underworld*.
2001	Publication of Salman Rushdie's New York novel *Fury*.
	On September 11, four U.S. airplanes hijacked by terrorists crash at the World Trade Center in New York City; in Shanksville, Pennsylvania; and at the Pentagon in Washington, D.C., killing nearly 3,000 U.S. citizens.
2002	Publication of Salman Rushdie's *Step Across This Line*.

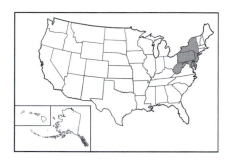

NOTES

Architecture

1. Spiro Kostof, *A History of Architecture: Settings and Rituals* (New York: Oxford University Press, 1985), 740.
2. Sylvia Hart Wright, *The Sourcebook of Contemporary North American Architecture: From Postwar to Postmodern* (New York: Van Nostrand Reinhold, 1989), 117.

Art

1. Edwin L. Wade, ed., *The Arts of the North American Indian: Native Traditions in Evolution* (New York: Hudson Hills Press, 1986), 55.
2. Ibid., 31.
3. Robert Bishop, *American Folk Sculpture* (New York: E. P. Dutton, 1974), 49, #62.
4. Ibid., 42, #54.
5. John Ebert, and Katherine Ebert, *American Folk Painters* (New York: Charles Scribner's Sons, 1975), 23.
6. Ibid.
7. Ibid., 30.
8. Whitney Museum of American Art, ed., *Two Hundred Years of American Sculpture* (New York: David R. Godine, 1976), 76.
9. Laura Rigal, *The American Manufactory: Art, Labor, and the World of Things in the Early Republic* (Princeton: Princeton University Press, 1998), 96.
10. Barbara Novak, *American Painting of the Nineteenth Century: Realism, Idealism, and the American Experience*, 2nd ed. (New York: Harper and Row, 1979), 229.
11. James M. Karl Bitter Dennis, *Architectural Sculpture, 1867–1915* (Madison: University of Wisconsin Press, 1967), 104.
12. Angela Miller, "Everywhere and Nowhere: The Making of the National Landscape," *American Literary History* 4, no. 2 (Summer 1992): 207–229.
13. Marilyn Stokstad, ed., *Art History*, rev. ed., vol. 2 (New York: Harry N. Abrams, 1999), 1096.

14. Abraham A. Davidson, *Early American Modernist Painting, 1910–1935*, 2nd ed. (New York: Da Capo Press, 1994), 18.

15. Bernard B. Pearlman, *Painters of the Ashcan School: The Immortal Eight* (New York: Dover Publications, 1979), 87.

16. John Loughery, *John Sloan: Painter and Rebel* (New York: Henry Holt and Co., 1995), 307.

17. Wade, *Arts*, 157.

18. Jill Johnston, *Jasper Johns: Privileged Information* (New York: Thames and Hudson, 1996), 282.

19. Jonathan Fineberg, *Art Since 1940: Strategies of Being* (Upper Saddle River, NJ: Prentice Hall, 1995), 384.

Ecology and Environment

1. This is the argument of many historians. See especially Fernand Braudel, *Capitalism and Material Life, 1400–1800* (New York: HarperCollins, 1973), and D. W. Meinig, *The Shaping of America: A Geographical Perspective on 500 Years of History: Volume 1, Atlantic America, 1492–1800* (New Haven: Yale University Press, 1986), xvi–xviii.

2. Tom Horton, "A Timely Perspective on the Bay: Events from Ages Past Continue to Shape the Region," *Baltimore Sun*, Jan. 16, 2004.

3. Karl W. Butzer, "The Indian Legacy in the American Landscape," in Michael P. Conzen, ed., *The Making of the American Landscape* (Boston: University of Chicago Press, 1990), 28.

4. Ralph H. Brown, *Historical Geography of the United States* (New York: Harcourt, Brace, 1949), 11.

5. William Cronin, *Changes in the Land: Indians, Colonists, and the Ecology of New England* (New York: Hill and Wang, 1983), 69. Though Cronin concentrates on the New England region, this approach also affected northern areas of the Mid-Atlantic, if not the entire region.

6. Peirce F. Lewis, "The Northeast and the Making of American Geographical Habits," in Conzen, *Making of the American Landscape*, 84.

7. Samuel P. Hays, *A History of Environmental Politics Since 1945* (Pittsburgh: University of Pittsburgh Press, 2000), 7.

8. Lewis, "Northeast," 88.

9. Hildegard Binder Johnson, "Towards a National Landscape," in Conzen, *Making of the American Landscape*, 128.

10. John A. Jakle, "Landscapes Redesigned for the Automobile," in Conzen, *Making of the American Landscape*, 296.

11. Ibid., 298.

12. Ibid., 299.

13. Michael Williams, "The Clearing of the Forests," in Conzen, *Making of the American Landscape*, 146.

14. Hays, *History of Environmental Politics*, 8.

15. M. L. Primack, "Land Clearing Under Nineteenth Century Techniques: Some Preliminary Calculations," *Journal of Economic History* 22 (1962): 485–486.

16. David R. Meyer, "The New Industrial Order," in Conzen, *Making of the American Landscape*, 250–251.

17. Chesapeake Bay Program, *The State of the Chesapeake Bay: A Report to the Citizens of the Bay*, July 2002, 9. Hereafter cited as *SCB*.

18. Chesapeake Bay Riparian Forest Buffer Initiative, *Riparian Forest Buffers: Linking Land and Water*, U.S. Environmental Protection Agency, EPA 903-R-99-002, March 1999, 1. We are particularly indebted to Lara Lutz, former public relations representative for the Save the Bay Foundation, for sources and information on the Chesapeake Bay region.

19. U.S. Environmental Protection Agency, *Mid-Atlantic Integrated Assessment (MAIA)*, available at http://www.epa.gov/maia/index.html.

20. *SCB*, 48.

21. Joe Matassino et al., eds., *State of the Delaware Estuary Report*, Partnership for the Delaware Estuary, 2002, 4.

22. Ibid.

23. http://www.horseshoecrab.com.

24. *SCB*, 25.

25. *The Cost of a Clean Bay: Assessing Funding Needs Throughout the Watershed*, Chesapeake Bay Commission Report, January 2003, 11.

26. Chesapeake Bay Program Forestry Workgroup, *Recommendations for the 2003 Directive on Expanded Riparian Forest Buffer Goals in the Chesapeake Watershed*, December 2003, 9.

27. Chesapeake Bay Commission, "Setting the Course: The Story of the Chesapeake 2000," special report, June 2000, 1.

28. Ibid.

29. *SCB*, 46.

30. "Smart Choices or Sprawling Growth: A Fifty-State Survey of Development," *Sierra Club Report on Sprawl*, September 2000, available at http://www.sierraclub.org/sprawl/50statesurvey.

31. Henry L. Diamond and Patrick F. Noonan, *Land Use in America* (Washington, DC: Island Press, 1996), xix.

32. "Growing Smart: A Program for Modernizing America's Laws Affecting Planning and the Management of Change," *Growing Smart* Newsletter (Chicago: American Planning Association, 1992).

33. Diamond and Noonan, *Land Use*, xix.

34. Ibid.

35. Edward K. Muller, "The Americanization of the City," in Conzen, *Making of the American Landscape*, 291.

36. Ibid.

37. *SCB*, 47.

38. Ibid.

39. Henry J. Bokuniewicz and Manfred P. Wolff, "Planning Long Island's Response to Rising Sea Level," in James E. Hickey Jr. and Linda A. Longmire, eds., *The Environment: Global Problems, Local Solutions* (Westport, CT: Greenwood Press, 1994), 248.

40. Ibid.

41. Terry L. Anderson and Bruce Yandle, *Agriculture and the Environment: Searching for Greener Pastures* (Stanford, CA: Hoover Institution Press, 2001), 41–42.

42. Matassino et al., *State of the Delaware Estuary Report*, 16.

43. The Trust for Public Land, http://www.tpl.org.

Ethnicity

1. Paul A. Wallace, "The Iroquois Confederacy," in *Indians in Pennsylvania* (Harrisburg: Pennsylvania Historical Museum Commission, 2000), 88–98; *Iroquois History*, http://www.tolatsga.org/iro.html; Daniel Richter, *Facing East from Indian Country* (Cambridge: Harvard University Press, 2001); *Mahican History*, http://www.dickshovel.com/mahican.html.

2. Richard White, *The Middle Ground: Indians, Empires, and Republics in the Great Lakes Region, 1650–1815* (Cambridge: Cambridge University Press, 1991), x.

3. Jane Merritt, *At the Crossroads: Indians and Empires on a Mid-Atlantic Frontier, 1700–1763* (Chapel Hill: University of North Carolina Press, 2003).

4. *Maryland Digital Immigration Library*, http://oriole.umd.edu/~mddlmddl/791/frameset.html.

5. Matthew S. Magda, *Welsh in Pennsylvania* (Harrisburg: Pennsylvania Historical and Museum Commission, 1986), http://www.phmc.state.pa.us/ppet/welsh.

6. Hasia Diner, *Erin's Daughters in America: Irish Immigrant Women in the Nineteenth Century* (Baltimore: Johns Hopkins University Press, 1984).

7. Kevin Kenny, *Making Sense of the Molly Maguires* (Oxford: Oxford University Press, 1998).

8. *African American History of Western New York*, http://www.math.buffalo.edu/~sww/0history/hwny.html.

9. *Traditions in Transition: Jewish Culture in Philadelphia, 1840–1940* (Philadelphia: Balch Institute for Ethnic Studies, 1989).

10. Joan Saverino, "'Domani Ci Zappa': Italian Immigration and Ethnicity in Pennsylvania," *Pennsylvania Folklife* 45 no. 1 (1995): 18.

11. Roger Horowitz and Mark J. Miller, "Immigrants in the Delmarva Poultry Processing Industry: The Changing Face of Georgetown, Delaware, and Environs," *JSRI Occasional Paper Number 37* (East Lansing: Julian Samora Research Institute, Michigan State University, 1999).

12. California is first, with 32 percent; from *Korean Population in the United States as Reflected in the 2000 U.S. Census*, www.calstatela.edu/centers/ckaks/census/kapopul2000.pdf.

13. *Maryland Digital Immigration Library*, http://oriole.umd.edu/~mddlmddl/791/frameset.html. On small business activity, see Kyeyoung Park, *The Korean American Dream: Immigrants and Small Business in New York City* (Ithaca: Cornell University Press, 1997).

14. These figures are the result of compilation of Census results for Delaware, Maryland, New Jersey, New York, Pennsylvania, and West Virginia, http://www.census.gov/main/www.cen2000.html.

15. Rakhmiel Peltz, "It Used to Be Like Jerusalem: South Philadelphia, Portal to the City and Enduring Jewish Community," in *Traditions in Transition: Jewish Culture in Philadelphia, 1840–1940* (Philadelphia: Balch Institute for Ethnic Studies, 1989), 59; Marilyn Harter, *Shopping for Identity: The Marketing of Ethnicity* (New York: Shocken, 2000).

Fashion

1. Lois W. Banner, *American Beauty* (New York: Alfred A. Knopf, 1983), 17.

2. "Appearance and Fashion," from "Women in America 1820–1842" and *Democracy in America* (June 2, 2003); online hypertext document at American Studies at University of Virginia, September 6, 2003, http://xroads.virginia.edu/~hyper/detoc/fem/appear.htm.

3. Jenna Weissman Joselit, *A Perfect Fit: Clothes, Character, and the Promise of America* (New York: Henry Holt, 2001), 116.

4. Ibid., 70.

5. Ibid., 73.

6. Shane White and Graham White, *Stylin': African American Expressive Culture from Its Beginning to the Zoot Suit* (Ithaca: Cornell University Press, 1998), 128.

7. Ibid., 119–121.

8. Ibid., 121.

9. Ibid., 187–191.

10. Banner, *American Beauty*, 29–34.

11. Joselit, *Perfect Fit*, 177–186.

12. Banner, *American Beauty*, 37–38.

13. White and White, *Stylin'*, 199–216.

14. Sarah Tomerlin Lee, ed., *American Fashion: The Life and Lines of Adrian, Mainbocher, McCardell, Norell, Trigere* (New York: Quadrangle/New York Times, 1975), 224.

15. Ibid., 368.

16. Ibid., 486.

17. Joselit, *Perfect Fit*, 189–190.

18. Patricia A. Cunningham and Susan Voso Lab, eds., *Dress and Popular Culture* (Bowling Green: Bowling Green State University Popular Press, 1991), 85–105.

Folklore

1. E. A. Smith *Myths of the Iroquois* (New York: Smithsonian Institute-Bureau of Ethnology, 1994), 10.

2. Arthur C. Parker, *Seneca Myth and Folk Tales* (Lincoln: University of Nebraska Press, 1989), xxxii.

3. Simon J. Bronner, *Popularizing Pennsylvania: Henry W. Shoemaker and the Progressive Uses of Folklore and History* (University Park: Pennsylvania State University Press, 1996), xiii, xiv.

4. Richard M. Dorson, *American Folklore* (Chicago: University of Chicago Press, 1959), 12.

5. Ibid.

6. Horace Wallace Binney, "Washington Irving: His Works, Genius, and Character," in Ralph M. Aderman, ed., *Critical Essays on Washington Irving* (Boston: G. K. Hall, 1990), 127–141.

7. Ibid.

8. Jenifer S. Banks, "Washington Irving: The Nineteenth Century American Bachelor," in Aderman, *Critical Essays on Washington Irving*, 141–142.

9. Ibid.

10. William L. Hedges, *Washington Irving: An American Study, 1802–1832* (Baltimore: Johns Hopkins University Press, 1965).

11. Ibid.

12. Brett Williams, *John Henry: A Bio-Bibliography* (Westport, CT: Greenwood Press, 1983).

13. Patrick W. Gainer, *Witches, Ghosts, and Signs: Folklore of the Southern Appalachians* (Grantsville: Seneca Books, 1975), 66–67.

14. B. A. Botkin, ed., *A Treasury of American Folklore: Stories, Ballads, and Traditions of the People* (New York: Crown Publishers, 1966), 722–724.

Food

1. Quoted in John L. Hess and Karen Hess, *The Taste of America* (1972; reprint, Champaign: University of Illinois Press, 2000), 107–108.

2. Peter Kalm, *The America of 1850*, quoted in Molly O'Neill, *New York Cookbook* (New York: Workman, 1992), 193.

3. *From Farm to Table: Making the Connection in the Mid-Atlantic Food System*, http://www .clagettfarm.org/Introduction.html.

Literature

1. David McCutchen, trans., *The Red Record: The Wallum Olum* (New York: Avery Publishing Group, 1993), 136.

2. Ibid., 26.

3. Reprinted in ibid., 148.

4. Jacob Steendam, *A Memoir of the First Poet in New Netherland. With His Poems Descriptive of the Colony* (The Hague: The Brothers Giunta D'Albani, 1861), 1–2.

5. Albert Cook Myers, ed., *Narratives of Early Pennsylvania, West New Jersey and Delaware, 1630–1707* (New York: Charles Scribner's Sons, 1912), 363.

6. Francis Daniel Pastorius, *A New Primmer*, New York, 1698, From the Original, now on deposit in Friends House, London (Boston: Massachusetts Historical Society, 1939), 85.

7. Clayton Coleman Hall, ed., *Narratives of Early Maryland, 1633–1684* (New York: Charles Scribner's Sons, 1910), 354.

8. Susan Castillo and Ivy Schweitzer, *The Literatures of Colonial America: An Anthology* (Cambridge, MA: Blackwell, 2001), 215.

9. Myers, *Narratives*, 300.

10. Ibid., 305.

11. Myra Jehlen and Michael Warner, eds., *The English Literatures of America, 1500–1800* (New York: Routledge, 1997), 1014.

12. Ibid., 1015.

13. Paul Lauter, gen. ed., *The Heath Anthology of American Literature*, 3rd ed. (Boston: Houghton Mifflin, 1998), 632.

14. Ibid.

15. Ola Elizabeth Winslow, *American Broadside Verse* (New Haven: Yale University Press, 1930), xviii.

16. Ibid., xxiii.

17. Lauter, *Heath Anthology*, 710.

18. Ibid., 688–689.

19. Ibid., 45–48.

20. Carla Mulford, *Only for the Eye of a Friend: The Poems of Annis Boudinot Stockton* (Charlottesville: University Press of Virginia, 1995), xv.

21. Ibid., 31, 152.

22. Ibid., 154, lines 61–66.

23. Allison Giffen, "Ann Eliza Bleecker," in *American Women Prose Writers to 1820*, ed. Carla Mulford, vol. 200 of *Dictionary of Literary Biography*. (Detroit: The Gale Group, 1999), 55–61.

24. Lauter, *Heath Anthology*, 1242.

25. Edward Wagenknecht, *Cavalcade of the American Novel* (New York: Henry Holt and Co., 1952), 8.

26. Ibid.

27. Lauter, *Heath Anthology*, 842.

28. Benjamin Franklin, *The Autobiography and Other Writings* (New York: Penguin Classics, 1986), 98.

29. Lauter, *Heath Anthology*, 890–891.

30. Quoted in ibid., 883.

31. J. Hector St. John de Crèvecoeur, *Letters from an American Farmer and Sketches of Eighteenth-Century America* (New York: Penguin Classics, 1986), 22, 51.

32. James Grossman, *James Fenimore Cooper* (William Sloane Associates, 1949), 28.

33. Donald A. Ringe, *Charles Brockden Brown*, rev. ed., Twayne's United States Authors Series (Boston: Twayne Publishers, 1991), 1.

34. Grossman, *Cooper*, 29.

35. Ibid., 102, 103.

36. James T. Callow, *Kindred Spirits: Knickerbocker Writers and American Artists, 1807–1855* (Chapel Hill: University of North Carolina Press, 1967), 3.

37. Jean Fagan Yellin, quoted in Lauter, *Heath Anthology*, 1837.

38. Ibid., 1839

39. Ibid., 1916.

40. Goldhurst, quoted in Lauter, *Heath Anthology*, 1441.

41. Contemporary Authors Online (Detroit: Gale 2002).

42. Merriam-Webster's *Encyclopedia of Literature*.

43. Michael Robertson, *Stephen Crane, Journalism, and the Making of Modern American Literature* (New York: Columbia University Press, 1997), 19.

44. David A. Copeland, *Colonial American Newspapers: Character and Content* (Newark: University of Delaware Press, 1997), 278.

45. George H. Douglas, *The Golden Age of the Newspaper* (Westport, CT: Greenwood Press, 1999), 31.

46. Lauren Kessler, *The Dissident Press* (Beverly Hills: Sage, 1984), 27, 36.

47. Hy B. Turner, *When Giants Ruled: The Story of Park Row, New York's Great Newspaper Street* (New York: Fordham University Press, 1999), 218.

48. Ibid.

49. Deborah Davis, *Katharine the Great: Katharine Graham and Her Washington Post Empire* (New York: Sheridan Square Press, 1979), 3.

50. Lynne Waldeland, *John Cheever*, Twayne's United States Authors Series (Boston: Twayne Publishers, 1979), 26.

51. Cary D. Wintz, ed., *Remembering the Harlem Renaissance* (New York: Garland Publishing, 1996), vii–viii.

52. Contemporary Authors Online, Gale 2002.

53. Ibid.

54. Thomas F. Merrill, *Allen Ginsberg*, Twayne's United States Authors Series (Boston: Twayne Publishers, 1988), 1–3.

55. Lawrence S. Friedman, *Understanding Cynthia Ozick* (Columbia: University of South Carolina Press, 1991), 1.

56. Contemporary Authors Online, Gale 2003.

57. Ibid.

Music

1. Edward Jablonski, *The Encyclopedia of American Music* (New York: Doubleday, 1981).

2. Kate Van Winkle Keller, "Secular Music to 1800," in David Nicholls, ed., *The Cambridge History of American Music* (New York: Cambridge University Press, 1999).

3. Charles H. Kaufman, *The Music of the Eighteenth Century New Jersey* (Newark: New Jersey Historical Commission, 1975), 11.

4. Ibid.

5. Weldon Wallace, "Maryland: Baltimore Musical Scene," in By Spaeth Sigmund and William J. Perlman, eds., *Music and Dance in the Southeastern States* (Gertrude Martine Rohrer, NY: Alectra, 1952).

6. Glenn Gunn Dillard, "Washington D.C.," in Sigmund and W. Perlman, *Music and Dance in the Southeastern States* (Gertrude Martine Rohrer, New York: Alectra, 1952), 142.

7. University of Pennsylvania Library Exhibitions Web site, http://www.library.upenn.edu/exhibits/rbm/ormandy/index.html.

8. Kate Van Winkle Keller, "Secular Music to 1800," in Nicholls, *The Cambridge History of American Music*.

9. Michael Broyles, "Art music from 1860–1920," in Nicholls, *The Cambridge History of American Music*, 230.

10. Gilbert Chase, *America's Music* (Chicago: University of Illinois Press, 1987).

11. Jablonski, *Encyclopedia of American Music*.

12. Jeffrey Magee, "Ragtime and Early Jazz," in Nicholls *Cambridge History of American Music*.

13. Kaufman, *The Music of the Eighteenth Century New Jersey*, 11.

14. Daniel Kingman, *American Music: A Panorama* (New York: Schirmer, 1979).

15. http://www.righteousbaberecord.com.

16. Juan Flores, "The Puerto Rican Roots of Hip Hop Culture," in Ray Allen and Lois Wilcken, eds., *Island Sounds in the Global City: Caribbean Popular Music and Identity in New York City* (New York: New York Folklore Society and Institute for Studies in American Music, Brooklyn College, 1998).

17. Keith C. Ward, "Musical Responses to HIV and AIDS," in James R. Heintz, ed., *Perspectives on American Music Since 1950* (New York: Garland, 1999).

18. Kyle Gann, *American Music in the Twentieth Century* (New York, Schirmer, 1997).

Religion

1. Douglas G. Jacobsen, *An Unprov'd Experiment: Religious Pluralism in Colonial New Jersey* (Brooklyn, NY: Carlson, 1991), 21.

2. Percentages and figures in Joseph J. Casino, "From Sanctuary to Involvement: A History of the Catholic Parish in the Northeast," in Jay P. Dolan, ed., *The American Catholic Parish: A History from 1850 to the Present*, vol. 1 (Mahwah, NJ: Paulist Press, 1987), 16, 23–24, 40.

3. Jewish percentages derived from Martin B. Bradley, Norman M. Green Jr., Dale E. Jones, Mac Lynn, and Lou McNeil, *Churches and Church Membership in the United States, 1990: An Enumeration by Region, State, and County Based on Data Reported for 133 Church Groupings* (Atlanta, GA: Glenmary Research Center, 1992).

4. Elaine K. Ellison and Elaine M. Jaffe, *Voices from Marshall Street: Jewish Life in a Philadelphia Neighborhood, 1920–1960* (Philadelphia: Camino Books, 1994), 95.

5. School percentages in Eli Lederhendler, *New York Jews and the Decline of Urban Ethnicity, 1950–1970* (Syracuse: Syracuse University Press, 2001), 106.

6. Figures for Muslims derived from Michael A. Kosegi and J. Gordon Melton, eds., *Islam in America: A Sourcebook* (New York: Garland, 1992).

7. Unless otherwise stated, all percentages are derived from Bradley et al., *Churches and Church Membership in the United States*.

8. George A. Kelly, *Inside My Father's House* (New York: Doubleday, 1989), 71.

9. Urban percentages derived from Bradley et al., *Churches and Church Membership in the United States*.

10. Lynn G. Johnson, "MAP/Churchmen Chart a City's Future," *United Church Herald* 10, no. 9 (September 1967): 13.

Sports and Recreation

1. Foster Rhea Dulles, *America Learns to Play: A History of Popular Recreation 1607–1940* (New York: D. Appleton–Century, 1940), 226.

2. Sol White and Jerry Malloy comps., *Sol White's History of Colored Base Ball, with Other Documents on the Early Black Game, 1886–1936* (Lincoln University of Nebraska Press, 1995), 31.

3. John Bowman and Joel Zoss, *Diamonds in the Rough: The Untold History of Baseball* (New York: Macmillan, 1989), 122.

4. Ibid., 172.

5. Stephen Jay Gould, *Triumph and Tragedy in Mudville: A Lifelong Passion for Baseball* (New York: W. W. Norton 2003), 256.

6. S. W. Pope, *Patriotic Games: Sporting Traditions in the American Imagination, 1876–1926* (Oxford: Oxford University Press, 1997), 98.

7. Ibid., 89.

8. Carl Prine, " 'King Football' Continues Long-Time Rule," *Pittsburgh Tribune-Review*, October 17, 2003.

9. Ashley Fantz, "Little League Baseball Not a Designated Hit Here," *Miami Herald*, August 31, 2003.

10. John Feinstein, *Civil War: Army vs. Navy: A Year Inside College Football's Purest Rivalry* (Back Bay Books, 1997).

11. Genio C. Scott, *Fishing in American Waters* (Secaucus, NJ: Castle Books, 1989, orig. pub. 1888), 61.

12. Dulles, *America Learns to Play*, 25–26.

13. Scott, *Fishing in American Waters*, 52.

BIBLIOGRAPHY

Abrahams, Roger D. *Afro-American Folktales: Stories from Black Traditions in the New World*. New York: Pantheon Books, 1985.

Andrews, Wayne. *Architecture in America: A Photographic History from the Colonial Period to the Present*. New York: HarperCollins, 1973.

Arnason, H. H. *History of Modern Art*. 3rd ed. New York: Harry N. Abrams, 1986.

Arthur, John A. *Invisible Sojourners: African Immigrant Diaspora in the United States*. Westport, CT: Praeger, 2000.

Banner, Lois W. *American Beauty*. New York: Alfred A. Knopf, 1983.

Besack, Michael R. *Aquaculture and the Environment in the United States*. Baton Rouge, LA: Aquacultural Society, 2002.

Bierhorst, John. *The Mythology of North America*. New York: Morrow, 1985.

Binder, Frederick, and David Reimers. *All the Nations Under Heaven: An Ethnic and Racial History of New York City*. New York: Columbia University Press, 1996.

Bishop, Robert. *American Folk Sculpture*. New York: E. P. Dutton, 1974.

Botkin, Benjamin Albert. *A Treasury of American Folklore*. New York: Crown, 1944.

Bowman, John, and Joel Zoss. *Diamonds in the Rough: The Untold History of Baseball*. New York: Macmillan, 1989.

Bradford Landau, Sarah, and Carl Condit. *The Rise of the New York Skyscraper, 1865–1913*. New Haven: Yale University Press, 1996.

Brunvand, Jan Harold. *American Folklore: An Encyclopedia*. New York: Garland, 1996.

Brown, Lester R. *Eco-Economy: Building an Economy for the Earth*. New York: W. W. Norton, 2001.

Brown, Ralph H. *Historical Geography of the United States*. New York: Harcourt, Brace, 1949.

Burke, Helen. *Foods from the Founding Fathers: Recipes from Five Colonial Seaports*. Hicksville, NY: Exposition Press, 1978.

Burnham Oliver, Valerie. *Fashion and Costume in American Popular Culture*. Westport, CT: Greenwood Press, 1996.

Cassidy, Frederic, chief ed. *The Dictionary of American Regional English*. 4 vols. Cambridge, MA: Belknap, 1985.

Castillo, Susan, and Ivy Schweitzer. *The Literatures of Colonial America: An Anthology*. Malden, MA: Blackwell, 2001.

Chase, Gilbert. *America's Music: From the Pilgrims to the Present (Music in American Life)*. Urbana: University of Illinois Press, 1992.

Coblentz, Elizabeth, with Kevin Williams. *The Amish Cook: Recollections and Recipes from an Old Order Amish Family*. Berkeley, CA: Ten Speed Press, 2002.

Collins, John J. *Native American Religions: A Geographical Survey*. Lewiston, NY: Edwin Mellen Press, 1991.

Condit, Carl. *American Building: Materials and Techniques from the Beginning of the Colonial Settlement to the President*. Chicago: University of Chicago Press, 1969.

Crawford, Richard. *America's Musical Life: A History*. New York: W. W. Norton, 2001.

Crystal, David. *The Cambridge Encyclopedia of Language*. Cambridge: Cambridge University Press, 1997.

Cunningham, Patricia A., and Susan Voso Lab, eds. *Dress and Popular Culture*. Bowling Green, KY: Bowling Green State University Popular Press, 1991.

Denby, David. *Awake in the Dark: Anthology of American Film Criticism, 1915 to the Present*. New York: Vintage Books, 1977.

Dockstader, Frederick J. *Weaving Arts of the North American Indian*. Revised ed. New York: HarperCollins, 1993.

Dolan, Jay P. *The American Catholic Experience: A History from Colonial Times to the Present*. Garden City, NY: Doubleday, 1985.

Dulles, Foster Rhea. *America Learns to Play: A History of Popular Recreation, 1607–1940*. New York: D. Appleton–Century, 1940.

Ebert, John, and Katherine Ebert. *American Folk Painters*. New York: Charles Scribner's Sons, 1975.

Elsaesser, Thomas, and Warren Buckland. *Studying Contemporary American Film: A Guide to Movie Analysis*. London: Oxford University Press, 2002.

Erdoes, Richard, and Alfonso Ortiz. *American Indian Myths and Legends*. New York: Pantheon Books, 1984.

Everson, William K. *American Silent Film*. New York: Oxford University Press, 1978.

Fein, Albert. *Frederick Law Olmsted and the American Environmental Tradition*. New York: George Braziller, 1972.

Gilbert, W. Kent. *Commitment to Unity: A History of the Lutheran Church in America*. Philadelphia: Fortress Press, 1988.

Golab, Caroline. *Immigrant Destinations*. Philadelphia: Temple University Press, 1977.

Gould, Stephen Jay. *Triumph and Tragedy in Mudville: A Lifelong Passion for Baseball*. New York: W. W. Norton, 2003.

Groff, Betty. *Betty Groff's Pennsylvania Dutch Cookbook*. New York: Macmillan, 1990.

Grushkin, Paul. *The Art of Rock*. New York: Abbeville, 1987.

Haberland, Wolfgang. *The Art of North America*. Art of the World. New York: Crown, 1964.

Harris, Cyril. *American Architecture: An Illustrated Encyclopedia*. New York: Norton Professional Books, 2002.

Harris, Lis. *Holy Days: The World of a Hasidic Family*. New York: Summit Books, 1985.

Hatch Nathan O. *The Democratization of American Christianity*. New Haven: Yale University Press, 1989.

Hawken, Paul. *The Ecology of Commerce: A Declaration of Sustainability*. New York: Harper, 1994.

Hickey, James E. Jr., and Linda A. Longmire, eds. *The Environment: Global Problems, Local Solutions*. Westport, CT: Greenwood Press, 1994.

Hill, John Gibson, and Pamela Church. *The Oxford Guide to Film Studies*. Oxford: Oxford University Press, 1998.

Hitchcock, Hugh Wiley. *Music in the United States: A Historical Introduction*. New York: Prentice Hall, 1970.

Jacobs, Lewis. *The Rise of the American Film: A Critical History*. New York: Teachers College Press, 1968.

Jehlen, Myra, and Michael Warner, eds. *The English Literatures of America, 1500–1800*. New York: Routledge, 1997.

Jennings, Francis, ed. *The History and Culture of Iroquois Diplomacy*. Syracuse, NY: Syracuse University Press, 1985.

Joselit, Jenna Weissman. *A Perfect Fit: Clothes, Character, and the Promise of America*. New York: Henry Holt, 2001.

Kimm, Silas Conrad. *The Iroquois: A History of the Six Nations of New York*. Reprint, New York: Fawcett, 1998.

Lannin, Joanne. *A History of Basketball for Girls and Women: From Bloomers to Big Leagues*. Minneapolis: Lerner Sports, 2000.

Lauter, Paul, gen. ed. *The Heath Anthology of American Literature*: 3rd ed. Boston: Houghton Mifflin, 1998.

Levenstein, Harvey A. *Paradox of Plenty: A Social History of Eating in Modern America*. New York: Oxford University Press, 1993.

Malinowski, Sharon, and Anna Sheets, eds. *The Gayle Encyclopedia of Native American Tribes*. Vol. 1. Detroit: Gale Research, 1998.

Marriott, Alice Lee, and Carol K. Rachlin. *American Indian Mythology*. New York: Crowell, 1968.

McIntosh, Elaine. *American Food Habits in Historical Perspective*. Westport, CT: Praeger, 1995.

Meinig, D. W. *The Shaping of America: A Geographical Perspective on 500 Years of History*. Vol. 1, *Atlantic America, 1492–1800*. New Haven: Yale University Press, 1986.

Melton, J. Gordon *Encyclopedia of American Religions*. 6th ed. Detroit: Gale Research, 1999.

Melton, J. Gordon, and Michael A. Kosegi, eds. *Islam in America: A Sourcebook*. New York: Garland, 1992.

Molles, Manuel C. *Ecology: Concepts and Applications*. New York: McGraw-Hill, 2001.

Museum of Modern Art. *American Folk Art*. New York: Arno Press, 1969.

Peterson, Robert. *Only the Ball Was White: A History of Legendary Black Players and All-Black Professional Teams*. Oxford: Oxford University Press, 1970.

Pope, S. W. *Patriotic Games: Sporting Traditions in the American Imagination, 1876–1926*. Oxford: Oxford University Press, 1997.

Portney, Paul R., and Robert N. Stavins, eds. *Public Policies for Environmental Protection*. Washington, DC: Resources for the Future, 2000.

Prichard, Robert W. *A History of the Episcopal Church*. Harrisburg, PA: Morehouse Publishing, 1999.

Pugh, Cedric D. J. *Sustainability, the Environment and Urbanization*. New York: Earthscan Publications, 1996.

Richey, Russell E., Kenneth E. Rowe, and Jean M. Schmidt, eds. *Perspectives in American Methodism: Interpretive Essays*. Nashville, TN: Abingdon Press, 1993.

Root, Waverley, and Richard de Rochemont. *Eating in America: A History*. New York: Morrow, 1976.

Roth, Leland. *American Architecture: A History*. Boulder: Westview Press, 1980.

———. *Concise History of American Architecture*. Boulder: Westview Press, 1980.

Salzman, Eric. *Twentieth Century Music: An Introduction*. 4th ed. New York: Prentice Hall, 2001.

Sandweiss, Martha A., ed. *Photography in Nineteenth-Century America*. Fort Worth, TX: Amon Carter Museum, 1991.

Schremp, Geraldine, and Gerry Schremp. *Celebration of American Food: Four Centuries in the Melting Pot*. Library of Congress Series. Golden, CO: Fulcrum Publishers, 1996.

Scott, Genio C. *Fishing in American Waters*. Secaucus, NJ: Castle Books, 1989.

Simpson, John Warfield. *Visions of Paradise: Glimpses of Our Landscape's Legacy*. Berkeley: University of California Press, 1999.

Stavins, R. N., ed. *Economics of the Environment*. New York: W. W. Norton, 2000.

Wang, Xinyang. *Surviving the City: The Chinese Immigrant Experience in New York City, 1890–1970*. Lanham, MD: Rowman and Littlefield, 2001.

Waters, Mary. *Black Identities: West Indian Immigrant Dreams and American Realities*. Cambridge, MA: Harvard University Press, 2001.

Whiffen, Marcus. *American Architecture since 1780: A Guide to the Styles*. Cambridge: MIT Press, 1992.

White, Shane, and Graham White. *Stylin': African American Expressive Culture from Its Beginning to the Zoot Suit*. Ithaca, NY: Cornell University Press, 1998.

Wilson, Jose. *American Cooking: The Eastern Heartland, New York, New Jersey, Pennsylvania, Ohio, Michigan, Indiana, Illinois*. New York: Time-Life, 1971.

Wolfram, Walt, and Natalie Schilling-Estes. *American English*. Oxford: Blackwell, 1998.

World Watch Institute. *The State of the World 2003*. New York: W. W. Norton, 2003.

INDEX

ABOUT THE EDITOR AND CONTRIBUTORS

ROBERT P. MARZEC, editor of this volume, is associate professor of English literature, postcolonial studies, global studies, and contemporary criticism at the State University of New York at Fredonia. He has completed a book-length project titled *Land and Empire: The Enclosure Movement, the Rise of the British Empire, and the Lost History of Inhabitancy*, for which he received a National Endowment for the Humanities award; and is currently at work on a second book project tentatively titled *Ethics and Literature in the Era of Globalization: Volume II of Land and Empire*. He has had articles published in *Boundary 2, Rhizomes,* and *Janus Head*. He is the founding editor of the journal *Crossings*.

CAFFILENE ALLEN is a part-time lecturer in the Professional Writing Program at the University of Maryland and holds a full-time position as a writer/editor with the U.S. Department of Agriculture. She holds a Ph.D. in colonial American literature and three master's degrees: one in Renaissance English, one in counseling, and one in public administration. All degrees are from Georgia State University in Atlanta.

CHRISTINE M. BATTISTA has a degree in communications, and is working toward her Ph.D. in literature. She is a graduate student at the State University of New York at Fredonia. She is currently working on a research project on Emma Goldman. She is the recipient of the Louis and David Adler Scholarship for excellence in Broadcasting and Journalism (2001).

JEREMY BONNER holds a Ph.D. in American history from the Catholic University of America in Washington, D.C., and is currently an independent scholar in Baltimore, Maryland. He has published on political and religious history in such journals as the *Journal of Mormon History* and *Anglican and Episcopal History*. He is currently working on a biography of Victor J. Reed (Catholic bishop of Oklahoma City and Tulsa, 1958–1971).

TIMOTHY FINNEGAN is the curator at the Adams Art Gallery in Dunkirk, New York. He received his B.A. in art history from the University of Wisconsin–Madison, specializing in American art movements of the twentieth century. He has curated shows of painting, sculpture, electronic media, printmaking, and ceramics.

GEOFFREY GRIFFIN has over ten years of experience as a sportswriter for newspapers while covering a variety of athletic events. He is also a published writer.

THOMAS S. HISCHAK is the author or editor of thirteen books on theater, film, and Tin Pan Alley, including *Word Crazy: Broadway Lyricists from Cohan to Sondheim, The American Musical Theatre Song Encyclopedia, Film It with Music: An Encyclopedic Guide to the American Movie Musical, American Theatre: A Chronicle of Comedy and Drama, Through the Screen Door: The Broadway Musical and the Movies*, and *The Oxford Companion to American Theatre*. He is also the author of fifteen published plays and a professor of theater at the State University of New York College at Cortland.

RUSSELL LEO is a Ph.D. student in the literature program at Duke University. He is currently working on a critical treatment of John Milton and seventeenth-century puritanisms and humanisms.

MICHAEL LOVAGLIO has an M.A. in English from State University of New York–Fredonia, where he was the recipient of the Rosa Parks Scholarship in 2000. He is currently writing for the *Village Times Herald*, the *Port Times-Record*, and the *Village Beacon-Record* on Long Island, New York.

DANIEL MALERK has an M.A. in English from State University of New York–Fredonia and teaches at Erie Community College in New York.

IAN MORLEY is an assistant professor based in the School of Design at Ming Chuan University in Taiwan. He has published work on a number of matters relating to the development of the environment in Britain after the industrial revolution, with his current interests being public health, civic design, and the development of modern town planning. In addition, he has presented aspects of his research at conferences in Asia, Europe, Oceania, and the United States.

ROBERT F. MOSS received a Ph.D. in English from the University of South Carolina. His recent publications include books and articles on food history and on the detective fiction of Raymond Chandler and Ross Macdonald. He lives in Charleston, South Carolina.

REBECCA ROEDER is a doctoral student in the Department of Linguistics at Michigan State University. Her research focuses on sociolinguistics and acoustic phonetics, especially with regard to urban dialects of American English in the United States.

KATHRYN WILSON is director of education and interpretation at the Historical Society of Pennsylvania in Philadelphia, where she has directed numerous ethnographic projects with local ethnic and immigrant communities. She has a Ph.D. in folklore and folklife from the University of Pennsylvania. Her research interests center on public culture, gender and ethnic identity, and the politics of the body.

EMILY WORKMAN is a graduate student at the University of Reno in literary studies and special education. She is a certified secondary English teacher in both New York and Nevada, holds a bachelor's degree in English and secondary education from the State University of New York at Fredonia, and has studied feminism and Victorian literature at Oxford University.

The Greenwood Encyclopedia of American Regional Cultures

The Great Plains Region, *edited by Amanda Rees*

The Mid-Atlantic Region, *edited by Robert P. Marzec*

The Midwest, *edited by Joseph W. Slade and Judith Yaross Lee*

New England, *edited by Michael Sletcher*

The Pacific Region, *edited by Jan Goggans with Aaron DiFranco*

The Rocky Mountain Region, *edited by Rick Newby*

The South, *edited by Rebecca Mark and Rob Vaughan*

The Southwest, *edited by Mark Busby*